Counselling and Resilience in School Community:

Contemporary Issues and Innovative Approaches

Eleni N. Nikolaou
https://orcid.org/0000-0003-1840-3433
University of the Aegean, Greece

IGI Global
Scientific Publishing
Publishing Tomorrow's Research Today

VP of Publishing Ethics & Research Integrity Melissa Wagner
Director of Acquisitions Mikaela Felty
Director of Book Development Jocelynn Hessler
Production Manager Mike Brehm
Cover Design Jose Rosado

Published in the United States of America by
IGI Global Scientific Publishing
701 East Chocolate Avenue
Hershey, PA, 17033, USA
Tel: 717-533-8845 | Fax: 717-533-7115
Website: https://www.igi-global.com E-mail: cust@igi-global.com

Library of Congress Cataloging-in-Publication Data

Names: Nikolaou, Eleni N. editor
Title: Counselling and resilience in school community : contemporary issues and innovative approaches / [edited by] Eleni Nikolaou.
Description: Hershey, PA : IGI Global Scientific Publishing, [2027] | Includes bibliographical references and index. | Summary: "The book illuminates the multiple ways in which counselling in school context can prevent the manifestation of emotional and behavioral difficulties. The provision of counselling-psychological services is also vital to promoting students' mental health, in preventing psychological disorders and in fostering psychosocial adaptation. Implementing preventive counselling interventions within school environment is crucial to enhancing resilience and wellbeing of all members of school community. In addition, it contributes to shaping school culture and the associated characteristics of school units for fostering resilience in school community"-- Provided by publisher.
Identifiers: LCCN 2026021818 (print) | LCCN 2026021819 (ebook) | ISBN 9798337394206 hardcover | ISBN 9798337394213 paperback | ISBN 9798337394220 ebook
Subjects: LCSH: School psychology | School mental health services | Students--Mental health
Classification: LCC LB1027.55 .C687 2027 (print) | LCC LB1027.55 (ebook)
LC record available at https://lccn.loc.gov/2026021818
LC ebook record available at https://lccn.loc.gov/2026021819

British Cataloguing in Publication Data
A Cataloguing in Publication record for this book is available from the British Library.

Table of Contents

Detailed Table of Contents

Overall, the chapter presents mentoring-oriented leadership as a useful framework for strengthening a sustainable and preventive school culture.

This study examines the professional well-being of preschool educators as a key factor in school resilience and the quality of the educational process. Through a literature review and qualitative research based on semi-structured interviews with ten kindergarten teachers in Rhodes, the study investigates the factors that enhance or undermine their professional well-being. The findings indicate that teachers associate well-being with emotional balance, job satisfaction, positive relationships with children and a balance between personal and professional life. At the same time, support from colleagues and school leaders functions as a reinforcing factor, while increasing bureaucracy, the demands of the educational system, and the lack of resources negatively affect their everyday professional experience. In conclusion, professional well-being emerges as a multidimensional and dynamic phenomenon that directly influences both educators themselves and the overall learning process.

In the school environment, where identities, attitudes, and values are formed, the need to prevent and address violence takes on particular importance. Nevertheless, the reality of education shows that violence remains a part of school life, often with gendered dimensions, a fact that makes its systematic study and effective management necessary. This study aims to help fill this gap by focusing on the views, experiences, and suggestions of high school students regarding gender-based violence in the school environment. The purpose of the study is to investigate how gender-based violence is understood and experienced in the school context through the narratives of high school students themselves. The research was conducted using a qualitative-interpretive approach, through semi-structured interviews with high school students in Rhodes, while the data were analyzed using thematic analysis. The results indicate that gender-based violence is recognized as behavior linked to gender and/or sexuality and manifests in multiple forms, with verbal violence being the most prevalent.

as a psychosocial protective resource that supports emotional regulation, social connectedness, belonging, and positive adaptation. Findings from an exploratory quantitative study involving preservice preschool teachers highlight the perceived value of music in fostering children's well-being and resilience. Building on the empirical findings and relevant literature, the chapter proposes the Music-Informed Preventive School Counselling and Resilience Framework, a multilevel model that positions music education as a resource for strengthening inclusive, supportive, and resilient school communities.

Attention-Deficit/Hyperactivity Disorder (ADHD) is one of the most common neurodevelopmental disorders of childhood, affecting not only the child but also the entire family system. Mothers of children with ADHD often experience increased levels of stress, parental burnout, and social pressure, while they are daily called upon to manage challenges related to their children's behavior. In this context, resilience constitutes a key factor in adaptation and psychosocial well-being. The present study investigates levels of resilience in a sample of 51 mothers of children with ADHD. The results indicated satisfactory levels of adaptive capacity. Additionally, resilience was found to be positively associated with specific coping strategies, particularly a positive approach. The findings suggest the presence of strong personal resources and stress-management abilities, despite the challenges associated with raising a child with ADHD. Strengthening resilience through targeted counseling and educational practices may significantly contribute to mothers' psychological empowerment.

This chapter explores the relationship between parenting practices and childhood aggression, highlighting the role of school counseling in fostering resilience. The authoritative parenting style (high warmth, reasonable control) functions protectively, limiting aggression and enhancing self-regulation. Conversely, the authoritarian style (low warmth, rigid control) and the permissive style (high warmth, absence of boundaries) constitute risk factors. Emphasis is placed on parental gender, family structure, and cultural context. Single parenthood, especially when accompanied by economic hardship, may lead to less effective parenting practices. School counseling emerges as a crucial intervention mechanism, supporting both parents and children while strengthening school-family collaboration in the prevention and management of aggression.

Preface

INTRODUCTION

Schools are increasingly understood not simply as places of academic instruction, but as complex communities in which educational, psychological, social, relational, and organizational processes intersect. Within these communities, students, teachers, families, school leaders, counselors, and wider stakeholders collectively shape the conditions that influence learning, well-being, belonging, and adaptation. Contemporary challenges—including changing family and social structures, increasing demands on educators, learning difficulties, gender-based violence, behavioral concerns, and the growing need for inclusive and preventive practices—require school communities to move beyond reactive approaches toward models that promote resilience, collaboration, and sustainable well-being. Against this background, *Counselling and Resilience in School Community: Contemporary Issues and Innovative Approaches* brings together diverse perspectives that illuminate how counseling and resilience can be embedded within the everyday life of schools.

The central premise of this volume is that resilience should not be viewed exclusively as an individual psychological characteristic. Rather, it is a dynamic and relational process that is influenced by organizational structures, interpersonal relationships, professional practices, family contexts, and the broader educational environment. Similarly, school counseling is presented throughout the volume not merely as an intervention for students experiencing difficulties, but as a multidimensional and preventive practice capable of strengthening relationships, supporting educators and families, promoting inclusion, addressing violence, and facilitating positive adaptation. The chapters therefore adopt complementary perspectives, ranging from systems theory and organizational learning to teacher–parent communication, mentoring leadership, professional well-being, inclusive education, citizen science, music, parenting, and family resilience.

This edited volume seeks to contribute to ongoing discussions about how school communities can become more supportive, inclusive, reflective, and resilient. The contributions combine theoretical analysis, empirical research, literature-based inquiry, and innovative conceptual frameworks, with particular attention to educational contexts in Greece and Cyprus while engaging with broader international scholarship. Collectively, the chapters emphasize the importance of whole-school approaches in which responsibility for well-being and resilience is shared across the school community. We hope that this volume will be valuable to researchers, educators, school counselors, psychologists, school leaders, teacher educators, policymakers, and other professionals seeking evidence-informed and context-sensitive approaches to contemporary challenges in education.

CHAPTER OVERVIEW

Chapter 1, "A Systems-Theoretical Perspective on Organizational Learning in the Greek Educational System: From Legislation to Resilient Schooling," by Exakousti-Petroula Angelakou, Stamatina Kioussi, and Anastassios Kodakos, establishes an organizational and systems-oriented foundation for understanding resilient schooling. The chapter examines the relationship between educational legislation, school culture, decision-making, organizational learning, counseling, and self-evaluation within Greek primary education. By combining longitudinal analysis of educational legislation with mixed-methods research, the authors demonstrate the continuing tension between compliance-oriented practices and deeper forms of organizational learning. Particular attention is given to communication, staff participation, reflective processes, and the development of conditions that can support more adaptive and resilient schools.

Chapter 2, "Communication between Teachers and Parents: The Role of Teachers in Cultivating Positive Relationships within the School Context," by Panagiotis Stamatis and Meropi Ntavlamanou, turns attention to the relational foundations of effective school communities. The chapter conceptualizes teacher–parent communication as a dynamic process shaped by cultural expectations, institutional structures, power relationships, and interpersonal competencies. It considers formal, informal, and digital communication practices and emphasizes the importance of trust, dialogue, cultural responsiveness, and collaboration. In doing so, it demonstrates how constructive school–family relationships can support student achievement, school cohesion, and teacher well-being.

Chapter 3, "Animals in the Primary School Classroom: Evidence-Based Benefits and Conditions for Implementation," by Georgia Ioannidou and Vasileios Papavasileiou, explores an innovative approach to supporting children's emotional and social development. The chapter reviews evidence concerning the potential contribution of classroom animals and structured animal-assisted programs to stress reduction, emotional regulation, social interaction, empathy, responsibility, motivation, and engagement. At the same time, it recognizes that such practices require careful planning and ethical implementation. Issues including allergies, phobias, hygiene, parental consent, appropriate animal selection, educational objectives, and animal welfare are therefore positioned as essential considerations for responsible practice.

Chapter 4, "School Leadership as Mentoring: A Relational and Preventive Approach to Teachers' Resilience," by Nikolaos Raptis and Nikolaos Psyrras, examines the role of school leadership in strengthening educators' capacity to adapt and thrive. The authors conceptualize resilience as a process shaped by organizational conditions rather than simply an individual attribute. Trust, psychological safety, reflective dialogue, mentoring, and collaborative learning are presented as important components of a supportive professional culture. The chapter also appropriately acknowledges that relational leadership cannot substitute for necessary structural reforms, thereby situating teacher resilience within the wider organizational context.

Chapter 5, "Preschool Teachers' Professional Well-Being as a Multidimensional Foundation of School Resilience," by Afroditi Ntouka and Eleni Nikolaou, focuses on the well-being of early childhood educators as a critical component of resilient educational environments. Drawing on literature and qualitative interviews with kindergarten teachers in Rhodes, the chapter examines factors that strengthen or undermine professional well-being. Emotional balance, job satisfaction, positive relationships, work–life balance, collegial support, and effective school leadership emerge as important resources, while bureaucracy, systemic demands, and resource limitations can create significant pressures. The chapter reinforces the understanding that the well-being of educators is closely connected to the quality and resilience of the educational environment as a whole.

Chapter 6, "The Prevention of Gender-Based Violence in the School Context: Students' Perspectives," by Maria Kouroutsidou, Katerina Karanikola, and Nikolaos Raptis, addresses one of the most pressing challenges facing contemporary school communities. Centering students' own perspectives, the chapter explores how gender-based violence is understood and experienced within the school environment. Through a qualitative-interpretive approach and thematic analysis of student interviews, the authors examine the forms through which violence manifests and the meanings students attach to these experiences. The chapter highlights the importance of listening to students and developing systematic preventive strategies that promote safety, respect, and gender-sensitive school cultures.

Chapter 7, "Motivation, Self-Regulation, and Teacher Practice: Innovative School-Based Interventions for Students with Learning Difficulties," by Maria Sofologi and Dimitra Katsarou, addresses inclusion through an integrated focus on motivation, self-regulation, and pedagogical practice. The chapter examines approaches including Universal Design for Learning, Multi-Tiered Systems of Support, co-regulation, metacognitive instruction, mindfulness, and technology-supported learning. By emphasizing teacher support and collaborative school cultures, the authors connect academic engagement with emotional regulation and resilience. The chapter consequently presents inclusive education as a collective school responsibility rather than an isolated set of interventions for individual learners.

Chapter 8, "From Nutrition Curriculum to School Resilience: A Counselling Approach Through Citizen Science," by Georgios Kritikos and Charistoula Chatzinikola, offers an innovative connection between curriculum, counseling, student participation, and resilience. The chapter reconceptualizes nutrition education as an opportunity for psychosocial and relational development and uses Citizen Science to position students as active co-researchers within their school communities. Through inquiry, reflection, and collaborative action, students can develop agency, collective efficacy, and school connectedness. School counselors are positioned as facilitators of psychological safety and interdisciplinary collaboration, illustrating the potential of curriculum-based approaches to contribute to whole-school resilience.

Chapter 9, "Music, Wellbeing, and School Counselling: Building Resilient School Communities," by Maria Argyriou, examines music as a psychosocial resource within preventive counseling and resilience-oriented education. The chapter explores the potential of musical engagement to promote emotional regulation, belonging, social connectedness, and positive adaptation. Drawing on literature and an exploratory quantitative study involving preservice preschool teachers, it develops the Music-Informed Preventive School Counselling and Resilience Framework. This contribution expands conventional understandings of counseling by demonstrating how creative and cultural practices can become meaningful resources for inclusive and supportive school communities.

Chapter 10, "Psychological Resilience of Mothers of Children with ADHD: An Empirical Study," by Kyriaki Tasiou and Eleni Nikolaou, extends the discussion of resilience beyond the immediate school environment to the family system. Focusing on mothers of children with ADHD, the chapter examines resilience and coping in the context of the demands associated with parenting a child with a neurodevelopmental condition. Findings from the study indicate satisfactory adaptive capacity and identify positive approaches to coping as an important correlate of resilience. The chapter highlights the potential contribution of counseling and educational practices to parental empowerment and emphasizes the importance of considering families as essential partners in supporting children's well-being.

Chapter 11, "Parenting Practices and Childhood Aggression: Fostering Resilience through School Counseling," by Eirini Tzovla, Marilena Mousoulidou, Andri Christodoulou, George Tsitsas, Angela Savvidou, and Theodoros Goutoglou, concludes the volume by examining the intersection of parenting, childhood aggression, resilience, and school counseling. The chapter considers how different parenting styles may function as protective or risk factors and highlights the influence of family structure, parental circumstances, and cultural context. School counseling is presented as an important mechanism for supporting both children and parents while strengthening school–family collaboration. In this way, the chapter reinforces the broader argument of the volume that resilience is most effectively fostered when educational and family systems work together.

CONCLUSION

Taken together, the chapters demonstrate that resilient school communities cannot be created through isolated programs or individual interventions alone. Resilience emerges through interconnected systems of relationships, organizational structures, professional practices, family partnerships, inclusive pedagogies, and preventive strategies. The contributions in this volume therefore encourage a shift from deficit-oriented approaches toward practices that identify and strengthen existing resources within students, educators, families, and school communities. Counseling, in this broader understanding, becomes an important mechanism for connecting these resources and supporting positive adaptation across multiple levels of the educational system.

A recurring theme across the volume is the importance of relationships. Whether the focus is on teacher–parent communication, mentoring leadership, professional well-being, student experiences of violence, inclusive teaching, participatory learning, music, parenting, or family resilience, supportive relationships emerge as fundamental conditions for well-being and sustainable educational development. At the same time, the chapters caution against placing responsibility for resilience solely on individuals. Organizational cultures, institutional policies, resources, leadership practices, and broader social conditions must also be addressed if schools are to develop genuinely resilient and inclusive environments. Effective counseling and resilience-building therefore require both interpersonal sensitivity and systemic awareness.

We offer this volume as a contribution to the continuing effort to understand and strengthen the resilience of school communities in a rapidly changing educational landscape. Its diverse perspectives demonstrate that innovative approaches can emerge when counseling is connected with organizational learning, inclusive education, family engagement, creative practice, participatory inquiry, leadership, and preventive action. We hope that the ideas and evidence presented here will stimulate further research, encourage reflective professional practice, and support the development of school environments in which students, educators, and families are not merely equipped to cope with challenges, but are enabled to grow, participate, belong, and flourish.

Chapter 1
A Systems-Theoretical Perspective on Organizational Learning in the Greek Educational System:
From Legislation to Resilient Schooling

Exakousti-Petroula Angelakou
http://orcid.org/0009-0004-2981-7708
University of the Aegean, Rhodes, Greece

Stamatina Kioussi
University of the Aegean, Rhodes, Greece

Anastassios Kodakos
University of the Aegean, Rhodes, Greece

ABSTRACT

This study examines the interrelationship between the legislative framework, school culture, decision premises, and mechanisms of school counseling and self-evaluation in shaping learning and resilient school organizations in Greek primary education. Methodologically, it combines longitudinal content analysis of educational legislation with a mixed-methods approach to organizational functioning and school culture. Original research instruments were developed, including a categorical system for legislative analysis based on dimensions of organizational complexity and mecha-

DOI: 10.4018/979-8-3373-9420-6.ch001

nisms of organizational self-diagnosis grounded in staff participation. The findings indicate that, despite policy emphasis on quality and evaluation, organizational learning remains largely oriented toward compliance and functional adaptation. The study further highlights the role of school culture and communication structures in fostering learning and resilience, while limited institutionalization of reflective processes constrains school development and the transition toward double-loop learning.

1. INTRODUCTION

The contemporary educational landscape operates within an environment of increasing institutional, social, and technological complexity (OECD, 2025; Selwyn, 2016;). Rapid societal transformation, growing student diversity, and expanding expectations regarding accountability, educational quality, inclusion, and effectiveness have fundamentally reshaped the conditions under which schools operate (Hargreaves, 2005). Consequently, schools can no longer be understood as linear organizations that simply implement externally prescribed policies. Rather, they function as complex social systems that continuously construct, reproduce, and transform internal structures of meaning in response to the complexity of their environment (Kodakos & Angelakou, 2016).

This transformation calls for a reconsideration of organizational resilience within educational research. Traditionally, resilience has been conceptualized either as an individual characteristic or as a process of adaptation to external challenges (Luthar, 2015; Masten, 2025; Rutter, 2006;). Although these perspectives have generated valuable insights, they provide only a partial explanation of how educational organizations preserve their coherence and functionality under conditions of sustained complexity. In this chapter, resilience is approached from a systems-theoretical perspective and conceptualized as an endogenous property of organizational systems. From this standpoint, resilience denotes the capacity of a school organization to maintain functional coherence and operational continuity while continuously reconstructing its internal decision premises and its relationship with the environment (Luhmann, 1995a). Rather than being reduced to adaptive performance, resilience emerges through the recursive processing of complexity, whereby the organization continuously reorganizes the conditions that enable its own functioning.

Within systems theory, resilience is understood as a second-order organizational function concerned with how the system observes, interprets, and regulates its own operations (Luhmann, 1995b; Willke, 2007). This perspective shifts the analytical focus from adaptation to organizational transformation by emphasizing the continuous reconfiguration of the conditions under which organizational action becomes possible. Consequently, resilience develops through reflective engagement with complexity rather than through linear processes of problem solving (Ungar, 2018). At the level of the school organization, this capacity is expressed in the maintenance of stable communicative structures despite ongoing pedagogical, social, and institutional change (Luhmann, 1995a).

According to Luhmann's theory of social systems, organizations are self-referential and operationally closed systems constituted through communication (Luhmann, 1995b). Their operation depends on the distinction between system and environment, through which environmental complexity is selectively processed and transformed into organizationally meaningful information. Communication therefore does not merely represent reality; it actively constitutes organizational reality through internally generated selections of meaning. These selections become stabilized through decision premises, understood as the rules, expectations, and interpretive schemes that structure organizational decision-making (Luhmann, 2000a; Willke, 1996). While stable decision premises provide continuity and reduce uncertainty, their transformation requires interventions that extend beyond immediate responses to address the underlying structures through which decisions are generated (Luhmann, 1995b). From this perspective, organizational learning is not confined to adaptation; rather, it entails the transformation of the conditions that shape organizational action (Argyris & Schön, 1978).

Building on this systems-theoretical perspective, Willke's (1996, 2007) concept of meta-learning highlights second-order learning as the capacity of organizations to reorganize their own processes of observation, reflection, and decision-making. Instead of concentrating on isolated improvements, meta-learning involves the critical examination of the cognitive and normative structures that guide organizational behavior. Organizational learning, therefore, becomes a continuous process of revising decision premises and reconstructing the communicative structures through which organizational meaning is generated. Although the distinction between single-loop and double-loop learning (Argyris & Schön, 1974) remains highly relevant, systems theory extends this discussion by focusing on the communicative conditions that make learning possible. Learning thus acquires a meta-operational dimension, emphasizing the continuous reconfiguration of the structures through which organizational decisions are produced (Luhmann, 1995b).

Within school organizations, counseling performs a function that extends beyond individual support. It operates as a mechanism of second-order observation by making implicit assumptions visible, broadening the range of communicative possibilities, and facilitating the reflective revision of organizational decision premises (Luhmann, 2000a; Willke, 2007). In doing so, counseling contributes not only to problem resolution but also to the development of organizational learning capacity and systemic resilience.

Teachers' Board constitutes a central decision premise within this process. Rather than acting solely as an implementer of educational policy, teachers actively participate in the construction, stabilization, and transformation of organizational decision premises. Professional collaboration, interpersonal trust, collective efficacy, and shared communicative practices form the organizational infrastructure through which decisions are maintained, questioned, or reconfigured (Bandura, 1997; Bryk & Schneider, 2002; Hoy & Tschannen-Moran, 1999). From this perspective, school culture is understood as a dynamic configuration of formal and informal expectations that shapes organizational decision-making (Schein, 2010). School self-evaluation complements this process by functioning as a mechanism of systemic self-observation. When viewed beyond accountability requirements, it becomes a reflective practice through which schools generate knowledge about their own functioning (MacBeath & McGlynn, 2004; OECD, 2013). Together with school counseling, self-evaluation establishes a continuous cycle of observation, reflection, and decision-making that supports organizational learning and strengthens systemic resilience (Fullan, 2007; 2025).

The Greek educational system provides a particularly relevant context for examining these processes because of its historically centralized governance structure, which has traditionally constrained organizational reflexivity. Although recent reforms have placed greater emphasis on evaluation, quality assurance, and school development, schools continue to operate predominantly within compliance-oriented frameworks shaped by external regulation. As a result, opportunities for endogenous organizational learning and the development of systemic resilience remain relatively limited (Angelakou, 2018).

Despite these developments, the relationship between the legislative framework, organizational decision premises, and school counseling has received only limited systematic attention within the Greek educational literature. Likewise, the conceptualization of schools as self-referential systems that generate resilience through organizational learning and the reflective processing of complexity remains insufficiently explored. This gap constrains both the theoretical advancement of systems-based approaches to organizational resilience and the development of evidence-informed strategies for sustainable school improvement within the Greek educational context.

Against this background, the present chapter adopts a systems-theoretical perspective on organizational learning grounded in Luhmann's theory of social systems and Willke's conception of meta-learning. It examines how the Greek legislative framework shapes the decision premises of school organizations and influences their capacity for organizational learning and resilience. Particular attention is given to the role of Teachers' Board as a critical decision premise, the transition from regulatory governance to School Development as a self-diagnostic process, and the contribution of school counseling to organizational reflexivity and systemic resilience.

The chapter contributes to the literature by reconceptualizing resilience as an endogenous organizational capacity rather than an externally prescribed policy outcome. Within this framework, School Development is understood as a second-order transformative process through which organizational learning, self-evaluation, and school counseling interact to strengthen systemic resilience by continuously reconstructing organizational meaning and decision premises.

2. THEORETICAL FRAMEWORK: LUHMANIAN SOCIAL SYSTEMS AND COMPLEXITY

2.1 Society as an Autopoietic System of Communication According to N. Luhmann

Niklas Luhmann's theory of social systems represents a fundamental epistemological shift in sociological thought by conceptualizing society as an autopoietic system constituted exclusively through communication. Within this theoretical framework, society is understood not as a collection of individuals, actions, or normative agreements, but as a continuously self-reproducing network of communicative operations. Rather than being grounded in actors or shared values, social order is recursively constituted through the ongoing production, reproduction, and stabilization of meaning (Luhmann, 1995b; Willke, 1996). Communication is therefore understood not merely as a medium for transmitting information but as the constitutive operation through which society reproduces itself.

Accordingly, a social system is defined not as an aggregate of individuals but as an operationally closed network of communication. Its identity is maintained through the continuous reproduction of the distinction between system and environment. This distinction does not imply separation from external reality; rather, it indicates that environmental complexity becomes meaningful only through internally generated communicative operations (Luhmann, 1995b). From this perspective, the environment possesses no independent significance for the system. Instead, it is constituted relationally through the system's own operations of observation and distinction. Consequently, what is identified as the environment is not given *a priori* but emerges through the system's communicative selections (Willke, 1996). The environment is therefore always system-relative and operationally constituted.

Within this conceptual framework, complexity represents the fundamental condition of all social systems. It refers to the excess of possible events and meanings relative to the system's capacity to process them simultaneously. Because no system can actualize every available possibility, selective operations become indispensable for sustaining communication. Complexity reduction is therefore not merely a strategic response to environmental demands but a constitutive requirement for systemic reproduction (Luhmann, 1995a; Willke, 1996). At the same time, every communicative selection excludes alternative possibilities, thereby introducing contingency as a structural characteristic of social reality. In systems theory, contingency does not denote randomness or instability. Rather, it expresses the openness of meaning and the existence of multiple possible configurations through which social order may be constituted (Luhmann, 1995a).

The stabilization of communication under conditions of contingency becomes analytically visible through Luhmann's concept of **double contingency**. Communication presupposes that each participant forms expectations not only about the actions of others but also about how others will interpret and respond to their own communicative contributions. This recursive orientation of expectations creates the conditions under which coordinated interaction becomes possible despite uncertainty. Consequently, social order emerges through the stabilization of expectations about expectations rather than through normative consensus (Luhmann, 1995a; Simon, 2010).

Within this framework, psychic and social systems are conceived as analytically distinct autopoietic systems. Psychic systems reproduce consciousness, whereas social systems reproduce communication. Individuals therefore do not constitute elements of social systems; rather, they belong to their environment. Despite this analytical distinction, the two systems remain structurally coupled, allowing reciprocal influence while preserving their respective operational closure (Luhmann, 1995b).

Structural coupling explains how operationally autonomous systems become mutually responsive without compromising their autonomy. Although psychic and social systems remain operationally closed, recurrent irritations enable each system to respond selectively to changes occurring in the other. Through this mechanism, social systems process environmental complexity while maintaining their own communicative logic.

From Luhmann's perspective, communication is constituted through the synthesis of three inseparable selections: information, utterance, and understanding. These selections do not occur as successive stages but form a single communicative event in which meaning emerges through their simultaneous integration. Communication is therefore inherently recursive, since every communicative operation establishes the conditions for subsequent communication (Luhmann, 1995a; Willke, 1996). Through this recursive reproduction, social systems maintain their autopoietic character. Society does not exist independently of communication; rather, it is continuously reproduced through ongoing communicative operations. Each communicative event simultaneously reproduces the very system that makes further communication possible.

Modern society is characterized by functional differentiation; whereby autonomous social subsystems operate according to internally specific communicative codes. Systems such as education, law, politics, science, and the economy reproduce themselves through binary distinctions that determine what counts as meaningful communication within their respective domains (Luhmann, 2003a). These communicative codes enable each subsystem to process complexity according to its own operational logic without requiring hierarchical coordination. Functional differentiation therefore replaces hierarchical forms of social integration with systemic specialization. Although individuals participate across multiple subsystems, they do not constitute their operations. Instead, each subsystem observes society from its own communicative perspective.

In summary, Luhmann's theory conceptualizes society as an autopoietic communication system that continuously reproduces itself through recursive meaning-making operations. Within this theoretical framework, communication, operational closure, the system–environment distinction, complexity, contingency, double contingency, structural coupling, and functional differentiation constitute the core analytical principles through which social systems reproduce their identity while processing environmental complexity. Complexity thus occupies a central position in systems theory, as it defines both the conditions and the limits of systemic reproduction. Building upon this premise, the following section examines complexity as a constitutive condition of social systems and explores its analytical significance for understanding organizational systems and organizational learning.

2.2 Complexity as a Constitutive Condition of Social Systems

Complexity constitutes a fundamental category in the systemic analysis of social phenomena. It refers to the surplus of possible relations within a system that exceeds its capacity for simultaneous actualization, thereby requiring continuous selective operations for system reproduction (Luhmann, 1995a). From this perspective, complexity is not defined by the number of elements, but by the structured multiplicity of relations that must be selectively processed in order for communication to continue.

Within the cybernetic tradition, complexity is understood less as a quantitative magnitude and more as relational density, where system behavior emerges from patterns of interconnection rather than from isolated elements (Magklaras, 2013; Wiener, 1948). Contemporary systems theory reinforces this view by emphasizing the non-reducibility of social phenomena to linear causal sequences (Jacobson & Wilensky, 2006). Social systems operate as networks of interdependent relations whose emergent properties cannot be derived from their individual components (Ramage & Shipp, 2009). Complexity, therefore, is intrinsically linked to emergence, insofar as systemic wholes exhibit properties that are not reducible to their parts.

In Luhmann's systems theory, complexity is structurally generated through the distinction between system and environment. The environment functions as a horizon of excess possibilities from which the system must select those relations that can be meaningfully processed (Luhmann, 1995b). Selection is therefore not an optional strategy but a constitutive condition of system reproduction. Each selection stabilizes meaning while simultaneously excluding alternative possibilities, thereby producing contingency as a structural feature of social reality (Willke, 1996). In this sense, contingency refers not to randomness but to the inherent openness of meaning within social systems. Social systems operate under conditions of nonlinearity, where interactions generate emergent effects that cannot be traced back to individual components. This nonlinearity reduces predictability and reinforces the necessity of selective processing as a structural requirement of communication (Flake, 1998 in Kodakos & Angelakou, 2017; Karsten, 2004).

Willke (1996) conceptualizes complexity as a structured, multidimensional phenomenon composed of five interrelated dimensions: objective, social, temporal, operative, and cognitive. These dimensions do not represent separate levels of reality but rather analytically distinct modes through which social systems process complexity and stabilize their operations.

- **The objective dimension** refers to the increasing variety of elements and relations within a system, where complexity intensifies as the number of possible interconnections expands, increasing the density of systemic interdependence within a given spatiotemporal context.
- **The social dimension** concerns functional differentiation and role specialization, which do not reduce complexity but instead increase it by multiplying interdependencies between roles and functions, since each function becomes dependent on the coordinated operation of others, thereby increasing demands for communication and coordination.
- **The temporal dimension** relates to the management of uncertainty through memory, expectation, and planning, whereby social systems stabilize "future presents" by selecting specific expectations and reducing the horizon of alternative futures, making temporal synchronization essential for communicative continuity.
- **The operative dimension** refers to the system's capacity for self-reorganization, whereby complexity becomes not only an external condition but also an internal resource enabling systems to modify their own structures, goals, and procedures through reflexive operations, thus underpinning their relative autonomy.
- **The cognitive dimension** represents the most advanced level of complexity, as it involves second-order observation, namely the observation of how

meaning is produced. Knowledge does not merely represent reality but actively contributes to its construction, while also transforming environmental complexity into processable information (Deutsch, 1969, in Willke, 1996) and translating it into action strategies (Etzioni, 1975, in Willke, 1996). This dimension therefore strengthens the system's capacity for self-reflexivity and self-thematization.

The strengthening of the cognitive dimension creates the conditions for a transition from functional adaptation to organizational learning. Within this framework, knowledge becomes embedded in communicative and institutional structures that enable continuous self-observation and the stabilization of operations. Organizational learning is therefore not limited to error correction or incremental adaptation, but extends to the transformation of the decision premises that structure organizational behavior (Argyris & Schön, 1978; Luhmann, 2018). Learning acquires a second-order character insofar as it concerns not only actions themselves, but also the conditions under which actions become possible (Willke, 2007). From this perspective, complexity is not merely a descriptive attribute of social systems but a constitutive condition that shapes how systems process information and stabilize their selections. The management of complexity requires the reflexive restructuring of decision-making frameworks. Within this analytical trajectory, organizational learning emerges as the key mechanism through which social systems process complexity at the level of decision premises. The following section therefore examines organizational learning as a second-order process that enables the restructuring of organizational decision structures and the stabilization of system operations under conditions of complexity.

2.3 Organizational Learning as a Mechanism for Processing Complexity and Restructuring Decision Premises

Building upon the systemic understanding of complexity developed in the preceding section, organizational learning may be understood as the primary mechanism through which organizations process experience, reduce uncertainty, and continuously reconstruct their internal structures under changing environmental conditions (Luhmann, 1995a; Weick, 1995). Through learning, experience is transformed into relatively stable yet continuously revisable forms of organizational knowledge that guide future decisions and actions (Argyris & Schön, 1978). From this perspective, organizations are conceived not as static structures of coordination but as communicative systems capable of processing information, making decisions, solving problems, and reorganizing their operations in response to environmental complexity (March & Simon, 1963; Simon, 1953, in Bouvier, 2013). Consequently, analytical attention shifts from the formal characteristics of organizational structures to the dynamic mechanisms through which decision-making capacities are maintained, revised, and continuously reconstructed.

The theoretical development of organizational learning has followed two principal trajectories. The first, associated primarily with Cyert and March(1963) and March and Simon (1993), conceptualizes learning as an adaptive process grounded in feedback mechanisms and in the comparison between expected and actual outcomes. Within this perspective, discrepancies are reduced by modifying organizational actions while leaving the underlying assumptions, values, and institutional arrangements largely unchanged. Organizational change therefore remains predominantly corrective, operating within established frameworks of action and decision-making rather than transforming the assumptions upon which they are based.

A more substantial theoretical shift was introduced by Argyris and Schön (1978), who reconceptualized organizational learning as a reflexive process directed not only toward organizational actions but also toward the assumptions that make those actions possible. Learning thus extends beyond error correction to encompass the critical examination of the cognitive and normative frameworks that organize organizational behavior. The knowledge generated through this reflexive activity does not remain at the individual level but gradually becomes institutionalized within organizational routines, rules, and communicative practices, thereby acquiring structural and normative significance. Organizational routines function simultaneously as repositories of accumulated experience and as mechanisms through which environmental complexity is selectively processed (Cyert & March, 1963). Learning should therefore be understood not as the simple accumulation of knowledge but as an ongoing organizational dynamic through which experience becomes structurally embedded and continuously shapes future organizational operations (Argyris & Schön, 1978; Dixon, 1994).

From a systems-theoretical perspective, this understanding acquires additional significance because organizations operate under conditions of irreducible complexity. As discussed in the previous section, complexity emerges from a surplus of possible relations that exceeds the system's capacity for complete processing, making selective operations indispensable for organizational continuity (Luhmann, 1995b). Learning extends these selective operations beyond immediate adaptation. Through recursive feedback, organizations not only modify their responses to environmental changes but also reconsider the criteria by which those changes are interpreted, evaluated, and incorporated into subsequent decisions (Argyris & Schön, 1978; March, 1991). In this respect, learning performs a dual function. It contributes to the stabilization of organizational action by reducing uncertainty while simultaneously enabling the revision of the interpretive frameworks within which decisions are generated. Consequently, organizations enhance their capacity to process complexity reflexively and to reorganize their own structures of meaning (Luhmann, 1995a; Weick, 1995).

The distinction between single-loop and double-loop learning reflects this dual function. In single-loop learning, discrepancies are corrected within existing rules, routines, and operational assumptions without questioning the broader framework that governs organizational behavior (Argyris, 1999). Learning therefore contributes to organizational stability by improving performance while leaving established decision premises unchanged. By contrast, double-loop learning involves the critical examination and transformation of the governing variables that shape organizational action, including underlying values, assumptions, norms, and interpretive frameworks (Argyris & Schön, 1978; Pedler et al., 1997). Rather than merely refining existing practices, it restructures the cognitive and normative conditions through which organizational decisions are produced. From a systems-theoretical perspective, such transformation represents not simply a change in organizational behavior but a revision of the communicative structures through which organizational meaning is generated and stabilized.

The transformative potential of learning becomes even more apparent when it is examined across different analytical levels. Rather than being confined to a single locus of activity, it develops through dynamic interactions between individual, collective, and organizational processes, allowing knowledge generated at one level to be interpreted, institutionalized, and reconstructed at another (Sun & Scott, 2003, in Kodakos et al., 2017). This multilevel perspective demonstrates that learning is an emergent systemic phenomenon rather than the simple aggregation of individual learning outcomes. At the individual level, learning refers to changes in knowledge, competencies, and behavior emerging through experience (Bigge, 1990; Gagné, 1975). At the collective level, it is constituted through collaborative practices, shared interpretations, and communicative interactions that gradually establish common frameworks for coordinated action (Lave & Wenger, 1991; Marquardt, 1996). At the organizational level, these shared understandings become embedded within formal structures, routines, procedures, and decision premises that transcend individual actors and acquire institutional continuity (Senge, 1990). Learning thus becomes progressively stabilized through organizational communication rather than remaining dependent upon individual knowledge alone.

Collectively, these multilevel dynamics illustrate how knowledge gradually acquires organizational status. Rather than being transferred linearly from individuals to organizations, it becomes institutionalized through communicative processes of interpretation, negotiation, diffusion, and stabilization that transform individual experience into collectively shared orientations for action (Nonaka & Takeuchi, 1995). Organizational learning therefore constitutes a continuous dynamic of systemic transformation through which shared meanings are generated, coordinated action is strengthened, and operational coherence is maintained under conditions of uncertainty and environmental change (Geissler, 1995).

From this perspective, the significance of organizational learning extends beyond improving organizational effectiveness. It is closely associated with the capacity of organizations to stabilize decision-making under conditions of increasing complexity and uncertainty (Cyert & March, 1963; March, 1991). Learning contributes not only to reducing uncertainty but also to transforming the interpretive frameworks through which uncertainty itself is recognized, evaluated, and processed (Senge, 1990). It therefore exceeds the character of a purely adaptive mechanism and assumes the form of a structural organizational function through which communicative systems continuously reproduce, revise, and reorganize the conditions of their own operation.

Nevertheless, the capacity to revise organizational decisions does not exhaust the developmental potential of organizational learning. Organizations may also develop the ability to reflect upon the very mechanisms through which learning, observation, and decision-making are organized. At this point, learning extends beyond the revision of organizational practices toward the examination of the conditions that make those practices possible. The object of reflection is no longer organizational action itself but the communicative frameworks through which observation, interpretation, learning, and decision-making are constituted (Luhmann, 1995b; Willke, 2007).

This transition marks the movement from organizational learning to organizational meta-learning. Whereas organizational learning primarily concerns the restructuring of organizational actions and decision premises, meta-learning focuses on the reflexive reconstruction of the cognitive and communicative conditions through which organizational decision premises are continuously produced, reproduced, and transformed. By shifting the focus from organizational adaptation to the observation of learning itself, meta-learning strengthens the organization's capacity for second-order observation, reflexive decision-making, and the continuous processing of complexity. The following section therefore examines meta-learning as the second-order organizational mechanism through which organizations reconstruct the frameworks of observation and decision-making that regulate their ongoing operations.

2.4 Meta-Learning as a Mechanism of Reflexive Regulation in Organizational Learning

Meta-learning (deutero-learning or, in certain theoretical traditions, triple-loop learning) refers to a form of second-order reflexivity through which organizational systems become capable of reflecting not only on their practices and assumptions but also on the communicative and cognitive frameworks that define what counts as knowledge, learning, and legitimate organizational action (Argyris & Schön, 1978; Flood & Romm, 1996). At this level, learning is no longer restricted to the modification of organizational action but extends to the reconfiguration of the conditions that render action meaningful and cognitively accessible (Weick, 1995). The differentiation of learning levels highlights the distinction between first-order and second-order learning processes. Whereas first-order learning primarily concerns behavioral adjustment, second-order learning introduces reflexive examination of the interpretive schemes through which experience acquires meaning in the first place (Argyris & Schön, 1978). Consequently, organizational learning presupposes relatively stabilized cognitive schemas that orient collective attention and define the relevance structures through which information is interpreted and processed (Walsh & Ungson, 1991; Weick, 1995).

Organizational knowledge should not be understood as a static repository of information. Rather, it emerges as a dynamic configuration of shared interpretations embedded within communicative routines, institutional practices, and stabilized patterns of interaction (Walsh & Ungson, 1991; Nonaka & Takeuchi, 1995; Nitschke, 2024). The transformation of experience into organizational knowledge is therefore understood as a process of collective sense-making through which meaning is communicatively stabilized, negotiated, and continuously reproduced over time (Davenport & Prusak, 2000; Tsoukas, 2005).

From a systems-theoretical perspective, Niklas Luhmann's theory of social systems redirects analytical attention from the substantive content of knowledge to the communicative conditions governing its production. Social systems generate meaning through recursive communication while simultaneously reducing environmental complexity through selective operations (Luhmann, 1995a). Learning presupposes this logic of selection, since every act of meaning production necessarily excludes alternative possibilities. Within this framework, decision premises—understood as stabilized expectations that guide organizational selections—define the boundaries within which communication, interpretation, and decision-making occur. Meta-learning concerns the reflexive reorganization of these premises rather than individual decisions themselves, focusing on the conditions that render organizational decisions possible, recognizable, and legitimate (Willke, 2007).

The concept of second-order observation further extends this perspective, referring to the capacity of a system to observe the distinctions and interpretive schemas through which it observes itself (Luhmann, 1995c). Applied to organizations, this implies the ability to reflect upon the criteria through which knowledge is validated and particular forms of organizational action become legitimate (Luhmann, 1995a; Weick, 1995). Meta-learning therefore should not be understood merely as an additional level of learning. Rather, it functions as a mechanism that reorganizes the conditions under which different forms of learning emerge, operate, and evolve (Argyris & Schön, 1978; Flood & Romm, 1996). From this perspective, meta-learning also performs a coordinating function between single-loop and double-loop learning. It shapes whether organizational deviations are treated as operational problems requiring corrective adjustments within existing structures or as indications that governing assumptions themselves require revision (Argyris & Schön, 1978; Kim & Callahan, 2013). Such reflexive coordination presupposes shared interpretive frameworks that enable collective meaning-making and the communicative processing of organizational experience (Tsoukas, 2005; Weick, 1995).

In the organizational learning literature, meta-learning is closely associated with organizational reflexivity and meta-level supervision, both of which extend reflection beyond experience itself to encompass the mechanisms through which learning is organized (Isaacs, 1993; Sun & Scott, 2003). Unlike knowledge-management approaches, meta-learning does not primarily focus on optimizing information flows. Rather, it concerns the reconfiguration of the communicative conditions through which knowledge acquires validity and organizational action becomes legitimate (Davenport & Prusak, 2000; Tsoukas, 2005). Under conditions of increasing complexity, organizational stability depends not only upon adaptation to environmental change but also upon the capacity to reorganize the interpretive structures through which complexity is perceived, interpreted, and processed (Vogus & Sutcliffe, 2007; Weick, 1995; Willke, 2007). From this perspective, organizational resilience emerges as a second-order systemic property grounded in the organization's capacity to transform its own mechanisms of self-observation, communicative self-description, and reflexive regulation (Luhmann, 1995b).

Meta-learning thus constitutes the highest level of reflexive regulation within organizational learning. Rather than merely supporting organizational adaptation, it enables social systems to reconstruct the communicative conditions under which knowledge, learning, and decision-making are produced and stabilized. In doing so, it strengthens the system's capacity for reflexive self-regulation, organizational resilience, and the continuous reproduction of organizational operations under conditions of uncertainty and environmental complexity.

3. THE SCHOOL UNIT CONTEXT AND SYSTEMS MODELING

3.1 The School Unit as a Field of Application of the Systems Approach

The systems approach conceptualizes the school unit as an open social system whose organizational functioning emerges through the continuous interaction between its internal structures and the broader social environment (Kodakos, 2010). Rather than constituting a closed administrative entity, the school unit operates as a complex organizational system in which educational reality is continuously produced and reproduced through communication, relationships, and organizational practices (Matsaggouras, 2007). Consequently, school organization is understood not as a static institutional structure but as a dynamic configuration of interdependent structures, processes, and relational patterns that continuously evolve under the influence of both internal and external conditions (Kodakos & Angelakou, 2016).

At the macro-systemic level, the school unit is embedded within a multilayered network of social systems, functioning simultaneously as a subsystem of the educational system and as an autonomous organizational entity (Kodakos & Angelakou, 2016). Its relationship with the environment is neither linear nor deterministic but characterized by dynamic interdependence and reciprocal influence. External demands are not mechanically incorporated into the organization. Rather, they are selectively interpreted and transformed through the school's internal structures, interpretive processes, and organizational logic, highlighting the active role of the school unit in shaping the conditions of its own operation (Kalavasis, 2013). In this respect, the school unit functions as an active mechanism for processing environmental complexity rather than as a passive recipient of external influences.

At the organizational level, the school unit may initially be approached as a system that transforms inputs into outputs. Inputs include human, material, financial, and informational resources that constitute the operational basis of the organization. Through internal processes of organization, coordination, and resource management, these inputs are transformed into educational outcomes extending beyond cognitive achievement to include the development of attitudes, values, and social competencies (Pashiardis, 2004, in Kodakos & Angelakou, 2016). Feedback mechanisms further support this process by facilitating continuous adaptation, self-regulation, and organizational adjustment in response to changing environmental conditions (Lunenburg, 2010).

Although the input–output perspective provides a useful analytical representation of organizational functioning, it remains insufficient for explaining how schools process meaning, uncertainty, and organizational complexity. For this reason, the present study adopts Luhmann's systems-theoretical perspective, which shifts analytical attention from the input–output logic to the communicative constitution and reproduction of social systems. Within this framework, the school unit is understood as an operationally closed communicative system whose fundamental element is neither action, behavior, nor resources, but communication itself. Communication constitutes the process through which organizational meaning is generated, relationships are reproduced, expectations are stabilized, and organizational structures are continuously reconstructed (Luhmann, 2003b). Consequently, school organization is constituted not primarily through administrative regulations but through recursive communicative processes that continuously produce and reproduce organizational meaning (Angelakou, 2019).

Within this framework, the relationship between the school unit and its environment is interpreted through the concept of structural coupling. The environment does not directly determine organizational functioning but operates as a source of perturbations that the system selectively processes according to its internally generated structures, symbolic codes, and distinctions (Luhmann, 2003a). Consequently, the school unit does not passively reflect external reality but actively constructs its own organizational interpretations and forms of meaning-making. Environmental complexity acquires significance only insofar as it becomes available for internal communicative processing (Qvortrup, 2005). Accordingly, organizational adaptation is understood not as a direct response to environmental demands but as an internally regulated process of communicative reconstruction.

At the level of internal organization, the school unit is constituted through differentiated roles, interactional processes, and communicative relationships, while organizational coherence derives from the functional interdependence of its constituent elements rather than from their homogeneity (Brinia, 2008; Kotsikis, 2003). Such differentiation inevitably increases organizational complexity, making communication and coordination indispensable conditions for maintaining organizational coherence. Systemic stability is therefore sustained through loosely coupled structures that simultaneously preserve organizational continuity while allowing adaptation to changing conditions (Simon, 2010). Internal complexity is consequently understood not as a dysfunctional condition but as a productive characteristic that enables the continuous reorganization of the school through the interaction between organizational and individual factors (Kodakos, 2010; Marzano, 2003). Complexity thus strengthens the adaptive, learning, and developmental capacities of the school organization.

A central dimension of the Luhmannian perspective lies in conceptualizing the school unit as a self-referential and autopoietic communicative system. Self-reference denotes the system's capacity to process information according to its own internally generated structures and distinctions, whereas autopoiesis refers to the continuous reproduction of the system through communication (Luhmann, 2003a; Qvortrup, 2005). This operation is accompanied by processes of self-observation through which the organization reflects upon its own communicative practices, evaluates its operations, and manages organizational complexity while preserving its systemic identity (Tasis, 2012). From this perspective, the school unit emerges as an evolving communicative system capable of continuously restructuring its communicative structures and organizational practices in response to environmental complexity (Angelakou, 2021).

Conceptualizing the school unit as an autopoietic communicative system shifts analytical attention from organizational structure to organizational learning. Within this perspective, learning is understood as the reflexive mechanism through which schools reconstruct their communicative structures, process environmental complexity, and strengthen their capacity for organizational development and resilience (Angelakou, 2018). The following section therefore examines the school unit as a learning organization and explores the role of organizational learning in processes of school development.

3.2 The School Unit as a Self-Referential System of Organizational Learning and Collective Intelligence

The conceptualization of the school unit as a learning organization is situated within the broader theoretical framework of organizational learning and systems theory, according to which organizations are understood not as static bureaucratic structures but as dynamic systems of knowledge production, communication, and decision-making (Argyris & Schön, 1978; Luhmann, 1995b; Senge, 1990). Within this epistemological perspective, the school unit is not approached merely as a mechanism for implementing externally prescribed educational policies; rather, it is understood as a self-referential organizational system that selectively processes environmental complexity through internal processes of communication, reflexivity, and meaning construction (Luhmann, 1995a; Willke, 1996). Consequently, the school unit's organizational functioning depends upon its capacity to transform experience into organizational knowledge and to embed such knowledge within stabilized yet continuously revisable structures of communication and decision-making (Argyris & Schön, 1978; Senge, 1990, in Kodakos & Angelakou, 2017).

Within this framework, the school unit constitutes a learning organization when the experience generated through everyday pedagogical, administrative, and social interactions does not remain fragmented or individually confined but is transformed into organizational knowledge that becomes embedded within routines, decision-making processes, and communicative structures (Huber, 1991; Nonaka & Takeuchi, 1995). Learning thus acquires an institutional and communicative character, transcending individual cognitive processes and becoming part of the organization's ongoing production and reproduction of meaning. In this sense, the school unit is not merely an organization that facilitates the learning of its members, but an organization that itself learns as a collective organizational entity (Bouvier, 2013, in Angelakou, 2018).

The constitution of the school unit as a learning organization presupposes the dynamic interconnection of individual, collective, and organizational forms of learning, allowing experience to acquire continuity and normative force through processes of communication, collaboration, and reflexivity (Sun & Scott, 2003). Professional learning communities, collaborative forms of experiential processing, and reflective professional practices function as mechanisms through which knowledge ceases to remain an individual cognitive resource and becomes an organizational capability for coordinated action (DuFour & Eaker, 1998; Wenger, 1998). Through these communicative processes, the organization develops forms of collective intelligence, understood as the capacity of its members to co-construct shared understandings and coordinated patterns of action (Georgiou, 2000, in Kodakos & Angelakou, 2017).

At this point, organizational memory acquires particular significance, as it is constituted through institutionalized practices, roles, procedures, cultural expectations, and communicative norms that stabilize experience and orient future organizational action (Hedberg, 1981; Walsh & Ungson, 1991). Organizational memory does not function as a passive repository of information; rather, it constitutes an active framework through which organizational experience is selectively interpreted, reconstructed, and incorporated into future decision-making, thereby shaping the organization's capacities for observation, communication, and meaning production (Hedberg, 1981; Walsh & Ungson, 1991; Weick, 1995). Through these processes, the school unit preserves organizational continuity while simultaneously acquiring the capacity to revise its practices under conditions of uncertainty and increasing environmental complexity (Luhmann, 1995b).

This dynamic is closely associated with double-loop learning, through which learning extends beyond the correction of organizational actions to the critical reconsideration of the assumptions, values, and organizational logics that guide those actions (Argyris & Schön, 1978). Within the school unit, double-loop learning becomes evident when professional communities critically examine not only teaching and administrative practices but also the interpretive frameworks through which educational reality itself is understood. Such reflexive processes enable the restructuring of organizational decision premises and strengthen the school unit's capacity for endogenous adaptation, organizational learning, and systemic resilience (Pedler et al., 1997; Senge, 1990).

The transition from a learning school unit to an *intelligent school* unit represents a qualitative advancement in organizational learning. This transition concerns the organization's capacity to reflect not only upon what it knows, but also upon the communicative processes through which knowledge is produced, organized, and utilized (Angelakou, 2018). From this perspective, organizational intelligence emerges not as the aggregate of the individual cognitive capacities of organizational members but as a systemic property arising from the coordinated processing of experience, the development of mechanisms of self-observation, and the strategic management of organizational knowledge (Marquardt, 1996; Willke, 1996).

The intelligent school unit is therefore constituted as a communicative system endowed with an enhanced capacity to understand both its internal operations and its relationship with the external environment (Kodakos & Angelakou, 2017). This capability is manifested through the school unit's ability to process uncertainty strategically, reconstruct its organizational structures reflexively, and collectively manage knowledge under changing environmental conditions (Willke, 1996). The school organization is no longer confined to the accumulation of experience; rather, it develops capacities for meta-observation and communicative self-regulation that enable it to redefine the conditions under which its own operations are organized (Bouvier, 2013; Willke, 2007). These capacities are closely associated with the development of collective intelligence, transcending the individual abilities of organizational members (Georgiou, 2000, in Angelakou, 2018).

Simultaneously, the intelligent school unit is characterized by the cultivation of communicative and organizational conditions that reinforce collaboration, reflexivity, and the collective production of knowledge. Professional trust, participatory decision-making, systematic feedback, experimentation, and continuous interaction with the external environment function as essential conditions for the development of organizational learning and self-regulation (Bryk & Schneider, 2002; Collinson et al., 2006; Marsick & Watkins, 2003). Likewise, collaborative cultures, knowledge-sharing practices, support for experimentation and calculated risk-taking, together with participatory and heterarchical forms of organization, expand the school's capacity for collective learning and organizational innovation (Fullan, 1996; Stoll & Fink, 1996; Sutton & Shouse, 2016). Under these conditions, school culture no longer functions exclusively as a mechanism for preserving organizational stability but becomes a dynamic context for the communicative processing of experience and the continuous reconstruction of organizational practices (Schein, 2010).

This systemic capacity is explicitly captured in the typology proposed by MacGilchrist, Myers, and Reed (2004, in Angelakou, 2018), according to which the intelligent school unit is constituted through interdependent forms of intelligence, including moral, emotional, reflective, collective, pedagogical, and systemic intelligence. Systemic intelligence assumes particular significance because it enables the school unit to develop systems thinking, self-organizing capacities, and networking mechanisms that strengthen coherence between organizational vision, strategic action, and collective learning. Through these processes, the school organization acquires the capacity to evaluate its own functioning, develop multidimensional understandings of organizational reality, and strategically redefine its future orientations (Luhmann, 1995b; Willke, 2007).

However, this evolutionary process is neither linear nor free from constraints. Organizations tend to develop stabilizing mechanisms, including defensive routines, rigid interpretive schemes, and standardized communicative patterns, which may restrict reflexive problem processing and reproduce established organizational logics (Argyris, 1999). Within school organizations, such mechanisms may reinforce bureaucratic conformity and constrain the development of more advanced forms of organizational learning, self-regulation, and collective intelligence. Consequently, the development of learning and intelligent school organizations presupposes institutional and communicative conditions that strengthen trust, collaboration, reflexive inquiry, and the collective processing of organizational experience (Bryk & Schneider, 2002; Hoy & Tschannen-Moran, 1999; Senge, 1990; Wenger, 1998;).

The school unit thus emerges as a systemically constituted knowledge organization that does not merely reproduce educational functions but continuously develops capacities for self-observation, organizational learning, and organizational transformation (Luhmann, 1995b; Willke, 2007). Organizational learning, collective knowledge production, communicative reflexivity, and organizational intelligence constitute complementary organizational functions through which the school unit processes environmental complexity, reconstructs its decision premises, and strengthens its systemic resilience (Argyris & Schön, 1978; Bouvier, 2013; Senge, 1990).

From this perspective, School Development cannot be conceptualized as a linear process of administrative or functional improvement but rather as a systemic process through which school organizations continuously reconstruct their communicative, cognitive, and organizational conditions. This perspective provides the theoretical foundation for examining the institutional mechanisms that support such reflexive organizational development, particularly self-evaluation, self-diagnostic inquiry, and school counseling within the contemporary Greek educational context (Dalin, 1998; MacBeath et al., 2005; Rolff, 2013; Schratz, 1993).

3.3 The Greek School Unit Between Bureaucratic Structuring and School Development

The operation of the school unit under conditions of increasing social and educational complexity renders the limitations of traditional bureaucratic forms of administration increasingly visible and foregrounds school development as a process of organizational transformation. Accelerated developments in science, technology, the economy, and broader social structures continuously reshape the operational environment of educational organizations, generating heightened uncertainty, functional differentiation, and environmental complexity that static and rule-oriented administrative models are unable to manage effectively (Fullan, 2020). Under these conditions, the school unit is required to develop mechanisms of organizational learning, reflexive adaptation, and the processing of environmental complexity in order to respond creatively to evolving educational demands (Qvortrup, 2005). This development necessitates a reconsideration of traditional conceptions of school organization and administration.

The effectiveness of school organizations no longer depends exclusively on administrative control or compliance with centrally prescribed regulations, but increasingly on their capacity to generate organizational learning, critically reflect upon organizational experience, and continuously reconstruct their decision-making processes in response to environmental complexity (Senge, 1990). Within this perspective, the school unit cannot be understood merely as a bureaucratic mechanism for implementing centrally designed educational policies, but rather as a communicative organization that develops internal capacities for collaboration, reflexive communication, and collective knowledge construction (Kodakos & Angelakou, 2016). Contemporary theories of school development therefore move beyond mechanistic and macro-administrative conceptions of schooling toward systemic and micropolitical perspectives that conceptualize the school unit as a relatively autonomous organizational system characterized by internal differentiation and the capacity for endogenous transformation (Dalin, 1998; Rolff, 1993). This theoretical shift reflects the growing need for school organizations to process environmental complexity through organizational learning and reflexive communication rather than through hierarchical regulation alone (Senge, 1990; Willke, 1996).

Within the Greek educational context, however, the development of such organizational autonomy remains significantly constrained by the historically centralized and bureaucratic structure of educational governance (Athanasoula-Reppa et al., 2008). Fundamental educational decisions are formulated at the central administrative level and transmitted to school units as binding regulations that substantially delimit the scope of local organizational discretion. Consequently, the school unit operates primarily as an implementing body for centrally determined educational policies rather than as an organization capable of generating autonomous organizational responses to its own educational conditions. Its operation therefore remains predominantly executive and administratively regulated, limiting opportunities for organizational learning, reflexive self-regulation, and endogenous organizational development (Kodakos & Angelakou, 2016).

This institutional configuration generates a persistent asymmetry between the formulation and implementation of educational reforms. Although reform initiatives frequently adopt, at the rhetorical level, principles such as school development, innovation, and school autonomy, their implementation commonly relies upon standardized administrative procedures that inadequately incorporate the specific needs, experiences, and organizational cultures of individual school units (Angelakou, 2018). Consequently, educational reforms often remain at the level of formal compliance without substantially transforming communicative structures, organizational routines, or the decision premises through which school organizations interpret and respond to educational challenges (Kodakos & Angelakou, 2016).

The predominance of centralized administrative regulation further reinforces bureaucratic stabilization within school organizations. The legislative and organizational framework of the Greek educational system predetermines significant aspects of school culture, organizational structures, and administrative practices

(Kodakos & Kioussi, 2009). Under such conditions, educational complexity is not transformed through internal organizational learning but rather reduced through standardized regulation and centralized administrative control (Luhmann, 1995b; Qvortrup, 2005). As a result, school units encounter considerable difficulty functioning as learning organizations capable of reflexively utilizing experience, generating collective intelligence, and strengthening their adaptive capacity under conditions of continuous change (Senge, 1990; Willke, 1996). This situation is further reinforced by the fragmented character of educational reforms and the strong influence of external policy actors, including European educational initiatives, international policy agendas, and successive governmental changes (Athanasoula-Reppa et al., 2008; Kodakos & Angelakou, 2016). Educational reforms are therefore frequently experienced as externally imposed requirements rather than as outcomes of internal organizational reflection and collective meaning-making (Angelakou, 2018). Consequently, opportunities for organizational learning and reflexive self-regulation remain limited, restricting the capacity of school organizations not only to improve their practices but also to critically reconsider the organizational assumptions and decision premises that shape their operation (Argyris & Schön, 1978).

This contradiction becomes particularly evident in contemporary policies concerning evaluation, self-evaluation, and school development. Although these policies formally introduce processes of reflection, planning, and collective evaluation, they are frequently incorporated into an already highly bureaucratic administrative framework that substantially limits their transformative potential. As a consequence, self-evaluation risks functioning primarily as a mechanism of accountability and administrative compliance rather than as a process supporting organizational learning, reflexive self-observation, and school development (Ball, 2003). School development, therefore, cannot be reduced to the implementation of technical or managerial improvement measures. Rather, it presupposes a more fundamental transformation of the organizational conditions under which school units operate (Harris & Jones, 2020; Fullan, 2020). Such transformation requires not only the introduction of new evaluation instruments but also the redesign of the communicative structures, collaborative practices, organizational routines, and decision premises through which schools produce, process, and utilize organizational knowledge (Datnow & Park, 2018; Hargreaves & O'Connor, 2018).

From this perspective, the principal challenge facing the Greek educational system extends beyond the more effective implementation of educational reforms. It concerns the creation of institutional and organizational conditions that enable school units to function as reflexive systems of organizational learning, self-regulation, and continuous development. Accordingly, strengthening functional autonomy, collaborative cultures, participatory decision-making, and organizational trust becomes a necessary precondition for enabling school units to develop systemic resilience, collective intelligence, and endogenous school development through continuous organizational learning and reflexive adaptation (Bryk & Schneider, 2002; Hoy & Tschannen-Moran, 1999; Willke, 1996;).

4. ORGANIZATIONS AS DECISION SYSTEMS: DECISION PREMISES IN NIKLAS LUHMANN'S THEORY

Regarding the introduction of new reform tools and a deeper redesign of the terms under which school units produce, process, and reproduce educational knowledge, Niklas Luhmann's organizational theory constitutes one of the most radical revisions of contemporary sociology of organizations, as it shifts the focus of analysis from the individual and action to the communicative processes that constitute social systems. Contrary to classical organizational theories, which perceive organizations as sets of people, roles, or power relations, Luhmann argues that organizations are not composed of persons but of communications and, more specifically, of decision communications (Luhmann, 2000c). This position is integrated into his general theoretical framework regarding autopoietic social systems, according to which social systems self-reproduce through their own operations, constantly producing the elements that constitute them (Maturana & Varela, 1980; Varela, 1979).

In this context, organizations constitute a distinct type of social system that reproduces itself through the linking of decisions to decisions. Organizational reality is not constituted by intentions or subjects, but by sequences of choices that make stability possible under conditions of uncertainty and complexity (Luhmann, 2005). The fundamental function of the organization is precisely the absorption of uncertainty through the institutionalization of communicative processes, which allow for the continuity of decision-making and the preservation of organizational cohesion.

This approach cannot be understood independently of Luhmann's general theory of social systems. He distinguishes three basic types of social systems: society, interaction systems, and organizations (Luhmann, 1992). Society constitutes the comprehensive social system, as it includes the total of all possible communications. Interaction systems are constituted through the physical presence of the participants, whereas organizations are constituted through decision communications. Contemporary society is characterized by functional differentiation; individual social subsystems—such as the economy, politics, law, science, or education—operate based on their own communicative codes and reproduce themselves self-referentially (Luhmann, 2012). Thus, the legal system operates with the code "legal/illegal," the economy with the code "payment/non-payment," and science with the code "truth/untruth." Organizations operate within these systems, translating their functional requirements into specific decision-making processes.

According to Luhmann, decisions are neither psychological acts nor products of individual will, but social communications. It is not the case that decisions are made first and then communicated; the decision itself is communication (Luhmann, 2000c). Consequently, it acquires a social existence only when it is integrated into the network of other decisions and becomes accepted as a basis for subsequent communications. The specificity of a decision lies in the fact that it simultaneously communicates both the selected option and the existence of alternative choices. Every decision declares that it could have been made differently. For this exact reason, decisions have an inherently paradoxical character (Luhmann, 2000c). On the one hand, they must appear binding and definitive; on the other hand, they are grounded in the existence of multiple possible alternatives.

This paradox renders decisions fragile forms of communication. In order to make them functionally manageable, organizations develop de-paradoxicalization mechanisms—that is, processes that obscure the contingency of choice and shift attention from the arbitrariness of the decision to the rationale or motivations accompanying it. A key mechanism of de-paradoxicalization is the personalization of the decision. Decisions are attributed to a "decision-maker," who is presented as a bearer of specialized knowledge or rational judgment (Luhmann, 2000c). As Becker and Haunschild (2003) point out, this process functions as an organizational fiction, since the decision appears as the result of individual intention rather than as a product of systemic communicative processes. The function of this fiction is not interpretive but legitimizing, as it allows the organization to continue the flow of decisions without questioning its own operational structure.

The concept that captures the structural operation of organizations in the most comprehensive way is that of "decision premises" (*Entscheidungsvoraussetzungen*). Influenced by H. Simon, Luhmann perceives organizational structures as products of previous decisions that determine the framework within which subsequent decisions are made (Luhmann, 2005; Simon, 1957). Decision premises do not constitute external constraints but internally produced forms of stabilization. Organizations themselves produce the conditions under which they operate and decide. The significance of this concept is fundamental because, without decision premises, every new decision would have to start from scratch. Organizations, however, survive precisely because they possess structures that reduce complexity and make certain choices more likely than others.

Luhmann distinguishes three basic types of decision premises: programs, communication channels, and personnel. Programmatic premises include rules, procedures, goals, and strategies that determine how decisions should be made (Luhmann, 2003c). Through these, organizations standardize their action and convert uncertainty into a repeatable process. Communication channels determine who can communicate with whom and in what manner. Hierarchy constitutes the most characteristic form of such a channel, without, however, exhausting the phenomenon, as informal communication networks also play an important role (March & Simon, 1958). Finally, personnel constitutes another critical decision premise, since decisions regarding hiring, promotion, or withdrawal determine the knowledge, values, and expectations integrated into organizational communication.

In his later works, Luhmann extends this concept by introducing the so-called "undecided" decision premises (Luhmann, 2000c). These are implicit structures that have not been explicitly institutionalized but nevertheless function as self-evident elements of organizational life. Organizational culture constitutes a prime example of such a premise. It consists of informal expectations, values, and shared assumptions that influence decision-making without appearing as direct decisions (Meyer & Rowan, 1977). Concurrently, cognitive routines—the ways in which an organization perceives its environment—function as sense-making schemata, that guide the categorization and interpretation of information (Weick, 1995). These undecided premises acquire particular importance because they operate invisibly, as self-evident mechanisms of stabilizing organizational reality.

The theory of decision premises is directly linked to the concept of uncertainty absorption, which Luhmann borrows from March and Simon (1958). Uncertainty absorption describes the process through which decisions render the reconsideration of previous uncertainties redundant. Every decision is based on a wealth of information, estimates, and potential consequences. Once made, however, subsequent decisions can take this for granted without needing to re-examine all the initial uncertainties (Luhmann, 2005). Organizational continuity becomes possible precisely because decisions function as stable premises for subsequent decisions. Without this process, organizations would collapse under the weight of complexity. Organizational stability, therefore, does not result from the elimination of uncertainty but from the capacity to manage it. Through programs, standardizations, communication channels, and cultural patterns, organizations convert uncertainty into stable forms of expectations. In this perspective, the critical question is not which decision is the "correct" one, but how the framework within which decisions become possible and functionally sustainable is organized.

Organizational change, whinin Luhmann's theoretical framework, is understood not as a product of complete control or strategic planning, but as an evolutionary process. Influenced by evolutionary approaches, Luhmann describes change through the interaction of three functions: variation, selection, and restabilization (Luhmann, 2000b). Variations occur when certain decisions deviate from established decision premises. These deviations function as potential innovations, which may either be rejected or integrated into organizational structures. Selection concerns the positive or negative acceptance of these deviations, whereas restabilization entails integrating these changes into the current network of expectations and communications. Change, therefore, is not completed with the appearance of a new structure; its functional stabilization within the system itself is required. This approach leads to a non-linear understanding of organizational change. Organizations do not change because they consciously decide to do so, but because the very premises that determine what can be decided are transformed. Planning and management are thus components of a broader evolutionary process that always remains inherently open to contingency and randomness (Seidl, 2005b). From this point of view, organizations appear as dynamic, self-referential systems that survive not by eliminating complexity, but by managing the uncertainties generated by their own environment (Roth, 2011).

Despite its significant influence, Luhmann's theory has received extensive criticism. A primary critique concerns the transfer of the concept of autopoiesis from biology to social theory. Researchers such as Fuchs and Hofkirchner (2009) and Mingers (2002) argue that Luhmann departs significantly from the original biological meaning of the term without adequately specifying the causal mechanisms producing social elements. At the same time, the departure from human action has been considered excessively structuralist and anti-humanistic. The emphasis on communicative self-production, according to his critics, limits the theory's capacity to account for agency, conflict, and power (Habermas, 1987). Jürgen Habermas, in particular, criticized Luhmann for disconnecting social analysis from any normative or emancipatory perspective. Furthermore, the theory has been accused of offering limited scope for practical intervention and management. Since organizations are presented as self-referential systems that process every external influence according to their own logic, the possibility of direct control or transformation seems significantly limited (Martens & Ortmann, 2006). Proponents of the theory counter, however, that this emphasis does not invalidate the possibility of intervention but rather illuminates the inherent limits and difficulties of organizational control.

Despite these criticisms, Luhmann's organizational theory remains an exceptionally powerful interpretive tool for unpacking organizational complexity. The concept of decision premises offers a particularly fertile theoretical framework for studying stability, culture, and change. Through this lens, organizations do not appear as simple aggregations of individuals or roles, but as dynamic systems of communications that self-reproduce through the continuous linking of decisions to subsequent decisions. Organizational stability is not the product of consensus or absolute control, but the result of the system's capacity to absorb uncertainty and convert complexity into functionally manageable forms of communication.

5. FROM DECISION PREMISES TO SCHOOL CULTURE: ITS SYSTEMIC MODELING WITHIN THE FRAMEWORK OF THE SCHOOL AS AN AUTOPOIETIC ORGANIZATION

The theoretical analysis of decision premises in the previous chapter demonstrated that, in Niklas Luhmann's systems theory, organizations are not constituted by persons but by networks of communicatively linked decisions. These decisions self-reproduce through the continuous management of complexity and uncertainty (Luhmann, 1984, 1995d, 2000c). Decision premises—namely programs, communication channels, and personnel—form the foundational organizational structures that allow for the continuity of decisions and the stabilization of organizational expectations (Luhmann, 2003c; Seidl & Becker, 2006). However, their importance extents far beyond the functional arrangement of organizations. The continuous interaction of these premises produces repetitive patterns of meaning, communication, and behavior, which gradually acquire cultural stability and constitute what is defined as school culture. From this perspective, culture is neither an external characteristic of the school nor a simple sum of individual attitudes and values; rather it is an emergent communicative phenomenon produced through the operation of the school as an autopoietic system of decisions (Martens, 2006; Piekarczyk, 2017).

This systemic understanding differs fundamentally from classical anthropological and organizational conceptions of culture. Early approaches treated culture as a set of socially transmitted values, symbols, and meanings that constitute collective forms of life (Geertz, 1973; Kluckhohn, 2017). In organizational studies, culture was primarily linked to shared values, rituals, and behavioral patterns that shape organizational identity and cohesion (Deal & Kennedy, 1982; Wilkins & Ouchi, 1983). Particularly significant was the contribution of Edgar Schein, who defined organizational culture as the pattern of basic assumptions that a group develops as it learns to cope with problems of external adaptation and internal integration (Schein, 1985, 2010). Despite their seminal importance, these views remained largely anthropocentric, as they perceived culture as a property of subjects or as a form of collective consciousness.

Luhmann's theory radically shifts the analytical focus from individuals to communication. Organizations are not composed of people but of communicative processes, whereas individuals belong to the environment of the social system rather than to the system itself (Luhmann, 1995a; Seidl, 2005c). Culture, therefore, is not understood as a psychological characteristic of the members but as a form of communicative stabilization. It functions as a web of expectations, interpretive schemata, and meanings that enables decisions to connect with one another, thereby facilitating the reproduction of the organization (Luhmann, 1997, 2000c). In this sense, culture operates as an "undecided" decision premise—that is, as an implicit background that determines which communications are considered acceptable, logical, and legitimate within the organization (Laermans, 2007; Luhmann, 1995c).

The significance of this approach becomes particularly evident in school organizations. The school is not merely an administrative institution for knowledge transmission, but a complex communicative system in which stable forms of meanings regarding learning, teaching, behavior, assessment, and authority are forged (Kluchert, 2009; Maslowski, 2001). School culture is not a static "climate" existing independently of organizational processes; it emerges through the continuous interaction of decisions, communicative practices, and structures of expectations. Pedagogical practices, forms of collaboration, rituals, conflict-management methods, and relationships among teachers, students, and administration constitute a dynamic network of communications through which specific dimensions of organizational reality are stabilized (MacGilchrist et al., 2004; Moloi, 2010).

In this context, school culture can only be fully understood through the operation of decision premises. Programmatic decisions, communication channels, and personnel do not represent merely administrative dimensions of organizational operation, but mechanisms for the production and reproduction of meaning. Programs include the rules, procedures, pedagogical goals, and strategies that determine how decisions are made (Luhmann, 2003c). Through these, the school standardizes its operation and produces stable forms of pedagogical and organizational behavior. For instance, a school organized around participatory forms of learning and collaborative processes fosters a fundamentally different culture from one operating under strictly hierarchical and exam-centered patterns (Mortimore, 1993; Scheerens, 1992).

Communication channels constitute the second basic category of decision premises determining who communicates with whom, in what way, and under what conditions. In the school environment, the relationships among the administration, teachers, students, and parents structure the flow of communications and decisively shape school culture. Concurrently, informal networks of collaboration, relations of trust, and forms of professional solidarity acquire particular importance, functioning as mechanisms of cultural stabilization. School culture is therefore constituted not only through formal hierarchical structures but also through informal communicative practices developed in daily school life (March & Simon, 1958; Seidl & Mormann, 2015).

The third decision premise, personnel, holds unique significance. In Luhmannian theory, decisions regarding the selection, evaluation, transfer, and professional development of staff are not merely administrative processes but core mechanisms of cultural reproduction (Luhmann, 2003c). Personnel functions as the primary vehicle for integrating organizational expectations into the daily practice of the school. Through teachers, leadership dynamics, professional relationships, and socialization processes, organizational decisions are converted into living pedagogical practices and cultural forms of behaviors. Teachers transmit not only cognitive content but also interpretive schemata, values, forms of authority, and patterns of collaboration. Every new hire or change in personnel composition introduces potential variations into the school's communication system, which may either be absorbed by the existing culture or lead to its transformation (Seidl, 2005a, 2007). Thus, personnel emerges as perhaps the most critical decision premise for the production, maintenance, and evolution of school culture.

Understanding school culture as an emergent systemic phenomenon allows for its modeling through decision premises. Consequently, a "three-dimensional model for mapping and capturing school culture" is proposed, organized around three basic axes: programmatic decisions, forms of communication, and personnel. The choice of a three-dimensional modeling holds theoretical significance because it captures the dynamic and interdependent nature of culture. The three axes do not operate autonomously but exist in a continuous feedback loop (Kioussi, 2025). Changes in programmatic structures affect communicative practices and personnel relations; correspondingly, changes in personnel or communication formats can transform the pedagogical and organizational strategies of the school. Culture emerges precisely from this continuous circular interaction of decision premises (Kioussi, 2025).

The theoretical foundation of this model is linked to contemporary theories of dynamic,multi-level culture. The multi-level model of Erez and Gati (2004) treats culture as an evolving and interactive phenomenon organized across multiple levels—individual, team, organizational, and national—operating through bidirectional top-down and bottom-up processes. This approach harmonizes with the Luhmannian logic of self-reference and the circularity of communications, recognizing that changes at one level affect the overall macro-structure of the system. Concurrently, the modelling utilizes elements from the dynamic theory of organizational culture by Ghinea and Bratianu (2012), according to which culture constitutes a dynamic and interdependent system of meaning that continuously evolves through organizational interactions (Ghinea & Bratianu, 2012). In contrast to static typological approaches, the proposed systemic model does not attempt to classify schools into predetermined cultural types, but to decode the processes through which culture is produced, stabilized, and transformed. The connection of the model to Schein's three-level framework, which distinguishes organizational culture into artifacts, espoused values, and deeper basic assumptions- is also vital (Schein, 1985, 2010). The systemic approach reinterprets these levels communicatively: artifacts, values, and assumptions are not treated as individual psychological states but as stabilized forms of organizational communication reproduced through decision premises.

The culmination of the proposed modelling is captured in the concept of a "Universally Appropriate/Holistically Adequate Culture," which describes a school where decision premises are in a state of functional equilibrium and mutual reinforcement. In this ideal cultural form, programs are clear and pedagogically coherent, communicative relations are participatory and open, and the personnel operates with shared values, professional trust, and a collective orientation. The school is thus transformed into a "living, self-evolving, and autopoietic system," possessing an enhanced capacity for organizational learning, uncertainty absorption, and adaptation to environmental shifts. This approach redefines school change not as an external intervention, but as a transformation of the very decision premises that generate culture. Educational reforms often fail because they attempt to alter formal procedures without affecting the underlying cultural and communicative structures of the organization. From a systemic perspective, sustainable change presupposes a transformation of the communicative expectations, forms of collaboration, and professional assumptions reproduced within the school.

In conclusion, Luhmann's systems theory offers an exceptionally powerful interpretive framework for understanding school culture as an emergent organizational phenomenon. Culture is neither a static set of values nor a psychological trait of school members, but the directproduct of interacting decision premises that organize the operation of the school as an autopoietic system of communication. Programs, communication channels, and especially personnel constitute a dynamic web of organizational structures through which the school produces and reproduces the configurations of meaning that ensure its continuity and stability. In particular, the decision premise concerning personnel emerges as the most vital mechanism of cultural reproduction and transformation, as it is through this premise that organizational expectations are integrated into daily pedagogical practice and converted into a living school reality.

6. METHODOLOGY

The present study adopts a qualitatively driven mixed-methods design, in which the qualitative approach constitutes the primary research orientation, while quantitative processing is employed complementarily to enhance the systematicity, comparability, and interpretive substantiation of the findings (Babbie, 2011; Cohen et al., 2008;). The selection of this methodological strategy is grounded in the nature of the research object; investigating the institutional and organizational mechanisms that shape school development, organizational learning, and systemic resilience presupposes an interpretive approach to social phenomena within their historical, institutional, and communicative context (Pourkos & Diafermos, 2010 in Angelakou, 2020). From this perspective, the study does not aim at the causal prediction of social phenomena, but rather at decoding the structures of communication, knowledge, and decision-making through which the educational system organizes the possibilities for operation, learning, and transformation within school units.

6.1 First Level of Analysis: Systemic Complexity and Learning/Resilient Organizations

In the first phase of the research, the object of analysis consists of the legislative framework governing Greek primary education. The epistemological foundation of the study is situated within the interpretive and systemic paradigm of organizational analysis and is theoretically grounded in Niklas Luhmann's theory of social systems (1995), as well as in Helmut Willke's theory of multiple complexity (1996, 2007). Within this framework, organizations are approached as self-referential and operationally closed systems of communication. These systems process environmental complexity through mechanisms of selection, self-observation, and reflexive restructuring of decision premises. Social systems theory is therefore not employed as a normative interpretive scheme, but rather as an analytical framework for identifying the communicative and cognitive mechanisms through which the educational system processes complexity and organizes the conditions of decision-making.

Consequently, the legislative framework is not treated merely as a normative body of regulations, but as an institutional mechanism for the constitution of organizational decision premises that shapes the possibilities of communication, learning, self-regulation, and transformation within school organizations. From this theoretical standpoint, the analysis of legislation aims to investigate the extent to which the Greek educational system facilitates or constrains the capacity of school organizations to develop forms of organizational learning, reflexive self-observation, and systemic resilience.

The research material includes the totality of legislative texts regulating the operation of Greek primary education from 1974 to the present, including laws, presidential decrees, ministerial decisions, and circulars. For reasons of methodological organization and diachronic comparability, the temporal scope of the analysis is structured into five analytical sub-periods (1974–1979, 1980–1989, 1990–1999, 2000–2009, and 2010–present). These periods function as analytical intersections for interpreting transformations in educational policy rather than as a strict historiographical periodization.

For the analysis of legislative texts, a combined application of qualitative and quantitative content analysis was employed, as this method enables the systematic, organized, and interpretive investigation of communicative material (Berelson, 1971 in Filias, 1996). From the perspective of the systemic approach, content analysis was not confined to the descriptive identification of thematic patterns. Instead, it functioned as a process of reconstructing the communicative schemas and institutional decision premises organizing school reality, thereby enabling the diachronic mapping of organizational and institutional transformations within the educational system. This approach enabled the systematic categorization of legislative material while simultaneously facilitating the interpretive investigation of the latent cognitive, communicative, and organizational structures underlying school operation. The primary unit of analysis was defined as the "theme," namely each autonomous semantic unit possessing complete meaning. This choice enabled the distinction between manifest and latent content, thereby allowing the identification not only of explicit normative formulations but also of the underlying organizational and cognitive structures embedded in the legislative framework.

For the systematic study of Greek primary education legislation, an original analytical system of categorical content analysis was constructed. This system operationalizes Willke's theory of multiple complexity into a functional analytical model for investigating organizational maturity, reflexivity, organizational learning, and systemic resilience within school organizations. More specifically, a multi-level categorical analytical framework was developed based on the five dimensions of complexity (objective, social, temporal, operative, and cognitive complexity). These dimensions are approached both as mechanisms for processing organizational uncertainty and as indicators of the quality and evolutionary maturity of social systems (Willke, 1996 in Angelakou, 2018; Angelakou, 2020).

Particular emphasis was placed on the cognitive dimension of complexity, which constituted the central analytical axis of the study, as it is directly associated with the capacity of organizations to produce reflexive knowledge, process uncertainty, and restructure their own decision premises. The prioritization of the cognitive dimension is grounded in the theoretical assumption that the possibilities of organizational learning, reflexivity, and resilience depend primarily upon the system's capacity to process knowledge and transform the very frameworks through which decisions are produced. From this perspective, the school unit is approached as a communicative system capable of developing mechanisms of cognitive self-observation, self-thematization, and transformation of its own cognitive and communicative structures (Willke, 1996).

The cognitive dimension was further specified into eleven (11) analytical subcategories concerning processes of organizational uncertainty forecasting and management, strategic utilization and reflexive management of knowledge, development of organizational self-awareness, collective action and collaborative communicative structures, organizational learning, social creativity, and the resolution of complex organizational problems.

The categorical analysis system was organized according to the principles of clarity, mutual exclusivity, internal coherence, and analytical systematicity, with the aim of ensuring the methodological validity and reliability of the analysis (Cohen et al., 2008). For data processing, procedures of typological and taxonomic analysis were employed, while analytic induction constituted the principal research strategy. This strategy enabled the dynamic formation of categories through a recursive interaction between theory and empirical material (Patton, 1990).

Coding procedures were conducted within a structured Excel environment, accompanied by the parallel recording of metadata for each unit of analysis, including time period, type of legislative text, year, legislative act number, and structural position within the document. The coding scheme was based on the distinction between explicit reference, latent reference, and absence of reference, thereby enabling the systematic representation of different levels of legislative meaning construction. The coding process was conducted iteratively and involved successive phases of preliminary coding, category refinement, and recoding procedures to strengthen analytical consistency.

Subsequently, the data were imported into the SPSS statistical package, where descriptive statistical techniques, including frequencies, percentages, and cross-tabulations, were applied to map the distribution of categories and facilitate the diachronic comparison of findings. Quantitative processing did not aim at the causal explanation of social phenomena. Rather, it functioned supportively to the interpretive logic of the research, strengthening the systematicity, comparability, and analytical substantiation of the findings.

The validity and reliability of the study were ensured through multi-level methodological triangulation (Thurmond, 2001), which included iterative coding procedures, independent verification of categorization by a second researcher, and methodological cross-validation of findings with focus-group data. The combined utilization of multiple levels of observation, reflexive control procedures, and cross-validation of research data strengthened the interpretive validity of the analysis and enabled the reflexive verification of the theoretical coherence of the interpretations produced.

6.2. Second Level of Analysis: Systemic Investigation of School Culture and Decision Premises

At this level, a mixed-methods research design was also adopted, integrating quantitative and qualitative data collection and analysis techniques to systemically investigate school culture as an emergent organizational phenomenon. The choice of this specific methodology was theoretically grounded in Niklas Luhmann's social systems theory, and particularly in the concept of organizations as self-referential decision systems (Luhmann, 2000a; 2018). The multifactorial, dynamic, and non-linear nature of school culture necessitated a multi-level research strategy capable of capturing both overt organizational structures and latent processes of sense-making and organizational self-observation (Creswell & Plano Clark, 2018).

The study was organized as an embedded single-case study design, according to Yin's (2018) typology, since the phenomenon under investigation was examined within its natural organizational context and in relation to the individual operational sub-units of the school organization. The choice of a case study was deemed methodologically appropriate due to the need for an in-depth investigation of the systemic operation of the school unit, its communication structures, and its decision-making processes. This specific strategy allowed for the analysis of organizational complexity under real operating conditions, without decoupling individual variables from the context within which they emerge (Merriam, 2009; Stake, 1995).

The overall research strategy followed a sequential explanatory mixed-methods design, in which quantitative data were collected and analyzed in the first stage, followed by a qualitative investigation aimed at providing an interpretive deepening and a systemic understanding of the findings (Creswell & Plano Clark, 2018). This specific design logic was deemed functionally more appropriate, as it enabled the initial mapping of the core decision premises and the subsequent analysis of the underlying mechanisms that shape the observed organizational dynamics.

6.2.1. The Sample

The research sample consisted of the entire teaching staff of the Teachers' Board of a secondary education school unit located in a semi-urban area, which constitutes the second largest general secondary education school unit in that specific regional district. The choice of this school unit was made to allow for a longitudinal, in-depth, and systemic investigation of the phenomenon of school culture within its natural organizational context.

The school unit served 300 students and had 40 teachers, as well as 4 educational support staff members. The sample included all permanent, substitute, and hourly general education teachers, as well as all remedial and parallel support special education teachers, which provided heterogeneity in terms of professional experience, specializations, and forms of participation in the school system.

For the collection of qualitative data, in addition to the participatory majority that comprised the Teachers' Board, 5 teachers participated in individual interviews (both permanent and substitutes) and 5 teachers participated in the focus-verification group.

Regarding the demographic characteristics of the sample, 11 men (27.5%) and 29 women (72.5%) participated. The sample included teachers of different specializations and levels of professional experience, a feature that enhanced the potential for a multi-level investigation of organizational perceptions and forms of making sense of school culture.

The choice of a single school organization was linked to the methodological logic of the embedded single-case study, since the phenomenon under investigation was treated as a complex and emergent organizational system requiring in-depth analysis and long-term observation. However, the limited sample size affects the generalizability of the results and restricts the statistical power of the quantitative analyses, particularly regarding the identification of variations among individual demographic groups.

This specific research choice was deemed theoretically and methodologically compatible with the systemic approach of the study, as it allowed for the analysis of school culture as an organizational phenomenon emerging through the communicative relations, decision premises, and processes of collective sense-making of the school system itself.

6.2.2. Quantitative Phase of the Research

In the first phase, first-order participatory observation was applied via a specially developed quantitative observation tool. The development of the tool was based on a process of theoretical and conceptual operationalization of the core concepts of Luhmann's theory, as well as on an analysis of existing organizational culture instruments (Ashkanasy et al., 2000).

The final instrument included 160 statements-variables, which were organized into three basic decision premises:

- Programmatic decisions.
- Personnel – values, attitudes, and forms of participation.
- Communicative structures and communication channels.

The initial development of the tool, which originally comprised over 200 variables, was followed by pilot testing to check for conceptual clarity, the internal consistency of the variables, and the functionality of the measurement scale. Successive revisions of the variables were carried out through theoretical recoding and the rewording of questions to limit conceptual overlap between categories.

A four-point Likert scale was used for data collection, allowing for the quantitative capturing of the perceived adequacy of each decision premise. The choice of this specific scale was based on its ability to support descriptive and correlational statistical analysis procedures while maintaining a high degree of comprehensibility for the participants, while simultaneously preserving the adequacy/inadequacy distinction in accordance with the systemic approach to the phenomenon under investigation.

Statistical analysis was conducted using SPSS software. Descriptive statistics techniques (means, standard deviations, frequency distributions) were applied, alongside an internal reliability analysis using Cronbach's Alpha coefficient to check the internal consistency of the individual axes of the instrument (Field, 2018). Furthermore, correlational analyses were performed between individual decision premises to investigate functional interactions among organizational parameters.

The quantitative phase of the research enabled the systematic mapping of perceived organizational adequacy and highlighted areas of functional stability or organizational weakness regarding the emergent phenomenon of school culture. Concurrently, it provided the necessary empirical foundation for the second, qualitative phase of the research.

6.2.3. Qualitative Phase of the Research

The second phase of the research was structured around a qualitative interpretive inquiry, utilizing second-order participatory observation, semi-structured interviews, and a focus group. The qualitative approach was deemed necessary due to the inability of quantitative data alone to capture the sense-making mechanisms, latent organizational practices, and self-observation processes of the system regarding the decision premises that shape the phenomenon of school culture.

Second-order participatory observation constituted the central methodological axis of the research. The concept of second-order observation stems directly from Luhmann's theory and concerns the observation of the way social systems themselves observe and describe themselves (Luhmann, 2000b). In contrast to first-order observation, which records events and behaviors, second-order observation focuses on the processes of meaning construction, interpretive practices, and the mechanisms of selection and exclusion of information by the organizational system itself.

The application of second-order observation was carried out by monitoring meetings of the Teachers' Board, recording interactions, and analyzing communication patterns. Particular emphasis was placed on:

- forms of organizational self-observation,
- mechanisms of complexity absorption,
- uncertainty management practices,
- forms of participation and detachment,
- as well as the informal communicative functions of the organization.

The observation recorded not only verbal interactions but also non-verbal elements such as pauses, silences, irony, humor, and shifts in communicative power, which were considered crucial for understanding organizational dynamics (Atkinson & Hammersley, 1994; Flick, 2014; Kioussi, 2025).

Concurrently, semi-structured interviews were conducted with teachers of the school unit. The choice of the semi-structured format was based on its capacity to combine thematic comparability with interpretive flexibility (Kvale & Brinkmann, 2009). The interview guide was organized around the core decision premises, while remaining open to the emergence of new thematic categories.

The interviews were audio-recorded, fully transcribed, and coded at multiple levels of analysis. Initially, open coding was applied, followed by axial coding, and subsequently selective coding. This process allowed for the emergence of secondary and tertiary decision premises that had not been anticipated in the original theoretical model.

The qualitative investigation concluded with a focus group, which functioned as a process of collective reflexive processing of the findings. This technique was used to investigate the negotiation of meaning among participants and to enhance the interpretive validity of the results (Morgan, 1997).

6.2.4. Qualitative Data Analysis

The analysis of the qualitative data was conducted through thematic analysis using NVivo software. The choice of thematic analysis was based on its ability to support the systematic identification, coding, and conceptual organization of recurring patterns of meaning (Braun & Clarke, 2006).

The analysis followed six successive stages:

1. Familiarization with the data.
2. Generation of initial codes.
3. Searching for thematic categories.
4. Reviewing thematic axes.
5. Defining and naming themes.
6. Synthesis and interpretation of the results.

The use of NVivo allowed for the creation of hierarchical thematic structures (tree nodes), the interconnection of different data types, and the detection of frequencies, convergences, and divergences between quantitative and qualitative findings. Moreover, it facilitated the process of methodological triangulation, through which data from different sources and collection methods were cross-referenced (Denzin, 1978).

6.2.5. Validity and Reliability of the Research

To enhance the validity and reliability of the research, multiple qualitative and quantitative control strategies were applied. In the quantitative phase, the internal consistency of the instrument was evaluated via Cronbach's Alpha, while the conceptual validity of the variables was checked through theoretical mapping against Luhmann's systemic model.

In the qualitative phase, the following procedures were applied:

- methodological triangulation,
- theoretical triangulation,
- reflexive memoing,
- and constant comparative analysis.

Additionally, the focus group functioned as a member-checking process, enhancing the interpretive reliability of the results (Lincoln & Guba, 1985).

Consequently, the choice of a mixed systemic methodology did not constitute a mere combination of data collection tools, but a methodological consequence of the theoretical assumption that school culture represents a complex, self-referential, and evolutionary social system. This specific strategy allowed for the investigation of both structural organizational characteristics and latent processes of sense-making, making a multi-level and systemically documented analysis of the phenomenon possible.

7. RESULTS

7.1 Capacities for Organizational Learning and Systemic Resilience of the Greek School Unit: Analysis of the Legislative Framework of Primary Education

7.1.1 The First Period of Analysis (1974–1979): The Legislative Framework and Decision-Making Premises

In the period 1974–1979, the cognitive dimension of complexity appears to be highly constrained within the legislative framework of Greek primary education. Specifically, only two (2) implicit references (1.5%) are identified, indirectly associated with processes of organizational learning and primarily concerning the formulation of the functional aims of primary and pre-primary education. These references are predominantly situated within the temporal dimension of complexity, as they are oriented toward future-oriented normative expectations, thereby indicating a minimal and functionally weak coupling between the cognitive and temporal horizons of meaning-making.

However, this coupling remains functionally weak and does not give rise to mechanisms of organizational self-observation or the reflexive reconfiguration of decision premises. The concept of learning is primarily constructed as a pedagogically defined and individually oriented objective, linked to the developmental trajectory of the student and the projection of their future social role, rather than as an inherent function of the school organization as an autopoietic communication system. Consequently, knowledge does not operate as a mechanism for reproducing or restructuring organizational decision premises, nor as a process of systemic reflexivity, but remains embedded within a normatively determined framework of administrative and pedagogical regulation.

From this perspective, the legislative framework of the period constructs the school unit primarily as an administratively hetero-determined mechanism for implementing predefined educational objectives, rather than as a learning system capable of internally producing knowledge, reflecting on its own operations, or reconfiguring decision-making premises. The limited presence of cognitive and reflexive mechanisms suggests that the processing of educational complexity is carried out mainly through regulatory standardization and externally imposed administrative control, rather than through endogenous processes of organizational learning and meaning production at the system level.

7.1.2 Second Period of Analysis (1980–1989): The Legislative Framework and Decision-Making Premises

A relative strengthening of the cognitive dimension of complexity can be observed in the period 1980–1989 compared to the preceding phase, although it does not yet constitute a coherent framework for organizational learning and reflexive self-regulation. Nineteen (19) implicit references (7.6%) were identified, clustered primarily within the subcategory of organizational learning, referring mainly to individual learning capacities and the pedagogical aims of primary education.

Most of these references are associated with the provisions of Law 1566/1985 concerning the development of skills, creative thinking, collaborative dispositions, and social competencies among students. These objectives exhibit a future-oriented normative trajectory and are thus primarily linked to the temporal dimension of complexity. However, learning continues to be conceptualized predominantly as an individual pedagogical process rather than as an organizational capability of the school system to reflect upon its own operations and to reconfigure its decision-making premises.

Although references to collaboration and collectivity are evident, they remain primarily oriented toward student socialization and do not translate into internal mechanisms of organizational learning or collective knowledge production at the level of the school unit. Consequently, collectivity is constructed more as a pedagogical objective than as a structure of communicative self-observation within the organization.

In parallel, early indications of an enhanced cognitive dimension emerge through provisions related to in-service teacher training. Professional development functions as a mechanism for adapting educational personnel to scientific, pedagogical, and institutional changes, as well as a channel for the introduction of new instructional and assessment practices. In this sense, an initial yet still weak coupling between the cognitive dimension and other dimensions of complexity becomes observable, particularly through the reconfiguration of professional roles and the introduction of educational innovations.

Nevertheless, despite the quantitative increase in the cognitive dimension compared to the 1974–1979 period, its development remains fragmented and functionally constrained. Stable mechanisms of organizational self-observation, strategic knowledge management, or collective reflexivity are not yet identifiable. The legislative framework continues to construct the school unit primarily as an administratively regulated institution for the implementation of educational policy, rather than as a learning system with an internalized capacity for the reflexive processing of experience and reconfiguration of decision-making premises.

7.1.3 Third Period of Analysis (1990–1999): The Legislative Framework and Decision-Making Premises

The period 1990–1999 marks a more advanced development of the cognitive dimension of complexity, as reflected in fifty-two (52) references (16.4%). This development indicates a reorientation of the legislative framework toward forms of school organization that incorporate communication processes, collaboration, professional learning, and collective coordination, thereby expanding the system's capacity to process organizational complexity.

The most frequently occurring subcategory concerns the development of communicative processes within and beyond the school unit. The legislative framework reinforces both internal communication among teachers, students, and administrative bodies, as well as external collaborations with institutional, social, and scientific actors. These processes are primarily associated with forms of collective coordination, cooperation, information exchange, and the management of operational aspects of school life. In parallel, an expansion of organizational learning is observed through in-service training activities, educational visits, collective activities, and collaborative pedagogical practices, which broaden opportunities for professional development and communicative interaction among members. However, learning continues to be predominantly framed as an individual pedagogical and professional process rather than as a formalized organizational function of reflexive experience processing and knowledge production by the school system itself. The emphasis remains largely on improving effectiveness and operational coordination within the school unit, rather than on establishing mechanisms of systemic self-observation and the reconfiguration of decision-making premises.

Of particular significance is the emergence of provisions related to problem-solving, social creativity, and knowledge governance. These regulatory elements indicate enhanced capacities for self-organization, collective action, and functional coordination within the school unit, primarily through the strengthened role of the teaching staff council and the development of collaborative planning and decision-making structures. This development suggests a partial shift toward more participatory and communicatively differentiated forms of organization, enabling a higher degree of internal processing of organizational experience.

Despite the substantial strengthening of the cognitive dimension, its development remains uneven and constrained with respect to the deeper reflexive and self-regulatory functions of the school organization. Most references still pertain to functional forms of cooperation and pedagogical coordination, while institutionalized mechanisms of organizational self-observation, strategic knowledge management, and systemic reflexivity remain absent. In this sense, the legislative framework of the period appears to move toward more collaborative and communicative forms of school organization, without yet fully constituting the school unit as a learning, reflexive, and cognitively self-regulating system.

7.1.4 Fourth Period of Analysis (2000–2009): The Legislative Framework and Decision-Making Premises

The period 2000–2009 is characterized by a further development of the cognitive dimension of complexity compared to earlier periods, as reflected in sixty-one (61) references (17.7%). This development indicates a gradual expansion of cognitive references within the legislative framework of Greek primary education; however, it does not yet give rise to a coherent or systemically integrated framework of organizational learning and reflexive self-regulation at the level of the school unit. Although the cognitive dimension becomes more prominently represented, it remains fragmented and primarily functionally oriented.

The most frequently occurring subcategory concerns communicative processes within the school unit and its interactions with external administrative, pedagogical, and support institutions. These processes are primarily associated with the coordination of educational work, the cultivation of a collaborative pedagogical climate, the implementation of school objectives, and the utilization of teaching practices and technological tools. Communication thus functions primarily as a mechanism of operational coherence and administrative coordination within the school unit, while secondarily contributing to the development of collective forms of action through school-based activities and cultural events.

In parallel, there is an increased presence of provisions related to in-service teacher training and pedagogical support, which are constructed as key mechanisms for adapting educational personnel to scientific, pedagogical, and technological developments. Within this context, elements of organizational learning and the reconfiguration of professional roles can be identified; however, these do not crystallize into stable institutional mechanisms of collective reflexivity or systemic processing of organizational experience. Knowledge continues to be framed predominantly as an instrument for improving the efficiency of educational practice, rather than as an autonomous organizational function of meaning production and reconfiguration of decision-making premises.

Furthermore, references emerge concerning knowledge control, self-evaluation, the forecasting of organizational change, and risk management. However, these functions remain largely concentrated at administrative levels and within predefined roles, without developing into collective or decentralized mechanisms of organizational self-observation. The self-regulatory capacity of the school unit thus appears constrained and dependent upon externally determined administrative structures.

Overall, the analysis of the 2000–2009 period reveals a clear quantitative and qualitative strengthening of the cognitive dimension of complexity compared to earlier phases, primarily through the expansion of communicative, collaborative, and training-related practices. Despite this expansion, the school unit continues to be constructed primarily as an administratively regulated institution for the implementation of educational policy, rather than as a fully reflexive, learning-oriented, and cognitively self-regulating organization.

7.1.5 Fifth Period of Analysis (2010–Present): The Legislative Framework and Decision-Making Premises

The period 2010–present exhibits the most significant development of the cognitive dimension of complexity compared to all preceding periods, accounting for 30.2% of total references and indicating a marked expansion of communicative, collaborative, and reflexive functions within the school unit. Across the dataset, references are identified across all eleven subcategories of the analytical framework, suggesting a qualitative shift toward a more complex and multilayered model of school organization. However, this development remains uneven, as references are predominantly concentrated in specific domains, particularly communicative processes, the development of collaborative networks, and forms of organizational learning associated with institutionally programmed interventions.

The subcategory of communicative processes continues to constitute the dominant axis of analysis, with relevant provisions extending both within the school unit and toward its external environment. Communication is no longer confined to internal coordination functions but is increasingly structured as a networked mechanism of collaboration involving other school units, educational authorities, local government, and social organizations. Within this context, the school unit is progressively embedded in institutionalized forms of inter-school collaboration, such as learning communities, which are recognized as mechanisms for collective professional development, the exchange of practices, and reinforcement of organizational learning. These structures signal a shift from isolated school functioning toward networked systems of knowledge production and reflexive practice.

In parallel, particular emphasis is placed on the development of participatory and socially oriented educational frameworks, most notably through the emergence of the "active citizen" paradigm. The relevant provisions integrate school learning into a broader normative and societal framework oriented toward the cultivation of democratic competencies, social responsibility, and participation in the public sphere. The incorporation of these elements strengthens the cognitive dimension of complexity, as it links learning processes to social action and to an institutional understanding of the school's role as an agent of social cohesion and civic formation.

A notably strengthened dimension also concerns organizational learning through mechanisms of evaluation, self-evaluation, and feedback on educational practice. Although these processes are frequently embedded within regulatory and administrative frameworks, they simultaneously function as spaces for reflexive practice and the collective interpretation of educational experience. However, knowledge production remains largely institutionally guided and does not fully crystallize as an autopoietic function of the school organization itself.

Furthermore, a significant enhancement is observed in the capacity to manage uncertainty and anticipate risks, most notably through initiatives related to crisis prevention, school violence management, mitigation of social inequalities, and support for vulnerable student populations. These practices are associated with the development of collaborative networks and interdisciplinary interventions, thereby reinforcing the systemic adaptability of the school unit in response to complex social environments.

Despite the clear expansion of the cognitive dimension during the 2010–present period, organizational learning and reflexivity continue to be activated primarily within institutionally predefined policy frameworks rather than as fully self-generated functions of the school system. Learning communities and active citizenship policies enhance the collective dimension of knowledge and participation; however, they remain embedded within an administratively regulated system of accountability and policy implementation.

In this sense, the legislative framework of the period conceptualizes the school unit as a system of high communicative and cognitive complexity, yet one that continues to operate within externally determined regulatory boundaries. The transition toward a fully self-regulating, reflexive, and learning-oriented organizational system remains ongoing, with school development being shaped as a process of institutionally supported but not yet fully endogenous systemic self-production.

7.2 Capacities for Organizational Learning and Systemic Resilience of the Greek School Unit: Findings From the Focus Group

Following the completion of the content analysis of the legislative framework governing Greek primary education, the present study proceeded to a qualitative triangulation of findings through a focus group involving headteachers of multi-unit primary school settings. This methodological choice is not intended to validate the findings of the content analysis; rather, it operates as a second-order observation mechanism through which it becomes possible to examine how institutional decision-making conditions are translated into organizational communicative structures, expectations, and practices at the level of the school unit.

Within the theoretical framework of N. Luhmann's social systems theory and H. Willke's concept of meta-learning, the focus group is not approached as a mere site for the elicitation of empirical accounts, but as a communicative environment in which forms of self-observation, feedback, and the reconfiguration of decision-making premises within the school organization become observable. The school unit is therefore not analyzed as a repository of knowledge, but as a communication system that generates and reproduces cognitive expectations through processes of meaning selection and processing.

Analysis of the data derived from the headteachers indicates that the cognitive dimension of complexity is not constituted as an individual attribute of knowledge, but as a systemic communicative function enabling the observation of the system's own decisions. Regular meetings of the teachers' board function as an internal second-order self-observation mechanism, through which the school unit does not merely assess the achievement of predefined goals, but re-examines the very criteria through which such goals are constructed. Within this perspective, feedback emerges as a process of reconfiguring decision-making premises rather than a simple corrective mechanism, while knowledge is not understood as a stable content but as a function of selecting among alternative courses of action through which the system reduces the complexity it itself generates.

Communication constitutes the central axis of the cognitive dimension, insofar as it expands the system's horizon of observation both internally and across systems. Inter-school collaborations, exchanges of pedagogical practices, and digital platforms (such as eTwinning and European networks) constitute a field of multiple and non-integrated observations of educational reality. However, these communicative flows do not culminate in unified organizational knowledge; rather, they amplify the heterogeneity of available cognitive perspectives. Communication thus functions not as a homogenizing mechanism, but as a mechanism for multiplying possible modes of observing both the system and its environment.

Professional development constitutes a key mechanism of structural coupling between the educational system and its scientific-pedagogical environment, through which new cognitive offerings are introduced and subsequently re-coded into pedagogical practices. Similarly, evaluation may function as a mechanism of reflexive self-observation, insofar as it enables the re-examination of evaluation criteria themselves, thereby contributing to the reconfiguration of decision-making premises.

Despite the strengthening of communicative, training-related, and feedback mechanisms, the school unit is not yet fully constituted as an autopoietic system of knowledge production. Learning continues to be attributed primarily to individual actors (teachers) rather than to the organizational system as a communicative whole. Consequently, the transition from "learning of members" to "learning of the system" remains partially incomplete, thereby limiting the stabilization of organizational learning as an endogenous function.

Overall, the findings of the focus group demonstrate that the school unit is developing an increasing capacity to process complexity through communication, professional development, and feedback, without yet having been fully constituted as a self-referential cognitive system. Organizational learning emerges as a dynamic yet only partially internalized function, remaining partly dependent on individual actors and on external institutional frameworks for knowledge activation. In this sense, the school unit may be understood as a system in an ongoing process of meta-learning, one that enhances its capacity for the reflexive processing of complexity without yet having stabilized learning as a permanent internal function of self-observation.

7.3 The Core Decision Premise of Personnel in School Culture: Quantitative and Qualitative Analysis

On a school-unit level and within the framework of Niklas Luhmann's systems theory, school personnel are not approached as a mere aggregate of individuals implementing administrative and pedagogical procedures, but as a fundamental decision premise through which the school system manages its cognitive and communicative complexity. Teachers function as agents of selection, processing, and stabilization of organizational meaning, directly influencing how the school self-observes, self-interprets, and reproduces its operational expectations.

The cognitive dimension of organizational complexity concerns the capacity of the school organization to simultaneously manage multiple demands, conflicting expectations, communicative uncertainties, and changing pedagogical conditions. Under this lens, the personnel functions as a core mechanism of complexity absorption, since stable forms of organizational continuity are produced through their values, attitudes, forms of participation, and communicative practices.

Consequently, for the purpose of empirically documenting the system's operational autopoiesis, methodological triangulation of the data was applied. The synthetic analysis of quantitative processing (SPSS), thematic coding (NVivo), and second-order observation allows for the mapping of the school unit's functional equilibrium against emerging sources of organizational entropy.

7.3.1. Quantitative Capturing and Descriptive Statistical Analysis

During the first stage of the empirical investigation, quantitative processing of the questionnaire data ($N = 40$) was carried out via SPSS software, aiming at the statistical mapping of the six grouped variables that constitute the sub-decision premises of the personnel. Measurement was conducted on a four-point Likert scale (1 = Never, 4 = Always), highlighting the following descriptive trends:

Table 1. Statistical Analysis of Grouped Variables of the Core Personnel Decision Premise

Sub-Decision Premises	N	Mean (*M*)	Standard Deviation (*SD*)	Min.	Max.
Professional Recognition / Appreciation	40	3.17	0.52	1.67	3.89
Professional Development / Improvement	40	3.10	0.36	1.80	3.80
Sense of Security / Friendly Environment	40	3.01	0.42	1.71	3.71
Willingness / Optimism / Positive Attitude	40	2.98	0.32	2.43	3.71
Teamwork / Integration	40	2.77	0.39	1.50	3.37
Professional Solidarity / Collaboration	40	2.76	0.34	2.00	3.50
Overall Core Personnel Premise	40	2.98	0.33	1.97	3.55

The descriptive indices demonstrate that the central tendencies of the responses cluster near the "Often" category, locating the Overall Core Personnel Decision Premise ($M = 2.98$, $SD = 0.33$) at the threshold of statistical and functional inadequacy.

An analytical approach to the individual values reveals that the highest mean scores are located in the premises of Professional Recognition ($M = 3.17$) and

Professional Development (M = 3.10). This finding substantiates the adequacy of the system's individual and structurally protected parameters. Conversely, the lowest means are recorded in those decision premises that presuppose collective and coordinated action, namely Teamwork ($M = 2.77$) and Professional Solidarity/ Collaboration ($M = 2.76$).

Additionally, checking for statistical differences based on the sociodemographic and professional characteristics of the sample (gender, age, education level, years of service, position of responsibility) via t-test and ANOVA criteria revealed a universal absence of statistical significance ($p > 0.05$). The limited values of the F-statistic combined with the small effect sizes certify a high degree of homogeneity in the participants' perceptions. This uniformity is interpreted systemically as a product of standardized professional socialization that neutralizes individual deviations, with the sole exceptions being some mild, non-significant trends of differentiation in Professional Development based on years of service ($p \approx 0.093$) and in Recognition based on age group ($p \approx 0.083$).

Final calculation of the internal consistency reliability index for this specific core decision premise yielded a Cronbach's alpha coefficient of ≈ 0.80, confirming the statistical coherence of the measurement tool (Table 1).

7.3.2. Checking Differences with Repeated Measures ANOVA

To investigate how the same sample of subjects evaluates the individual decision premises, a repeated-measures analysis of variance (Repeated Measures ANOVA) was applied, since the measurements constitute dependent variables within the same system.

The analysis yielded statistically significant results, F (5, 195) = 15.16, $p < 0.001$, which documents that teachers substantially differentiate their assessments depending on the functional nature of each respective premise.

Pairwise comparisons (*post hoc* tests) applying the Bonferroni correction revealed the following statistically significant deviations:

- The sub-premise of Professional Recognition ($M = 3.18$) showed a statistically significant superiority over the corresponding premises of Collaboration ($M = 2.76$) and Teamwork ($M = 2.77$) ($p < 0.001$).
- Similarly, Professional Development ($M = 3.11$) recorded significantly higher values compared to the same two collective decision premises ($p < 0.001$).
- Furthermore, the sub-premises of Positive Attitude ($M = 2.98$) and Sense of Security ($M = 3.01$) were found to be statistically superior to Collaboration and Teamwork ($p < 0.01$).

This specific statistical pattern confirms the existence of an internal functional asymmetry, as teachers evaluate more positively the individually sustainable and institutionally safeguarded premises of their professional role, while appearing cautious toward practices that presuppose systematic collective action.

7.3.3 Thematic Analysis of Qualitative Data (NVivo) and Second-Order Observation

The qualitative analysis of the semi-structured interviews via NVivo software allowed for the hierarchization of data based on the frequency of occurrence of coded references, highlighting the prior decision premises that determine the system's operation.

7.3.4. Professional Recognition, Appreciation, and the "Symbol of Inclusion"

The sub-premise of Professional Recognition and Appreciation emerged as the most decisive, gathering 28 references. In systemic terms, recognition functions as a "symbol of inclusion," validating the subject's functional contribution and reinforcing organizational cohesion (Luhmann, 1995a). The qualitative findings show that this premise is produced mainly informally, in the form of moral rewards from the Administration and the student body (*"I received it as praise..."*).

However, its adequacy is judged as partial, since a structural rift is detected in its coupling with the broader environment: while internal recognition ensures functional normalcy (23 references), 5 references record a complete lack of recognition from external systems, such as central politics (*"There is a degradation of the public school"*). The absence of external institutional validation introduces elements of entropy, constituting a deficit in structural coupling.

7.3.5. Professional Solidarity, Collaboration, and Team Integration

The sub-premises of Collaboration (19 references) and Teamwork (14 references) highlight, through thematic analysis and second-order observation, the formation of "islands of high teamwork" within the organization. This trend is identified preeminently in one specific specialty subgroup, which is conceptualized as the stable functional core of the school unit: (*"This group of Specialty is its strength..."*).

Conversely, however, qualitative observation recorded a functional asymmetry, as subgroups reproduce informal rivalries based on the symbolic promotion of their projects (*"A very clear clash is observed... informal competition over which project will be promoted more"*). In addition, deficient support is observed at the level of mentoring toward newly appointed teachers, as senior teachers tend to perceive the need for guidance as a professional weakness, opting instead for communicative isolation.

7.3.6. Professional Development, In-Service Training, and Attitudes Toward Change

The sub-premise of Professional Development (17 references) emerged as a crucial mechanism for managing external complexity. This trend is reflected in the voluntary participation of teachers in in-school training sessions outside working hours, a fact that demonstrates an advanced capacity for self-regulation.

Regarding Change, the focus group redefined the findings, clarifying that any hesitation is not due to ideological refusal, but is purely functional: it is directly linked to inadequate state training and the fear of error (*"Whatever we do is done superficially... if you provide the adequate equipment, I will change").* In contrast, attitudes toward mandatory evaluation are uniformly defensive. The focus group fully validated the quantitative inadequacy, equating the process with *"psychological pressure"* and a *"threat to labor rights."* This stance constitutes a typical defensive routine aimed at safeguarding the system's professional autonomy against logics foreign to it.

7.3.7. Friendly Environment, Sense of Security, and Student-Centeredness

The sense of a Friendly Environment and Security (16 references) constitutes a strong decision premise, which is confirmed by second-order observation through the pleasant atmosphere, humour, and integration rituals (e.g., farewell events).

However, qualitative deepening brought to light a serious internal rift, as the sense of psychological safety is directly threatened by phenomena of student delinquency (*"A large percentage of teachers experience bullying... threatened psychologically and emotionally"*). This finding stands in sharp contrast to the strong Student-Centeredness of the personnel (11 references for Willingness/Positive Attitude). As confirmed by the focus group, teachers maintain a genuine interest in the students (*"We have the student as our focus... we are not merely bureaucratic"*), a fact that generates a systemic contradiction: the personnel absorbs the complexity of the students' problems, while simultaneously experiencing communicative fatigue and personal exposure.

7.3.8. Systemic Synthetic Evaluation

Summarizing the findings of the quantitative and qualitative analysis, the Core Personnel Decision Premise is characterized by a deep structural ambiguity, moving between marginal inadequacy and partial adequacy.

On the one hand, the school system demonstrates high levels of horizontal social cohesion and internal solidarity, deploying humour and informal networks of trust as mechanisms to balance pressures. On the other hand, however, the lack of stable structures of external recognition, the absence of systematic institutional mentoring, and the psychological burden from managing student delinquency introduce significant entropy into the system.

Consequently, this core decision premise appears oriented primarily toward maintaining internal stability and defending the organization, presenting deficits in terms of collective reflection and its institutional evolution.

8. CONCLUSIONS

Modern school units, when approached through a systems-theoretical perspective, cannot be adequately conceptualized as static administrative entities or hierarchical organizations of instructional delivery. Rather, they operate as autopoietic and operationally closed communicative systems that reproduce themselves through the continuous selection and reduction of environmental complexity. In this sense, the school system does not passively absorb external demands; it actively constructs the meaning of these demands through internally generated communicative operations, thereby transforming environmental irritations into stabilized decision premises that define its own operational reality. The core function of the system lies in its capacity to filter, codify, and re-articulate environmental stimuli into communicative selections that acquire internal validity. Cognition, therefore, is not an individual attribute but a distributed systemic operation embedded in recursive communicative expectations. Within this framework, organizational learning cannot be reduced to training, skill acquisition, or policy implementation. It must instead be understood as the continuous, recursive reconfiguration of decision premises through which the system observes, differentiates, and re-observes its own operations.

This study has sought to theorize organizational learning in Greek primary education by constructing a conceptual bridge between macro-level institutional differentiation and micro-level organizational communication. At the macro level, legislative evolution is interpreted as an ongoing intensification of communicative complexity and institutional expectations. At the micro level, the school unit functions as a selective interpretive system in which these expectations are not directly implemented but are reconstructed through the core personnel decision premises—values, beliefs, professional orientations, and participation structures—which collectively constitute the emergent form of school culture and condition the system's trajectory toward resilience.

At the macro-institutional level, the historical trajectory of Greek educational governance demonstrates a persistent amplification of regulatory density, institutional differentiation, and communicative expansion. However, this expansion is not accompanied by an equivalent intensification of internal self-referential observation mechanisms. Instead, hetero-referential expectations increasingly exceed the system's reflexive absorption capacity. As a result, the cognitive dimension of complexity becomes structurally instrumentalized: knowledge is predominantly mobilized not as a reflexive medium of system reconfiguration, but as a stabilizing mechanism for pre-existing organizational operations.

From the perspective of Helmut Willke's theory of meta-learning, this condition reflects a structural conflation between first-order adaptive learning and second-order reflexive learning. While the system demonstrates a capacity for localized adaptation, meta-learning remains fragmented and institutionally dispersed. It appears only intermittently through mechanisms such as professional development, evaluation regimes, and counselling structures. However, these mechanisms do not converge into a stable systemic property of organizational self-observation. Instead, they remain externally introduced functional differentiations that are only loosely coupled with the system's internal logic of meaning production. Consequently, the educational system can be characterized as semi-reflexive: it generates learning effects at the level of individuals and groups but fails to stabilize learning as an enduring property of organizational self-reference. This condition is reinforced by the dominance of hetero-referential decision premises, whereby key organizational expectations are produced externally through centralized governance structures. Within this configuration, accountability and quality assurance mechanisms do not primarily function as reflexive triggers, but rather as instruments of compliance, thereby converting potential learning processes into procedural adaptation rather than systemic self-transformation.

These macro-level dynamics are not merely structural abstractions; they are concretely inscribed in the micro-operations of the school unit. Here, the personnel's decision premise functions as a living communicative structure through which external complexity is selectively processed and transformed into internally meaningful action. Rather than constituting a stable organizational resource, this premise operates as a structurally ambivalent mechanism that simultaneously enables operational continuity and generates localized communicative strain.

Under conditions of intensified institutional pressure and environmental uncertainty, school organizations tend to develop a cultural configuration oriented toward adaptation, defensive stabilization, and operational survival. Within this configuration, collaborative practices remain weakly institutionalized, as collective coordination has not yet been fully stabilized as an organizational expectation. Instead, cooperation emerges in informal, contingent, and relationally embedded forms, shaped by trust, proximity, and situational necessity rather than formal organizational design. This condition is further reinforced by multiple systemic tensions, including the defensive reception of external evaluation regimes, which are frequently interpreted as intrusive hetero-referential interventions rather than opportunities for reflexive learning. Combined with organizational opacity, insufficient mentoring infrastructures, and high personnel mobility, these conditions hinder the stabilization of communicative expectations. At the same time, increasing psychosocial demands associated with student complexity place additional burdens on teachers without equivalent institutional support, resulting in communicative saturation and a gradual reliance on individualized decision-making processes.

Paradoxically, however, the same decision premise that generates fragility also enables continuity. The school system demonstrates a latent capacity for adaptive resilience through informal communicative structures that compensate for the absence of formal institutional integration. "Islands of high teamwork," particularly within subject-based subgroups, function as localized condensations of trust and coordination, partially reconstructing systemic coherence in an otherwise fragmented organizational environment. Similarly, the strong student-centered orientation of teaching practice ensures the continuity of the system's functional core even under conditions of strain.

Informal communicative practices—ranging from collegial humour to everyday rituals of coordination—operate as latent stabilizing mechanisms that absorb tension and translate systemic overload into manageable meaning structures. In parallel, voluntary engagement in professional development and gradual technological adaptation indicate the presence of endogenous learning capacities that are not fully dependent on external coercion but emerge from within the communicative logic of the organization itself.

The integration of macro- and micro-level findings suggests that systemic resilience and school development should not be treated as separate or sequential outcomes, but rather as co-emergent effects of a single underlying mechanism: the system's capacity for self-observation. Resilience, in this sense, is not a stable organizational attribute but an emergent communicative property that arises when the system succeeds in transforming everyday communication into second-order observations of its own functioning.

Crucially, however, this transformation remains only partially realized. The existing communicative resources—trust, student-centeredness, and adaptive innovation—constitute important preconditions for reflexive stabilization, yet they remain insufficiently institutionalized as systemic structures. What is missing is not communicative capacity, but the institutional closure of reflexivity. A genuine transition toward resilient schooling therefore does not require further increases in regulatory complexity. Rather, it requires a reconfiguration of the system's internal architecture of observation. First, generalized institutional trust must replace personalized and contingent relational stability, enabling the emergence of stable communicative expectations through which organizational knowledge can be consistently produced and circulated. Second, structural couplings between the educational system and its institutional environment must be redefined. Mechanisms such as evaluation, counselling, and professional development should no longer operate primarily as instruments of compliance or external accountability. Instead, they must be reconceptualized as second-order observation mechanisms that connect individual experience, organizational practice, and institutional expectations within a unified reflexive framework.

In theoretical terms, school development must be understood as a non-linear, recursive, and continuously negotiated tension between hetero-referential regulation and self-referential organization. The decisive condition for systemic transformation is the institutional stabilization of reflexivity at the level of micro-decision premises. Only when this threshold is reached does the school system cease to operate primarily as an adaptive survival structure and begins to function as a self-referentially stabilized system of resilient schooling.

REFERENCES

Angelakou, E.-P. (2018). *School development as a self-referential process of improvement of the organizational learning and intelligence: The example of post - dictatorship Greece.* [Doctoral dissertation, University of the Aegean]. National Archive of PhD Theses. https://doi.org/DOI: 10.12681/eadd/43701

Angelakou, E.-P. (2019). The communication system in school operation and development: The case of Greek educational legislation. In C. Kalloniatis, C.-N. Anagnostopoulos, D. Papageorgiou, A. Kitsiou, & M. Sideri (Eds.), *International Conference on Cultural Informatics, Communication & Media Studies e-Proceedings, 1*(1). National Documentation Center. http://dx.doi.org/DOI: 10.12681/cicms.2733

Angelakou, E.-P. (2020). Commitments of the educational legal framework to the communication system: A systemic study of the "communication complexity" of Greek primary educational organizations. In A. Kodakos & P. Stamatis (Eds.), *Communication and education, Vol. 3: Issues of theory and research methodology of communication in education* (pp. 187–205). Diadrasi.

Angelakou, E.-P. (2021). The "adaptation" of Greek primary school to a social environment of increasing communicative complexity. In A. Kodakos & F. Kalavasis (Series Eds.), *Topics in Educational Design, Vol 12: Educational engineering of communication and its media in the design and development of educational organizations* (pp. 182–200). Diadrasi.

Argyris, C. (1999). *On organizational learning* (2nd ed.). Blackwell Publishers.

Argyris, C., & Schön, D. A. (1974). *Theory in practice: Increasing professional effectiveness.* Jossey-Bass.

Argyris, C., & Schön, D. A. (1978). *Organizational learning: A theory of action perspective.* Addison-Wesley.

Ashkanasy, N. M., Broadfoot, L. E., & Falkus, S. (2000). Questionnaire measures of organizational culture. In Ashkanasy, N. M., Wilderom, C. P. M., & Peterson, M. F. (Eds.), *Handbook of organizational culture and climate* (pp. 131–145). Sage.

Athanasoula-Reppa, A. (2008). *Educational administration and organizational behavior: The pedagogy of educational administration.* Ellin.

Atkinson, P., & Hammersley, M. (1994). Ethnography and participant observation. In Denzin, N. K., & Lincoln, Y. S. (Eds.), *Handbook of qualitative research* (pp. 248–261). Sage.

Babbie, E. (2011). *Introduction to social research* (G. Vogiatzis, Trans.; K. Zafeiropoulos, Ed.-Intro.). Kritiki.

Ball, S. J. (2003). The teacher's soul and the terrors of performativity. *Journal of Education Policy, 18*(2), 215–228. DOI: 10.1080/0268093022000043065

Bandura, A. (1997). *Self-efficacy: The exercise of control.* W H Freeman/Times Books/ Henry Holt & Co.

Becker, M. C., & Haunschild, A. (2003). The impact of boundaryless carries on organizational decision making. An analysis from the perspective of Luhmann's theory on social system. *International Journal of Human Resource Management, 14*(5), 713–727. DOI: 10.1080/0958519032000080767

Bigge, M. (1990). *Learning theories for teachers* (Kantas, A., & Chantzi, A., Trans.). Patakis.

Bouvier, A. (2013). *Management and cognitive sciences (A. Kodakos & F. Kalavasis* (Theofylaktopoulou, E., Koitsanou, E., & Papazachariou, T. Eds. & Trans.). Diadrasi.

Braun, V., & Clarke, V. (2006). Using thematic analysis in psychology. *Qualitative Research in Psychology, 3*(2), 77–101. DOI: 10.1191/1478088706qp063oa

Brinia, V. (2008). *Management of educational units and education.* Stamoulis.

Bryk, A. S., & Schneider, B. (2002). *Trust in schools: A core resource for improvement.* Russell Sage Foundation.

Cohen, L., Manion, L., & Morrison, K. (2008). *Research methods in education (5th compl* (Kyranakis, S., Mavrakis, M., & Mitsopoulou, C. Eds. & Trans.). Metaichmio.

Collinson, V., Cook, T. F., & Conley, S. (2006). Organizational learning in schools and school systems: Improving learning, teaching, and leading. *Theory into Practice, 45*(2), 107–116. DOI: 10.1207/s15430421tip4502_2

Creswell, J. W., & Plano Clark, V. L. (2018). *Designing and conducting mixed methods research* (3rd ed.). Sage.

Cyert, R. M., & March, J. G. (1963). *A behavioral theory of the firm.* Prentice-Hall.

Dalin, P. (1998). *School development: Theories and strategies: An international handbook.* Cassell.

Datnow, A., & Park, V. (2018). *Professional collaboration with purpose: Teacher learning towards equitable and excellent schools.* Routledge., DOI: 10.4324/9781351165884

Davenport, T. H., & Prusak, L. (2000). *Working knowledge: How organizations manage what they know*. Harvard Business School Press.

Deal, T., & Kennedy, A. (1982). *Corporate cultures: The rites and rituals of corporate life*. Wesley.

Denzin, N. K. (1978). *The research act: A theoretical introduction to sociological methods* (2nd ed.). McGraw-Hill.

Dixon, N. (1994). *The organizational learning cycle: How we can learn collectively*. McGraw-Hill.

DuFour, R., & Eaker, R. (1998). *Professional learning communities at work: Best practices for enhancing student achievement*. National Education Service.

Erez, M., & Gati, E. (2004). A dynamic, multi-level model of culture: From the micro level of the individual to the macro level of a global culture. *Applied Psychology, 53*(4), 583–598. DOI: 10.1111/j.1464-0597.2004.00190.x

Filias, V. (1996). *Introduction to the methodology and techniques of social research*. Gutenberg.

Flick, U. (2014). *An introduction to qualitative research* (5th ed.). Sage.

Flood, R. L., & Romm, N. R. A. (1996). Contours of diversity management and triple-loop learning. *Kybernetes, 25*(7/8), 154–163. DOI: 10.1108/03684929610149747

Fuchs, C., & Hofkirchner, W. (2009). Autopoiesis and critical social theory. *Kybernetes, 38*(6), 1112–1129.

Fullan, M. (1996). Turning systemic thinking on its head. *Phi Delta Kappan, 77*(6), 420–423.

Fullan, M. (2007). *The new meaning of educational change* (4th ed.). Teachers College Press.

Fullan, M. (2020). *Leading in a culture of change* (2nd ed.). Jossey-Bass.

Gagné, R. M. (1975). *Essentials of learning for instruction*. Dryden Press.

Geertz, C. (1973). *The interpretation of cultures*. Basic Books.

Geissler, H. (1995). *Organisationslernen und Wissensmanagement* [Organizational learning and knowledge management]. R. Oldenbourg Verlag.

Ghinea, V. M., & Bratianu, C. (2012). Organizational culture modeling. *Management & Marketing*, 7(2), 257–276.

Habermas, J. (1987). *The theory of communicative action, Volume 2: Lifeworld and system.* Beacon Press.

Hargreaves, A. (2005). Educational change takes ages: Life, career and generational factors in teachers' emotional responses to educational change. *Teaching and Teacher Education, 21*(8), 967–983. DOI: 10.1016/j.tate.2005.06.007

Hargreaves, A., & O'Connor, M. T. (2018). *Collaborative professionalism: When teaching together means learning for all.* Corwin. DOI: 10.4135/9781506328133

Harris, A., & Jones, M. (2020). COVID-19 – School leadership in disruptive times. *School Leadership & Management, 40*(4), 243–247. DOI: 10.1080/13632434.2020.1811479

Hedberg, B. (1981). How organizations learn and unlearn. In Nystrom, P. C., & Starbuck, W. H. (Eds.), *Handbook of organizational design: Adapting organizations to their environment* (Vol. 1, pp. 3–27). Oxford University Press.

Hoy, W. K., & Tschannen-Moran, M. (1999). Five faces of trust: An empirical confirmation in urban elementary schools. *Journal of School Leadership, 9*(3), 184–208. DOI: 10.1177/105268469900900301

Huber, G. P. (1991). Organizational learning: The contributing processes and the literatures. *Organization Science, 2*(1), 88–115. DOI: 10.1287/orsc.2.1.88

Isaacs, W. N. (1993). Taking flight: Dialogue, collective thinking, and organizational learning. *Organizational Dynamics, 22*(2), 24–39. [REMOVED HYPERLINK50 FIELD] https://doi.org/DOI: 10.1016/0090-2616(93)90051-2

Jacobson, M. J., & Wilensky, U. (2006). Complex systems in education: Scientific and educational importance and implications for the learning sciences. *Journal of the Learning Sciences, 15*(1), 11–34. DOI: 10.1207/s15327809jls1501_4

Kalavasis, F. (2013). Routes of networks and/or reasoning. In A. Kodakos & F. Kalavasis (Series Eds.), *Topics in Educational Planning* (Vol. 6: *Social networking and schools: Bridges and meanings)* (pp. 129–148). Atrapos.

Karsten, J. (2004). *Teaching about complexity in primary and secondary schools: An exploration of new approaches to ecosystem education* [Doctoral dissertation, McGill University]. McGill University Repository.

Kim, J. H., & Callahan, J. L. (2013). Finding the intersection of the learning organization and learning transfer: The significance of leadership. *European Journal of Training and Development, 37*(2), 183–200. DOI: 10.1108/03090591311301680

Kioussi, S. (2025). A systems approach to school culture as a factor in effective school development [Doctoral dissertation, University of the Aegean]. National Archive of PhD Theses. https://doi.org/DOI: 10.12681/eadd/60580

Kluchert, G. (2009). Schulkultur(en) in historischer Perspektive: Einführung in das Thema. *Zeitschrift für Pädagogik, 55*(3), 326–333.

Kluckhohn, C. (2017). *Mirror for man: The relation of anthropology to modern life* (1st ed.). Routledge., DOI: 10.4324/9781315107127

Kodakos, A. (2010). Systemic educational leadership. In F. Kalavasis & A. Kodakos (Series Eds.), *Topics in educational planning, Vol. 4: Communication and governance of educational systems,* (pp. 75–92). Diadrasi.

Kodakos, A., & Angelakou, E.-P. (2016). From school theories to school development. In A. Kodakos & F. Kalavasis (Series Eds.), *Topics in educational planning, Vol. 8: Systemic educational development: Technological and pedagogical interweaving,* (pp. 29–65). Diadrasi.

Kodakos, A., & Angelakou, E.-P. (2017). The portrait of an intelligent school: The example of Greece. In A. Kodakos & F. Kalavasis (Series Eds.), *Topics in educational planning, Vol. 9: The school as an intelligent, hybrid, and moral entity* (pp. 85–117). Diadrasi.

Kodakos, A., Angelakou, E.-P., & Oikonomidi, E. (2017, August 22–25). *School development as development of organizational learning and change: A systemic approach* [Conference presentation]. *European Conference on Educational Research (ECER)*, Copenhagen, Denmark.

Kotsikis, V. (2003). *Educational administration and policy.* Ellin.

Kvale, S., & Brinkmann, S. (2009). *InterViews: Learning the craft of qualitative research interviewing* (2nd ed.). Sage.

Laermans, R. (2007). Theorizing culture, or reading Luhmann against Luhmann. *Cybernetics & Human Knowing, 14*(2–3), 67–83.

Lave, J., & Wenger, E. (1991). *Situated learning: Legitimate peripheral participation.* Cambridge University Press. DOI: 10.1017/CBO9780511815355

Lincoln, Y. S., & Guba, E. G. (1985). Naturalistic inquiry. *Sage (Atlanta, Ga.).*

Luhmann, N. (1984). *Soziale Systeme: Grundriss einer allgemeinen Theorie.* Suhrkamp.

Luhmann, N. (1992). Organisation. In Küpper, W., & Ortmann, G. (Eds.), *Mikropolitik: Rationalität, Macht und Spiele in Organisationen* (pp. 165–185). Westdeutscher Verlag.

Luhmann, N. (1995a). *Social Systems* (Bednarz, J.Jr, & Baecker, D., Trans.). Stanford University Press.

Luhmann, N. (1995b). *Theory of social systems* (Karkatsoulis, P., & Makrydimitris, A., Eds.). Sakkoulas. (Original work published 1984)

Luhmann, N. (1995c). Kultur als historischer Begriff. In Luhmann, N. (Ed.), *Gesellschaftsstruktur und Semantik IV* (pp. 31–54). Suhrkamp.

Luhmann, N. (1995d). The paradox of observing systems. *Cultural Critique*, *31*(31), 37–55. DOI: 10.2307/1354444

Luhmann, N. (1997). *Die Gesellschaft der Gesellschaft*. Suhrkamp.

Luhmann, N. (2000a). *Organisation und Entscheidung*. Westdeutscher Verlag. DOI: 10.1007/978-3-322-97093-0

Luhmann, N. (2000b). *Die Gesellschaft der Gesellschaft*. Suhrkamp.

Luhmann, N. (2000c). *Organization and decision*. Cambridge University Press.

Luhmann, N. (2003a). Organization. In Bakken, T., & Hernes, T. (Eds.), *Autopoietic organization theory: Drawing on Niklas Luhmann's social systems perspective* (pp. 31–52). Copenhagen Business School Press.

Luhmann, N. (2003b). *The reality of the mass media* (Zeri, P., Trans.). Metaichmio. (Original work published 1996)

Luhmann, N. (2003c). *Funktionen und Folgen formaler Organisation* (4th ed.). Suhrkamp Verlag.

Luhmann, N. (2005). *Soziale Systeme: Grundriß einer allgemeinen Theorie* (7th ed.). Suhrkamp.

Luhmann, N. (2012). *Theories of distinction: Redescribing the descriptions of modernity*. Stanford University Press.

Luhmann, N. (2018). *Organization and decision (D. Baecker* (Barrett, R. Ed. & Trans.). Cambridge University Press. (Original work published 2000), DOI: 10.1017/9781108560672

Lunenburg, F. C. (2010). Schools as open systems. *Schooling*, *1*(1), 1–5.

Luthar, S. S. (2015). Resilience in development: A synthesis of research across five decades. In Cicchetti, D., & Cohen, D. J. (Eds.), *Wiley*. Developmental psychopathology, DOI: 10.1002/9780470939406.ch20

MacBeath, J., & McGlynn, A. (2004). *Self-evaluation. What's in it for schools?* RoutledgeFalmer., DOI: 10.4324/9780203018668

MacBeath, J., Schratz, M., Meuret, D., & Jakobsen, L. B. (2005). *Self-evaluation in the European school: How things have changed* (Deligianni, M., Trans.). Metaixmio.

MacGilchrist, B., Myers, K., & Reed, J. (2004). *The intelligent school* (2nd ed.). Sage. DOI: 10.4135/9781446216484

Magklaras, V. (2013). *Theories of social systems: Parsons, Luhmann, Habermas*. Sideris.

March, J. G. (1991). Exploration and exploitation in organizational learning. *Organization Science*, *2*(1), 71–87. DOI: 10.1287/orsc.2.1.71

March, J. G., & Simon, H. A. (1958). *Organizations*. Wiley.

March, J. G., & Simon, H. A. (1963). *Organizations*. Wiley.

March, J. G., & Simon, H. A. (1993). *Organizations* (2nd ed). Oxford.

Marquardt, M. J. (1996). *Building the learning organization: Mastering the five elements for corporate learning*. Davies-Black Publishing.

Marsick, V. J., & Watkins, K. E. (2003). Demonstrating the value of an organization's learning culture: The dimensions of the learning organization questionnaire. *Advances in Developing Human Resources*, *5*(2), 132–151. DOI: 10.1177/1523422303005002002

Martens, W. (2006). The distinctions within organizations: Luhmann from a cultural perspective. *Organization*, *13*(1), 83–108. DOI: 10.1177/1350508406059643

Martens, W., & Ortmann, G. (2006). Organisationen in der Systemtheorie Niklas Luhmanns. *Zeitschrift für Soziologie*, *35*(2), 115–139.

Marzano, R. J. (2003). *What works in schools: Translating research into action*. ASCD.

Maslowski, R. (2001). *School culture and school performance: An explorative study into the organizational culture of secondary schools and their effects* [Doctoral dissertation, University of Twente]. Twente University Press.

Maslowski, R. (2006). A review of inventories for diagnosing school culture. *Journal of Educational Administration*, *44*(1), 6–35. DOI: 10.1108/09578230610642638

Masten, A. (2025). *Ordinary magic. Resilience in development* (2nd ed.). Guilford Press.

Matsaggouras, H. (2007). *Theory and practice of teaching: The school classroom—Space, group, discipline, method*. Grigoris.

Maturana, H. R., & Varela, F. J. (1980). *Autopoiesis and cognition: The realization of the living*. Reidel. DOI: 10.1007/978-94-009-8947-4

Maurer, K. (2010, February). Communication and language in Niklas Luhmann's systems theory. *Pandaemonium Germanicum,* 1–21. https://doi.org/DOI: 10.1590/S1982-88372010000200002

Merriam, S. B. (2009). *Qualitative research: A guide to design and implementation*. Jossey-Bass.

Meyer, J. W., & Rowan, B. (1977). Institutionalized organizations: Formal structure as myth and ceremony. *American Journal of Sociology*, *83*(2), 340–363. DOI: 10.1086/226550

Mingers, J. (2002). Can social systems be autopoietic? Assessing Luhmann's social theory. *The Sociological Review*, *50*(2), 278–299. DOI: 10.1111/1467-954X.00367

Moloi, K. C. (2010). How can schools build learning organisations in difficult education contexts? *South African Journal of Education*, *30*(4), 621–633. DOI: 10.15700/saje.v30n4a392

Morgan, D. L. (1997). *Focus groups as qualitative research* (2nd ed.). Sage. DOI: 10.4135/9781412984287

Mortimore, P. (1993). School effectiveness and the management of effective Learning and teaching. *School Effectiveness and School Improvement*, *4*(4), 290–310. DOI: 10.1080/0924345930040404

Nitschke, P. (2024). Berger & Luckmann (1966): The Social Construction of Reality. In Hoffjann, O., & Sandhu, S. (Eds.), *Schlüsselwerke für die Strategische Kommunikationsforschung*. Springer VS., DOI: 10.1007/978-3-658-45292-6_29

Nonaka, I., & Takeuchi, H. (1995). *The knowledge-creating company: How Japanese companies create the dynamics of innovation*. Oxford University Press. DOI: 10.1093/oso/9780195092691.001.0001

OECD. (2013). *Synergies for better learning: An international perspective on evaluation and assessment*. OECD Publishing.

OECD. (2025). *Education at a Glance 2025: OECD Indicators*. OECD Publishing.

Patton, M. Q. (1990). Qualitative evaluation and research methods. *Sage (Atlanta, Ga.)*.

Pedler, M., Burgoyne, J., & Boydell, T. (1997). *The learning company: A strategy for sustainable development* (2nd ed.). McGraw-Hill.

Piekarczyk, A. (2017). Organisation Culture from Systems Theory of Organisation Perspective. In Nedelko, Z., & Brzozowski, M. (Eds.), *Exploring the Influence of Personal Values and Cultures in the Workplace* (pp. 39–52). IGI Global., DOI: 10.4018/978-1-5225-2480-9.ch003

Qvortrup, L. (2005). Society's education system: An introduction to Niklas Luhmann's pedagogical theory. *Seminar. International Journal (Toronto, Ont.)*, *1*(1), 1–21.

Ramage, M., & Shipp, K. (2009). *Systems thinkers*. Springer., DOI: 10.1007/978-1-84882-525-3

Rolff, H.-G. (1993). *Wandel durch Selbstorganisation: Theoretische Grundlagen und praktische Hinweise für eine bessere Schule*. Juventa.

Rolff, H.-G. (2013). Schulleitung und Schulentwicklung. In Rolff, H.-G. (Ed.), *Schulentwicklung kompakt: Modelle, Instrumente, Perspektiven* (pp. 10–29). Beltz.

Roth, S. (2011). Les deux révolutions de l'autopoïèse: De la biologie à l'organisation. *Revue Internationale de Psychosociologie*, *17*(43), 179–204.

Rutter, M. (2006). Implications of resilience concepts for scientific understanding. *Annals of the New York Academy of Sciences*, *1094*(1), 1–12. DOI: 10.1196/annals.1376.002

Scheerens, J. (1992). *Effective schooling*. Cassell.

Schein, E. H. (1985). *Organizational culture and leadership*. Jossey-Bass.

Schein, E. H. (2010). *Organizational culture and leadership* (4th ed.). Jossey-Bass.

Seidl, D. (2005a). Organisational change and the concept of autopoiesis. In Czarniawska, B., & Sevón, K. (Eds.), *Global ideas: How ideas, objects and practices travel in the global economy* (pp. 133–146). Copenhagen Business School Press.

Seidl, D. (2005b). The basic concepts of Luhmann's theory of social systems. In Seidl, D., & Becker, K. H. (Eds.), *Niklas Luhmann and organization studies*. Liber & Copenhagen Business School Press.

Seidl, D. (2005c). *Organisational Identity and Self-Transformation: An Autopoietic Perspective*. Liber & Copenhagen Business School Press.

Seidl, D. (2007). Organisational identity and self-transformation: An autopoietic perspective. In Berthoin Antal, A., Dierkes, M., Child, J., & Nonaka, I. (Eds.), *Handbook of organizational learning and knowledge* (pp. 85–107). Oxford University Press.

Seidl, D., & Becker, K. H. (2006). Organizations as distinction generating and processing systems: Niklas Luhmann's contribution to organization studies. *Organization, 13*(1), 9–35. DOI: 10.1177/1350508406059635

Seidl, D., & Mormann, H. (2015). Niklas Luhmann as organization theorist. In Adler, P., du Gay, P., Morgan, G., & Reed, M. (Eds.), *The Oxford Handbook of Sociology, Social Theory, and Organization Studies: Contemporary Currents* (pp. 125–157). Academic., DOI: 10.1093/oxfordhb/9780199671083.013.0007

Selwyn, N. (2016). *Education and Technology: Key Issues and Debates* (2nd ed.). Bloomsbury Academic.

Senge, P. M. (1990). *The fifth discipline: The art and practice of the learning organization*. Century / Doubleday.

Simon, F. B. (2010). *Introduction to the systems theory of organizations* (Makrydimitris, A., Trans.). Sakkoulas.

Simon, H. A. (1957). *Administrative behavior: A study of decision-making processes in administrative organization* (2nd ed.). Macmillan.

Stake, R. E. (1995). The art of case study research. *Sage (Atlanta, Ga.)*.

Stoll, L., & Fink, D. (1996). *Changing our schools: Linking school effectiveness and school improvement*. Open University Press.

Sun, P., & Scott, J. (2003). Exploring the divide: Organizational learning and learning organization. *The Learning Organization, 10*(4), 202–215. DOI: 10.1108/09696470310476972

Sutton, P., & Shouse, A. W. (2016). Building a culture of collaboration in schools. *Phi Delta Kappan, 97*(7), 69–73. DOI: 10.1177/0031721716641653

Tasis, T. (2012, April–June). The dialogue between Habermas and Luhmann. *Theseis*, 119.

Thurmond, V. A. (2001). The point of triangulation. *Journal of Nursing Scholarship*, *33*(3), 253–258. DOI: 10.1111/j.1547-5069.2001.00253.x

Tsoukas, H. (2005). *Complex knowledge: Studies in organizational epistemology*. Oxford University Press.

Ungar, M. (2018). Systemic resilience: Principles and processes for a science of change in contexts of adversity. *Ecology and Society*, *23*(4), art34. Advance online publication. DOI: 10.5751/ES-10385-230434

Varela, F. G. (1979). *Principles of biological autonomy*. North Holland.

Vogus, T. J., & Sutcliffe, K. M. (2007). Organizational resilience: Toward a theory and research agenda. In *Proceedings of the 2007 IEEE International Conference on Systems, Man and Cybernetics* (pp. 3418–3422). IEEE. https://doi.org/DOI: 10.1109/ICSMC.2007.4414160

Walsh, J. P., & Ungson, G. R. (1991). Organizational memory. *Academy of Management Review*, *16*(1), 57–91. DOI: 10.2307/258607

Weick, K. E. (1995). *Sensemaking in organizations*. Sage Publications.

Wenger, E. (1998). *Communities of practice: Learning, meaning, and identity*. Cambridge University Press. DOI: 10.1017/CBO9780511803932

Wiener, N. (1948). *Cybernetics: Or, Control and Communication in the Animal and the Machine*. MIT University Press.

Wilkins, A., & Ouchi, W. (1983). Efficient cultures: Exploring the relationship between culture and organizational performance. *Administrative Science Quarterly*, *28*(3), 468–8. DOI: 10.2307/2392253

Willke, H. (1996). *Introduction to Systems Theory* (Livos, N., Trans.). Kritiki Publications.

Willke, H. (2007). *Smart governance: Governing the global knowledge society*. Campus Verlag.

Yin, R. K. (2018). *Case study research and applications: Design and methods* (6th ed.). Sage.

ADDITIONAL READING

Kioussi, S., & Kodakos, A. (2023). A systems approach to school culture in the light of Niklas Luhmann's theory. In V. Chiou, L. Geunis, O. Holz, N. O. Ertukr, J. Ratkowska-Pasikowska, F. Shelton (Eds), *Contemporary challenges in education. Paradoxes and illuminations.* Waxmann.

Kioussi, S., & Kodakos, A. (2025). A systems research 1st order observation tool on major factors influencing teachers' school culture. In V. Chiou, L. Geunis, O. Holz, N. O. Ertukr, J. RatkowskaPasikowska, F. Shelton (Eds), *Research and evidence-based perspectives in education. Diverse discourse, connected conversations.* Waxmann.

Kodakos, A. (2014). The communication system of society and the role of the body: An attempt at a historical systemic approach to communication. In Kodakos, A., & Stamatis, P. (Eds.), *Non-verbal communication in education: Theory and practice* (Vol. 1, pp. 41–86). Diadrasi.

Kodakos, A. (2018). Diagnosis model of systemic competence and applications in systemic school development: An emerged proposal. In A. Kodakos & F. Kalavasis (Series Eds), *Topics in educational design, Vol. 10: Developments models schools: Applications of the systemic approach and its educational engineering* (pp. 127-152). Diadrasi.

Kodakos, A. (2023). The development of learning educational organizations as a systemic process of transition from the state of unorganized to the state of organized complexity. In A. Kodakos & F. Kalavasis (Series Eds), *Topics in educational design, Vol.13: The engineering of transition in educational design and development of school units: Theories, systems, processes, functions, models, tools, programs, technologies* (pp. 37-51). Diadrasi.

Kodakos, A., Papadosifou, M., & Angelakou, E.-P. (2019). From partial quality to complexity as an indicator of organizational flexibility. In A. Kodakos & F. Kalavasis (Series Eds.), *Topics in educational design, Vol. 11: Complexity in the design and development of educational units* (pp. 55–76). Diadrasi.

Larios-Hernandez, G. (2021). Premises of digital transformation in autopoietic organization: A framework proposal. In Malgorzata, P. (Ed.), *Handbook of Research on Autopoiesis and Self-Sustaining Processes for Organizational Success* (1st ed., pp. 325–345). Business Science Reference., DOI: 10.4018/978-1-7998-6713-5.ch016

Martens, W. (2006). The distinctions within organizations: Luhmann from a cultural perspective. *Organization*, *13*(1), 83–108. DOI: 10.1177/1350508406059643

Maslowski, R. (2006). A review of inventories for diagnosing school culture. *Journal of Educational Administration*, *44*(1), 6–35. DOI: 10.1108/09578230610642638

Seidl, D., & Becker, K. H. (2006). Organizations as distinction generating and processing systems: Niklas Luhmann's contribution to organization studies. *Organization*, *13*(1), 9–35. DOI: 10.1177/1350508406059635

KEY TERMS AND DEFINITIONS

Autopoietic System: A system that continuously reproduces its own organization and constituent elements through a operationally closed cycle of internal interactions (intra-systemic communications), thereby maintaining its identity while remaining structurally coupled with its environment.

Cognitive Dimension of Complexity: A dimension of complexity referring to the system's capacity for self-regulation and self-steering through the production, processing, and utilization of knowledge.

Collective Reflection: A collective process of reflexive processing of experience and practice, through which members of an organization jointly examine and interpret their actions, assumptions, and outcomes in order to generate shared understanding and inform future practice.

Decision Premises: The structural conditions of an organization that are themselves the product of prior decisions. Functioning as a "duality of structure," they simultaneously constrain and enable organizational action by limiting choices to facilitate the absorption of uncertainty. Luhmann categorizes these into three explicit, decided types: programmatic decisions (regulations and goals), communication channels (formal and informal lines of authority), and personnel (membership and role assignments), which are collectively operationalized through organizational positions.

Double-Loop Learning: The capacity of individuals, groups, or organizations to critically re-examine existing conditions, reformulate underlying assumptions and policies, and accordingly transform their actions, thereby expanding their capabilities and fostering collective intelligence and reflective organizational development.

Educational Legislation: The body of laws, regulations, and formal policy frameworks that govern the structure, operation, and accountability of educational systems and institutions, defining the conditions under which educational organizations function.

Educational System: A social formation and societal subsystem characterized by a distinct structure and mode of operation, existing in dynamic interrelation and structural coupling with other social systems and subsystems —such as the political, economic, and cultural systems— both at the national and global levels.

Environment: Everything that exists external to the system and is not constituted as part of its internal operations, while nonetheless serving as a continuous source of complexity, stimuli, and structural coupling conditions.

Learning/Intelligent Organization: An organizational model structured in such a way as to absorb, generate, and utilize knowledge in order to foster innovation, adaptability, and continuous development, while simultaneously enhancing and facilitating the learning capacities of its members through ongoing processes of organizational transformation aimed at strengthening effectiveness and operational efficiency.

Meta-Learning: The capacity to learn about the learning process itself, achieved when organizations, groups, or individuals develop the ability to distinguish between, selectively employ, and effectively benefit from single-loop and double-loop learning processes.

Non-Decision Premises: structural frameworks within an organization that have not been established by an explicit, official act of decision-making. Instead, they emerge as structural by-products of ongoing communication. They operate beneath the organization's conscious awareness, being taken for granted and stripped of their perceived contingency. Luhmann distinguishes two primary forms: organizational culture (implicit norms governing how decisions are handled) and cognitive routines (internalized schemata used to perceive, categorize, and respond to environmental stimuli).

Organizational Complexity: A property of a system that may refer either to the number and diversity of its constituent elements (variety) or to the degree of unpredictability associated with the system's behavior and developmental trajectories (variability).

Organizational Learning: A higher-order form of learning encompassing both individual and collective learning processes occurring within and across organizational contexts, through which organizations develop, transform, and reproduce their structures, practices, and decision-making capacities.

Organizational Resilience: The capacity of an organization to maintain its functional coherence and operational closure under conditions of increased complexity, through the dynamic reconfiguration of decision premises and the continuous restructuring of its structural couplings with the environment, thereby ensuring the persistence and adaptive continuity of its communicative operations over time.

School Culture: An emerging autopoietic phenomenon, shaped by the dynamic interplay of programmatic, communicative, and value-driven decision premises. It manifests as an emergent phenomenal truth, conditioned by its interaction with decision premises that define what is deemed known, permissible, and feasible within the school organization. At the same time, it functions as a meaning-giving mechanism that regulates how the school relates both to itself and to its social environment.

School Development: A systematic, goal-oriented, and self-referential process through which the members of a school organization consciously pursue transformative improvement in the functioning, self-regulation, and self-governance of the organization.

School Unit: A distinct organizational entity operating within the broader social formation of the educational system, constituted through structured communicative, administrative, and pedagogical processes.

Second-Order Observation: The cybernetic process of "observing observers" or observing the distinctions used by an observing system. It shifts the analytical lens to *how* the system is being seen and by whom. In organizational analysis, this methodology allows a system (or researcher) to reflect upon its own blind spots, deconstruct its taken-for-granted decision premises, and expose the contingency of its internal realities.

Self-Referential School Unit: A school organization that continuously reproduces and restructures its own constitutive elements to maintain its organizational coherence and operational continuity over time.

Self-Referential System: A system that observes, evaluates, and reflects upon its own operations to regulate and manage both internal and environmental complexity through recursive self-observation processes.

Social Subsystems: Functionally differentiated subsystems of society constituted through specialized communicative operations.

Social System: A system of recursively reproduced values, meanings, and structural configurations composed of differentiated subsystems, representing the highest level of differentiation within the global social system.

System (in Social Systems Theory): A set of elements and the structured relations among these elements and their properties, such that they constitute a coherent whole engaged in continuous communication and structural coupling with its external environment.

Systems Approach: An interdisciplinary worldview oriented toward transdisciplinary collaboration among diverse scientific domains, aiming to conceptually and analytically address the organized complexity of the world.

Chapter 2
Communication Between Teachers and Parents:
The Role of Teachers in Cultivating Positive Relationships Within the School Context

Panagiotis J. Stamatis
http://orcid.org/0000-0002-9459-7156
University of the Aegean, Rhodes, Greece

Meropi J. Ntavlamanou
Primary Education Directorate of Dodecanese, Greece

ABSTRACT

This chapter examines teacher–parent communication as a foundational dimension of contemporary educational practice, emphasizing its pedagogical, psychosocial, and institutional significance. Drawing on international literature, it conceptualizes communication as a multidimensional and dynamic process that transcends information exchange and is embedded in cultural norms, power relations, and school structures. The teacher is positioned as a central mediator and collaborative partner whose attitudes, competencies, and communication strategies decisively influence parental engagement and student outcomes. The analysis explores formal, informal, and digital modalities of communication, as well as theoretical models of collaboration, associated challenges, and culturally responsive practices. The chapter concludes that systematic, dialogical, and trust-based communication enhances student achievement, strengthens school cohesion, and supports teachers' professional well-being, thereby contributing to sustainable and inclusive educational environments.

DOI: 10.4018/979-8-3373-9420-6.ch002

INTRODUCTION

Effective communication between schools and families is one of the most critical issues in contemporary educational policy and practice, as it has a significant impact on students' academic success, social integration, and emotional well-being. Schools and families are key agents in a child's socialization. The relationship between them shapes the context in which a child's learning and psychosocial skills develop (Epstein, 2018; Jeynes, 2017).

International literature has gradually moved away from traditional, linear communication models, adopting more complex, dynamic and interactive approaches that recognize parents as equal partners in the learning process (Goodall & Montgomery, 2014; Pushor, 2015). Teachers play a pivotal role in this context, forming relationships of trust and mutual respect with families through their communication practices (Stamatis, 2015).

This chapter, based on related literature and research findings, explores communication between teachers and parents as a key mechanism for fostering positive, functional, and collaborative relationships within the school context. Particular emphasis is placed on the role of teachers as key mediators of the communication process, with a decisive influence on the scope and quality of parental engagement (Willemse et al., 2018). The chapter's specific objectives are:

a) To provide a conceptual clarification of communication in the school environment;
   (b) To highlight the importance of communication for school–family collaboration;
   (c) Presenting and critically evaluating the main forms of communication developing in contemporary educational practice.

Numerous empirical studies demonstrate that communication between teachers and parents is one of the most consistent predictors of students' academic success and adjustment to school life (Stamatis & Nikolaou, 2020). Such research shows that even brief and limited communication between teachers and parents can lead to statistically significant improvements in school performance and student participation in school events. One example is Kraft and Rogers' (2015) research, which showed that systematically sending short, targeted messages from teachers to parents reduced secondary school students' failure rates and increased their school attendance.

Similar findings have been reported in experimental intervention studies, which have shown that an improvement in the quality of communication between schools and families was associated with higher levels of student engagement, more positive attitudes towards school, and improved behavior (Kraft & Dougherty, 2013). Researchers also emphasize that the quality and style of communication, rather than just its frequency, play a critical role in its effectiveness (Stamatis & Stavropoulou, 2018).

Large cross-national studies in developing education systems confirm that systematic communication between schools and families is associated with higher learning achievement, even when controlling for socioeconomic factors (Li et al., 2023). These findings support the view that communication acts as a mechanism to compensate for social inequalities.

In a school environment, communication between teachers and parents is an ongoing, dynamic, socially determined process involving the exchange of information, meanings, and emotions. The main goal is to support the child's learning and all-round development. It is not a neutral process of information transmission, but a predominantly pedagogical practice influenced by school culture, the expectations of those involved, and the wider socio-cultural context (Pushor, 2015; Murray et al., 2015).

Current literature highlights three main forms of school-family communication: formal/informal, informal/informal, and digital. Rather than competing with each other, these forms complement each other, and their effectiveness depends on them being used consciously and in balance within an overall school-family collaboration strategy (Goodall & Montgomery, 2014). More specifically, the mentioned forms of school-family communication are:

1. *Formal communication*, which includes institutionalized, planned practices such as parent meetings, written communications and progress reports. Empirical research shows that this format ensures the transparency, clarity and institutional validity of information. However, it is often characterized by limited interaction and a one-sided flow of information (Watkins, 1997). Its effectiveness is enhanced when accompanied by opportunities for dialogue and feedback.
2. *Informal communication*, which manifests itself through brief daily contacts, telephone conversations or informal messages, has been shown to be critical in building trusting and close relationships. Qualitative and quantitative studies show that parents perceive direct, personal communication as a sign of professional interest and pedagogical care. This enhances cooperation and reduces conflict with teachers (Vickers & Minke, 1995; Gelfer, 1991).

3. In recent years, *digital communication* has become increasingly important, with people using emails, educational platforms, and instant messaging apps. Empirical studies demonstrate that digital communication increases the frequency of contact between schools and families and enables parents who find it difficult to respond to traditional forms of communication due to professional or social constraints to participate more easily (Hidayat & Arini, 2022). At the same time, experimental

research has shown that targeted digital communication interventions can measurably improve student achievement and stimulate engagement with school (Forsström et al., 2025). However, it has been pointed out in the literature that uncritical or excessive use of digital media may lead to misunderstandings, ambiguity of boundaries and professional strain for teachers (Russell & Qiu, 2024). Therefore, effective digital communication requires clear pedagogical planning, commonly accepted rules and teacher training.

A series of empirical studies confirm the above findings while also highlighting the specifics of the institutional and organizational framework (Stamatis & Nikolaou, 2022). While teachers acknowledge the importance of communicating with parents, they also identify barriers such as a lack of time, an absence of systematic training, and unclear role expectations (Stamatis & Chatzinikola, 2021). Nevertheless, studies demonstrate that, when based on relationships of trust, mutual respect and professionalism, communication is instrumental in shaping a positive school climate and enhancing parental engagement (Pasiardis, 2016).

In conclusion, the majority of research findings suggest that school-family communication is not a single, homogeneous practice, but rather a complex web of forms and strategies whose effectiveness depends on pedagogical orientation, teachers' skills, parents' receptiveness to cooperation, and the institutional framework within which these parameters develop.

THEORETICAL FRAMEWORK OF SCHOOL-FAMILY COMMUNICATION: THE ROLE OF THE TEACHER IN SHAPING POSITIVE RELATIONSHIPS

In the modern educational environment, the role of the teacher is not only to transmit information to parents, but also to act as a mediator and an essential partner of the family. A teacher ensures effective, mutually acceptable and beneficial communication between the school and the family. This reflects a broader pedagogical approach in which children's learning and development are seen as the result of collective responsibility and the co-construction of relationships between school and family (Pushor, 2015).

As a mediator, the teacher must bridge the differences in value systems, expectations and communication practices that are often evident in the school and family environments. This mediating function is particularly important in environments of cultural, linguistic or socio-economic heterogeneity, where the risk of misinterpretation and conflict increases (Baraldi & Gavioli, 2023). Consequently, teachers act as mediators of communication, facilitating dialogue, fostering mutual understanding, and promoting trusting relationships with parents.

The literature indicates that the quality of the relationship between teachers and parents often acts as a critical mediator between communication and students' learning and behavioral outcomes. Studies have shown that positive, collaborative relationships between teachers and parents are associated with increased student engagement, improved school adjustment and more positive social behavior (Sheridan et al., 2012; Kim et al., 2013). Similarly, experimental studies demonstrate that interventions, which enhance collaborative teacher-parent communication indirectly but consistently, improve student achievement by enhancing the quality of the relationship (Kraft & Dougherty, 2013).

At the same time, as an essential partner of the family, the teacher is expected to recognize and utilize parental knowledge, experience and expectations, while avoiding hierarchical or paternalistic practices. According to the "working with parents" theory, meaningful collaboration requires parents to participate equally in pedagogical decision-making processes, as well as ensuring their views and experiences are systematically recognized and considered (Pushor, 2015). Research findings confirm that trust and willingness to collaborate with the teacher are enhanced when parents perceive the teacher as an ally rather than a controlling agent (Kuusimäki et al., 2019).

The role of the teacher as a mediator in situations of tension or conflict between school and family is of particular importance. Studies focusing on school conflict management demonstrate that the way in which teachers communicate with parents can either de-escalate tensions or exacerbate those (Yu & Wang, 2023). Teacher mediation competence is therefore directly linked to active listening skills, empathy, and pedagogically informed communication. In summary, the teacher's role as mediator and family partner is pivotal in developing effective communication between school and family. For this reason, effectively exercising this role requires institutional support, appropriate organizational structures and systematic teacher training in interpersonal relationship management, communication and cooperative learning.

The approach to the role of the teacher as a school mediator and family partner emphasizes the importance of interpersonal relationships, communication skills, and a professional attitude in establishing a positive and supportive framework for cooperation between the school and the family. However, teachers' professional activity is not carried out in isolation, but is embedded in broader theoretical, organizational and institutional contexts which substantially impact the definition, organization and implementation of collaboration with parents.

In this context, international literature focuses on specific models of teacher-parent collaboration. These models function as conceptual tools for understanding, designing and evaluating communication and collaboration practices in the school environment. These models play a key role in contemporary educational research and policy-making as they provide structured frameworks for improving school-family communication. Organizations such as the OECD and UNESCO recognize school-family collaboration as a critical factor in developing educational quality, social cohesion, and student well-being (OECD, 2018; UNESCO, 2021). From this perspective, theoretical collaboration models serve as both interpretive frameworks and guides for formulating, implementing and evaluating educational policies and their practical applications. The most prominent models of teacher–parent collaboration are the parental engagement model, the collaboration/partnership model, and the ecosystem model. These highlight the models' theoretical starting points, the degree of parental involvement, and the role of the teacher in shaping school–family communication (Epstein, 2018; Goodall & Montgomery, 2014; Thompson, 2019).

More specifically, the parental engagement model developed by Epstein (2018) has significantly influenced educational research and policy design in Europe and North America. Emphasis is placed on the six types of engagement, which are embedded in national strategies that promote systematic parental information, parental involvement in school life and connections between schools and families. Meta-analyses of international literature show that organized parental engagement is linked to positive academic and social outcomes, especially for students from disadvantaged backgrounds (Jeynes, 2017).

Unlike 'engagement' approaches, the collaborative or partnership model promotes equal participation of schools and families in decision-making and shared responsibility for students' learning. This model is linked to contemporary participatory educational practices that encourage dialogue, transparency, and parental involvement (Goodall & Montgomery, 2014).

Research findings from international studies suggest that schools adopting collaborative communication models exhibit greater trust, improved conflict management, and a more positive school climate (Kuusimäki et al., 2019). Also, studies have shown that parental involvement is enhanced when teachers adopt collaborative attitudes and recognize the value of parental involvement, even in school settings with limited institutional resources (Stamatis & Chatzinikola, 2021).

The ecosystem model of cooperation, related to the theory of ecological systems, has significantly impacted policies aimed at including and supporting students with diverse social, cultural, and learning characteristics. In this context, school–family communication is viewed as an ongoing, multi-level interaction process, in which the teacher plays a pivotal role as a liaison between the school and the family (Thompson, 2019).

International studies show that interventions based on the ecosystem model, which take the socio-cultural context of families into account, promote sustainable and meaningful forms of cooperation (Sheridan et al., 2012).

Linking teacher–parent collaboration models to educational policies and empirical evidence shows that effective school–family communication is not an individual practice, but a process shaped by institutions and culture. Teachers are called upon to operate within these contexts, utilizing theoretical models as tools for professional reflection and pedagogical planning.

Communication between schools and families is a multidimensional pedagogical and psychosocial mechanism that decisively influences both students' learning paths and the climate of relations within school communities. From a pedagogical perspective, communication is not merely the transmission of information; it is an interactive process involving the negotiation of meanings and the joint development of educational practices, with the teacher playing a central role.

Effective teacher-parent communication at this level supports the learning process by enhancing coherence between school expectations and family practices. Research shows that systematic, quality communication improves school performance, reduces incidents of school violence, and fosters positive attitudes towards school (Garcés-Prettel et al., 2020). Through pedagogically sensitive communication practices, the teacher assumes the roles of guide and coordinator, translating students' pedagogical needs into messages that parents can understand and integrating family perspectives into school work.

At the same time, school-family communication has strong psychosocial dimensions, as it is linked to the emotional climate, trust, and sense of acceptance among those involved. The quality of communication influences students' psychosocial adjustment, particularly when characterized by empathy, mutual respect, and acknowledgement of family needs (Kapetanovic & Skoog, 2021). In this context, teachers are required to demonstrate emotional intelligence and active listening skills in order to address sensitive issues related to school and family life.

The psychosocial well-being of teachers is particularly important. Although the increased frequency and digitization of communication with families facilitates collaboration, it can burden teachers emotionally if clear boundaries and institutional support are lacking (Kuusimäki et al., 2019). Therefore, the pedagogical dimension of communication is inextricably linked to the need to develop psychosocial skills and support mechanisms for educational staff.

School-family communication is considered a vital aspect of pedagogical cooperation and social cohesion. Studies have shown that the quality of relationships between teachers and parents is influenced by cultural factors, socioeconomic inequalities, and the level of teachers' pedagogical training (Stamatis, 2013). At the same time, there is a growing emphasis on strengthening the school as a 'learning community', where communication serves to enhance the trust and psychosocial security of all members (Mavrogiorgos, 2016).

The pedagogical and psychosocial dimensions of school-family communication emphasize the multifaceted role of teachers as both pedagogical professionals and agents of emotional and social mediation. Investment in communication skills, institutional support, and cultivating a culture of cooperation are crucial for forming positive, sustainable relationships within the school context. School-family collaboration therefore requires the development of trusting and respectful relationships, where communication is a vital mechanism for fostering pedagogical partnerships and social cohesion within the school community (Kassotakis & Flouris, 2018).

A teacher's attitudes and values are critical to developing meaningful and functional communication with parents. Contemporary pedagogical literature emphasizes that school-family communication is not neutral, but is significantly impacted by teachers' perceptions of family involvement and participation in school life. A positive attitude towards parents, based on recognizing the complementary nature of the roles of schools and families, fosters trust and a willingness to collaborate (Palts & Harro-Loit, 2015).

At a fundamental level, communication between teachers and parents is based on principles such as mutual respect, equality, transparency, and shared responsibility for the child's educational journey. When teachers adopt values of democratic participation and inclusion, communication becomes a means of empowering parents and a tool for building trusting relationships, particularly in socially and culturally diverse school environments (Gisewhite et al., 2021). Conversely, reticent or controlling attitudes may act as inhibitors, limiting parental involvement and reinforcing conflictual dynamics.

Professional communication skills are a key element of a teacher's pedagogical competence. The ability to clearly articulate messages, adapt speech for different communication styles, manage challenging conversations, and provide pedagogically supportive feedback has been associated with more positive parental attitudes towards school (Hamm & Mousseau, 2023). These skills cannot be taken for granted; they require systematic training and integration into initial and ongoing teacher education.

Greek-language literature highlights that teachers' attitudes and communication skills are influenced by the institutional framework and professional culture of the school. Studies emphasize the importance of strengthening training support to enable teachers to effectively communicate with parents from diverse social and cultural backgrounds (Stamatis, 2015a).

Therefore, the quality of school-family cooperation is determined by an interrelated whole of attitudes, values and communication skills. Empathy, respect and active listening are fundamental psychosocial dimensions of teacher–parent communication and prerequisites for building trusting relationships. Empathy is the teacher's ability to understand parents' feelings, concerns and expectations without prejudice or judgement. Research indicates that empathic communication enhances parents' sense of acceptance and reduces conflict (Kapetanovic & Skoog, 2021). Respect is expressed through language choice, tone of speech and recognition of parental experience as a valuable source of knowledge for the child. Literature emphasizes that treating parents as equal interlocutors rather than passive recipients of information enhances their commitment to school collaboration (Al-Mahdi, 2019). Respect therefore serves as a basis for inclusive and co-responsible communication.

Active listening is inextricably linked to the previous two concepts and is a key skill for teachers in their dialogue with parents. It involves listening carefully, rephrasing, clarifying, and acknowledging the interlocutor's feelings. Studies show that active listening reduces parental defensiveness and creates a climate of cooperation, particularly in cases of difficulty or crisis (Romanovska & Novak, 2024).

Empathy and active listening are recognized as essential skills for addressing the diverse needs of families and promoting positive mental health. Research indicates that cultivating these skills enhances a teacher's pedagogical authority and contributes to creating a positive school climate (Matsangouras, 2017; Stamatis & Nikolaou, 2022a). Therefore, empathy, respect, and active listening are central to a teacher's professional identity and to effective collaboration between schools and families.

WAYS AND MEANS OF COMMUNICATION BETWEEN TEACHERS AND PARENTS

Communication between teachers and parents is a multidimensional pedagogical process that goes beyond the mere exchange of information. It presupposes relations of cooperation, mutual respect, and shared responsibility. International literature consistently highlights that the chosen forms of communication directly influence parental engagement, trust in the school, and ultimately, students' success and well-being at school (Bordalba & Bochaca, 2019).

In most educational systems, each teacher is expected to facilitate a 'mixed model of communication' with parents, combining face-to-face, written and digital communication practices. This approach considers socio-economic, cultural, linguistic and other factors, and is considered critical for including families with different levels of access, digital literacy and experience of the school system (Solano, 2022). Despite their weaknesses, each form of communication has important strengths, which are discussed in more detail below.

Digital technologies have emerged as a key driver in reshaping communication between schools and families, particularly following the experience of the 2019–2020 global pandemic, during which these technologies were widely adopted. Communication platforms, educational applications, and learning management systems have enabled continuous information sharing and increased parents' involvement in school life (Chen & Rivera-Vernazza, 2023).

Research shows that digital platforms can facilitate regular, personalized communication, provided they are used with pedagogical criteria and clear boundaries, thereby enhancing trust and collaboration between teachers and parents (Hsu & Chen, 2023). However, there is a risk of reproducing inequalities due to the digital divide, as families with limited access or low digital literacy may be excluded from new forms of communication.

The communicative role of the modern educator is therefore extremely important, requiring the development of digital communication skills, the selection of appropriate tools, and the cultivation of a culture of collaboration that incorporates not only the technological dimension, but also pedagogical and ethical principles.

Face-to-face communication is widely regarded as the cornerstone of a strong teacher-parent relationship, as it fosters interpersonal closeness and emotional understanding. Face-to-face meetings between teachers and parents provide a space for meaningful dialogue, the negotiation of mutual expectations and the joint addressing of difficulties (Hirst, 2021).

On issues such as school adjustment, behavior, or learning difficulties in particular, physical presence facilitates active listening and empathy, which enhance the sense of alliance between school and family (Shao, 2021). At the same time, school events and open activities facilitate informal communication, strengthening community ties and promoting inclusivity.

Written and digital communication offers stability and accuracy, as well as the opportunity for reflection. Written information remains available and can be reused by teachers and parents. The effectiveness of written communication also depends on clarity, linguistic simplicity, and respect for parents' time and needs. Email and school platforms that accept written messages are also widely used for updates, feedback and coordinating actions, which enhances a sense of continuity in collaboration (Richardson, 2022).

Literature emphasizes the importance of communication between teachers and parents that considers families' cultural backgrounds and avoids technocratic or evaluative formulations that could elicit defensive responses (Erdreich, 2021). Teachers who are more informed are aware that communication in writing and digitally does not operate independently, but instead works in tandem with face-to-face practices. This creates an integrated and flexible way of communicating that improves collaboration between schools and families.

CHALLENGES AND DIFFICULTIES IN TEACHER-PARENT COMMUNICATION

Despite the importance of cooperation between schools and families, communication between teachers and parents is often characterized by difficulties, tensions and mismatched expectations. International literature shows that these challenges are not solely the result of individual factors, but are also linked to institutional, social and cultural contexts that influence how those involved perceive their roles and responsibilities (Özmen et al., 2016). In multicultural, school-based settings in particular, communication may be hindered by language barriers, stereotypes, and parents' negative experiences of the education system. This necessitates the development of conflict prevention and management strategies.

Communication between teachers and parents is widely known as being critical to students' academic and socio-emotional development. Despite its importance, this communication is often hindered by factors relating to the structure and organization of the school, as well as the interpersonal dynamics within the school community. These factors are multifaceted and interdependent, making communication a complex and challenging process.

At an organizational level, teachers' limited time and increased workload are key barriers to systematic and meaningful communication with parents. The absence of regular, institutionalized communication structures often results in sporadic or ad hoc contact, mainly initiated when problems or crises arise (Stamatis, 2019). This practice reinforces the perception of communication as a mechanism for resolving difficulties rather than a means of prevention and cooperation, and associates it with negative emotions such as anxiety and worry.

At the institutional level, power imbalances and differing views on the roles and responsibilities of schools and families can lead to conflict. Teachers tend to view communication as a professional obligation governed by pedagogical objectives and specific boundaries, whereas parents often see it as a way of getting individual attention and an immediate response to their requests (Dor, 2018). These divergent expectations can lead to misinterpretations and mutual frustration, potentially resulting in conflicts with teachers.

At the interpersonal level, emotional and psychological factors can have a significant impact on the quality of communication. Parents' anxiety about their children's progress and teachers' burnout can reduce their willingness to engage in meaningful dialogue. Previous negative experiences of working with the school can also reinforce defensive attitudes, suspicion, and reduced trust, making it difficult to develop open and collaborative communication (Stefanova & Nikolova, 2019). Overall, communication difficulties are not the fault of individuals, but are a product of complex organizational and interpersonal conditions.

Conflicts and misunderstandings in communication between teachers and parents are an unavoidable part of school life, particularly when the issues being discussed are highly emotional, such as school performance, behavior, or learning difficulties. Contemporary research suggests that conflicts often arise from incomplete, unclear or delayed communication, rather than solely from conflicting views (Stamatis & Nikolaou, 2019).

Avoiding difficult discussions or delaying informing parents can lead to tension building up and conflict escalating. When parents are unexpectedly informed of issues concerning their children, they may perceive the communication as threatening or punitive, which can lead to defensive or aggressive reactions (Stamatis, 2013). In contrast, timely and proactive communication has been associated with a reduced likelihood of misunderstandings, and with creating a climate of cooperation and trust (Conus & Fahrni, 2017).

A central aspect of conflict management is the emotional dimension of conflicts. Active listening, empathy and avoiding critical or judgmental language are key communication skills that facilitate dialogue and mutual understanding (Li, Ochoa & McWayne, 2023). Clearly presenting the school's pedagogical goals in a documented manner helps to clarify expectations and reduce tension.

At the same time, the literature emphasizes the importance of a collaborative approach to conflict management. When parents are treated as equal partners in their children's learning and are involved in decision-making, conflict is less likely to occur and trust with teachers is strengthened. Conflict management is therefore not just a technical issue, but a pedagogical process requiring communication skills, reflection, and institutional support.

Cultural and social differences are a critical factor affecting the quality and effectiveness of communication between schools and families, particularly in multicultural educational environments. Families differ in terms of their socioeconomic backgrounds, educational attainment, language practices and cultural perceptions of education. These factors shape their expectations and influence their participation in school communication (Joshi et al., 2005).

Over the past decade, international research has suggested that parents from minority or immigrant groups often find communication with the school unclear or uneven, particularly in the absence of language support or cultural sensitivity on the part of the school (Dor, 2018). Using institutional or academic language without adequate explanation can act as a deterrent, limiting parents' ability to participate meaningfully in school dialogue.

At the same time, stereotypical perceptions and low expectations of families from different social or cultural backgrounds can perpetuate inequalities and have a negative impact on the quality of communication. Contemporary socio-pedagogical approaches argue that these difficulties cannot be attributed solely to families' 'cultural differences', but are related to how school communication is organized and the power relations inherent in the school's institutional framework (Elbers & de Haan, 2014).

Adopting culturally responsive communication practices, such as acknowledging families' experiences and knowledge, being flexible in the means and modes of communication used, and cultivating teachers' intercultural competence, has been linked to increased parental engagement and the creation of more inclusive school communities. When recognized as a pedagogical resource rather than a problem, diversity can substantially improve communication and school-family cooperation.

GOOD PRACTICES AND STRATEGIES TO ENHANCE COMMUNICATION

Effective communication between teachers and parents requires systematic planning and the implementation of strategies based on the pedagogical principles of cooperation, trust and involvement. According to international literature, effective communication practices are linked to a positive school culture, improved student learning, and the empowerment of the school community as a whole (Boonk et al., 2018).

These strategies go beyond merely transmitting information; they aim to establish channels of two-way communication, recognizing parents as equal partners in the learning process. In this context, the teacher's role transforms, moving from that of a mere information provider to that of a relationship coordinator and pedagogical mediator (Epstein, 2018).

Trust is a key component of the relationship between teachers and parents, as well as being a prerequisite for meaningful cooperation. According to international research, trust develops through consistent, reliable and fair longitudinal experiences in the interactions of school community members (Tschannen-Moran, 2014). It is not a static state, but rather a dynamic process that requires constant cultivation.

The quality of communication plays a key role in shaping a climate of trust. Using clear, understandable, non-judgmental language and avoiding technocratic or vague language helps reduce communication barriers and fosters respect (Sheridan et al., 2019). Regular feedback and continuous, timely information exchange between teachers and parents helps to prevent tensions and misunderstandings.

Empathy and active listening are particularly important communication skills. When parents feel that their views and concerns are heard without prejudice, their sense of psychological safety increases and collaborative problem solving becomes easier (Wentzel, 2015). Understanding different experiences and expectations can reduce power imbalances and build bridges of understanding.

Trust is further strengthened by establishing stable and predictable communication practices. Scheduled meetings, clear cooperation frameworks and transparent decision-making processes help create a stable foundation for collaboration (Bryk & Schneider, 2002). Within this framework, cooperation becomes institutionalized and ceases to depend on individual dispositions.

Parental involvement in school life is a central pillar of contemporary educational policy and research, as it is associated with numerous advantages for children and the wider school community. International literature highlights that parental involvement is multifaceted, encompassing various forms of engagement within and beyond the school environment (Hill & Tyson, 2009).

Practices that encourage participation in flexible and accessible ways, taking into account the varying social, cultural, and professional circumstances of families, are considered effective. Adopting inclusive strategies reduces exclusions and enhances a sense of collective identity and participation (Pushor & Ruitenberg, 2005). In this context, participation is not viewed as an obligation, but rather as an opportunity for meaningful contribution.

Effective practices encourage participation in flexible and accessible ways that consider the various social, cultural and professional circumstances of families. Adopting inclusive strategies reduces exclusions and enhances a sense of collective identity and participation (Stamatis & Nikolaou, 2016). In this context, participation is not viewed as an obligation, but rather as an opportunity for meaningful contribution.

It is particularly important to recognize parents as bearers of knowledge and experience. When schools utilize the skills and experiences of families, a sense of parity is fostered, as well as a framework for the co-creation of educational practices (Auerbach, 2012). Transitioning from passive participation to meaningful collaboration strengthens school culture and enhances the sustainability of educational interventions.

Furthermore, systematic parental involvement in school life has been linked to positive academic and socio-emotional outcomes for students. Research suggests that aligning school and family expectations improves learning consistency and engagement with school (Fan & Chen, 2001). Parental involvement is therefore not just a communication practice, but a fundamental component of a democratic and collaborative educational community.

BENEFITS OF EFFECTIVE COMMUNICATION

According to international literature, when communication is systematic, two-way and based on trust, the quality of learning improves, the school climate improves and the educational project becomes more sustainable (Boonk et al., 2018). These benefits do not operate in isolation, but rather feed off each other to create a positive cycle of development and collaboration. Communication acts as a structural coherence mechanism that links the school's pedagogical practices with the family environment, creating an integrated framework of support for the educational process. Effective communication between teachers and parents produces benefits that extend to three interrelated levels: a) the student level; b) the school community level; and c) the teacher level. More specifically, effective communication:

a) At the student's level, effective school-family communication contributes to their academic progress and emotional development. Indeed, effective school-family communication is a key contributor to both academic progress and emotional development in terms of the student's learning path. Clear, organized communication enables teachers and parents to align their goals and expectations, creating a stable, supportive learning environment.

Research has also shown that students whose parents maintain regular communication with the school are more engaged with school, perform better and are more consistent in their schoolwork (Hill & Tyson, 2009). At the same time, students' emotional well-being is enhanced when they perceive collaboration and support from both the school and their family. This enhances students' sense of security and self-esteem within the school community, where they experience emotional stability. This emotional stability acts as a protective factor against anxiety, feelings of alienation at school, and learning difficulties, particularly during times of transition or increased demands (Wilder, 2014).

b) At the level of the school community, i.e. collectively, effective communication enhances cohesion and functionality. Communication at this level not only concerns the relationship between teachers and parents, but also shapes a culture of cooperation, inclusiveness and shared responsibility.

Schools that invest in functional and institutionalized communication mechanisms develop stronger social capital, reduce conflict, and foster a sense of belonging among pupils, parents, and teachers. Effective communication that supports active parental involvement in school life promotes democratic practices and strengthens the collective identity of the school community (Sheldon & Van Voorhis, 2004). In multicultural school environments, communication is particularly important as it functions as a tool for inclusion, bridging social and cultural differences and contributing to the creation of a school that is open and accessible to all families (Epstein, 2018).

(c) At the teacher level, effective communication has an impact on the quality of relationships with parents, which directly influences professional satisfaction, self-efficacy, and mental resilience (Nikolaou & Stamatis, 2023). Positive, collaborative relationships with families are associated with lower levels of job-related stress and burnout because teachers feel supported and recognized in their work

(Skaalvik & Skaalvik, 2017; Ntavlamanou, 2024). Conversely, poor or conflicting communication can lead to professional fatigue and disengagement from the school environment (Collie et al., 2015). Therefore, investing in communication is not only about improving learning outcomes, but also about ensuring the professional well-being and sustainability of the teaching role in the modern school (Nikolaou & Stamatis, 2022).

CONCLUSIONS

The extended analysis of teacher–parent communication confirms that it constitutes a foundational pillar of effective schooling, shaping not only students' academic trajectories but also the psychosocial climate and organizational coherence of school communities. Communication between schools and families emerges from the literature as a complex, multidimensional process that transcends the mere transmission of information. It is embedded in pedagogical values, power relations, cultural expectations, and institutional structures, all of which interact to determine its quality and impact. Consequently, effective communication should be understood as a pedagogical practice in its own right, requiring intentional design, professional competence, and sustained institutional support.

A central conclusion of the reviewed research is that the role of the teacher is decisive in shaping the nature and outcomes of school–family communication. Teachers act not only as conveyors of information but as mediators, relationship builders, and partners of families. Their attitudes, values, and communication skills strongly influence parents' willingness to engage with the school and to participate meaningfully in their children's education. When teachers adopt inclusive, respectful, and collaborative approaches, communication becomes a vehicle for trust-building and shared responsibility. Conversely, hierarchical, formalistic, or defensive communication practices tend to reinforce distance, mistrust, and conflict, limiting the potential benefits of school–family collaboration.

The findings further indicate that the effectiveness of communication is closely linked to its qualitative characteristics rather than its frequency alone. Empathy, active listening, clarity of language, and transparency consistently emerge as key factors in fostering positive relationships. Communication that acknowledges parents' experiences and perspectives, and that frames difficulties as shared challenges rather than individual failures, is more likely to lead to constructive cooperation. In this sense, communication functions as a relational bridge that aligns school expectations with family practices, thereby creating continuity in students' learning and socio-emotional development.

The coexistence of multiple forms of communication—formal, informal, and digital—highlights the need for a balanced and context-sensitive communication strategy. Formal communication provides structure, accountability, and institutional legitimacy, while informal communication strengthens interpersonal bonds and reinforces trust. Digital communication, increasingly prominent in contemporary education, offers flexibility, immediacy, and broader accessibility, particularly for parents facing time or logistical constraints. However, the literature also cautions that digital tools are not pedagogically neutral. Without clear boundaries, shared norms, and adequate training, they may contribute to misunderstandings, professional overload, and the reproduction of social inequalities. Therefore, their integration must be guided by pedagogical intent and ethical considerations rather than technological convenience alone.

Another important conclusion concerns the theoretical models that inform school–family collaboration. Parental engagement, partnership, and ecosystem models provide valuable frameworks for conceptualizing communication practices and clarifying the teacher's role within them. Evidence suggests that models emphasizing reciprocity, shared decision-making, and sensitivity to families' socio-cultural contexts are particularly effective in promoting inclusion and sustainability. In contrast, approaches that reduce communication to formal compliance or unidirectional information flow tend to limit parental agency and the transformative potential of collaboration. The alignment of communication practices with broader educational policies and institutional cultures is therefore crucial for their long-term effectiveness.

The challenges identified in teacher–parent communication underscore that difficulties are rarely attributable to individual shortcomings alone. Time constraints, workload pressures, ambiguous role expectations, cultural and linguistic differences, and emotional factors such as anxiety or burnout all shape communication dynamics. Conflicts often arise from delayed, unclear, or problem-focused communication rather than from inherent disagreement. Proactive, timely, and dialogical communication is shown to mitigate tensions and foster a climate of mutual understanding. Importantly, culturally responsive communication practices can counteract exclusionary dynamics, enabling schools to engage families from diverse backgrounds as partners rather than marginal participants.

Finally, the benefits of effective communication extend across multiple levels of the educational system. At the student level, it supports academic achievement, engagement, emotional security, and resilience. At the level of the school community, it enhances social cohesion, democratic participation, and a shared sense of purpose. At the teacher level, positive communication with parents contributes to professional satisfaction, self-efficacy, and reduced burnout. These interrelated benefits create a virtuous cycle in which strong relationships reinforce educational quality and institutional sustainability.

In conclusion, school-family communication should be recognized as a strategic and ethical priority within contemporary education. Investing in teachers' communication competencies, establishing supportive institutional frameworks, and cultivating a culture of trust and collaboration are essential for building positive, enduring relationships between schools and families. When grounded in pedagogical intentionality and relational ethics, communication becomes a powerful mechanism for promoting equity, well-being, and educational success within the school context.

REFERENCES

Al-Mahdi, O. (2019). *Family–School Connections: Different Theoretical Perspectives and their Implications for Teacher Education. Humanities and Social Sciences Review, 2*(4), 13–23. https://j.ideasspread.org/index.php/hssr/article/view/350

Auerbach, S. (2012, Ed.). *School Leadership for Authentic Family and Community Partnerships: Research Perspectives for Transforming Practice*. Routledge.

Baraldi, C., & Gavioli, L. (2023). Mediation and dialogue in multilingual and multicultural contexts. In Gavioli, L., & Wadensjö, C. (Eds.), *The Routledge Handbook of Public Service Interpreting* (pp. 1–14). Routledge.

Boonk, L., Gijselaers, H. J. M., Ritzen, H., & Brand-Gruwel, S. (2018). A review of the relationship between parental involvement indicators and academic achievement. *Educational Research Review, 24*, 10–30. DOI: 10.1016/j.edurev.2018.02.001

Bordalba, M. M., & Bochaca, J. G. (2019). Digital media for family–school communication? Parents' and teachers' beliefs. *Computers & Education, 132*, 44–62. DOI: 10.1016/j.compedu.2019.01.006

Bryk, A. S., & Schneider, B. (2002). *Trust in Schools: A Core Resource for Improvement*. Russell Sage Foundation.

Chen, J. J., & Rivera-Vernazza, D. E. (2023). Communicating Digitally: Building Preschool Teacher–Parent Partnerships via Digital Technologies during COVID-19. *Early Childhood Education Journal, 51*(7), 1189–1203. DOI: 10.1007/s10643-022-01366-7 PMID: 35789788

Collie, R. J., Shapka, J. D., & Perry, N. E. (2015). School climate and social–emotional learning: Predicting teacher stress, job satisfaction, and teaching efficacy. *Journal of Educational Psychology, 104*(4), 1189–1204. DOI: 10.1037/a0029356

Conus, X., & Fahrni, L. (2017). Routine communication between teachers and parents from minority groups: An endless misunderstanding? *Educational Review, 71*(2), 234–256. DOI: 10.1080/00131911.2017.1387098

Dor, A. (2018). Parent–teacher Communication: The Case of Diverse Family Patterns. *Education and Society (Melbourne), 36*(1), 5–20. DOI: 10.7459/es/36.1.02

Elbers, E., & de Haan, M. (2014). Parent–teacher conferences in Dutch culturally diverse schools: Participation and conflict in institutional context. *Learning, Culture and Social Interaction, 3*(4), 252–266. DOI: 10.1016/j.lcsi.2014.01.004

Epstein, J. L. (2018). *School, Family, and community Partnerships: Preparing Educators and Improving Schools*. Routledge., DOI: 10.4324/9780429494673

Fan, X., & Chen, M. (2001). Parental Involvement and Students' Academic Achievement: A Meta-Analysis. *Educational Psychology Review, 13*(1), 1–22. DOI: 10.1023/A:1009048817385

Forsström, S., Morten, M., Munthe, E., Alvarez-Galvan, J.-L., & Houldsworth, L. (2025). The impact of digital technologies on students' learning: Results from a literature review. *OECD Education Working Paper No. 335*. https://dx.doi.org/ DOI: 10.1787/19939019

Garcés-Prettel, M., Santoya-Montes, Y., & Jiménez-Osorio, J. (2020). Influence of family and pedagogical communication on school violence. *Media Education Research Journal, 63*(28), 73–82. DOI: 10.3916/C63-2020-07

Gelfer, J. I. (1991). Teacher–Parent Partnerships: Enhancing Communications. *Childhood Education, 67*(3), 164–167. DOI: 10.1080/00094056.1991.10521602

Gisewhite, R. A., Jeanfreau, M. M., & Holden, C. L. (2021). A call for ecologically-based teacher–parent communication skills training in pre-service teacher education programmes. *Educational Review, 73*(5), 597–616. DOI: 10.1080/00131911.2019.1666794

Goodall, J., & Montgomery, C. (2014). Parental involvement to parental engagement: A continuum. *Educational Review, 66*(4), 399–410. DOI: 10.1080/00131911.2013.781576

Hamm, J. E., & Mousseau, A. D. S. (2023). Predicting Parent Trust Based on Professionals' Communication Skills. *Education Sciences, 13*(4), 350. DOI: 10.3390/educsci13040350

Hidayat, H., & Arini, F. D. (2022). Exploring Factors of the Parent–Teacher Partnership Affecting Learning Outcomes: Empirical Study in the Early Childhood Education Context. *International Journal of Instruction, 15*(4), 411–434. https://www.e-iji.net/dosyalar/iji_2022_4_23.pdf. DOI: 10.29333/iji.2022.15423a

Hill, N. E., & Tyson, D. F. (2009). Parental involvement in middle school: A meta-analytic assessment of the strategies that promote achievement. *Developmental Psychology, 45*(3), 740–763. DOI: 10.1037/a0015362 PMID: 19413429

Hirst, J. C. (2021). *Perspectives on the Use of Technology as a Home–School Communication and Parent Partnership Tool*. Walden University Scholar Works. https://scholarworks.waldenu.edu/cgi/viewcontent.cgi?article=11992&context=dissertations

Hsu, P. C., & Chen, R. S. (2023). Analyzing the Mechanisms by Which Digital Platforms Influence Family–School Partnerships among Parents of Young Children. *Sustainability (Basel), 15*(24), 16708. Advance online publication. DOI: 10.3390/su152416708

Jeynes, W. H. (2017). A Meta-Analysis on the Relationship between Character Education and Student Achievement and Behavioral Outcomes. *Education and Urban Society*, *51*(1), 33–71. DOI: 10.1177/0013124517747681

Joshi, A., Eberly, J., & Konzal, J. (2005). Dialogue across cultures: Teachers' perceptions about communication with diverse families. *Multicultural Education*, *13*(2), 11–15. https://www.researchgate.net/publication/286896219_Dialogue_across_cultures_Teachers'_perceptions_about_communication_with_diverse_families

Kapetanovic, S., & Skoog, T. (2021). The Role of the Family's Emotional Climate in the Links between Parent–Adolescent Communication and Adolescent Psychosocial Functioning. *Research on Child and Adolescent Psychopathology*, *49*(2), 141–154. DOI: 10.1007/s10802-020-00705-9 PMID: 32960375

Kassotakis, M., & Flouris, G. (2018). *School and family: Dimensions of cooperation and communication*. Gutenberg.

Kim, E. M., Sheridan, S. M., Kwon, K., & Koziol, N. (2013). Parent beliefs and children's social-behavioral functioning: The mediating role of parent–teacher relationships. *Journal of School Psychology*, *51*(2), 175–185. DOI: 10.1016/j.jsp.2013.01.003 PMID: 23481083

Kraft, M. A., & Dougherty, S. M. (2013). The Effect of Teacher–Family Communication on Student Engagement: Evidence from a Randomized Field Experiment. *Journal of Research on Educational Effectiveness*, *6*(3), 199–222. DOI: 10.1080/19345747.2012.743636

Kraft, M. A., & Rogers, T. (2015). The underutilized potential of teacher-to-parent communication: Evidence from a field experiment. *Economics of Education Review*, *47*, 49–63. DOI: 10.1016/j.econedurev.2015.04.001

Kuusimäki, A.-M., Uusitalo-Malmivaara, L., & Tirri, K. (2019). Parents' and Teachers' Views on Digital Communication in Finland. *Education Research International*, *2019*(9), 1–7. DOI: 10.1155/2019/8236786

Li, L.-W., Ochoa, W., McWayne, C. M., Priebe Rocha, L., & Hyun, S. (2023). "Talk to me": Parent–teacher background similarity, communication quality, and barriers to school-based engagement among ethnoculturally diverse Head Start families. *Cultural Diversity & Ethnic Minority Psychology*, *29*(2), 267–278. DOI: 10.1037/cdp0000497 PMID: 34735169

Mavrogiorgos, G. (2016). School-family cooperation in the modern educational context. *Review of Educational Issues*, *22*, 45–60. https://ejournals.epublishing.ekt.gr/index.php/epaggelmatiki/article/view/12645

Murray, E., McFarland-Piazza, L., & Harrison, L. J. (2015). Changing patterns of parent–teacher communication and parent involvement from preschool to school. *Early Child Development and Care*, *185*(7), 1031–1052. DOI: 10.1080/03004430.2014.975223

Nikolaou, E. N., & Stamatis, P. J. (2022). Preservice Preschool Teachers' perspectives on the Psychological Well-being of Pre-schoolers. *The International Journal of Childbirth Education*, *3*(2), 1–8. DOI: 10.33422/ijce.v3i2.313

Nikolaou, E. N., & Stamatis, P. J.Eleni N. NikolaouPanagiotis J. Stamatis. (2023). Promoting Teacher Psychological Well-Being: Implications for School Mental Health and Teacher Training. *US-China Education Review B*, *13*(4), 213–222. DOI: 10.17265/2161-6248/2023.04.001

Ntavlamanou, M. (2024). Occupational Burnout of Greek Primary Education Teachers. European. *Journal of Education and Pedagogy*, *5*(6), 46–51. DOI: 10.24018/ejedu.2024.5.6.893

OECD. (2018). *Education at a glance 2018: OECD indicators*. OECD Publishing., DOI: 10.1787/eag-2018-

Özmen, F., Akuzum, C., Zincirli, M., & Selcuk, G. (2016). The Communication Barriers between Teachers and Parents in Primary Schools. *Eurasian Journal of Educational Research*, *16*(66), 27–46. https://dergipark.org.tr/en/pub/ejer/issue/42424/510769. DOI: 10.14689/ejer.2016.66.2

Palts, K., & Harro-Loit, H. (2015). PARENT-TEACHER COMMUNICATION PATTERNS CONCERNING ACTIVITY AND POSITIVE-NEGATIVE ATTITUDES. *Trames*, *19*(2), 139–154. https://www.kirj.ee/public/trames_pdf/2015/issue_2/Trames-2015-2-139-154.pdf

Pushor, D. (2015). Walking Alongside: A Pedagogy of Working with Parents and Family in Canada. *Teaching Education*, *42*(4), 5–26. DOI: 10.1108/S1479-368720150000025008

Pushor, D., & Ruitenberg, C. (2005). *Parent engagement and leadership*. Dr. Stirling McDowell Foundation for Research into Teaching., https://mcdowellfoundation.ca/wp-content/uploads/2025/08/134_parent_engagement.pdf

Romanovska, L., & Novak, M. (2024). THE ROLE OF TEACHER-STUDENT RELATIONSHIPS IN PROVIDING SOCIAL AND PSYCHOLOGICAL SUPPORT TO PARTICIPANTS OF THE EDUCATIONAL PROCESS. *Social Work Education*, *11*(2), 308–319. DOI: 10.25128/2520-6230.24.2.11

Russell, W., & Qiu, H. (2024). The Dynamics of Parent–Teacher Relationships and Their Impact on Student Success. *Iranian Journal of Educational Sociology*, *7*(1), 212–218. DOI: 10.61838/kman.ijes.7.1.21

Shao, X. (2021). *The implementation of digital communication (DC) in parent–teacher partnership in China: teachers' and parents' views*. Oxford University Research Archive. https://ora.ox.ac.uk/objects/uuid:ea270492-e1d2-4f14-ad66-8dae0f021c28

Sheldon, S. B., & Van Voorhis, F. L. (2004). Partnership programs in U.S. schools: Their development and relationship to family involvement outcomes. *School Effectiveness and School Improvement*, *15*(2), 125–148. DOI: 10.1076/sesi.15.2.125.30434

Sheridan, S. M., Smith, T. E., Kim, E. M., Beretvas, S. N., & Park, S. (2012). A Meta-Analysis of Family–School Interventions and Children's Social–Emotional Functioning: Moderators and Components of Efficacy. *Review of Educational Research*, *89*(2), 296–332. DOI: 10.3102/0034654318825437

Skaalvik, E. M., & Skaalvik, S. (2017). Motivated for teaching? Associations with school goal structure, teacher self-efficacy, job satisfaction and emotional exhaustion. *Teaching and Teacher Education*, *67*, 152–160. DOI: 10.1016/j.tate.2017.06.006

Solano, M. (2022). *Communicating Effectively: An Exploration of Communication Methods between Parents and Teachers with Mixed Methods*. West Chester University. https://digitalcommons.wcupa.edu/all_doctoral/156/

Stamatis, P. J. (2013). *Communication in Education*. Diadrassi Publications.

Stamatis, P. J. (2015). *Preschool and Early Elementary School Pedagogy: Communicative Dimensions of Educational Procedure*. Diadrassi Publications.

Stamatis, P. J. (2015a). From Kindergarten to Primary School: Communication Activities for a Smoother Transition of Preschoolers. *The International Journal of Early Childhood Learning*, *21*(3-4), 1–8. DOI: 10.18848/2327-7939/CGP/v21i3-4/48449

Stamatis, P. J. (2019). Communication relations among parents and preschoolers: Thoughts, comments and suggestions. In Nata, R. V. (Ed.), *Progress in Education* (Vol. 60, pp. 83–106). Nova Science Publishers.

Stamatis, P. J., & Chatzinikola, M. (2021). Advantages and Reasons Hindering the Communication between Teachers and Parents: An Empirical Study. *European Journal of Education and Pedagogy*, *2*(2), 43–48. DOI: 10.24018/ejedu.2021.2.2.79

Stamatis, P. J. & Nikolaou, E. N. (2016). Communication and collaboration between school and family for addressing bullying. *International Journal of Criminology and Sociology, 5, 99-104. Special Issue "Adjustment of Learners' Violent Behaviour in a School Context"*. Lifescience Global https://doi.org/DOI: 10.6000/1929-4409.2016.05.09

Stamatis, P. J., & Nikolaou, E. N. (2019). Parents' Perceptions about Bullying. In Ancho, I. V., & Krizna, K. R. (Eds.), *School Violence: Risk factors, prevention and challenges* (pp. 97–115). Nova Science Publishers.

Stamatis, P. J., & Nikolaou, E. N. (2020). *Communication and Mental Health Promotion in Early Childhood Education*. Nova Science Publishers. DOI: 10.52305/QXVD5566

Stamatis, P. J., & Nikolaou, E. N. (2022). *The 21st-century Kindergarten. Communication and counselling issues in preschool and early elementary school education*. Gutenberg.

Stamatis, P. J., & Nikolaou, E. N. (2022a). *Counseling and Communication in Education*. Diadrassi Publications.

Stamatis, P. J., & Stavropoulou, E. J. (2018). Communication styles of preschool and early primary school teachers during teaching activities. In Stamatis, P. J., & Nikolaou, E. N. (Eds.), *Violent Communication and Bullying in Early Childhood Education* (pp. 35–55). Nova Science Publishers.

Stefanova, E., & Nikolova, N. (2019). Overcoming the barriers in teacher–parent communication. In *Proceedings of EDULEARN19 Conference* (pp. 1107–1116). https://doi.org/DOI: 10.21125/edulearn.2019.0349

Thompson, B. (2019). Characteristics of Parent–Teacher E-Mail Communication. *Communication Education*, *57*(2), 201–223. DOI: 10.1080/03634520701852050

Tschannen-Moran, M. (2014). *TRUST MATTERS: LEADERSHIP for SUCCESSFUL SCHOOLS*. Jossey-Bass.

UNESCO. (2021). *Reimagining our futures together: a new social contract for education*. International Commission on the Futures of Education., DOI: 10.54675/ASRB4722

Vickers, H. S., & Minke, K. M. (1995). Exploring parent–teacher relationships: Joining and communication to others. *School Psychology Quarterly*, *10*(2), 133–150. DOI: 10.1037/h0088300

Watkins, T. J. (1997). Teacher Communications, Child Achievement, and Parent Traits in Parent Involvement Models. *The Journal of Educational Research*, *91*(1), 3–14. DOI: 10.1080/00220679709597515

Wentzel, K. R. (2015). Teacher-Student Relationships, Motivation, and Competence at School. In Rubie-Davies, C. M. (Ed.), *The Routledge International Handbook of Social Psychology of the Classroom* (pp. 167–176). Routledge.

Wilder, S. (2014). Effects of parental involvement on academic achievement: A meta-synthesis. *Educational Review*, *66*(3), 377–397. DOI: 10.1080/00131911.2013.780009

Willemse, T. M., Thompson, I., Vanderlinde, R., & Mutton, T. (2018). Family–school partnerships: A challenge for teacher education. Journal of Education for Teaching. *Journal of Education for Teaching*, *44*(4), 1–6. DOI: 10.1080/02607476.2018.1465545

Yu, G., & Wang, C. (2023). Teacher as Mediator: How Teacher Interacts with Parents of the Victim and Agent in School Conflict. *Contrastive Pragmatics*, *4*(1), 1–30. DOI: 10.1163/26660393-bja10070

Chapter 3

Animals in the Primary School Classroom: Evidence-Based Benefits and Conditions for Implementation

Georgia Ioannidou
http://orcid.org/0000-0003-0899-6124
University of the Aegean, Rhodes, Greece

Vasileios Papavasileiou
University of the Aegean, Rhodes, Greece

ABSTRACT

The presence of animals in primary school classrooms, either through certified programs involving a trained handler or as resident classroom animals, is increasingly discussed as a supportive practice that may enhance the learning environment. Studies report reduced stress, improved emotional regulation, and more positive mood, factors associated with better attention and persistence during classroom activities. Animals can also facilitate social interaction, promoting cooperation, empathy, and responsibility through simple, structured care routines. In addition, fewer conflicts and more consistent rule-following have been described when interactions are brief, planned, and integrated into instruction. In literacy-related activities, such as reading to a dog, increased motivation and self-confidence have been reported. Successful implementation requires clear educational aims, parent/guardian information and consent procedures, hygiene rules, provisions for allergies and phobias, careful selection of the animal, and ongoing attention to animal welfare.

DOI: 10.4018/979-8-3373-9420-6.ch003

INTRODUCTION

The everyday realities of primary education demonstrate that learning is not an exclusively cognitive process; rather, it unfolds within specific emotional and social contexts. Contemporary interdisciplinary scholarship suggests that emotional processes influence core functions associated with school performance, including attention, working memory, decision-making, and social judgment, and that a deeper understanding of the role of emotion can improve the design of learning environments. (Immordino-Yang & Damasio, 2007). Within this framework, the capacity for emotion regulation has been empirically linked to indicators of early academic success. For example, in a study involving kindergarten children, emotion regulation was associated both with teachers' reports of classroom productivity and with standardized measures of early literacy and mathematics skills (Graziano et al., 2007). At the level of educational policy and systems, the growing emphasis on social and emotional competencies is also reflected in large-scale international initiatives. The OECD Survey on Social and Emotional Skills (SSES), for instance, examines, among other issues, how competencies such as perseverance and empathy are related to educational and broader developmental outcomes, thereby underscoring the importance of the school environment in fostering these skills (OECD, 2024).

In the search for practices that support well-being and a positive classroom climate, the presence of animals in the classroom has attracted growing interest. Internationally, such approaches are generally situated under the umbrella of Animal-Assisted Interventions (AAI), namely structured, goal-oriented interventions that incorporate animals into health, educational, and human services. More specifically, in educational settings, several forms of implementation can be identified: (a) certified programs involving an animal and a handler conducted within the school context; (b) animal-assisted education activities with explicit instructional objectives, such as literacy development or the enhancement of social skills; and (c) resident or classroom animals, which are incorporated into the school routine through established rules of interaction and care. This distinction is not merely terminological; rather, it is associated with different aims, varying degrees of structure and evidentiary support, as well as different organizational and supervisory requirements (IAHAIO, 2018).

Against this background, animal-assisted interventions in educational contexts are typically implemented with aims related to attention, classroom behavior, well-being, and socio-emotional functioning, although recent systematic evidence also points to marked heterogeneity across study populations, intervention characteristics, outcome domains, and measurement approaches (Moe et al., 2025). This heterogeneity is compounded by broader methodological and terminological inconsistency within the AAI literature (Santaniello et al., 2020). For this reason, detailed reporting of what is actually implemented in the classroom is essential if findings are to be compared meaningfully and synthesized more reliably (Hoffmann et al., 2014).

The most consistent positive findings regarding dog-assisted interventions in school settings primarily concern socio-emotional and behavioral indicators, such as stress reduction, positive social interaction, and aspects of classroom climate, which appear to support greater student engagement in classroom activities (Wintermantel et al., 2024; Meixner & Kotrschal, 2022).

More specifically, in targeted educational applications, animal-assisted education interventions have been linked to positive changes in the school experience and in aspects of social interaction among children aged 4 to 14 years, suggesting that the animal may function as a "shared point of reference" that facilitates communication and collaboration (Morgan, 2024).

Of particular interest are also studies examining biological markers of stress. In a randomized controlled trial conducted in a school setting, children's participation in brief, repeated sessions with a dog were associated with favorable changes in salivary cortisol, supporting the view that the presence of an animal may serve as a stress-regulating factor within the school routine (Meints et al., 2022).

In the area of literacy, "Reading-to-a-dog" (RTD) programs are typically organized as practices in which the student reads aloud to a non-judgmental "audience" and are often associated with enhanced motivation and self-confidence. Moreover, such programs have been linked to favorable changes in processes that make reading a more positive experience, including reduced anxiety and increased willingness to participate, thereby facilitating systematic practice (Hall et al., 2016).

At the same time, international literature emphasizes that the multiplicity of terms surrounding animal-assisted interventions often creates confusion regarding what is actually being implemented, who holds responsibility, and how a given initiative should be evaluated. IAHAIO explicitly notes that the coexistence of multiple and differing terminologies has contributed to conceptual ambiguity and that clearer definitions and guidance are required, particularly with respect to the welfare of the animals involved (IAHAIO, 2018).

In a similar vein, studies conducted in school settings exhibit substantial heterogeneity in terms of research design, type of intervention, and outcome measures. This variability makes the use of clearer protocols and more systematic documentation especially important, so that meaningful comparison across studies and more robust synthesis of findings can be achieved (Brelsford et al., 2017).

CONCEPTUAL FRAMEWORK AND TERMINOLOGY

For the purposes of this chapter, Animal-Assisted Interventions (AAI) are understood primarily in line with the IAHAIO definition as goal-directed and structured interventions that intentionally incorporate animals into health, educational, and human service settings in order to produce beneficial or therapeutic effects for humans (IAHAIO, 2018). In practical terms, however, AAI should not be equated with just any animal presence in school, but rather with a programmed, designed, and ideally evaluated practice involving clear aims, defined roles, and appropriate supervision (López-Cepero, 2020). This clarification is especially important in a field where support-animal terminology is often used inconsistently, including in educational contexts, and where clearer operational distinctions have therefore been recommended (Howell et al., 2022). Within this framework, IAHAIO distinguishes Animal-Assisted Education (AAE), Animal-Assisted Activity (AAA), Animal-Assisted Therapy (AAT), and Animal-Assisted Coaching (AAC), with AAE typically being the most central category in primary education (IAHAIO, 2018). In implementation terms, school-based programs also differ according to who leads them and who assumes responsibility for the animal, with IAHAIO's training guidelines distinguishing activity-based from professionally led services (IAHAIO, 2022).

A more specialized form of AAE is represented by literacy programs such as RTD, which have been associated with gains in reading motivation and a more positive reading-related experience. (Jalongo, 2005; Goodmon et al., 2021). Another distinct application is the resident or classroom animal, namely an animal incorporated into the everyday routine of the classroom under established rules of interaction and care. This form is often referred to by public agencies as a "class pet." For example, the CDC explicitly addresses as school-based scenarios both "class pets" and animals used in hands-on learning activities (CDC, 2024).

The present chapter focuses on educational applications, namely AAE, AAA, and related practices, rather than on situations in which a child is accompanied by a service animal as a reasonable accommodation or support measure related to disability. In many regulatory frameworks, a service animal is defined as a dog individually trained to perform specific tasks or duties for a person with a disability (U.S. Department of Justice, ADA, 2011). Furthermore, the literature on AAI emphasizes that therapy animals involved in interventions or visits must be clearly distinguished from service animals and emotional support animals, as these categories differ in terms of purpose, context, and role (Linder et al., 2017).

A classical framework for interpreting the positive effects associated with the presence of an animal in the classroom is provided by social support theory, according to which the experience of support buffers stress and mitigates the negative impact of stressful life events (Cohen & Wills, 1985). Within the school context, this perspective suggests that the animal may function as a stable, neutral, and predictable stimulus that fosters a sense of safety and calm, that is, as a particular form of social presence that supports students' emotional equilibrium during demanding or anxiety-provoking activities. (Ein et al., 2018; Polheber & Matchock, 2014).

In the scientific discussion concerning the underlying mechanism, it has been proposed that human interaction with animals may be associated with psychobiological processes that promote calmness, social openness, and trust. More specifically, Beetz et al. (2012) argue that several of the psychological and psychophysiological effects of human–animal interaction, such as reductions in stress-related parameters and the enhancement of social processes, may be linked to activation of the oxytocin system.

A second, complementary theoretical pathway suggests that positive emotional experiences in the classroom are not merely "pleasant" in nature but may temporarily broaden the scope of attention and thought and, over time, contribute to the development of psychological and social resources (Fredrickson, 2001). Within this framework, the presence of an animal, when structured and pedagogically integrated, may serve as a positive affective stimulus that supports participation, persistence, and students' willing engagement in activities such as reading and collaborative tasks.

Attention Restoration Theory posits that directed attention is susceptible to fatigue and that certain experiences, particularly those characterized by "soft fascination", can facilitate the recovery of attentional capacity (Kaplan, 1995). Applied to the classroom context, this perspective suggests that brief, planned contact with, or the presence of, an animal may function as a "micro-restorative break," helping to restore concentration before or during cognitively demanding tasks without diverting from the pedagogical objective.

Research on the effects of natural stimuli suggests that contact with elements of nature may be associated with positive emotional responses and reduced stress; a classic example is Ulrich's (1984) study, in which exposure to a natural landscape was linked to more favorable recovery indicators. On a broader theoretical level, the biophilia hypothesis proposes that human beings possess an innate, evolutionarily grounded affinity for living systems (Wilson, 1984). Although the classroom is not a natural environment, the presence of an animal may introduce an element of "living nature" that supports positive mood and calmness, particularly when the interaction is gentle, predictable, and brief.

One of the most well-documented findings in the literature on human–animal interaction is the "social catalyst effect," according to which dogs can increase the likelihood of social contact and conversation among people (McNicholas & Collis, 2000). In the school context, this effect may translate into more frequent opportunities for social initiative, collaboration, and the emergence of a shared point of reference, the animal itself, which often reduces awkwardness and facilitates communication among children and between children and teachers.

From the perspective of Self-Determination Theory (SDT), the quality of motivation is enhanced when basic psychological needs, namely relatedness, competence, and autonomy, are satisfied (Ryan & Deci, 2000). In this light, the presence of an animal may be understood as supporting primarily the need for relatedness, by fostering a warm and positive relational context, and the need for competence, by providing a safe setting for practicing skills such as reading or presenting without a pronounced sense of evaluation; as a result, it may strengthen students' intrinsic willingness to participate. For a more comprehensive application of the theory, however, such as the design of activities that also promote autonomy through choice and self-direction, the broader contemporary framework of SDT may be drawn upon (Ryan & Deci, 2017).

A further positive pathway concerns the development of empathy and an ethical orientation toward living beings. Research in humane education has examined programs aimed at fostering care for and respect toward animals, documenting improvements in attitudes toward the proper treatment of animals and, in some cases, a generalization of these effects to empathy toward other human beings (Ascione, 1997; Ascione & Weber, 1996). Within the classroom, accordingly, simple and structured care routines, implemented through clearly defined roles, rules, and supervision, may function as a practical "laboratory" for cultivating responsibility, empathy, and a cooperative disposition.

Overall, the theoretical background supports a multifactorial model according to which the presence of an animal may (a) reduce stress and enhance positive affect, (b) support the restoration of attention, (c) function as a social catalyst, and (d) strengthen motivation through relatedness and competence, while at the same time (e) providing opportunities for the development of empathy and responsibility.

EVIDENCE OF BENEFITS IN PRIMARY EDUCATION

Dog-assisted interventions may exert a regulatory effect on stress, with supporting evidence documented through biomarkers such as salivary cortisol. More specifically, interventions lasting longer than 15 minutes have been associated with statistically significant reductions in cortisol, underscoring duration as a critical factor influencing effect size (Peña-Jorquera et al., 2025). Consistent with this line of evidence, in a school-related clinical–educational context, the presence of a volunteer therapy dog during a psychosocial intervention has been linked to lower within-session activity of the hypothalamic–pituitary–adrenocortical axis (HPA), as reflected in cortisol measurements, thereby supporting the view that the animal's presence may produce a measurable reduction of stress at the time of the intervention (Schuck et al., 2024).

The evidence regarding well-being in school-based applications is not limited to biomarkers but also includes qualitative data reflecting the experiences of children and the wider school community. Participation in school-based dog-assisted reading programs has been associated with a more positive overall experience, a stronger sense of achievement, and indications of enhanced perceived well-being, particularly through positive emotions and increased engagement in the reading task (Henderson et al., 2020). In a broader range of school professionals, therapy dogs have likewise been perceived as making a positive contribution to the reduction of anxiety and heightened arousal, while also facilitating students' emotional and behavioral regulation within the school environment (Baird et al., 2023).

In school-based applications involving structured activities, there is evidence to suggest that systematic interaction with a dog may support both well-being and social inclusion. In particular, the focus on the animal's nonverbal communication appears to facilitate the expression of emotions and behaviors that may not readily emerge under other school conditions, thereby promoting children's psychological well-being and socio-emotional development (Correale et al., 2017). Extending this perspective to more targeted school settings that provide intensive support, the case study by Farrand and Jung (2025), conducted in a Tier 3 classroom (i.e., a setting providing the most intensive level of individualized support within a multi-tiered system of supports), indicates, through the triangulation of observations, student feedback, and an interview with the teacher/handler, that the systematic integration of a therapy dog can strengthen dimensions of emotional support and contribute positively to the overall well-being of the learning environment.

Although school-based applications vary considerably, positive effects on well-being appear more frequently when contact with the animal is of sufficient duration rather than merely fleeting, is repeated consistently over time, for example, in weekly sessions conducted across several weeks and is embedded within a structured framework featuring clearly defined activities. In particular, a duration exceeding 15 minutes emerges as a practical factor associated with more favorable cortisol regulation (Peña-Jorquera et al., 2025). These beneficial effects seem to be further strengthened when implementation is carefully organized, with stable collaboration and communication between the school and handlers, as well as with clear pedagogical planning, including defined goals, a session protocol, and systematic observation and evaluation, so that the presence of the animal can be translated into meaningful experiences of well-being and emotional expression within the classroom (Henderson et al., 2020; Correale et al., 2017).

Beyond the indications derived from cortisol measures and qualitative reports of well-being, it is important to clarify why stress reduction has direct pedagogical significance in primary education. During the school years, stress is not merely an "emotion," but a biopsychological state organized by the brain that affects adaptation and behavior in the classroom (McEwen, 2007). At the level of cognitive functioning, the literature indicates that stress can undermine prefrontal cortical processes, that is, mechanisms supporting working memory, inhibitory control, and cognitive regulation, skills that children draw upon daily in activities such as reading, problem solving, and rule-following (Arnsten, 2009). At a more integrative level, a meta-analysis of acute stress has shown that it burdens core executive functions, including working memory and cognitive flexibility, both of which are essential for smooth transitions and for remaining on task (Shields, Sazma, & Yonelinas, 2016). At the same time, the literature on stress and learning emphasizes that stress may critically impair memory retrieval, with immediate implications for situations in which students are asked to demonstrate what they know (Vogel & Schwabe, 2016).

At a developmental level, stress regulation in childhood also relies on social mechanisms, since systems of self-regulation are still maturing and the presence of support may therefore function as a regulatory factor in children's stress responses. The phenomenon of social buffering describes the capacity of a "significant other" to reduce activation of the HPA axis under challenging conditions; from this perspective, animal-assisted interventions may be understood as a distinctive form of supportive presence when implemented with clear structure, predictability, and appropriate boundaries (Gunnar & Quevedo, 2007; Hostinar et al., 2014). Illustratively, in a controlled experiment with children aged 7–12 years, the presence of the child's own pet dog during the established Trier Social Stress Test for Children (TSST-C) functioned as a regulatory factor for perceived stress, while more active yet calm interaction, for example, increased petting, was associated with a more favorable cortisol response profile (Kertes et al., 2017). This finding is pedagogically valuable because it supports an important practical principle: the beneficial effect lies not merely in the presence of a dog, but in the opportunity for calm, voluntary, and appropriately guided interaction, which may operate as a "regulatory break" before or during demanding school activities. Consequently, stress reduction may be regarded as a central mechanism through which animal-assisted interventions support the everyday functioning of the classroom, facilitating readiness to learn and more sustained student engagement.

The presence of an animal may function as a shared point of reference and strengthen the sense of "groupness" within the classroom, thereby contributing to a more positive social climate, greater social inclusion, and the reshaping of social roles, with the role of the "caregiver" often emerging as a unifying element for the group (Mombeck & Avsar, 2024). From a primary-education perspective, this pattern is pedagogically meaningful because shared care and responsibility can be organised through simple, structured routines that create a common purpose, thereby increasing opportunities for cooperation, positive peer interaction, and inclusive participation in everyday classroom life.

The socio-emotional dimensions of the school years concern not merely "good behavior," but a broader set of competencies that enable the child to participate consistently in the learning process, to relate effectively to peers and adults, and to respond to the demands of the classroom. The concept of socio-emotional competence encompasses (a) awareness and understanding of emotions, (b) emotion regulation and management, (c) prosocial skills, and (d) motivation and persistence in activities, all of which are associated with school readiness and school adjustment (Denham, 2006).

Within the field of Social and Emotional Learning (SEL), one of the most widely used organizing frameworks is the CASEL 5 model, which identifies five interrelated domains: self-awareness, self-management, social awareness, relationship skills, and responsible decision-making (CASEL, 2020). At the same time, it has been emphasized that SEL does not belong exclusively to formal programs but is most effective when embedded in everyday classroom practices, routines, relationships, and the broader culture of the school (Jones & Bouffard, 2012). This perspective is especially relevant in primary education, where socio-emotional functioning is closely linked to student engagement, as supportive relationships with teachers and peers are associated with motivation, goal orientation, and interest in school, that is, with the kind of participatory energy that mobilizes the child within everyday learning activities (Wentzel, 1998). For this reason, interventions that strengthen classroom climate, relationships, and emotional safety may exert a broader influence on students' school trajectories, even when they do not directly target academic skills.

The presence of an animal in the classroom, whether as part of an organized Animal-Assisted Education (AAE) activity or a structured reading program, may function as a context for SEL, insofar as it creates authentic, recurring social situations in which children can practice a range of core competencies. In terms of self-awareness, children learn to recognize when they feel excited or anxious and to translate these feelings into appropriate behavior before approaching the animal. With regard to self-management, routines of "calm approach," waiting one's turn, and following simple rules of contact foster impulse control and persistence in structured processes. At the level of social awareness and empathy, observing signs of the animal's comfort or discomfort and discussing its needs and boundaries can strengthen children's capacity to adopt the perspective of the "other." Similarly, relationship skills may be cultivated through small-group activities with assigned roles, for example, reading, keeping time, or reminding peers of the rules, which promote cooperation and positive interaction. Finally, responsible decision-making is supported through choices related to animal welfare, such as determining when to stop an activity and how to protect the animal's space and calm, thereby providing concrete examples of responsibility in practice (CASEL, 2020; Jones & Bouffard, 2012).

A useful perspective is that socio-emotional benefits are not merely immediate or short-term. The literature indicates that school-based SEL programs can produce positive effects that are sustained over time (Taylor et al., 2017), thereby reinforcing the view that interventions which improve the emotional and social context of learning may generate cumulative gains for students' overall school experience. Moreover, high-quality reviews have linked SEL to academic outcomes, confirming that socio-emotional competencies do not operate in opposition to learning, but rather in conjunction with it (Corcoran et al., 2018). Finally, the socio-emotional dimensions of classroom life cannot easily be separated from the role of the teacher. The literature emphasizes that teachers' socio-emotional competence and well-being directly shape the quality of classroom interactions and the overall classroom climate; accordingly, any practice, including animal-assisted interventions, is likely to be more effective when embedded within a culture of emotional support, clear routines, and positive relationships (Schonert-Reichl, 2017).

The integration of classroom animals over the course of a school year has been associated with greater gains in indicators of social skills and social competence, as well as reductions in certain problematic behaviors, according to teachers' reports, while parents' reports likewise indicate increases in prosocial behaviors in comparison with classrooms without an animal (McCullough et al., 2021). Particularly important in this case is that the study does not focus on momentary or short-term exposure, but rather examines the longer-term incorporation of classroom animals, an approach that aligns more closely with the realities of school practice and with broader goals of socio-emotional development.

Structured animal-assisted activity programs implemented within primary school classrooms have been associated with greater improvements in children's social functioning, including increases in social skills and reductions in problematic behaviors relative to waitlist groups, as reflected in standardized measures of social skills and behavior such as the Social Skills Rating System (O'Haire et al., 2013). For primary education, this finding is particularly valuable because it links the presence of animals in the school setting to specific and measurable social outcomes, rather than merely to general impressions of calmness or improved atmosphere.

The consistent presence of a dog in the classroom has been associated with increased empathy toward animals and, according to teachers' evaluations, with higher levels of social inclusion and fewer aggressive behaviors compared with classrooms without a dog (Hergovich et al., 2002). More broadly, the presence of animals in the classroom and, in particular, organized humane education may function as a framework for cultivating empathy toward both animals and humans by strengthening perspective-taking, the recognition of needs and boundaries, and prosocial dispositions. In school-based humane education programs involving direct child–animal interaction, increases in indicators of empathy have likewise been documented within the broader context of socio-emotional learning (Ngai et al., 2021).

Empathy does not appear to be necessarily confined to animal-directed attitudes. A school-based program centered on animals and nature over the course of an academic year has been associated with positive changes in both major forms of human-directed empathy, cognitive and affective, with a particularly strong effect on affective empathy (Samuels & Onuoha-Jackson, 2023). In a more traditional school-based humane education context involving repeated animal visits, increased self-reported empathy and more positive attitudes toward animals have likewise been documented among students in the early grades, supporting the view that systematic, experiential forms of engagement can translate into more favorable humane attitudes (Nicoll et al., 2008). Complementing these findings, the literature further indicates that children's emotional bonds with animals, such as attachment, are associated with indices of compassion and caregiving and predict more positive attitudes toward animals, thereby reinforcing the idea that caring roles constitute a practical pathway for fostering empathy and responsibility (Hawkins & Williams, 2017).

A further positive pathway concerns skills that indirectly support the quality of peer relationships, such as emotion understanding. Scandurra et al. (2021) evaluated an AAE intervention involving dogs with children aged 6–7 years, consisting of five bimonthly sessions, and found improved emotion comprehension in the intervention group compared with the control group, with the benefit maintained at a three-month follow-up. Given that emotion understanding is regarded as critical for the quality of peer interaction, this finding supports a constructive educational mechanism. The presence of an animal may be pedagogically leveraged to strengthen socio-cognitive skills associated with cooperation, conflict resolution, and empathy.

The evidence regarding social effects also includes direct observation of classroom behaviors, beyond teacher- and parent-reported rating scales. More specifically, in the presence of guinea pigs, students have been observed to display more positive social behaviors, greater social approach, and more positive affect compared with control conditions involving toys or other objects (O'Haire et al., 2013). Regardless of the specific sample, the contribution of this study lies in its documentation of the social gains associated with the presence of an animal through behavioral indicators in an authentic school setting, that is, through what children actually do, such as social approach, contact, and the expression of positive affect, rather than only through what they report feeling.

In primary education, consistent participation, smooth transitions, and positive relationships constitute a foundation for learning. Effective classroom management has been associated, albeit with small but consistent effect sizes, with academic, behavioral, and socio-emotional outcomes, particularly when preventive and relationship-centered practices are emphasized. Within this framework, the presence of an animal in the classroom may be understood as a complementary condition that supports classroom climate and facilitates the educational process. This perspective is further reinforced by observational school-based research employing systematic video recording and behavioral coding, in which the presence of a dog in the classroom has been associated with a more homogeneous social profile within the group, reduced behavioral extremes such as aggression and hyperactivity, and greater social inclusion of children who had previously been more withdrawn. Notably, despite the interest elicited by the animal, greater attention directed toward the teacher has also been recorded, supporting the view that the presence of a dog may enhance classroom cohesion and improve the conditions for teaching and learning (Kotrschal & Ortbauer, 2003).

The presence of a schooldog, that is, a dog that regularly accompanies the teacher, has been associated with positive changes in students' school experience that relate directly to classroom climate, including a more positive attitude toward school and an increase in positive emotions connected with learning over the course of the school year. Such enhancement of positive effects and attitudes toward learning may, in turn, indirectly facilitate cooperation, persistence, and more stable, calm participation in classroom life (Beetz, 2013). From a more practical perspective, one indicator of classroom functioning is the frequency with which repeated verbal reminders or prompts are required for the completion of a structured activity. In this regard, the presence of a well-trained dog has been associated with a reduced need for both general and task-specific prompts relative to control conditions, suggesting that it may facilitate more automatic adherence to instructions and, consequently, a smoother flow of classroom activity (Gee et al., 2010). Along similar lines, the presence of a dog during the performance of motor tasks has been linked to better compliance with instructions, reinforcing the view that a calm dog may function as a stabilizing factor for on-task behavior (Gee et al., 2009). More broadly, interaction with a dog and/or the dog's presence has been associated with enhanced performance by children on tests of attention and concentration; pedagogically, this may translate into more time spent on task and less distractibility that might otherwise disrupt the flow of instruction (Hediger & Turner, 2014).

Field-based evidence suggests that the presence of animals in the classroom is a widespread practice and is used by teachers as a means of enhancing classroom climate. It has been documented that a substantial proportion of classrooms house animals, primarily small vertebrates, and that the principal reasons reported for doing so relate to enjoyment and the creation of experiential, "hands-on" learning opportunities, a finding consistent with the role of animals as regulators of classroom atmosphere and as catalysts for positive engagement (Rud & Beck, 2003). In a similar vein, teachers describe multiple ways of integrating animals into instruction and attribute to their presence positive effects on socio-emotional dimensions, such as empathy, which are in turn associated with a more cooperative and positive classroom climate (Daly & Suggs, 2010). Extending this picture, primary-school implementations within programs have been associated with improvements in motivation and peer relationships, as well as with more positive classroom behavior and an overall enhancement of interactions, as reflected in observations and participant reports (Sorin et al., 2015).

For the presence of an animal to function as a positive factor in classroom climate, rather than merely as a "pleasant interruption," the implementation literature emphasizes the importance of its organized integration into the school ecosystem through clear goals, alignment with the school's needs, and broad support from the school community. In this regard, Grové et al. (2021) highlight that therapeutic dog programs that operate effectively in school settings rely on flexible design, staff communication and training, and whole-school support, features that, in practical terms, foster a stable and predictable framework for interaction and, consequently, a calmer classroom climate. Taken together, the evidence in primary education suggests that the presence of a dog, and/or other classroom animals, may be associated with improved teaching conditions through (a) the reduction of behavioral extremes and the strengthening of classroom cohesion, (b) the enhancement of attention and concentration together with easier compliance with instructions, and (c) the promotion of a more positive school experience that supports everyday cooperation and participation.

The presence of animals in school-based programs may strengthen students' sense of connectedness and belonging at school, that is, the feeling of being accepted and of having a meaningful place within the school community (Fedor, 2018), a dimension of psycho-emotional significance given that school belonging has been associated with more positive academic, behavioral, and psychological outcomes (Štremfel et al., 2024).

In this respect, the regular presence of a school dog has been linked to a more positive attitude toward school and to enhanced positive emotions associated with learning over the course of the school year, while a more favorable profile has also been observed on standardized measures of classroom climate and school experience; together, these factors may be understood as a psycho-emotional foundation that facilitates engagement and persistence (Beetz, 2013). A similar dynamic is evident in RTD practices, which are often described as low-evaluative-pressure environments in which the student experiences greater emotional safety to try, to expose themselves to the task, and to persist, precisely because the animal functions as a non-judgmental "audience." This dimension is especially critical in the early grades, where fear of making mistakes and feelings of embarrassment can strongly affect participation (Steel et al., 2021; Steel, 2023).

Experiential humane education involving interaction with animals may constitute a clear pathway for the development of empathy and specific dimensions of socio-emotional competence. (Thompson & Gullone, 2003)

Empathy-oriented humane education training has been associated with increases in children's empathy toward animals, supporting the view that structured caregiving- and perspective-taking activities can cultivate empathy-related skills and responsible attitudes. (Angantyr et al., 2016)

At the same time, animal- and nature-focused school-based animal welfare education has been associated with improvements in empathy-related and humane-attitude outcomes among primary school students. (Hawkins et al., 2017; Williams et al., 2022). This perspective is further supported by evidence indicating that stronger emotional attachment to pets in childhood and adolescence is associated with more compassionate responding and higher affective empathy, suggesting that caregiving roles may serve as a practical route to the cultivation of empathy and responsibility. (Bosacki et al., 2022)

More broadly, a systematic review reports that the strength of the child–companion animal bond has been linked to psychosocial outcomes such as empathy, although findings vary across studies and measures. (Groenewoud et al., 2023)

At the same time, in school contexts where animal care is organized collaboratively, shared care routines have been described as fostering experiences of bonding and belongingness, while also strengthening peer relationships through common practices of responsibility and care. (Pinto & Foulkes, 2015).

Animal-assisted applications may also be understood as practices that shape the psycho-emotional climate at the level of the school community, particularly when they are designed to support not only students' well-being but also the adults who implement the programme through stable routines and a shared culture. This emphasis on adults is not incidental. In primary education, teacher stress has been conceptualised as a meaningful occupational phenomenon with classroom-relevant consequences, influencing how everyday demands are appraised and managed during instruction and transitions (Kyriacou, 2001). Relatedly, work on teacher self-efficacy and job stress indicates that teachers' perceived capacity to manage classroom demands is closely linked to their job satisfaction and stress-related outcomes, suggesting that classroom practices which protect predictability and reduce avoidable friction may indirectly support adult functioning (Klassen & Chiu, 2010). In addition, teachers' emotion-regulation ability has been associated with burnout-related indicators and job satisfaction, reinforcing the relevance of interventions that support calm, predictable interactional environments for both students and staff (Brackett et al., 2010).

Against this background, school-based dog programmes can be framed as potentially contributing to teacher and staff experience when they are implemented in structured, time-efficient ways. Teachers' accounts of working with dogs in schools describe perceived benefits that extend beyond students to everyday classroom processes and staff morale, while also highlighting that such programmes require clarity of purpose and practical coordination to remain feasible within school routines. (Lewis et al., 2023) Similarly, qualitative evidence focusing on teachers' lived experiences has emphasised perceived value for classroom de-escalation and behaviour management, alongside the need for clearly bounded interactions and role clarity to avoid implementation drift. (Kelsey, 2021) Complementing these experiential accounts, structured dog-based activities have also been associated with short-term improvements in educators' mood-related indicators in early childhood educational contexts, suggesting that teacher-level effects may be measurable when animal presence is organised and predictable. (Fujisawa et al., 2022) Taken together, these strands support the view that animal-assisted practices may contribute to a calmer and more supportive school climate at the level of the adults as well as the students, but that this potential is most likely to be realised when implementation is planned and resourced rather than ad hoc (Leos et al., 2022).

In contemporary educational research, school engagement is conceptualized as a multidimensional construct, encompassing behavioral, emotional, and cognitive engagement, and as a critical lever linked to participation, persistence, and, ultimately, children's learning trajectories (Fredricks, Blumenfeld, & Paris, 2004). From this perspective, animal-assisted interventions in school settings are of particular interest not only because of their potential academic effects, but also because they appear to directly influence classroom behaviors such as willingness to participate, time on task, and attitudes toward learning. In line with this view, participation in an AAE program involving dogs has been associated with improvements in indicators of everyday engagement in schoolwork, including work attitude, pleasant behavior, emotional stability, and social behavior, according to teachers' evaluations, while students themselves have reported higher levels of self-confidence. These indicators are especially valuable because they capture practical dimensions of classroom participation, such as remaining engaged in the activity, exerting effort, and persisting with the task (Verhoeven et al., 2023).

Academic engagement can also be captured directly through the measurement of on-task behaviors in reading contexts. In this regard, reading aloud to a dog within a visitation-based program has been associated with increases in on-task behavior and with the maintenance of these improvements over time, thereby highlighting changes at the level of task performance itself, that is, in what the student actually does during the activity, rather than merely in general impressions (Bassette & Taber-Doughty, 2013). Similarly, the integration of therapy dogs into school-based reading programs has been linked to increased interest and motivation, as well as to enhanced attention and focus, with staff and volunteers reporting that students are better able to remain on task during reading activities as part of the everyday school routine (Kirnan et al., 2016).

In the field of literacy, particular emphasis has been placed on research designs that distinguish the effect of an animal's presence from that of additional attention or the novelty of the situation by employing multiple comparison groups (e.g., dog, adult, teddy bear, control group). Within such designs, improvements in reading-related performance indicators, such as rate, accuracy, and comprehension, have been interpreted as consistent with enhanced concentration and persistence during the activity, especially when the intervention involves repeated practice (le Roux et al., 2014). In a similar vein, under school-based cross-over conditions, reading in the presence of a therapy dog has been associated with improvements in aspects of reading performance linked to concentration, including word and punctuation recognition as well as adherence to line breaks, compared with reading in the presence of a human companion (Wohlfarth et al., 2014).

In the earliest school grades, where engagement in learning is strongly shaped by emotion, for example, fear of making mistakes or hesitation about reading aloud, RTD interventions have been associated with improved well-being and greater engagement in reading, with particularly noticeable changes among more vulnerable children. At the same time, primary teachers' perceptions converge in suggesting that RTD is linked to reduced anxiety, increased motivation and self-confidence, and a more positive attitude toward reading (Steel, 2022; Steel et al., 2021). This pattern is further supported by findings from a pilot dog-assisted reading program involving children aged 6–11 years, in which higher attendance and more consistent participation in sessions, even reaching full attendance, were recorded, alongside parent reports of increased willingness to read at home, thereby highlighting the role of the animal as a motivating factor and a facilitator of sustained engagement (Uccheddu et al., 2019).

In primary education, progress in reading is shaped not only by systematic practice and the teaching of strategies, but also by how children experience reading itself, for example, in terms of self-confidence, anxiety, and attitudes toward or enjoyment of the activity. Reading self-efficacy has been identified as a malleable construct that can be strengthened through intervention and is theoretically associated with increased engagement in reading, insofar as its enhancement may translate into greater effort and persistence (Unrau et al., 2017). Consistent with this perspective, in a large sample of primary school children, reading self-efficacy was found to be positively associated with reading fluency and its development, particularly when assessed through more specific indicators (Peura et al., 2019). At the same time, reading as a source of anxiety is a well-documented phenomenon among students with reading difficulties and may be negatively related to indicators of fluency and comprehension; accordingly, it is pedagogically meaningful for school-based interventions to target, even indirectly, the reduction of reading-related tension and the strengthening of self-confidence (Fishstrom et al., 2024).

In school-based applications, dog-assisted reading programs have been associated with improvements in children's attitudes toward reading, even when reading fluency does not necessarily improve to the same extent. More specifically, positive changes in children's reading attitudes have been documented through instruments such as the Elementary Reading Attitude Survey (ERAS) (Coffman et al., 2023). Similarly, in short-term practice programs, the presence of a dog has been linked to the maintenance of a positive attitude toward reading, in contrast to the declines observed in control groups on ERAS subscales, thereby suggesting a protective effect on reading attitude (Lenihan et al., 2016). At a more experiential level, the rationale underlying these interventions is the creation of a non-judgmental audience and a positive routine that allows the child to remain engaged in the activity with greater ease and persistence, an aim that is fully consistent with the broader view that confidence and self-efficacy function as key drivers of engagement in reading (Unrau et al., 2017).

Beyond attitudes, there is also evidence suggesting that the presence of a dog may be associated with increased relaxation during reading. In Fung's (2019) pilot study involving three third-grade students with lower reading achievement, participants demonstrated greater relaxation during dog-assisted reading sessions, as measured through heart rate variability (HRV), together with improvements in reading fluency following the program. This type of evidence is important, because it indicates that such programs do not function merely as a source of motivation, but may also alter the immediate psychophysiological context in which the child reads, thereby making reading a more sustainable and manageable experience.

At the level of skill development, dog-assisted reading interventions have been associated with higher performance among students with reading difficulties when compared with alternative conditions such as reading with an adult, with a teddy bear, or with no intervention, with the benefits also being maintained at follow-up (le Roux et al., 2015). Complementing these findings, the broader body of quantitative research conducted in school settings has also been synthesized in a meta-analysis on the effects of dogs on learning, which includes reading-related outcomes (Reilly et al., 2020). At the same time, the positive effects of RTD programs are documented more convincingly when implementation is grounded in clear design, appropriate measures, and careful description of delivery characteristics. Even when quantitative differences are not particularly pronounced over a short duration, students and teachers consistently report a positive experience, especially with regard to reading as an activity in itself (Steel, 2024; Steel, 2023). For school-based design, this translates in practical terms into short but regular sessions, a predictable framework, an emphasis on enjoyment and self-confidence, and realistic monitoring indicators, such as ERAS for attitudes and oral reading fluency (ORF), a performance-based measure typically derived from a timed read-aloud (e.g., rate and accuracy), as has already been implemented in published studies (Coffman et al., 2023).

Executive functions (EF) refer to a set of higher-order cognitive processes that enable the child to remain goal-directed, inhibit impulses, hold and manipulate information in working memory, and shift flexibly between rules or activities (Diamond, 2013; Best & Miller, 2010). The "unity and diversity" model further suggests that EF comprise both a common underlying component (common EF) and distinct elements, such as inhibition, updating/working memory, and shifting/cognitive flexibility, a distinction that is pedagogically useful because different school activities place different demands on these subsystems (Friedman & Miyake, 2017). Within primary education, EF are closely linked to school readiness and classroom learning through their role in self-regulation and attentional control and therefore constitute a plausible target and outcome when examining practices designed to improve the learning environment (Blair & Raver, 2015).

A central assumption in this field is that interaction with an animal may support executive skills indirectly by creating conditions that facilitate cognitive control, including lower levels of tension and stress, more positive affect, greater willingness to engage, and a calmer context in which the child can exercise inhibition, persistence, and flexibility (Tepper et al., 2023). More specifically, the relationship between human–animal interaction and executive functions has been examined primarily through three approaches: (a) pet ownership or an ongoing relationship with a companion animal, (b) the presence of an animal during the administration of executive function tasks, and (c) participation in organized animal-assisted services or programs. Within this framework, the presence of an animal during the performance of cognitive tasks has been associated with better performance in specific executive processes, such as flexibility and inhibition, that is, in skills of direct relevance to educational practice (Tepper et al., 2023).

Under conditions in which the presence of a real dog is compared with that of a toy dog during the administration of executive-function tasks, better performance has been reported on tasks requiring cognitive flexibility (set shifting) and inhibition, as well as faster completion of set-shifting and sustained-attention tasks (Becker, 2014). Beyond reading-related applications, school-based dog-assisted interventions have also been associated with improvements in cognitive skills such as spatial ability. More specifically, a brief, repeated dog-assisted intervention (20 minutes, twice weekly for four weeks) has been linked to higher spatial-ability performance both immediately after the intervention and at short-term follow-up. Given that spatial thinking constitutes an important foundation for mathematical and scientific learning and is functionally related to the attention and working-memory processes involved in complex school tasks, such findings further support the view that animal-assisted interventions may, under appropriate conditions, enhance aspects of cognitive functioning that are educationally significant (Brelsford et al., 2022).

The international literature on animal-assisted interventions extends beyond the general student population and includes studies examining outcomes in children with specific psychosocial difficulties, an area of particular relevance to schools because improvements in regulation, self-perception, and emotional functioning may indirectly facilitate participation in learning. In children with ADHD, randomized evidence from the P.A.C.K. (Positive Assertive Cooperative Kids) intervention indicates that the canine-assisted version was associated with a greater reduction in ADHD symptom severity compared with the same psychosocial intervention delivered without a dog (Schuck, Emmerson, Fine, & Lakes, 2015). In a related randomized study focusing on self-perception, dog-assisted intervention was linked to more positive changes in self-esteem relative to a comparison condition without a dog (Schuck et al., 2018). At the level of immediate stress regulation, findings based on acute cortisol responses during psychosocial sessions further suggest that the presence of a therapy dog may be associated with a distinct, more regulated response profile in children with ADHD (Schuck et al., 2024). Complementing this evidence, a school-based case study of animal-assisted education with a dog reported improvements in classroom concentration and social-communicative functioning over an academic year, alongside a reduction in the observed severity of ADHD-related classroom difficulties (Juríčková et al., 2020). Taken together, these findings are pedagogically meaningful because they suggest that animal-assisted approaches may support not only students' willingness to participate but also their readiness to engage in structured classroom activities, including guided practice, rule-following, and cooperative work.

With regard to depression in childhood, the evidence within the field of Animal-Assisted Interventions (AAI) more often concerns depressive symptoms rather than formal clinical diagnoses, particularly in contexts involving trauma or abuse. In a group therapeutic intervention for children and adolescents with a history of sexual abuse, the groups that included therapy dogs showed reductions in trauma-related symptoms, including depressive symptoms, with particularly favorable outcomes observed in the dogs + therapeutic stories condition (Dietz, Davis, & Pennings, 2012). In a similar vein, systematic reviews indicate that, in trauma-exposed populations, AAI and AAT interventions are frequently associated with improvements in internalizing symptoms, including depressive indicators (O'Haire, Guérin, & Kirkham, 2015), while a review of AAT for children and adolescents with, or at risk for, mental health difficulties likewise highlights positive findings for canine-assisted approaches in trauma-related settings (Hoagwood, Acri, Morrissey, & Peth-Pierce, 2017). More recently, a systematic review examining AAT for the reduction of anxiety in children and adolescents also summarized favorable evidence for dog-assisted groups, in which lower levels of depression were reported in comparison with groups without a dog (Brandão et al., 2025). Taken together, these findings may be interpreted as indicating that animal-assisted interventions, when they are structured and embedded within a supportive framework, can promote positive emotional change in children with heightened vulnerability.

Animal-assisted activities may support first-grade children during school entry by helping them manage the increased demands of the transition from kindergarten, particularly with respect to anxiety and stress. The findings suggest that educational settings could consider animal-assisted approaches as one option for reducing transition-related anxiety and stress. In particular, a rabbit-assisted intervention that begins in kindergarten and continues into the first school year may offer continuity and familiarity in both the environment and the intervention approach, potentially strengthening its supportive effect during the preschool-to-school transition. The authors also propose that similar approaches may be relevant to other educational transitions later in development (Iváncsik et al., 2025).

FROM EVIDENCE TO PRACTICE

The implementation of a school-based animal program is more usefully understood as a staged process rather than as a one-off initiative. The EPIS (Exploration, Preparation, Implementation, Sustainment) model conceptualizes this trajectory from exploration and preparation to implementation and sustainment, emphasizing that each phase is characterized by distinct needs, barriers, and facilitating factors (Aarons, Hurlburt, & Horwitz, 2011). At the same time, the implementation literature underscores that success depends not merely on good intentions, but on the presence of supportive structures, such as training, supervision, feedback mechanisms, and monitoring data, which enable the program to operate consistently and sustainably within the school setting (Fixsen et al., 2005).

Planning is strengthened when a brief theory of change is clearly articulated, namely, what is done, why it is expected to help, and how its effects will be identified, and when the suitability of the practice for the specific school context is taken into account. The Consolidated Framework for Implementation Research (CFIR) emphasizes that the adoption of a given practice is shaped by characteristics of the intervention itself, the external and internal school environment, the individuals involved, and the implementation process (Damschroder et al., 2009). In practical terms, this means that the intervention must fit within the school timetable, involve clearly defined roles, and be supported by school leadership. A policy-oriented implementation guide further suggests that programs operate more smoothly when they are delivered in a consistent "dose", that is, in a brief, repeated, and predictable manner, and according to a commonly accepted protocol, before any attempt is made to expand or institutionalize them (Tennessee Department of Education, 2025).

For the program to remain functional, a minimal yet clearly defined organizational structure is required, including the selection of an appropriate model (e.g., visits/AAE, a schooldog, or a classroom animal), the designation of responsible personnel, the establishment of basic rules of interaction, and concise documentation. In this regard, distinguishing between student outcomes and implementation indicators is particularly useful, as it helps clarify what is working and why. The concept of implementation outcomes, such as acceptability, feasibility, fidelity, penetration, and sustainability, thus serves as a bridge between program design and the educational or psychosocial benefits that may follow (Proctor et al., 2011). At the same time, monitoring implementation quality is essential in order to determine whether the intervention was delivered as intended. The fidelity framework proposes that elements such as dosage, core intervention components, quality of delivery, and participant responsiveness should be systematically tracked (Carroll et al., 2007). At the school level, this can be achieved through a light-touch system of recording and feedback, as recommended in the literature on the evaluation of school-based intervention implementation (Schultes et al., 2023).

Finally, implementation is strengthened when a One Health/One Welfare perspective is explicitly adopted, that is, when equal attention is given to both human and animal well-being. In this respect, evaluation should avoid treating human benefit as something to be achieved at the animal's expense and should instead be designed so as to promote mutually positive conditions (Hediger et al., 2019). The need for standards of good practice in the field of AAI has likewise been identified as a priority, in order to ensure that applications are both high in quality and comparable across contexts (Brelsford et al., 2020). At the level of everyday school practice, basic routines of hygiene and spatial boundaries further contribute to the stability and predictability of implementation (CDC, 2009).

Animal welfare is not a peripheral concern but a fundamental precondition for ensuring that educational and psycho-emotional benefits are sustainable over time. The ethical perspective of "dual benefit" emphasizes that the use of animals in school settings must avoid instrumentalization and instead incorporate institutional oversight and accountability, so that the practice remains both ethically coherent and operationally stable (Fossati, 2026). At the level of implementation, professionals in the field likewise identify animal welfare as a foundation of both quality and effectiveness, stressing the need for adequate knowledge of animal behavior, the adaptation of working conditions to the animal's needs, and immediate responsiveness to signs of distress. In practical terms, this perspective translates into measures that prevent fatigue and help maintain a positive framework of interaction (Ameli et al., 2023).

Contemporary approaches to animal welfare have shifted from a narrow emphasis on the absence of suffering toward a broader view that also includes the possibility of positive experiences. The Five Domains Model provides an evaluative framework that explicitly incorporates the dimension of human interactions, thereby enabling a more holistic assessment of the impact of the school environment on the animal (Mellor et al., 2020). With specific regard to intervention dogs, the literature further emphasizes that welfare is strongly influenced by social and environmental factors such as the quality of the relationship with the handler, the degree of control and predictability afforded to the animal, and the availability of opportunities for rest or withdrawal. In practical terms, this perspective supports the use of brief, repeated sessions rather than prolonged, uncontrolled presence, as well as the provision of a "safe space" to which the animal can retreat when needed (Glenk & Foltin, 2021).

Health and safety are better supported when basic standards are established for the handler–animal team. Guidelines issued by a public authority in New York describe minimum criteria, including appropriate temperament and basic obedience, regular veterinary examination and health documentation, grooming prior to visits, and practices designed to reduce microbial risks, as well as organizational provisions such as the designation of a responsible liaison, record keeping, and an incident-reporting system, all of which contribute to the stability and transparency of a school-based program (New York State Department of Agriculture and Markets, 2019). Within this framework, hygiene functions as a mechanism that makes the intervention more predictable and therefore more beneficial for the school community. The NASPHV Compendium on Animals in Public Settings includes specific guidance for schools, such as informing parents, supervising interactions, defining appropriate areas, avoiding food spaces, and ensuring cleaning and disinfection, while also identifying handwashing as the single most important preventive measure (NASPHV, 2023).

In the same vein, broader reviews suggest that when simple hygiene protocols are implemented, such programs can operate with relative safety without undermining their psychosocial character (Bert et al., 2016). At the same time, an inclusive approach requires explicit provision for allergies and asthma. School policy models emphasize the need for an organized framework of management, including identification, communication, action plans, and staff preparedness, so that the presence of an animal does not create new forms of exclusion (BSACI, 2024). This concern is further reinforced by environmental exposure studies showing that dog and cat allergens may be present in school settings, thereby underscoring the importance of routine cleaning, adequate ventilation, and clear spatial boundaries (Sheehan et al., 2017; Niesler et al., 2016). In a similar practical vein, guidance from patient organizations highlights measures such as designated zones, cleaning and ventilation practices, consistent handwashing, and timely communication as ways of reconciling potential benefits with the protection of vulnerable students (Allergy &

Anaphylaxis Australia, 2024). Ultimately, the positive impact of such interventions is more likely to be sustained when participation is safe and voluntary, supported by procedures for information-sharing and consent, as well as by the explicit right not to participate within a broader school policy on well-being. In this respect, sector-wide standards and organisational policies for animal-assisted interventions emphasise clearly delineated roles, written procedures, and structured mechanisms for managing foreseeable challenges, helping to ensure the experience remains consistently positive (Standards of Practice for Animal-Assisted Interventions, 2021; Pet Partners, 2017), while public guidance likewise underlines that severe fear of animals or allergies may require alternative arrangements in order for implementation to remain genuinely inclusive (New York State Department of Agriculture and Markets, 2019).

DISCUSSION AND CONCLUDING REMARKS

Overall, the evidence discussed in this chapter converges on the view that classroom-based animal presence in primary education is most reliably associated with socio-emotional and behavioural benefits that matter for day-to-day instruction, namely a calmer affective tone, more positive peer interaction, and smoother participation in classroom activity. These effects are best understood as improvements in the relational and organisational conditions of learning rather than as direct, uniform gains in academic attainment. This interpretation aligns with broader evidence that the quality of teacher–student relationships predicts longer-term school trajectories (Hamre & Pianta, 2001) and with interaction-focused frameworks that foreground emotional support, classroom organisation, and instructional support as key levers for engagement (Pianta et al., 2012). It is also consistent with models of the prosocial classroom that emphasise socio-emotional processes as foundational to classroom functioning (Jennings & Greenberg, 2009) and with accounts of socio-emotional competence as a core pathway to positive adjustment in school-aged children (Domitrovich et al., 2017).

A second overarching implication is that benefits depend strongly on how animal-based practices are embedded in school life. Developers' perspectives on school implementation repeatedly highlight the importance of clear aims, feasible integration into the timetable, staff preparation and guidance, and leadership support for sustained delivery (Forman et al., 2009). For this reason, practical formats that preserve predictability and instructional coherence, such as brief, repeated small-group sessions focused on regulation and cooperation, RTD activities designed to strengthen the reading experience or classroom animals embedded within structured care routines, are more likely to be viable and educationally meaningful.

This emphasis on structured implementation is compatible with guidance in the school-based human–animal interaction literature, which argues that educational gains often occur indirectly through climate, relationships, and engagement, and that clearer specification of programme components is essential for interpretability and replication (Gee et al., 2017; Griffin et al., 2019).

To support sustainability without overburdening schools, evaluation can remain intentionally light, provided it is systematic and formative. Implementation research in education has shown that documenting core features such as dosage, adherence to essential components, and quality of delivery helps distinguish programme effects from implementation variability and supports iterative improvement over time (Century et al., 2010; Moore et al., 2015). In school terms, this can be achieved through brief session logs and periodic team reflection rather than intensive measurement regimes.

System-level integration remains the most robust route to stability. When animal-based practices are positioned within a whole-school wellbeing and SEL strategy, rather than as standalone "add-ons", they are more likely to generate shared language, consistent routines, and sustained commitment. Whole-school SEL implementation models provide practical steps for vision-setting, selection, implementation, and monitoring (Meyers et al., 2019), while leadership and community processes are central to cultivating climates of trust, empathy, and respect (Patti et al., 2015; Weissberg, 2019). Framing such practices in relation to broader educational aims, cognitive, intrapersonal, and interpersonal competencies, also aligns them with contemporary accounts of transferable "life and work" skills (National Research Council, 2012).

Finally, sustainable implementation is inseparable from ethics, safety, and inclusion. Clear school policies, an explicit right not to participate, and basic hygiene routines support predictability and protect vulnerable students, while a One Health/One Welfare orientation reinforces that educational benefit cannot be pursued at the expense of animal welfare (NASPHV, 2023; American Veterinary Medical Association, n.d.). Taken together, the chapter supports the position that animals in primary classrooms can constitute a pedagogically valuable and socially enabling practice when delivered through clear goals, stable structure, proportionate documentation, and ethically robust safeguards, conditions that also make programmes more comparable and, therefore, more readily learnable across schools (Century et al., 2010; Skivington et al., 2021).

REFERENCES

Aarons, G. A., Hurlburt, M., & Horwitz, S. M. (2011). Advancing a conceptual model of evidence-based practice implementation in public service sectors. *Administration and Policy in Mental Health, 38*(1), 4–23. DOI: 10.1007/s10488-010-0327-7

Allergy & Anaphylaxis Australia. (2024). *Support dogs in school and the risk to students with allergy.* https://allergyfacts.org.au/support-dogs-in-school-and-the-risk-to-students-with-allergy/

Ameli, K., Braun, T. F., & Krämer, S. (2023). Animal-assisted interventions and animal welfare—An exploratory survey in Germany. *Animals (Basel), 13*(8), 1324. Advance online publication. DOI: 10.3390/ani13081324

American Veterinary Medical Association. (n.d.). *Animal-assisted interventions: Guidelines.* https://www.avma.org/resources-tools/animal-health-and-welfare/service-emotional-support-and-therapy-animals/animal-assisted-interventions-guidelines

Angantyr, M., Hansen, E. M., Eklund, J. H., & Malm, K. (2016). Reducing sex differences in children's empathy for animals through a training intervention. *Journal of Research in Childhood Education, 30*(3), 273–281. DOI: 10.1080/02568543.2016.1178198

Arnsten, A. F. T. (2009). Stress signalling pathways that impair prefrontal cortex structure and function. *Nature Reviews. Neuroscience, 10*(6), 410–422. DOI: 10.1038/nrn2648

Ascione, F. R. (1997). Humane education research: Evaluating efforts to encourage children's kindness and caring toward animals. *Genetic, Social, and General Psychology Monographs, 123*(1), 57–77. https://api.semanticscholar.org/CorpusID:142398952

Ascione, F. R., & Weber, C. V. (1996). Children's attitudes about the humane treatment of animals and empathy: One-year follow-up of a school-based intervention. *Anthrozoos, 9*(4), 188–195. DOI: 10.2752/089279396787001455

Baird, R., Berger, E., & Grové, C. (2023). Therapy dogs and school wellbeing: A qualitative study. *Journal of Veterinary Behavior, 68*, 15–23. DOI: 10.1016/j.jveb.2023.08.005

Bassette, L. A., & Taber-Doughty, T. (2013). The effects of a dog reading visitation program on academic engagement behavior in three elementary students with emotional and behavioral disabilities: A single case design. *Child and Youth Care Forum*, *42*(3), 239–256. DOI: 10.1007/s10566-013-9197-y

Becker, J. L. (2014). Presence of a dog on executive functioning and stress in children with emotional disorders. *ETD Collection for Fordham University.* https://research.library.fordham.edu/dissertations/AAI3629239

Beetz, A. (2013). Socio-emotional correlates of a schooldog-teacher-team in the classroom. *Frontiers in Psychology*, *4*. Advance online publication. DOI: 10.3389/fpsyg.2013.00886

Beetz, A., Uvnäs-Moberg, K., Julius, H., & Kotrschal, K. (2012). Psychosocial and psychophysiological effects of human-animal interactions: The possible role of oxytocin. *Frontiers in Psychology*, *3*. Advance online publication. DOI: 10.3389/fpsyg.2012.00234

Bert, F., Gualano, M. R., Camussi, E., Pieve, G., Voglino, G., & Siliquini, R. (2016). Animal assisted intervention: A systematic review of benefits and risks. *European Journal of Integrative Medicine*, *8*(5), 695–706. DOI: 10.1016/j.eujim.2016.05.005

Best, J. R., & Miller, P. H. (2010). A developmental perspective on executive function. *Child Development*, *81*(6), 1641–1660. DOI: 10.1111/j.1467-8624.2010.01499.x

Blair, C., & Raver, C. C. (2015). School readiness and self-regulation: A developmental psychobiological approach. *Annual Review of Psychology*, *66*(1), 711–731. DOI: 10.1146/annurev-psych-010814-015221

Bosacki, S., Tardif-Williams, C. Y., & Roma, R. P. S. (2022). Children's and adolescents' pet attachment, empathy, and compassionate responding to self and others. *Adolescents (Basel, Switzerland)*, *2*(4), 493–507. DOI: 10.3390/adolescents2040039

Brackett, M. A., Palomera, R., Mojsa-Kaja, J., Reyes, M. R., & Salovey, P. (2010). Emotion-regulation ability, burnout, and job satisfaction among British secondary-school teachers. *Psychology in the Schools*, *47*(4), 406–417. DOI: 10.1002/pits.20478

Brandão, C., Sampaio, M., Sousa-Gomes, V., Fávero, M., & Moreira, D. (2025). Effects of animal-assisted therapy for anxiety reduction in children and adolescents: A systematic review. *Journal of Clinical Medicine*, *14*(1), 287. DOI: 10.3390/jcm14010287

Brelsford, V. L., Dimolareva, M., Gee, N. R., Rowan, E., & Meints, K. (2022). Can dog-assisted and relaxation interventions boost spatial ability in children with and without special educational needs? A longitudinal, randomized controlled trial. *Frontiers in Pediatrics*, *10*, 886324. Advance online publication. DOI: 10.3389/fped.2022.886324

Brelsford, V. L., Meints, K., Gee, N. R., & Pfeffer, K. (2017). Animal-assisted interventions in the classroom—A systematic review. *International Journal of Environmental Research and Public Health*, *14*(7), 669. DOI: 10.3390/ijerph14070669

Brelsford, V. L., Meints, K., Gee, N. R., & Pfeffer, K. (2020). Best practice standards in animal-assisted interventions: How the field can move forward. *Animals (Basel)*, *10*(10), 1853. DOI: 10.3390/ani10101853

British Society for Allergy & Clinical Immunology. (2024). *Model policy for allergy management at school.* https://www.bsaci.org/wp-content/uploads/2024/01/Model-Policy-for-allergy-at-management-at-school-v2.1-090124.pdf

Carroll, C., Patterson, M., Wood, S., Booth, A., Rick, J., & Balain, S. (2007). A conceptual framework for implementation fidelity. *Implementation Science : IS*, *2*(1), 40. Advance online publication. DOI: 10.1186/1748-5908-2-40

Centers for Disease Control and Prevention. (2009). *Appendix D: Guidelines for animals in school and child-care settings. In Compendium of measures to prevent disease associated with animals in public settings.* https://www.cdc.gov/mmwr/preview/mmwrhtml/rr5805a5.htm

Centers for Disease Control and Prevention. (2024). Resources for schools and daycares. *Healthy Pets, Healthy People.* https://www.cdc.gov/healthy-pets/schools-daycares/index.html

Century, J., Rudnick, M., & Freeman, C. (2010). A framework for measuring fidelity of implementation: A foundation for shared language and accumulation of knowledge. *The American Journal of Evaluation*, *31*(2), 199–218. DOI: 10.1177/1098214010366173

Coffman, A. N., Bernstein, E. R., Davies, S. C., & Justice, A. F. (2023). The Impact of a Canine-Assisted Reading Program on Readers Needing Extra Practice. *The Reading Teacher*, *76*(6), 724–734. DOI: 10.1002/trtr.2192

Cohen, S., & Wills, T. A. (1985). Stress, social support, and the buffering hypothesis. *Psychological Bulletin*, *98*(2), 310–357. DOI: 10.1037/0033-2909.98.2.310

Collaborative for Academic, Social, and Emotional Learning (CASEL). (2020). *CASEL's SEL framework* (CASEL 5). https://casel.org/casel-sel-framework-11-2020/

Corcoran, R. P., Cheung, A. C. K., Kim, E., & Xie, C. (2018). Effective universal school-based social and emotional learning programs for improving academic achievement: A systematic review and meta-analysis of 50 years of research. *Educational Research Review*, *25*, 56–72. https://api.semanticscholar.org/CorpusID:149185325. DOI: 10.1016/j.edurev.2017.12.001

Correale, C., Crescimbene, L., Borgi, M., & Cirulli, F. (2017). Development of a dog-assisted activity program in an elementary classroom. *Veterinary Sciences*, *4*(4), 62. DOI: 10.3390/vetsci4040062

Daly, B., & Suggs, S. (2010). Teachers' experiences with humane education and animals in the elementary classroom: Implications for empathy development. *Journal of Moral Education*, *39*(1), 101–112. DOI: 10.1080/03057240903528733

Damschroder, L. J., Aron, D. C., Keith, R. E., Kirsh, S. R., Alexander, J. A., & Lowery, J. C. (2009). Fostering implementation of health services research findings into practice: A consolidated framework for advancing implementation science. *Implementation Science : IS*, *4*(1), 50. DOI: 10.1186/1748-5908-4-50

Denham, S. A. (2006). Social–emotional competence as support for school readiness: What is it and how do we assess it? *Early Education and Development*, *17*(1), 57–89. https://psycnet.apa.org/doi/10.1207/s15566935eed1701_4. DOI: 10.1207/s15566935eed1701_4

Diamond, A. (2013). Executive functions. *Annual Review of Psychology*, *64*(1), 135–168. DOI: 10.1146/annurev-psych-113011-143750

Dietz, T. J., Davis, D., & Pennings, J. (2012). Evaluating animal-assisted therapy in group treatment for child sexual abuse. *Journal of Child Sexual Abuse*, *21*(6), 665–683. DOI: 10.1080/10538712.2012.726700

Domitrovich, C. E., Durlak, J. A., Staley, K. C., & Weissberg, R. P. (2017). Social-emotional competence: An essential factor for promoting positive adjustment and reducing risk in school children. *Child Development*, *88*(2), 408–416. DOI: 10.1111/cdev.12739

Ein, N., Li, L., & Vickers, K. (2018). The effect of pet therapy on the physiological and subjective stress response: A meta-analysis. *Stress and Health*, *34*(4), 477–489. DOI: 10.1002/smi.2812

Farrand, K. M., & Jung, J. Y. (2025). Exploring how a therapy dog intervention in a Tier 3 classroom influences mental health components of well-being: A case study. *Behavioral Sciences (Basel, Switzerland)*, *15*(11), 1585. DOI: 10.3390/bs15111585

Fedor, J. (2018). Animal-assisted therapy supports student connectedness. *NASN School Nurse, 33*(6), 355–358. DOI: 10.1177/1942602X18776424

Fishstrom, S., Capin, P., Fall, A. M., Roberts, G., Grills, A. E., & Vaughn, S. (2024). Understanding the relation between reading and anxiety among upper elementary students with reading difficulties. *Annals of Dyslexia, 74*(1), 123–141. DOI: 10.1007/s11881-024-00299-7

Fixsen, D. L., Naoom, S. F., Blase, K. A., Friedman, R. M., & Wallace, F. (2005). *Implementation research: A synthesis of the literature.* University of South Florida, Louis de la Parte Florida Mental Health Institute, National Implementation Research Network. https://fpg.unc.edu/sites/fpg.unc.edu/files/resource-files/NIRN-MonographFull-01-2005.pdf

Forman, S. G., Olin, S. S., Hoagwood, K. E., Crowe, M., & Saka, N. (2009). Evidence-based interventions in schools: Developers' views of implementation barriers and facilitators. *School Mental Health, 1*(1), 26–36. DOI: 10.1007/s12310-008-9002-5

Fossati, P. (2026). Correlated subjects: Relational ethics and veterinary legal accountability in animal-assisted interventions. *Animals (Basel), 16*(1), 92. DOI: 10.3390/ani16010092

Fredricks, J. A., Blumenfeld, P. C., & Paris, A. H. (2004). School engagement: Potential of the concept, state of the evidence. *Review of Educational Research, 74*(1), 59–109. DOI: 10.3102/00346543074001059

Fredrickson, B. L. (2001). The role of positive emotions in positive psychology: The broaden-and-build theory of positive emotions. *The American Psychologist, 56*(3), 218–226. DOI: 10.1037/0003-066X.56.3.218

Friedman, N. P., & Miyake, A. (2017). Unity and diversity of executive functions: Individual differences as a window on cognitive structure. *Cortex, 86*, 186–204. DOI: 10.1016/j.cortex.2016.04.023

Fujisawa, H., Kumasaka, T., & Kudo, K. (2022). Effects of animal-assisted activities on stress reduction in nursery school teachers. *International Medical Journal, 29*(5), 269–272. DOI: 10.1016/j.pedn.2017.05.006

Fung, S.-C. (2019). Effect of a canine-assisted read aloud intervention on reading ability and physiological response: A pilot study. *Animals (Basel), 9*(8), 474. DOI: 10.3390/ani9080474

Gee, N. R., Crist, E. N., & Carr, D. N. (2010). Preschool children require fewer instructional prompts to perform a memory task in the presence of a dog. *Anthrozoos, 23*(2), 173–184. DOI: 10.2752/175303710X12682332910051

Gee, N. R., Griffin, J. A., & McCardle, P. M. (2017). Human–animal interaction research in school settings: Current knowledge and future directions. *AERA Open*, *3*(3), 1–9. DOI: 10.1177/2332858417724346

Gee, N. R., Sherlock, T. R., Bennett, E. A., & Harris, S. L. (2009). Preschoolers' adherence to instructions as a function of presence of a dog and motor skills task. *Anthrozoos*, *22*(3), 267–276. DOI: 10.2752/175303709X457603

Glenk, L. M., & Foltin, S. (2021). Therapy dog welfare revisited: A review of the literature. *Veterinary Sciences*, *8*(10), 226. DOI: 10.3390/vetsci8100226

Goodmon, L. B., Burnett, P. R., Pack, R., & Powell, R. (2021). The effect of a dog assisted reading program on the reading ability and motivation of children with dyslexia. *Human Animal Interactions Bulletin*, *9*(2), 1–26. DOI: 10.1079/hai.2021.0031

Graziano, P. A., Reavis, R. D., Keane, S. P., & Calkins, S. D. (2007). The role of emotion regulation in children's early academic success. *Journal of School Psychology*, *45*(1), 3–19. DOI: 10.1016/j.jsp.2006.09.002

Griffin, J. A., Hurley, K., & McCune, S. (2019). Human–animal interaction research: Progress and possibilities. *Frontiers in Psychology*, *10*, 2803. Advance online publication. DOI: 10.3389/fpsyg.2019.02803

Groenewoud, D., Enders-Slegers, M. J., Leontjevas, R., van Dijke, A., de Winkel, T., & Hediger, K. (2023). Children's bond with companion animals and associations with psychosocial health: A systematic review. *Frontiers in Psychology*, *14*, 1120000. DOI: 10.3389/fpsyg.2023.1120000

Grové, C., Henderson, L., Lee, F., & Wardlaw, P. (2021). Therapy dogs in educational settings: Guidelines and recommendations for implementation. *Frontiers in Veterinary Science*, *8*, 655104. DOI: 10.3389/fvets.2021.655104

Gunnar, M., & Quevedo, K. (2007). The neurobiology of stress and development. *Annual Review of Psychology*, *58*(1), 145–173. DOI: 10.1146/annurev.psych.58.110405.085605

Hall, S. S., Gee, N. R., & Mills, D. S. (2016). Children Reading to Dogs: A Systematic Review of the Literature. *PLoS One*, *11*(2), e0149759. Advance online publication. DOI: 10.1371/journal.pone.0149759

Hamre, B. K., & Pianta, R. C. (2001). Early teacher–child relationships and the trajectory of children's school outcomes through eighth grade. *Child Development*, *72*(2), 625–638. DOI: 10.1111/1467-8624.00301

Hawkins, R. D., & Williams, J. M. (2017). Childhood attachment to pets: Associations between pet attachment, attitudes to animals, compassion, and humane behaviour. *International Journal of Environmental Research and Public Health, 14*(5), 490. DOI: 10.3390/ijerph14050490

Hawkins, R. D., & Williams, J. M. (2017). Assessing effectiveness of a nonhuman animal welfare education program for primary school children. *Journal of Applied Animal Welfare Science, 20*(3), 240–256. DOI: 10.1080/10888705.2017.1305272

Hediger, K., Meisser, A., & Zinsstag, J. (2019). A One Health research framework for animal-assisted interventions. *International Journal of Environmental Research and Public Health, 16*(4), 640. DOI: 10.3390/ijerph16040640

Hediger, K., & Turner, D. C. (2014). Can dogs increase children's attention and concentration performance? A randomised controlled trial. *Human Animal Interactions Bulletin, 2*(2), 21–39. DOI: 10.1079/hai.2014.0010

Henderson, L., Grové, C., Lee, F., Trainer, L., Schena, H., & Prentice, M. (2020). An evaluation of a dog-assisted reading program to support student wellbeing in primary school. *Children and Youth Services Review, 118*, 105449. Advance online publication. DOI: 10.1016/j.childyouth.2020.105449

Hergovich, A., Monshi, B., Semmler, G., & Zieglmayer, V. (2002). The effects of the presence of a dog in the classroom. *Anthrozoos, 15*(1), 37–50. DOI: 10.2752/089279302786992775

Hoagwood, K. E., Acri, M., Morrissey, M., & Peth-Pierce, R. (2017). Animal-assisted therapies for youth with or at risk for mental health problems: A systematic review. *Applied Developmental Science, 21*(1), 1–13. DOI: 10.1080/10888691.2015.1134267

Hoffmann, T. C., Glasziou, P. P., Boutron, I., Milne, R., Perera, R., Moher, D., Altman, D. G., Barbour, V., Macdonald, H., Johnston, M., Lamb, S. E., Dixon-Woods, M., McCulloch, P., Wyatt, J. C., Chan, A.-W., & Michie, S. (2014). Better reporting of interventions: Template for intervention description and replication (TIDieR) checklist and guide. *BMJ (Clinical research ed.), 348*. DOI: 10.1136/bmj.g1687

Hostinar, C. E., Sullivan, R. M., & Gunnar, M. R. (2014). Psychobiological mechanisms underlying the social buffering of the hypothalamic–pituitary–adrenocortical axis: A review of animal models and human studies across development. *Psychological Bulletin, 140*(1), 256–282. DOI: 10.1037/a0032671

Howell, T. J., Nieforth, L., Thomas-Pino, C., Samet, L., Agbonika, S., Cuevas-Pavincich, F., Fry, N. E., Hill, K., Jegatheesan, B., Kakinuma, M., MacNamara, M., Mattila-Rautiainen, S., Perry, A., Tardif-Williams, C. Y., Walsh, E. A., Winkle, M., Yamamoto, M., Yerbury, R., Rawat, V., & Bennett, P. (2022). Defining Terms Used for Animals Working in Support Roles for People with Support Needs. *Animals (Basel)*, *12*(15), 1975. Advance online publication. DOI: 10.3390/ani12151975

Immordino-Yang, M. H., & Damasio, A. (2007). We Feel, Therefore We Learn: The Relevance of Affective and Social Neuroscience to Education. *Mind, Brain and Education : the Official Journal of the International Mind, Brain, and Education Society*, *1*(1), 3–10. DOI: 10.1111/j.1751-228X.2007.00004.x

International Association of Human-Animal Interaction Organizations. (2018). *The IAHAIO definitions for animal assisted intervention and guidelines for wellness of animals involved in AAI* (White paper; updated for 2018). https://iahaio.org/wp/wp-content/uploads/2021/01/iahaio-white-paper-2018-english.pdf

International Association of Human-Animal Interaction Organizations. (2022). *IAHAIO international guidelines for minimum standards for education and training in animal-assisted interventions (AAI).* https://iahaio.org/wp/wp-content/uploads/2022/11/iahaio-educational-standards_final.pdf

Iváncsik, R., Podráczky, J., Molnár, M., Stromájer, G. P., & Csima, M. (2025). The role of animal-assisted intervention in supporting the preschool-to-school transition. *International Journal of Early Childhood*, *57*(3), 667–686. DOI: 10.1007/s13158-024-00414-0

Jalongo, M. R. (2005). "What are all these dogs doing at school?": Using therapy dogs to promote children's reading practice. *Childhood Education*, *81*(3), 152–158. DOI: 10.1080/00094056.2005.10522259

Jennings, P. A., & Greenberg, M. T. (2009). The prosocial classroom: Teacher social and emotional competence in relation to student and classroom outcomes. *Review of Educational Research*, *79*(1), 491–525. DOI: 10.3102/0034654308325693

Jones, S. M., & Bouffard, S. M. (2012). Social and emotional learning in schools: From programs to strategies and commentaries. *Child Policy Nexus*, *26*(4), 1–33. DOI: 10.1002/j.2379-3988.2012.tb00073.x

Juríčková, V., Bozděchová, A., Machová, K., & Vadroňová, M. (2020). Effect of animal assisted education with a dog within children with ADHD in the classroom: A case study. *Child & Adolescent Social Work Journal*, *37*(6), 677–684. DOI: 10.1007/s10560-020-00716-x

Kaplan, S. (1995). The restorative benefits of nature: Toward an integrative framework. *Journal of Environmental Psychology*, *15*(3), 169–182. DOI: 10.1016/0272-4944(95)90001-2

Kelsey, R. M. (2021). Teachers' lived experiences regarding the use of therapy dogs as a behavior management strategy: A phenomenological study (Doctoral dissertation, Drexel University). DOI: 10.17918/00000359

Kertes, D. A., Liu, J., Hall, N. J., Hadad, N. A., Wynne, C. D. L., & Bhatt, S. S. (2017). Effect of pet dogs on children's perceived stress and cortisol stress response. *Social Development*, *26*(2), 382–401. DOI: 10.1111/sode.12203

Kirnan, J. P., Siminerio, S., & Wong, Z. (2016). The impact of a therapy dog program on children's reading skills and attitudes toward reading. *Early Childhood Education Journal*, *44*(6), 637–651. DOI: 10.1007/s10643-015-0747-9

Klassen, R. M., & Chiu, M. M. (2010). Effects on teachers' self-efficacy and job satisfaction: Teacher gender, years of experience, and job stress. *Journal of Educational Psychology*, *102*(3), 741–756. DOI: 10.1037/a0019237

Kotrschal, K., & Ortbauer, B. (2003). Behavioral effects of the presence of a dog in a classroom. *Anthrozoos*, *16*(2), 147–159. DOI: 10.2752/089279303786992170

Kyriacou, C. (2001). Teacher stress: Directions for future research. *Educational Review*, *53*(1), 27–35. DOI: 10.1080/00131910120033628

le Roux, M., Swartz, L., & Swart, E. (2015). The effect of an animal-assisted reading programme on word recognition and spelling skills of grade 3 children. *Tydskrif vir Geesteswetenskappe*, *55*(2), 289–303. DOI: 10.17159/2224-7912/2015/V55N2A9

le Roux, M. C., Swartz, L., & Swart, E. (2014). The effect of an animal-assisted reading program on the reading rate, accuracy and comprehension of Grade 3 students: A randomized control study. *Child and Youth Care Forum*, *43*(6), 655–673. DOI: 10.1007/s10566-014-9262-1

Lenihan, D., McCobb, E., Diurba, A., Linder, D., & Freeman, L. (2016). Measuring the effects of reading assistance dogs on reading ability and attitudes in elementary schoolchildren. *Journal of Research in Childhood Education*, *30*(2), 252–259. DOI: 10.1080/02568543.2016.1143896

Leos, R. A., Cuccaro, P. M., Herbold, J. R., & Hernandez, B. F. (2022). Exploring School Staff Perceptions Relating to Animals and Their Involvement in Interventions to Support Mental Health. *International Journal of Environmental Research and Public Health*, *19*(12), 7126. DOI: 10.3390/ijerph19127126

Lewis, H., Godfrey Oostendorp, J., & Knight, C. (2023). Tales of the unexpected: Teacher's experiences of working with children and dogs in schools. *Human-Animal Interactions, 11*(1), 1–11. DOI: 10.1079/hai.2023.0040

Linder, D. E., Mueller, M. K., Gibbs, D. M., Siebens, H. C., & Freeman, L. M. (2017). Animal-assisted interventions: A national survey of health and safety policies in hospitals, eldercare facilities, and therapy animal organizations. *American Journal of Infection Control, 45*(8), 883–887. DOI: 10.1016/j.ajic.2017.04.287

López-Cepero, J. (2020). Current status of animal-assisted interventions in scientific literature: A critical comment on their internal validity. *Animals (Basel), 10*(6), 985. Advance online publication. DOI: 10.3390/ani10060985

McCullough, A., Ruehrdanz, A., Garthe, R., Hellman, C., & O'Haire, M. (2021). Measuring the social, behavioral, and academic effects of classroom pets on third and fourth-grade students. *Human Animal Interactions Bulletin, 9*(1), 1–21. DOI: 10.1079/hai.2021.0023

McEwen, B. S. (2007). Physiology and neurobiology of stress and adaptation: Central role of the brain. *Physiological Reviews, 87*(3), 873–904. DOI: 10.1152/physrev.00041.2006

McNicholas, J., & Collis, G. M. (2000). Dogs as catalysts for social interactions: Robustness of the effect. *British Journal of Psychology, 91*(1), 61–70. DOI: 10.1348/000712600161673

Meints, K., Brelsford, V. L., Dimolareva, M., Maréchal, L., Pennington, K., Rowan, E., & Gee, N. R. (2022). Can dogs reduce stress levels in school children? effects of dog-assisted interventions on salivary cortisol in children with and without special educational needs using randomized controlled trials. *PLoS One, 17*(6), e0269333. Advance online publication. DOI: 10.1371/journal.pone.0269333

Meixner, J., & Kotrschal, K. (2022). Animal-assisted interventions with dogs in special education—A systematic review. *Frontiers in Psychology, 13*, 876290. Advance online publication. DOI: 10.3389/fpsyg.2022.876290

Mellor, D. J., Beausoleil, N. J., Littlewood, K. E., McLean, A. N., McGreevy, P. D., Jones, B., & Wilkins, C. (2020). The 2020 Five Domains Model: Including Human–Animal Interactions in assessments of animal welfare. *Animals (Basel), 10*(10), 1870. Advance online publication. DOI: 10.3390/ani10101870

Meyers, D. C., Domitrovich, C. E., Dissi, R., Trejo, J., & Greenberg, M. T. (2019). Supporting systemic social and emotional learning with a schoolwide implementation model. *Evaluation and Program Planning*, *73*, 53–61. DOI: 10.1016/j.evalprogplan.2018.11.005

Moe, I., Ho, P. J., Andersson, M., Karlberg, S., Lidfors, L., Sampaio, F., & Feldman, I. (2025). Effectiveness of animal-assisted services for school-aged children: A systematic review. *European Child & Adolescent Psychiatry*, *34*(10), 3017–3033. DOI: 10.1007/s00787-025-02740-7

Mombeck, M. M., & Albers, T. (2024). The Impact of a School Dog on Children's Social Inclusion and Social Climate in a School Class. *European Journal of Investigation in Health, Psychology and Education*, *14*(1), 1–17. DOI: 10.3390/ejihpe14010001

Moore, G. F., Audrey, S., Barker, M., Bond, L., Bonell, C., Hardeman, W., Moore, L., O'Cathain, A., Tinati, T., Wight, D., & Baird, J. (2015). Process evaluation of complex interventions: *Medical Research Council guidance. BMJ (Clinical Research Ed.)*, *350*(mar19 6), h1258. Advance online publication. DOI: 10.1136/bmj.h1258

Morgan, S. (2024). Animal assisted education and social communication competency: Systematic literature review. *Discover Education*, *3*(1), 258. Advance online publication. DOI: 10.1007/s44217-024-00357-7

National Association of State Public Health Veterinarians Animal Contact Compendium Committee. (2023). *Compendium of measures to prevent disease associated with animals in public settings.* https://nasphv.org/Documents/AnimalsInPublicSettings2023.pdf

National Research Council. (2012). *Education for life and work: Developing transferable knowledge and skills in the 21st century.* The National Academies Press. https://www.nationalacademies.org/projects/DBASSE-CFE-10-06

New York State Department of Agriculture and Markets. (2019). *Guidance for handlers and facilities using therapy dogs.* https://agriculture.ny.gov/system/files/documents/2020/03/therapydogguidance.pdf

Ngai, J. T. K., Yu, R. W. M., Chau, K. K. Y., & Wong, P. W. C. (2021). Effectiveness of a school-based programme of animal-assisted humane education in Hong Kong for the promotion of social and emotional learning: A quasi-experimental pilot study. *PLoS One*, *16*(3), e0249033. Advance online publication. DOI: 10.1371/journal.pone.0249033

Nicoll, K., Trifone, C., & Samuels, W. E. (2008). An in-class, humane education program can improve young students' attitudes toward animals. *Society & Animals, 16*(1), 45–60. DOI: 10.1163/156853008X269881

Niesler, A., Ścigała, G., & Łudzeń-Izbińska, B. (2016). Cat (Fel d 1) and dog (Can f 1) allergen levels in cars, dwellings and schools. *Aerobiologia, 32*(3), 571–580. DOI: 10.1007/s10453-016-9433-7

O'Haire, M. E., Guérin, N. A., & Kirkham, A. C. (2015). Animal-assisted intervention for trauma: A systematic literature review. *Frontiers in Psychology, 6*. Advance online publication. DOI: 10.3389/fpsyg.2015.01121

O'Haire, M. E., McKenzie, S. J., Beck, A. M., & Slaughter, V. (2013). Social behaviors increase in children with autism in the presence of animals compared to toys. *PLoS One, 8*(2), e57010. Advance online publication. DOI: 10.1371/journal.pone.0057010

O'Haire, M. E., McKenzie, S. J., McCune, S., & Slaughter, V. (2013). Effects of animal-assisted activities with guinea pigs in the primary school classroom. *Anthrozoos, 26*(3), 445–458. DOI: 10.2752/175303713X13697429463835

OECD. (2024). Nurturing Social and Emotional Learning Across the Globe: Findings from the OECD Survey on Social and Emotional Skills 2023. OECD Publishing. https://www.oecd.org/en/publications/nurturing-social-and-emotional-learning-across-the-globe_32b647d0-en.html

Patti, J., Senge, P., Madrazo, C., & Stern, R. (2015). Developing socially, emotionally, and cognitively competent school leaders and learning communities. In Durlak, J. A., Domitrovich, C. E., Weissberg, R. P., & Gullotta, T. P. (Eds.), *Handbook of social and emotional learning: Research and practice* (pp. 438–452). Guilford Press.

Peña-Jorquera, H., Hernández-Jaña, S., Sanchez-Martinez, J., Espinoza-Puelles, J. P., Martínez-Flores, R., Barreto-Schuch, F., Yáñez-Sepúlveda, R., Delgado-Floody, P., Ferrari, G., Sadarangani, K. P., Cancino-López, J., Bento-Torres, J., Espinoza-Salinas, A., Stamatakis, E., & Cristi-Montero, C. (2025). Dog companionship and cortisol levels in youth: A systematic review and meta-analysis. *Social Science & Medicine, 369*, 117815. Advance online publication. DOI: 10.1016/j.socscimed.2025.117815

Peura, P., Aro, T., Viholainen, H., Räikkönen, E., Usher, E. L., Sorvo, R., & Aro, M. (2019). Reading self-efficacy and reading fluency development among primary school children: Does specificity of self-efficacy matter? *Learning and Individual Differences, 73*, 67–78. DOI: 10.1016/j.lindif.2019.05.007

Pianta, R. C., Hamre, B. K., & Allen, J. P. (2012). Teacher–student relationships and engagement: Conceptualizing, measuring, and improving the capacity of classroom interactions. In Christenson, S. L., Reschly, A. L., & Wylie, C. (Eds.), *Handbook of research on student engagement* (pp. 365–386). Springer., DOI: 10.1007/978-1-4614-2018-7_17

Pinto, L. E., & Foulkes, D. (2015). Well-Being and Human-Animal Interactions in Schools: The Case of "Dog Daycare Co-Op". *Brock Education Journal, 24*(2). Advance online publication. DOI: 10.26522/brocked.v24i2.395

Polheber, J. P., & Matchock, R. L. (2014). The presence of a dog attenuates cortisol and heart rate in the Trier Social Stress Test compared to human friends. *Journal of Behavioral Medicine, 37*(5), 860–867. DOI: 10.1007/s10865-013-9546-1

Proctor, E., Silmere, H., Raghavan, R., Hovmand, P., Aarons, G., Bunger, A., Griffey, R., & Hensley, M. (2011). Outcomes for implementation research: Conceptual distinctions, measurement challenges, and research agenda. *Administration and Policy in Mental Health, 38*(2), 65–76. DOI: 10.1007/s10488-010-0319-7

Reilly, K. M., Adesope, O. O., & Erdman, P. (2020). The effects of dogs on learning: A meta-analysis. *Anthrozoos, 33*(3), 339–360. DOI: 10.1080/08927936.2020.1746523

Rud, A. G.Jr, & Beck, A. M. (2003). Companion animals in Indiana elementary schools. *Anthrozoos, 16*(3), 241–251. DOI: 10.2752/089279303786992134

Ryan, R. M., & Deci, E. L. (2000). Self-determination theory and the facilitation of intrinsic motivation, social development, and well-being. *The American Psychologist, 55*(1), 68–78. DOI: 10.1037/0003-066X.55.1.68

Ryan, R. M., & Deci, E. L. (2017). *Self-determination theory: Basic psychological needs in motivation, development, and wellness.* Guilford Press. DOI: 10.1521/978.14625/28806

Samuels, W. E., & Onuoha-Jackson, N. (2023). Learning to care: An in-school humane education program improves affective and cognitive empathy among lower-elementary students. *International Journal of Educational Research Open, 5*, 100292. Advance online publication. DOI: 10.1016/j.ijedro.2023.100292

Santaniello, A., Dicé, F., Carratú, R. C., Amato, A., Fioretti, A., & Menna, L. F. (2020). Methodological and terminological issues in animal-assisted interventions: An umbrella review of systematic reviews. *Animals (Basel), 10*(5), 759. DOI: 10.3390/ani10050759

Scandurra, C., Santaniello, A., Cristiano, S., Mezza, F., Garzillo, S., Pizzo, R., Menna, L. F., & Bochicchio, V. (2021). An animal-assisted education intervention with dogs to promote emotion comprehension in primary school children—The Federico II model of healthcare zooanthropology. *Animals (Basel), 11*(6), 1504. Advance online publication. DOI: 10.3390/ani11061504

Schonert-Reichl, K. A. (2017). Social and emotional learning and teachers. *The Future of Children, 27*(1), 137–155. DOI: 10.1353/foc.2017.0007

Schuck, S. E. B., Emmerson, N. A., Fine, A. H., & Lakes, K. D. (2015). Canine-assisted therapy for children with ADHD: Preliminary findings from the Positive Assertive Cooperative Kids Study. *Journal of Attention Disorders, 19*(2), 125–137. DOI: 10.1177/1087054713502080

Schuck, S. E. B., Johnson, H. L., Abdullah, M. M., Stehli, A., Fine, A. H., & Lakes, K. D. (2018). The role of animal assisted intervention on improving self-esteem in children with attention deficit/hyperactivity disorder. *Frontiers in Pediatrics, 6*, 300. Advance online publication. DOI: 10.3389/fped.2018.00300

Schuck, S. E. B., Zeiler, C. N., Stehli, A., Steinhoff, L. A., Stokes, R. Y., Jeffrey, S. E., & Granger, D. A. (2024). Acute salivary cortisol response in children with ADHD during psychosocial intervention with and without therapy dogs. *Frontiers in Psychiatry, 15*, 1476522. Advance online publication. DOI: 10.3389/fpsyt.2024.1476522

Schultes, M. T. (2023). An introduction to implementation evaluation of school-based interventions. *European Journal of Developmental Psychology, 20*(1), 189–201. DOI: 10.1080/17405629.2021.1976633

Sheehan, W. J., Permaul, P., Petty, C. R., Coull, B. A., Baxi, S. N., Gaffin, J. M., Lai, P. S., Gold, D. R., & Phipatanakul, W. (2017). Association Between Allergen Exposure in Inner-City Schools and Asthma Morbidity Among Students. *JAMA Pediatrics, 171*(1), 31–38. DOI: 10.1001/jamapediatrics.2016.2543

Shields, G. S., Sazma, M. A., & Yonelinas, A. P. (2016). The effects of acute stress on core executive functions: A meta-analysis and comparison with cortisol. *Neuroscience and Biobehavioral Reviews, 68*, 651–668. DOI: 10.1016/j.neubiorev.2016.06.038

Skivington, K., Matthews, L., Simpson, S. A., Craig, P., Baird, J., Blazeby, J. M., Boyd, K. A., & Moore, L. (2021). A new framework for developing and evaluating complex interventions: Update of Medical Research Council guidance. *BMJ (Clinical Research Ed.), 37*, n2061. Advance online publication. DOI: 10.1136/bmj.n2061

Sorin, R., Brooks, T., & Lloyd, J. (2015). The impact of the Classroom Canines program on children's reading, social and emotional skills, and motivation to attend school. *The International Journal of Literacies*, *22*(2), 23–35. DOI: 10.18848/2327-0136/CGP/v22i02/48840

Steel, J. (2023). Reading to Dogs in schools: A controlled feasibility study of an online Reading to Dogs intervention. *International Journal of Educational Research*, *117*, 102117. Advance online publication. DOI: 10.1016/j.ijer.2022.102117

Steel, J. (2024). Children's wellbeing and reading engagement: the impact of reading to dogs in a Scottish Primary 1 classroom. *Education 3-13*, *52*(3), 375–390. https://doi.org/DOI: 10.1080/03004279.2022.2100442

Steel, J. (2024). Reading to Dogs as a form of animal-assisted education: Are positive outcomes supported by quality research? *Literacy*, *58*(1), 102–119. DOI: 10.1111/lit.12345

Steel, J., Williams, J. M., & McGeown, S. (2021). Reading to dogs in schools: An exploratory study of teacher perspectives. *Educational Research*, *63*(3), 279–301. DOI: 10.1080/00131881.2021.1956989

Štremfel, U., Šterman Ivančič, K., & Peras, I. (2024). Addressing the sense of school belonging among all students? A systematic literature review. *European Journal of Investigation in Health, Psychology and Education*, *14*(11), 2901–2917. DOI: 10.3390/ejihpe14110190

Taylor, R. D., Oberle, E., Durlak, J. A., & Weissberg, R. P. (2017). Promoting positive youth development through school-based social and emotional learning interventions: A meta-analysis of follow-up effects. *Child Development*, *88*(4), 1156–1171. DOI: 10.1111/cdev.12864

Tennessee Department of Education. (2025). *School therapy dog implementation guide.* https://www.tn.gov/content/dam/tn/education/health-%26-safety/School_Therapy_Dog_Implementation_Guide.pdf

Tepper, D., Shnookal, J., Howell, T., & Bennett, P. (2023). Can interacting with animals improve executive functions? A systematic review. *Animals (Basel)*, *13*(13), 2080. Advance online publication. DOI: 10.3390/ani13132080

Thompson, K. L., & Gullone, E. (2003). Promotion of empathy and prosocial behaviour in children through humane education. *Australian Psychologist*, *38*(3), 175–182. DOI: 10.1080/00050060310001707187

Ulrich, R. S. (1984). View through a window may influence recovery from surgery. *Science*, *224*(4647), 420–421. DOI: 10.1126/science.6143402

Unrau, N. J., Rueda, R., Son, E., Polanin, J. R., Lundeen, R. J., & Muraszewski, A. K. (2017). Can reading self-efficacy be modified? A meta-analysis of the impact of interventions on reading self-efficacy. *Review of Educational Research*, *88*(2), 167–204. DOI: 10.3102/0034654317743199

U.S. Department of Justice, Civil Rights Division. (2011). *ADA requirements: Service animals.* ADA.gov. https://www.ada.gov/resources/service-animals-2010-requirements/

Verhoeven, R., Butter, R., Martens, R., & Enders-Slegers, M.-J. (2023). Animal-assisted education: Exploratory research on the positive impact of dogs on behavioral and emotional outcomes of elementary school students. *Children (Basel, Switzerland)*, *10*(8), 1316. Advance online publication. DOI: 10.3390/children10081316

Vogel, S., & Schwabe, L. (2016). Learning and memory under stress: Implications for the classroom. *npj Science of Learning, 1*. DOI: 10.1038/npjscilearn.2016.11

Weissberg, R. P. (2019). Promoting the social and emotional learning of millions of school children. *Perspectives on Psychological Science*, *14*(1), 65–69. DOI: 10.1177/1745691618817756

Wentzel, K. R. (1998). Social relationships and motivation in middle school: The role of parents, teachers, and peers. *Journal of Educational Psychology*, *90*(2), 202–209. https://psycnet.apa.org/doi/10.1037/0022-0663.90.2.202. DOI: 10.1037/0022-0663.90.2.202

Williams, J. M., Padilla Cardoso, M., Zumaglini, S., & Finney, A. L. (2022). "Rabbit Rescuers": A school-based animal welfare education intervention for young children. *Anthrozoos*, *35*(1), 55–73. DOI: 10.1080/08927936.2021.1944561

Wilson, E. O. (1984). *Biophilia*. Harvard University Press. DOI: 10.4159/9780674045231

Wintermantel, L., Grové, C., Henderson, L., & Laletas, S. (2024). Social and emotional therapy dog-assisted interventions in mainstream school settings: A systematic review. *Educational and Developmental Psychologist*, *41*(1), 74–90. DOI: 10.1080/20590776.2023.2256444

Wohlfarth, R., Mutschler, B., Beetz, A., & Schleider, K. (2014). An investigation into the efficacy of therapy dogs on reading performance in 6–7 year old children. *Human Animal Interactions Bulletin*, *2*(2), 60–73. DOI: 10.1079/hai.2014.0013

Chapter 4
School Leadership as Mentoring:
A Relational and Preventive Approach to Teachers' Resilience

Nikolaos Raptis
University of the Aegean, Rhodes, Greece

Nikolaos Psyrras
http://orcid.org/0009-0008-2454-8122
University of the Aegean, Rhodes, Greece

ABSTRACT

This chapter examines school leadership as a mentoring-oriented, relational, and preventive approach to teachers' resilience. It argues that resilience should not be regarded only as an individual capacity, but as a process shaped by organizational conditions and supportive professional culture. Based on literature, the chapter highlights the importance of trust, reflective dialogue, psychological safety, and collaborative learning. It suggests that mentoring-oriented leadership can support teachers' professional engagement and long-term resilience by creating emotionally supportive and collaborative school environments. Moreover, it recognizes that relational leadership cannot replace broader structural and systemic changes. Overall, the chapter presents mentoring-oriented leadership as a useful framework for strengthening a sustainable and preventive school culture.

DOI: 10.4018/979-8-3373-9420-6.ch004

INTRODUCTION

Teaching in contemporary school environments has become increasingly complex and demanding. Teachers are expected to respond not only to academic needs, but also to students' emotional, behavioural, and psychosocial difficulties. At the same time, they work in educational environments characterized by constant change, increased accountability, inclusive education policies, and growing administrative demands (Gu, 2014; Hascher et al., 2021). As a result, teaching is recognized as an emotionally demanding and professionally complex occupation.

These conditions have brought teachers' wellbeing and resilience to the forefront of educational research. In recent years, increasing levels of stress, emotional exhaustion, and burnout among teachers have become a major concern internationally (Collie et al., 2012; Schaufeli, 2015). Many teachers struggle to maintain their professional motivation and emotional balance while trying to respond to the challenges of school life. For this reason, resilience is considered an essential dimension of teachers' professional sustainability and effectiveness (Beltman et al., 2011; Mansfield et al., 2016).

However, contemporary literature no longer approaches resilience as an individual trait. Current research emphasizes that resilience is a dynamic and relational process that develops through the interaction between personal capacities and supportive professional environments (Gu, 2014; Ungar, 2011). In other words, teachers do not become resilient on their own. Their resilience is influenced by the quality of relationships, the school climate, and the organizational conditions in which they work.

At the same time, wellbeing and resilience appear to be closely connected. Hascher et al. (2021) argue that resilience supports the maintenance and development of wellbeing, while wellbeing itself functions as an important psychological resource that helps teachers respond adaptively to professional challenges. This relationship highlights the importance of supportive school environments. Research shows that factors such as collegial relationships, trust, collaboration, and administrative support function as important protective resources for teachers (Daniilidou & Platsidou, 2018; Munezero et al., 2026).

Within this framework, the role of school leadership becomes particularly important. Leadership not only influences school management and instructional processes, but also shapes the relational and emotional conditions of teachers' professional experiences. Studies have shown that supportive leadership practices contribute to trust, collective efficacy, professional commitment, and teachers' wellbeing (Hallinger & Heck, 2010; Leithwood et al., 2008). More recent research also suggests that leadership affects resilience indirectly through the development of supportive organizational relationships and positive school climates (Cilek et al., 2025).

Furthermore, mentoring and coaching approaches in educational leadership are receiving increasing attention. These approaches emphasize reflective dialogue, active listening, professional support, and psychological safety (Aguilar, 2013; Knight, 2017). Mentoring, in particular, is closely associated with supportive professional relationships and the development of professional identity. Nevertheless, most studies focus mainly on mentoring as a process for developing school leaders themselves. Less attention has been given to conceptualizing school leadership more broadly as a mentoring-oriented practice that supports the resilience and wellbeing of teachers.

The chapter explores teacher resilience and wellbeing from a systemic and relational perspective, emphasizing the protective role of organizational and personal conditions within school environments. It further examines school leadership as a relational resource and connects mentoring and coaching approaches with contemporary educational leadership literature. Building on these perspectives, the chapter proposes a conceptual framework of school leadership as mentoring and discusses its implications for school counselling and sustainable school cultures.

It begins by examining teacher wellbeing and resilience in contemporary school contexts, with particular emphasis on the protective factors associated with professional sustainability. Then, it explores the relational role of school leadership and the contribution of mentoring and coaching approaches. Building on these perspectives, the chapter conceptualizes school leadership as a mentoring-oriented relational practice that may enhance teachers' wellbeing and resilience through trust, reflective dialogue, and a collaborative school culture. Finally, it discusses the implications of the proposed framework for preventive school counselling practices, leadership development, and the promotion of sustainable school environments.

TEACHER WELLBEING AND RESILIENCE IN CONTEMPORARY SCHOOLS

The Changing Nature of Teachers' Work

Teaching has always been a demanding profession. However, over recent decades the complexity of teachers' work has increased significantly. Teachers are expected not only to support students' academic development, but also to address their emotional, behavioural, and social needs within diverse school communities. At the same time, schools operate in environments shaped by continuous reforms, accountability pressures, inclusion policies, and administrative expectations (Day & Gu, 2013; Gu, 2014).

Teachers are required to manage classroom relationships, support students experiencing psychological difficulties, communicate with families, and maintain professional effectiveness under conditions of uncertainty. These demands often create emotional stress and intensify feelings of stress and exhaustion (Hargreaves, 2001; Kyriacou, 2000). In many educational systems, increasing accountability has further expanded teachers' workload and professional responsibilities (Gu & Day, 2013).

Within this context, teacher wellbeing has emerged as a significant concern in educational research and policy. Studies report growing levels of emotional exhaustion, stress, and professional burnout among teachers (Collie et al., 2012; Schaufeli, 2015). Burnout is associated with chronic work-related stress, reduced professional satisfaction, emotional fatigue, and difficulties in maintaining motivation and engagement (Khamisa et al., 2015). Such conditions affect not only teachers' personal wellbeing, but also their professional commitment and long-term retention in the profession.

Research also shows that many teachers remain committed and professionally engaged, despite the challenges of contemporary school life. Gu and Day (2013) argue that teachers sustain their professional commitment through a strong sense of moral purpose and positive school environments. This perspective has contributed to a growing shift in the literature from deficit-oriented approaches, which focus on stress and burnout, towards approaches that examine teachers' strengths and professional sustainability.

As a result, resilience has become a central concept in research on teachers' professional practice. Rather than focusing only on risk and vulnerability, research examines how teachers manage challenges, adapt to demanding circumstances, and maintain their professional commitment over time (Beltman et al., 2011; Mansfield et al., 2016). Recent research suggests that resilience should be understood within the organizational and relational contexts of schools rather than as an individual characteristic. Factors such as school climate, collegial relationships, leadership support, and professional culture significantly influence teachers' daily professional experiences and their ability to respond effectively to diversity (Gu, 2014; Munezero et al., 2026). Within this context, wellbeing and resilience are viewed as essential dimensions of teachers' professional sustainability and long-term commitment.

Teacher Wellbeing and Resilience

Teacher wellbeing is generally understood as a multidimensional concept that reflects teachers' emotional, psychological, social, and professional functioning within their work environments. Research suggests that wellbeing is not limited to the absence of stress or burnout. Instead, it is associated with positive professional experiences, emotional balance, job satisfaction, a sense of purpose, and supportive professional relationships (Hascher et al., 2021). Within educational contexts, teacher wellbeing is also connected with motivation, professional commitment, and teaching effectiveness (Shu, 2022).

Teacher resilience is similarly conceptualized as a multidimensional and dynamic process. Earlier approaches described resilience as a personal trait or individual capacity (Atkinson et al., 2009; Jacelon, 1997). However, contemporary perspectives emphasize that resilience develops through the interaction between personal and contextual resources (Masten, 2016; Masten & Barnes, 2018). From this perspective, resilience refers to teachers' capacity to adapt positively to professional challenges and sustain their professional identity despite demanding working conditions (Gu & Day, 2013). Consequently, resilience is increasingly regarded as a relational and context-dependent process rather than exclusively individual.

The relationship between wellbeing and resilience has attracted considerable attention in the literature. Hascher et al. (2021), through the AWaRE model, describe resilience as a process that supports the maintenance and development of wellbeing. Similarly, Mansfield et al. (2016) argue that wellbeing functions both as an outcome of resilience and as a resource that enables teachers to respond adaptively to professional demands. Ainsworth and Oldfield (2019) further suggest that both individual and contextual factors influence teachers' wellbeing, job satisfaction, and resilience. Therefore, emotional experiences, cognitive appraisals, and the availability of contextual resources play an important role in teachers' ability to cope with professional challenges. As a result, supportive school environments are particularly essential for sustaining both wellbeing and resilience.

Protective Factors and Relational Resilience

Recent perspectives on teacher resilience emphasize the importance of professional relationships and organizational conditions. Although personal characteristics such as self-efficacy, optimism, and emotional regulation remain important, resilience is widely understood as a process that develops within social contexts (Masten, 2016; Ungar, 2011).

Evidence indicates that teachers are more likely to sustain motivation and professional commitment when they work in environments characterized by trust, collaboration, and supportive relationships. Positive collegial interactions and opportunities for professional dialogue contribute to emotional adjustment and professional engagement (Bryk, 2010; Kools & Stoll, 2016). Similarly, a supportive school culture appears to strengthen teachers' capacity to manage uncertainty and respond effectively to challenges over time. Professional recognition and relational trust also function as important protective resources. Tschannen-Moran and Hoy (2000) argue that trust promotes cooperation and openness within school organizations. In schools where teachers experience respect and psychological safety, professional collaboration becomes more sustainable and emotionally supportive. Such relational conditions reduce feelings of isolation and contribute to a stronger sense of professional identity and collective efficacy.

Research on professional wellbeing further highlights the importance of organizational resources in reducing emotional exhaustion. According to the Job Demands-Resources framework, supportive organizational conditions may mitigate the negative effects of work-related demands and strengthen motivation and engagement (Bakker & Demerouti, 2017). Therefore, emotional support, constructive feedback, and opportunities for professional learning operate not only as resources for professional development, but also as protective factors for teachers' wellbeing and resilience.

This relational perspective shifts attention away from resilience as an exclusively individual responsibility. Instead, resilience is increasingly understood as embedded within the everyday culture of schools and the quality of professional interactions within them.

SCHOOL LEADERSHIP AS A RELATIONAL RESOURCE

Instructional and Collaborative Leadership

School leadership has a strong influence on teachers' ongoing professional experiences. Beyond administrative responsibilities, school leaders shape the school climate, the quality of professional relationships, and the opportunities teachers have for collaboration and growth (Wang'ombe, 2023). Recent studies continue to demonstrate that leadership influences school improvement through organizational and relational processes rather than through direct control approaches. Teachers are more motivated to remain professionally engaged when school leaders encourage participation, collaboration, and shared responsibility (Alzouebi et al., 2025; Dreer, 2024; Heinla & Kuurme, 2024; Ma & Marion, 2024). Supportive leadership practices appear to reduce work-related stress and strengthen teachers' job satisfaction in demanding school environments.

Instructional leadership remains one of the central approaches in educational leadership research. Earlier models focused mainly on supervision and instructional coordination. However, more recent perspectives emphasize professional learning, collaboration, reflective dialogue, and professional growth (Harris et al., 2022; Liu & Hallinger, 2018). Thus, leadership is widely conceptualized as a process that supports teachers' professional learning and strengthens organizational capacity rather than focusing solely on performance monitoring.

At the same time, collaborative leadership approaches emphasize participation, professional trust, and shared responsibility within school communities (Hallinger

& Heck, 2010). In this way, leadership is viewed less as an individual role and more as a collective process that develops through communication and collaborative problem-solving. Teachers working in collaborative environments report stronger professional relationships and lower levels of isolation (Ma & Marion, 2024). Such conditions appear especially significant in schools facing uncertainty, increased workload, and emotional pressure.

Recent studies also suggest that trust-based leadership practices contribute positively to teachers' wellbeing and resilience (Cilek et al., 2025; Keravnos & Lipsou, 2026). For instance, Cilek et al. (2025) found that teachers' wellbeing and resilience mediate the relationship between principals' trust in teachers and leadership for learning. Similarly, recent systematic reviews indicate that collaborative school cultures and supportive leadership practices strengthen professional commitment and emotional adjustment in school settings (Wilson Heenan et al., 2023; Gámez-Genovart et al., 2025). Leadership cannot be regarded only as a managerial and administrative function. It also shapes the relational conditions within which teachers work, interact, and sustain their professional identities. This relational dimension becomes particularly important when considering how schools can support teachers' resilience in complex and changing educational environments.

Leadership and Professional Relationships

Trust plays an essential role in teachers' professional experiences within schools. Teachers are more willing to collaborate, exchange ideas, and participate in school life when they feel respected and supported by school leaders (Tschannen-Moran & Hoy, 2000). Relationships based on trust also facilitate communication and help teachers discuss difficulties more openly. Recent evidence suggests that supportive leadership relationships are associated with higher levels of wellbeing and professional engagement. Teachers who feel trusted by school leaders often report stronger motivation, greater professional confidence, and a stronger sense of belonging within the school community (Keravnos & Lipsou, 2026). Consistent with this, Cilek et al. (2025) found that teachers' wellbeing and resilience influence the relationship between principals' trust in teachers and leadership for learning.

Professional relationships also affect the way teachers experience daily school life. In schools where communication is open and supportive, teachers are more likely to share concerns and participate in professional dialogue. Such environments strengthen collaboration and reduce feelings of professional isolation (Edmondson & Lei, 2014). In contrast, limited communication and excessive control increase stress and emotional pressure (Aloia & McTigue, 2019).

In recent years greater attention has been given to the relational aspects of school leadership. In particular, school leaders are expected not only to coordinate organizational processes, but also to create professional environments characterized by trust, support, collaboration, and open communication (Harris et al., 2022; Keravnos & Lipsou, 2026). In such contexts, teachers feel professionally valued and actively involved in school life. Studies further suggest that a supportive school culture is linked to stronger professional commitment, greater job satisfaction, and lower levels of emotional exhaustion among teachers (Dreer, 2024; Heinla & Kuurme, 2024).

In addition, relational leadership practices appear closely connected with teachers' wellbeing and resilience. Opportunities for professional dialogue and constructive feedback strengthen teachers' sense of belonging and confidence (Ma & Marion, 2024). Additionally, collaborative school environments encourage teachers to seek support, exchange experiences, and participate more actively in professional learning processes (Kools & Stoll, 2016). These relational conditions seem particularly important in contemporary school contexts, where teachers work under conditions of uncertainty, emotional pressure, and professional demands.

From this perspective, leadership influences teachers not only through formal structures or administrative responsibilities, but also through the social and professional interactions that emerge within the school environment. School leaders' approaches to communication, teacher support, and the management of professional challenges appear to have a significant impact on teachers' wellbeing and resilience.

Supporting Teachers' Resilience Through Leadership

Research over the last decade has shown that school leadership is closely related to teachers' wellbeing and resilience. Supportive leadership practices influence professional performance along with teachers' emotional experiences and long-term engagement with their work. Teachers working in schools characterized by trust, collaboration, and supportive communication report higher levels of wellbeing and stronger professional commitment (Heinla & Kuurme, 2024; Keravnos & Lipsou, 2026).

Furthermore, leadership shapes the ways in which teachers respond to stress and demanding working conditions. School leaders who encourage participation and promote professional learning contribute to supportive school environments (Dreer, 2024). Such conditions are particularly significant in contemporary school settings, where teachers are required to manage demanding workloads and professional responsibilities. Recent studies further suggest that leadership influences resilience indirectly through relational and organizational processes. For instance, Cilek et al. (2025) demonstrated that teachers' wellbeing and resilience mediate the relationship between principals' trust in teachers and leadership for learning, emphasizing the role of supportive school relationships in fostering resilience. In addition, Wilson Heenan et al. (2023) found that collaborative leadership practices strengthen teachers' professional commitment and adjustment, while Gámez-Genovart et al. (2025) highlighted the contribution of collective efficacy and shared professional support to resilient school environments.

The relationship between leadership and resilience can be explained through the availability of organizational resources within schools. According to the Job Demands-Resources framework, leadership support and constructive feedback function as crucial resources, helping reduce emotional exhaustion (Bakker & Demerouti, 2017). However, school environments characterized by limited support and weak professional relationships may increase stress and contribute to reduced professional commitment. These findings support the view that resilience should not be regarded only as an individual characteristic. Teachers' ability to adapt and sustain their commitment over time is connected to the relational and organizational conditions of school life (Beltman et al., 2011; Mansfield et al., 2016). From this perspective, school leadership can be viewed as an important source of professional and emotional support that strengthens teachers' wellbeing and resilience through everyday interactions, collaboration, and supportive school culture.

MENTORING AND COACHING IN EDUCATIONAL LEADERSHIP

Defining Mentoring and Coaching

Mentoring and coaching are widely discussed in educational leadership and teacher professional development. Both approaches aim to support professional growth and reflective practice within schools. Although the two concepts are closely connected, the literature distinguishes between them according to their focus, structure, and the type of support they provide (Luong, 2025; Stokes et al., 2021).

Mentoring is described as a professional relationship based on guidance, support, and shared experience. In educational settings, a mentor helps another professional navigate challenges, reflect on practice, and develop confidence in their role (Sweeney & LeBoeuf, 2023). The process is not limited to instructional advice or technical support; it also includes emotional encouragement and support for professional identity development (Rickard et al., 2025). Recent approaches present mentoring as a holistic process connected to wellbeing and long-term engagement with the profession (Mantzourani et al., 2022; Quinn et al., 2025). While mentoring is typically associated with long-term relational support and professional development, coaching is more commonly linked to targeted improvement and goal-oriented professional learning.

Coaching is generally conceptualized as a more focused and structured form of professional support. In particular, it is associated with the improvement of specific practices, instructional skills or professional goals (King & Winn, 2017). Within schools, coaching involves reflective conversations, feedback, collaborative problem-solving, and support for professional learning (Hoang et al., 2024). Rather than positioning one person as the expert who provides solutions, coaching tends to encourage reflection and self-directed learning (Silverii et al., 2024).

Although mentoring and coaching differ conceptually and functionally, they share several common characteristics. Both are based on communication, trust, collaboration, and reflective dialogue (Sahlberg & Stringer, 2023). Furthermore, both approaches create opportunities for professional exchange and supportive interaction within school communities. For this reason, the literature treats mentoring and coaching as complementary practices that contribute to collaborative professional cultures rather than as separate processes (Stokes et al., 2021). Therefore, within school environments mentoring and coaching are connected not only with professional learning, but also with teachers' emotional experiences and professional sustainability. Supportive professional relationships, opportunities for reflection, and constructive dialogue may help teachers manage professional demands more effectively and maintain stronger engagement with their work over time.

Mentoring as a Relational and Reflective Practice

Mentoring in educational settings is increasingly viewed as a relational process rather than a technical form of professional guidance. Contemporary approaches emphasize mentoring as a process developed through supportive professional relationships characterized by trust, communication, empathy, and reflective dialogue (Aguilar, 2013; Sweeney & LeBoeuf, 2023). In school organizations, mentoring creates opportunities for teachers to discuss professional experiences openly, reflect on challenges, and receive emotional and professional support in demanding working environments.

Unlike approaches that focus on evaluation or performance management, mentoring is associated with professional encouragement and collaborative learning. The mentor's role is not limited to transferring knowledge or providing instructional advice. Instead, mentoring involves listening and helping teachers make sense of professional experiences and daily school challenges (Rickard et al., 2025). This relational dimension appears particularly essential in contemporary school environments, where teachers experience emotional pressure, professional uncertainty, and increased organizational demands.

Reflective dialogue is considered one of the central dimensions of mentoring practice. Schön (2017) describes reflection as a process through which professionals examine their experiences and critically evaluate their professional perspectives and practices. Within mentoring relationships, reflective conversations allow teachers to explore difficulties, rethink classroom practices, and develop greater professional awareness (Grimmett et al., 2018; Lipton & Wellman, 2024). Reflection further supports teachers in connecting theory with practice and in addressing complex situations in a more reflective way.

Research additionally suggests that reflective professional dialogue contributes positively to teachers' confidence and professional identity. Teachers who participate in supportive mentoring relationships report feeling more capable of managing challenges and maintaining professional motivation over time (Mantzourani et al., 2022). Opportunities for open discussion and collaborative reflection may reduce feelings of professional isolation and strengthen teachers' sense of belonging in the school community. Such experiences seem to be especially important for early-career teachers, but they are also relevant for experienced teachers working under challenging professional conditions. Moreover, mentoring contributes to the development of safe and supportive school environments. Specifically, psychological safety refers to professional environments in which individuals feel comfortable discussing mistakes and seeking support without fear of negative judgment (Edmondson & Lei, 2014). Under such conditions, teachers are more willing to communicate honestly and engage actively in collaborative learning practices. As a result, trust is strengthened and more supportive professional relationships are developed within the school community.

Recent studies highlight the reciprocal nature of mentoring relationships. Contemporary mentoring models move away from hierarchical approaches in which one professional is positioned exclusively as the expert. Instead, mentoring is increasingly approached as a collaborative and reciprocal learning process that supports dialogue and mutual professional growth (Conner & Walker, 2025; Harrison et al., 2024; Hogue et al., 2025). This perspective is consistent with broader relational approaches to educational leadership, where professional learning is understood as collective and socially constructed. The contribution of mentoring extends beyond individual professional development. Supportive mentoring practices may influence the wider school culture by strengthening collaboration and collective learning (Shen et al., 2026). In schools where reflective dialogue and professional support are encouraged, teachers appear more willing to exchange ideas and participate in professional learning communities (Kools & Stoll, 2016). Such collaborative school environments may provide important professional and emotional support that helps teachers maintain their wellbeing and resilience over time.

In this context, mentoring extends beyond a structured form of professional guidance and becomes a relational process that contributes to teachers' long-term professional sustainability. Mentoring encourages trust, reflective dialogue, emotional support, and collaborative interaction among professionals. These conditions can help teachers respond more effectively to professional demands while maintaining their engagement and professional identity. As school environments become increasingly demanding, relational forms of support such as mentoring may become particularly important for promoting teachers' wellbeing and sustaining their resilience.

Mentoring and Leadership Development

Current approaches to educational leadership emphasize the value of professional dialogue and shared learning in school communities. Accordingly, mentoring is linked to processes that support both professional development and leadership growth (Harris et al., 2022; Klar & Brewer, 2013; Leontopoulos et al., 2025). Through mentoring relationships, teachers and school leaders have opportunities to share experiences and reflect on professional challenges in a more open and supportive way. Such interactions encourage reflective thinking and professional dialogue while helping professionals navigate the interpersonal relationships and organizational dimensions of school life (Klar & Brewer, 2013; Rickard et al., 2025). This perspective is closely related to collaborative and distributed approaches to leadership. The literature views leadership as a collective process shaped through collaboration and responsibility in school communities (Spillane, 2006; Hallinger & Heck, 2010). In this context, mentoring supports school culture where teachers are encouraged to exchange perspectives and participate in collective professional learning processes (Morcom & MacCallum, 2022). In this way, leadership is connected not only with decision-making, but also with the ability to encourage dialogue and strengthen collaboration within the school environment.

Research further suggests that mentoring may influence the wider professional culture of schools. For example, in schools where reflective conversations and professional exchange are fostered, teachers feel more comfortable seeking support and collaborating with colleagues (Kools & Stoll, 2016; Shen et al., 2026). Such conditions may reduce feelings of professional isolation, particularly in demanding school contexts characterized by emotional pressure and organizational uncertainty. Professional support and opportunities for collaborative reflection can contribute to the development of a stronger sense of professional belonging and greater collective efficacy in schools.

Mentoring can provide important support for school leaders as well. School leaders frequently work under conditions characterized by emotional pressure, conflict management, and organizational complexity. Reflective dialogue and supportive professional relationships may help school leaders respond more effectively to these challenges while maintaining constructive relationships with teachers and colleagues (Conner & Walker, 2025; Tahir & Safder, 2025). Additionally, Leontopoulos et al. (2025) indicate that mentoring relationships may support the development of leaders' reflective capacity, emotional awareness, and professional confidence.

Viewed from this perspective, mentoring is not limited to a formal professional development strategy. Instead, it reflects a broader relational approach to leadership based on trust, dialogue, reflection, and professional support. These practices could help schools develop a collaborative professional culture that strengthen teachers' wellbeing, professional learning, and resilience over time (Aguilar, 2013; Sahlberg & Stringer, 2023).

School Leadership as Mentoring: A Relational and Preventive Framework for Teachers' Resilience

Reframing School Leadership as Mentoring

In recent years educational leadership has become steadily associated with relational and supportive approaches rather than exclusively administrative responsibilities. School leaders are expected to coordinate organizational processes and instructional practices, but also to support teachers emotionally and professionally in demanding school environments (Harris et al., 2022; Keravnos & Lipsou, 2026). In this context, mentoring provides a useful perspective for reconsidering the role of school leadership in contemporary school organizations.

Traditional leadership models emphasized supervision, accountability, and organizational control. Although these dimensions remain characteristics of school leadership, the literature places greater emphasis on communication, collaboration, trust, and professional support (Hallinger & Heck, 2010; Liu & Hallinger, 2018). Teachers working in complex educational environments require opportunities for dialogue and reflection rather than formal evaluation or performance monitoring. As a result, leadership is commonly perceived as a relational practice that shapes the professional experiences and interactions in schools. From this perspective, mentoring offers a meaningful framework for understanding leadership as a form of relational support. Mentoring is not limited to formal guidance or technical assistance. It involves supportive professional relationships through which individuals exchange experiences and strengthen professional confidence (Aguilar, 2013; Sweeney & LeBoeuf, 2023). In the school context, such relationships may help teachers feel emotionally supported, particularly in periods characterized by workload pressure and organizational change.

Viewing school leadership through a mentoring perspective shifts attention away from hierarchical models of authority toward approaches based on dialogue and collaborative professional learning. School leaders who adopt mentoring-oriented practices are more likely to encourage participation and reflective communication in school communities (Knight, 2017; Rickard et al., 2025). Such practices contribute to more supportive professional environments in which teachers feel more comfortable participating in collective learning processes. This perspective is connected with relational approaches to resilience. Evidence suggests that teachers' resilience develops through supportive organizational conditions and professional relationships (Gu, 2014; Ungar, 2011). Consequently, school leadership may function as a protective relational resource when it promotes trust and collaboration in the school environment. Therefore, mentoring-oriented leadership practices could contribute not only to professional development, but also to teachers' wellbeing and long-term professional sustainability.

Reframing leadership as mentoring does not imply that school leaders become mentors in every professional interaction. Rather, it suggests that mentoring principles such as reflective dialogue, supportive communication, professional encouragement, and collaborative learning may shape leadership practices more broadly. In this sense, leadership becomes less connected with control and more associated with the creation of professional conditions that support teachers' growth and resilience. Furthermore, this approach is consistent with collaborative and distributed perspectives on educational leadership. Professional learning and school improvement are now viewed as collective processes that emerge through interaction and shared responsibility (Kools & Stoll, 2016; Spillane, 2006). Mentoring-oriented leadership may strengthen these processes by encouraging professional relationships and creating space where teachers can exchange experiences.

Recent discussions on educational leadership further emphasize the need for leadership approaches that extend beyond traditional administrative functions and respond to the increasing complexity of contemporary school environments. Leadership 4.0 perspectives suggest that effective school leadership involves not only organizational coordination and technological adaptation but also the development of relational, ethical, and collaborative school cultures that support professional learning and participation (Psyrras, 2026). Similarly, emerging research on artificial intelligence integration in education highlights the importance of school leaders' capacity to foster supportive environments in which teachers can engage with innovation while maintaining professional confidence and wellbeing (Raptis & Psyrras, 2026). These perspectives reinforce the argument that leadership is increasingly associated with relational support, shared learning, and the cultivation of conditions that enable teachers to adapt constructively to change.

It is a fact that in demanding educational environments, teachers experience emotional pressure, professional uncertainty, and high organizational expectations. Under such conditions, relational forms of leadership become essential. School leaders who encourage supportive communication and professional dialogue can help reduce feelings of isolation and strengthen teachers' confidence and engagement with their work (Dreer, 2024; Heinla & Kuurme, 2024). Therefore, through daily interactions and collaborative practices, leadership can contribute to the development of a school culture that supports both professional learning and resilience.

Within this relational framework, school leadership as mentoring emphasizes supportive professional relationships based on dialogue, trust, and collaboration. In these contexts, teachers feel more confident in expressing concerns and participate in professional dialogue, experiences that can contribute positively to wellbeing and resilience. Figure 1 presents the proposed conceptual framework of mentoring-oriented school leadership as a relational and preventive approach to teachers' resilience.

Figure 1. Mentoring-Oriented Leadership Framework for Teacher Resilience

Mentoring-Oriented Leadership Practices

(dialogue, trust, support, reflection)

↓

Relational Conditions

(Psychological safety, collegial trust,

professional belonging)

↓

Professional Processes

(Reflective dialogue, collaboration,

collective learning, empowerment)

↓

Teacher Wellbeing

↓

Teacher Resilience

↓

Sustainable and Preventive School Culture

Relational Trust and Psychological Safety

Trust is widely regarded as one of the foundational characteristics of effective school communities. In educational settings, trust develops through daily interactions shaped by respect, consistency, openness, and professional care (Bryk & Schneider, 2002). When teachers feel that school leaders value their perspectives, they are more likely to participate in collaboration and collective school processes. Furthermore, trust supports open communication and creates conditions that facilitate meaningful and open professional dialogue among educators.

Closely connected to trust is the concept of psychological safety. Edmondson (1999) explains psychological safety as the perception that individuals can express concerns and share ideas without fear of criticism or humiliation. In schools this sense of safety allows teachers to communicate honestly about classroom challenges and professional difficulties. Instead of avoiding uncertainty, teachers feel more comfortable seeking support and engaging in reflective discussion with colleagues. Research suggests that a psychologically safe school culture encourages collaboration and professional learning. Hargreaves and O'Connor (2018) note that collaborative professionalism depends on relationships characterized by openness and mutual respect. Similarly, Louis (2010) argues that relational trust strengthens professional community and supports collective engagement within schools. Teachers working in such environments are generally more willing to exchange experiences and participate in problem-solving processes.

School leadership has a crucial role in shaping these relational conditions. Leadership practices based on dialogue and active listening contribute to stronger professional relationships in school organizations (Fullan, 2017; Shields, 2010). Teachers tend to feel more professionally respected when school leaders encourage participation and maintain supportive communication. In contrast, school environments defined by excessive control or limited communication increase emotional pressure and professional distance among staff members.

Teachers' wellbeing and resilience are influenced by the quality of relational conditions within schools. Evidence suggests that supportive professional environments can help reduce emotional exhaustion while strengthening teachers' sense of professional competence and belonging (Skaalvik & Skaalvik, 2018). In addition, opportunities for collegial support and reflective interaction may help teachers cope more effectively with stress and remain professionally engaged under demanding working conditions (Wolgast & Fischer, 2017). In leadership approaches that prioritize mentoring, trust and psychological safety play a central role in supporting collaborative learning and the development of resilient school culture.

Reflective Support and Professional Empowerment

Reflective support is an important dimension of mentoring-oriented leadership. In contemporary school environments, teachers work under conditions of emotional pressure and increasing organizational demands. Under such conditions, opportunities for reflection and supportive dialogue become especially important. Reflective interactions allow teachers to discuss challenges openly, reconsider professional practices, and develop greater awareness of their experiences (Schön, 2017). Unlike leadership approaches based mainly on evaluation and control, mentoring-oriented leadership emphasizes dialogue, active listening, and professional encouragement (Ollila et al., 2025). School leaders who support reflective communication contribute to environments where teachers feel respected and emotionally supported (Aguilar, 2013). These conditions may play a supportive role in contexts marked by heavy workloads and emotional pressure.

Professional empowerment is strongly associated with reflective support and professional dialogue. Teachers tend to remain professionally engaged when they feel that their opinions are valued and their professional contribution is recognized (Leat et al., 2015; McArdle & Coutts, 2010). Opportunities for participation and professional autonomy strengthen confidence and support teachers' professional identity (Day & Gu, 2013). Supportive professional relationships can also reduce feelings of isolation while promoting collaborative learning and reflective professional practice.

Additionally, reflective dialogue strengthens teachers' professional adaptability. Through collaborative reflection, teachers can examine classroom experiences and explore alternative approaches to professional challenges (Lipton & Wellman, 2024). Such processes may enhance teachers' sense of competence and improve their ability to respond constructively to uncertainty and change. Therefore, reflection operates not only as a professional learning process, but also as a relational and emotional resource that supports wellbeing and resilience.

Furthermore, mentoring-oriented leadership supports professional empowerment by encouraging teacher voice and collaborative participation within the school community (Ollila et al., 2025; Savas et al., 2025). In school environments characterized by supportive communication, teachers tend to feel more comfortable expressing concerns and sharing professional experiences. These conditions enhance trust, psychological safety, and collective engagement in the school community (Dreer-Goethe, 2026; Savas et al., 2025). In contrast, environments defined by excessive control and limited dialogue weaken professional confidence and reduce opportunities for collaboration. The connection between reflective support and resilience becomes evident in challenging school contexts. Teachers who participate in supportive professional environments are more capable of maintaining long-term professional engagement and commitment. Constructive feedback, emotional support, and chances for professional dialogue function as important protective resources that enhance teachers' wellbeing and resilience (Mansfield et al., 2016; Munezero et al., 2026).

Consequently, reflective support and professional empowerment should be recognized as central components of supportive school leadership. These relational conditions influence teachers' professional experiences and their ability to respond effectively to daily challenges. Therefore, mentoring-oriented leadership contributes to resilience by fostering professional environments based on reflection, collaboration, and ongoing support.

Collective Learning and Shared Responsibility

Contemporary school organizations require teachers to respond continuously to professional, emotional, and organizational challenges. In such contexts, resilience cannot be considered only as an individual capacity. Specifically, studies emphasize that resilience develops through collective and relational processes in schools (Hascher et al., 2021; Gu, 2014). Therefore, collaborative school culture may serve as a significant protective environment that supports teachers' wellbeing and long-term engagement with their work. Teachers are more likely to stay professionally engaged when they reflect on challenges and participate in shared professional learning processes (Kools & Stoll, 2016). In this case, professional learning extends beyond the acquisition of instructional knowledge and becomes a relational process based on trust and mutual support.

Professional learning communities contribute significantly to this process. Collaborative reflection and professional dialogue allow teachers to discuss classroom experiences and share concerns (DuFour & Fullan, 2013). Supportive professional interactions can foster a stronger sense of connection among teachers while helping to reduce professional isolation. Their importance becomes even greater in school environments where emotional demands and uncertainty are common features of professional life. As a result, school organizations defined by collaboration and professional support may create conditions that enhance teachers' resilience and long-term professional engagement. Additionally, shared responsibility is equally important in mentoring-oriented leadership. For instance, in schools where teachers actively participate in decision-making and problem-solving, professional commitment and collective efficacy tend to become stronger (Hallinger & Heck, 2010). When school leadership promotes participation and acknowledges teachers' experiences and professional perspectives, teachers tend to develop a stronger sense of professional recognition and inclusion. These relational conditions can foster trust and contribute to a more supportive and emotionally secure school environment. Teachers working in schools that encourage communication and collegial support are more willing to exchange experiences and seek assistance when facing difficulties (Gu, 2014; Kools & Stoll, 2016). These collaborative interactions could enhance professional belonging and contribute to a more supportive school culture. In contrast, limited opportunities for collaboration and professional dialogue may increase emotional pressure in school organizations.

In mentoring-oriented leadership, collective learning and shared responsibility function as significant relational dimensions of supportive school culture. Leadership practices that encourage professional dialogue and reflective interaction appear particularly essential for sustaining teachers' wellbeing, professional engagement, and resilience in complex educational contexts. From this perspective, mentoring-oriented leadership can be further perceived as a preventive and relational approach that contributes to the development of supportive and resilient school culture.

Preventive Leadership and Sustainable School Culture

Schools today operate under demanding and unstable conditions. Teachers are expected to address academic expectations while managing emotional and social challenges in school contexts. At the same time, constant reforms and workload demands can gradually affect teachers' motivation and professional commitment. For this reason, the discussion surrounding teacher resilience has shifted from individual coping strategies to the wider organizational and relational conditions that shape teachers' professional experiences (Gu & Day, 2013; Hascher et al., 2021). Preventive leadership does not focus solely on managing problems after they appear. Instead, it aims to create school conditions that support teachers before stress and emotional exhaustion become deeply rooted. Supportive communication, trust, reflective dialogue and collegial collaboration can serve as protective factors that enhance teachers' professional experiences and emotional wellbeing (Fullan, 2007).

Preventive approaches to school leadership place emphasis on the creation of organizational conditions that support teachers before professional difficulties become unmanageable. Within this framework, leadership is associated more with the cultivation of professional relationships that encourage trust and mutual support rather than with supervision and control. Such relational conditions may strengthen teachers' emotional adjustment and reduce feelings of professional isolation (Aguilar, 2013; Kools & Stoll, 2016). In schools where communication remains open and supportive, teachers tend to develop stronger professional commitment and a greater willingness to participate in collective professional processes. Collegial trust and collaborative interaction contribute to environments where teachers feel professionally acknowledged and socially connected (Hargreaves & O'Connor, 2018). By contrast, organizational environments marked by distance, limited participation, and weak collegial relationships may intensify emotional strain and reduce professional engagement.

Supportive organizational practices appear to influence teachers' capacity to sustain resilience over time. Chances for reflective participation, constructive professional dialogue, and collaborative support may boost teachers' sense of professional confidence and emotional security (Cilek et al., 2025; Keravnos & Lipsou, 2026). These experiences highlight that resilience can be regarded not only as a result of individual adaptive capacities, but also as a process influenced by the relational and organizational conditions in school communities.

Accordingly, mentoring-oriented leadership extends beyond administrative coordination and becomes part of a broader effort to cultivate supportive and resilient school communities. School leaders who promote reflective dialogue and collegial collaboration contribute to more supportive professional environments. Such forms of professional support may help teachers maintain motivation, emotional balance, and long-term professional engagement.

School Counselling and Teachers' Resilience

In modern school environments, teachers are expected to support students academically and emotionally while working under demanding organizational conditions (Dollarhide & Saginak, 2011). Evidence suggests that emotionally supported teachers are more capable of responding constructively to students' needs and participating in collaborative preventive practices (Gámez-Genovart et al., 2025; Hascher et al., 2021). In contrast, emotional exhaustion and professional isolation may weaken teachers' capacity to identify students' difficulties and engage effectively in supportive school processes. Thus, resilience should not be framed only as an individual coping capacity, but as a relational and organizational process shaped by school culture and professional relationships (Gu, 2014; Munezero et al., 2026).

In this framework, school counselling can play a significant preventive role in strengthening supportive school contexts. School counselling models highlight the importance of collaboration among teachers, principals, school counsellors, psychologists, and other support professionals (Sink, 2005; Weist et al., 2003). Collaborative practices among professionals may improve communication and promote more effective responses to students' emotional and behavioural difficulties. Additionally, interdisciplinary support systems can positively influence teachers' professional confidence and emotional wellbeing.

Furthermore, leadership practices based on active listening and psychological safety can help teachers feel more comfortable discussing challenges and seeking support when needed (Savas et al., 2025). In school environments where supportive dialogue is encouraged, teachers are more willing to collaborate with counsellors and participate in problem-solving processes. Similarly, approaches to mental health promotion emphasize that a supportive school culture influences both student and teacher wellbeing (Weist et al., 2014). Therefore, preventive school counselling is not limited to individual therapeutic intervention. Instead, it involves the development of relational conditions that promote emotional safety, collaboration, inclusion, and professional support across the school community. Overall, mentoring-oriented leadership and preventive school counselling share common goals related to wellbeing, resilience, and sustainable school culture. By strengthening trust and collaboration, schools can create environments in which teachers feel emotionally supported and professionally valued.

IMPLICATIONS FOR MENTORING-ORIENTED LEADERSHIP AND PREVENTIVE SCHOOL PRACTICE

Contemporary school environments require forms of support that extend beyond administrative and instructional management. Teachers are expected to respond to emotional and social challenges while maintaining professional effectiveness under conditions of continuous change. In such contexts, teacher wellbeing and resilience cannot be perceived only as individual responsibilities. Instead, they are closely connected to the relational and organizational conditions that influence daily professional experiences in schools (Gu, 2014; Hascher et al., 2021).

This perspective highlights important implications for mentoring-oriented leadership and preventive school practice. Current approaches in educational research emphasize the value of practices that foster supportive and collaborative school environments (Cefai & Cavioni, 2014). From this perspective, supporting teachers' wellbeing is related to preventive school practice, since teachers' emotional experiences influence professional relationships and the broader quality of school life. The discussion presented in this chapter suggests that mentoring-oriented leadership may contribute positively to the development of supportive school environments. Leadership practices based on dialogue, trust, reflective communication, and professional support can boost teachers' emotional security. In other words, teachers who feel professionally respected and supported are more willing to discuss challenges and participate in collaborative professional processes (Kools & Stoll, 2016; Keravnos & Lipsou, 2026).

According to the framework proposed in this chapter, mentoring-oriented leadership highlights the importance of relational conditions in sustaining teachers' professional engagement. Opportunities for collegial reflection and collaborative learning function as protective conditions that help teachers respond to demanding professional situations more effectively and constructively (Mansfield et al., 2016). In contrast, school organizations characterized by isolation and weak professional relationships may lead to higher levels of emotional exhaustion and lower professional commitment over time.

Furthermore, the present discussion includes implications for leadership preparation and professional development. Educational leadership programs traditionally emphasize management, instructional supervision, and organizational effectiveness. However, contemporary school environments additionally require relational and emotionally responsive leadership practices. Therefore, leadership preparation and professional development initiatives need to place greater emphasis on:

- reflective communication and active listening,
- mentoring and supporting professional dialogue,
- emotional awareness and relational leadership,
- collaborative problem-solving practices,
- the development of psychologically safe school environments.

Such competencies can help school leaders create a professional culture that supports teachers' wellbeing and long-term resilience. Similarly, professional learning in schools could benefit from approaches that encourage participation and reflective interaction rather than focusing exclusively on technical improvement. Teachers appear more able to sustain motivation and professional commitment when they participate in supportive professional communities characterized by trust and shared responsibility (Hargreaves & O'Connor, 2018).

Overall, the discussion of this chapter highlights the importance of approaching resilience as a relational and preventive process in school organizations. Mentoring-oriented leadership offers a framework through which schools can develop supportive professional relationships and create conditions that foster teachers both emotionally and professionally. Against this background, preventive school practices are connected with leadership approaches that encourage trust and collaboration in school organizations. Such relational practices contribute to more supportive and sustainable school environments where teachers feel professionally valued and more capable of maintaining long-term engagement with their work.

LIMITATIONS AND FUTURE DIRECTIONS

Although mentoring-oriented leadership offers a useful conceptual framework for supporting teachers' resilience, several limitations should be acknowledged. First, the approach discussed in this chapter is theoretical and literature-based. Therefore, future empirical research is needed to examine how mentoring-oriented leadership is experienced by teachers in different educational contexts. Qualitative studies could explore teachers' perceptions of supportive leadership, reflective dialogue, and psychological safety in schools. In addition, quantitative research may examine whether mentoring-oriented leadership practices influence teacher wellbeing and resilience.

Second, mentoring-oriented leadership may be shaped by cultural and organizational contexts. School leaders do not act independently of broader educational systems. Their capacity to support teachers is influenced by workload, accountability demands, available resources, and policy expectations. For this reason, future research should examine how mentoring-oriented leadership can be implemented in schools with different levels of autonomy, resources, and institutional support. Comparative studies across educational systems could provide valuable insights into the contextual factors that enable or restrict relational leadership practices.

Third, it is important to avoid idealizing mentoring-oriented leadership as a solution to all problems associated with teacher stress and resilience. While supportive leadership can create more positive professional environments, it cannot fully address challenges such as understaffing, heavy workloads, ongoing policy changes, and limited access to mental health support. Therefore, future discussions should connect relational leadership with broader organizational and systemic reforms. Teacher resilience needs to be supported not only through interpersonal care but also through fair working conditions and sustainable educational policies.

Finally, future research could further examine the role of school counsellors, psychologists, and other professionals in strengthening mentoring-oriented leadership practices. Collaboration between school leaders and counselling professionals may help schools develop more coherent preventive strategies for teacher wellbeing. Such collaboration could include training in communication skills, reflective supervision, stress prevention, and the identification of professional distress. In this way, mentoring-oriented leadership may become part of a collaborative and preventive school culture that promotes resilience and wellbeing.

CONCLUSION

In contemporary school contexts, resilience has emerged as a central concern due to the growing emotional, organizational, and professional demands placed on teachers. However, resilience should not be interpreted simply as teachers' ability to endure pressure or adapt individually to difficult working conditions. Such approaches risk placing responsibility solely on teachers rather than addressing school systems and organizational structures. This chapter argued that resilience is connected to the relational and organizational conditions that shape teachers' professional experiences.

In this context, the chapter examined mentoring-oriented leadership as a relational and preventive approach to teachers' wellbeing and resilience. Leadership was examined not only as a managerial or instructional process, but also as a practice that promotes trust, communication, collaboration, and psychological safety in school communities. Supportive professional relationships and reflective dialogue can boost teachers' professional engagement and emotional security, particularly in demanding school environments. However, mentoring-oriented leadership should not be regarded as a universal solution to the structural difficulties schools currently face. Heavy workloads, accountability pressures, staff shortages, and policy instability cannot be addressed only through supportive leadership practices or collaborative school cultures. Relational support is essential, but it cannot replace broader organizational and systemic change. For this reason, approaches to resilience that focus exclusively on individual adaptability or interpersonal support may fail to address the broader structural conditions that shape teachers' professional experiences.

The chapter suggests that mentoring-oriented leadership offers a meaningful framework for reconsidering the role of school leadership in modern school environments. Leadership practices grounded in trust, dialogue, reflective support, and collaboration may contribute to a school culture in which teachers feel respected, emotionally supported, and more connected to the professional community. Such environments promote professional agency, inclusion, collaboration, sustainability, and meaningful educational innovation across diverse school contexts. Ultimately, resilience may be conceptualized not simply as an individual capacity to cope with adversity, but as a professionally and socially constructed process influenced by the relational and organizational conditions of contemporary educational environments.

REFERENCES

Aguilar, E. (2013). *The art of coaching: Effective strategies for school transformation*. John Wiley & Sons.

Ainsworth, S., & Oldfield, J. (2019). Quantifying teacher resilience: Context matters. *Teaching and Teacher Education*, *82*, 117–128. DOI: 10.1016/j.tate.2019.03.012

Aloia, L. S., & McTigue, M. (2019). Buffering against sources of academic stress: The influence of supportive informational and emotional communication on psychological well-being. *Communication Research Reports*, *36*(2), 126–135. DOI: 10.1080/08824096.2019.1590191

Alzouebi, K., Al Hammadi, D. Y., Ankit, A., & Abu Khurma, O. (2025). School innovation: Building a culture through leadership and stakeholder engagement. *Societies (Basel, Switzerland)*, *15*(4), 77. DOI: 10.3390/soc15040077

Atkinson, P. A., Martin, C. R., & Rankin, J. (2009). Resilience revisited. *Journal of Psychiatric and Mental Health Nursing*, *16*(2), 137–145. DOI: 10.1111/j.1365-2850.2008.01341.x

Bakker, A. B., & Demerouti, E. (2017). Job demands–resources theory: Taking stock and looking forward. *Journal of Occupational Health Psychology*, *22*(3), 273–285. https://psycnet.apa.org/doi/10.1037/ocp0000056. DOI: 10.1037/ocp0000056

Beltman, S., Mansfield, C., & Price, A. (2011). Thriving not just surviving: A review of research on teacher resilience. *Educational Research Review*, *6*(3), 185–207. DOI: 10.1016/j.edurev.2011.09.001

Bryk, A., & Schneider, B. (2002). *Trust in schools: A core resource for improvement*. Russell Sage Foundation.

Bryk, A. S. (2010). Organizing schools for improvement. *Phi Delta Kappan*, *91*(7), 23–30. DOI: 10.1177/003172171009100705

Cefai, C., & Cavioni, V. (2014). *Social and emotional education in primary school: Integrating theory and research into practice*. Springer. DOI: 10.1007/978-1-4614-8752-4

Cilek, A., Kılınç, A. Ç., Erdoğan, O., Arslan, K., & Sezgin, F. (2025). Linking principal support and teacher resilience to teacher leadership in Türkiye: The mediating role of teacher work engagement. *Educational Management Administration & Leadership*, •••, 17411432241308679.

Collie, R. J., Shapka, J. D., & Perry, N. E. (2012). School climate and social–emotional learning: Predicting teacher stress, job satisfaction, and teaching efficacy. *Journal of Educational Psychology*, *104*(4), 1189–1204. https://psycnet.apa.org/doi/10.1037/a0029356. DOI: 10.1037/a0029356

Conner, T., & Walker, A. (2025). Reciprocal Mentoring: The Secret to Thriving Change Leadership Partnerships. *Alabama Journal of Educational Leadership*, *12*, 74–93.

Daniilidou, A., & Platsidou, M. (2018). Teachers' resilience scale: An integrated instrument for assessing protective factors of teachers' resilience. *Hellenic Journal of Psychology*, *15*(1), 15–39.

Day, C., & Gu, Q. (2013). *Resilient teachers, resilient schools: Building and sustaining quality in testing times*. Routledge. DOI: 10.4324/9780203578490

Dollarhide, C. T., & Saginak, K. A. (2011). *Comprehensive school counseling programs: K-12 delivery systems in action*. Pearson Higher Ed.

Dreer, B. (2024). Teachers' well-being and job satisfaction: The important role of positive emotions in the workplace. *Educational Studies*, *50*(1), 61–77. DOI: 10.1080/03055698.2021.1940872

Dreer-Goethe, B. (2026). Moments that matter: How critical incidents shape the well-being of student teachers during their practicum. *Research Papers in Education*, •••, 1–25. DOI: 10.1080/02671522.2026.2659788

DuFour, R., & Fullan, M. (2013). *Cultures built to last: Systemic PLCs at work TM*. Solution Tree Press.

Edmondson, A. (1999). Psychological safety and learning behavior in work teams. *Administrative Science Quarterly*, *44*(2), 350–383. DOI: 10.2307/2666999

Edmondson, A. C., & Lei, Z. (2014). Psychological safety: The history, renaissance, and future of an interpersonal construct. *Annual Review of Organizational Psychology and Organizational Behavior*, *1*(1), 23–43. DOI: 10.1146/annurev-orgpsych-031413-091305

Fullan, M. (2007). *Leading in a culture of change*. John Wiley & Sons.

Gámez-Genovart, M., Oliver-Trobat, M. F., & Rosselló-Ramon, M. R. (2025). Research on teacher well-being: A systematic review. *Teaching and Teacher Education*, *168*, 105264. DOI: 10.1016/j.tate.2025.105264

Grimmett, H., Forgasz, R., Williams, J., & White, S. (2018). Reimagining the role of mentor teachers in professional experience: Moving to I as fellow teacher educator. *Asia-Pacific Journal of Teacher Education, 46*(4), 340–353. DOI: 10.1080/1359866X.2018.1437391

Gu, Q. (2014). The role of relational resilience in teachers' career-long commitment and effectiveness. *Teachers and Teaching, 20*(5), 502–529. DOI: 10.1080/13540602.2014.937961

Gu, Q., & Day, C. (2013). Challenges to teacher resilience: Conditions count. *British Educational Research Journal, 39*(1), 22–44. DOI: 10.1080/01411926.2011.623152

Hallinger, P., & Heck, R. H. (2010). Collaborative leadership and school improvement: Understanding the impact on school capacity and student learning. *School Leadership & Management, 30*(2), 95–110. DOI: 10.1080/13632431003663214

Hargreaves, A. (2001). *Changing teachers, changing times: Teachers' work and culture in the postmodern age*. Teachers College Press.

Hargreaves, A., & O'Connor, M. T. (2018). *Collaborative professionalism: When teaching together means learning for all*. Corwin Press. DOI: 10.4135/9781506328133

Harris, A., Jones, M., & Ismail, N. (2022). Distributed leadership: Taking a retrospective and contemporary view of the evidence base. *School Leadership & Management, 42*(5), 438–456. DOI: 10.1080/13632434.2022.2109620

Harrison, H. F., Kinsella, E. A., Loftus, S., DeLuca, S., McGovern, G., Belanger, I., & Eugenio, T. (2024). "Nurturing a trusting learning community": Perceptions of relationships in a health professions education peer mentorship program. *International Journal of Mentoring and Coaching in Education, 13*(1), 55–72. DOI: 10.1108/IJMCE-08-2022-0065

Hascher, T., Beltman, S., & Mansfield, C. (2021). Teacher wellbeing and resilience: Towards an integrative model. *Educational Research, 63*(4), 416–439. DOI: 10.1080/00131881.2021.1980416

Heinla, E., & Kuurme, T. (2024). The impact of school culture, school climate, and teachers' job satisfaction on the teacher-student relationship: A case study in four Estonian schools. *Research Papers in Education, 39*(3), 439–465. DOI: 10.1080/02671522.2022.2150883

Hoang, K., Grow, H. M., Rooholamini, S. N., McPhillips, H., Selling, S. K., Rassbach, C. E., & Blankenburg, R. (2024). Impact of longitudinal coaching on pediatric residents' professional identity formation: A multi-institution qualitative study. *Academic Pediatrics, 24*(5), 866–874. DOI: 10.1016/j.acap.2024.04.012

Hogue, B., Xue, M., & Wessel-Powell, C. (2025). A self-study of bi-directional mentoring relationships within an early literacy methods course. *Studying Teacher Education, 21*(3), 318–341. DOI: 10.1080/17425964.2025.2552649

Jacelon, C. S. (1997). The trait and process of resilience. *Journal of Advanced Nursing, 25*(1), 123–129. DOI: 10.1046/j.1365-2648.1997.1997025123.x

Keravnos, N., & Lipsou, E. (2026). Relational trust and principal well-being: Extending the job demands–resources framework in school leadership. *Educational Management Administration & Leadership, 17411432261446399*, 17411432261446399. Advance online publication. DOI: 10.1177/17411432261446399

Khamisa, N., Oldenburg, B., Peltzer, K., & Ilic, D. (2015). Work related stress, burnout, job satisfaction and general health of nurses. *International Journal of Environmental Research and Public Health, 12*(1), 652–666. DOI: 10.3390/ijerph120100652

King, M., & Winn, D. (2017). Cross institutional peer coaching: A case study. In *Beyond mentoring* (pp. 93–106). Chandos Publishing., DOI: 10.1016/B978-0-08-101294-9.00008-8

Klar, H. W., & Brewer, C. A. (2013). Successful leadership in high-needs schools: An examination of core leadership practices enacted in challenging contexts. *Educational Administration Quarterly, 49*(5), 768–808. DOI: 10.1177/0013161X13482577

Knight, J. (2017). *The impact cycle: What instructional coaches should do to foster powerful improvements in teaching*. Corwin Press.

Kools, M., & Stoll, L. (2016). *What makes a school a learning organisation?* OECD Publishing., DOI: 10.1787/5jlwm62b3bvh-

Kyriacou, C. (2000). *Stress-busting for teachers*. Nelson Thornes.

Leat, D., Reid, A., & Lofthouse, R. (2015). Teachers' experiences of engagement with and in educational research: What can be learned from teachers' views? *Oxford Review of Education, 41*(2), 270–286. DOI: 10.1080/03054985.2015.1021193

Leithwood, K., Harris, A., & Hopkins, D. (2008). Seven strong claims about successful school leadership. *School Leadership & Management, 28*(1), 27–42. DOI: 10.1080/13632430701800060

Leontopoulos, S., Skenderidou, I., Stafylis, N., Papageorgiou, K., & Skenderidis, P. (2025). MENTORING AND COACHING IN EDUCATIONAL LEADERSHIP: FOSTERING REFLECTIVE AND STRATEGIC SCHOOL LEADERS. *European Journal of Education Studies, 12*(12). Advance online publication. DOI: 10.46827/ejes.v12i12.6341

Lipton, L., & Wellman, B. (2024). *Mentoring Matters: A Practical Guide to Learning-Focused Relationships, (Establish a learning-focused mentor-teacher relationship).* Solution Tree Press.

Liu, S., & Hallinger, P. (2018). Principal instructional leadership, teacher self-efficacy, and teacher professional learning in China: Testing a mediated-effects model. *Educational Administration Quarterly, 54*(4), 501–528. DOI: 10.1177/0013161X18769048

Louis, K. S. (2010). *Learning from leadership: Investigating the links to improved student learning*. Wallace Foundation.

Luong, G. Y. (2025). The effectiveness of mentoring, coaching, and induction practices for early career teachers: A scoping review. *Teaching and Teacher Education, 163*, 105065. DOI: 10.1016/j.tate.2025.105065

Ma, X., & Marion, R. (2024). How does leadership affect teacher collaboration? Evidence from teachers in US schools. *School Effectiveness and School Improvement, 35*(2), 116–141. DOI: 10.1080/09243453.2024.2330533

Mansfield, C. F., Beltman, S., Broadley, T., & Weatherby-Fell, N. (2016). Building resilience in teacher education: An evidenced informed framework. *Teaching and Teacher Education, 54*, 77–87. DOI: 10.1016/j.tate.2015.11.016

Mantzourani, E., Chang, H., Desselle, S., Canedo, J., & Fleming, G. (2022). Reflections of mentors and mentees on a national mentoring programme for pharmacists: An examination into relationships, personal and professional development. *Research in Social & Administrative Pharmacy, 18*(3), 2495–2504. DOI: 10.1016/j.sapharm.2021.04.019

Masten, A. S. (2016). Resilience in developing systems: The promise of integrated approaches. *European Journal of Developmental Psychology, 13*(3), 297–312. DOI: 10.1080/17405629.2016.1147344

Masten, A. S., & Barnes, A. J. (2018). Resilience in children: Developmental perspectives. *Children (Basel, Switzerland), 5*(7), 98. DOI: 10.3390/children5070098

McArdle, K., & Coutts, N. (2010). Taking teachers' continuous professional development (CPD) beyond reflection: Adding shared sense-making and collaborative engagement for professional renewal. *Studies in Continuing Education, 32*(3), 201–215. DOI: 10.1080/0158037X.2010.517994

Morcom, V., & MacCallum, J. (2022). Mentoring experienced teachers to change their practice: A sociocultural perspective for professional learning and development. *Learning, Culture and Social Interaction, 34*, 100627. DOI: 10.1016/j.lcsi.2022.100627

Munezero, E., Tóth, E., & Hódi, Á. (2026). A systematic review on teacher resilience assessment: Trends, foci, and implications. *Hungarian Educational Research Journal*, 063-2026. DOI: 10.1556/063.2026.00425

Ollila, J., Mankki, V., & Räihä, P. (2025). Collaboration and control: Insights into principals' role in establishing teacher mentoring in Finnish schools. *Professional Development in Education*, •••, 1–18. DOI: 10.1080/19415257.2025.2567260

Psyrras, N. (2026). Leadership 4.0 in education: Beyond technology. *Management in Education, 08920206261440720*, 08920206261440720. Advance online publication. DOI: 10.1177/08920206261440720

Quinn, J. F., Cola, P. A., Cooper, M., & Miller, C. (2025). Development of a survey tool to assess emotional and social behavioral competencies of science technology engineering math and medicine (STEMM) graduate students. *PLoS One*, *20*(9), e0328308. DOI: 10.1371/journal.pone.0328308

Raptis, N. G., & Psyrras, N. (2026). Integrating artificial intelligence in primary education: empirical insights of school leadership perspectives. In *Artificial Intelligence in Education* (Vol. 2, No. 3, pp. 18-32). Emerald Publishing Limited. DOI: 10.1108/AIIE-06-2025-0149

Rickard, M., Ackermann, D. M., Schnitzler, M., & Kozlowski, D. (2025). Emotional intelligence as a component of surgical coaching: A scoping review. *Journal of Surgical Education*, *82*(1), 103316. DOI: 10.1016/j.jsurg.2024.103316

Sahlberg, P., & Stringer, A. (2023). Coaching for professional learning of early career teachers. In *International Encyclopedia of Education* (pp. 144–152). Elsevier Ltd., DOI: 10.1016/B978-0-12-818630-5.04011-2

Savaş, G., Arslan, K., Dolapcı, E., Erdoğan, O., & Kılınç, A. Ç. (2025). Leadership for learning, teacher epistemic curiosity and psychological safety: Promoting professional learning. *Educational Management Administration & Leadership, 17411432251355389*, 17411432251355389. Advance online publication. DOI: 10.1177/17411432251355389

Schaufeli, W. B. (2015). Engaging leadership in the job demands-resources model. *Career Development International*, *20*(5), 446–463. DOI: 10.1108/CDI-02-2015-0025

Schön, D. A. (2017). *The reflective practitioner: How professionals think in action*. Routledge., DOI: 10.4324/9781315237473

Shen, J., Shi, Q., & Zhang, S. (2026). Teacher induction and collaboration: Investigating the role of school instructional leadership, mentoring, and collaborative school culture. *Journal of Educational Change*, *27*(1), 1–29. DOI: 10.1007/s10833-026-09541-y

Shields, C. M. (2010). Transformative leadership: Working for equity in diverse contexts. *Educational Administration Quarterly*, *46*(4), 558–589. DOI: 10.1177/0013161X10375609

Shu, K. (2022). Teachers' commitment and self-efficacy as predictors of work engagement and well-being. *Frontiers in Psychology*, *13*, 850204. DOI: 10.3389/fpsyg.2022.850204

Silverii, H., Cain, M. P., Ahn, J., Fernandez, N., Lendvay, T., Gupta, A., Joyner, B., Kieran, K., Shnorhavorian, M., & Merguerian, P. (2024). Putting the coach in the game: Current and future state of surgical coaching in pediatric urology. *Journal of Pediatric Urology*, *20*(4), 608–e1. DOI: 10.1016/j.jpurol.2024.03.004

Sink, C. A. (2005). *Contemporary school counseling: Theory, research, and practice*. Lahaska Press.

Skaalvik, E. M., & Skaalvik, S. (2018). Job demands and job resources as predictors of teacher motivation and well-being. *Social Psychology of Education*, *21*(5), 1251–1275. DOI: 10.1007/s11218-018-9464-8

Spillane, J. P. (2006). Towards a theory of leadership practice: A distributed perspective. In *Rethinking schooling* (pp. 208–242). Routledge.

Stokes, P., Fatien Diochon, P., & Otter, K. (2021). "Two sides of the same coin?" Coaching and mentoring and the agentic role of context. *Annals of the New York Academy of Sciences*, *1483*(1), 142–152. DOI: 10.1111/nyas.14316

Sweeney, P. J., & LeBoeuf, J. (2023). Enabling Medical Leaders Through Mentoring. *Clinics in Sports Medicine*, *42*(2), 219–231. DOI: 10.1016/j.csm.2022.11.006

Tahir, A., & Safder, M. (2025). Relationship between Reflective Teaching and Teachers' Burnout at Public Secondary School Level. *Journal of Sustainable Education*, 15-24. DOI: 10.71257/jse.v2i2.4743

Tschannen-Moran, M., & Hoy, W. K. (2000). A multidisciplinary analysis of the nature, meaning, and measurement of trust. *Review of Educational Research*, *70*(4), 547–593. DOI: 10.3102/00346543070004547

Ungar, M. (2011). The social ecology of resilience: Addressing contextual and cultural ambiguity of a nascent construct. *The American Journal of Orthopsychiatry, 81*(1), 1–17. https://psycnet.apa.org/doi/10.1111/j.1939-0025.2010.01067.x. DOI: 10.1111/j.1939-0025.2010.01067.x

Wang'ombe, T. (2023). The role of educational leadership in fostering a positive school culture and enhancing teacher retention. *European Journal of Education, 1*(1), 31–43.

Weist, M. D., Evans, S. W., & Lever, N. A. (Eds.). (2003). *Handbook of school mental health: Advancing practice and research* (pp. 1–7). Kluwer Academic/Plenum Publishers. DOI: 10.1007/978-0-387-73313-5

Wilson Heenan, I., De Paor, D., Lafferty, N., & Mannix McNamara, P. (2023). The impact of transformational school leadership on school staff and school culture in primary schools—A systematic review of international literature. *Societies (Basel, Switzerland), 13*(6), 133. DOI: 10.3390/soc13060133

Wolgast, A., & Fischer, N. (2017). You are not alone: Colleague support and goal-oriented cooperation as resources to reduce teachers' stress. *Social Psychology of Education, 20*(1), 97–114. DOI: 10.1007/s11218-017-9366-1

Chapter 5
Preschool Teachers' Professional Well-Being as a Multidimensional Foundation of School Resilience

Afroditi Vasileios Ntouka
http://orcid.org/0009-0009-2423-0533
University of the Aegean, Rhodes, Greece

Eleni Nikolaos Nikolaou
http://orcid.org/0000-0003-1840-3433
University of the Aegean, Rhodes, Greece

ABSTRACT

This study examines the professional well-being of preschool educators as a key factor in school resilience and the quality of the educational process. Through a literature review and qualitative research based on semi-structured interviews with ten kindergarten teachers in Rhodes, the study investigates the factors that enhance or undermine their professional well-being. The findings indicate that teachers associate well-being with emotional balance, job satisfaction, positive relationships with children and a balance between personal and professional life. At the same time, support from colleagues and school leaders functions as a reinforcing factor, while increasing bureaucracy, the demands of the educational system, and the lack of resources negatively affect their everyday professional experience. In conclusion, professional well-being emerges as a multidimensional and dynamic phenomenon that directly influences both educators themselves and the overall learning process.

DOI: 10.4018/979-8-3373-9420-6.ch005

THE CONCEPT OF WELL-BEING

Interest in the concept of well-being dates to ancient Greece (Angner, 2011). Over time, the concept has endured and is now a central topic of discussion in the social sciences. According to Alezandrova (2017: 3-4), "concern for human well-being lies at the very root of modern social science. Social science thus began its life as a form of knowledge formally dedicated to the advancement of well-being."

Of particular interest is the fact that well-being, as a concept, is now at the center of research, not only in the social sciences but across most scientific disciplines. Among these disciplines are psychology (Kim, Doiron, Warren & Donaldson, 2018; Rusk & Water, 2013; Wang, Guo & Yang, 2023), sociology, philosophy, literature, health, communication, media, public policy, and education (Eger & Maridal, 2015), all of which emphasize the substantive analysis and recognition of the meaning and essence of the concept.

However, the complexity of the concept prevents a single definition from being universally accepted across all scientific disciplines. According to Hone and colleagues (2016), most researchers and research teams agree that there are theoretical, conceptual, and functional models of well-being and that it is a multidimensional phenomenon. Cann et al. (2021) consider that the concept of well-being consists of four basic dimensions: cognitive, subjective, physical-psychological, and social. For Mercer and Gregersen (2020), well-being comprises the physical, emotional, cognitive/intellectual, and spiritual dimensions, while for Ryan & Deci (2011), well-being is the open and healthy functioning of the individual.

One definition of well-being states that it can be understood through the feelings individuals experience, how they react on a personal and social level, and how they ultimately evaluate their lives as a whole (Michaelson et al., 2012). Based on this definition, it appears that well-being refers to all those elements related to emotions and behaviors, knowledge, and relationships (Jarden & Roache, 2023).

Research on the concept of well-being indicates that there is a difference between how academics and non-academics perceive the concept. For non-academics, well-being concerns values such as mental health, a sense of self-worth, work-life balance, and inner harmony (Crisp, 2014). In contrast, academic research also highlights the substantive significance of the relationships that well-being shapes or influences (Delle Fave et al., 2011).

Cultural differences are also evident in the conceptual approach to the concept of well-being. According to research, Chinese students cite optimism and satisfaction as important aspects of well-being, whereas for European students, mental health is not particularly important (Hone et al., 2016). This finding is also confirmed by Uchida et al. (2015), who report that in East Asia, well-being is directly linked to social harmony—that is, conformity to social norms—while in European and American countries, well-being is more closely associated with individual achievements.

All definitions of the concept of well-being converge on the fact that it is a positive emotional state in which specific environmental factors, personal needs, and individual expectations coexist (Aelterman et al., 2007).

Dimensions of Well-being

Well-being is a multifactorial concept that has been the subject of intense research in recent years, not only as a field of study but also as an indicator of quality of life, resilience, and social cohesion. In contrast to earlier conceptions that defined it primarily as the absence of illness or discomfort, the contemporary view encompasses a broad range of subjective, psychological, physical, and social parameters (Lomas et al., 2021).

This multifaceted approach is essential, as well-being is not understood as a static state, but as a dynamic process influenced by personal, interpersonal, and structural factors. Based on this observation, theoretical models have been developed that seek to capture its core dimensions and explain the mechanisms that enhance it.

The scientific literature converges on the view of well-being as a multidimensional concept. Although approaches differ in terms of formulation and focus, several studies identify six main dimensions:

Physical well-being: Refers to good physical condition, vitality, and the absence of pain or physical exhaustion. It constitutes the foundation for an individual's active participation in everyday life activities (WHO, 2015).

Emotional well-being: Relates to emotional stability, the ability to manage stress, and the experience of positive emotions (Keyes & Waterman, 2022). Self-awareness and emotional regulation are considered critical factors of this dimension.

Psychological well-being: Includes a sense of purpose in life, autonomy, personal growth, and decision-making ability. Ryff & Singer (2015) confirm the importance of these parameters across populations of different ages and socioeconomic backgrounds.

Social well-being: Refers to the quality of relationships, social acceptance, and the sense of belonging to groups or communities. Social support is considered a predictive factor for both mental and physical health (Helliwell et al., 2020).

Professional well-being: Concerns job satisfaction, a sense of meaning at work, and the balance between professional and personal life. Under conditions of increasing job insecurity, this dimension has gained particular importance (Grant et al., 2021).

Spiritual/existential well-being: Although less measurable, it relates to a sense of meaning, inner peace, and personal connection with broader values or metaphysical beliefs (Fisher, 2020).

It is important to note that these dimensions do not operate independently. On the contrary, they interact with one another, forming a complex system that is continuously shaped by both external and internal factors.

CLARIFICATION OF THE CONCEPT OF "PROFESSIONAL WELL-BEING"

Teachers' well-being has attracted significant scholarly attention in recent decades, particularly in light of the significant increase in cases of sick leave and voluntary resignation among teachers across different cultural and national contexts. Indeed, it is widely accepted in academic discourse that the teaching profession is inherently demanding and full of challenges, resulting in increased exposure to stress, burnout, and, more broadly, a high attrition rate. Well-being goes beyond the simplistic notion of merely the absence of illness in the workplace. It encompasses the concept of teachers functioning in a healthy and effective manner in their professional roles. Specifically, while the concepts of physical, psychological, and mental health primarily concern the absence of dysfunction, well-being is more accurately characterized by teachers' ability to cultivate a positive yet dynamic balance between their available resources and the myriad challenges and demands they face (environmental, social, personal, physical, intellectual, and psychological) (Benevene et al., 2020).

In this subsection, the concept of occupational well-being will be introduced and examined in greater detail. However, before defining the concept, it is necessary to clarify the confusion that often exists between the concepts of occupational well-being and job satisfaction. Occupational well-being has often been examined in comparison to occupational burnout and work-related stress. In fact, according to research by Pakarinen et al. (2010), it was found that student performance is negatively affected by teacher stress. For Kourkouni (2020), the concept of job satisfaction is encompassed within the concept of professional well-being, and according to Schina (2016), job satisfaction serves as an indicator of professional well-being.

Job satisfaction can be examined based on teachers' responses to questions regarding working conditions, relationships with colleagues and the principal, as well as organizational issues related to school operations (Kourkouni, 2020) . Furthermore, professional well-being is not the opposite of work-related stress. A teacher who does not feel stressed does not necessarily experience professional well-being (Mercer & Gregersen, 2020). According to Pagán-Castaño, Maseda-Moreno, and Santos-Rojo (2019), professional well-being has three dimensions: teachers' subjective experiences and work performance, mental and physical health, and the relationships built between employees and supervisors. According to recent research, job satisfaction is part of professional well-being, but the two are by no means synonymous (Van

Horn et al., 2004). Workplace well-being is a fluid concept, as it can change from day to day and moment to moment (Cann et al., 2021; Mercer & Gregersen, 2020) and cannot be considered synonymous with or opposed to the concepts with which it is so often confused. Just as with the definition of well-being, there is no universally accepted definition of occupational well-being.

The first definition of occupational well-being was formulated in 1984 by Diener, who defined it as a psychological experience involving an objective evaluation of life circumstances and current conditions and a subjective evaluation of life's meaning and satisfaction. It is of utmost importance for an individual's life, work, and social interactions (Cui, 2022).

According to Acton et al. (2015), teacher well-being can be defined as the individual's—that is, the teacher's—sense of personal work fulfillment, completion, successful purpose, and happiness, which is constructed through the collaborative process with colleagues and students. Aelterman et al. (2007) and Brichero et al. (2009) agree that professional well-being is a positive emotional state resulting from the harmony between the set of specific environmental factors and the personal needs and expectations of teachers.

Well-being, as a combination of professional and personal development, constitutes an ideal environment in which teachers feel effective (Day & Gu, 2009) and, above all, useful and productive in what they offer. In recent years, research interest has shifted toward a positive definition of well-being and is no longer focused primarily on the identification and treatment of stress, but rather on the factors that influence and promote well-being. Teachers' well-being and positive job satisfaction contribute to their effectiveness, as well as to the maintenance of that effectiveness.

Professional well-being is not a given state that characterizes a teacher throughout their entire career (Pot, 2017). However, it is directly related to school effectiveness and depends to a large extent on the good physical, mental, and emotional well-being of teachers (Anastassopoulos, 2018). Furthermore, it is influenced by various factors, such as the quality of school leadership, social support, and a sense of belonging to a community (Kusma et al., 2012).

Alagaraja (2020) argues that teachers experience well-being when they find meaning and purpose in their work, as this strengthens their commitment and engagement in the educational context. It also increases when they interact positively with colleagues and supervisors or principals, and when their personal beliefs and values align with those of the school where they work.

Finally, the concept of well-being has been found to be closely related to the quality of interpersonal relationships among students, colleagues, and family members, while also being positively associated with improved academic performance among students. Well-being is a complex and multidimensional phenomenon that encompasses cognitive, emotional, physical, and mental components, and incorporates dispositional, personal, organizational, and environmental factors (Benevene et al., 2020).

Models of Professional Well-Being

One of the earliest models referring to professional well-being is Karasek's Job Demand-Control Model, introduced in 1979. The model examines two factors that are considered to influence employees. These are the job itself—that is, the responsibilities employees are required to perform daily—and the employee's independence/freedom to define the parameters of their work and take initiatives (Pomaki & Anagnostopoulou, 2003).

Another model that attempted to examine professional well-being is the Job Characteristics Model proposed by Hackman and Oldham in 1980. This model was used to measure employee motivation and includes five core job characteristics. Specifically, it includes skill variety, task identity, task significance, feedback, and autonomy. These characteristics are believed to lead to the development of critical psychological states, such as the perceived significance and effectiveness of work, as experienced by employees, as well as knowledge of the actual results of their work activity. These psychological states, in turn, are expected to affect employees' professional well-being either positively or negatively (Johns & Saks, 2005).

To the above models was added the Demand–Control–Social Support Model, which introduced the variable of social support as a determining factor influencing employees' professional well-being (Karasek & Theorell, 1990). Subsequently, Van et al. (2004) proposed a work-related well-being model based on the models of Ryff and Warr. Specifically, they adopted three dimensions from Ryff's model—emotional, social, and professional well-being—and two dimensions from Warr's model—cognitive and psychosomatic well-being. In this way, they constructed a five-dimensional model of well-being.

According to Saaranen et al. (2007), teachers' professional well-being is based on four parameters: (a) working conditions, (b) workload (worker and work), (c) working community, and (d) professional competence and opportunities for professional development. More specifically, working conditions are associated with the work environment, the suitability of the workplace, the existence of disturbing noise and noise pollution, adequate technological infrastructure, and proper ergonomic arrangements (Hallinger, 2003; Hoy & Miskel, 2005). Workload refers to the number of students in the classroom, class size, and non-teaching duties. These organizational parameters (Devos et al., 2007) affect teachers' professional well-being, since excessive workload negatively impacts teachers' overall health, making them less productive and effective (Harter et al., 2002).

Regarding the working community, this dimension refers to psychosocial parameters such as work demands, social support, atmosphere, and collaboration, all of which can influence workplace relationships. Educational reforms, which often negatively affect teachers' psychology, are also considered part of the working community (Aelterman et al., 2007). Finally, according to the creators of the model, professional competence concerns the improvement of professional skills, teachers' active participation, and positive engagement with the profession (Saaranen et al., 2007). Essentially, professional competence could be understood as teachers' ability to cope with forthcoming difficulties and successfully overcome them.

Finally, Collie et al. (2012) argue that professional well-being should be examined through the dimensions of workload well-being, organisational well-being, and student interaction well-being. Workload well-being concerns issues related to workload and associated work pressure, organisational well-being refers to teachers' perceptions of the school, school leadership, and the overall culture characterizing the school unit, while the final dimension concerns teachers' interactions with their students. It is worth noting that, although the two models consist of five and three dimensions respectively, all of these dimensions are interconnected (OECD, 2020).

Factors Influencing Teachers' Professional Well-being

Regarding the factors that influence teachers' professional well-being, the literature suggests that individual factors play a dominant role, such as personality, personal style, psychological resilience, adaptability, and self-efficacy (Ji, 2022). Equally decisive are school-related factors, which pertain to school culture, school climate, the work environment, administrative organization, teacher compensation, and opportunities for professional development (Skaalvik & Skaalvik, 2018). Furthermore, the influence of the community and the developmental conditions of the local society, as well as political and economic factors, should not be overlooked (Ji, 2022).

Some of these factors include self-esteem, social and emotional skills, emotional intelligence, fatigue, burnout, and stress, and finally, certain relational factors. More specifically, self-esteem refers to how individuals evaluate their own abilities and potential in the learning process (Ross et al., 2012). Furthermore, teachers' self-esteem has a positive influence on their teaching behavior and on learning outcomes in general (Roberts et al., 2019).

Social and emotional competencies and emotional intelligence refer to teachers' social and emotional knowledge, skills, and attitudes, which contribute to their effectiveness in the workplace (MacCallum et al., 2015). They also help teachers recognize, process, and regulate their emotions so they can effectively manage their stress, thereby increasing their well-being and overall performance in the classroom (Fernandez–Molina et al., 2019).

Regarding fatigue, stress, and burnout, a review of the literature reveals that these are the factors most extensively studied in relation to teachers' well-being. In fact, it has been found that teachers' stress levels are particularly high and, correspondingly, their well-being is at low levels compared to the general population (Education Support Partnership, 2019). Some of the factors contributing to these issues among teachers include ever-increasing bureaucracy, a lack of time for planning, the exclusion of early childhood educators from decision-making processes, etc. In fact, research suggests that if teachers' stress and fatigue are not addressed, they can very easily be led to burnout (Bermejo–Toro et al., 2016; Wolf et al., 2015).

Furthermore, with regard to relational factors, these refer to undesirable behaviors on the part of students and their parents, a lack of management, and ineffective leadership in difficult situations—in the classroom, in the school building, regarding logistical equipment, etc. In other words, they concern situations that fall within the broader school context and are capable of influencing teachers' well-being and their instructional effectiveness (Cherkowski, 2018; Katidou, 2019). The climate and culture of the school could also be included among these factors (OECD, 2014).

Another factor that influences teachers' professional well-being is professional commitment. Professional commitment refers to teachers' ability to carry out any responsibility they undertake, while simultaneously experiencing pleasant and positive emotions. They should be active and dedicated to their professional duties, yet at the same time, they should feel a sense of satisfaction and not feel pressured or burdened (Wefald et al., 2012).

According to Aeltermna et al. (2007), since professional well-being is equated with a positive emotional state, it arises from the harmonious coexistence of specific environmental factors, personal needs, and teachers' expectations. They also note that measuring teachers' well-being could be considered a measure of the quality of the education provided. Furthermore, Warr (2007) argues that teachers who have the space and opportunities for personal development experience higher levels of professional well-being.

Conversely, if they do not clearly understand their role within the school context, their professional well-being is consequently negatively affected (Travers, 2010). In this regard, the school principal also plays a decisive role; they should trust their teaching staff and provide them with opportunities to participate in and contribute to the organization and administration of the school (Pashiardis, 2004).

It is clear from the above that the literature has identified several factors that influence teachers' professional well-being. Therefore, professional well-being should not be taken for granted, as in many cases it is determined by teachers' needs and expectations. In other words, while working conditions may be the same for all teachers working in a school, their professional well-being will not be the same for everyone (Pot, 2017). In summary, the factors influencing teachers' professional well-being are work-related stress, interpersonal relationships, transformational leadership, social support, and self-efficacy (Cuil & Mui, 2023).

Therefore, it is easy to see that teachers' professional well-being arises, exists and is maintained at a positive level when teachers work in a positive work environment, where their health and safety are ensured, and when they interact positively and are supported by colleagues and senior administrators (Brownett et al., 2021; Pot, 2017). Thus, teachers become effective, innovative, creative, and productive; they feel committed and strive to contribute as much as possible to the teaching and educational process.

A literature review of the factors influencing teachers' professional well-being provides insights into the complex nature of their well-being and the various individual factors that influence it. The analysis of relevant research highlights the importance of managing both individual and organizational challenges with the aim of enhancing teachers' positive professional experience.

The key findings of the review indicate that workplace factors play a critical role in teachers' professional well-being. Factors such as work-related stress require the provision of a supportive and pleasant work environment that fosters the continuous development and recognition of teachers' work. The review also highlights the value of interpersonal relationships and social support in enhancing teachers' professional well-being. Positive social relationships, whether with colleagues or students, foster a sense of belonging and strengthen bonds in the workplace. The development of a culture of cooperation and respect contributes to teachers' emotional resilience and overall professional satisfaction. At the same time, the importance of personal characteristics that influence teachers' well-being is highlighted (Cuil & Mui, 2023). Self-efficacy, as a key individual characteristic, is linked to mental well-being and job satisfaction. Promoting self-care strategies and providing support for managing stress and professional challenges are important steps in maintaining teachers' well-being.

RESEARCH METHODOLOGY

This study sought to examine the well-being of preschool teachers in order to determine how it is promoted, supported, and addressed, with a specific focus on their professional well-being. Furthermore, the study aimed to highlight the importance of professional well-being in the educational process, which is believed to significantly and qualitatively influence the planning, implementation, and outcomes of teaching.

Research Questions

Research questions provide the framework for the research process and guide the research. Essentially, they involve translating the research objective into specific questions that will yield concrete answers (Cohen et al., 2008). In the context of this postdoctoral dissertation, the research questions formulated are as follows:

- What do preschool teachers themselves know about their professional well-being?
- What importance do preschool teachers themselves attach to their professional well-being?
- What level of professional well-being is considered ideal?
- Do preschool teachers recognize the importance of promoting and addressing their professional well-being?
- How is the professional well-being of preschool teachers supported?
- Which suggestions for improving professional well-being do preschool teachers agree with?

This study will attempt to answer the above questions.

Data Collection Tool and Method

A semi-structured interview was used as the data collection instrument for the present study. The interview constitutes the most widespread and valuable research tool in qualitative methodology (Liargovas, 2023), as it enables interaction and communication between the researcher and the participants, while also eliciting useful information related to the issue under investigation (Cohen et al., 2008). According to Iosifidis (2003), the interview allows the researcher to understand and examine social behaviors as well as participants' perceptions through their own views and experiences. Essentially, through the interview process, it becomes possible to understand people's lived experiences and the meaning they themselves attribute to the phenomenon under investigation (Seidman, 2013).

More specifically, a semi-structured interview consisting of fifteen (15) questions was employed. The semi-structured interview may be characterized as semi-directive, since the questions are predetermined in terms of number, sequence, and content, thereby defining the framework of the interview. At the same time, it allows for the discussion of additional issues that may emerge during the interview process. In other words, it provides flexibility, enabling the researcher to explore the topic more thoroughly and in depth (Liargovas et al., 2023), without the interviewee perceiving that they are being guided (Griva & Stamou, 2014).

Through the semi-structured interview, teachers were invited to respond regarding how they personally experience professional well-being and which factors they believe enhance it or generate negative emotions that adversely affect their professional well-being. The views of teachers themselves, as a social group, are considered particularly important, since they can reveal possible subjective motives and perspectives (Robson, 2007).

Research Sample

The term "sample" refers to a smaller number of individuals who constitute part of the total population and may be considered representative of that population (Martin, 2008). Based on the available time, resources, and sources, the researcher decides how many and which individuals will form part of the sample, while still aiming to ensure the reliability and validity of the research findings (Liargovas, 2023). Sampling seeks the generalization of research results, and for this reason the researcher carefully selects the sampling method.

For the purposes of the present study, the sample for the semi-structured interviews consisted of preschool education teachers working on the island of Rhodes. Specifically, the sample included ten kindergarten teachers, and purposive sampling was employed, a non-probability sampling technique in which participants are selected based on the researcher's judgment and knowledge. The researcher's knowledge is considered crucial, given that the sample members were not selected randomly, thus minimizing the margin of error in the findings (Liargovas, 2023).

Regarding the demographic characteristics of the sample, all ten participating kindergarten teachers were women. Two of them were head teachers, two were permanent kindergarten teachers, one was newly appointed, and the remaining five were substitute teachers. The head teachers had more than twenty years of teaching experience and were expected to retire within two years. The permanent teachers had more than ten years of experience, while the newly appointed teacher had been working as a permanent teacher for the last two years, after previously serving as a substitute teacher for three years. The substitute teachers had more than five years of professional experience. In terms of professional qualifications, eight of the kindergarten teachers in the sample, excluding the head teachers, held at least one postgraduate degree, whereas the head teachers had attended only professional seminars. Finally, regarding their family status, nine of the kindergarten teachers were married and had children, while only one substitute teacher was unmarried and had no children.

Research Procedure

The semi-structured interviews were conducted over a period of one month, specifically during January 2024. The researcher visited the workplace of the ten (10) kindergarten teachers who participated in the study, following a telephone conversation to arrange the exact time of the meeting. The interviews lasted approximately 15 minutes on average, depending on the participants' responses and their willingness to provide additional information regarding the issue under investigation.

Research Ethics and Research Integrity

This study was designed and conducted in strict accordance with the principles of ethics and research integrity governing social and educational research involving human subjects. Research involving human subjects must be conducted exclusively in accordance with ethical principles, such as participant autonomy, beneficence, justice, and non-maleficence, both for participants and researchers. The ethical principles in research refer to the ethical implications that conducting a study may have and its effects on society (Liargovas, 2023).

Regarding research ethics, this refers to the set of guidelines that must be followed. That is, the set of rules that govern the relationships between researchers and participants and primarily regulate how researchers should behave toward participants (Isaris & Pourkos, 2015).

In conducting this study, all ethical and deontological considerations relevant to scientific research were adhered to. Specifically, the participants were informed in writing about the topic and purpose of the study, and after their anonymity was confirmed, they signed the corresponding document, thereby consenting to participate in the study. In addition, the participants were provided with the researcher's contact information so that they could contact her at any time and if they wished to be informed of the study's results.

More specifically, the questionnaire was sent along with the Informed Consent Form, which explained in a clear and understandable manner:

- the purpose of the study
- its methodological nature
- the duration of participation
- its voluntary nature
- guarantees of anonymity and confidentiality
- the right to withdraw at any time without any consequences.

The researcher ensured that there was no form of pressure or influence regarding participation. The participants were professional preschool educators with no hierarchical or other relationship of dependence on the researcher.

It was also important to clarify that the participants would not be evaluated in any way for their responses and that their participation would in no way affect their position or professional reputation. This was particularly crucial, given that the study addressed issues of emotional well-being and job satisfaction—issues that may involve subjective sensitivities.

The researcher ensured that the survey responses would be used exclusively for analysis purposes and would not be shared or transferred to third parties. The data were stored using coding and pseudonymization to protect the participants' identities. Furthermore, it was agreed that each participant had the right to access, correct, or withdraw her responses at a later stage, as stipulated by the European General Data Protection Regulation (GDPR, EU Regulation 2016/679).

Beyond the technical and legal considerations, the research process was designed with respect for the participants' personal dignity and psychological well-being. The researcher was sensitive to potential emotional exhaustion or fatigue resulting from recalling unpleasant experiences, and for this reason adopted a supportive and empathetic approach throughout the investigation.

In accordance with scientific ethics, the following rules were also observed:

- Avoidance of falsification, selective use, or interpretation of data to support hypotheses.
- Presentation of results with accuracy and transparency.
- Documentation of the analytical process to ensure the validity and reliability of the interpretation (analytical traceability).

Finally, participants were given the opportunity, if they so desired, to be informed of the key findings and to access a non-technical summary of the results, in the context of knowledge sharing and scientific reciprocity toward practitioners.

The overall philosophy of the research approach is fully aligned with contemporary scientific ethics, which is not limited merely to compliance with procedural rules, but aims to create a relationship of trust and equality between the researcher and the research subject (Nind et al., 2021). The researcher operated with a focus on authentic engagement, respect for the participants' voices, and transparency in the research process, seeking not only to gather data but also to preserve the human dimension of the research.

RESULTS

Regarding the first question ("What does well-being mean to you?"), the teachers' responses did not differ significantly. The preschool teachers were asked about the concept of well-being and, more specifically, what it meant to them personally. Most participants answered that well-being refers to a healthy emotional and mental state ("A healthy physical and mental condition"). In addition, all participants referred to the existence of positive emotions associated with the profession they had chosen to pursue. They mentioned feelings such as euphoria, inner emotional uplift, and satisfaction, especially pleasant emotions arising from their interaction with children ("a proper way of life that brings us joy, happiness, satisfaction, and all these related emotions"). Some preschool teachers also defined well-being as the balance between professional and personal life ("it refers me to the concept of pleasure and satisfaction; being satisfied both personally and professionally"), approaching the definition of well-being as it has been shaped through the study of the relevant literature.

In the second question ("What do you consider to be the ideal level of well-being at work? Can you describe it?"), the participants were asked to express their views regarding the ideal level of well-being in their work environment. With the exception of one preschool teacher who stated that an ideal level of well-being cannot exist ("I do not believe there is an ideal level in our work"), the remaining participants described an environment that generates exclusively positive emotions ("Coming to work with pleasure, feeling motivated to work, and enjoying myself during working hours"). They described an environment free from tensions and conflicts ("there should be no tensions; what I have planned should be accomplished satisfactorily—ideally may not be possible, but satisfactorily—whether regarding collegial relationships or relationships with colleagues") and, above all, referred enthusiastically to a pleasant environment that promotes creative and enjoyable activities both for themselves and for the children, free mainly from conflicts with colleagues and parents.

In the third question ("Can you describe an experience that you would characterize as ideal for your well-being at work?"), the preschool teachers were asked to describe an experience that positively contributed to their professional well-being. Although they initially found it difficult to answer, after receiving clarification from the researcher, all participants recalled an experience or memory that filled them with pleasant emotions whenever they thought about it ("I think it has to do with when I first started truly listening to the children and when I took on a secondary role in the classroom. That was when teaching became magical for me"). Some participants also referred to effective collaboration with colleagues and cooperation without conflicts and tensions as a pleasant experience ("Generally, through relationships with colleagues and through the various activities we do, I think positive emotions are created"), which contributes both to their professional well-being and to their effectiveness in the educational process.

In the following question ("Describe how you feel about your job, e.g., are you satisfied with the school where you work? Would you change it?"), participants were asked to describe their feelings regarding their work. It is worth noting that all participants used a single word that best expressed their feelings, such as happy, fulfilled, complete, and satisfied ("I am satisfied regarding the environment and the cooperation with colleagues, and I would hardly change it"; "Generally speaking, I am satisfied. I would change the school infrastructure"). The researcher attempted to elicit more detailed responses through follow-up questions, but the additional information obtained revealed that participants felt very fortunate about the profession they had chosen and could not imagine themselves doing another job ("It is my whole life; I cannot imagine myself doing anything else").

In the fifth question ("Do you believe there is a balance between your personal and professional life?"), the preschool teachers were asked about the level of balance between their personal and professional lives. Considering that nine of the teachers were married and only one did not have children, all participants stated that the profession of preschool teacher allows them to maintain a relatively good balance between personal and professional life ("Yes. It is something I strive for without favoring one over the other"). Working with children, which fills them with positive emotions, along with a work schedule that coincides with the hours their own children are at school, were identified as the two primary reasons for maintaining this balance. The preschool teacher who was unmarried and without family obligations also stated that she maintained a satisfactory balance between her professional and personal life.

In the following question ("If such a balance exists, are you satisfied with this situation? Please justify your answer"), participants were asked whether they were satisfied with the balance they had previously described. All participants stated that they were satisfied with this balance ("Yes, I make sure this balance exists because I would not be able to perform adequately in either area without it"). However, they added that this balance has begun to be disrupted in recent years due to the increasing demands imposed by the Ministry of Education ("If you do not take into account the recent changes taking place in kindergartens, such as skills workshops, afternoon training seminars, etc., one could say that our well-being is still maintained at good levels"). These demands include mandatory afternoon training sessions, the daily planning of skills workshops, and other obligations that teachers cannot avoid. Nevertheless, these responsibilities have not yet significantly disrupted the balance between their professional and personal lives.

In the seventh question ("Is it possible for you to take a break or rest period during work when you need it?"), participants were asked about the possibility of taking breaks during working hours. Naturally, taking breaks in a kindergarten setting is almost impossible ("No. During working hours, absolutely not"), especially when a teacher works alone and there is no colleague available to replace her even briefly. Therefore, all participants stated that they could not take breaks during work, while some added that any break would come at the expense of their colleagues ("Only by burdening another colleague").

In the eighth question ("Do the available educational tools—printed, material, or digital—affect the teaching process and your teaching effectiveness?"), participants were asked about the educational materials available in their classrooms and the extent to which these resources affect their teaching practices. Only one preschool teacher stated that she did not rely on available materials but instead on her imagination and attempted to work based on that ("I know what exists in my classroom and I try to work with those materials based on my imagination and the children's abilities"). The remaining participants stated that the continuous reduction of educational materials, combined with the increasing demands of the Ministry of Education, creates serious difficulties in their teaching process and overall classroom performance. They are required to carry out activities and complete skills workshops without having the appropriate means and materials ("Yes, it affects it. I believe we would like more digital tools. We would probably need them for a more effective educational process, and printed materials are always necessary to attract children's attention because children need more colors, more materials, and more stimuli"). Nine preschool teachers reported that the current conditions in kindergartens negatively affect their professional well-being.

In the following question ("Do you believe that your principal or school director supports you, and how does their attitude affect your well-being?"), participants were asked how the behavior of their supervisors influences their professional well-being and whether they feel supported. All ten preschool teachers agreed that effective cooperation with their supervisor has a significant impact on their professional well-being ("Very much. First of all, she trusts us, and I think that is our greatest strength—the trust she shows us. It is not that she leaves us alone and is indifferent; rather, we feel trusted"). None of the participants reported experiencing problems with their supervisor. On the contrary, they described excellent cooperation without conflicts, which contributes to effective and productive work ("We are like a family; she is like our older sister. Honestly, support from the supervisor is everything"). However, these responses may partly be explained by the fact that most participants were permanent teachers whose relationships with their supervisors had been built on stable foundations. Nevertheless, the relevant literature indicates that teachers' professional well-being can be disrupted by negative relationships with supervisors or school directors, as discussed in the theoretical section of the present study.

In the following question ("Do you believe that you meet your supervisor's expectations? Why or why not?"), participants were asked whether they believed they met their supervisors' expectations. All preschool teachers answered positively, relying mainly on the non-verbal communication of their supervisors. They explained that the reactions of their supervisors, both verbal and non-verbal, did not indicate dissatisfaction or disagreement regarding the lessons they implemented ("Because I receive this feedback"). On the contrary, they stated that they had developed a positive relationship resembling a family bond ("You are talking about a school where we all care deeply for one another").

In the eleventh question ("Do you participate in voluntary activities such as Erasmus or eTwinning related to school actions outside working hours? Why or why not?"), participants were asked about their participation in voluntary activities taking place outside working hours. Most preschool teachers, especially permanent staff members, responded positively ("Yes, of course, if necessary and if it benefits the children"). In contrast, substitute teachers stated that since they do not know in which school they will work during the following academic year, they are reluctant to participate in such programs ("At the moment, no. I have participated in eTwinning before, but currently the conditions were not favorable for me personally, and mainly because I do not know which school I will be in next year").

In the twelfth question ("What motivates you to give your best in teaching?"), participants were asked about the reasons motivating them to perform at their highest level in teaching. The most common response was the sense of responsibility ("I think it is the sense of responsibility. We are the first building block at such an important age, and it is very important to feel that the foundation you are laying is solid") toward the children and their progress by the end of the school year ("I think it is the result you see at the end"). Comparing the cognitive, emotional, and social level of children at the beginning and end of the school year made participants feel highly effective, which generated pleasant emotions and increased their professional well-being. From the beginning of the school year, they commit themselves to meeting both curriculum requirements and the needs of the children in their classrooms. Positive outcomes reward them and motivate them to achieve even greater results.

In the thirteenth question ("Do you consider your commute to and from work to be free from stress?"), participants were asked whether they experienced stress while traveling to or from work. Responses varied depending on family circumstances and the distance each teacher had to travel. Specifically, teachers who traveled longer distances stated that there were days when they felt stressed, mainly about arriving on time, adverse weather conditions, or unresolved issues involving parents from the previous day ("No. The commute is unfortunately a major issue because I live in Rhodes city, so yes, it is stressful for me"; "It is not completely stress-free. We rush to arrive on time, wondering if we forgot something, but not to a great extent"). Regarding the return journey home, only one preschool teacher reported feeling stressed because she had a young child and needed to leave work promptly to collect her child from school. She also mentioned that some parents repeatedly arrive late to pick up their children, creating additional stress ("When dismissal time approaches, I become anxious because I worry that not all parents will arrive on time, and then I will also be late picking up my daughter from school. Of course, this also has to do with personality").

The fourteenth question ("Do you believe you are adequately paid? Why or why not?") concerned participants' views regarding how salary affects their professional well-being. All preschool teachers stated that they were not adequately compensated considering the quality of their teaching and the hours they devote to their work. They believe that preschool teachers are particularly undervalued given the working conditions, the increase in responsibilities, and their final salary ("I believe not. The enormous responsibility of my work, as well as the workload I bring home to be effective in my classroom, deserves greater compensation"). Only one participant added that although they are not adequately paid, given the current economic conditions in Greece, preschool teachers' salaries could still be considered relatively satisfactory ("Within the Greek context, yes, I believe I am relatively well paid compared to the salaries of others").

Finally, the interview concluded with the question of whether participants felt comfortable speaking with the School Counselor about problems they encounter at work ("Do you feel comfortable discussing work-related problems with the School Counselor? Why or why not?"). Responses varied depending on whether the participants were substitute or permanent teachers. Substitute preschool teachers stated that although they had met the School Counselor, they did not feel particularly comfortable communicating with her about potential problems. This was attributed to the temporary nature of their employment, since they may belong to another school district the following academic year and therefore work with a different School Counselor ("Yes, I have met her and she is very polite. However, I do not know whether I would contact her if a problem arose. Next year I may be in another district and meet another School Counselor"). In contrast, permanent preschool teachers stated that they had already communicated with the School Counselor regarding difficulties encountered during teaching and had developed a particularly friendly relationship with her ("We have very good cooperation, and I believe this is exactly how it should be, because that is the role of school counselors. In every difficulty there should be good cooperation to solve problems").

LIMITATIONS OF THE STUDY

Regarding the limitations, it can be stated that the present study, although it provides important qualitative insights into the professional well-being of preschool teachers, presents certain limitations that should be taken into account when interpreting the findings:

Sample size and composition: The study was based on a limited number of participants, which restricts the generalizability of the results. Although diversity was sought, the proportions of gender, age, years of experience, or workplace location may not be fully representative of the overall population of preschool teachers.

Data collection method: Although the use of semi-structured interviews provides depth, it relies exclusively on subjective narratives and personal interpretations. It is possible that some participants provided socially desirable responses or avoided openly expressing negative experiences, especially when these were related to colleagues or school leadership.

Lack of longitudinal data: The study is cross-sectional, meaning that it captures opinions and experiences at a single point in time. It cannot reflect the development of participants' well-being over time or across different stages of their professional lives.

Focus exclusively on preschool education: Although this was an intentional choice, it limits the possibility of comparative analysis with teachers from other educational levels, such as primary or secondary education.

Limited consideration of organizational factors: The study focuses on the personal and interpersonal dimensions of well-being but does not examine in depth institutional or policy-related factors (e.g., job stability, professional development, evaluation), which often strongly influence teachers' psychological condition.

RECOMMENDATIONS FOR FUTURE RESEARCH

Based on the above limitations and the findings of the present study, the following recommendations for future research are proposed:

Expansion of the sample at a national level: Conducting similar research in the future with a larger and geographically diverse sample would allow for more generalizable conclusions and could highlight potential regional or cultural differences in the perception of well-being.

Combination with quantitative methods: The integration of quantitative tools (e.g., well-being scales, burnout or job satisfaction measures) could enhance the reliability of the findings and enable the statistical examination of relationships between variables.

Longitudinal design: Studying teachers' professional well-being across different stages of their careers (e.g., early, mid-career, burnout phase) would provide meaningful data for understanding the factors that lead to well-being or decline.

In-depth exploration of the role of leadership: Investigating the relationship between school administration and professional well-being—especially through empathetic or participatory leadership—could enrich the theoretical understanding of organizational influences.

Comparative approach across educational levels or countries: Comparing findings with data from teachers in primary or secondary education, or even across different educational systems (e.g., within EU countries), could highlight the impact of institutional and cultural contexts on professional well-being.

Participatory/empowerment methodologies: Future research could adopt approaches in which teachers themselves co-shape research questions or interventions, actively contributing to the understanding and improvement of their well-being (e.g., action research, co-design, focus groups).

Linking findings to educational policy and professional development: Connecting the findings with the content of training programs (e.g., those provided by national educational bodies) could lead to more targeted policies for supporting teachers.

Teachers play a fundamental role in shaping and advancing the educational system, constituting a central factor in social development and national well-being. Their contribution is critical, as it is directly linked to the implementation of educational policies and the achievement of curriculum goals, while they significantly influence students' academic and personal development (Huang, 2021).

According to Feuerbach, the essence of life and happiness stems from common causes, suggesting that personal aspirations for growth and success are grounded in the institution of education and the cultivation of abilities (Liu, 1984). From this perspective, strengthening teachers' professional skills and improving the quality of their teaching practices emerge as cornerstones for the advancement of the educational system (Liu, 2023; Zhao, 2022).

CONCLUSIONS

Despite its limitations, the findings of the present study highlight the importance of maintaining high levels of professional well-being among preschool educators. In relation to the research questions of the study, the following conclusions may be drawn:

1. Preschool educators appear to be familiar with the concept of professional well-being and are able to define and describe it. Professional well-being is per-

ceived as a positive emotional state, particularly when there is balance between professional and personal life.

2. Through their responses during the semi-structured interviews, the participants identified relationships with colleagues, relationships with their supervisor or head teacher, and the availability of educational resources in the kindergarten setting as the main factors affecting their professional well-being, since these factors influence their ability to design and implement teaching activities. In addition, another factor affecting their professional well-being appears to be the distance they are required to travel to and from work. Salary, however, does not seem to influence them significantly, as all participants stated that they would choose the same profession regardless of earning more or less money. Finally, their employment status also has a considerable impact on their professional well-being. Whether they are substitute or permanent teachers directly affects their sense of professional well-being.

3. The participants describe the ideal level of well-being as a set of conditions that can exist within an environment dominated exclusively by positive emotions. Such an environment is built upon healthy relationships with colleagues and especially with the school head, the physical condition of the kindergarten facilities, the commuting distance from home, and the availability of materials necessary for the implementation of teaching activities.

4. Substitute kindergarten teachers experience professional well-being differently from permanent teachers. On the one hand, substitute teachers reported feeling professional well-being in relation to their profession; on the other hand, uncertainty regarding the following school year generates increased anxiety and stress. This uncertainty affects their professional well-being and consequently their overall teaching effectiveness. In contrast, permanent kindergarten teachers feel greater job security and plan their teaching with greater confidence, which contributes to maintaining their professional well-being.

The general conclusion of this study could serve as the starting point for an ongoing search for ways to develop, improve, and manage the overall well-being—and particularly the professional well-being—of preschool educators. Consequently, all necessary conditions should be established to promote changes and innovations in the educational process that lead to improved learning outcomes. Therefore, the present study could serve as a starting point for larger-scale research with a broader sample.

PROPOSALS FOR THE UTILIZATION OF THE RESEARCH FINDINGS

The findings of the present study portray a dynamic and emotionally committed educational staff that nevertheless requires greater institutional and psychological support. Moreover, the findings are consistent with the international literature emphasizing the importance of organizational well-being policies within the educational community (Hargreaves, 2019; Lomas et al., 2021).

The utilization of these findings could aim at maintaining preschool educators' positive relationship with their profession while simultaneously addressing the factors of stress and fatigue that appear to affect their daily functioning. Furthermore, the findings reveal that the professional well-being of preschool educators is not solely an individual matter, but is shaped through a complex system of interactions involving school climate, relationships with colleagues and administrative staff, organizational culture, and the demands of the educational framework.

From this perspective, the adoption of a systemic approach to school counseling becomes necessary, viewing teachers' well-being as a fundamental prerequisite for school resilience and effective educational functioning. School counseling can contribute substantially through interventions that strengthen collaboration, professional empowerment, psychosocial support, and the prevention of professional burnout.

At the same time, fostering a supportive and participatory school environment can strengthen educators' sense of security, acceptance, and professional satisfaction. Therefore, the professional well-being of kindergarten teachers affects not only their personal and professional functioning, but is also directly connected to the overall quality of the educational process and the creation of resilient school communities.

REFERENCES

Aelterman, A., Engels, N., Van Petegem, K., & Verhaeghe, J. P. (2007). The wellbeing of teachers in Flanders: The importance of a supportive school culture. *Educational Studies, 33*(3), 285–298. DOI: 10.1080/03055690701423085

Alagaraja, M. (2020). Wellbeing in the workplace: A new conceptual model and implications for practice. In Dhiman, S. (Ed.), *The Palgrave handbook of workplace well-being* (pp. 1–22). Palgrave Macmillan. DOI: 10.1007/978-3-030-02470-3_69-1

Anastassopoulos, A. (2018). *Teacher well-being: Dimensions and interconnections with the role of the principal-leader and the school climate* (Master's thesis, Hellenic Open University, School of Humanities, Studies in Education Program).

Angner, E. (2011). The evolution of eupathics: The historical roots of subjective measures of wellbeing. *International Journal of Wellbeing, 1*(1), 4–41. https://doi .org/XXXX. DOI: 10.5502/ijw.v1i1.14

Angner, E. (2011). The evolution of eupathics: The historical roots of subjective measures of wellbeing. *International Journal of Wellbeing, 1*(1), 4–41. DOI: 10.5502/ijw.v1i1.14

Benevene, P., De Stasio, S., & Fiorilli, C. (2020). Well-being of school teachers in their work environment. *Frontiers in Psychology, 11*, 1239. Advance online publication. DOI: 10.3389/fpsyg.2020.01239 PMID: 32903655

Bermejo-Toro, L., Prieto-Ursua, M., & Hernandez, V. (2016). Towards a model of teacher well-being: Personal and job resources involved in teacher burnout and engagement. *Educational Psychology, 36*(3), 481–501. DOI: 10.1080/01443410.2015.1005006

Brownett, T., Wilson, V., & Bowden, A. (2021). Wellbeing at work. In Manley, K., Wilson, V., & Oye, C. (Eds.), *International practice development in health and social care* (2nd ed., pp. 220–236). John Wiley & Sons. DOI: 10.1002/9781119698463.ch16

Cann, R. F., Riedel-Prabhakar, R., & Powell, D. (2021). A model of positive school leadership to improve teacher wellbeing. *International Journal of Applied Positive Psychology, 6*(3), 195–218. DOI: 10.1007/s41042-020-00045-5

Cherkowski, S. (2018). Positive teacher leadership: Building mindsets and capacities to grow wellbeing. *International Journal of Teacher Leadership, 9*(1), 63–78.

Cohen, L., Manion, L., & Morrison, K. (2008). *Research methods in education* (Kyrianakis, S., Mavrakis, M., Mitsopoulou, C., Bithara, P., & Filopoulou, M., Trans.). Metaichmio Publications.

Crisp, R. (2014). Well-being. In Zalta, E. N. (Ed.), *The Stanford encyclopedia of philosophy*. Stanford University., https://plato.stanford.edu/archives/win2014/entries/well-being/

Cui, L. (2022). The role of teacher-student relationships in predicting teachers' occupational wellbeing, emotional exhaustion, and enthusiasm. *Frontiers in Psychology*, *13*, 896813. Advance online publication. DOI: 10.3389/fpsyg.2022.896813 PMID: 35664194

Day, C., & Gu, Q. (2009). Teacher emotions: Well being and effectiveness. In Schutz, P. A., & Zembylas, M. (Eds.), *Advances in teacher emotion research: The impact on teachers' lives* (pp. 15–31). Springer. DOI: 10.1007/978-1-4419-0564-2_2

Delle Fave, A., Brdar, I., Freire, T., Vella-Brodrick, D., & Wissing, M. P. (2011). The eudaimonic and hedonic components of happiness: Qualitative and quantitative findings. *Social Indicators Research*, *100*(2), 185–207. DOI: 10.1007/s11205-010-9632-5

Devos, G., Bouckenooghe, D., Engels, N., Hotton, G., & Aelterman, A. (2007). An assessment of well- being of principals in Flemish primary schools. *Journal of Educational Administration*, *45*(1), 33–61. DOI: 10.1108/09578230710722449

Education Support Partnership. (2019). *Health survey 2017: The mental health and wellbeing of education professionals in the UK*. YouGov. https://www.educationsupport.org.uk/sites/default/files/education_staff_health_survey_2017.pdf

Eger, R. J., & Maridal, J. H. (2015). A statistical meta-analysis of the wellbeing literature. *International Journal of Wellbeing*, *5*(1), 45–74. DOI: 10.5502/ijw.v5i2.4

Fernandez-Molina, M., Hernandez-Prados, M. A., & Belmonte, M. L. (2019). Teacher emotional competence and well-being in the educational context. *International Journal of Environmental Research and Public Health*, *16*(20), 4065. Advance online publication. DOI: 10.3390/ijerph16204065

Fisher, J. W. (2020). Reconsidering spiritual well-being: Complexity, plurality and practice. *Religions*, *11*(1), 26. Advance online publication. DOI: 10.3390/rel11010026

Grant, C. A., Gardner, K., Cavendish, W., & Moltzen, R. (2021). The professional wellbeing of educators: A review. *Educational Research Review*, *34*, 100411. Advance online publication. DOI: 10.1016/j.edurev.2021.100411

Griva, E., & Stamou, A. G. (2014). *Investigating bilingualism in the school environment: Perspectives of teachers, students, and immigrant parents*. Kyriakidis Publications.

Hackman, J. R., & Oldham, G. R. (1980). *Work redesign*. Addison-Wesley.

Hallinger, P. (2003). Leading educational change: Reflections on the practice of instructional and transformational leadership. *Cambridge Journal of Education*, *33*(3), 329–352. DOI: 10.1080/0305764032000122005

Hargreaves, A. (2019). *Teacher well-being: Its meaning and its measurement* (OECD Education Working Papers No. 213). OECD Publishing. https://doi.org/ DOI: 10.1787/c1aa7a2d-en

Harter, J. K., Schmidt, F. L., & Keyes, C. L. M. (2002). Well-Being in the workplace and its relationship to Business Outcomes: A review of the Gallup studies. In Keyes, C. L., & Haidt, J. (Eds.), *Flourishing: The positive person and the good life* (pp. 205–224). American Psychological Association.

Helliwell, J. F., Layard, R., Sachs, J., & De Neve, J. E. (2020). World happiness report 2020. *Sustainable Development Solutions Network*. https://worldhappiness.report/ed/2020

Hone, L., Schofield, G., & Jarden, A. (2016). Conceptualizations of wellbeing: Insights from a prototype analysis on New Zealand workers. *New Zealand Journal of Human Resource Management*, *12*(1), 97–118.

Hoy, W. K., & Miskel, C. G. (2005). *Educational administration: Theory, research, and practice* (7th ed.). McGraw-Hill.

Iosifidis, T. (2003). *Analysis of qualitative data in the social sciences*. Kritiki Publications.

Isaris, P., & Pourkos, M. (2015). *Qualitative research in the social sciences*. National and Kapodistrian University of Athens, Department of Philosophy, Pedagogy and Psychology.

Jarden, A., & Roache, A. (2023). What is wellbeing? *International Journal of Environmental Research and Public Health*, *20*(6), 5006. Advance online publication. DOI: 10.3390/ijerph20065006 PMID: 36981914

Ji, Y. (2022). Teacher well-being: A literature review. *Frontiers in Psychology*, *13*, 903513. Advance online publication. DOI: 10.3389/fpsyg.2022.903513

Johns, G., & Saks, A. M. (2005). *Organizational Behaviour* (6th ed.). Pearson Education Canada Inc.

Karasek, R., & Theorell, T. (1990). *Healthy work: Stress, productivity, and the reconstruction of working life*. Basic Books.

Karasek, R. A. (1979). Job demands, job decision latitude, and mental strain: Implications for job redesign. *Administrative Science Quarterly*, *24*(2), 285–308. DOI: 10.2307/2392498

Katidou, E. (2019). *Teachers' well-being: Shaping factors and dimensions in primary education* (Master's thesis, University of Western Macedonia, School of Education, Department of Primary Education, Postgraduate Program).

Keyes, C. L. M., & Waterman, M. B. (2022). Pathways to flourishing: The dynamic interplay of psychological and social well-being. *The Journal of Positive Psychology*, *17*(2), 100–115. DOI: 10.1080/17439760.2021.1884477

Kim, H., Doiron, K., Warren, M. A., & Donaldson, S. I. (2018). The international landscape of positive psychology research: A systematic review. *International Journal of Wellbeing*, *8*(1), 50–70. DOI: 10.5502/ijw.v8i1.651

Kourkouni, A. (2020). *Professional well-being and factors affecting it: Perceptions of permanent and substitute primary education teachers* (Master's thesis, Hellenic Open University, Patras, Greece).

Kusma, B., Groneberg, D. A., Nienhaus, A., & Mache, S. (2012). Determinants of day care teachers' job satisfaction. *Central European Journal of Public Health*, *20*(3), 191–198. DOI: 10.21101/cejph.a3700 PMID: 23285519

Liargovas, P. (2023). *Introduction to scientific research*. Papazisis Publications.

Liargovas, P., Dermatis, Z., & Komninos, D. (2023). *Research methodology and scientific writing* (2nd ed.). Tziolas Publications.

Liu, Z. (2023). Transforming teaching: Wellbeing and professional practice. *Frontiers in Psychology*, *14*, 1192148. DOI: 10.3389/fpsyg.2023.1192148 PMID: 37397297

Lomas, T., Waters, L., Williams, P., Oades, L. G., & Kern, M. L. (2021). The dynamics of wellbeing: A systems approach. *The Lancet. Public Health*, *6*(7), e508–e513. DOI: 10.1016/S2468-2667(21)00025-9

Mercer, S., & Gregersen, T. (2020). *Teacher wellbeing*. Oxford University Press.

Michaelson, J., Mahony, S., & Schifferes, J. (2012). *Measuring wellbeing: A guide for practitioners*. New Economics Foundation.

Nind, M., Wiles, R., Bengry-Howell, A., & Crow, G. (2021). Ethical challenges in the researcher-participant relationship: Reflective ethical decision-making in qualitative research. *Qualitative Research*, *21*(2), 261–276. DOI: 10.1177/1468794118796365

OECD. (2020). *Supporting teachers' well-being: Insights from TALIS 2018*. OECD Publishing., DOI: 10.1787/53e2b1bd-

Pagán-Castaño, E., Sánchez-García, J., Garrigos-Simon, F. J., & Guijarro-García, M. (2021). The influence of management on teacher well-being and the development of sustainable schools. *Sustainability (Basel)*, *13*(6), 2909. DOI: 10.3390/su13052909

Pakarinen, E., Kiuru, N., Lerkkanen, M., Poikkeus, A., Siekkinen, M., & Nurmi, J. (2010). Classroom organization and teacher stress predict learning motivation in kindergarten children. *European Journal of Psychology of Education*, *25*(3), 281–300. DOI: 10.1007/s10212-010-0025-6

Pashiardis, P. (2004). *Educational leadership: From the period of benevolent indifference to the modern era*. Metaichmio Publications.

Pomaki, G., & Anagnostopoulou, T. (2003). A test and extension of the demand/control/social support model: Prediction of wellness/health outcomes in Greek teachers. *Psychology & Health*, *18*(4), 537–550. DOI: 10.1080/0887044031000147256

Pot, F. D. (2017). Workplace innovation and wellbeing at work. In Oeij, P., Rus, D., & Pot, F. (Eds.), *Workplace innovation: Aligning perspectives on health, safety and well-being* (pp. 95–110). Springer. DOI: 10.1007/978-3-319-56333-6_7

Robson, C. (2007). *Real world research: A resource for social scientists and practitioner-researchers*. Gutenberg - G. & K. Dardanos.

Ross, S. W., Romer, N., & Horner, R. H. (2012). Teacher well-being and the implementation of schoolwide positive behavior interventions and supports. *Journal of Positive Behavior Interventions*, *20*(10), 1–12.

Rusk, R. D., & Waters, L. E. (2013). Tracing the size, reach, impact, and breadth of positive psychology. *The Journal of Positive Psychology*, *8*(3), 207–221. DOI: 10.1080/17439760.2013.777766

Ryan, R. M., & Deci, E. L. (2017). *Self-determination theory: Basic psychological needs in motivation, development, and wellness*. Guilford Press. DOI: 10.1521/978.14625/28806

Ryff, C. D. (1989). Happiness is everything, or is it? Explorations on the meaning of psychological well-being. *Journal of Personality and Social Psychology*, *57*(6), 1069–1081. DOI: 10.1037/0022-3514.57.6.1069

Ryff, C. D., & Singer, B. H. (2015). Know thyself and become what you are: A eudaimonic approach to psychological well-being. *Journal of Happiness Studies*, *16*(1), 3–20. DOI: 10.1007/s10902-013-9504-1

Saaranen, T., Tossavainen, K., Turunen, H., & Vertio, H. (2007). Occupational well-being of school staff members: A structural equation model. *Health Education Research*, *22*(2), 248–260. DOI: 10.1093/her/cyl073 PMID: 16880218

Schina, E. M. (2016). *The professional well-being of primary education teachers and the factors determining it* (Master's thesis, University of Peloponnese, Department of Social and Educational Policy, Postgraduate Program: Educational Programs and Material - Formal, Informal and Distance Education).

Seidman, I. (2013). *Interviewing as qualitative research: A guide for researchers in education and the social sciences*. Teachers College Press.

Skaalvik, E. M., & Skaalvik, S. (2018). Job demands and job resources as predictors of teacher motivation and well-being. *Social Psychology of Education*, *21*(5), 1251–1275. DOI: 10.1007/s11218-018-9464-8

Travers, C. J. (2010). Current knowledge on the nature, prevalence, sources and potential impact of teacher stress. In Leka, T., & Houdmont, J. (Eds.), *Occupational health psychology* (pp. 23–54). Wiley-Blackwell.

Uchida, Y., Ogihara, Y., & Fukushima, S. (2015). Cultural construal of wellbeing: Theories and empirical evidence. In Glatzer, W., Camfield, L., Møller, V., & Rojas, M. (Eds.), *Global handbook of quality of life*. Springer. DOI: 10.1007/978-94-017-9178-6_38

Van Horn, J., Taris, T. W., Schaufeli, W. B., & Schreurs, P. J. G. (2004). The structure of occupational well-being: A study among Dutch teachers. *Journal of Occupational and Organizational Psychology*, *77*(3), 365–375. DOI: 10.1348/0963179041752718

Wang, F., Guo, J., & Yang, G. (2023). Study on positive psychology from 1999 to 2021: A bibliometric analysis. *Frontiers in Psychology*, *14*, 1101157. DOI: 10.3389/fpsyg.2023.1101157 PMID: 36935984

Warr, P. (1990). The measurement of well-being and other aspects of mental health. *Journal of Occupational Psychology*, *63*(3), 193–210. DOI: 10.1111/j.2044-8325.1990.tb00521.x

Warr, P. (2007). *Road improvement and poverty reduction in Laos*. Australian Agricultural and Resource Economics Society.

Wefald, A. J., Mills, M. J., Smith, M. R., & Downey, R. G. (2012). A comparison of three job engagement measures: Examining the factorial and criterion-related validity. *Applied Psychology. Health and Well-Being*, *4*(1), 67–90. DOI: 10.1111/j.1758-0854.2011.01059.x PMID: 26286971

Wolf, S., Torrente, C., McCoy, M., Rasheed, D., & Aber, J. L. (2015). Cumulative risk and teacher well-being in the Democratic Republic of the Congo. *Comparative Education Review*, *59*(4), 717–742. DOI: 10.1086/682902

World Health Organization. (2015). [*A European policy framework supporting action across government and society for health and well-being*. World Health Organization, Regional Office for Europe.]. *Health*, •••, 2020.

Zhao, Q. (2022). On the role of teachers' professional identity and well-being in their professional development. *Frontiers in Psychology*, *13*, 913708. DOI: 10.3389/fpsyg.2022.913708 PMID: 35719489

Chapter 6
The Prevention of Gender-Based Violence in the School Context: Students' Perspectives

Maria Kouroutsidou
http://orcid.org/0000-0002-0345-541X
University of the Aegean, Rhodes, Greece

Katerina Karanikola
University of the Aegean, Rhodes, Greece

Nikolaos G Raptis
University of the Aegean, Rhodes, Greece

ABSTRACT

In the school environment, where identities, attitudes, and values are formed, the need to prevent and address violence takes on particular importance. Nevertheless, the reality of education shows that violence remains a part of school life, often with gendered dimensions, a fact that makes its systematic study and effective management necessary. This study aims to help fill this gap by focusing on the views, experiences, and suggestions of high school students regarding gender-based violence in the school environment. The purpose of the study is to investigate how gender-based violence is understood and experienced in the school context through the narratives of high school students themselves. The research was conducted using a qualitative-interpretive approach, through semi-structured interviews with high school students in Rhodes, while the data were analyzed using thematic analysis.

DOI: 10.4018/979-8-3373-9420-6.ch006

The results indicate that gender-based violence is recognized as behavior linked to gender and/or sexuality and manifests in multiple forms, with verbal violence being the most prevalent.

INTRODUCTION

At the international level, the discussion on gender-based violence in the school environment is framed by the concept of School-Related Gender-Based Violence (SRGBV), which is used to describe phenomena such as sexual harassment, sexism, misogynistic behavior, and other forms of gender-based abuse experienced by girls, boys, and non-binary individuals in school, with disproportionate impacts on girls and students who do not conform to dominant gender norms. Although the term has been extensively studied in low- and middle-income countries, it remains largely invisible in the scientific and institutional discourse of high-income countries, despite the documented presence of the phenomenon there as well. This absence is linked to stereotypes and misconceptions that foster the illusion that schools in these societies are free from such problems (Wescott & Roberts, 2025).

Despite international recognition of the issue's importance, research in Greece shows limited engagement with gender-based violence in schools. While school bullying has been extensively addressed in the literature, the gender dimension remains under-explored, with very few relevant studies (Artinopoulou et al., 2016; Bouna, 2018). This creates a significant knowledge gap, which hinders our understanding of children's experiences and the development of effective interventions.

In school, where young people's identities, attitudes, and values are formed, the need to eliminate violence takes on even greater significance. However, reality shows that violence remains an integral part of school life, often manifesting with gendered nuances, a fact that makes it necessary to study and address it in depth. Experiences and suggestions from high school students regarding gender-based violence.

Through the views, experiences, and suggestions of high school students regarding gender-based violence, this project seeks to highlight an experiential dimension of the phenomenon that is often absent from academic discourse. The voices of adolescents are crucial, as they reflect not only their experience as victims or witnesses of violence, but also their perceptions of the role of the school community and the possible solutions that can be implemented.

GENDER-BASED VIOLENCE IN THE SCHOOL SETTING

All children have the right to a safe and supportive school environment that allows them to grow, succeed, and reach their full potential. Nevertheless, many students, particularly in developing countries, experience daily forms of gender-based violence—both direct and indirect—that significantly impact their social lives and educational trajectories (Murgor, Korir, & Ogoma, 2020).

Violence in the school environment constitutes a violation of children's fundamental rights and is a complex, multifactorial phenomenon with a strong gender dimension. In most cases, its roots lie in gender inequalities, dominant social norms, and the discrimination that is perpetuated and reproduced within society (UNESCO, Plan International, & Mahidol University, 2014). Sex-based school-related violence (SRGBV) is recognized as a global phenomenon, observed in diverse social and cultural settings and affecting millions of children, families, and communities. Its occurrence is not linked to a single institution or culture, but to broader structures and norms that reproduce gendered power relations (UNESCO & UN Women, 2016).

At the same time, gender-based violence in schools is linked to broader social phenomena, such as domestic violence or its portrayal in the media, and calls for critical reflection on the role of schools and the professionals involved. As Silkenbeumer and Pérez (2010) emphasize, although many schools implement violence prevention initiatives, there is a significant lack of a coherent framework for reflection and professional guidance that could enhance their effectiveness.

DEFINITION OF GENDER-BASED SCHOOL VIOLENCE

Gender-based school violence (SRGBV) refers to any act or threat of sexual, physical, or psychological abuse that occurs within or around the school environment and is linked to gender norms and stereotypes, which are reinforced by unequal power relations (UNESCO & UN Women, 2016). It is not limited to the physical school setting but can also occur on the way to or from school, at home, in the community, or in the digital space. This violence can occur between students, from teachers or other staff members toward students, from students toward teachers, as well as among school staff members (UNGEI, 2020).

In terms of the forms it can take, school-related gender-based violence (SRGBV) includes sexual, physical, and psychological violence (UNESCO, 2019). Specifically, sexual violence can manifest as unwanted sexual contact, sexual harassment, rape or attempted rape, coercion, sexual comments and jokes, as well as the sharing of sexual content (UNESCO & UN Women, 2016). Physical violence involves assaults, beatings, corporal punishment, and destruction of personal property, while psychological violence manifests itself through verbal or emotional abuse, social exclusion, or intimidation (UNESCO, 2019).

In addition, Leach (2008) distinguishes between direct and indirect gender-based violence: the former is characterized by a clear sexual dimension, such as in cases of sexual harassment, touching, verbal abuse, intimidation, or forced sexual acts. The latter, also known as symbolic gender-based violence, includes less visible forms that are reproduced through everyday school practices, such as the application of gender-differentiated punishments.

In many school settings, gender-based violence is perceived by male and female students as a normal and expected part of daily life, within a widespread culture of tolerance or silence toward violence (UNGEI, 2024). As Heiliger (2001) points out, even behaviors such as physical altercations or verbal attacks are often not recognized as forms of violence but are considered expected or developmentally normal. The normalization of these behaviors not only makes it difficult to recognize them as forms of violence but also acts as a deterrent to reporting them, thereby allowing them to persist (UNGEI, 2024).

Key factors contributing to the occurrence of school-related gender-based violence (SRGBV) include structural and power-based inequalities between women and men, girls and boys, as well as harmful social perceptions of masculinity and patriarchy (UNGEI, 2024). Social and cultural stereotypes systematically attribute more power to men and boys, perpetuating narratives that legitimize violence (UNGEI, 2020). According to Heiliger (2001), the social acceptance of aggression as a means of affirming male identity reinforces deeply rooted notions of dominance and renders the use of violence a socially acceptable expression of masculine behavior. At the same time, however, Silkenbeumer and Pérez (2010) point out that simply equating violence with masculinity is insufficient, as it overlooks the common functions and deeper structures of violence across both genders. An analysis of the relationship between gender and violence requires a nuanced approach that takes social and cultural contexts into account.

Furthermore, school violence can serve as a means of shaping gender identity. This occurs, for example, through sexist comments made by boys toward girls or the exclusion of female students who deviate from traditional appearance standards (UNGEI, 2020). Bouna's qualitative study (2018) highlights that many students perceive violent behavior as "natural" or "inevitable" in men, while participation in violent acts is often a means of fulfilling their social role. The expression of various forms of violence thus contributes to the perpetuation of gender hierarchies.

Finally, the absence of an adequate institutional framework and the lack of dialogue on issues of gender and sexuality exacerbate the vulnerability of students who belong to the LGBTQI+ community (UNGEI, 2020). In this context, it is worth noting that the school, as an institutional and social space, plays an active role in the construction and enforcement of gender identities. As Silkenbeumer and Pérez (2010) note, it is a space where certain forms of femininity and masculinity are recognized and reinforced, while others are questioned or rejected. These processes interact with class, cultural, and generational factors and shape expectations regarding the behavior of both students and teachers.

However, despite the documented prevalence and social characteristics of gender-based violence in schools, its dimension as a gendered phenomenon is often downplayed in the literature. In many studies, only sexual violence is recognized as gender-based, as it primarily affects girls, while other forms—such as psychological or physical violence—are not included in the same framework (Burton, 2005).

THE ROLE OF TEACHERS AND THE SCHOOL COMMUNITY

The prevention and management of school violence, including incidents with a gender-based dimension, require the collective involvement of all members of the school community. Teachers, principals, students, and parents are called upon to actively contribute to the creation of a safe, supportive, and inclusive environment capable of preventing or limiting the occurrence of violent behavior (Panagiotopoulos & Mousidou, 2014). It is, therefore, important for all members of the school community to collaborate effectively, forming a united front against violence, with consistent attitudes and clear messages that reinforce a positive and protective school climate (Murgor, Korir, & Ogoma, 2020).

However, as Kokkidu and Mygdanis (2024) point out, teachers are called upon to meet increased demands, without always having the necessary resources to support students experiencing complex social situations, such as poverty or domestic violence. Despite these difficulties, the importance of the role of the school and teachers, as well as the crucial contribution of parents and guardians, is highlighted within the context of a comprehensive approach to preventing and addressing violence and bullying in the school environment.

Teachers

Teachers play a pivotal role in creating a safe educational environment. Their ability to identify problems early on, intervene effectively, and build trusting relationships with students strengthens the school's educational climate. Their empathy and social sensitivity contribute to strengthening the student community and fostering solidarity. In this context, it is crucial that they promote open dialogue, encouraging the honest expression of thoughts and feelings. Inaction in the face of incidents of violence can be interpreted as tolerance and reinforce a sense of impunity (UNESCO, 2019).

With regard to the gender dimension of violence, all teachers need training to reflect on their personal attitudes and expectations regarding gender. Awareness of stereotypical perceptions is essential to prevent them from influencing the learning experiences and performance of boys and girls. Although male teachers can play a positive role in preventing gender-based violence, the international literature also documents cases of their involvement in incidents of sexual abuse or exploitation, particularly in developing countries, without the imposition of sanctions—a phenomenon that is, however, in the minority (Kouroutsidou & Raptis, 2021).

Today's teachers must possess the skills to identify educational inequalities and take action to ensure the equal participation of all students. Promoting gender equality within the school and taking a clear stance against forms of gender-based violence are key aspects of their professional role (Council of Europe, 2019). Their emergence as agents of change is crucial for the transition to a school environment free from gender-based discrimination and violence (Murgor et al., 2020).

The Principal

International literature highlights the critical role of the school principal in preventing and addressing violence within the school environment. The principal is considered a central figure in school administration and plays a decisive role in fostering a positive and supportive school climate, which directly influences the likelihood of aggressive behaviors (Cornell & Huang, 2016). School climate can either mitigate or reinforce violent behaviors depending on how relationships, norms, and expectations are structured within the educational community. In this context, promoting collaboration among all members of the school community is a key responsibility of school leadership, aimed at preventing and addressing violence effectively (Crawford & Burns, 2022). Establishing clear, fair, and consistent behavioral expectations in cooperation with teachers further strengthens preventive efforts.

Beyond crisis management, the principal is expected to adopt a proactive and accessible leadership role, ensuring that students feel comfortable seeking support when needed. Maintaining a calm and supportive stance is essential for the effective handling of bullying incidents and for preventing escalation. In addition, school leaders are encouraged to engage teachers and parents in the organization of collaborative school activities (Epstein et al., 2019). Student participation in such activities enhances creativity, emotional expression, and peer interaction, while also strengthening social relationships within the school community. These processes contribute to improved school engagement and a reduction in deviant or aggressive behaviors (Wang & Degol, 2016).

Students

Students play a crucial role in preventing school and gender-based violence, as they are not only recipients but also active participants in such interventions. Their involvement in structured experiential activities can strengthen positive behaviors and reduce aggressive tendencies. Evaluation findings from the "Stark ohne Gewalt" program indicate that students reported a reduction in aggressive behaviors following participation, while female students demonstrated significant increases in empathy and self-confidence, particularly through engagement in arts-based workshops characterized by supportive and positive relational environments (Kröger, Klann, & Kaps, 2009).

At the same time, reliance on student self-reports in program evaluation highlights the importance of systematically integrating students' perspectives into the design, implementation, and assessment of educational interventions. Research emphasizes that student voice is essential for developing democratic and inclusive school environments, as it enables more accurate and meaningful evaluations of educational practices (Gillett-Swan & Baroutsis, 2023).

Beyond participation in prevention programs, contemporary research underscores the complexity of student involvement in school violence, which cannot be adequately understood through the binary categorization of "perpetrator" and "victim." Instead, involvement is often fluid and context-dependent, with students occupying multiple or shifting roles over time (Armitage, 2021). Empirical studies further show that a considerable proportion of students involved in aggressive behaviors have also experienced victimization, highlighting the cyclical and reciprocal nature of peer violence in school settings (Modecki et al., 2020).

In addition, peer dynamics research identifies a broader range of participant roles, including defenders, reinforcers, outsiders, and passive bystanders, all of which play a significant role in either sustaining or disrupting bullying processes (Chow et al., 2022). These roles are structurally embedded within classroom social systems and influence group norms, peer reinforcement patterns, and behavioral outcomes.

Understanding these differentiated roles is essential for effective prevention, as successful interventions must address not only direct victims and perpetrators but also the wider peer ecology that maintains or challenges violent behavior (Gaffney et al., 2021).

Students' Experiences with Gender-Based Violence in the School Environment

Research on gender-based violence in school contexts highlights its multidimensional and cross-cultural nature, with evidence consistently pointing to both gendered patterns of victimization and variation across forms of violence. A qualitative study conducted by Tristiana et al. (2023) among adolescent girls in Indonesia illustrates that students may experience multiple intersecting forms of violence, including verbal, physical, sexual, and online abuse. These experiences are often accompanied by emotional consequences such as guilt, shame, and helplessness, which contribute to silence and difficulties in seeking support.

Quantitative evidence from European contexts supports these findings while also emphasizing gender-differentiated patterns of victimization. For instance, research in Germany indicates that girls are more frequently exposed to verbal, social, and sexual harassment, whereas boys report higher levels of physical violence and exposure to direct aggression (Melzer & Schubarth, 2006). Notably, some forms of violence, particularly sexual harassment, tend to be normalized or minimized, especially in relation to female students.

Similar patterns are observed in the Greek educational context. Empirical findings by Buna (2018) suggest that boys are more often involved in physical and verbal aggression, while girls report higher exposure to relational and indirect forms of bullying. Cyberbullying emerges as a shared domain of victimization and perpetration, reflecting the expansion of violent behaviors into digital spaces.

These patterns are further corroborated by large-scale national evidence. The study by Artinopoulou, Bampali, and Nikolopoulos (2016), based on a sample of over 36,000 students, confirms statistically significant gender differences in experiences of violence from both peers and teachers. While boys report higher levels of physical victimization, girls more frequently experience relational forms of mistreatment. Importantly, the findings also highlight the broader psychological impact of victimization, including emotional distress, social withdrawal, and reduced help-seeking behaviors, underscoring the long-term consequences of school violence on students' well-being.

RESEARCH METHODOLOGY

Originality and Significance of the Research

Gender-based violence in the school environment constitutes an experience that, although affecting a significant number of children—primarily girls—often remains underreported or insufficiently recognized. Despite the extensive research interest in school violence and bullying within Greek literature, the gender dimension of these phenomena remains relatively underexplored. Existing studies in the Greek language appear limited in number and scope (Artinopoulou et al., 2016; Bouna, 2018), and as Kouroutsidou and Raptis (2021) note, the issue has not yet been examined to the extent required by its social and educational significance.

The present study seeks to address this research gap by focusing on students' personal experiences, perceptions, and suggestions. In doing so, it aims to contribute to a more nuanced, experiential understanding of gender-based violence within the school context, foregrounding adolescents' perspectives and lived realities.

Purpose of the Research and Research Questions

The purpose of the present study is to explore high school students' views, experiences, and suggestions regarding gender-based violence in the school environment.

This objective is addressed through the following research questions:

1. How do students perceive the concept of gender-based violence within the school environment?
2. How do students evaluate the role of the school, parents, and teachers in the prevention and management of gender-based violence?
3. What actions do students propose for the prevention and management of gender-based violence in schools?

Research Approach

The design of the present study was determined by its purpose and the research questions formulated (Cohen, Manion, & Morrison, 2008). To explore high school students' views, experiences, and suggestions regarding gender-based violence in the school environment, a qualitative-interpretive approach was adopted. This approach focuses on understanding how individuals construct and interpret their social reality within specific contexts (Mason, 2011).

Qualitative research methods enable an in-depth and dynamic exploration of social phenomena, emphasizing the meanings and interpretations that individuals attribute to their experiences (Vrasidas, 2014). In this framework, attention is given to everyday experiences emerging from participants' natural settings, while the researcher acts as the primary instrument of data collection and interpretation (Isari & Pourkos, 2015).

Sampling

In qualitative research, the aim of sampling is not statistical generalization, but the in-depth understanding of the phenomenon under investigation. The process of sample selection significantly influences the quality of the data and, consequently, the validity of the conclusions (Patton, 2002; Isari & Pourkos, 2015).

In the present study, convenience sampling was employed, a strategy in which participants are selected based on their availability and the researcher's ease of access to them (Patton, 2002). A total of ten students (five boys and five girls) from the first, second, and third grades of high schools in Rhodes participated in the study. This approach was chosen for practical reasons, including participant accessibility and the facilitation of data collection, although it is widely acknowledged as a non-probability sampling method that prioritizes feasibility over representativeness (Isari & Pourkos, 2015).

Data Collection and Analysis

Within the context of the present study, the semi-structured interview was selected as the primary data collection tool, as it facilitates the in-depth exploration of students' experiences, perceptions, and values regarding gender-based violence in the school environment. It provides the researcher with the opportunity to approach the phenomenon under study through the personal perspective of the participants, highlighting their own voices. The interactive nature of the interview allows for the flexible adaptation of the process in real time and for a focus on themes that may not have been anticipated in advance (Isari & Pourkos, 2015).

The analysis of the qualitative data was conducted through thematic analysis, which involves a systematic process of identifying, organizing, and interpreting recurring patterns of meaning within the dataset, allowing access to collective ways of meaning-making and shared experiences (Braun & Clarke, 2012). The researcher identifies a variety of patterns, placing emphasis on those directly related to the research questions, which consequently guide the analytical process. Thematic analysis does not approach themes as "ready-made" categories that are simply revealed, but rather as constructions that emerge through the research process itself. It constitutes a flexible methodological approach that can be adapted to different theoretical frameworks.

PRESENTATION OF THE RESEARCH FINDINGS

Students' Views on the Concept of Gender-Based Violence

In the first research question, students were asked to describe what they understand when they hear the term "gender-based violence." Their responses indicate that, for most participants, this concept is directly associated with gender or sexuality and is perceived as a form of mistreatment and offense. They associated it with behaviors expressed because someone is a boy or a girl. As they stated, "it is violence coming from boys toward girls or from girls toward boys" (S1), "gender-based violence is when someone behaves badly toward another person because they are a boy or a girl" (S2), and "gender-based violence is when someone treats another person badly because they are a boy or because they are a girl. For example, when they insult or make fun of them" (S3).

In the same context, several students emphasized that "gender-based violence is when I either comment negatively on you, push you, or psychologically abuse you because you are a girl or because you are a boy" (S1), while some pointed out that "it is when there is any kind of violence between genders, between girls and boys" (S4). Others referred directly to the dimension of discrimination, stating that it is "the existence of discrimination depending on each person's gender" (S3), or that "I did not know what gender-based violence was… I understood that it is when a man imposes himself on a woman" (S9). Similarly, it was mentioned that it concerns "violence that occurs because someone is different in terms of their gender" (S5), or that it is expressed "when someone is treated badly simply because they are a girl or a boy" (S7).

The dimension of sexuality was also reflected in the students' responses, as several participants pointed out that "the negative behaviors experienced by some individuals" occur "because of their gender or sexual orientation" (S10). There were also students who admitted that they had never encountered the term before, stating: "gender-based violence… I have never heard of it. In some way, both genders are degraded. And mainly from the male toward the female" (S6).

Beyond the definition itself, the majority of students focused on the forms that gender-based violence may take. They referred to several different types, with verbal violence being the most frequently mentioned, followed by physical, psychological, and sexual violence. As participants stated, "it can be verbal or physical" (S1), "there is verbal violence. There is physical violence as well. And emotional, let's say. Psychological, emotional" (S2), while others emphasized that it is "mainly verbal, but also physical assaults" (S7). One characteristic example referred to the image of "a couple who may be married, where the man abuses the woman, beats her, but also demeans her and shouts at her, which is both physical and verbal violence" (S8). This perception was further reinforced by the observation that "physical, verbal, psychological… all of these exist at school" (S8), and that "there is verbal, physical, psychological violence… and sexual harassment" (S9). In some cases, participants also referred to verbal attacks and comments associated with appearance or humiliation, such as when "insulting someone is verbal violence… and within the genders there are many people who try to belittle others through negative comments about appearance and everything else" (S4).

Finally, a large proportion of the responses placed emphasis on stereotypes regarding men and women and their connection to power, strength, and gender identity. Several students observed that "some people believe that their gender is stronger and more important" (S1) and that "men must be superior, and they feel the need to demonstrate this" (S4). Some described this more directly, stating that "it happens more often from boys toward girls because boys believe they are better than girls" (S5), or "when the woman does not have the power to speak..." (S6). In the same context, participants mentioned that "it is when one gender uses stereotypical ideas for its own benefit" (S1), that "there are stereotypes... people judge what is different" (S2), and that "perhaps one person tries to prove that they are better than the other... so that it appears that the entire gender group has this weakness" (S3). Furthermore, it was stated that "usually men exercise physical violence... because they are physically stronger and believe that women cannot defend themselves" (S7). In other cases, violence was associated with the imposition of a "male role," as reflected in statements such as "usually the man abuses the woman... he tries to demonstrate the male role" (S8), or "I believe it happens because they try, in some way, to impose themselves and demonstrate the male role within their marriage" (S3). Similar perceptions were reflected in statements such as "by nature, men are stronger... in the past there was the idea that they were superior" (S9), and "society has instilled the idea that men are stronger; stereotypes exist" (S10).

Students' Experiences with Gender-Based Violence in the School Environment

The second research question explored the forms of gender-based violence that students had experienced or observed within the school environment and the ways in which these forms were associated with gender. The responses were numerous and varied; however, almost all participants focused on verbal violence, which they described as the most common form. As they characteristically noted: "Most incidents are verbal, such as teasing and comments" (S2), "Usually it happens through words and mocking" (S1), and "Nowadays it is mostly verbal, through comments and insults" (S4). In addition, several students added that verbal violence often includes "sexist comments... which are violence, but people become so used to them that they seem normal" (S10).

According to the narratives of most students, verbal violence is primarily expressed through comments and mockery targeting appearance, body image, or clothing. Some students specifically mentioned that there are "comments about appearance, about the body... which can be very hurtful" (S4), while others emphasized that "mockery and comments about appearance are bullying" (S6). In the same context, participants also referred to "mocking the way someone dresses or their body"

(S8) as a common phenomenon, while it was further noted that "students who dress in a more 'feminine' way… are criticized" (S2).

The targeting of students who display a different gender expression or sexual orientation was also strongly reflected in the participants' accounts. The majority of responses included relevant examples. As described by the students: "In my class, they used to comment on a student because he was homosexual… they said offensive things about his sexuality" (S4), "when there is a boy with more feminine behavior… all the boys will go and make fun of him" (S3), or "a boy who was more feminine was constantly mocked" (S9). Similar incidents were mentioned by other participants, who stated that "they may mock a boy who behaves in a more feminine way" (S6, S7), while one student commented that "yes, such things happen, these kinds of issues are observed… boys targeting more feminine boys" (S3). Likewise, another student explained: "A boy who is a little more feminine… gets mocked" (S2). In the same context, it was emphasized that "they target students who appear more vulnerable… because of their appearance, opinions, or sexual orientation" (S8), while another participant referred to the "isolation of students because of their appearance or because they hold different views on sexual matters" (S10).

Beyond verbal violence and targeting, a significant number of students also referred to physical violence. Most participants agreed that this form of violence is observed mainly among boys. As they stated: "mostly boys get into fights" (S2), "among boys it is more common to fight physically" (S7), and "physical assaults usually come from boys… they have this physical strength" (S6). Furthermore, it was noted that "boys find it easier to engage in physical violence. That is how they have been raised" (S10). Nevertheless, several students emphasized that girls are also involved, although less frequently: "At first I thought boys showed more aggression… but I have also seen girls fighting physically" (S3), and "there are fights, mostly among boys, but girls also fight sometimes" (S8). One student additionally stated: "boys are more violent… but girls can also fight or engage in verbal violence" (S3).

At the same time, several students underlined that there are differences between genders in the ways violence is expressed. As they noted: "boys are more physical, girls more verbal" (S3), "boys usually fight physically, while girls mostly use words" (S2), and "boys may fight through physical assaults, whereas girls tend to do it more through comments" (S4). In the same context, one participant observed that "boys engage more in physical fights, while girls express it more verbally—because girls do not have the same physical strength" (S1).

Finally, fewer students referred specifically to sexual harassment and sexist comments, although they emphasized that these constitute existing forms of violence. As participants stated: "sexist comments about girls have been heard" (S4), "boys make sexist comments toward girls. Of course that is violence" (S10), "there is also sexual harassment" (S9), and "sexist comments and insinuations have been made"

(S8). Some students clarified that "in my school at least, no sexual violence has occurred" (S6), or that "I have not seen sexual violence at school" (S9). At the same time, several participants focused on the attitudes of peers, observing a tendency to normalize such behaviors, stating that "there are certain teasing behaviors that are not considered real violence… hearing a comment is seen as normal" (S7), or that "teasing exists, but many students consider it a joke" (S5). On the other hand, some participants emphasized that "sexist comments are violence, but nowadays they are so common that people see them as something ordinary" (S10).

Students' Views on the Role of the School Community in Addressing Gender-Based Violence

In the third research question, students were asked to evaluate the role of the school, parents, teachers, and classmates in the prevention and management of gender-based violence. Their responses highlighted different experiences and perspectives, revealing a variety of ways in which such incidents are either addressed or neglected.

The majority of students focused on the attitudes of teachers, pointing out their contradictory responses. As participants stated: "some teachers react appropriately… but there are also some who are indifferent" (S3), "some teachers ignore it and pay no attention" (S4), and "some teachers react properly… others do nothing" (S9). At the same time, it was mentioned that "the teachers saw it, but they did not say anything. They considered it a joke" (S1), or that "there are teachers who are indifferent, they simply teach their lesson and leave" (S4). On the other hand, some students emphasized that "teachers tried to talk to the students involved… but it had no result" (S10), while others noted that "teachers intervene… and there have even been suspensions" (S8). In certain narratives, it was also reported that "there are teachers who genuinely care… and try to talk with the students" (S9), or that "some teachers will help, while others remain indifferent" (S5).

Several students also referred to institutional shortcomings, mainly emphasizing the lack of supervision. As they reported: "there were no teachers on duty… there was nobody there at that moment" (S6), "there is nobody supervising" (S7), "there is not enough supervision during breaks" (S9), or even that "these incidents happen because there is nobody to stop them" (S9). Some participants added that "they do not pay attention. They will not engage in discussion; they simply hear what happened and move on without dealing with it" (S4). Nevertheless, there were also cases in which the school intervened: "they came afterward and separated them" or "they were punished with suspension" (S1).

Particular emphasis was placed by many students on the role of parents. As they stated, "parents play a major role… they should intervene whether the child is exercising or experiencing violence" (S7), while others underlined that "parents can give advice… but children usually prefer not to involve them" (S6). One participant mentioned that "parents should cultivate proper behavior and equality between genders" (S3). Many responses connected violence with the family environment, noting that "many individuals reproduce what they observe in the family environment" (S5), "if parents hit their children, then those children do the same" (S1), or that "those who exercise violence learn it from their family… or face family-related problems" (S9). Within the same context, one participant referred to "people who have learned such behaviors because that is what their parents taught them" (S4), while another observed that "if someone displays negative behavior, it may originate from the home environment or from harmful peer groups" (S6).

The majority of students also emphasized the importance of cooperation between school and family. Their responses indicated that "parents should take a position and communicate with the school administration" (S10), and that "parents should cooperate with the school in order to be aware of their children's behavior" (S8). Some participants added that "parents should be informed… although many children do not speak openly" (S9), or that "parents and teachers can work together to find a solution" (S1). In the same context, one student highlighted that "teachers should inform parents…" (S5), while another emphasized that "cooperation is necessary… otherwise parents and teachers perceive things differently" (S2). Finally, one participant stressed that "yes, I believe it is important in order for the problem to be solved" (S7).

The responses also reflected the dimension of empathy, or more frequently, the lack of it. Some students referred to the minimization of the seriousness of such incidents, stating that "they said nothing… the teachers saw it… they considered it funny" (S2), or that "people do not understand how serious it would be if something similar happened to their own child or to someone close to them. They simply do not realize how serious it is" (S7). Regarding peers, the descriptions indicated that students often adopt an indifferent stance: "they were just watching and laughing" (S1), "I was standing far away, I looked for a moment and then stopped paying attention" (S1), and "the students who observed the incident… did not care. They heard about it and moved on" (S4). Another student added that "other students usually support the person exercising violence… it is very rare for someone to tell them to stop" (S9).

DISCUSSION AND CONCLUSIONS OF THE RESEARCH

Students' Views on the Concept of Gender-Based Violence

The students' descriptions indicate that the concept of gender-based violence is directly associated with gender and sexuality, while at the same time recognizing multiple forms of expression and stereotypical perceptions that sustain it.

The students' narratives converge on the view that gender-based violence is understood as targeted behavior attributed to gender and/or sexuality. Participants described situations in which individuals become recipients of mistreatment, devaluation, or offensive behavior precisely "because they are a boy or a girl" or because of their sexual orientation. This understanding is aligned with the definition of school-related gender-based violence as acts or threats of sexual, physical, or psychological abuse associated with gender norms and unequal power relations (UNESCO & UN Women, 2016), and is consistent with the conceptualization of gender as a socially and culturally constructed category embedded within institutions and power relations (Meissner, 2008). At a comparative level, research findings from German schools demonstrate that students' definitions of "what constitutes violence" are strongly mediated by gender roles and cultural representations of what is considered "acceptable," thereby confirming the distinctly gendered dimension of such perceptions (Melzer & Schubarth, 2006).

At the same time, students recognized a broad spectrum of forms of gender-based violence, with verbal violence emerging most prominently. Participants referred to derogatory or ironic comments regarding appearance and clothing, as well as to physical, psychological, and sexual forms of violence. This typology is consistent with international conceptualizations of gender-based violence (UNESCO, 2019; UNESCO & UN Women, 2016; WHO, 2002) and, particularly in relation to its verbal dimension, may also be interpreted through the concept of symbolic violence, namely invisible and socially normalized practices of power reproduced through language and cultural mechanisms (Bourdieu, 1991). On a theoretical level, the verbal and sexist dimension has been identified as a typical manifestation of gender-based violence within the school environment (Heiliger, 2001). Comparatively, empirical studies document both its widespread occurrence and the gendered forms it assumes, with verbal and indirect violence appearing frequent and differentiated according to gender (Bouna, 2018; Melzer & Schubarth, 2006; Sakka & Markos, 2013).

Furthermore, the students' narratives consistently reflected persistent gender stereotypes: men were portrayed as "stronger" or "superior," while the exercise of violence was associated with the demonstration or imposition of a "male role." This pattern is linked to harmful perceptions of masculinity and patriarchal hierarchies that reproduce gender-based violence (UNGEI, 2020; UNGEI, 2024), as well as to theoretical approaches concerning normative masculinities and gendered power structures (Connell, 2006). At a theoretical level, the process of socialization highlights the role of significant adults—parents and teachers—in shaping and reinforcing, or alternatively discouraging, specific gendered behaviors (Kouroutsidou & Raptis, 2021). In line with this perspective, quantitative findings indicate that adolescents more frequently attribute aggression to boys—often perceiving it as "expected"—while associating girls with indirect or verbal forms of violence, a pattern that reflects the aforementioned hierarchies (Sakka & Markos, 2013).

Finally, although the term "gender-based violence" was not familiar to all participants, the students' descriptions demonstrated a clear recognition of the related practices and their connection to gender hierarchies. The international literature emphasizes the need for greater terminological clarity and institutional cultivation of the concept of school-related gender-based violence, so that such practices may be systematically named and recognized (UNESCO & UN Women, 2016). The relevant discussion also highlights an additional difficulty: the gendered dimension of violence is often underestimated, as only sexual violence tends to be explicitly recognized as gender-based, whereas other forms, such as psychological or physical violence, are not always clearly included within the same framework (Burton, 2005).

Overall, students' views on gender-based violence are aligned with international definitions, recognize multiple forms of expression—with particular emphasis on the verbal dimension—and are mediated by stereotypical gender expectations.

Students' Experiences with Gender-Based Violence in the School Environment

The students' descriptions reveal that gender-based violence within the school environment is experienced in multiple ways and manifests itself at different levels, ranging from verbal and physical violence to sexual harassment. Their experiences reveal not only gender-based differentiations but also the normalization of many behaviors, a factor that renders the recognition and management of violence particularly complex.

The students' narratives highlighted verbal violence as the most widespread form, with frequent references to teasing, insults, and sexist comments. The international literature defines verbal violence as offensive or degrading language aimed at humiliation and intimidation (UNESCO, 2019), while Tillmann et al. (1999) emphasize that it may lead to serious psychological consequences. The United Nations (2006) further underlines that systematic verbal abuse functions as a mechanism of psychological degradation, negatively affecting the victim's social integration. At the empirical level, similar experiences were documented in the qualitative study conducted by Tristiana et al. (2023), in which female students described systematic verbal harassment by classmates, while Melzer and Schubarth (2006) recorded higher levels of exposure to verbal harassment among girls compared to boys. In the SPEAK! study (Maschke & Stecher, 2021), more than half of the students reported sexist or sexual comments within the school environment, thus confirming the extent of the phenomenon.

Another central finding concerns the targeting of students who do not conform to dominant gender norms, particularly boys displaying a more "feminine" gender expression, as well as references to sexuality serving as grounds for mockery or social exclusion. This phenomenon may be understood on two interconnected levels: at the level of peer groups and at the level of broader social structures. Gugel (2018) notes that adolescent peer groups tend to reject deviant behaviors, reproduce hierarchies, and unite against what is perceived as "different," thereby intensifying processes of targeting and exclusion. At the same time, Schröttle (2010) emphasizes that forms of violence associated with gender or sexuality do not constitute isolated acts of aggression, but rather reproduce social inequalities, as they are rooted in patriarchal and heteronormative structures of power. Furthermore, it has been pointed out that the absence of an institutional framework and open dialogue regarding issues of gender and sexuality increases the vulnerability of LGBTQI+ students (UNGEI, 2020), while the school, as an institution, actively contributes to the construction and enforcement of gender identities by reinforcing certain forms of masculinity and femininity while rejecting others (Silkenbeumer & Pérez, 2010). Comparative studies strongly highlight patterns of gender-based targeting and the frequent exposure of girls to verbal or sexual harassment (Bouna, 2018; Maschke & Stecher, 2021; Melzer & Schubarth, 2006; Tristiana et al., 2023), while the normalization of sexist comments as "jokes" is also extensively documented (Maschke & Stecher, 2021). Nevertheless, the aforementioned studies do not explicitly address targeting based on sexual orientation or non-conforming gender expression.

Physical violence was described by the students as more common among boys, although conflicts between girls were not excluded. This finding may be interpreted in light of theoretical approaches, as Tillmann et al. (1999) define physical violence as a form of physical coercion that causes or threatens to cause bodily harm, emphasizing that its social acceptance and interpretation vary according to cultural norms and historical conditions. Within the same framework, Hagemann-White (2020) underlines that perceptions of male identity and power often legitimize the use of violence as an "expected" means of asserting dominance, a perception associated with the belief that physical aggression constitutes an inherent characteristic of masculinity. Thus, the perception of physical violence as an "expected" male behavior may be viewed as a product of social stereotypes that sustain such practices. In this regard, both international and Greek literature reinforce this finding: Melzer and Schubarth (2006) document high levels of boys' involvement in physical conflicts, while Bouna

(2018) reports that physical violence is attributed to boys as a characteristic form of behavior, in contrast to the more indirect conflicts associated with girls (e.g., hair-pulling). Similar findings are presented in the nationwide study conducted by Artinopoulou, Bampali, and Nikolopoulos (2016), in which boys reported higher levels of exposure to physical violence.

The students' testimonies also revealed clear gender differentiations regarding the ways violence is expressed: boys were more strongly associated with physical aggression, whereas girls were associated with verbal or indirect forms of conflict. This distinction may be interpreted through the social dimension of gender roles, since, as Connell (2006) argues, cultural norms shape normative forms of masculinity and femininity, thereby defining different standards of "acceptable" behavior for boys and girls. In Bouna's study (2018), boys were more frequently identified as perpetrators of threats and physical assaults, whereas girls tended to employ irony or indirect practices. Similarly, Melzer and Schubarth (2006), as well as the SPEAK! study (Maschke & Stecher, 2021), document differentiated patterns of experiences according to gender, which are associated with social norms and stereotypical expectations.

Sexual harassment and sexist comments, although reported less frequently in comparison with other forms of violence, were nevertheless identified by students as existing experiences within the school environment. UN Women (2015) defines sexual violence as any act of a sexual nature expressed without the individual's clear, free, and informed consent, emphasizing that it may take verbal, physical, or symbolic forms. Similarly, the WHO (2002) points out that such practices may originate from any individual and may occur within any social context, including schools. At the empirical level, the study conducted by Tristiana et al. (2023) records testimonies from girls who experienced sexual assaults by classmates and, in certain cases, by teachers, while both the SPEAK! study (Maschke & Stecher, 2021) and the study by Hofherr and Kindler (2018) reveal that a significant proportion of students have experienced sexual harassment, with girls being more frequently exposed to unwanted contact and comments. Within the Greek context, Bouna (2018) reports that boys appear more frequently as perpetrators of sexual insults, whereas girls report more experiences involving sexist comments.

Finally, a crucial finding concerns the normalization of gender-based violence, as many incidents—particularly sexist comments—are not recognized as forms of violence, but are instead perceived as "jokes" or as part of everyday life. This dimension may be interpreted through the concept of symbolic violence (Bourdieu, 1991), according to which practices of power are expressed through socially acceptable forms and internalized by individuals as part of the natural order of things, thereby reinforcing the reproduction of gender inequalities. At the empirical level, Melzer and Schubarth (2006) document that sexual harassment is often not recognized as violence, but rather as teasing or joking, while in the SPEAK! study (Maschke & Stecher, 2021), students described sexist comments and unwanted behaviors as "normal." Similarly, Bouna (2018) emphasizes that tolerance toward sexist manifestations within the school environment contributes to the perpetuation of stereotypical gender perceptions and undermines the recognition of violence as a social problem.

Overall, the students' experiences consistently confirm stable gendered patterns and the normalization of violence: the predominance of verbal violence, gender-based differentiations in the expression of violence, the targeting of individuals who deviate from dominant norms, and the treatment of sexist behaviors as "jokes."

REFERENCES

Armitage, R. (2021). Bullying in children: Impact on child health. *BMJ Paediatrics Open*, *5*(1), e001336. DOI: 10.1136/bmjpo-2020-000939 PMID: 33782656

Artinopoulou, B., Theodoros Babalis, T., & Vasilios Nikolopoulos, V. (2016). *Nationwide survey on school violence and bullying in primary and secondary education*. Ministry of Education, Research and Religious Affairs.

Bourdieu, P. (1991). *Language and symbolic power (J. B. Thompson* (Raymond, G., & Adamson, M. Eds. & Trans.). Harvard University Press., https://monoskop.org/images/4/43/Bourdieu_Pierre_Language_and_Symbolic_Power_1991.pdf

Braun, V., & Clarke, V. (2012). Thematic analysis. In H. Cooper, P. M. Camic, D. L. Long, A. T. Panter, D. Rindskopf, & K. J. Sher (Eds.), *APA handbook of research methods in psychology: Vol. 2. Research designs: Quantitative, qualitative, neuropsychological, and biological* (pp. 57–71). American Psychological Association. https://doi.org/DOI: 10.1037/13620-004

Burton, P. (2005). *Suffering at school: Results of the Malawi gender-based violence in schools survey*. National Statistics Office.

Chow, A. R. W., Pingault, J.-B., & Baldwin, J. R. (2022). Early risk factors for joint trajectories of bullying victimization and perpetration. *European Child & Adolescent Psychiatry*, *32*(9), 1723–1731. DOI: 10.1007/s00787-022-01989-6 PMID: 35469033

Connell, R. W. (2006). *Social gender*. Epikentro.

Cornell, D., & Huang, F. (2016). Authoritative school climate and high school student risk behavior: A cross-sectional multi-level analysis of student self-reports. *Journal of Youth and Adolescence*, *45*(11), 2246–2259. DOI: 10.1007/s10964-016-0424-3 PMID: 26781806

Council of Europe. (2019). *Gender mainstreaming toolkit for education*. Council of Europe.

Crawford, C., & Burns, R. (2022). School culture, racial composition, and preventing violence: Evaluating punitive and supportive responses to improving safety. *Social Sciences (Basel, Switzerland)*, *11*(7), 270. DOI: 10.3390/socsci11070270

Dimitra Sakka, D., & Aris Markos, A. (2013). From the adolescents' perspective: Violence and aggression at school in relation to ethnocultural background and gender. *Scientific Yearbook of the School of Philosophy. Developmental Psychology*, *1*, 127–162.

Epstein, J. L., & Sheldon, S. B. (2019). The importance of evaluating programs of school, family, and community partnerships. *Aula Abierta, 48*(1), 31–42. DOI: 10.17811/rifie.48.1.2019.31-42

Gaffney, H., Farrington, D. P., & Ttofi, M. M. (2021). School-based anti-bullying programs: A meta-analysis. *Aggression and Violent Behavior, 58*, 101611. DOI: 10.1016/j.avb.2020.101611

Gillett-Swan, J., & Baroutsis, A. (2023). Student voice and teacher voice in educational research: A systematic review of 25 years of literature. *Oxford Review of Education, 50*(4), 533–551. DOI: 10.1080/03054985.2023.2257132

Gugel, G. (2018). Warum sind Menschen gewalttätig? Ursachen von Aggression und Gewalt. *Bürger & Staat, 68*(3), 113–119. https://www.buergerundstaat.de/3_18/gewalt.pdf

Hagemann-White, C. (2020). *Gewalt und Geschlecht: Gewaltverhältnisse & Gewaltdynamiken.* Universitätsklinikum Ulm, Klinik für Kinder- und Jugendpsychiatrie/Psychotherapie (KJPP). https://www.academia.edu/71972478/Hagemann_White_2020_Gewalt_und_Geschlecht

Heiliger, A. (2001). Gewalt in der Schule: Geschlechterdifferenzierung und Handlungsperspektiven. *Pädagogisches Forum, 6*, 448–453.

Hofherr, S., & Kindler, H. (2018). Sexuelle Übergriffe in Schulen aus der Sicht von Schülerinnen und Schülern: Zusammenhänge zum Erleben von Schule und der Bereitschaft zur Hilfesuche. In Andresen, S., & Tippelt, R. (Eds.), *Sexuelle Gewalt in Kindheit und Jugend: Theoretische, empirische und konzeptionelle Erkenntnisse und Herausforderungen erziehungswissenschaftlicher Forschung* (pp. 95–110). Beltz Juventa., DOI: 10.25656/01:22311

Isari, F., & Michalis Pourkos, M. (2015). *Qualitative research methodology.* Association of Greek Academic Libraries. https://hdl.handle.net/11419/5826

Kröger, C., Klann, N., & Kaps, M. (2009). „Stark ohne Gewalt": Evaluation eines innovativen Ansatzes zur schulischen Gewaltprävention. *Beratung Aktuell, 10*(2), 3–23.

Leach, F. (2008). Gender violence in schools in the developing world. *Commonwealth Education Partnerships, 2008*, 28–31.

Maria Kokkidou, M., & Georgios Mygdanis, G. (2024). School bullying, victimization and intervention proposals. *Culture - Journal of Culture in Tourism. Art Education, 4*(2), 33–43. DOI: 10.12681/hjre.19440

Maria Kouroutsidou, M., & Nikolaos Raptis, N. (2021). *Gender violence and educational institutions: Teachers as social reformers. The case of the Dodecanese.* Goni Publications.

Marsden, N., Link, J., & Büllesfeld, E. (2015). Personas und stereotype Geschlechterrollen. In Marsden, N., & Kempf, U. (Eds.), *Gender-UseIT: HCI, usability und UX unter Gendergesichtspunkten* (pp. 91–104). De Gruyter Oldenbourg.

Maschke, S., & Stecher, L. (2021). *Sexualisierte Gewalt in der Erfahrung Jugendlicher: Erweiterungsstudie Berufliche Schulen. Kurzbericht.* Arbeitsgruppe „Speak". https://www.uni-marburg.de/de/fb21/erzwinst/arbeitsbereiche/aew/forschung/speak/kurzbericht-speak-berufliche-schulen_maschke-stecher.pdf

Mason, J. (2011). *Conducting qualitative research* (E. Dimitriadou, Trans., & N. Kyriazi, Ed.). Pedio.

Meissner, H. (2008). *Die soziale Konstruktion von Geschlecht: Erkenntnisperspektiven und gesellschaftstheoretische Fragen.* Freie Universität Berlin. https://www.fu-berlin.de/sites/gpo/soz_eth/Geschlecht_als_Kategorie/Die_soziale_Konstruktion_von_Geschlecht_____Erkenntnisperspektiven_und_gesellschaftstheoretische_Fragen/hanna_meissner.pdf

Melzer, W., & Schubarth, W. (2006). *Gewalt als soziales Problem an Schulen: Untersuchungsergebnisse und Präventionsstrategien.* Verlag Barbara Budrich. https://doi.org/DOI: 10.25656/01:16061

Modecki, K. L., Minchin, J., Harbaugh, A. G., Guerra, N. G., & Runions, K. C. (2020). Bullying and victimization across contexts. *The Journal of Adolescent Health, 66*(2), 203–210. DOI: 10.1016/j.jadohealth.2014.06.007 PMID: 25168105

Murgor, J. C., Korir, R. R., & Ogoma, S. O. (2020). In-school gender-based violence in public primary schools in one municipality, Kenya. *International Journal of Education and Research, 8*(6), 1–16.

Panagiotopoulos, G., & Moysidou, E. (2014). Conclusions. In Vergidis, D., Panagiotopoulos, G., & Moysidou, E. (Eds.), *Violence in the school environment: A journey through the schools of the Regional Directorate of Education of Western Greece* (pp. 255–266). Peloponnisos.

Patton, M. Q. (2002). *Qualitative research and evaluation methods* (3rd ed.). Sage.

Schröttle, M. (2010). Kritische Anmerkungen zur These der Gendersymmetrie bei Gewalt in Paarbeziehungen. *Gender – Zeitschrift für Geschlecht. Kultur und Gesellschaft, 2*(1), 133–151.

Silkenbeumer, M., & Vazquez Perez, R. (2010). *Gewalt und Geschlecht an Schulen: Analysen, Positionen, Praxishilfen.* Max-Traeger-Stiftung. https://www.gew.de/index.php?eID=dumpFile&t=f&f=24453&token=f77ae32eff309a4d6110e1c8a350aaeab5fb4d4f&sdownload=

Tillmann, K.-J., Holler-Nowitzki, B., Holtappels, H. G., Meier, U., & Popp, U. (1999). *Schülergewalt als Schulproblem: Verursachende Bedingungen, Erscheinungsformen und pädagogische Handlungsperspektiven.* Juventa.

Tristiana, R. D., Pratiwi, I. N., Wulansari, D., Yusuf, A., & Sulistyono, R. E. (2023). Adolescents' experience of gender-based violence: A qualitative study. *International Journal of Public Health Science, 12*(2), 822–830. DOI: 10.11591/ijphs.v12i2.22614

UNESCO. (2019). *Behind the numbers: Ending school violence and bullying.* UNESCO., DOI: 10.54675/TRVR4270

UNESCO. (2021). *The journey towards comprehensive sexuality education: Global status report.* UNESCO. https://unesdoc.unesco.org/ark:/48223/pf0000377963

UNESCO & UN Women. (2016). *Global guidance on addressing school-related gender-based violence.* UNESCO., DOI: 10.54675/VFOP6248

UNESCO, Global Education Monitoring Report Team. (2020). *Global education monitoring report 2020: Gender report – A new generation: 25 years of efforts for gender equality in education.* UNESCO. https://unesdoc.unesco.org/ark:/48223/pf0000374514

United Nations. (2006). *World report on violence against children.* United Nations. https://violenceagainstchildren.un.org/sites/violenceagainstchildren.un.org/files/document_files/world_report_on_violence_against_children.pdf

https://www.ungei.org/sites/default/files/A-whole-school-approach-to-prevent-school-related-gender-based-violence-Minimum-Standards-and-Monitoring-Framework-2019-eng.pdf

United Nations Girls' Education Initiative. (2020). *Frequently asked questions: School-related gender-based violence.* UNGEI. https://www.ungei.org/publication/frequently-asked-questions-school-related-gender-based-violence

United Nations Girls' Education Initiative. (2024). *Prevention of sexual violence in education settings: White paper.* UNGEI. https://www.ungei.org/sites/default/files/202410/Prevention%20Of%20Sexual%20Violence%20In%20Education%20Settings%20White%20Paper.pdf

Vrasidas, C. (2014). *Introduction to qualitative research.* CARDET Press.

Wang, M. T., & Degol, J. L. (2016). School climate: A review of the construct, measurement, and impact on student outcomes. *Educational Psychology Review, 28*(2), 315–352. DOI: 10.1007/s10648-015-9319-1

Wescott, S., & Roberts, S. (2025). On the utility of the concept of 'school-related gender-based violence' (SRGBV) in the context of escalating gendered violence in schools. *Critical Studies in Education*, 1–19. Advance online publication. DOI: 10.1080/17508487.2025.2514278

Women, U. N. (2015). *A framework to underpin action to prevent violence against women.* UN Women. https://www.unwomen.org/sites/default/files/Headquarters/Attachments/Sections/Library/Publications/2015/Prevention_Framework_unwomen_nov2015.pdf

World Health Organization. (2002). *World report on violence and health* (Krug, E., Dahlberg, L., Mercy, J., Zwi, A., & Lozano, R., Eds.). World Health Organization., https://apps.who.int/iris/handle/10665/42495

Chapter 7
Motivation, Self-Regulation, and Teacher Practice:
Innovative School-Based Interventions for Students with Learning Difficulties

Maria Sofologi
http://orcid.org/0000-0003-0380-2220
University of Ioannina, Greece

Dimitra Katsarou
http://orcid.org/0000-0001-8690-0314
University of the Aegean, Rhodes, Greece

ABSTRACT

This chapter explores how self-regulation, motivation, and inclusive teaching practices support students with ADHD, ASD, and SLD. It examines evidence-based approaches, including UDL, MTSS, co-regulation, metacognitive instruction, mindfulness, and technology-supported learning. Emphasizing teacher support, inclusive pedagogy, and collaborative school cultures, the chapter proposes an integrative framework to enhance engagement, emotional regulation, resilience, academic success, and long-term participation in inclusive educational environments.

DOI: 10.4018/979-8-3373-9420-6.ch007

1. INTRODUCTION

Self-regulation is widely regarded as a foundational construct in contemporary educational psychology due to its central role in academic achievement, emotional adjustment, behavioral functioning, and sustained learning engagement. Within educational contexts, self-regulation refers to the capacity to deliberately monitor, evaluate, and adapt one's cognitive processes, emotions, motivation, attention, and behavior in order to achieve goal-directed outcomes and participate effectively in learning activities. This construct is particularly significant for students with learning difficulties, including Attention Deficit Hyperactivity Disorder (ADHD), Autism Spectrum Disorder (ASD), Specific Learning Disorder (SLD), Developmental Co-ordination Disorder (DCD), and developmental language disorders, where persistent challenges in executive functioning, inhibitory control, working memory, emotional regulation, and attentional flexibility often compromise classroom participation and academic performance (Diamond, 2013; Sofologi et al., 2025).

In response to increasing classroom diversity, educational systems are progressively shifting toward inclusive paradigms that prioritize equity, participation, and meaningful learning for all students (Katsarou, 2024). Historically, intervention approaches have tended to focus on remediation of academic deficits or the management of observable behaviours, often overlooking the underlying self-regulatory processes that shape learning, engagement, and persistence. However, contemporary research increasingly indicates that self-regulatory difficulties represent a core mechanism underlying academic underachievement, behavioural disengagement, social exclusion, and emotional distress among learners with learning difficulties (Yang et al., 2022). As a result, there is a growing emphasis on integrative educational approaches that address cognitive, emotional, motivational, and behavioural regulation within authentic instructional contexts.

Theoretical frameworks from social-cognitive theory, self-determination theory, executive functioning research, and sociocultural perspectives provide a robust foundation for understanding self-regulation as a dynamic and contextually embedded process. Zimmerman (2000) conceptualizes self-regulated learning as a dynamic cyclical model involving forethought, performance, self-monitoring, and self-reflection, highlighting the role of strategic and metacognitive processes in learning. Complementarily, self-determination theory posits that optimal motivation and sustained engagement arise when learners experience autonomy, competence, and relatedness within supportive environments (Deci et al., 2000). Collectively, these perspectives position self-regulation not as a fixed individual trait, but as a developable capacity shaped through interaction with instructional practices, social relationships, and classroom ecology.

For students with learning difficulties, the development of self-regulation is often more complex due to heterogeneous profiles of neurocognitive functioning, sensory processing, emotional reactivity, and attentional control. Nevertheless, accumulating evidence suggests that self-regulatory capacities can be meaningfully enhanced through intentional pedagogical design, structured scaffolding, co-regulatory teacher–student interactions, and inclusive classroom environments that provide predictability, emotional safety, and opportunities for guided autonomy (Gehle et al., 2023). Within this framework, teachers assume a pivotal role not only as transmitters of knowledge but also as active regulators of learning processes, shaping how students manage attention, persist through challenges, and develop motivational resilience.

Accordingly, this chapter provides a critical examination of self-regulation and motivation in students with learning difficulties within inclusive educational settings. It explores theoretical foundations alongside practical implications for classroom practice, whole-school inclusive models, professional learning for teachers, and systemic implementation challenges. The analysis adopts an integrative perspective in which cognitive, emotional, motivational, and social dimensions of learning are understood as interdependent and mutually reinforcing processes that collectively shape educational outcomes.

1.1 Cognitive and Emotional Self-Regulation in Students With Learning Difficulties

Self-regulation is a complex, multidimensional construct that refers to the dynamic coordination of cognitive, emotional, motivational, and behavioral systems in order to support goal-directed learning and adaptive functioning. Within contemporary educational psychology, it is increasingly conceptualized as a higher-order regulatory system encompassing planning, attentional control, working memory, inhibitory processes, self-monitoring, and reflective evaluation, all of which are essential for effective academic engagement and sustained learning performance (Zimmerman & Schunk, 2011; Diamond, 2013).

A critical distinction in the contemporary literature concerns cognitive self-regulation and emotional self-regulation, which operate as functionally distinct yet highly interdependent systems. Cognitive self-regulation involves executive processes such as maintaining task-relevant information in working memory, selectively allocating attention, inhibiting automatic or irrelevant responses, and flexibly shifting strategies in response to changing task demands. Emotional self-regulation, by contrast, refers to the capacity to monitor, modulate, and adapt emotional responses—such as frustration, anxiety, or excitement—in ways that preserve cognitive engagement and facilitate persistence in learning tasks. Recent empirical research increasingly emphasizes that disruptions in emotional regulation directly impair cognitive efficiency by reducing attentional capacity and working-memory performance, thereby affecting academic outcomes (Gehle et al., 2022).

Students with learning difficulties, including ADHD, ASD, and SLD, frequently present with co-occurring impairments in both cognitive and emotional domains of regulation. In ADHD, robust evidence indicates significant deficits in inhibitory control, sustained attention, and working memory, which manifest in impulsivity, distractibility, inconsistent task completion, and poor behavioral persistence (Sofologi et al., 2025). Importantly, recent experimental and neurocognitive research has further demonstrated that these executive-function deficits are closely linked to difficulties in emotion regulation, particularly under conditions requiring cognitive control or frustration tolerance (Smith et al., 2023).

Similarly, students with Autism Spectrum Disorder (ASD) often exhibit challenges in cognitive flexibility, sensory integration, and adaptive emotional responding. Difficulties managing uncertainty, transitions, and sensory overload are frequently associated with heightened emotional reactivity and behavioral dysregulation in classroom contexts (American Psychiatric Association, 2022). These emotional challenges are not isolated phenomena but are closely tied to executive demands, particularly in situations requiring shifting attention, adapting to change, or interpreting complex social and instructional cues.

Students with Specific Learning Disorders (SLD) experience additional regulatory challenges linked to persistent academic failure and heightened cognitive load during reading, writing, and mathematical tasks. Empirical evidence suggests that repeated exposure to academic difficulty can significantly undermine motivational regulation, increase emotional distress, and reduce persistence, thereby reinforcing cycles of disengagement and avoidance (Meltzer, 2018). Over time, these experiences contribute to diminished academic self-efficacy and weakened strategic engagement. From a neurocognitive standpoint, executive functions constitute the primary mechanisms underlying cognitive self-regulation. Working memory supports the active maintenance and manipulation of information; inhibitory control enables suppression of irrelevant impulses and distractions; and cognitive flexibility facilitates adaptive shifting between strategies and representations. Meta-analytic and experimental studies consistently demonstrate that impairments in these executive systems are strongly associated with academic underachievement and reduced classroom functioning, particularly in neurodevelopmental populations (Diamond, 2013; Sankalaite et al., 2021).

Importantly, contemporary research highlights that cognitive and emotional regulation are not independent systems but are structurally and functionally integrated. Experimental findings indicate that improvements in executive control processes such as working memory and inhibition can lead to measurable gains in emotional regulation capacities, suggesting shared underlying neural and cognitive mechanisms (Groves et al., 2022). This interaction underscores the importance of integrated intervention models that simultaneously target cognitive control and emotional regulation processes.

Furthermore, sociocultural theory further expands this perspective by emphasizing that self-regulation is initially externally mediated through social interaction and gradually internalized through guided participation with more knowledgeable others (Vygotsky, 1978). Within educational contexts, this process is operationalized through co-regulation, whereby teachers actively scaffold both cognitive strategies and emotional responses during learning. Co-regulatory interactions—such as modelling problem-solving, supporting emotional reframing, and guiding attentional focus—are essential for students who have not yet developed autonomous regulatory capacities.

Recent empirical work supports the effectiveness of instructional and digital interventions targeting executive functions and emotion regulation in students with ADHD and related learning difficulties. For example, randomized controlled trials have demonstrated that targeted training of working memory and inhibitory control can lead to measurable improvements in both cognitive performance and emotional regulation outcomes, although effects vary depending on intervention design and intensity (Groves et al., 2022). Similarly, systematic reviews of cognitive training interventions indicate that structured executive-function training can yield improvements in attentional control and academic functioning, particularly when embedded within educational contexts.

The classroom environment also plays a decisive role in shaping regulatory development. High-stress, unpredictable, or punitive learning environments have been shown to exacerbate emotional dysregulation and reduce cognitive efficiency, particularly among vulnerable learners (Shanker, 2016). In contrast, structured, predictable, and emotionally supportive environments enhance both cognitive control and emotional stability by reducing extraneous cognitive load and supporting sustained engagement. Emerging research on educational technology further highlights its potential role in supporting self-regulation. Digital scaffolds, adaptive learning platforms, self-monitoring tools, and gamified systems have been shown to enhance attentional control, persistence, and engagement among students with executive-function difficulties, particularly when combined with explicit instructional support (Cho et al., 2021; Stalmach et al., 2023). However, evidence consistently indicates that such tools are most effective when embedded within relational, teacher-mediated pedagogical frameworks rather than used as standalone interventions.

In synthesis, cognitive and emotional self-regulation should be understood as interdependent, developmentally sensitive, and contextually mediated processes that are shaped through continuous interaction between neurocognitive systems, emotional experiences, social relationships, and instructional environments. For students with learning difficulties, effective educational intervention requires integrated, evidence-based approaches that simultaneously address executive functioning, emotional regulation, motivation, and environmental support systems. This perspective aligns with contemporary empirical findings demonstrating that improvements in cognitive control processes can produce downstream benefits in emotional regulation and academic functioning, particularly when supported by structured, relational, and inclusive educational practices (Diamond, 2013; Groves et al., 2022; Zimmerman & Schunk, 2011).

1.2 The Role of Motivation in Students With Learning Difficulties

Motivation constitutes a fundamental determinant of learning, shaping not only academic engagement and persistence but also emotional resilience, behavioral regulation, and long-term educational trajectories among students with learning difficulties. Contemporary educational psychology increasingly rejects earlier deficit-oriented perspectives that emphasized cognitive impairment or behavioral dysregulation in isolation, and instead highlights motivation as a central explanatory mechanism influencing how students interpret academic demands, sustain effort, and respond to failure within school contexts (Ryan & Deci, 2020). Students who repeatedly encounter academic struggle, social exclusion, or negative evaluative experiences are particularly vulnerable to the development of maladaptive motivational patterns, including reduced self-efficacy, avoidance behaviors, and diminished persistence.

From a theoretical standpoint, motivation is best understood as a multidimensional and dynamic construct encompassing intrinsic interest, goal orientation, expectancy-value beliefs, emotional engagement, and persistence over time. Self-determination theory provides a particularly influential framework, proposing that optimal motivation arises when the basic psychological needs for autonomy, competence, and relatedness are adequately satisfied within learning environments (Deci et al., 2000). These needs are especially salient for students with learning difficulties, who frequently experience schooling contexts characterized by high external control, repeated correction, and limited opportunities for meaningful participation or autonomous decision-making.

The motivational profiles of students with specific learning and neurodevelopmental profiles further illustrate the complexity of these processes. Students with Attention Deficit Hyperactivity Disorder (ADHD) often exhibit altered reward processing, heightened sensitivity to immediate reinforcement, and reduced tolerance for delayed gratification, which can significantly undermine sustained engagement in conventional instructional tasks (Barkley, 2015). In such contexts, traditional pedagogical approaches that rely heavily on delayed rewards, repetitive practice, or passive learning structures may fail to maintain attention and effort, thereby increasing disengagement.

Similarly, students with Specific Learning Disorders (SLD) frequently internalize repeated academic failure as evidence of low competence, which can lead to learned helplessness, reduced academic self-concept, and avoidance of challenging tasks. Over time, these experiences may significantly erode intrinsic motivation and contribute to disengagement from academic learning. For students with Autism Spectrum Disorder (ASD), motivational challenges are often intertwined with social communication differences, sensory sensitivities, and difficulties in processing complex or unpredictable social learning environments, all of which may influence classroom participation and emotional investment in learning activities (American Psychiatric Association, 2022).

On the other hand, Bandura's (1997) theory of self-efficacy offers a complementary lens for understanding motivational processes in students with learning difficulties. Self-efficacy refers to learners' beliefs about their capacity to organize and execute actions required to achieve desired outcomes. Empirical research consistently demonstrates that strong self-efficacy beliefs are associated with greater persistence, adaptive strategy use, emotional resilience, and academic achievement. Conversely, repeated experiences of failure may progressively weaken self-efficacy, resulting in reduced effort, avoidance of challenging tasks, and diminished engagement with learning opportunities.

Within classroom contexts, motivation is significantly shaped by the quality of instructional design and teacher-student interactions. A substantial body of research indicates that motivationally supportive classrooms are associated with improved engagement, persistence, and self-regulatory behavior among students with learning difficulties (Chu et al., 2020). Such environments typically prioritize mastery-oriented learning goals, formative feedback, and individual progress rather than normative comparison or competitive performance structures. In these settings, teachers play a crucial role in reinforcing effort, providing structured guidance, and supporting incremental progress, thereby strengthening motivational resilience. Autonomy-supportive teaching practices represent one of the most empirically validated approaches for enhancing intrinsic motivation. Within autonomy-supportive environments, teachers actively promote student agency through meaningful choice, explanation of task relevance, encouragement of independent problem-solving, and acknowledgement of student perspectives (Ryan & Deci, 2020). Importantly, autonomy support is not synonymous with reduced structure; rather, it reflects a pedagogical balance between guidance and agency. Empirical studies indicate that when students with attentional and learning difficulties are provided with structured autonomy, they demonstrate higher engagement, improved persistence, and enhanced self-regulatory functioning (Chu et al., 2020).

Motivation is also deeply embedded within relational and affective dimensions of schooling. Positive teacher-student relationships contribute significantly to students' sense of belonging, emotional security, and willingness to engage in cognitively demanding tasks. In contrast, environments characterized by criticism, relational conflict, or emotional neglect are associated with increased anxiety, behavioral dysregulation, and academic disengagement. Accordingly, relational trust and emotional attunement are increasingly recognized as core components of motivational development in inclusive education. Contemporary strengths-based and inclusive pedagogical approaches further challenge traditional deficit-oriented models of motivation. Rather than focusing primarily on remediation of weaknesses, strengths-based frameworks emphasize the identification and development of students' abilities, interests, and potential areas of competence. Students with learning difficulties often demonstrate diverse strengths, including creativity, visual-spatial reasoning, persistence, problem-solving abilities, and technological skills. Instructional practices that integrate these strengths into learning tasks contribute significantly to intrinsic motivation, identity development, and sustained engagement.

Instructional models such as project-based learning, inquiry-based instruction, collaborative learning structures, and multimodal assessment approaches have been shown to enhance motivational engagement by increasing relevance, autonomy, and competence development. Research suggests that such approaches are particularly effective for students with ADHD and ASD, as they provide opportunities for active engagement, contextualized learning, and meaningful participation (Hattie, 2009). These pedagogical strategies reduce reliance on narrow, performance-based evaluation systems and instead foster deeper engagement with learning processes.

In addition, gamified learning environments have emerged as a promising innovation for supporting motivation in students with learning difficulties. Gamification incorporates structured game elements such as immediate feedback, goal progression, reward systems, and collaborative challenges into educational contexts. Empirical evidence indicates that gamified interventions can improve attention, persistence, and emotional engagement, particularly for learners with executive-function and attentional challenges (Cho et al., 2021). The effectiveness of such interventions is closely linked to their capacity to provide immediate reinforcement and visible indicators of progress, which are particularly beneficial for students who struggle with delayed reward processing.

Motivational processes are also shaped by broader sociocultural and contextual influences. Culturally responsive educational practices emphasise that students' motivation is influenced by identity, language, family expectations, and social belonging. Inclusive classrooms that actively validate diversity and promote cultural responsiveness are more likely to enhance students' sense of belonging and intrinsic motivation, thereby supporting both emotional wellbeing and academic engagement.

In conclusion, motivation in students with learning difficulties is better understood as a fluid and context-sensitive process rather than a stable individual characteristic. It develops through ongoing interactions between learners' cognitive and emotional profiles and the educational environments in which they participate, including teaching approaches, interpersonal relationships, and broader school culture. Educational settings that deliberately foster autonomy, competence, social connectedness, and strengths-oriented participation are more likely to enhance motivation, support the development of self-regulation, and contribute to positive long-term academic outcomes (Deci et al., 2000; Ryan et al., 2020; Zimmerman & Schunk, 2011).

2. INCLUSIVE EDUCATIONAL FRAMEWORKS AND SCHOOL-WIDE APPROACHES

Motivation is widely recognized as a foundational driver of learning engagement, academic persistence, achievement, and emotional wellbeing. In the context of students with learning difficulties, motivational processes are often significantly shaped by cumulative experiences of academic struggle, corrective feedback, social marginalization, and constrained opportunities for autonomy within classroom settings. Over time, these experiences may contribute to disengagement from learning, diminished academic self-concept, and the internalization of low competence beliefs, which further weaken participation and persistence.

Self-determination theory provides a robust theoretical lens for understanding motivational development in this population. Deci et al., (2000) argue that intrinsic motivation is optimally supported when the basic psychological needs of autonomy, competence, and relatedness are satisfied. Within educational contexts, these needs are particularly critical for students with learning difficulties, who are often exposed to highly structured or externally controlled learning environments that limit self-directed engagement, reduce perceived competence through repeated failure, and restrict opportunities for meaningful peer connection and belonging.

These motivational challenges are evident across different learner profiles. Students with Attention Deficit Hyperactivity Disorder (ADHD) frequently encounter learning environments characterized by frequent behavioral correction and externally imposed regulation, which may undermine autonomy and reduce intrinsic engagement. Students with Specific Learning Disorders (SLD) often experience persistent academic difficulties that can erode perceptions of competence and foster feelings of helplessness. Similarly, students with Autism Spectrum Disorder (ASD) may encounter barriers in social reciprocity, peer interaction, and classroom belonging, all of which can negatively impact relatedness and emotional engagement within school contexts.

Bandura's (1997) concept of self-efficacy further deepens the understanding of motivational processes in students with learning difficulties. Self-efficacy refers to learners' beliefs about their ability to successfully organize and execute actions required to achieve specific goals. High levels of self-efficacy are associated with sustained effort, adaptive strategy use, resilience in the face of difficulty, and effective recovery from setbacks. Conversely, repeated academic failure can gradually undermine self-efficacy beliefs, increasing avoidance behaviors, reducing persistence, and contributing to motivational withdrawal. Within classroom practice, teachers exert a decisive influence on students' motivational trajectories. Instructional environments that prioritize excessive performance comparison, punitive correction, or rigid behavioral control may inadvertently intensify anxiety and disengagement. In contrast, classrooms that emphasize mastery, effort, strategic learning, and collaborative engagement are more likely to foster resilience, persistence, and adaptive motivation. Empirical evidence indicates that autonomy-supportive instructional practices are strongly associated with improved engagement and self-regulatory outcomes among students with attentional and learning difficulties (Chu et al., 2020).

Autonomy-supportive pedagogy involves providing students with meaningful choices, encouraging learner voice, acknowledging emotional experiences, and fostering participation in decision-making processes related to learning. Such practices enhance students' sense of agency and ownership over learning activities. Importantly, autonomy support should not be interpreted as a reduction in structure; rather, it reflects a balanced instructional approach that combines clear expectations and scaffolding with opportunities for independent and meaningful engagement. The relational dimension of motivation is equally significant. Positive and supportive teacher–student relationships are strongly associated with increased emotional security, classroom belonging, and willingness to engage in cognitively demanding tasks. Students who perceive their teachers as respectful, consistent, and emotionally responsive are more likely to persist in the face of difficulty and maintain engagement during challenging learning experiences. Conversely, relational conflict or perceived rejection may contribute to emotional withdrawal, anxiety, and behavioral disengagement.

Recent developments in educational research have increasingly emphasized strengths-based approaches to motivation. Traditional models of special education have often been grounded in deficit-oriented perspectives that focus primarily on remediation of weaknesses and reduction of difficulties. In contrast, strengths-based pedagogical frameworks highlight students' existing abilities, interests, and cognitive assets. Many students with learning difficulties demonstrate notable strengths, including creativity, problem-solving skills, visual-spatial reasoning, persistence, empathy, technological aptitude, and deep interest in specific domains.

Integrating these strengths into instructional design has been shown to significantly enhance motivation and engagement. Learning approaches such as project-based learning, inquiry-based instruction, collaborative group work, and multimodal assessment strategies provide opportunities for students to demonstrate competence in diverse ways. These approaches also support identity development by enabling students to experience success and recognition beyond traditional academic performance measures. Gamification represents another increasingly prominent strategy for enhancing motivation in learners with learning difficulties. By incorporating game-design elements such as structured feedback systems, progression levels, rewards, challenges, and collaborative tasks, gamified learning environments can significantly increase engagement and persistence. Empirical research indicates that gamification can improve attention, task completion, and sustained motivation, particularly among students with ADHD and other attentional or executive-functioning challenges (Cho et al., 2021). The provision of immediate feedback and visible progress is especially beneficial for learners who experience difficulties with delayed reinforcement and sustained effort regulation. Motivation is also profoundly influenced by broader sociocultural and contextual factors. Culturally responsive pedagogical approaches recognize that students' identities, linguistic backgrounds, family expectations, and lived experiences play a critical role in shaping engagement and participation. Inclusive educational environments that actively validate diversity and promote a sense of belonging contribute significantly to motivational resilience, emotional wellbeing, and sustained academic engagement.

In summary, motivation in students with learning difficulties should be conceptualized as a dynamic and contextually embedded process rather than a fixed individual trait. It emerges from the interaction between learners' cognitive and emotional characteristics and the environments in which learning occurs. Educational systems that intentionally foster autonomy, competence, relatedness, and strengths-based participation create optimal conditions for the development of motivation, engagement, and self-regulated learning.

2.1 Systemic Inclusive Education for Supporting Students With Learning Difficulties

Inclusive education has progressively evolved from a narrow placement-based perspective toward a broader systemic and rights-based framework that emphasizes participation, equity, accessibility, emotional wellbeing, and responsiveness to learner diversity. Contemporary inclusive schools are no longer expected merely to accommodate students with learning difficulties within mainstream classrooms;

rather, they are increasingly required to cultivate educational environments that actively promote academic engagement, self-regulation, social participation, emotional resilience, and positive identity development. This paradigm shift reflects growing recognition that educational success is deeply interconnected with students' experiences of belonging, psychological safety, and meaningful participation within school communities (Meyer et al., 2014).

Students with learning difficulties frequently encounter barriers that extend beyond academic performance alone. Difficulties related to executive functioning, attentional regulation, emotional processing, communication, and social interaction may contribute to exclusionary experiences, low self-esteem, reduced classroom participation, and fragmented support provision. Consequently, inclusive education requires systemic approaches that address both learning and psychosocial development simultaneously. Contemporary research increasingly highlights that inclusive schooling is most effective when it promotes collaborative, flexible, and relationship-centered educational cultures that support the diverse cognitive, emotional, and motivational needs of learners (Gehle et al., 2023).

One of the most influential frameworks informing contemporary inclusive practice is Universal Design for Learning (UDL). Rooted in principles of accessibility and learner variability, UDL proposes that curriculum and instruction should be designed proactively to accommodate diverse learning profiles through multiple means of engagement, representation, and expression (Meyer et al., 2014). Rather than implementing reactive accommodations only after difficulties emerge, UDL encourages educators to anticipate learner diversity from the outset and to create flexible learning environments that minimize barriers to participation.

For students with learning difficulties, UDL practices may involve multimodal teaching approaches, visual scaffolding, assistive technologies, differentiated pacing, flexible assessment opportunities, and student-centered instructional pathways. Such practices not only improve accessibility but also strengthen self-regulatory functioning by reducing cognitive overload and promoting strategic engagement. Importantly, UDL aligns closely with theories of self-regulated learning because it emphasizes learner agency, reflective participation, and autonomy-supportive educational practices (Zimmerman & Schunk, 2011). When students are provided with multiple pathways for accessing and demonstrating learning, they are more likely to experience competence, motivation, and sustained engagement.

Another key framework within inclusive education is the Multi-Tiered System of Supports (MTSS), which prioritizes prevention, early identification, and progressively intensive support across academic, behavioral, emotional, and social domains. This model is based on the assumption that learning and behavioral difficulties should be addressed early and systematically through tiered levels of intervention, rather than through delayed responses or deficit-focused approaches. At Tier 1, universal supports are implemented across the entire school population and typically include the establishment of a positive and inclusive classroom climate, explicit instruction of behavioral and academic expectations, whole-school social-emotional learning (SEL) programs, and classroom-based strategies that promote self-regulation and engagement. Tier 2 supports are designed for students who are at risk and require targeted, small-group interventions, while Tier 3 interventions provide intensive, individualized support tailored to specific and complex learner needs (Sugai & Horner, 2009; McIntosh & Goodman, 2016).

Empirical research consistently shows that school-wide frameworks such as Positive Behavioral Interventions and Supports (PBIS) and SEL-based programs are associated with improved school climate, stronger emotional wellbeing, reduced behavioral incidents, and increased instructional time (Bradshaw, Mitchell, & Leaf, 2010; Durlak et al., 2011). These outcomes highlight the effectiveness of preventative and systems-based approaches in fostering supportive learning environments for diverse learners, including those with learning difficulties and neurodevelopmental disorders. Importantly, these approaches mark a clear shift away from traditional punitive or exclusionary disciplinary models, which have often disproportionately affected students with learning and behavioral challenges. Instead of focusing on punishment or behavioral correction alone, contemporary inclusive education frameworks emphasize relational trust, emotional safety, restorative practices, and collaborative problem-solving. This shift aligns with broader educational goals of equity and participation, ensuring that students are supported to develop adaptive behaviors and self-regulation skills within inclusive and supportive school communities (Osher et al., 2010; Gregory, Clawson, Davis, & Gerewitz, 2016).

Trauma-sensitive educational approaches have also gained increasing importance within inclusive school reform. Many students with learning difficulties experience chronic stress associated with repeated academic failure, social rejection, sensory overload, and ongoing corrective feedback. Over time, these experiences may negatively affect emotional regulation, self-efficacy, motivation, and school participation. Trauma-sensitive schools recognize that emotional wellbeing and learning are inseparable processes and therefore prioritize emotional safety, predictability, relational consistency, and psychologically supportive environments (Shanker, 2016). Teachers working within trauma-sensitive frameworks seek to understand behavior as communication rather than solely as misconduct, thereby promoting empathy and supportive intervention rather than punishment.

Equally important within inclusive educational models is the role of interdisciplinary collaboration. Effective inclusion depends on strong partnerships among teachers, school psychologists, speech and language therapists, occupational therapists, special educators, families, and school leaders. Collaborative professional relationships enhance consistency across interventions and support a more holistic understanding of students' cognitive, emotional, social, and motivational profiles. Family-school collaboration is particularly valuable because families possess essential knowledge regarding students' strengths, emotional triggers, coping strategies, interests, and self-regulatory patterns. Schools that actively involve families in planning and decision-making processes are often more successful in promoting inclusive participation and long-term student wellbeing.

Whole-school approaches emphasizing restorative practices have also demonstrated substantial relevance for students with learning difficulties. Restorative educational models prioritize relationship repair, empathy development, accountability, and social understanding rather than relying primarily on exclusionary discipline. Such approaches are closely aligned with co-regulation theory because they recognize that students develop emotional regulation and social competence through supportive interpersonal interactions. Restorative practices contribute to stronger school connectedness, improved emotional safety, and more inclusive peer relationships. Importantly, sustainable inclusive education cannot be achieved without addressing teacher wellbeing and organizational culture. Teachers working within highly demanding educational contexts frequently experience emotional exhaustion, stress, and professional burnout, all of which may negatively affect classroom climate and relational responsiveness. Inclusive school reform therefore requires organizational structures that support teacher wellbeing through collaborative planning opportunities, ongoing professional learning, reflective supervision, and supportive leadership practices. Educational leaders play a critical role in establishing school cultures characterized by inclusion, trust, emotional safety, and shared responsibility for student success.

Ultimately, inclusive education should not be conceptualized merely as the physical placement of students with learning difficulties within mainstream classrooms. Rather, it represents the development of educational systems that actively promote dignity, belonging, accessibility, emotional wellbeing, participation, and meaningful engagement for all learners. Contemporary inclusive models increasingly recognize that students thrive academically and emotionally when schools cultivate responsive, relational, and flexible learning environments capable of supporting diverse strengths, needs, and identities.

2.2 Enhancing Self-Regulatory Competence Through Classroom-Based Practices

Practical classroom strategies for enhancing self-regulation must be grounded in an understanding that regulation is shaped through the interaction of cognitive, emotional, social, motivational, and environmental processes. Contemporary research increasingly demonstrates that isolated behavior-management interventions are insufficient for addressing the complex needs of students with learning difficulties. Effective classroom practices instead involve integrated and relational approaches that support strategic thinking, emotional safety, participation, and adaptive coping (Meltzer, 2018). One of the most strongly supported approaches involves explicit instruction in self-regulated learning strategies. Embedded strategy instruction integrates planning, monitoring, reflection, and problem-solving directly into everyday academic tasks rather than teaching regulation as a separate intervention (Dignath et al., 2008). Teachers model metacognitive processes through think-aloud strategies, guided questioning, and reflective dialogue. Such approaches help students understand how effective learners organize information, monitor comprehension, evaluate progress, and adapt strategies during challenging tasks.

Research indicates that explicit metacognitive instruction significantly improves academic achievement and self-regulatory competence among students with learning difficulties (Zimmerman et al., 2011). Students with SLD, for example, often struggle to identify ineffective strategies or recognize misunderstandings during reading and writing activities. Through scaffolded reflection and strategic modeling, teachers support the development of independent learning processes. Visual supports remain particularly important for children with executive-function difficulties because they reduce working-memory demands and increase predictability. Visual schedules, task organizers, graphic organizers, color-coded systems, and step-by-step instructions externalize information that may otherwise overwhelm attentional systems. Such strategies are especially beneficial for students with ADHD and ASD who may experience difficulties organizing information, transitioning between activities, or maintaining attentional focus.

The physical and sensory classroom environment also significantly influences self-regulation. Overstimulating and unpredictable learning spaces may increase anxiety, sensory overload, and dysregulation among students with learning difficulties. Consequently, inclusive classrooms increasingly incorporate sensory-sensitive practices such as flexible seating arrangements, quiet regulation areas, movement opportunities, and reduced visual clutter. Such environmental modifications support emotional comfort and attentional engagement. Movement-based interventions have gained increasing support within educational research because physical activity contributes positively to executive functioning, emotional regulation, and sustained attention (Diamond, 2013). Short movement breaks, stretching routines, standing workstations, and outdoor learning activities help students regulate arousal and maintain concentration. These strategies are particularly valuable for students with ADHD and sensory-processing differences who may struggle with prolonged sedentary instruction.

Mindfulness-based interventions have increasingly been recognized as valuable practices within classroom contexts. These approaches cultivate students' awareness of their thoughts, emotions, and bodily sensations while also strengthening attentional control and emotional regulation. Empirical evidence indicates that school-based mindfulness programs can reduce stress, improve attention, and enhance classroom behavior, particularly among students with attentional and emotional regulation difficulties (Zoogman et al., 2015; Zenner et al., 2014). In practical terms, brief mindfulness strategies such as breathing exercises, grounding techniques, and short reflective pauses embedded within daily classroom routines can meaningfully support students' self-regulatory capacities.

However, emotional regulation is deeply embedded in interpersonal processes and cannot be fully understood in isolation from relationships. Co-regulation therefore plays a central role in effective classroom practice, as students often require adult support before they are able to regulate independently. Teachers who respond with emotional calmness during moments of dysregulation, validate students' feelings, and guide them through structured problem-solving contribute to emotionally secure learning environments that foster adaptive coping. From a sociocultural perspective, Vygotsky (1978) emphasizes that higher-order psychological functions first emerge through social interaction before being internalized, highlighting the importance of guided support in the development of self-regulation.

Collaborative learning approaches further strengthen self-regulatory development by providing structured opportunities for peer interaction and shared meaning-making. Activities such as cooperative learning, peer tutoring, and group-based problem-solving encourage students to articulate their thinking processes, negotiate strategies, and monitor both individual and collective participation. Research suggests that such collaborative structures not only enhance academic engagement but also support metacognitive awareness and social connectedness, both of which are closely linked to self-regulation (Johnson & Johnson, 2009; Laal & Laal, 2012).

In addition, technology-supported interventions offer promising tools for promoting self-regulation and motivation in inclusive classrooms. Digital supports such as visual schedules, self-monitoring applications, adaptive learning platforms, reminders, and gamified learning environments can assist students in organizing their learning, maintaining focus, and sustaining engagement. Evidence suggests that technology-enhanced interventions can improve executive functioning and learning outcomes when used as structured pedagogical tools rather than stand-alone solutions (Schmid et al., 2014; Kim et al., 2018). Importantly, technology should complement, rather than replace, relational and teacher-mediated instructional practices.

Overall, effective self-regulation interventions depend on consistency and intentionality across classroom routines and instructional design. Students are more likely to internalize self-regulatory strategies when opportunities for planning, reflection, emotional awareness, and strategic problem-solving are systematically embedded within everyday learning experiences. This aligns with research indicating that repeated practice within supportive and structured environments is essential for the development and transfer of self-regulatory skills across contexts (Dignath & Büttner, 2008; Panadero, 2017). The following table summarizes evidence-based classroom strategies commonly associated with improved self-regulation and motivational engagement.

Table 1. Evidence-Based Classroom Strategies for Supporting Self-Regulation and Motivation

Strategy	Description	Impact on Students With Neurodevelopmental Disorders
Embedded metacognitive instruction	Explicit teaching of planning, monitoring, and reflection during academic activities	Improves independent learning and strategic thinking
Visual supports and organizers	Use of schedules, prompts, graphic organizers, and visual task breakdowns	Reduces cognitive overload and improves organization
Co-regulation practices	Supportive teacher guidance during emotional or behavioral dysregulation	Enhances emotional safety and adaptive coping
Mindfulness activities	Breathing exercises, grounding strategies, and reflective awareness	Strengthens attentional and emotional regulation
Flexible sensory environments	Quiet spaces, flexible seating, and movement opportunities	Reduces stress and sensory overload
Collaborative learning	Peer-mediated learning and cooperative problem-solving	Strengthens social participation and motivation
Gamified learning systems	Feedback-based and interactive learning technologies	Increases engagement and persistence
Autonomy-supportive instruction	Student choice and collaborative decision-making	Enhances intrinsic motivation and self-efficacy

Ultimately, classroom strategies are most effective when they are embedded within relational, inclusive, and emotionally responsive pedagogical frameworks. Self-regulation develops not through isolated interventions but through consistent participation in supportive educational environments.

2.3 Educator Professional Development for Inclusive and Self-Regulated Learning Environments

Effective development of self-regulation in inclusive classrooms depends strongly on the quality and sustainability of educator professional development. Current research consistently shows that isolated behaviour management strategies are insufficient to meet the complex cognitive, emotional, and motivational needs of learners with learning difficulties and neurodevelopmental disorders. Instead, effective practice requires teachers to adopt integrated, developmentally informed, and relationally responsive pedagogical approaches that are continuously supported through structured professional learning systems (Meltzer, 2018; Gehle et al., 2023).

A central component of classroom practice involves explicit instruction in self-regulated learning strategies. Rather than being taught as a separate skill, self-regulation is most effective when embedded within academic instruction through planning, monitoring, organization, and reflection activities (Dignath & Büttner, 2008). Teachers support this process by modelling cognitive and metacognitive strategies using think-aloud, guided practice, and scaffolded instruction, enabling students to gradually internalize effective learning behaviors such as goal setting, self-monitoring, and adaptive strategy use (Zimmerman, 2000). However, successful implementation of these approaches depends on teachers' professional knowledge and conceptual understanding of learning processes. Many educators report limited training in executive functioning, emotional regulation, and neurodevelopmental conditions, which can constrain their ability to effectively support diverse learners (Meltzer, 2018). As a result, professional development must move beyond procedural training and instead foster a deeper understanding of self-regulation as a dynamic, context-dependent process shaped through interaction, instruction, and social experience (Vygotsky, 1978; Zimmerman, 2000).

High-quality professional learning therefore requires interdisciplinary knowledge, integrating insights from educational psychology, cognitive science, and inclusive pedagogy. When teachers understand how executive functions, attention, and emotional regulation influence learning, they are more likely to adopt strengths-based and supportive interpretations of student behavior rather than punitive or deficit-based perspectives (Meltzer, 2018). This shift is critical for building inclusive classroom environments characterized by emotional safety, relational trust, and adaptive instructional support.

Research also emphasizes that effective professional development must be sustained, collaborative, and embedded within practice. Short-term workshops alone are insufficient to produce meaningful changes in teaching behavior. Instead, ongoing coaching, peer collaboration, reflective dialogue, and classroom-based inquiry have been shown to be more effective in supporting long-term pedagogical change and the consistent application of inclusive strategies (Desimone & Garet, 2015; Gehle et al., 2023). Teacher wellbeing is another essential dimension of professional development. Educators working with students with complex learning and behavioral needs often experience high levels of emotional and cognitive demand, increasing the risk of stress and burnout. This can reduce emotional availability and affect classroom interactions. Research highlights the importance of supporting teacher emotional regulation and resilience, as teacher wellbeing is closely linked to student engagement and classroom climate (Jennings & Greenberg, 2009; Shanker, 2016).

At a systemic level, implementation challenges such as large class sizes, time constraints, high curricular demands, and accountability pressures can limit the application of inclusive and self-regulation-focused practices. These structural constraints indicate that successful inclusion requires not only teacher competence but also institutional support, policy alignment, and adequate resourcing. School leadership plays a key role in shaping the conditions for effective professional development. Leadership practices that promote collaboration, shared responsibility, and a sustained commitment to inclusion are associated with stronger implementation of evidence-based instructional practices. Conversely, compliance-driven school cultures can limit teacher autonomy and reduce opportunities for reflective practice and innovation.

An additional challenge lies in balancing structure and flexibility in classroom practice. While structured routines and predictable environments support students with executive functioning difficulties, inclusive education also requires teachers to adapt instruction to individual learner needs. Developing this balance is a key professional skill that must be cultivated through sustained training and reflective practice. Finally, culturally responsive pedagogy is essential in ensuring equity in inclusive education. Teachers must be supported to understand how culture, language, identity, and socioeconomic background influence student motivation and behavior. Without this awareness, there is a risk of misinterpreting differences through deficit-based assumptions. Culturally responsive teaching therefore strengthens the effectiveness of inclusive and self-regulation-oriented practices (Gay, 2018).

In summary, effective educator professional development for inclusive and self-regulated learning environments must be sustained, practice-based, and interdisciplinary. It should integrate insights from educational psychology, executive functioning research, motivational theory, and culturally responsive pedagogy to equip teachers with the knowledge and skills needed to support diverse learners effectively in inclusive classroom settings.

3. CONCLUSION: REFRAMING SELF-REGULATION AND MOTIVATION AS FOUNDATIONS OF INCLUSIVE LEARNING

The growing complexity of contemporary classrooms requires a reconsideration of how educational success is conceptualized for students with learning difficulties and neurodevelopmental disorders. This chapter has demonstrated that self-regulation and motivation are not peripheral factors influencing academic achievement but represent fundamental processes through which learners engage with knowledge, manage challenges, and develop their identities as capable participants in educational communities. Students' difficulties with attention, emotional control, strategic learning, and persistence should therefore not be interpreted solely as individual limitations. Instead, they reflect dynamic interactions between learner characteristics, instructional conditions, social relationships, and institutional structures. A comprehensive understanding of these interactions provides the basis for developing inclusive educational practices that promote not only academic progress but also autonomy, resilience, and lifelong learning capacities (Zimmerman, 2000; Ryan & Deci, 2020).

A central argument emerging from this chapter is that self-regulation should be positioned as a core educational outcome rather than an assumed prerequisite for learning. Traditional educational models have often expected students to arrive at school with sufficient levels of attention control, emotional regulation, strategic awareness, and independent learning skills. However, contemporary developmental perspectives demonstrate that these competencies are gradually constructed through guided experiences, social interaction, and intentional instructional support. For students with learning difficulties, this developmental pathway may require additional scaffolding due to differences in executive functioning, cognitive processing, emotional responsiveness, and previous educational experiences (Diamond, 2013; Zimmerman & Schunk, 2011). Consequently, schools have a responsibility not only to accommodate existing regulatory differences but also to actively teach and cultivate the processes that enable students to become increasingly independent learners.

The conceptualization of self-regulation as a developmental and socially mediated capacity represents an important shift from earlier perspectives that viewed regulation primarily as an internal characteristic of the individual. Social-cognitive and sociocultural theories emphasize that learners acquire regulatory strategies through observation, interaction, feedback, and participation within meaningful contexts (Bandura, 1997; Vygotsky, 1978). This perspective has profound implications for inclusive education because it highlights the importance of the learning environment in shaping students' regulatory growth. Rather than asking why some students fail to regulate their behaviour or emotions, educators must consider how classroom structures, relationships, and teaching practices either support or restrict the development of regulatory competence.

The relationship between cognitive control and emotional adjustment is particularly significant in this regard. Learning requires students to coordinate multiple processes, including maintaining attention, managing information, responding flexibly to changing demands, and regulating emotional reactions to difficulty. When these systems are disrupted, students may experience a cycle in which academic challenges generate frustration, frustration reduces engagement, and reduced engagement limits opportunities for success. Over time, these experiences may influence students' self-perceptions and willingness to participate in learning activities. Understanding this reciprocal relationship reinforces the need for educational approaches that address cognitive and emotional dimensions simultaneously rather than treating them as separate areas of intervention (Groves et al., 2022).

Motivation provides the essential link between students' regulatory capacities and their willingness to apply them. The development of self-regulated learning requires not only strategic knowledge but also the desire and confidence to engage in strategic behaviour. Within self-determination theory, motivation is strengthened when educational environments support learners' experiences of autonomy, competence, and connection with others (Deci et al., 2000; Ryan & Deci, 2020). These principles are especially relevant for students who have experienced repeated academic difficulties, as such experiences may influence how they interpret challenges and evaluate their own abilities. When students perceive themselves as unsuccessful learners, they may gradually reduce effort, avoid challenging tasks, or disengage from academic opportunities. Therefore, creating conditions in which students experience meaningful progress and personal agency is essential for rebuilding positive motivational orientations.

This perspective requires educators to reconsider the meaning of engagement and disengagement in classrooms. Behaviors commonly interpreted as lack of motivation may represent complex responses to inaccessible tasks, limited confidence, emotional stress, or previous experiences of failure. A student who avoids participation may not necessarily lack interest in learning but may be protecting themselves from anticipated difficulty or negative evaluation. Recognizing these underlying processes allows teachers to move beyond behavioural interpretation toward more supportive and responsive educational decision-making. Such an approach aligns with strengths-based perspectives that emphasize identifying learners' abilities, interests, and sources of competence rather than focusing exclusively on areas of difficulty (Meltzer, 2018).

The integration of motivational principles within inclusive education also challenges schools to reconsider traditional approaches to achievement and assessment. Systems that prioritize comparison, competition, and standardized outcomes may unintentionally reinforce feelings of inadequacy among students who learn differently. In contrast, environments that emphasize individual growth, strategic improvement, and meaningful contribution provide greater opportunities for students to develop confidence and persistence. Mastery-oriented approaches encourage learners to view challenges as opportunities for development and support the gradual construction of adaptive beliefs about learning (Bandura, 1997). Therefore, inclusive education requires not only changes in instructional techniques but also changes in the underlying values and assumptions that define successful learning.

A major implication of this chapter is that inclusive education must be understood as an ecological process involving multiple interconnected levels of support. Although classroom practices are essential, sustainable inclusion cannot depend exclusively on individual teachers. Whole-school cultures, leadership structures, professional collaboration, family partnerships, and policy frameworks all influence whether students experience genuine participation and belonging. Contemporary inclusive frameworks emphasize that effective educational systems anticipate learner diversity and establish supportive structures before difficulties become barriers to achievement (Meyer et al., 2014). This represents a movement away from reactive intervention toward proactive design, where accessibility and flexibility are embedded within everyday educational practice.

Within this broader framework, teachers occupy a particularly influential position because they translate inclusive principles into students' daily experiences. Their role extends beyond delivering curriculum content to include facilitating emotional security, supporting strategic thinking, and creating motivationally supportive learning environments. Teachers act as external regulators who gradually transfer responsibility to students through modelling, scaffolding, feedback, and guided independence. This process reflects the principle of co-regulation, whereby students initially rely on interpersonal support before developing more autonomous regulatory capacities (Vygotsky, 1978). For learners with significant regulatory challenges, these relationships may represent a critical pathway through which confidence, competence, and independence develop.

However, expecting teachers to fulfil this complex role without adequate preparation is unrealistic. Professional development must therefore become a central component of inclusive educational reform. Effective teacher learning requires more than awareness of diagnostic categories or lists of classroom strategies. Instead, educators need deeper conceptual knowledge regarding how learning, motivation, executive functioning, and emotional development interact. They also require opportunities to apply this knowledge through collaborative inquiry, coaching, reflection, and ongoing professional dialogue (Desimone & Garet, 2015; Gehle et al., 2023). Such approaches support teachers in moving from reactive classroom management toward proactive instructional design.

Teacher wellbeing must also be considered a fundamental condition for successful inclusion. Supporting students with complex learning and behavioural needs involves significant emotional labour, and educators require institutional systems that protect their own capacity for regulation and responsiveness. Research demonstrates that teacher emotional wellbeing influences classroom relationships, instructional quality, and students' social-emotional experiences (Jennings & Greenberg, 2009). Consequently, inclusive education should recognize that supporting learners and supporting educators are interconnected priorities rather than separate objectives.

The chapter has further illustrated that innovation, including technology-enhanced learning and gamified approaches, offers valuable opportunities when implemented within appropriate pedagogical frameworks. Digital resources can provide additional pathways for personalization, feedback, organization, and engagement; however, their effectiveness depends on purposeful integration with teacher guidance and relational support. Technology should therefore be viewed as an extension of inclusive pedagogy rather than a substitute for human interaction. The future of educational innovation lies in combining technological possibilities with evidence-based instructional practices that maintain the central importance of teacher-student relationships.

Looking ahead, research and practice must continue moving toward integrated models that recognize the complexity of learning difficulties and the multiple pathways through which students develop competence. Future educational approaches should investigate how self-regulation interventions can be adapted across diverse cultural contexts, how student perspectives can inform inclusive design, and how schools can establish sustainable systems that support both learners and educators. Greater attention should also be directed toward understanding how strengths-based approaches can reshape students' identities and challenge assumptions regarding ability, achievement, and participation.

Ultimately, this chapter advances the view that self-regulation and motivation represent foundational dimensions of inclusive learning rather than specialized concerns limited to particular student populations. Every learner develops within relationships, environments, and systems that influence opportunities for success. For students with learning difficulties, inclusive education must therefore create conditions in which regulation, motivation, and competence can emerge through meaningful participation and appropriate support. The purpose of education is not simply to help students overcome difficulties but to create environments where diverse learners can develop their capacities, recognize their strengths, and participate fully in academic and social life.

By positioning teachers as facilitators of regulation, designers of motivating environments, and contributors to inclusive transformation, educational systems can move toward a more comprehensive understanding of student success. The future of inclusive education depends on recognizing that learning is simultaneously cognitive, emotional, social, and motivational. When schools intentionally cultivate these interconnected dimensions, students with learning difficulties are provided not only with opportunities to achieve academically but also with the foundations required for independence, resilience, and meaningful lifelong engagement with learning.

4. FUTURE DIRECTIONS: ADVANCING RESEARCH AND PRACTICE IN SELF-REGULATION, MOTIVATION, AND INCLUSIVE EDUCATION

The evolving landscape of inclusive education highlights the need for continued theoretical refinement, empirical investigation, and practical innovation in understanding and supporting self-regulation and motivation among students with learning difficulties and neurodevelopmental disorders. Although significant progress has been made in identifying effective classroom practices and inclusive frameworks, future developments must move beyond fragmented intervention models toward integrated, sustainable, and context-sensitive approaches. The complexity of students' cognitive, emotional, motivational, and social experiences requires educational systems to adopt multidimensional perspectives that recognize self-regulation as a developmental process shaped through interactions among learners, educators, families, and broader institutional environments (Zimmerman, 2000; Ryan & Deci, 2020).

One important direction for future research involves developing more comprehensive models that integrate cognitive, emotional, motivational, and contextual dimensions of self-regulation. Existing research has frequently examined executive functioning, emotional regulation, or motivation as separate constructs; however, evidence increasingly demonstrates that these processes operate as interconnected systems influencing learning engagement and achievement. Future studies should therefore investigate how these domains interact over developmental trajectories and how changes in one area influence outcomes in others. Longitudinal research designs will be particularly valuable for examining how self-regulatory competencies develop across childhood and adolescence, how educational experiences contribute to these changes, and which factors promote resilience among students with diverse learning profiles (Diamond, 2013; Zimmerman & Schunk, 2011).

A second critical direction concerns the need for more personalized and adaptive approaches to intervention. Students with learning difficulties represent a highly heterogeneous population, with considerable variation in cognitive profiles, emotional needs, communication abilities, sensory experiences, and motivational characteristics. Future educational research should therefore prioritize individualized frameworks that move beyond diagnostic categories and consider students' unique strengths, preferences, and learning contexts. Advances in educational assessment, digital learning analytics, and adaptive technologies may provide opportunities to identify individual regulatory patterns and design more responsive instructional supports. However, personalization should remain grounded in inclusive principles, ensuring that individualized approaches do not contribute to segregation or reinforce deficit-based interpretations of learner differences.

The role of technology in supporting self-regulation represents another significant area for future exploration. Digital tools, artificial intelligence-supported learning platforms, virtual environments, and adaptive feedback systems offer promising opportunities to enhance engagement, organization, metacognitive awareness, and independent learning. Future research should examine not only whether technological interventions are effective but also the conditions under which they produce meaningful educational benefits. Particular attention should be given to the role of teacher mediation, accessibility, ethical considerations, data privacy, and equitable access. Technology should be conceptualized as a complement to relational pedagogy rather than a replacement for human interaction, as supportive teacher-student relationships remain fundamental to motivation, emotional security, and learning development (Cho et al., 2021; Stalmach et al., 2023).

Future research should also further investigate the role of teacher professional development in sustaining inclusive and self-regulation-oriented educational practices. While numerous evidence-based strategies have been identified, implementation remains inconsistent due to differences in teacher preparation, institutional support, workload demands, and available resources. Future professional learning models should move away from short-term, knowledge-transfer approaches and instead emphasize continuous, collaborative, practice-based development. Coaching, reflective supervision, interdisciplinary collaboration, and professional learning communities may provide more effective pathways for supporting teachers' capacity to design responsive learning environments (Desimone & Garet, 2015). Research should also examine how teacher beliefs, emotional regulation, and professional identity influence the implementation of inclusive practices, given that educators' perceptions of students strongly shape classroom interactions and expectations.

Another important area for future development involves strengthening the role of students' voices in educational research and practice. Historically, interventions for students with learning difficulties have often been designed from adult perspectives, with limited consideration of learners' own experiences and interpretations. Future inclusive education research should increasingly adopt participatory approaches that position students as active contributors to decision-making processes. Understanding how students perceive support strategies, classroom environments, motivation, and barriers to participation can provide valuable insights for designing more meaningful and effective educational practices. Student agency should therefore become a central consideration in the development of self-regulation interventions, aligning with motivational theories emphasizing autonomy and ownership of learning (Deci et al., 2000).

The importance of culturally responsive and socially inclusive approaches also requires greater attention. Research on self-regulation and motivation has frequently been conducted within specific cultural and educational contexts, limiting the generalizability of findings across diverse populations. Future investigations should examine how cultural values, language backgrounds, family expectations, and social identities influence students' motivational beliefs and regulatory development. Inclusive education must recognize that learning does not occur independently from students' cultural and social experiences. Culturally responsive pedagogies can contribute to stronger belonging, identity development, and engagement by ensuring that educational practices reflect and respect learner diversity (Gay, 2018).

At the systemic level, future educational reform should focus on creating sustainable structures that support inclusion beyond individual classrooms. Although teacher practices are essential, long-term improvement requires supportive leadership, adequate resources, interdisciplinary collaboration, and policy frameworks aligned with inclusive values. Future research should examine how schools successfully implement whole-school approaches, including Universal Design for Learning (UDL), Multi-Tiered Systems of Support (MTSS), social-emotional learning initiatives, and restorative practices. Understanding the organizational conditions that enable effective implementation will be critical for translating evidence-based knowledge into sustainable educational change (Meyer et al., 2014; McIntosh & Goodman, 2016).

Furthermore, future studies should place greater emphasis on evaluating long-term outcomes associated with self-regulation and motivation interventions. While many existing studies demonstrate improvements in short-term academic engagement or behavioural outcomes, less is known about whether these gains transfer across settings and continue throughout students' educational trajectories. Research should examine whether early development of self-regulatory competence contributes to later academic achievement, social participation, emotional wellbeing, and transition success into adulthood. Such evidence would strengthen the argument that self-regulation should be considered a fundamental educational priority rather than a supplementary intervention target.

In conclusion, the future of inclusive education depends on developing integrated approaches that recognize self-regulation and motivation as central components of human learning and development. Future progress requires collaboration among researchers, educators, policymakers, families, and students to create educational systems that are flexible, responsive, and grounded in evidence. By combining advances in educational psychology, neuroscience, technology, and inclusive pedagogy, future practices can move toward more personalized, equitable, and sustainable models of education. Ultimately, the goal is not merely to improve students' ability to cope with educational demands but to transform learning environments so that all students are empowered to participate, achieve, and develop as confident and autonomous lifelong learners.

REFERENCES

American Psychiatric Association. (2022). *Diagnostic and statistical manual of mental disorders* (5th ed., text rev.). American Psychiatric Publishing.

Bandura, A. (1997). *Self-efficacy: The exercise of control*. W. H. Freeman.

Cho, H. J., Levesque-Bristol, C., & Yough, M. (2021). International students' self-determined motivation, beliefs about classroom assessment, learning strategies, and academic adjustment in higher education. *Higher Education, 81*(6), 1215–1235. DOI: 10.1007/s10734-020-00608-0

Chu, L., Li, P., & Yu, M. (2020). The longitudinal effect of children's self-regulated learning on reading habits and well-being. *International Journal of Educational Research, 104*, 101673. Advance online publication. DOI: 10.1016/j.ijer.2020.101673

Deci, E. L., & Ryan, R. M. (2000). The "what" and "why" of goal pursuits: Human needs and the self-determination of behavior. *Psychological Inquiry, 11*(4), 227–268. DOI: 10.1207/S15327965PLI1104_01

Desimone, L. M., & Garet, M. S. (2015). Best practices in teachers' professional development in the United States. Psychology. *Social Education, 7*(3), 252–263. DOI: 10.25115/psye.v7i3.515

Diamond, A. (2013). Executive functions. *Annual Review of Psychology, 64*(1), 135–168. DOI: 10.1146/annurev-psych-113011-143750 PMID: 23020641

Dignath, C., Buettner, G., & Langfeldt, H. P. (2008). How can primary school students learn self-regulated learning strategies most effectively? A meta-analysis on self-regulation training programmes. *Educational Research Review, 3*(2), 101–129. DOI: 10.1016/j.edurev.2008.02.003

Dignath, C., & Büttner, G. (2008). Components of fostering self-regulated learning among students. A meta-analysis on intervention studies at primary and secondary school level. *Metacognition and Learning, 3*(3), 231–264. DOI: 10.1007/s11409-008-9029-x

Elias, M. J., Zins, J. E., & Weissberg, R. P. (1997). *Promoting social and emotional learning: Guidelines for educators*. Association for Supervision and Curriculum Development.

Gehle, M., Trautner, M., & Schwinger, M. (2023). Motivational self-regulation in children with mild learning difficulties during middle childhood: Do they use motivational regulation strategies effectively? *Journal of Applied Developmental Psychology, 84*, 101487. Advance online publication. DOI: 10.1016/j.appdev.2022.101487

Gehle, R., Dörrenbächer, S., & Perels, F. (2023). Teachers' promotion of self-regulated learning in inclusive classrooms: Current developments and future directions. *Teaching and Teacher Education, 125*, 104054. DOI: 10.1016/j.tate.2023.104054

Hattie, J. (2009). *Visible learning: A synthesis of over 800 meta-analyses relating to achievement.* Routledge.

Jennings, P. A., & Greenberg, M. T. (2009). The prosocial classroom: Teacher social and emotional competence in relation to student and classroom outcomes. *Review of Educational Research, 79*(1), 491–525. DOI: 10.3102/0034654308325693

Johnson, D. W., & Johnson, R. T. (2009). An educational psychology success story: Social interdependence theory and cooperative learning. *Educational Researcher, 38*(5), 365–379. DOI: 10.3102/0013189X09339057

Katsarou, D. (2024). The Play as a Mediator of Learning and Psychosocial Empowerment of Children with Learning Difficulties. In L. Ioannidou & a. Argyriadi (Eds), *Building Mental Resilience in Children: Positive Psychology, Emotional Intelligence, and Play* (pp 332-346). IGI Global. DOI: 10.4018/979-8-3693-8312-4.ch013

Katsarou, D., Mantsos, E., Papadopoulou, S., Sofologi, M., Efthymiou, E., Vasileiou, I., Megari, K., Theodoratou, M., & Kougioumtzis, G. (2025). Exploring AI technology in grammar performance testing for children with learning disabilities. *Education Sciences, 15*(3), 351–365. DOI: 10.3390/educsci15030351

Laal, M., & Laal, M. (2012). Collaborative learning: What is it? *Procedia: Social and Behavioral Sciences, 31*, 491–495. DOI: 10.1016/j.sbspro.2011.12.092

Meltzer, L. (Ed.). (2018). *Executive function in education: From theory to practice.* Guilford Publications.

Meyer, A., Rose, D. H., & Gordon, D. (2014). *Universal design for learning: Theory and practice.* CAST.

Montague, M. (2008). Self-regulation strategies to improve mathematical problem solving for students with learning disabilities. *Learning Disability Quarterly, 31*(1), 37–44. DOI: 10.2307/30035524

Panadero, E. (2017). A review of self-regulated learning: Six models and four directions for research. *Frontiers in Psychology*, *8*, 422. DOI: 10.3389/fpsyg.2017.00422 PMID: 28503157

Pintrich, P. R. (2004). A conceptual framework for assessing motivation and self-regulated learning in college students. *Educational Psychology Review*, *16*(4), 385–407. DOI: 10.1007/s10648-004-0006-x

Reeve, J., & Cheon, S. H. (2021). Autonomy-supportive teaching: Its malleability, benefits, and potential to improve educational practice. *Educational Psychologist*, *56*(1), 54–77. DOI: 10.1080/00461520.2020.1862657

Ryan, R. M., & Deci, E. L. (2020). Intrinsic and extrinsic motivation from a self-determination theory perspective: Definitions, theory, practices, and future directions. *Contemporary Educational Psychology*, *61*, 101860. DOI: 10.1016/j.cedpsych.2020.101860

Sankalaite, S., Huizinga, M., Dewandeleer, J., Xu, C., De Vries, N., Hens, E., & Baeyens, D. (2021). Strengthening executive function and self-regulation through teacher-student interaction in preschool and primary school children: A systematic review. *Frontiers in Psychology*, *12*, 718262. DOI: 10.3389/fpsyg.2021.718262 PMID: 34489822

Shanker, S. (2016). *Self-reg: How to help your child (and you) break the stress cycle and successfully engage with life*. Penguin.

Smith, T. E., Thompson, A. M., & Maynard, B. R. (2022). Self-management interventions for reducing challenging behaviors among school-age students: A systematic review. *Campbell Systematic Reviews*, *18*(1), e1223. DOI: 10.1002/cl2.1223 PMID: 36913185

Sofologi, M., Katsarou, D., Efthymiou, E., Kougioumtzis, G., Argyriadis, A., Kamari, A., Mantsos, E., & Megari, K. (2025). Unrevealing the pattern of interrelationships among learning behaviors, executive functions and social functioning in preschool age children. In Megari, K. (Ed.), *Clinical applications of pediatric neuropsychology from infancy to adolescence* (pp. 107–118). IGI Global. DOI: 10.4018/979-8-3693-9689-6.ch005

Stalmach, A., D'Elia, P., Di Sano, S., & Casale, G. (2023). Digital learning and self-regulation in students with special educational needs: A systematic review of current research and future directions. *Education Sciences*, *13*(10), 1051. DOI: 10.3390/educsci13101051

Trautner, M., & Schwinger, M. (2020). Integrating the concepts self-efficacy and motivation regulation: How do self-efficacy beliefs for motivation regulation influence self-regulatory success? *Learning and Individual Differences*, *80*, 101890. Advance online publication. DOI: 10.1016/j.lindif.2020.101890

Trautner, M., Schwinger, M., & Otterpohl, N. (2020). Effects of school-based self-regulation interventions on academic outcomes: A meta-analytic review. *Metacognition and Learning*, *15*(3), 315–344. DOI: 10.1007/s11409-020-09232-1

Vygotsky, L. S. (1978). *Mind in society: The development of higher psychological processes*. Harvard University Press.

Yang, D., Chen, P., Wang, H., Wang, K., & Huang, R. (2022). Teachers' autonomy support and student engagement: A systematic literature review of longitudinal studies. *Frontiers in Psychology*, *13*, 925955. DOI: 10.3389/fpsyg.2022.925955 PMID: 36072024

Zenner, C., Herrnleben-Kurz, S., & Walach, H. (2014). Mindfulness-based interventions in schools—A systematic review and meta-analysis. *Frontiers in Psychology*, *5*, 603. DOI: 10.3389/fpsyg.2014.00603 PMID: 25071620

Zimmerman, B. J. (2000). Attaining self-regulation: A social cognitive perspective. In Boekaerts, M., Pintrich, P. R., & Zeidner, M. (Eds.), *Handbook of self-regulation* (pp. 13–39). Academic Press., DOI: 10.1016/B978-012109890-2/50031-7

Zimmerman, B. J., & Schunk, D. H. (2011). *Self-regulated learning and performance: An introduction and an overview. Handbook of self-regulation of learning and performance*. Routledge.

Zoogman, S., Goldberg, S. B., Hoyt, W. T., & Miller, L. (2015). Mindfulness interventions with youth: A meta-analysis. *Mindfulness*, *6*(2), 290–302. DOI: 10.1007/s12671-013-0260-4

Chapter 8
From Nutrition Curriculum to School Resilience:
A Counselling Approach Through Citizen Science

Georgios Kritikos
http://orcid.org/0000-0002-1390-977X
University of the Aegean, Rhodes, Greece

Charistoula Chatzinikola
http://orcid.org/0000-0002-1670-0496
University of the Aegean, Rhodes, Greece

ABSTRACT

Contemporary school communities face complex educational and psychosocial challenges that require integrated approaches to student well-being and resilience. This chapter proposes a counselling-informed framework that reconceptualizes the nutrition curriculum as a pathway for fostering school resilience. Grounded in ecological and multisystem resilience theory, the chapter positions nutrition education as a curriculum-embedded domain that supports psychosocial and relational development. Through participatory Citizen Science methodologies, students engage as co-researchers investigating food-related practices within their school communities. Inquiry, reflection, and collaborative action strengthen student agency, collective efficacy, and school connectedness, while school counsellors facilitate psychological safety and interdisciplinary collaboration. By linking curriculum, counselling, and participatory pedagogy, the chapter offers a whole-school perspective on resilience building.

DOI: 10.4018/979-8-3373-9420-6.ch008

INTRODUCTION

Contemporary school communities operate within increasingly complex social, emotional, and health-related environments that directly influence students' academic engagement and psychosocial development. In this context, resilience has been widely recognized as a multidimensional construct referring not only to individual coping capacity but also to the adaptive functioning of systems, including families, schools, and communities (Masten & Motti-Stefanidi, 2020; Ungar, 2012). School resilience, therefore, reflects the school community's ability to foster protective processes, promote well-being, and sustain supportive relationships in the face of adversity. School counselling plays a central role in cultivating such processes, as it integrates preventive, developmental, and systemic interventions aimed at enhancing students' personal, social, and academic growth (Gibson et al., 2022; Kirk eta al., 2025).

Within comprehensive school counselling frameworks, resilience-building is not limited to crisis intervention; it is embedded in everyday educational practices that strengthen self-efficacy, belongingness, emotional regulation, and collaborative problem-solving (Kirk et al., 2025; Masten & Motti-Stefanidi, 2020). From a systemic perspective, school counsellors function as coordinators of interdisciplinary collaboration, facilitators of reflective dialogue, and advocates for inclusive school climates. This systemic positioning enables counselling professionals to connect health education, psychosocial support, and community engagement into coherent resilience-oriented strategies.

Nutrition education, although traditionally situated within health promotion, represents a powerful yet underutilized domain for resilience-building in school settings. Research consistently highlights the interconnections between nutrition, cognitive functioning, emotional well-being, and academic performance (Basch, 2011). Dietary behaviors are shaped by complex ecological influences, including family practices, socioeconomic conditions, cultural norms, and school environments (Sadownik, 2023). Addressing nutrition through a systemic lens, therefore, aligns closely with counselling approaches that consider students within interconnected relational and environmental systems.

When integrated into school counselling initiatives, nutrition education can move beyond knowledge transmission toward empowerment-oriented practice. By fostering critical awareness of food choices, body image, peer influence, and media representations, counsellors can support students in developing agency, self-regulation, and adaptive decision-making skills, core components of resilience (Masten & Motti-Stefanidi, 2020). Moreover, nutrition-related projects can serve as platforms for strengthening peer collaboration and school connectedness, both of which are recognized as protective factors in resilience research (Ungar, 2012).

Participatory methodologies such as Citizen Science further enhance this potential by engaging students actively in inquiry and knowledge production (Bonney et al., 2009). In school settings, participatory nutrition projects promote experiential learning, student voice, collective problem-solving, and shared responsibility. Through collaboration between counsellors and educators, students assume active roles that strengthen self-efficacy, agency, and school connectedness, all of which support resilient school communities.

Within this systemic and participatory perspective, the nutrition curriculum functions as a bridge between health promotion and school counselling. Rather than remaining an isolated curriculum component focused primarily on knowledge acquisition or behavioral change, it becomes part of a broader resilience-oriented strategy grounded in interdisciplinary collaboration, reflective dialogue, and meaningful student engagement. Contemporary resilience research emphasizes that adaptive capacity emerges through interactions among individual competencies, supportive relationships, and institutional conditions (Masten & Motti-Stefanidi, 2020; Ungar, 2012). Consequently, curriculum domains that are closely connected to students' everyday experiences can serve as important contexts for activating resilience processes. Nutrition-related learning is particularly relevant in this regard, as food practices are embedded within family routines, peer interactions, cultural norms, and school environments.

Participatory methodologies such as Citizen Science further strengthen this potential by engaging students as active contributors to inquiry and knowledge production rather than passive recipients of information (Bonney et al., 2009). At the same time, school counsellors play a crucial role in facilitating psychologically safe environments that encourage participation, dialogue, and inclusion (Gibson et al., 2022; Edmondson, 1999). This chapter therefore reframes the nutrition curriculum as a counselling-informed pathway for fostering resilience through participatory Citizen Science. Drawing on systemic theory, it examines the interconnections among resilience, school counselling, and nutrition-related learning, while proposing a practical framework for implementing participatory, resilience-focused initiatives within school settings. By integrating curriculum, counselling, and participatory pedagogy, the chapter contributes to ongoing discussions on innovative whole-school approaches.

LITERATURE REVIEW

Resilience in School Contexts

Resilience has evolved from being conceptualized as an individual trait to being understood as a dynamic, multisystemic process that emerges through interactions among individuals and their environments (Masten & Motti-Stefanidi, 2020; Ungar, 2012). Contemporary resilience research emphasizes adaptive capacity across interconnected systems, including family, school, and community structures (Masten & Motti-Stefanidi, 2020). Within educational settings, resilience is increasingly framed as both a student-level and institutional-level construct.

At the individual level, resilience involves competencies such as emotional regulation, problem-solving skills, self-efficacy, and adaptive coping strategies (Masten & Motti-Stefanidi, 2020). At the relational level, supportive peer relationships and positive student–teacher interactions serve as protective factors. At the institutional level, resilience is reflected in school climate, inclusive practices, collaborative leadership, and the capacity to respond constructively to stressors or crises.

The school environment functions as a critical developmental context in which protective processes can either be strengthened or undermined. Ecological systems theory (Sadownik, 2023) underscores that students' adaptive functioning is shaped by nested environmental systems. Accordingly, resilience-building initiatives must address not only individual competencies but also relational and institutional conditions.

Recent global disruptions, including public health crises, economic instability, and social fragmentation, have further underscored the need for resilience-oriented school models. Whole-school approaches that integrate academic, social, and health dimensions are increasingly recommended to support adaptive capacity across systems (Masten & Motti-Stefanidi, 2020).

Despite growing attention to resilience in education, most literature emphasizes psychosocial interventions, social-emotional learning, or crisis response, while limited attention has been given to curriculum domains such as nutrition education as pathways for resilience activation within systemic and participatory frameworks. Although resilience research, school counselling, and participatory methodologies have developed in parallel, their integration within health-related curricula remains underexplored.

The Role of School Counselling in Resilience Building

School counselling is increasingly recognized as a key lever for resilience-building within school communities, particularly when resilience is understood as a multisystemic process rather than an individual attribute. Comprehensive counselling frameworks conceptualize school counsellors as professionals who support student development proactively through prevention, skill-building, and systemic collaboration (Gibson et al., 2022). This positioning aligns closely with contemporary resilience theory, which emphasizes that adaptive functioning is strengthened when protective processes are activated across contexts, including classroom practices, peer relationships, family, school partnerships, and the institutional climate (Masten & Motti-Stefanidi, 2020).

Within a whole-school perspective, school counselling contributes to resilience in three interrelated ways. First, at the individual level, counsellors support students' self-regulation, coping, and decision-making, promoting competencies such as self-efficacy and reflective capacity, core mechanisms consistently highlighted in resilience research (Bandura, 1990; Masten & Motti-Stefanidi, 2020). Second, at the relational level, counselling practice strengthens protective relationships by fostering peer support, improving student–teacher communication, and creating psychologically safe spaces where students can engage without fear of stigma. Psychological safety is critical for participation and learning, especially when interventions require students to share experiences or negotiate group processes (Edmondson, 1999). Third, at the institutional level, counsellors contribute to resilience by coordinating initiatives, facilitating interdisciplinary planning, and supporting school climate through preventive and developmental programming embedded in school structures (Kirk et al., 2025).

From an ecological standpoint, the counsellor's systemic role is particularly important because school challenges are rarely isolated. Students' well-being is shaped by nested systems and their interactions (Sadownik, 2023). Consequently, resilience-oriented counselling does not focus solely on individual "fixes," but also on strengthening the conditions that allow adaptive functioning to emerge, supportive norms, inclusive practices, and coordinated responses to student needs. In practice, this means that school counsellors often function as bridges between students, teachers, administrators, and families, translating psychosocial needs into actionable school practices and policy-relevant dialogue.

Counselling's contribution becomes even more salient in the context of innovation and change. Implementing contemporary, participatory approaches, such as Citizen Science projects embedded in curriculum, requires stakeholder engagement, contextual fit, and sustained support. Implementation research suggests that long-term adoption of new practices depends not only on the quality of the intervention design but also on the quality of implementation processes, including training, coaching, and alignment with organizational routines (Kirk et al., 2015). In school settings, counsellors are well placed to provide this kind of relational and organizational scaffolding, particularly when interventions touch sensitive domains such as nutrition, health, and identity.

Importantly, resilience-oriented counselling is strengthened when it adopts a strengths-based and culturally responsive stance. Social-ecological perspectives argue that resilience is negotiated and culturally shaped, requiring sensitivity to contextual meanings, resources, and constraints (Ungar, 2012). For nutrition-related initiatives, this is especially relevant: dietary practices carry cultural and socioeconomic meanings that can inadvertently become sources of stigma if approached prescriptively. Counsellors can protect psychological safety and promote inclusive engagement by ensuring that school initiatives emphasize inquiry, reflection, and empowerment rather than moralization.

Finally, school counselling aligns naturally with whole-school improvement efforts, particularly when schools aim to cultivate adaptive capacity amid contemporary stressors. Educational change scholarship highlights that sustainable innovation involves iterative collaboration, shared vision, and attention to system dynamics (Fullan, 2005). When counselling services participate in school development planning, rather than operating only as ancillary support, they can help institutionalize resilience-building practices and ensure that innovative approaches become part of the school's ongoing culture.

Nutrition Curriculum and Psychosocial Development

The nutrition curriculum has traditionally been framed within health promotion paradigms that emphasize knowledge acquisition, behavior modification, and the prevention of diet-related conditions. While such approaches have contributed significantly to public health goals, they often conceptualize nutrition as a discrete instructional topic rather than as a curriculum-embedded domain with broader psychosocial and developmental implications. As a result, the everyday role of nutrition-related learning in shaping students' cognitive, emotional, and social experiences within school contexts has remained relatively underexplored.

Emerging research suggests that dietary practices are closely linked not only to physical health outcomes but also to cognitive functioning, emotional regulation, and social participation (Basch, 2011; Masten & Motti-Stefanidi, 2020). When nutrition is approached as part of the curriculum rather than as an isolated health message, it becomes embedded in routines, interactions, and learning environments that shape students' adaptive functioning on a daily basis.

At the cognitive level, adequate and consistent nutrition has been associated with improved attention, memory, and classroom engagement. Basch (2011) highlights that nutritional status significantly influences learning readiness, particularly among students experiencing socioeconomic disadvantage. Energy instability resulting from irregular meals or high-sugar intake can lead to fluctuations in concentration and mood, which, in turn, affect academic performance, classroom behavior, and peer relationships. From a curriculum perspective, these effects extend beyond individual outcomes to influence classroom climate and collective learning processes.

Beyond cognitive functioning, the nutrition curriculum intersects with processes of identity formation and social belonging. During middle childhood and adolescence, food-related practices are shaped by peer norms, media influences, body image discourses, and family routines. These influences operate within interconnected ecological systems that extend beyond individual choice (Sadownik, 2023). When nutrition is treated as a socially situated curriculum domain, it offers students opportunities to critically examine how personal habits are shaped by social expectations, cultural meanings, and institutional arrangements. This perspective aligns with social-ecological models of resilience, which emphasize the dynamic interplay between personal agency and contextual resources (Ungar, 2012).

Developmental research further indicates that health-related decision-making is closely connected to emerging autonomy and self-concept during adolescence. According to self-determination theory, autonomy, competence, and relatedness constitute fundamental psychological needs that support motivation, engagement, and well-being (Deci & Ryan, 2000). Nutrition curricula that rely predominantly on prescriptive or normative messaging risk undermining autonomy by positioning students as passive recipients of expert knowledge. In contrast, curriculum approaches that incorporate inquiry, reflection, and dialogue can support autonomous decision-making, strengthen self-efficacy, and foster a sense of ownership over learning.

Food-related experiences are also deeply intertwined with emotional regulation. Patterns such as emotional eating, restrictive practices, or social comparison around food often reflect underlying psychosocial processes rather than isolated behavioral choices. Although school-based nutrition curricula are not clinical interventions, they can provide structured opportunities for guided reflection on how dietary habits intersect with mood, stress, and social pressure. When facilitated in psychologically safe learning environments, such reflection can enhance metacognitive awareness, emotional literacy, and adaptive coping strategies—capacities central to resilience development (Masten & Motti-Stefanidi, 2020).

Importantly, the nutrition curriculum also operates at an institutional level through the school food environment. Cafeteria policies, food availability, marketing practices, and informal norms communicate implicit messages about values, inclusion, and care. These environmental dimensions of the curriculum shape students' everyday experiences and perceptions of institutional support. Whole-school approaches to health promotion suggest that aligning curriculum content with environmental conditions enhances both sustainability and impact (Masten & Motti-Stefanidi, 2020). When students are invited to examine, discuss, and potentially influence these conditions through participatory inquiry, the nutrition curriculum shifts from a focus on individual behavior change toward collective agency and institutional engagement.

Despite these connections, the literature reveals a persistent gap between nutrition curricula and psychosocial resilience frameworks. Many school-based nutrition initiatives emphasize knowledge or behavioral outcomes without linking them to social-emotional development or counselling processes, while resilience and school counselling research often overlooks curriculum-based domains as sites for resilience activation.

This conceptual separation represents a missed opportunity. When embedded within systemic counselling and participatory methodologies, the nutrition curriculum can support self-regulation, reflective awareness, collaborative problem-solving, and school connectedness. Rather than functioning as a peripheral health topic, food-related learning can become part of broader developmental processes linked to identity, agency, and belonging.

Citizen Science and Participatory Approaches in Education

Citizen Science refers to the active involvement of non-professional participants in scientific inquiry, data collection, and knowledge production (Bonney et al., 2009). Initially associated with environmental and ecological research, Citizen Science has increasingly expanded into educational contexts, where it functions not only as a research methodology but also as a pedagogical approach that promotes engagement, collaboration, and critical thinking.

In school settings, participatory approaches grounded in Citizen Science principles reposition students as contributors to knowledge rather than passive recipients of information. This shift aligns with constructivist learning theories, which emphasize that knowledge is co-constructed through experience, reflection, and social interaction. By engaging students in authentic inquiry processes, formulating questions, collecting data, analyzing findings, and presenting conclusions, Citizen Science fosters ownership and experiential learning.

From a psychosocial perspective, participatory methodologies are closely linked to empowerment and agency. When students perceive that their voices matter and that their findings can influence real-world practices, their sense of competence and self-efficacy increases (Bandura, 1990). Such experiences are directly connected to resilience processes, as adaptive functioning is strengthened when individuals believe they can meaningfully influence their environment (Masten & Motti-Stefanidi, 2020).

Moreover, participatory inquiry supports relational resilience. Collaborative research tasks require communication, negotiation, and shared decision-making, reinforcing social bonds and collective efficacy. Collective efficacy, defined as a group's shared belief in its ability to achieve desired outcomes (Bandura, 1990), is particularly relevant in school communities where peer influence strongly shapes behavior. When students work together to investigate issues such as school food environments or dietary patterns, they practice collective problem-solving that extends beyond the specific topic of nutrition.

Citizen Science also aligns with democratic education principles by promoting inclusivity and shared responsibility. Students from diverse backgrounds can contribute experiential knowledge, thereby validating multiple perspectives and fostering cultural responsiveness. Such inclusivity is consistent with social-ecological resilience frameworks, which emphasize access to resources, recognition, and meaningful participation as core protective processes (Ungar, 2012).

In addition, participatory approaches contribute to metacognitive development. Reflection on research processes, what was discovered, how conclusions were reached, and what implications emerge, supports critical thinking and self-awareness. These capacities enhance students' ability to navigate complexity and uncertainty, competencies increasingly recognized as essential in contemporary educational environments.

Despite its growing prominence, the integration of Citizen Science into school counselling frameworks remains underexplored. Much of the educational literature highlights its impact on scientific literacy or environmental awareness, while less attention has been given to its potential as a resilience-building mechanism embedded in psychosocial practice. This gap becomes particularly evident in domains such as nutrition education, where participatory inquiry could bridge health knowledge with identity development, agency, and institutional engagement.

By integrating Citizen Science methodologies into systemic counselling processes, schools can create structured opportunities for students to explore health-related behaviors within supportive relational contexts. This integration allows participatory inquiry to function not only as an instructional innovation but also as a developmental intervention that activates resilience across individual, relational, and institutional levels.

Synthesis: Toward an Integrated Resilience-Oriented Framework

The reviewed literature highlights four converging strands. First, resilience is increasingly understood as a multisystemic process shaped by individual competencies, relational supports, and institutional structures (Masten & Motti-Stefanidi, 2020; Ungar, 2012). Second, school counselling provides a systemic framework that can coordinate preventive and developmental initiatives across these levels (Gibson et al., 2022; Kirk et al., 2025). Third, nutrition education influences cognitive, emotional, and social functioning, yet it is rarely conceptualized as a resilience mechanism within counselling practice. Fourth, participatory approaches such as Citizen Science promote agency, collective efficacy, and reflective learning, processes central to adaptive functioning.

Although each of these strands has developed robustly within its respective field, the literature suggests limited cross-fertilization among them. Resilience research rarely examines curriculum-based health domains as mechanisms for activating protective processes. School counselling scholarship has paid limited attention to participatory pedagogies as tools for systemic resilience design. Similarly, nutrition education and Citizen Science are seldom situated within comprehensive counselling frameworks that explicitly address psychological safety, relational dynamics, and institutional embedding.

This fragmentation points to a conceptual gap with direct implications for school practice. Contemporary school communities face complex challenges that require integrative, rather than compartmentalized, responses. Health-related behaviors, psychosocial development, and student participation are deeply interconnected within everyday school life, suggesting the need for frameworks that acknowledge and operationalize these interdependencies.

School Connectedness and Climate as Resilience Pathways

A key mechanism through which school-based interventions contribute to resilience is the strengthening of school connectedness and school climate. School connectedness is commonly defined as students' beliefs that adults and peers in the school care about their learning and about them as individuals. Large-scale evidence indicates that stronger connectedness is associated with reduced risk behaviors and improved well-being, suggesting that it operates as a protective factor within adolescents' broader ecological context. For example, McNeely et al. (2002) analyzed data from the National Longitudinal Study of Adolescent Health and found that students' perceptions of being cared for and feeling part of the school were linked to lower levels of substance use, violence, and early sexual initiation. In resilience terms, this points to the value of interventions that increase relational trust, belonging, and supportive adult-student relationships, domains where school counsellors have direct influence through preventive programming, consultation, and climate-oriented initiatives.

School climate research further clarifies the institutional conditions that support adaptive functioning. Thapa et al. (2013) synthesize school climate scholarship and highlight core dimensions including safety, relationships, teaching and learning, institutional environment, and school improvement processes. These dimensions align closely with multisystem resilience perspectives, which frame resilience as the capacity of systems to organize resources and relationships to promote positive adaptation. Importantly, school climate is not merely an "atmosphere" variable; it is shaped by day-to-day practices, norms, and participatory structures. Within the proposed framework, student-led inquiry and collective action around nutrition can be understood as a climate intervention insofar as it strengthens participation, voice, and shared responsibility. The counsellor's facilitation role is therefore not only psychosocial but also institutional: supporting climate-relevant processes such as psychological safety, inclusive dialogue, and constructive collaboration across stakeholder groups.

Whole-School Health Promotion and Integration With Academic Aims

The proposed model also aligns with whole-school health promotion frameworks. A major reference point is the World Health Organization's Health Promoting Schools (HPS) approach, which emphasizes integrated action across curriculum, school environment, and family/community partnerships. A Cochrane review of interventions based on the HPS framework reports benefits for certain health outcomes (including physical activity and, in some cases, dietary behaviors), although effects vary by context and implementation quality (Langford et al., 2014). The review underscores a core lesson highly relevant to the present chapter: sustainable outcomes depend on coordinated, system-level implementation rather than isolated lessons.

From a counselling-informed perspective, the HPS framework provides a useful backdrop for positioning nutrition initiatives within whole-school development rather than as "extra" programming. The counsellor can play a coordinating and boundary-spanning role consistent with HPS principles, supporting coherent planning, facilitating family communication, and helping staff interpret the initiative as linked to student readiness to learn. This linkage is supported by evidence that health and learning are intertwined. When nutrition projects are framed as supporting attention, emotional regulation, and engagement, they become easier to align with school improvement priorities and thus more likely to be sustained.

Social-Emotional Learning Evidence as an Adjacent Justification

Another complementary literature is social-emotional learning (SEL). While SEL is not identical to resilience, meta-analytic findings demonstrate that universal school-based SEL interventions can improve social-emotional skills, attitudes, behavior, and academic performance, suggesting that developmental competencies can be strengthened through coordinated school efforts. Durlak et al. (2011) synthesized evidence from 213 school-based SEL programs and reported improvements across social-emotional and academic outcomes. Importantly, they also noted that implementation quality moderated effects, which aligns with the chapter's emphasis on systemic planning, psychological safety, and institutional embedding.

A follow-up meta-analysis focusing on longer-term effects found that SEL programs can show sustained benefits over time (Taylor et al., 2017). This is particularly relevant for the current chapter because it suggests that resilience-relevant processes (e.g., self-regulation, relational skills, problem-solving) can be cultivated through structured educational experiences and maintained beyond immediate implementation. Positioning participatory nutrition inquiry within a counselling framework that explicitly targets agency, reflective capacity, and collective efficacy parallels the mechanisms emphasized in SEL research, while offering a distinctive entry point through a tangible, culturally meaningful domain (food and everyday routines).

Nutrition, Cognition, and Academic Engagement

To strengthen the chapter's mechanism argument, it is helpful to highlight a robust sub-literature on nutrition and cognitive/academic outcomes. Basch (2011) provides an influential synthesis linking health disparities and educational achievement, noting that nutrition-related factors can influence students' readiness to learn. More specifically, breakfast research provides evidence-informed insights into how dietary practices relate to cognition and classroom functioning. Hoyland et al. (2009) systematically reviewed studies on breakfast and cognitive performance and reported that breakfast consumption is generally associated with benefits relative to skipping breakfast, with some variation depending on nutritional status and study design. Complementing this work, Adolphus et al. (2013) reviewed the effects of breakfast on behavior and academic performance, emphasizing that breakfast can influence in-class behavior and school performance outcomes, while also pointing to the need for ecologically valid measures.

Within the present chapter, these findings can be used cautiously, not to claim that a counselling-led nutrition project will directly raise grades, but to justify why nutrition is a legitimate topic for resilience-oriented school development. If nutrition-related routines influence energy regulation, attention, and mood, then participatory inquiry into the school food environment can be framed as part of a broader strategy for supporting students' functional capacities and engagement. This makes the intervention more defensible to school leadership and teachers who prioritize learning outcomes, and it strengthens the conceptual coherence between health education and resilience-building.

Citizen Science Learning Outcomes and Youth Agency

A frequent critique of Citizen Science in education is that outcomes are assumed rather than articulated. The citizen science field has increasingly responded with frameworks and reviews focused on learning and developmental outcomes. Bonney et al. (2009) established citizen science as a tool for expanding scientific knowledge and literacy, and later work has called for clearer outcome pathways. For example, Bonney et al. (2014) highlight the need for scalable design principles and evaluation approaches. A systematic review from Finger et al. (2023) examined educational and scientific outcomes in citizen science research, illustrating both the promise of citizen science and the variability in reported outcomes.

For youth-focused citizen science, Ballard et al. (2017) provide particularly relevant evidence, showing how youth participation can support environmental science learning and conservation agencies. Although the domain differs from nutrition, the underlying mechanism, youth agency developed through authentic inquiry and community-relevant action, transfers well. In the proposed counselling-informed model, participatory nutrition inquiry can be positioned similarly as an agency-building practice that strengthens students' sense of competence, voice, and collective impact. This strengthens the chapter's "innovative approaches" alignment with the edited volume while grounding claims in an emerging but increasingly rigorous evidence base.

Equity and Food-Related Vulnerability in the School Community

Finally, a resilience-oriented approach must acknowledge that food practices are shaped by socioeconomic conditions, cultural contexts, and, in some cases, food insecurity. While the chapter appropriately avoids deficit framing, adding an explicit equity lens strengthens both scientific and ethical positioning. School counsellors can use participatory inquiry to surface structural influences, such as affordability, accessibility, and marketing, without individualizing blame. This approach aligns with social-ecological resilience perspectives, emphasizing that resilience is negotiated through access to resources and recognition in context (Ungar, 2012). In practical terms, an equity lens supports trauma-informed facilitation (e.g., avoiding public disclosure of food scarcity), encourages culturally responsive dialogue with families, and motivates system-level actions that are feasible within local constraints (e.g., improving breakfast availability, revising canteen options, or creating student-led informational campaigns that respect cultural diversity).

GUIDELINES FOR SCHOOL COUNSELLORS: IMPLEMENTING RESILIENCE-ORIENTED NUTRITION PROJECTS

Integrating nutrition education into a resilience-oriented school counselling framework requires intentional planning, systemic coordination, and sensitivity to the psychosocial dynamics of the school community. The following practice-oriented guidelines are designed to support school counsellors in implementing participatory, resilience-focused nutrition initiatives within diverse educational contexts.

Initiating a Systemic Project: Positioning Nutrition Within a Resilience Framework

The successful implementation of a resilience-oriented nutrition initiative requires systemic positioning rather than isolated activity planning. School counsellors are uniquely situated to frame nutrition education not merely as a health promotion topic but as an entry point into broader psychosocial development and whole-school resilience building. Contemporary resilience theory emphasizes that adaptive capacity emerges from interactions among individual, relational, and institutional systems (Masten & Motti-Stefanidi, 2020; Ungar, 2012). Therefore, interventions addressing health behaviors should be embedded within these interconnected systems rather than treated as stand-alone activities.

Reframing Nutrition as a Psychosocial Construct

Nutrition should be conceptualized as a multidimensional construct linked to emotional regulation, cognitive functioning, academic engagement, and peer relationships. Research indicates that physical well-being, including dietary habits, significantly influences concentration, energy regulation, and school performance (Basch, 2011). Moreover, food-related behaviors are embedded in social and ecological contexts shaped by family patterns, socioeconomic conditions, and cultural norms (Sadownik, 2023).

From a counselling perspective, reframing nutrition as a psychosocial and ecological phenomenon aligns with developmental and preventive school counselling models (Gibson et al., 2022). This positioning supports an integrative approach where health education becomes part of a broader resilience-enhancing strategy rather than a moralizing or behavior-control initiative.

Conducting Systemic Mapping

A systemic project begins with ecological awareness. Bronfenbrenner's ecological systems theory (Sadownik, 2023) highlights that student behavior is shaped by nested environmental systems, including family, school, peer networks, and community structures. Accordingly, school counsellors should engage in brief contextual mapping processes that identify protective and risk factors within the school ecosystem.

This may include reviewing school well-being indicators, exploring teacher observations, facilitating brief student discussions, and identifying existing health or SEL initiatives. Such mapping reflects a strengths-based orientation, which emphasizes recognizing existing assets and protective mechanisms within school communities (Kirk et al., 2025; Ungar, 2012).

Aligning With Institutional Priorities

Institutional alignment enhances both feasibility and sustainability. Whole-school resilience approaches emphasize coordinated action rather than fragmented programming (Masten & Motti-Stefanidi, 2020). When nutrition initiatives are linked to academic performance, student engagement, and school climate, they are more likely to receive administrative support.

School counsellors can explicitly connect the initiative to social-emotional learning objectives, preventive counselling frameworks, and school improvement plans. Framing the project within a comprehensive counselling model reinforces its legitimacy and coherence within institutional structures (Kirk et al., 2025).

Building an Interdisciplinary Micro-Team

Resilience research consistently underscores the importance of relational networks and collaborative processes in fostering adaptive capacity (Ungar, 2012). Establishing a small interdisciplinary team distributes responsibility and models cooperative functioning at the adult level.

Collaboration among counsellors, teachers, and administrators reflects multi-system resilience principles, where adaptive functioning is strengthened through coordinated system responses (Masten & Motti-Stefanidi, 2020).

Clarifying Resilience-Oriented Goals

Goal framing is critical. Resilience-oriented interventions focus on strengthening protective processes such as self-regulation, agency, connectedness, and collective efficacy (Masten & Motti-Stefanidi, 2020). Therefore, objectives should explicitly reference developmental capacities rather than merely behavioral outcomes.

For example, rather than focusing exclusively on modifying eating habits, the initiative may aim to enhance students' self-regulation, reflective capacity, and collaborative responsibility through participatory nutrition inquiry. Such reframing ensures conceptual alignment with resilience theory and comprehensive school counselling practice (Kirk et al., 2025).

Ensuring Psychological Safety in Participatory Inquiry

Participatory nutrition projects, particularly those grounded in Citizen Science methodologies, require careful attention to psychological safety. Because food-related discussions may intersect with issues of body image, socioeconomic status, cultural identity, and family practices, they can evoke vulnerability, comparison, or even stigma. School counsellors, therefore, play a critical role in ensuring that participatory inquiry unfolds within a trauma-informed, strengths-based, and developmentally appropriate framework.

Establishing a Safe and Inclusive Climate

Psychological safety refers to a shared belief that the group is safe for interpersonal risk-taking (Edmondson, 1999). In school-based participatory projects, this includes students' confidence to express ideas, share experiences, and reflect openly without fear of ridicule or marginalization.

At the outset of the project, counsellors should facilitate the co-construction of group norms, such as respectful listening, non-judgmental language, confidentiality where appropriate, and recognition of diverse family and cultural practices. Such norm-setting reflects trauma-informed educational principles, which emphasize predictability, trust, empowerment, and emotional safety (McCance-Katz, 2018). Establishing clear relational boundaries reduces anxiety and promotes inclusive participation.

Avoiding Moralization and Stigmatization

Nutrition education can unintentionally adopt moralistic tones (e.g., "good" vs. "bad" food), which may reinforce shame or social comparison. From a counselling perspective, it is essential to frame dietary behaviors as contextual and modifiable rather than as indicators of personal worth.

Strengths-based counselling approaches emphasize recognizing competencies, resources, and adaptive efforts rather than deficits (Kirk et al., 2025; Ungar, 2012).

Accordingly, discussions should focus on patterns and choices rather than labels, avoid public comparison of students' habits, recognize cultural diversity in dietary practices, and normalize variability in routines. This approach reduces stigma and aligns the project with resilience-building principles that prioritize protective processes over risk-focused narratives (Masten & Motti-Stefanidi, 2020).

Addressing Body Image and Peer Dynamics

Adolescence, in particular, is a developmental stage marked by heightened sensitivity to peer evaluation and body-related concerns. Food-related inquiry may trigger self-consciousness or teasing if not carefully facilitated.

School counsellors should monitor group interactions for subtle forms of exclusion or mockery, intervene promptly in cases of teasing, separate discussions of health from appearance, and reinforce that resilience involves self-care, not conformity. Linking nutrition explicitly to energy, concentration, and well-being, rather than weight or appearance, supports adaptive self-concepts and reduces risk of body-related stigma.

Facilitating Reflective Dialogue

Participatory inquiry becomes developmentally meaningful when accompanied by guided reflection. Reflective dialogue supports metacognition, emotional awareness, and meaning-making, key resilience mechanisms (Masten & Motti-Stefanidi, 2020).

Counsellors can use structured prompts such as "What surprised you about our findings?", "How do your eating habits affect your mood during the school day?", and "What makes it difficult to change certain habits?" This process encourages students to contextualize behaviors within broader ecological systems (Sadownik, 2023) rather than internalizing responsibility in isolating ways.

Supporting Autonomy and Empowerment

Self-determination theory highlights that autonomy, competence, and relatedness are fundamental psychological needs supporting intrinsic motivation and well-being (Deci & Ryan, 2000). In participatory projects, counsellors can nurture these needs by allowing students to choose research questions, assigning flexible roles based on strengths, validating contributions, and encouraging collaborative problem-solving. When students experience ownership over the inquiry process, they are more likely to internalize learning and develop self-efficacy, an essential component of resilience (Masten & Motti-Stefanidi, 2020).

Integrative Perspective

Ensuring psychological safety transforms a nutrition project from a content-focused activity into a resilience-supportive developmental experience. By integrating trauma-informed awareness, strengths-based facilitation, and participatory dialogue, school counsellors create conditions in which students can explore health-related behaviors without fear of judgment. Within such environments, participatory inquiry strengthens not only knowledge acquisition but also emotional regulation, agency, and connectedness, core dimensions of school resilience.

Facilitating Student Agency and Collective Efficacy

A central objective of participatory nutrition initiatives grounded in Citizen Science is to activate student agency. Within resilience theory, agency is understood as the individual's perceived capacity to influence their environment and make meaningful decisions (Masten & Motti-Stefanidi, 2020; Ungar, 2012). In school contexts, agency is not merely a personal trait but a relational and systemic process that emerges when students are granted voice, responsibility, and authentic participation. School counsellors play a pivotal role in cultivating such conditions.

In traditional health education models, students often assume passive roles as recipients of expert knowledge. By contrast, Citizen Science methodologies reposition students as co-researchers who generate questions, collect data, interpret findings, and propose actions (Bonney et al., 2009). This epistemological shift, from transmission to co-construction, has profound implications for resilience development. When students actively investigate their own dietary habits and school food environments, they begin to perceive themselves as capable contributors rather than subjects of regulation.

From a counselling perspective, facilitating agency involves more than delegating tasks. It requires intentional scaffolding that supports autonomy while maintaining psychological containment. Self-determination theory posits that autonomy, competence, and relatedness are essential psychological needs that foster intrinsic motivation and well-being (Deci & Ryan, 2000). In participatory nutrition projects, counsellors can nurture autonomy by inviting students to formulate research questions that reflect their lived experiences. Competence is strengthened when students are guided in designing manageable research tools and interpreting results meaningfully. Relatedness develops through collaborative inquiry and shared responsibility.

Collective efficacy represents a further layer of resilience. Bandura (1990) conceptualized collective efficacy as a group's shared belief in its capacity to organize and execute actions required to achieve desired outcomes. Within school communities, collective efficacy is closely associated with improved climate, cooperation, and adaptive functioning. When students collaborate to analyze dietary patterns or advocate for healthier school practices, they engage in a shared problem-solving process that reinforces group competence. The counsellor's role here is to facilitate constructive dialogue, manage conflict, and ensure equitable participation so that collective processes remain inclusive rather than dominated by a few voices.

Importantly, fostering agency does not imply transferring full responsibility to students without guidance. Adolescents, in particular, benefit from structured facilitation that integrates reflection and emotional processing. The counsellor supports students in connecting research findings to broader ecological influences, such as peer pressure, marketing strategies, family routines, and school policies (Sadownik, 2023). This ecological contextualization prevents oversimplified interpretations and reduces the likelihood of self-blame, reinforcing a systemic understanding of behavior instead.

Opportunities for public presentation, such as sharing findings with school leadership or younger students, further consolidate both individual and collective efficacy. When students see their work acknowledged and potentially influencing institutional decisions, they experience a tangible sense of impact. This recognition strengthens their perception of belonging and reinforces the adaptive cycle linking participation to resilience (Masten & Motti-Stefanidi, 2020).

Moreover, facilitating agency within nutrition projects contributes to the development of transferable competencies. Students practice critical thinking, negotiation, leadership, and reflective communication, skills that extend beyond health education into broader academic and social domains. By intentionally integrating these competencies into counselling objectives, the initiative aligns with comprehensive developmental counselling frameworks (Gibson et al., 2022; Kirk et al., 2025).

Ultimately, student agency and collective efficacy are not incidental by-products of participatory projects; they are core resilience mechanisms intentionally activated through structured facilitation. When school counsellors embed Citizen Science methodologies within a supportive relational climate, nutrition education becomes a vehicle for empowering students to recognize their capacity to influence both personal habits and collective school practices. In doing so, the intervention strengthens adaptive capacity at individual and systemic levels.

Managing Resistance and Systemic Barriers

The implementation of participatory, resilience-oriented initiatives within school settings rarely unfolds without challenges. Schools are complex organizations shaped by institutional routines, competing priorities, cultural norms, and resource constraints. From a systemic perspective, resistance should not be interpreted as obstruction but as a natural response within adaptive systems undergoing change (Fullan, 2005).

School counsellors, positioned at the intersection of student support and institutional processes, are uniquely equipped to navigate these dynamics constructively.

Resistance may emerge at multiple levels. Teachers may perceive the initiative as an additional workload within already demanding schedules. Administrators may prioritize measurable academic outcomes over preventive or developmental programming. Parents may express concerns about the framing of nutrition-related discussions, particularly when they perceive it as judgmental or culturally insensitive. Recognizing these reactions as systemic responses rather than individual opposition allows counsellors to adopt a collaborative rather than confrontational stance.

Implementation science emphasizes that sustainable school-based interventions depend on contextual fit, stakeholder buy-in, and gradual integration into existing structures (Kirk et al., 2015). Accordingly, school counsellors should frame nutrition projects not as external innovations but as complementary extensions of ongoing educational goals. Drawing explicit connections between dietary habits, concentration, emotional regulation, and academic performance can help bridge perceived divides between health and learning (Basch, 2011). When stakeholders recognize alignment with institutional priorities, resistance often diminishes.

Another critical factor involves the cultural meaning of food. Nutrition practices are deeply embedded in family traditions, socioeconomic realities, and cultural identities. A resilience-oriented approach must therefore avoid prescriptive messaging and instead emphasize inquiry, reflection, and contextual understanding (Ungar, 2012). Counsellors can facilitate informational sessions for parents that clarify the project's participatory, non-judgmental nature. Transparent communication reduces misunderstanding and fosters trust between school and family systems.

Time constraints represent a common structural barrier. Rather than introducing stand-alone sessions, counsellors may collaborate with subject teachers to embed project components within existing curricula, such as science, social studies, or language classes. This integrative strategy aligns with whole-school approaches to well-being, highlighting the importance of cross-sector collaboration in promoting resilience (Masten & Motti-Stefanidi, 2020). By distributing responsibilities and aligning objectives, the intervention becomes part of the institutional fabric rather than an isolated add-on.

At times, resistance may manifest subtly through passive disengagement or minimal participation. In such cases, relational leadership becomes crucial. Transformational leadership research suggests that shared vision, dialogue, and incremental success experiences increase collective commitment to change (Leithwood & Jantzi, 2005). School counsellors can support small, visible wins, such as a successful student presentation or positive classroom feedback, that demonstrate the project's value. These early successes function as reinforcing feedback loops within the system, gradually shifting perceptions.

Importantly, managing systemic barriers also involves counsellors maintaining reflexivity. Practitioners must consider their own assumptions about nutrition, health, and resilience, ensuring that their facilitation remains culturally responsive and developmentally appropriate. A systemic counselling orientation recognizes that change is co-constructed through relationships rather than imposed through authority.

Ultimately, resistance should be conceptualized as part of the adaptive process of institutional transformation. By addressing barriers through dialogue, alignment, collaboration, and cultural sensitivity, school counsellors can transform potential obstacles into opportunities to strengthen relational trust and systemic coherence. In doing so, the very process of navigating resistance becomes an enactment of resilience at the institutional level.

Embedding the Intervention in the School Counselling Program

For participatory nutrition initiatives to contribute meaningfully to school resilience, they must extend beyond short-term projects and become embedded within the broader school counselling framework. Sustainability is not achieved through repetition alone but through structural integration, relational continuity, and alignment with institutional vision. From a systemic counselling perspective, embedding an intervention involves anchoring it within policies, routines, and shared professional practices (Kirk et al., 2025).

Comprehensive school counselling models emphasize preventive and developmental programming delivered through coordinated, data-informed planning (Gibson et al., 2022). Positioning participatory nutrition projects within this framework enhances their legitimacy and ensures coherence with existing social-emotional learning, well-being, or prevention initiatives. Rather than functioning as an isolated thematic unit, the intervention becomes part of a continuum of services that promote self-regulation, decision-making skills, collaboration, and student voice.

Institutional embedding also strengthens multisystem resilience. According to resilience theory, adaptive capacity increases when protective processes are reinforced across interconnected systems (Masten & Motti-Stefanidi, 2020). When nutrition-related inquiries are linked to counselling objectives, classroom practices, family engagement, and school policy discussions, they activate reinforcing loops that extend beyond individual classrooms. For example, reflective sessions facilitated by the counsellor may connect with SEL modules on emotional awareness, while student-led proposals may inform school-level health policies. These cross-level connections contribute to institutional coherence.

Documentation plays a crucial role in sustainability. Counsellors can record implementation steps, student reflections, and observed changes in engagement or climate. Even without formal research measurement, systematic documentation supports reflective practice and institutional memory. Over time, such documentation may inform annual planning cycles, contributing to iterative refinement and scalability.

Embedding the intervention also requires cultivating adult capacity. Professional development discussions or brief collaborative meetings can help teachers understand the psychosocial rationale underpinning the project. When educators recognize links between nutrition, attention regulation, and classroom climate (Basch, 2011), they are more likely to integrate resilience-supportive language and practices into daily routines. This distributed ownership aligns with whole-school approaches to mental health and well-being, which emphasize shared responsibility rather than reliance on specialized personnel alone (Masten & Motti-Stefanidi, 2020).

Family engagement further consolidates institutional integration. Informational meetings or newsletters that explain the initiative's participatory, non-prescriptive nature foster transparency and trust. Recognizing families as partners rather than targets reinforces the model's ecological orientation (Sadownik, 2023; Ungar, 2012). Such collaboration supports continuity between school and home systems, strengthening the broader resilience ecology.

Finally, embedding the intervention requires a forward-looking orientation. Rather than treating each project cycle as an endpoint, counsellors can frame participatory nutrition inquiry as part of an ongoing culture of reflective, student-centered engagement. Subsequent cohorts of students may adapt or expand previous projects, creating a legacy of institutional learning. Over time, the school community develops not only healthier habits but also a shared identity as an adaptive, participatory system.

In this sense, sustainability is less about maintaining a specific activity and more about cultivating a resilient process. When participatory nutrition initiatives are structurally integrated into the counselling program and aligned with whole-school priorities, they contribute to enduring institutional resilience, manifested through collaborative problem-solving, inclusive dialogue, and collective efficacy.

ETHICAL, EQUITY, AND REFLECTIVE-EVALUATION CONSIDERATIONS FOR A PRACTICE-ORIENTED MODEL

Ethical Facilitation: Confidentiality, Consent, and Non-Stigmatizing Participation

Even when a project is framed as inquiry-based learning, students may disclose sensitive information, such as family routines, financial constraints, dieting behaviors, or peer teasing related to appearance. A counselling-informed approach, therefore, treats ethical facilitation as an active component of resilience building rather than an administrative formality. At the start of the project, counsellors can establish clear participation norms and discuss the difference between "sharing experiences" and "sharing private details." In group settings, the emphasis should be on patterns and systems (e.g., "What makes breakfast hard on school mornings?") rather than on personal confession.

A trauma-informed stance supports this process by prioritizing choice, predictability, and emotional safety (Brunzell et al., 2015; McCance-Katz, 2018). In practice, this can mean offering multiple ways to participate (speaking, writing, anonymous notes, small-group work), allowing students to opt out of personal sharing, and ensuring that any student-generated data (e.g., class surveys about snack choices) is aggregated and discussed at the group level. The counsellor's responsibility is to protect students from unintended exposure, including subtle forms of stigma that can emerge when "healthy eating" is treated as a moral virtue. This is consistent with psychological safety research, which links a non-punitive climate to learning and participation (Edmondson, 1999).

Equity-by-Design: Using Inquiry to Surface Structural Constraints

A systemic framework is particularly useful for avoiding a common pitfall in school nutrition work: over-emphasizing "individual choice" while under-emphasizing structural constraints. Students' food practices are shaped by affordability, access, time, marketing, cultural norms, and school routines. When these constraints remain implicit, students experiencing disadvantage may feel judged, while students with greater resources may interpret health behaviors as purely individual achievements.

Equity-by-design means building the project around questions that naturally reveal structural influences. Examples include: "How do time schedules shape breakfast?" "How does the school canteen menu reflect what is easy to sell?" "What kinds of food are advertised to young people and why?" The counsellor's role is to help students interpret findings through an ecological lens (Ungar, 2012), distinguishing between controllable micro-choices and broader environmental conditions that require collective action. This approach supports resilience by cultivating realistic agency: students learn to identify feasible changes (e.g., preparing a simple, affordable breakfast plan; negotiating a classroom snack policy) while also understanding when advocacy and system-level collaboration are needed (e.g., canteen offerings, school breakfast availability).

Equity-by-design also includes cultural responsiveness. Food is intertwined with identity; therefore, "healthy" cannot be treated as a single, culture-neutral template. Counsellors can actively invite multiple cultural perspectives on meals and routines, framing diversity as a resource for learning rather than a deviation from a norm. This aligns with social-ecological resilience perspectives that emphasize recognition and access to resources as part of adaptive capacity (Ungar, 2012).

Practical Data Stewardship in Student-Led Inquiry

Citizen Science-inspired projects often involve collecting information: observations of the school food environment, photos of labels, simple snack logs, or short surveys. Even when the project is not designed as formal research, the presence of "data" can create privacy risks if not managed responsibly. A practice-oriented approach can therefore adopt light-touch data stewardship routines: avoid collecting identifying information when it is not necessary; store class materials in a secure teacher/counsellor space; and agree that photos of peers are not used without explicit permission.

When student work is presented to the broader school community, the counsellor can guide students toward ethical presentation practices: use aggregated results; avoid naming individuals or families; and frame findings as opportunities for improvement rather than "exposing problems." This also supports institutional trust, which is crucial for sustaining the initiative over time. In the citizen science literature, attention to participant outcomes and learning is increasingly paired with attention to responsible design and evaluation (Bonney et al., 2014; Finger et al., 2023). The same principle applies here: the quality of the participatory process is a core outcome in itself.

Reflective Evaluation Without Formal Instruments

Implementation science indicates that sustainability depends on "learning while doing," including monitoring fit, fidelity, and responsiveness (Kirk et al., 2015). For school counsellors, this can be operationalized through three simple layers of reflection.

First, process indicators: attendance/participation patterns, student role distribution (who speaks, who leads, who withdraws), and quality of group norms. These indicators help the counsellor assess psychological safety and inclusion (Edmondson, 1999). Second, proximal developmental indicators: short reflective prompts collected at key points (e.g., "One thing I learned about how my environment influences food choices..."), shifts in students' language from blame to systems thinking, and examples of student-initiated problem-solving. These can be aligned with the framework's intended mechanisms (agency, collective efficacy, reflective capacity). Third, school-level indicators: small observable changes such as a class agreement about snacks, a canteen conversation initiated by students, or a teacher adopting supportive routines (e.g., allowing a brief "breakfast check-in" during morning homeroom).

The value of these indicators is not that they "prove effectiveness" in a research sense, but that they create feedback loops for improving the intervention. For example, if reflection notes reveal rising comparison or shame, the counsellor can reframe discussions toward energy and well-being rather than body image. If participation becomes dominated by a few students, roles can be rotated to strengthen inclusion. If teachers report time pressure, the project can be re-embedded into existing lessons rather than added as extra sessions. In this way, reflective evaluation functions as a resilience practice at the adult-system level: the school learns to adapt the initiative rather than abandon it when constraints appear.

Strengthening the Case for Sustainability: Linking Youth Agency to Institutional Learning

Finally, sustainability can be framed as a developmental process for the school system. Citizen science scholarship suggests that participation can produce learning and agency outcomes, particularly when youth see their work connected to real-world action (Ballard et al., 2017). Reviews also suggest that participant outcomes may include self-efficacy, skills, and civic engagement, although results vary and depend on design quality (Bela et al., 2016; Peter et al., 2019). Translating this into the school context, the goal is not to turn students into "junior nutritionists" but to create a repeatable school routine in which students practice inquiry, dialogue, and collective problem-solving around a concrete topic that matters in everyday life.

When the school counselling program institutionalizes this routine, through annual cycles, documentation, and shared leadership with teachers, the school builds an organizational memory for participatory resilience work. Over time, this can generalize beyond nutrition: the same participatory-counselling infrastructure can be applied to other topics linked to contemporary school challenges (digital well-being, bullying prevention, climate anxiety, inclusion). In that sense, the nutrition project serves as a manageable entry point for a broader culture of participatory resilience within the school community.

DISCUSSION

The present chapter proposes a systemic and participatory framework that integrates nutrition education, school counselling, and Citizen Science as interrelated mechanisms for strengthening school resilience. The discussion that follows situates this framework within the broader literature and reflects on its theoretical and practical implications.

Theoretical Integration and Contribution

One of the central contributions of this chapter lies in bridging conceptual domains that are often treated separately in educational research. While resilience theory emphasizes multisystem adaptive processes (Masten & Motti-Stefanidi, 2020; Ungar, 2012), and school counselling frameworks advocate preventive and developmental programming (Kirk et al., 2025), health-related curriculum domains, such as nutrition education, are rarely conceptualized as resilience-activating mechanisms.

By positioning nutrition education within a systemic counselling framework and operationalizing it through participatory Citizen Science methodologies, the proposed model expands the scope of resilience-oriented practice. It suggests that resilience does not emerge solely through targeted psychosocial interventions but can also be cultivated through curriculum-embedded, inquiry-based experiences that enhance agency, collaboration, and reflective awareness.

Furthermore, the model contributes to multisystem resilience theory (Masten & Motti-Stefanidi, 2020) by illustrating how protective processes can be activated simultaneously at individual (self-regulation, agency), relational (collective efficacy), and institutional (school climate, participatory governance) levels through a single integrated initiative.

Implications for Counselling Practice

The framework redefines the role of school counsellors from reactive support providers to systemic facilitators of resilience design. Rather than intervening only in response to identified difficulties, counsellors are positioned as architects of participatory learning environments that proactively cultivate adaptive competencies.

This shift aligns with contemporary counselling paradigms emphasizing prevention, strengths-based practice, and systemic coordination (Kirk et al., 2025). It also suggests that counselling services can meaningfully intersect with curricular domains, thereby expanding their influence beyond traditional individual or small-group formats.

Importantly, the participatory structure requires counsellors to adopt facilitative and reflective roles, ensuring psychological safety while encouraging student voice. Such positioning reinforces counselling's relational core and strengthens trust within the school community.

Institutional and Cultural Considerations

Implementing participatory nutrition initiatives within diverse school contexts requires sensitivity to institutional culture and sociocultural diversity. Food practices are deeply embedded in family traditions, socioeconomic conditions, and identity narratives. Therefore, resilience-oriented nutrition education must avoid prescriptive or deficit-based framing.

From a social-ecological perspective (Ungar, 2012), resilience is contextually negotiated. Initiatives that succeed in one cultural setting may require adaptation in another. Institutional readiness, leadership support, and collaborative climate significantly influence sustainability (Fullan, 2005).

The model thus underscores the importance of cultural responsiveness, transparent communication with families, and gradual integration within existing school structures.

LIMITATIONS AND FUTURE DIRECTIONS

As a conceptual and practice-oriented framework, the proposed model has limitations. It has not yet been empirically tested across varied educational contexts, and its effectiveness may depend on counsellor training, institutional support, and available time resources. Additionally, participatory processes require careful facilitation to prevent unintended peer comparison or stigmatization.

Future research may explore empirical assessment of resilience outcomes associated with participatory nutrition initiatives, longitudinal impact on school climate, cross-cultural adaptations of the framework, and the role of counselling leadership in sustaining institutional resilience.

Despite these limitations, the framework offers a theoretically grounded and practically adaptable approach to integrating health education within resilience-oriented school development.

CONCLUSION

Strengthening resilience within school communities requires approaches that move beyond fragmented, short-term interventions and toward integrated, systemic practice embedded in everyday school life. This chapter proposed that the nutrition curriculum, when enacted through participatory methodologies and coordinated within comprehensive school counselling frameworks, can function as a meaningful pathway for cultivating adaptive capacity at individual, relational, and institutional levels. Rather than treating nutrition education as a peripheral or purely health-oriented component, the chapter reframed it as a curriculum-embedded domain with significant psychosocial and developmental relevance.

By situating resilience within curriculum processes, the proposed framework expands prevailing understandings of how adaptive capacities are fostered in schools. Resilience is not conceptualized as an outcome of isolated psychosocial programs alone, but as an emergent property of learning environments that promote agency, reflection, collaboration, and shared responsibility. Through structured participatory inquiry, students engage not only with food-related knowledge but also with relational processes that support self-regulation, critical awareness, and collective problem-solving. In this sense, the nutrition curriculum becomes a lived context through which resilience is practiced rather than merely taught.

Central to this reconceptualization is the systemic role of school counselling. Throughout the chapter, school counsellors were positioned not only as providers of individual support but as facilitators of resilience-oriented environments. By ensuring psychological safety, supporting student voice, coordinating interdisciplinary collaboration, and embedding participatory initiatives into broader school planning, counsellors contribute to creating conditions in which adaptive processes can emerge organically. This expanded role highlights school counselling as a form of systemic leadership that connects curriculum, pedagogy, and well-being into a coherent whole-school approach.

The integration of Citizen Science methodologies further strengthens this perspective by operationalizing participation as a core resilience mechanism. Through inquiry-based and collaborative practices, students are positioned as contributors to knowledge and school improvement rather than passive recipients of instruction. This participatory stance reinforces agency, collective efficacy, and school connectedness—key protective processes associated with resilient school communities. Importantly, Citizen Science functions here not simply as an instructional innovation, but as a counselling-informed strategy that supports inclusive participation and reflective dialogue within safe relational contexts.

In an era characterized by social complexity, health-related challenges, and rapidly evolving educational demands, schools are increasingly expected to cultivate not only academic achievement but also adaptive, collaborative, and reflective communities. The framework presented in this chapter responds to these expectations by offering an integrative model that links curriculum, counselling practice, and participatory pedagogy. By embedding resilience-building processes within the nutrition curriculum, the proposed approach aligns with contemporary calls for whole-school strategies that address well-being, equity, and sustainability.

Ultimately, resilience is not built through isolated programs or prescriptive interventions, but through sustained relational and systemic processes that permeate school culture. When nutrition education is reimagined as part of a broader ecosystem of support, participation, and shared meaning-making, it can contribute significantly to the development of empowered and adaptive school communities. By conceptualizing the nutrition curriculum as a counselling-led, participatory domain, this chapter advances a holistic perspective on resilience that is both theoretically grounded and practically relevant for contemporary educational settings.

REFERENCES

Adolphus, K., Lawton, C. L., & Dye, L. (2013). The effects of breakfast on behavior and academic performance in children and adolescents. *Frontiers in Human Neuroscience, 7*, 425. DOI: 10.3389/fnhum.2013.00425 PMID: 23964220

Ballard, H. L., Dixon, C. G. H., & Harris, E. M. (2017). Youth-focused citizen science: Examining the role of environmental science learning and agency for conservation. *Biological Conservation, 208*, 65–75. DOI: 10.1016/j.biocon.2016.05.024

Bandura, A. (1990). Perceived self-efficacy in the exercise of personal agency. *Journal of Applied Sport Psychology, 2*(2), 128–163. DOI: 10.1080/10413209008406426

Basch, C. E. (2011). Healthier Students Are Better Learners: A Missing Link in School Reforms to Close the Achievement Gap. *The Journal of School Health, 81*(10), 593–598. DOI: 10.1111/j.1746-1561.2011.00632.x PMID: 21923870

Bela, G., Peltola, T., Young, J. C., Balázs, B., Arpin, I., Pataki, G., Hauck, J., Kelemen, E., Kopperoinen, L., van Herzele, A., Keune, H., Hecker, S., Suškevičs, M., Roy, H. E., Itkonen, P., Külvik, M., László, M., Basnou, C., Pino, J., & Bonn, A. (2016). Learning and the transformative potential of citizen science. *Conservation Biology, 30*(5), 990–999. DOI: 10.1111/cobi.12762 PMID: 27185104

Bonney, R., Cooper, C. B., Dickinson, J., Kelling, S., Phillips, T., Rosenberg, K. V., & Shirk, J. (2009). Citizen science: A developing tool for expanding science knowledge and scientific literacy. *Bioscience, 59*(11), 977–984. DOI: 10.1525/bio.2009.59.11.9

Bonney, R., Shirk, J. L., Phillips, T. B., Wiggins, A., Ballard, H. L., Miller-Rushing, A. J., & Parrish, J. K. (2014). Next Steps for Citizen Science. *Science, 343*(6178), 1436–1437. DOI: 10.1126/science.1251554 PMID: 24675940

Brunzell, T., Waters, L., & Stokes, H. (2015). Teaching with strengths in trauma-affected students: A new approach to healing and growth in the classroom. *The American Journal of Orthopsychiatry, 85*(1), 3–9. DOI: 10.1037/ort0000048 PMID: 25642652

Deci, E. L., & Ryan, R. M. (2000). The "What" and "Why" of Goal Pursuits: Human Needs and the Self-Determination of Behavior. *Psychological Inquiry, 11*(4), 227–268. DOI: 10.1207/S15327965PLI1104_01

Durlak, J. A., Weissberg, R. P., Dymnicki, A. B., Taylor, R. D., & Schellinger, K. B. (2011). The Impact of Enhancing Students' Social and Emotional Learning: A Meta-Analysis of School-Based Universal Interventions. *Child Development*, *82*(1), 405–432. DOI: 10.1111/j.1467-8624.2010.01564.x PMID: 21291449

Edmondson, A. C. (1999). Psychological Safety and Learning Behavior in Work Teams. *Administrative Science Quarterly*, *44*(2), 350–383. DOI: 10.2307/2666999

Finger, L., Sprinks, J., van den Born, R. J. G., & van den Berg, L. (2023). The science of citizen science: A systematic literature review on educational and scientific outcomes. *Frontiers in Education*, *8*, 1226529. DOI: 10.3389/feduc.2023.1226529

Fullan, M. (2005). The Meaning of Educational Change: A Quarter of a Century of Learning. In Lieberman, A. (Ed.), *The Roots of Educational Change: International handbook of educational change* (pp. 202–216). Springer., DOI: 10.1007/1-4020-4451-8_12

Gibson, E. M., Certion, C. B., & Aldridge, L. D. (2022). The ASCA national model. In Edwards, C. N., & Graham, M. A. (Eds.), *Foundations of School Counseling: Innovation in Professional Practice* (pp. 57–72). Springer Publishing., DOI: 10.1891/9780826187536.0004

Hoyland, A., Dye, L., & Lawton, C. L. (2009). A systematic review of the effect of breakfast on the cognitive performance of children and adolescents. *Nutrition Research Reviews*, *22*(2), 220–243. DOI: 10.1017/S0954422409990175 PMID: 19930787

Kirk, M. A., Kelley, C., Yankey, N., Birken, S. A., Abadie, B., & Damschroder, L. (2015). A systematic review of the use of the Consolidated Framework for Implementation Research. *Implementation Science : IS*, *11*(1), 72. DOI: 10.1186/s13012-016-0437-z PMID: 27189233

Kirk, S., VanMeter, C., & van Asselt, K. W. (2025). School Counselor and Principal Relationship as a Predictor of ASCA National Model Implementation. *Professional School Counseling*, *29*(1b), 2156759X251365244. Advance online publication. DOI: 10.1177/2156759X251365244

Langford, R., Bonell, C. P., Jones, H. E., Pouliou, T., Murphy, S. M., Waters, E., Komro, K. A., Gibbs, L. F., Magnus, D., & Campbell, R. (2014). The WHO Health Promoting School framework for improving the health and well-being of students and their academic achievement. *Cochrane Database of Systematic Reviews*, *2014*(4), CD008958. Advance online publication. DOI: 10.1002/14651858.CD008958.pub2 PMID: 24737131

Leithwood, K., & Jantzi, D. (2005). A Review of Transformational School Leadership Research 1996–2005. *Leadership and Policy in Schools, 4*(3), 177–199. DOI: 10.1080/15700760500244769

Masten, A. S., & Motti-Stefanidi, F. (2020). Multisystem Resilience for Children and Youth in Disaster: Reflections in the Context of COVID-19. *Adversity and Resilience Science, 1*(2), 95–106. DOI: 10.1007/s42844-020-00010-w PMID: 32838305

McCance-Katz, E. F. (2018). The Substance Abuse and Mental Health Services Administration (SAMHSA): New Directions. *Psychiatric Services (Washington, D.C.), 69*(10), 1046–1048. DOI: 10.1176/appi.ps.201800281 PMID: 30099944

McNeely, C. A., Nonnemaker, J. M., & Blum, R. W. (2002). Promoting School Connectedness: Evidence from the National Longitudinal Study of Adolescent Health. *The Journal of School Health, 72*(4), 138–146. DOI: 10.1111/j.1746-1561.2002.tb06533.x PMID: 12029810

Peter, M., Diekötter, T., & Kremer, K. (2019). Participant Outcomes of Biodiversity Citizen Science Projects: A Systematic Literature Review. *Sustainability (Basel), 11*(10), 2780. DOI: 10.3390/su11102780

Sadownik, A. R. (2023). Bronfenbrenner: Ecology of human development in ecology of collaboration. In Sadownik, A. R., & Višnjić Jevtić, A. (Eds.), *Re) theorising more-than-parental involvement in early childhood education and care* (pp. 83–95). Springer., DOI: 10.1007/978-3-031-38762-3_4

Taylor, R. D., Oberle, E., Durlak, J. A., & Weissberg, R. P. (2017). Promoting Positive Youth Development Through School-Based Social and Emotional Learning Interventions: A Meta-Analysis of Follow-Up Effects. *Child Development, 88*(4), 1156–1171. DOI: 10.1111/cdev.12864 PMID: 28685826

Thapa, A., Cohen, J., Guffey, S., & Higgins-D'Alessandro, A. (2013). A Review of School Climate Research. *Review of Educational Research, 83*(3), 357–385. DOI: 10.3102/0034654313483907

Ungar, M. (2012). *The Social Ecology of Resilience: A Handbook of Theory and Practice*. Springer., DOI: 10.1007/978-1-4614-0586-3

Chapter 9
Music, Wellbeing, and School Counselling:
Building Resilient School Communities

Maria Argyriou
http://orcid.org/0000-0002-4178-1136
University of the Aegean, Rhodes, Greece

ABSTRACT

This chapter examines the contribution of music education to preventive school counseling, well-being promotion, and resilience development in contemporary educational settings. Drawing on perspectives from music education, resilience theory, and school counseling, it explores how musical engagement can function as a psychosocial protective resource that supports emotional regulation, social connectedness, belonging, and positive adaptation. Findings from an exploratory quantitative study involving preservice preschool teachers highlight the perceived value of music in fostering children's well-being and resilience. Building on the empirical findings and relevant literature, the chapter proposes the Music-Informed Preventive School Counselling and Resilience Framework, a multilevel model that positions music education as a resource for strengthening inclusive, supportive, and resilient school communities.

1. INTRODUCTION

The promotion of children's wellbeing, mental health, and resilience has emerged as a central priority within contemporary educational research, policy, and practice. Increasingly, educational quality is understood as extending beyond academic

DOI: 10.4018/979-8-3373-9420-6.ch009

achievement to encompass emotional wellbeing, social connectedness, participation, belonging, and positive developmental outcomes (OECD, 2017, 2020; Keeley, 2021; World Health Organization, 2022). Schools are therefore recognised not only as sites of learning but also as environments capable of strengthening the protective factors that support healthy development, inclusion, and positive adaptation.

Contemporary resilience scholarship similarly conceptualises resilience as a dynamic and multisystemic process that emerges through interactions among individuals, relationships, institutions, and broader sociocultural contexts rather than as a fixed personal characteristic (Ungar, 2021; Southwick et al., 2023). Within this perspective, protective factors such as emotional competence, self-efficacy, social support, participation, and positive identity development play a crucial role in promoting wellbeing and adaptive functioning (Bandura, 1997; Masten, 2021; Goldstein & Brooks, 2023; Theron, 2023). Ecological approaches further emphasise that children's development is shaped by interconnected systems of relationships operating across family, school, community, and policy contexts (Bronfenbrenner & Morris, 2007).

Parallel to these developments, a growing body of international research highlights the contribution of music education to children's emotional, social, cognitive, and psychosocial development. Music-based experiences have been associated with emotional expression and regulation, self-confidence, social connectedness, belonging, creativity, empathy, and psychological wellbeing (Hallam & Himonides, 2022; Barrett et al., 2019, 2022; Welch et al., 2020). Research in early childhood settings further suggests that musical engagement can support social and emotional competence, collaborative participation, and positive peer relationships, all of which are recognised as important contributors to child wellbeing (Jia, 2024; Argyriou, 2025). Studies have also demonstrated the value of music for fostering intercultural understanding, cultural identity, inclusion, and participation among diverse groups of learners (Argyriou, 2025; Henley, 2025; Lorenzo de Reizabal, 2022).

Recent evidence further indicates that music may function as a protective psychosocial resource that strengthens resilience and wellbeing by supporting emotional regulation, adaptive coping, and positive self-perceptions (Saarikallio et al., 2020; Feng & Wang, 2025). Despite these documented benefits, music remains largely peripheral within school counselling frameworks and preventive educational policies, where its contribution is often viewed primarily through artistic or curricular lenses.

The chapter adopts a protective factors perspective, proposing that music education can be understood as a multidimensional educational resource that contributes to wellbeing and resilience through emotional, social, cultural, and relational processes. Combining theoretical analysis with findings from an exploratory quantitative study involving preservice preschool teachers, the chapter examines perceptions of music's contribution to children's confidence, emotional development, belonging, creativity, social interaction, and wellbeing. Building upon the theoretical and empirical findings, it proposes the Music-Informed Preventive School Counselling and Resilience Framework, a multilevel model illustrating how music may contribute to protective processes operating across individual, relational, school, and policy dimensions, thereby supporting more inclusive, resilient, and wellbeing-oriented educational environments.

2. SCHOOL COUNSELLING, WELLBEING AND RESILIENCE: CONTEMPORARY PERSPECTIVES

2.1 School Counselling in the Twenty-First Century

School counselling has become an increasingly important component of contemporary educational systems as schools are expected to support not only academic achievement but also students' emotional, social, and psychological wellbeing (Kolbert et al., 2022; World Health Organization, 2022). Growing concerns regarding children's mental health, social adjustment, and educational participation have reinforced the need for comprehensive school-based support systems that promote positive development and prevent psychosocial difficulties before they become more deeply established (OECD, 2017, 2020; Keeley, 2021). Consequently, contemporary school counselling has evolved beyond its traditional remedial role towards a broader preventive and developmental orientation that seeks to enhance wellbeing, resilience, inclusion, and educational success for all learners (Goodman-Scott & Ockerman, 2023; Sink, 2005).

Current approaches to school counselling are strongly influenced by ecological and systemic perspectives that recognise the interconnected nature of children's developmental experiences. Drawing on bioecological theory, development is understood as the result of ongoing interactions among individuals, relationships, institutions, and wider social contexts (Bronfenbrenner & Morris, 2007). Accordingly, school counsellors increasingly operate across multiple levels of the educational ecosystem, collaborating with teachers, families, school leaders, and community stakeholders to create supportive learning environments (Kolbert et al., 2022; Goodman-Scott & Ockerman, 2023). This perspective aligns closely with contemporary resilience scholarship, which conceptualises resilience as a dynamic and multisystemic process emerging from interactions between individuals and their environments rather than as a fixed personal characteristic (Ungar, 2021; Southwick et al., 2023).

The developmental focus of contemporary school counselling is also closely associated with inclusive education and educational equity. School counsellors contribute to fostering environments characterised by belonging, participation, emotional safety, and social support, particularly for students who may experience vulnerability or marginalisation (Cefai et al., 2018; Kakos, 2025). Such responsibilities extend beyond individual interventions and include preventative programmes, whole-school wellbeing initiatives, consultation, and collaborative support structures designed to strengthen student engagement and positive school experiences (Goodman-Scott & Ockerman, 2023).

Recent scholarship further emphasises the importance of strengths-based approaches that focus on identifying and cultivating protective factors rather than merely addressing deficits or risk. Within this perspective, self-efficacy, competence, social connectedness, and positive identity development are viewed as important resources that support adaptive functioning and positive development (Bandura, 1997; Masten, 2021; Goldstein & Brooks, 2023). As educational systems increasingly prioritise wellbeing and resilience, school counselling has become a key mechanism through which schools can promote holistic development and build supportive, inclusive, and resilient educational communities.

2.2 Student Wellbeing in Contemporary Education

Student wellbeing has become a central concern within contemporary educational research and policy, reflecting a growing recognition that educational quality extends beyond academic achievement to encompass emotional, psychological, social, and developmental outcomes (OECD, 2017, 2020; Keeley, 2021; World Health Organization, 2022). Increasingly, schools are expected to support learners' holistic development by creating environments that promote positive relationships, participation, inclusion, and healthy developmental trajectories. Within this perspective, wellbeing is viewed not merely as the absence of difficulties but as a positive state that enables children and young people to thrive, develop their capabilities, and engage meaningfully in educational and social life (Fegter & Fattore, 2024; Ravi, 2026).

Contemporary understandings conceptualise wellbeing as a multidimensional construct encompassing emotional wellbeing, psychological functioning, social connectedness, physical health, educational engagement, and opportunities for participation (OECD, 2020; Keeley, 2021; World Health Organization, 2022). Such perspectives emphasise that children's developmental experiences are shaped by multiple interacting factors and therefore require holistic educational approaches that address cognitive, emotional, social, and relational dimensions simultaneously (Bronfenbrenner & Morris, 2007; Fegter & Fattore, 2024).

Research consistently demonstrates strong associations between wellbeing and educational outcomes. Students who experience higher levels of wellbeing are more likely to demonstrate engagement, motivation, persistence, positive social relationships, and successful participation in learning environments (OECD, 2017; Khine et al., 2021). Conversely, reduced wellbeing and poor mental health are associated with lower educational participation, behavioural difficulties, social withdrawal, and diminished academic engagement (World Health Organization, 2022; Keeley, 2021). These findings reinforce the view that wellbeing constitutes a foundational condition for learning, development, and long-term educational success.

Relationships occupy a particularly important position within contemporary wellbeing frameworks. Supportive interactions with teachers, peers, families, and wider school communities contribute significantly to children's sense of belonging, emotional security, and educational engagement (Theron, 2023; Goldstein & Brooks, 2023). Educational environments characterised by inclusion, participation, and positive social relationships are more likely to foster adaptive functioning and positive developmental outcomes, particularly among students experiencing vulnerability or disadvantage (Cefai et al., 2018; Kakos, 2025).

These developments have important implications for school counselling and preventive educational practice. Contemporary approaches increasingly recognise that promoting wellbeing requires not only individual support but also the cultivation of supportive school cultures, positive relationships, and opportunities for meaningful participation across the educational community (Kolbert et al., 2022; Goodman-Scott & Ockerman, 2023). Such perspectives align closely with contemporary resilience theory, which emphasises the role of protective environments in fostering positive adaptation and healthy development.

2.3 Resilience as a Dynamic Ecological and Multisystemic Process

Resilience has become one of the most influential concepts in contemporary educational, developmental, and counselling research. While early perspectives often conceptualised resilience as an individual capacity to overcome adversity, contemporary scholarship increasingly understands it as a dynamic, ecological, and multisystemic process emerging through interactions among individuals and the environments in which they live, learn, and develop (Masten, 2021; Ungar, 2021; Southwick et al., 2023). Within this perspective, resilience is not viewed as a fixed personal characteristic but as an adaptive process supported by access to protective relationships, opportunities, resources, and supportive social contexts (Theron, 2023; Goldstein & Brooks, 2023).

A major development within resilience theory has been the shift from deficit-oriented explanations towards strengths-based and ecological approaches. Contemporary scholars emphasise that positive adaptation is fostered not only by individual competencies but also by the availability of supportive systems that promote wellbeing and development (Masten, 2021; Ungar, 2021). Resilience therefore emerges through the interaction of biological, psychological, social, cultural, and institutional processes, making it inherently multisystemic in nature (Southwick et al., 2023).

The bioecological model of human development provides an important conceptual foundation for understanding these processes. According to Bronfenbrenner and Morris (2007), development occurs through reciprocal interactions between individuals and multiple environmental systems. Schools represent one of the most influential developmental contexts because they provide access to social relationships, participation opportunities, routines, expectations, and learning experiences that shape children's developmental trajectories. Consequently, resilience is increasingly understood as a characteristic of educational ecosystems as much as of individual learners (Theron, 2023).

Recent educational research highlights the importance of school environments in promoting resilience and positive adaptation. Supportive relationships, inclusive practices, opportunities for participation, emotional safety, and a strong sense of belonging have all been identified as key protective factors associated with positive developmental outcomes (Cefai et al., 2018; Kakos, 2025; Goldstein & Brooks, 2023). Such findings reinforce the view that resilience is strengthened when children experience environments that foster connection, competence, and meaningful engagement.

The relationship between resilience and wellbeing is particularly significant. Contemporary scholarship increasingly recognises wellbeing as both a protective factor and an outcome of resilience processes. Positive emotions, social connectedness, participation, and supportive relationships contribute to adaptive functioning, while resilient adaptation, in turn, supports long-term wellbeing and healthy development (World Health Organization, 2022; Masten, 2021; Southwick et al., 2023). This ecological and strengths-based understanding of resilience provides an important foundation for contemporary preventive and developmental approaches to school counselling and educational practice.

2.4 Preventive and Developmental Models of School Counselling

The growing emphasis on wellbeing, resilience, and positive development has contributed to a substantial reconceptualisation of school counselling during recent decades. Contemporary approaches increasingly move beyond remedial and crisis-oriented models towards preventive, developmental, and strengths-based frameworks that seek to promote positive outcomes for all learners rather than focusing exclusively on the remediation of difficulties (Kolbert et al., 2022; Goodman-Scott & Ockerman, 2023). This shift reflects broader developments within educational psychology, resilience research, and public health, all of which emphasise the importance of strengthening protective factors before significant psychosocial difficulties emerge (Masten, 2021; Goldstein & Brooks, 2023; World Health Organization, 2022).

Preventive school counselling is grounded in ecological understandings of human development. According to Bronfenbrenner and Morris (2007), developmental outcomes emerge through reciprocal interactions between individuals and multiple environmental systems, including families, schools, peer groups, communities, and wider sociocultural structures. Consequently, contemporary counselling frameworks increasingly recognise that promoting wellbeing requires more than individual intervention; it requires the cultivation of supportive educational environments that foster positive relationships, participation, inclusion, and meaningful engagement (Ungar, 2021; Theron, 2023; Kakos, 2025). Within this perspective, schools function not merely as instructional settings but as developmental ecosystems that shape children's emotional, social, and psychological trajectories.

The preventive orientation of school counselling is closely aligned with contemporary resilience theory. Resilience is increasingly understood as a dynamic process supported by access to protective relationships, supportive institutions, and opportunities for positive participation (Masten, 2021; Ungar, 2021; Southwick et al., 2023). Educational environments characterised by belonging, emotional safety, social support, and inclusion contribute significantly to resilient adaptation and positive developmental outcomes (Cefai et al., 2018; Goldstein & Brooks, 2023). Consequently, contemporary counselling approaches seek to strengthen protective factors such as self-efficacy, social connectedness, emotional competence, participation, and positive identity development, all of which have been associated with improved wellbeing and adaptive functioning (Bandura, 1997; Masten, 2021).

Developmental models of school counselling further emphasise that support should be available across all stages of students' educational journeys rather than only in response to crises. Such models advocate universal and school-wide approaches that promote wellbeing, belonging, and social-emotional development for the entire student population (Kolbert et al., 2022; Goodman-Scott & Ockerman, 2023). This orientation aligns with international evidence demonstrating that positive educational experiences are associated with enhanced engagement, motivation, participation, and long-term wellbeing (OECD, 2017, 2020; Keeley, 2021).

Within this preventive and developmental paradigm, music education emerges as a particularly promising educational resource. A growing body of research indicates that musical engagement supports many of the protective factors identified within contemporary resilience and wellbeing frameworks, including emotional expression, self-regulation, social connectedness, belonging, creativity, confidence, empathy, and positive identity development (Hallam & Himonides, 2022; Barrett et al., 2019, 2022; Welch et al., 2020). Music-based experiences have also been associated with emotional wellbeing, adaptive coping, and social participation, suggesting that music can function as a psychosocial resource that supports positive development across diverse educational contexts (Saarikallio et al., 2020; Feng & Wang, 2025; Jia, 2024).

Importantly, music possesses characteristics that make it particularly compatible with preventive approaches. Unlike interventions targeted only at specific groups, musical activities can be implemented universally and inclusively within everyday educational practice. Through singing, movement, collaborative music-making, listening, improvisation, and creative expression, children are provided with opportunities to participate actively, build relationships, experience competence, and develop a sense of belonging (Barrett et al., 2022; Argyriou, 2025; Henley, 2025). Such experiences correspond closely to the protective mechanisms identified within ecological and multisystemic models of resilience.

From this perspective, music education may be conceptualised not merely as an artistic subject but as a developmental and preventive resource capable of supporting wellbeing and resilience across individual, relational, and institutional levels. Integrating music within broader school counselling and wellbeing initiatives therefore represents a promising avenue for strengthening protective processes, promoting positive development, and contributing to more inclusive and resilient educational communities.

3. MUSIC EDUCATION AS A RESOURCE FOR MENTAL HEALTH, WELLBEING, AND RESILIENCE

3.1 Music, Emotional Development and Wellbeing

The growing recognition of children's wellbeing and mental health as central educational priorities has intensified scholarly interest in the contribution of music education to psychosocial development. Contemporary research increasingly conceptualises music not merely as an artistic discipline but as a multidimensional educational practice that supports emotional, social, cognitive, and developmental growth across diverse educational contexts (Barrett et al., 2022; Hallam & Himonides, 2022; Welch et al., 2020). Through singing, listening, movement, improvisation, and creative musical participation, children engage in experiences that facilitate emotional expression, self-awareness, communication, and meaning-making, all of which are closely associated with positive developmental outcomes and wellbeing.

One of the most widely recognised contributions of music education concerns its role in supporting emotional development and emotional regulation. Emotional competence constitutes a key protective factor associated with wellbeing, resilience, and positive adaptation throughout childhood and adolescence (Masten, 2021; Goldstein & Brooks, 2023; Theron, 2023). Musical engagement provides developmentally appropriate opportunities for children to recognise, express, and regulate emotions through non-verbal and multimodal forms of communication. Rhythm, melody, movement, and musical interaction create emotionally rich learning environments in which children can explore feelings, develop self-awareness, and strengthen adaptive coping capacities (Barrett et al., 2019; Saarikallio et al., 2020).

Research further suggests that music functions as an important resource for emotional self-regulation and psychological wellbeing. Musical experiences are frequently associated with mood management, emotional expression, relaxation, reflection, and stress reduction (Saarikallio et al., 2020; Hallam & Himonides, 2022). Recent evidence indicates that engagement in music-based activities may strengthen emotional resilience and contribute positively to wellbeing by supporting adaptive emotional responses and enhancing self-perceptions of competence and agency (Feng & Wang, 2025). Such findings align closely with resilience theory, which emphasises the importance of emotional regulation and self-efficacy as protective mechanisms that support positive adaptation in the face of developmental challenges (Bandura, 1997; Ungar, 2021).

The educational significance of these processes is particularly evident during early childhood, a developmental period characterised by rapid emotional, social, and cognitive growth. Music provides children with safe and supportive environments in which they can experience, communicate, and reflect upon emotions while participating actively in meaningful learning experiences (Barrett et al., 2022; Jia, 2024). Through collaborative music-making, singing, and movement activities, children are afforded opportunities to experience success, develop confidence, and build positive self-concepts, all of which contribute to wellbeing and healthy development (Argyriou, 2025; Barrett et al., 2019).

Contemporary wellbeing frameworks increasingly conceptualise wellbeing as a multidimensional construct encompassing emotional functioning, social relationships, participation, engagement, belonging, and life satisfaction (OECD, 2017, 2020; Keeley, 2021; World Health Organization, 2022). Music appears uniquely positioned to support many of these dimensions simultaneously. Studies consistently associate musical participation with positive affect, social engagement, self-esteem, emotional competence, and educational participation (Hallam & Himonides, 2022; Welch et al., 2020; Jia, 2024). Furthermore, music offers accessible and inclusive forms of participation that transcend linguistic, cultural, and academic barriers, making it particularly valuable within increasingly diverse educational settings (Argyriou, 2025; Henley, 2025).

From a preventive and developmental perspective, these characteristics render music highly relevant to contemporary approaches to school counselling and wellbeing promotion. Emotional awareness, confidence, adaptive coping, participation, and positive self-development are central objectives of contemporary educational practice and resilience-oriented intervention (Kolbert et al., 2022; Goodman-Scott & Ockerman, 2023; Masten, 2021). By fostering these protective factors through engaging and universally accessible experiences, music education may be understood not simply as an enrichment activity but as a valuable psychosocial resource capable of supporting mental health promotion, wellbeing enhancement, and resilience-building within contemporary educational environments.

3.2 Music, Belonging, Inclusion and Resilience

Beyond its contribution to emotional development, music functions as a powerful social, cultural, and educational resource that supports belonging, inclusion, participation, and resilience. Contemporary resilience scholarship increasingly emphasises that positive adaptation emerges not solely from individual characteristics but through interactions among individuals, relationships, institutions, and broader sociocultural environments (Masten, 2021; Ungar, 2021; Southwick et al., 2023). Consequently, access to supportive relationships, meaningful participation, positive identities, and inclusive communities has become central to contemporary understandings of wellbeing and resilience (Theron, 2023; Goldstein & Brooks, 2023). Within this context, music education offers distinctive opportunities to strengthen many of the protective factors associated with healthy development and positive adaptation.

Music occupies a unique position within educational environments because it is inherently relational. Musical participation frequently involves cooperation, synchronisation, shared attention, collective expression, and reciprocal interaction among participants (Barrett et al., 2022; Welch et al., 2020). Through singing, movement, ensemble activities, improvisation, and collaborative music-making, learners engage in experiences that foster empathy, communication, trust, and social connectedness. Such interactions contribute to the development of positive peer relationships and supportive social networks, which contemporary resilience research consistently identifies as among the most important protective factors promoting wellbeing and adaptive functioning (Masten, 2021; Theron, 2023; Goldstein & Brooks, 2023). In educational settings, these experiences may strengthen students' sense of belonging and participation while simultaneously supporting emotional security and social engagement.

Belonging has emerged as a particularly important dimension of contemporary educational wellbeing frameworks. Research increasingly demonstrates that students who experience a strong sense of belonging within school communities are more likely to demonstrate engagement, motivation, persistence, positive self-perceptions, and adaptive coping capacities (OECD, 2017, 2020; Keeley, 2021). Music appears especially effective in fostering belonging because participation is based upon shared experiences, collective achievement, and mutual contribution rather than solely upon academic performance. Musical activities create opportunities for children to contribute meaningfully to group processes, experience recognition from peers and teachers, and develop positive social identities within supportive educational communities (Barrett et al., 2019; Jia, 2024). These experiences align closely with ecological understandings of resilience, which emphasise the importance of connectedness and participation as foundations of positive development (Ungar, 2021).

Music also contributes significantly to educational inclusion. Unlike many learning activities that depend heavily upon linguistic competence, literacy skills, or conventional academic achievement, music provides multiple pathways for participation and success. Children with diverse abilities, cultural backgrounds, developmental profiles, and learning needs can engage meaningfully in musical experiences through singing, movement, listening, improvisation, composition, and creative expression (Henley, 2025; Barrett et al., 2022). Such opportunities promote recognition, acceptance, and participation while reducing barriers that may otherwise limit engagement. Inclusive musical experiences therefore, contribute to educational environments characterised by equity, accessibility, and social participation, all of which are recognised as important conditions supporting wellbeing and resilience (Cefai et al., 2018; Kakos, 2025).

The cultural dimensions of music further reinforce these contributions. Music functions as a carrier of cultural memory, identity, and collective meaning, enabling learners to connect with their own cultural heritage while simultaneously engaging with the traditions and perspectives of others (Argyriou, 2025; Burnard & Randles, 2022). Through culturally responsive musical experiences, children develop greater appreciation of diversity, intercultural understanding, and respect for multiple forms of cultural expression. Such experiences support identity formation and cultural inclusion while contributing to educational environments that value diversity and participation. Contemporary educational research increasingly recognises these dimensions as essential components of equitable and inclusive schooling (Henley, 2025; Kakos, 2025).

Importantly, contemporary resilience theory conceptualises resilience as a multisystemic process operating across interconnected levels of experience, including individual, relational, institutional, and community systems (Ungar, 2021; Southwick et al., 2023). Music appears particularly valuable because it simultaneously strengthens protective processes across all of these levels. At the individual level, musical engagement supports emotional expression, confidence, creativity, and self-efficacy (Bandura, 1997; Hallam & Himonides, 2022). At the relational level, it promotes empathy, cooperation, belonging, and social connectedness (Barrett et al., 2022; Welch et al., 2020). At the institutional level, music contributes to inclusive school cultures characterised by participation, engagement, and positive relationships (Cefai et al., 2018). At the community and cultural levels, it facilitates identity formation, cultural continuity, and collective participation (Argyriou, 2025; Burnard & Randles, 2022).

Recent empirical evidence supports this integrated perspective. Studies indicate that musical engagement contributes positively to emotional well-being, social participation, confidence, identity development, and adaptive coping capacities, all of which are closely associated with resilience and positive development (Feng & Wang, 2025; Shen & Yang, 2025; Jia, 2024). Consequently, music should be understood not merely as a curricular subject but as a developmental and preventive educational resource that strengthens a network of interconnected protective factors. From a school counselling perspective, these contributions are particularly significant because they align closely with contemporary priorities concerning belonging, inclusion, participation, well-being, and the promotion of resilience. Music, therefore, represents a valuable component of holistic educational approaches that seek to foster supportive, inclusive, and resilient school communities.

4. METHODOLOGICAL FRAMEWORK

4.1 Research Design and Context

The present study employed an exploratory quantitative cross-sectional survey design to investigate preservice preschool teachers' perceptions regarding the contribution of music education to children's psychosocial development, wellbeing, and resilience. Exploratory quantitative approaches are particularly appropriate when examining educational phenomena that remain insufficiently investigated and when the aim is to identify patterns, tendencies, and professional beliefs rather than establish causal relationships (Creswell & Creswell, 2024; Cohen et al., 2018; Johnson et al., 2020). Survey research is widely used in teacher education because it enables the systematic examination of participants' perceptions, attitudes, and pedagogical understandings across defined populations (Aydoğdu & Ayanoğlu, 2020; Aksoy, 2026).

The study was conducted at the Department of Preschool Education Sciences and Educational Design of the University of the Aegean, Greece, within the broader context of undergraduate teacher education. Contemporary teacher preparation programmes increasingly emphasise not only pedagogical knowledge but also competencies related to inclusion, emotional development, wellbeing, and child-centred educational practice (European Commission, 2023; OECD, 2023). Within this context, music education is frequently conceptualised as a holistic pedagogical approach capable of supporting multiple dimensions of child development, including emotional, social, cognitive, and communicative growth (Welch et al., 2020; Barrett et al., 2022; Bulut, 2020; Bilir-Seyhan & Ocak-Karabay, 2018).

The selection of preservice preschool teachers as participants was particularly relevant because these future educators will be responsible for designing and implementing learning experiences within early childhood settings. Their perceptions are therefore likely to influence future classroom practices and the extent to which music-based approaches are incorporated into educational environments. Examining these perceptions contributes to broader discussions concerning teacher preparation, professional identity development, and the educational value of music within contemporary early childhood education (Burnard & Randles, 2023; McFerran & Hense, Koike & Rickwood, 2018).

The study was informed by a protective factors perspective derived from contemporary theories of wellbeing and resilience. Rather than focusing on developmental difficulties, the research explored participants' perceptions regarding the contribution of music education to psychosocial resources associated with positive adaptation, emotional competence, belonging, creativity, and social connectedness (Masten, 2021; Ungar, 2021; Southwick et al., 2023). This strengths-based orientation aligns with current international educational priorities that emphasise mental health promotion, resilience, social-emotional learning, and preventative approaches to child development (WHO, 2022; UNICEF, 2021; UNESCO, 2021). Consequently, the study sought to generate empirical evidence capable of informing contemporary discussions concerning music education, wellbeing, resilience, and preventive school counselling.

4.2 Participants and Sampling Strategy

The study involved sixty-six (N = 66) undergraduate students enrolled in the Department of Preschool Education Sciences and Educational Design at the University of the Aegean. Participants were preservice preschool teachers preparing for professional careers within early childhood education settings. The participants represented a population particularly relevant to the aims of the study because they were engaged in university-level coursework related to child development, pedagogy, educational design, and music education. Through their studies, participants had been exposed to contemporary theoretical perspectives concerning holistic child development, inclusive educational practices, and the pedagogical applications of music within preschool contexts. Their responses therefore reflected developing professional understandings rather than solely personal opinions.

A convenience sampling strategy was employed. Convenience sampling involves the selection of participants who are readily accessible to the researcher and is widely used within educational research, particularly in exploratory studies conducted within university settings (Cohen et al., 2018). The decision to utilise convenience sampling was based on practical considerations related to participant accessibility and the exploratory nature of the investigation. Although convenience sampling does not permit statistical generalisation to broader populations, it is considered appropriate when the objective is to explore perceptions, attitudes, and experiences within a specific educational context (Creswell & Creswell, 2024). In the present study, the purpose was not to generate nationally representative findings but rather to obtain meaningful insights into how future preschool educators perceive the contribution of music education to children's psychosocial development.

Participants were informed about the purpose of the study and invited to participate voluntarily. No incentives were offered for participation, and respondents retained the right to withdraw from the study at any stage. Participation was based entirely upon informed consent and individual willingness to contribute to the research process.

The sample provides a valuable perspective on future educational practice because preservice teachers occupy a transitional position between higher education and professional teaching. Their perceptions offer insight into how contemporary teacher education programmes may influence future pedagogical understandings concerning music, wellbeing, resilience, and holistic child development. While the findings should be interpreted within the limitations associated with a single-institution sample, they nevertheless contribute meaningfully to emerging discussions concerning the role of music education in fostering psychosocial protective factors within early childhood educational settings.

4.3 Research Instrument

Data were collected through a structured questionnaire specifically designed to investigate preservice preschool teachers' perceptions regarding the contribution of music education to children's psychosocial development, wellbeing, and resilience. The questionnaire was administered electronically using Google Forms, a platform widely employed in educational research due to its accessibility, efficiency, and capacity to facilitate anonymous participation and data management (Barrett, Flynn, Brown & Welch, 2019; Creswell & Creswell, 2024).

Questionnaires are among the most frequently used instruments in educational research for examining beliefs, attitudes, perceptions, and self-reported experiences (Cohen et al., 2018). Their structured format enables researchers to gather comparable data from multiple participants whilst ensuring consistency across responses. In the present study, the use of a questionnaire was considered particularly appropriate because the primary objective was to explore participants' perceptions concerning the developmental and educational value of music rather than to measure behavioural outcomes directly. The instrument was organised into nine thematic sections designed to capture different dimensions of participants' perceptions regarding music education and child development. These sections reflected key concepts emerging from the literature on music education, wellbeing, resilience, creativity, emotional development, and psychosocial learning. The questionnaire therefore sought to align empirical data collection with the theoretical framework developed in the preceding chapters (Dollman, 2023).

The first section collected demographic information, including participants' academic characteristics and background variables relevant to the study. Demographic data provide important contextual information that enables researchers to interpret findings more accurately and describe the sample comprehensively (Cohen et al., 2018).

The second section explored participants' general perceptions regarding the educational value of music in early childhood settings. Items examined the extent to which respondents viewed music as an important pedagogical resource capable of supporting children's overall development. These questions were informed by contemporary scholarship that conceptualises music as a multidimensional educational practice contributing to cognitive, emotional, social, and cultural learning (Welch et al., 2020; Barrett et al., 2022).

The third section focused on confidence-building and self-esteem. Participants were asked to evaluate the extent to which music education contributes to children's self-confidence, self-expression, initiative-taking, and willingness to participate in educational activities. These dimensions were included because self-confidence is consistently recognised as a protective factor associated with positive adaptation and resilience (Masten, 2021; Theron, 2023).

The fourth section examined perceptions concerning children's sense of belonging and social inclusion. Questions investigated whether musical experiences support participation, cooperation, acceptance, and the development of positive peer relationships. The inclusion of this dimension was informed by research demonstrating that belonging represents a significant predictor of educational engagement, wellbeing, and resilience (OECD, 2017;2018; WHO, 2022).

The fifth section addressed emotional development and emotional intelligence. Participants evaluated the extent to which music facilitates emotional awareness, emotional expression, empathy, emotional regulation, and understanding of feelings. These constructs are particularly relevant because emotional competence is widely recognised as a foundational component of both wellbeing and resilience (Saarikallio et al., 2020).

The sixth section focused on creativity and imaginative development. Music education has frequently been associated with creative thinking, divergent problem-solving, innovation, and self-expression (Burnard, 2012). Consequently, participants were invited to reflect upon the extent to which music contributes to children's creative capacities and imaginative engagement.

The seventh section explored social interaction and communication. Respondents evaluated whether music-based activities promote collaboration, communication skills, mutual respect, group participation, and interpersonal understanding. These dimensions were included because social connectedness has consistently been identified as a central protective factor supporting wellbeing and resilience across developmental contexts (Ungar, 2021; Barrett et al., 2022).

The eighth section examined perceptions of music as a contributor to children's overall wellbeing and holistic development. Questions focused on broader developmental outcomes, including happiness, engagement, positive emotional experiences, motivation, and quality of participation in educational settings. This section reflected contemporary multidimensional conceptualisations of wellbeing promoted by international organisations such as the OECD and WHO (OECD, 2017; 2018).

The final section provided opportunities for participants to express broader views regarding the role of music in early childhood education and its potential contribution to positive educational experiences. This concluding section enabled respondents to reflect upon the overall significance of music within preschool learning environments.

Research questionnaire primarily utilised Likert-type response scales, allowing participants to indicate levels of agreement with specific statements. Likert scales are widely recognised as effective instruments for measuring perceptions and attitudes because they enable the quantification of subjective viewpoints whilst preserving response variability (Cohen et al., 2018; Creswell & Creswell, 2024). In addition, selected items employed multiple-choice formats to gather supplementary information regarding participants' educational perspectives and experiences.

The development of the instrument was informed by contemporary literature concerning music education, wellbeing, resilience, creativity, emotional development, and social-emotional learning. Particular attention was given to ensuring alignment between questionnaire items, research questions, and the theoretical constructs discussed throughout the chapter. Such alignment contributes to content validity by ensuring that the instrument adequately represents the domains under investigation (Creswell & Creswell, 2024).

Overall, the questionnaire was designed to provide a comprehensive overview of preservice teachers' perceptions regarding the contribution of music education to multiple dimensions of children's psychosocial development. By examining confidence, belonging, emotional competence, creativity, social interaction, and wellbeing simultaneously, the instrument enabled the collection of data directly relevant to the study's broader objective of exploring music as a potential source of psychosocial protective factors associated with resilience and preventative educational practice.

As the questionnaire was developed specifically for the purposes of the present exploratory study, emphasis was placed on conceptual alignment with the research questions and theoretical framework rather than on the development of a standardised psychometric instrument. The questionnaire was designed to capture participants' perceptions across multiple dimensions associated with music education, wellbeing, resilience, and psychosocial development. Consequently, the findings should be interpreted as exploratory indicators of preservice teachers' perceptions rather than as measurements derived from a validated psychometric scale.

4.4 Data Collection and Analysis Procedures

Data collection was conducted during the academic year at the Department of Preschool Education Sciences and Educational Design, University of the Aegean. Participation was voluntary, and all participants received detailed information regarding the purpose of the study, confidentiality procedures, and their right to withdraw at any stage without penalty. Informed consent was obtained prior to participation in accordance with established ethical principles governing educational research (Cohen et al., 2018; Creswell & Creswell, 2024; Israel & Hay, 2021).

The questionnaire was distributed electronically through Google Forms. Online survey methods have become widely accepted in educational and social science research because they facilitate efficient data collection, increase accessibility, support participant anonymity, and reduce administrative burden (Zimba & Gasparyan, 2023). The use of a digital platform enabled participants to complete the questionnaire at a convenient time and location, thereby reducing barriers to participation and supporting higher response rates among university students (Bhalerao, 2015; Creswell & Creswell, 2024). No personally identifiable information was collected, further supporting anonymity and minimising potential response bias (Dillman et al., 2014). Upon completion of the data collection period, responses were exported into spreadsheet format and screened for completeness, consistency, and potential recording errors. Preliminary data screening is considered an essential stage of quantitative analysis because it contributes to data quality and enhances the credibility of subsequent findings (Becker, 2020; Tian et al., 2025).

Given the exploratory nature of the study and its focus on preservice teachers' perceptions, descriptive statistical analysis was employed as the primary analytical approach. Descriptive statistics are widely recommended for exploratory educational studies because they enable researchers to summarise patterns within datasets and provide an accessible overview of participants' attitudes, perceptions, and experiences (Cohen et al., 2018; Creswell & Creswell, 2024). Analysis focused on frequencies, percentages, and response distributions across questionnaire items related to confidence, emotional competence, creativity, belonging, social interaction, wellbeing, and resilience.

The interpretation of findings was informed by the theoretical framework developed in the preceding chapters. Statistical patterns were examined in relation to contemporary theories of wellbeing, resilience, emotional development, and protective factors (Masten, 2021; Ungar, 2021; WHO, 2022). Rather than seeking causal explanations, the analysis aimed to identify dominant tendencies within participants' responses and generate empirical insights into how future preschool educators conceptualise the contribution of music education to children's psychosocial development, wellbeing, and resilience. Such an approach is consistent with recommendations for exploratory quantitative research designed to generate foundational knowledge and inform subsequent investigation (Creswell & Creswell, 2024).

4.5 Ethical Considerations

Ethical integrity was maintained throughout all stages of the research process in accordance with internationally recognised principles governing educational research, including voluntary participation, informed consent, confidentiality, anonymity, and responsible data management (Cohen et al., 2018; Israel & Hay, 2021). Prior to participation, all respondents received information regarding the purpose of the study, the nature of their involvement, and the intended use of the collected data. Participation was entirely voluntary, and participants retained the right to withdraw at any stage without penalty or adverse consequences. Informed consent was obtained before access to the questionnaire was granted. Particular attention was devoted to protecting participants' privacy. No personally identifiable information was collected, and all responses were submitted anonymously through the online survey platform. Anonymity was considered especially important because it encouraged honest responses and reduced the likelihood of social desirability bias (Head, 2020). Confidentiality was maintained throughout data collection, storage, analysis, and reporting, and all information was used exclusively for academic and research purposes.

The study was conducted in accordance with the principles of the General Data Protection Regulation (GDPR) of the European Union. Participants were informed about data handling procedures, storage practices, and the manner in which findings would be reported. Since no identifying information was collected, the potential risks associated with privacy or confidentiality breaches were minimal. Because the participant group consisted of university students, particular care was taken to ensure that participation was not perceived as obligatory or linked to academic assessment. The voluntary nature of participation was emphasised throughout the research process in order to minimise potential power imbalances between researchers and participants (Kushwaha, Yadav, Sonker & Devi, 2024). Furthermore, the study focused exclusively on educational perceptions and professional beliefs rather than sensitive personal experiences or psychological assessment. Consequently, the research was considered low risk. Overall, the study adhered to contemporary standards of educational research ethics by safeguarding participants' rights, dignity, autonomy, and wellbeing while ensuring the responsible generation and dissemination of academic knowledge.

4.6 Methodological Limitations

Several methodological limitations should be considered when interpreting the findings of this study. First, the research relied exclusively on self-reported questionnaire data. Although participant perceptions provide valuable insight into professional beliefs and educational understandings, they do not necessarily reflect actual classroom practices or direct developmental outcomes (Cohen et al., 2018). Consequently, the findings should be interpreted as indicators of preservice teachers' perceptions rather than evidence of the effects of music education on children. Second, the study was conducted within a single higher education institution and employed convenience sampling. While appropriate for exploratory educational research, this approach limits the generalisability of findings beyond the specific population examined (Creswell & Creswell, 2024). Educational contexts and teacher preparation programmes may differ across institutions and countries, potentially influencing participants' views. Third, the cross-sectional design captured perceptions at a single point in time and therefore cannot account for changes that may occur throughout teacher education or professional practice. Longitudinal research could provide deeper insight into the evolution of educators' beliefs concerning music, wellbeing, and resilience. An additional limitation concerns the absence of direct child data. The study examined future educators' perceptions rather than children's actual experiences, wellbeing, or developmental outcomes. Future research could incorporate classroom observations, teacher interviews, and child-centred measures to provide a more comprehensive understanding of music's contribution to psychosocial development. Finally, the questionnaire did not undergo formal psychometric validation procedures, such as pilot testing, expert review, or internal consistency reliability analysis. Although the instrument was informed by the relevant literature and aligned with the study's conceptual framework, future studies may strengthen its methodological robustness through systematic validation procedures.

Despite these limitations, the study provides valuable empirical insight into how future preschool educators conceptualise the relationship between music education, wellbeing, resilience, and preventive educational practice.

5. FINDINGS

The present study sought to explore preservice preschool teachers' perceptions regarding the contribution of music education to children's psychosocial development, wellbeing, and resilience. More specifically, the investigation examined how future educators perceive the role of music in supporting confidence, emotional development, belonging, inclusion, creativity, social interaction, and overall wellbeing within early childhood educational contexts. The findings revealed a remarkably consistent pattern of positive responses across all investigated dimensions, indicating a broad consensus concerning the developmental value of music education. Participants overwhelmingly recognised music as a meaningful educational resource capable of fostering emotional, social, and psychological growth while simultaneously strengthening several protective factors associated with positive adaptation and resilience.

These findings are particularly significant when interpreted in light of contemporary ecological and multisystemic perspectives on wellbeing and resilience, which emphasise the importance of supportive relationships, meaningful participation, emotional competence, and inclusive educational environments (Masten, 2021; Ungar, 2021; Southwick et al., 2023; Theron, 2023). To provide an overview of the main findings, **Table 1** summarises participants' responses across the principal dimensions investigated in the study. The results indicate consistently high levels of agreement regarding the contribution of music education to children's psychosocial development, wellbeing, and resilience. At the same time, the findings reveal a notable discrepancy between participants' recognition of music's educational value and their own perceived preparedness to implement music-based pedagogies within educational settings.

Table 1. Summary of Participants' Perceptions Regarding the Contribution of Music Education to Children's Psychosocial Development, Wellbeing, and Resilience

Dimension	Positive Responses (%)
Confidence and self-esteem	96.9
Emotional development	98.5
Emotional regulation	86.4
Belonging and inclusion	95.4
Creativity and imagination	97.0
Social interaction and cooperation	93.9
Wellbeing	95.4
Educatinal value of music	92.4

continued on following page

Table 1. Continued

Dimension	Positive Responses (%)
Limited practical experience	78.8
Low confidence in implementation	86.4

As shown in **Table 1**, participants reported overwhelmingly positive perceptions concerning the developmental contribution of music education. The highest levels of agreement were observed in relation to emotional development, creativity, confidence, wellbeing, and inclusion, suggesting a broad consensus regarding the value of music as a developmental and educational resource. These findings provide the foundation for the more detailed analyses presented in the following sections.

5.1 Perceived Contribution of Music Education to Children's Confidence

One of the most prominent findings of the study concerns participants' perceptions regarding the contribution of music education to the development of children's confidence and self-esteem. The results revealed that 96.9% of participants believed that music education contributes positively to children's self-confidence, indicating a strong consensus among preservice preschool teachers regarding the empowering role of musical experiences in early childhood settings. Participants perceived music as providing opportunities for active participation, self-expression, achievement, and social recognition, all of which contribute to positive self-perceptions and feelings of competence.

These perceptions are consistent with contemporary understandings of self-efficacy and positive development, which emphasise the importance of mastery experiences, participation, and supportive learning environments in fostering confidence and resilience (Bandura, 1997; Bandura & Wessels, 1997; Masten, 2021). Participants frequently associated musical activities with opportunities for children to experience success, communicate ideas, and engage meaningfully in classroom life. Such experiences were perceived as particularly beneficial for children who may be hesitant to participate in more conventional academic activities, suggesting that music offers alternative pathways for engagement and achievement (Argyriou, 2025b).

The findings further indicate that participants view music as an inclusive educational resource capable of supporting children with diverse abilities, learning profiles, and cultural backgrounds. Through singing, movement, musical games, improvisation, and collaborative activities, children are encouraged to participate actively and contribute to shared experiences. These opportunities may strengthen feelings of competence and belonging while supporting the development of positive identities and self-worth (Argyriou & Tapsis, 2025; Lici, Avdulaj, Argyriou & Lamaj, 2026).

An additional finding concerns participants' own perceptions of preparedness to implement music-based activities. Although 92.4% recognised the educational value of music, 78.8% reported limited prior practical experience in music education, while 86.4% expressed low confidence regarding the organisation and implementation of music activities. Furthermore, despite 89.5% having received university-level instruction in music education, many respondents continued to report uncertainty about applying this knowledge in practice. These findings suggest a gap between theoretical understanding and pedagogical confidence, highlighting the need for more applied and practice-oriented experiences within teacher education programmes. This finding is particularly relevant because teacher self-efficacy has been consistently associated with instructional decision-making, innovation, and willingness to implement creative pedagogical approaches (Cefai, Bartolo, Cavioni & Downes, 2018; Leriou, 2023). Strengthening practical musical competencies during teacher preparation may therefore increase future educators' confidence and improve the integration of music-based learning experiences within preschool classrooms.

Participants also emphasised the importance of positive feedback and collaborative participation in supporting children's confidence. Musical activities were perceived as creating opportunities for affirmation, recognition, and constructive encouragement, all of which contribute to positive self-esteem and motivation. Such experiences are especially significant during early childhood, when self-concepts are still developing and remain highly responsive to supportive social interactions (Argyriou, 2021; Makris, Welch & Himonides, 2022; Argyriou, 2025c). The Figure 1., synthesises participants' perceptions and relevant literature regarding the developmental mechanisms linking music education, competence, belonging, and positive adaptation.

Figure 1. Supportive contexts to children's confidence, self-esteem and resilience

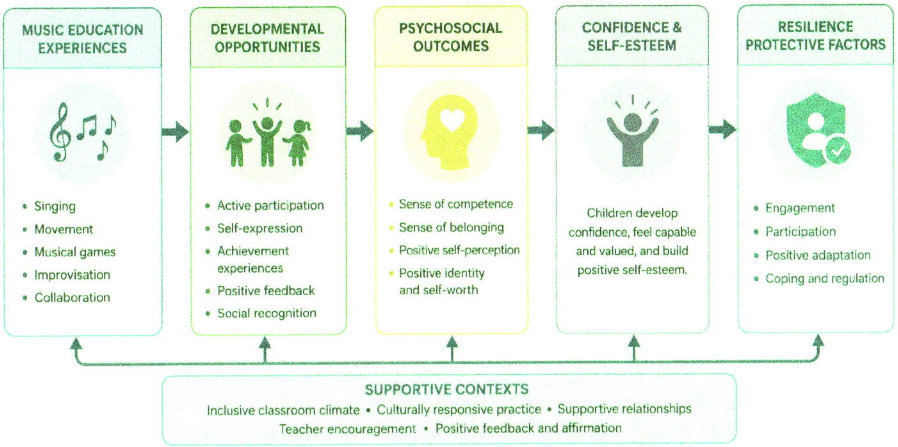

From a resilience perspective, these findings suggest that music education may contribute to the development of important protective factors associated with positive adaptation. Contemporary resilience theory emphasises that confidence emerges through supportive environments that provide opportunities for competence-building, participation, and meaningful engagement (Masten, 2021; Ungar, 2021). The participants' responses indicate that music education may offer precisely such opportunities, enabling children to experience achievement, express themselves creatively, and participate confidently within supportive educational communities.

Overall, the findings indicate that preservice preschool teachers perceive music education as a significant contributor to children's confidence, self-esteem, and positive self-development. At the same time, the results reveal a need for stronger practical preparation in music education within teacher education programmes. Together, these findings support the view that music can function as a valuable developmental and preventative resource that promotes confidence, participation, and positive psychosocial outcomes during early childhood.

5.2 Music Education and Emotional Development

The findings indicate that preservice preschool teachers perceive music education as a highly effective means of supporting children's emotional development, emotional expression, and emotional wellbeing. Across the relevant questionnaire items, participants expressed overwhelmingly positive views regarding the capacity of music to facilitate emotional awareness, communication, and regulation. In particular, 98.5% of respondents reported that children's mood and emotional responsiveness are positively influenced by engagement in musical activities, while 86.4% believed that music helps children process and manage emotions within supportive educational environments. Participants perceived music as providing opportunities for children to recognise, express, and communicate emotions that may otherwise be difficult to verbalise. Through singing, movement, musical games, listening activities, and creative musical experiences, children are encouraged to explore emotional states and engage actively with their feelings. Such experiences were viewed as contributing to emotional awareness and emotional literacy, both of which are widely recognised as important dimensions of child wellbeing and psychosocial development (Argyriou, 2021; Váradi, 2022; Argyriou, 2025c; Argyriou, 2025a).

The findings further suggest that participants regard music as an important resource for emotional regulation. Musical engagement was perceived as helping children reduce emotional tension, manage stress, and restore emotional balance through structured and enjoyable experiences. This perception aligns with contemporary research demonstrating that music can support mood regulation and emotional self-management across childhood and adolescence (Smith, 2021; Jia, 2024). Within educational settings, such functions are particularly valuable because emotional regulation is closely associated with positive learning experiences, social adjustment, and psychological wellbeing.

Participants also recognised that music may evoke a wide range of emotional responses. Approximately 89.4% acknowledged that musical experiences can generate diverse emotions, including joy, excitement, sadness, frustration, and anger. Importantly, however, respondents viewed music as a constructive medium through which these emotions can be explored and understood. Rather than avoiding difficult emotions, music was perceived as creating safe opportunities for emotional exploration and expression. This finding reflects contemporary perspectives that conceptualise music as both an emotional stimulus and an emotional resource capable of supporting emotional growth and self-understanding (Saarikallio et al., 2020).

Another noteworthy finding concerns the perceived contribution of music to empathy and interpersonal understanding. Participants reported that collaborative musical activities encourage children to listen to others, share experiences, and engage in collective forms of expression. Such processes may support the development of empathy, perspective-taking, and prosocial behaviour, all of which are important components of social-emotional competence (Barrett et al., 2022). These interpersonal dimensions are especially relevant in preschool settings, where foundational social and emotional skills are still emerging.

From a resilience perspective, the findings suggest that music education may contribute to the development of protective emotional resources. Contemporary resilience theory highlights emotional competence and self-regulation as key factors supporting positive adaptation and coping (Masten, 2021). By providing opportunities for emotional expression, understanding, and regulation, music may strengthen children's capacity to respond constructively to challenges while maintaining psychological wellbeing. Figure 2 synthesises participants' perceptions and relevant literature regarding the role of musical engagement in supporting emotional competence, socio-emotional development, and positive adaptation.

Figure 2. Supportive Educational Environments to children's emotional development, emotional regulation, wellbeing, and resilience

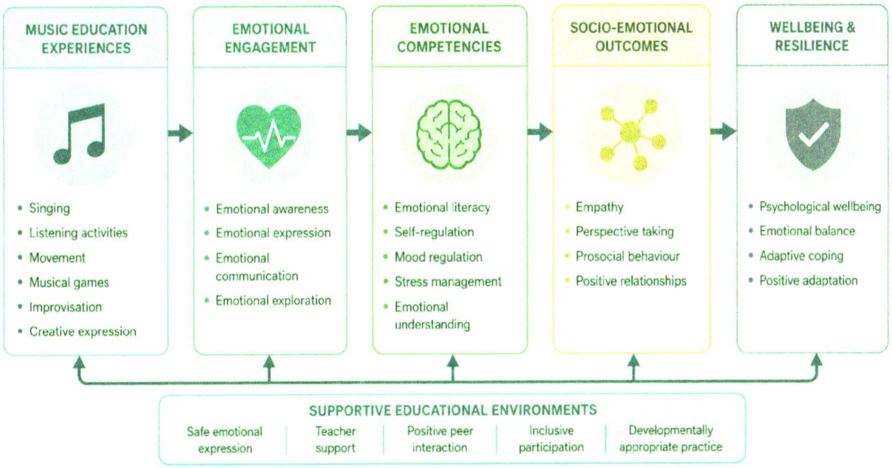

Findings indicate that preservice preschool teachers perceive music education as a powerful medium for supporting emotional expression, emotional awareness, empathy, and emotional regulation. The exceptionally high levels of agreement recorded across relevant items suggest that future educators recognise music as a significant contributor to children's emotional wellbeing and psychosocial development. These findings reinforce the broader argument that music education can function as a valuable preventative and developmental resource within educational approaches aimed at promoting wellbeing and resilience.

5.3 Music Education, Belonging, and Social Inclusion

A further significant finding concerns participants' perceptions regarding the contribution of music education to children's sense of belonging, social inclusion, and interpersonal connectedness. Across the relevant questionnaire items, preservice preschool teachers consistently identified music as a powerful medium for fostering participation, strengthening peer relationships, and promoting inclusive educational environments. These findings are particularly important given the growing recognition of belonging as a key protective factor associated with wellbeing, educational engagement, and resilience (Bronfenbrenner & Morris, 2007; Crawford, 2020; Brown, Douthwaite, Donnelly & Olaniyan, 2025).

Participants overwhelmingly perceived group musical experiences as opportunities for children to develop social bonds and experience meaningful participation within classroom communities. Through singing, movement, musical games, rhythmic activities, and collaborative performances, children are encouraged to interact with peers, coordinate actions, share responsibilities, and engage in collective experiences. Such activities create shared social spaces in which participation and cooperation become central components of learning (Campayo & Cabedo, 2017; Barrett et al., 2022; Welch et al., 2020).

Particularly noteworthy is the finding that 93.9% of respondents viewed music as an effective tool for promoting social cohesion among children from diverse cultural and linguistic backgrounds. Participants recognised that music can transcend verbal barriers and create opportunities for communication, cooperation, and mutual understanding through shared experiences. This perception aligns with international research highlighting the contribution of music to intercultural dialogue, social inclusion, and community building (Welch, Biasutti, MacRitchie, McPherson & Himonides, 2020; Argyriou, 2025b).

The findings further suggest that participants perceive music as supporting inclusive educational practices. Musical activities offer multiple modes of participation through movement, rhythm, listening, singing, improvisation, and creative expression, allowing children with different abilities and learning profiles to engage meaningfully in classroom life. Consequently, music was viewed as a resource capable of reducing barriers to participation and strengthening inclusive educational environments (Atkinson & Robson, 2012; Koç, & Sungurtekin, 2023).

Participants also expressed strong support for the use of multicultural musical repertoires in preschool education, with 89.4% recognising their value in fostering cultural understanding and respect for diversity. Such perceptions are consistent with contemporary educational priorities emphasising intercultural dialogue, global citizenship, and appreciation of cultural plurality (Argyriou, 2025a; Argyriou & Lici, 2026). Through exposure to diverse musical traditions, children may develop openness, empathy, and positive attitudes towards difference while simultaneously strengthening their own cultural identities.

From a resilience perspective, these findings are particularly significant because social belonging and connectedness are recognised as central protective factors supporting positive adaptation and wellbeing (Ungar, 2021; Masten, 2021). Music education appears to contribute to these processes by creating opportunities for participation, acceptance, collaboration, and shared achievement. Similarly, contemporary school counselling frameworks emphasise belonging, positive peer relationships, and inclusive school climates as essential components of preventative approaches to student wellbeing (ASCA, 2003; Carey & Dimmitt, 2021).

Findings indicate that preservice preschool teachers perceive music education as a significant contributor to children's sense of belonging, social inclusion, intercultural understanding, and community participation. The consistently high levels of agreement suggest that future educators recognise music as a powerful social resource capable of fostering inclusive educational environments and strengthening protective relational factors associated with wellbeing and resilience.

5.4 Music Education and Creativity

Creativity emerged as another highly valued dimension of music education within the participants' responses. Preservice preschool teachers consistently perceived music as a powerful catalyst for imagination, originality, spontaneity, and creative thinking. The findings revealed that 89.4% of participants believed that music education supports children's imagination and spontaneity, while 93.9% recognised its contribution to the development of creative thinking. These results indicate a strong consensus regarding the developmental value of music beyond artistic learning and highlight its perceived contribution to broader cognitive, emotional, and psychosocial growth.

Participants viewed music as uniquely positioned to encourage exploration, experimentation, improvisation, and self-expression. Through singing, movement, musical games, storytelling, rhythmic activities, and creative play, children are provided with opportunities to generate ideas, make choices, and engage actively in meaning-making processes. Such experiences were perceived as fostering creative agency by encouraging children to become active participants rather than passive recipients of learning experiences (Burnard & Randles, 2022; Papageorgi, Saunders, Himonides & Welch, 2022; Kanellou & Argyriou, 2026).

The findings further suggest that participants associate musical creativity with motivation and engagement. Music was perceived as stimulating curiosity, sustaining attention, and encouraging active participation in learning. These perceptions align with contemporary educational research highlighting the relationship between creative learning environments, intrinsic motivation, and positive educational engagement (Khine, Zandvliet & Fraser, 2021; Argyriou & Tapsis, 2026). Musical activities frequently combine cognitive, emotional, social, and physical dimensions of participation, creating rich and meaningful learning experiences that support children's enthusiasm for learning (Argyriou & Lici, 2026). Importantly, participants appeared to recognise creativity not merely as an artistic outcome but as a broader developmental capacity associated with flexibility, innovation, and adaptive thinking. This interpretation is particularly relevant when considered through the lens of resilience theory. Creativity and resilience share several common characteristics, including openness to new experiences, problem-solving, flexibility, and the capacity to respond constructively to challenges (Masten, 2021). Musical activities often encourage children to explore alternatives, experiment with ideas, and engage collaboratively in solving creative challenges, thereby supporting adaptive developmental processes.

From an ecological perspective, creativity may function as a protective factor because it expands the range of resources available to children when responding to developmental demands and everyday challenges (Ungar, 2021). Music education contributes to this process by creating environments in which children can express themselves freely, explore possibilities, and experience personal agency through imaginative engagement. Such opportunities may strengthen confidence, autonomy, and positive identity development while supporting broader processes of wellbeing and resilience. Participants also emphasised the role of music in fostering spontaneity and originality within psychologically safe environments. Musical play encourages experimentation without excessive evaluation, allowing children to take creative risks and develop confidence in their own ideas and abilities. These experiences contribute not only to creative development but also to self-esteem and positive self-perception.

Findings indicate that preservice preschool teachers perceive music education as a highly effective means of fostering imagination, spontaneity, creative thinking, and active engagement in learning. The exceptionally positive responses recorded across relevant items suggest that future educators recognise creativity as one of the most important developmental contributions of music education. Viewed through the lens of resilience theory, creativity may be understood not only as an educational outcome but also as a psychosocial resource that supports adaptive thinking, personal agency, and positive developmental trajectories.

5.5 Music Education, Wellbeing, and Resilience

The findings presented across the previous sections collectively suggest that preservice preschool teachers perceive music education as a multidimensional educational resource capable of supporting children's wellbeing and resilience. Rather than influencing a single developmental domain, music was consistently associated with a range of interconnected outcomes, including confidence, emotional competence, social belonging, inclusion, creativity, and positive engagement. Taken together, these findings indicate that future educators view music not merely as an artistic subject but as a holistic pedagogical practice that contributes to children's overall development and psychosocial wellbeing.

A notable pattern emerging from the data is the consistency with which participants associated music education with positive developmental outcomes. Across all thematic areas, respondents reported exceptionally high levels of agreement regarding the contribution of music to children's confidence, emotional expression, social participation, and creative development. These perceptions align with contemporary understandings of wellbeing, which conceptualise positive development as the interaction of emotional, social, psychological, and educational dimensions rather than the absence of difficulties alone (OECD, 2018; World Health Organization, 2022; Learning & Well-Being, 2020).

Findings suggest that music contributes to wellbeing through multiple pathways. Participants perceived musical engagement as supporting emotional expression and regulation, fostering positive relationships, strengthening social participation, and creating opportunities for achievement and self-expression. These experiences are widely recognised as important protective factors associated with positive developmental outcomes and psychological wellbeing (Welch & McPherson, 2018; Feng & Wang, 2025). The high levels of agreement recorded throughout the study indicate that future educators recognise music as a meaningful contributor to these processes. The findings are equally significant when viewed through the lens of resilience theory. Contemporary resilience research emphasises that resilience is not a fixed individual trait but a dynamic process supported by access to protective resources embedded within relationships, educational environments, and social contexts (Masten, 2021; Ungar, 2021). Confidence, emotional competence, belonging, creativity, and positive social relationships are consistently identified as key protective factors associated with positive adaptation. Importantly, these are the same developmental outcomes most strongly associated with music education by the participants in the present study.

From this perspective, music education may be understood as a developmental resource that supports resilience by strengthening both individual and relational protective factors. Through participation in singing, movement, musical games, improvisation, and collaborative activities, children are provided with opportunities to experience competence, connection, expression, and achievement within supportive educational environments. These experiences may contribute to the development of the psychosocial resources required for positive adaptation and long-term wellbeing.

The findings also have important implications for contemporary approaches to school counselling and preventative education. Developmental models of school counselling increasingly emphasise the promotion of protective factors, emotional wellbeing, social connectedness, and positive school climates rather than focusing exclusively on intervention after difficulties emerge (ASCA, 2003; Carey & Dimmitt, 2012; 2021). The participants' responses suggest that music education may support many of these objectives by providing engaging and inclusive opportunities for participation, communication, emotional expression, and relationship building.

Findings indicate that preservice preschool teachers perceive music education as a significant contributor to children's wellbeing and resilience. By supporting confidence, emotional competence, belonging, creativity, and social connectedness, music appears to strengthen a network of interconnected protective factors associated with positive developmental trajectories. These findings provide the empirical foundation for the conceptual framework proposed in the following chapter, which positions music education as a resource capable of supporting preventative and developmental approaches to school counselling across individual, relational, school, and policy dimensions.

6. DISCUSSION

The findings of the present study contribute to a growing body of international scholarship that positions music education as a multidimensional educational practice with significant implications for children's well-being, resilience, inclusion, and holistic development. While music has traditionally been justified within educational systems primarily through artistic, aesthetic, or cultural arguments, the results of this study support a broader conceptualization in which music functions as a developmental resource capable of strengthening psychosocial protective factors associated with positive adaptation and well-being (Hallam & Himonides, 2022; Barrett et al., 2022; Welch et al., 2020).

A particularly important contribution of the findings lies in their alignment with contemporary ecological and multisystemic understandings of resilience. Current resilience scholarship has moved decisively beyond individualistic interpretations and increasingly conceptualises resilience as a dynamic process emerging through interactions among personal resources, supportive relationships, educational environments, and wider sociocultural systems (Masten, 2021; Ungar, 2021; Southwick et al., 2023; Theron, 2023). Viewed through this lens, music education appears to operate not merely as a curricular activity but as a context through which multiple protective processes can be activated simultaneously. The participants consistently associated musical engagement with confidence, emotional competence, belonging, creativity, participation, and social connectedness, all of which have been identified within resilience literature as significant contributors to positive developmental outcomes (Goldstein & Brooks, 2023; Masten, 2021).

The findings also reinforce contemporary understandings of well-being as a multidimensional construct encompassing emotional, psychological, social, and participatory dimensions of development (OECD, 2017, 2020; Keeley, 2021; World Health Organization, 2022). Rather than supporting a single aspect of development, music appears capable of contributing across multiple well-being domains simultaneously. This observation is particularly significant because contemporary educational policy increasingly advocates integrated approaches that recognize the interdependence of emotional health, social participation, educational engagement, and positive developmental trajectories (Department of Education, 2023; Fegter & Fattore, 2024). The participants' perceptions suggest that music provides opportunities for children to experience meaningful participation, positive relationships, self-expression, and achievement within supportive educational environments, thereby contributing to several dimensions of well-being concurrently.

The findings further support research highlighting the central role of emotional competence within both resilience and well-being frameworks. Emotional awareness, emotional regulation, and emotional expression are increasingly recognized as foundational capacities supporting adaptive functioning, social relationships, and psychological health (Saarikallio et al., 2020; Váradi, 2022; Feng & Wang, 2025). Participants consistently perceived music as facilitating these processes through developmentally appropriate and engaging forms of participation. This perception is particularly relevant within early childhood education, where opportunities for non-verbal communication and emotional exploration play a crucial role in supporting children's socio-emotional development (Barrett et al., 2022; Jia, 2024; Pérez-Moreno et al., 2026). Consequently, music may provide an accessible pedagogical medium through which emotional literacy and emotional self-regulation can be fostered within everyday educational practice.

Equally significant is the strong emphasis participants placed on belonging, inclusion, and social connectedness. Contemporary educational research consistently identifies belonging as one of the strongest predictors of educational engagement, well-being, and positive adaptation (OECD, 2017; Brown et al., 2025; Nijs, 2025). The present findings suggest that music may contribute uniquely to belonging because participation is grounded in shared experiences, collective achievement, cooperation, and mutual contribution rather than solely in academic performance. Such observations resonate with ecological theories of development, which emphasize the importance of supportive relational environments in shaping developmental outcomes (Bronfenbrenner & Morris, 2007). Through collaborative music-making, children encounter opportunities to develop positive peer relationships, experience recognition, and participate meaningfully within classroom communities, thereby strengthening relational protective factors associated with resilience and well-being (Welch et al., 2020; Barrett et al., 2022; Henley, 2025).

The participants' support for multicultural and inclusive musical experiences also reflects broader international concerns regarding educational equity, diversity, and intercultural understanding. Music possesses a unique capacity to facilitate communication across linguistic, cultural, and social boundaries, enabling children to engage with diverse perspectives while simultaneously affirming their own identities and cultural backgrounds (Argyriou, 2025a; Burnard & Randles, 2022; Crawford, 2020). In increasingly diverse educational settings, such experiences may contribute to more inclusive school cultures characterized by participation, mutual respect, and social cohesion. These dimensions are particularly relevant given contemporary policy priorities emphasizing inclusion, cultural diversity, and global citizenship education (Kakos, 2025; United Nations Office for Disaster Risk Reduction, 2023).

Another important implication concerns the relationship between creativity and resilience. Contemporary scholarship increasingly recognizes creativity as more than an artistic outcome, positioning it instead as a developmental resource associated with flexibility, problem-solving, adaptability, and innovation (Burnard, 2012; Burnard & Randles, 2022; Randles & Burnard, 2023). The participants' perceptions suggest that musical experiences create environments in which children are encouraged to experiment, improvise, make decisions, and explore alternative possibilities. Such opportunities may strengthen adaptive capacities that are central to resilience processes, particularly in contexts characterized by uncertainty and change (Ungar, 2021; Southwick et al., 2023).

Perhaps the most significant implication emerging from the findings concerns the relationship between music education and contemporary preventive approaches to school counseling. Developmental models of school counselling increasingly focus on strengthening protective factors and promoting well-being before difficulties emerge (Carey & Dimmitt, 2012, 2021; Goodman-Scott & Ockerman, 2023). The outcomes most strongly associated with music by participants correspond closely to the competencies targeted within preventative counseling frameworks, including emotional competence, self-efficacy, belonging, social connectedness, participation, and positive identity development. These convergences suggest that music education may represent an important, yet underutilized, resource within whole-school approaches to wellbeing promotion and resilience-building.

Taken together, the findings support a reconceptualization of music education as a developmental and preventive educational resource operating across emotional, social, cultural, and relational domains. Rather than functioning solely as an artistic subject, music appears capable of strengthening an interconnected network of protective factors that support well-being, resilience, inclusion, and positive development. This interpretation provides the theoretical rationale for the music-informed preventive school counseling and resilience framework proposed in the following section and supports the broader argument that music should occupy a more central position within contemporary well-being-oriented educational policy and practice.

7. MUSIC-INFORMED PREVENTIVE SCHOOL COUNSELLING AND RESILIENCE FRAMEWORK

The findings of the present study, interpreted alongside contemporary scholarship on wellbeing, resilience, school counselling, and music education, support the development of a Music-Informed Preventive School Counselling and Resilience Framework. This framework conceptualises music education not merely as an artistic discipline but as a multidimensional developmental resource capable of strengthening psychosocial protective factors associated with wellbeing, resilience, and positive adaptation. It responds to contemporary educational priorities that increasingly emphasise preventative approaches to child development, mental health promotion, social inclusion, and holistic education (Department of Education, 2023).

Contemporary school counselling has progressively evolved from predominantly reactive and remedial models towards preventative and developmental approaches that seek to strengthen protective factors before significant difficulties emerge (ASCA, 2023; Carey & Dimmitt, 2021). Within this paradigm, educational experiences that foster emotional competence, belonging, confidence, positive relationships, creativity, and active participation are regarded as essential contributors to children's wellbeing and healthy development. The findings of the present study suggest that music education contributes meaningfully to each of these domains. Participants consistently perceived music as fostering self-confidence, emotional expression, social connectedness, creativity, intercultural understanding, and positive engagement. These outcomes correspond closely to the protective factors identified within contemporary resilience theory and preventative school counselling frameworks (Masten, 2021; Ungar, 2021; WHO, 2022).

The framework is grounded in ecological and developmental understandings of resilience. Drawing upon Bronfenbrenner (2007) ecological systems theory and Ungar's ecological model of resilience (2021), it conceptualises wellbeing and resilience as dynamic processes emerging through interactions among individuals, relationships, educational environments, and broader social systems. Consequently, music is understood not as a single intervention or isolated educational activity but as a developmental resource operating simultaneously across multiple ecological levels.

At the individual level, music contributes to the development of personal competencies that support wellbeing and resilience. The findings demonstrated that participants perceived music as strengthening children's confidence, emotional awareness, creativity, motivation, self-expression, and positive self-concept. Such competencies have long been recognised as important protective factors associated with positive developmental adaptation (Masten, 2021; Çalış, Tan, Maç & Turan, 2022). Through participation in singing, movement, listening, improvisation, composition, and creative musical play, children encounter opportunities to experience mastery, develop self-efficacy, regulate emotions, and construct positive identities. These experiences contribute directly to psychological wellbeing by fostering agency, competence, autonomy, and emotional self-regulation.

Beyond the individual level, music functions as a relational resource that supports the development of positive interpersonal relationships. The findings revealed strong participant agreement regarding music's contribution to belonging, inclusion, empathy, communication, cooperation, and social interaction. Contemporary resilience research consistently identifies supportive relationships as among the most powerful protective factors available to children (Masten, 2021; Ungar, 2021). Musical activities encourage collaboration, shared participation, collective achievement, and mutual understanding. Through these experiences, children strengthen peer relationships, develop social connectedness, and experience meaningful inclusion within educational communities. Music therefore contributes not only to individual development but also to the relational networks through which resilience is nurtured and sustained.

The framework further recognises the school environment as a critical context for the promotion of wellbeing and resilience. Educational settings function as developmental ecosystems capable of either supporting or constraining children's psychosocial development (Bronfenbrenner & Morris, 2007; Kakos, 2025). The findings suggest that music contributes positively to classroom climate by fostering participation, creativity, emotional safety, engagement, inclusion, and collaborative learning. Musical activities create opportunities for children to contribute actively, experience recognition, and participate in supportive educational communities. In doing so, music strengthens the environmental conditions necessary for the development of positive school cultures and wellbeing-oriented educational practices. Within preventative school counselling frameworks, such environments are particularly important because they simultaneously reduce risk factors and strengthen protective processes (American School Counselor Association, 2023).

Importantly, the framework extends beyond the classroom to the policy and systemic level. International organisations including UNESCO, the OECD, and the WHO increasingly advocate for educational policies that prioritise wellbeing, inclusion, creativity, mental health promotion, and social-emotional learning (OECD, 2018; United Nations Office for Disaster Risk Reduction, 2023; World Health Organization, 2022). Despite these priorities, music education is frequently positioned as a supplementary subject rather than as a strategic contributor to holistic child development. The present framework proposes that music should be recognised as an important educational resource capable of advancing many of the objectives currently pursued through wellbeing-oriented educational policy. Strengthening music education within curricula, teacher education programmes, school-wide wellbeing initiatives, and interdisciplinary collaborations may therefore contribute to more comprehensive approaches to child development and educational wellbeing.

A central feature of the framework is its recognition that resilience emerges not through a single mechanism but through the interaction of multiple protective factors operating across interconnected developmental systems. Confidence, emotional competence, belonging, creativity, positive relationships, inclusion, participation, and engagement do not function independently. Rather, they reinforce one another and collectively contribute to children's capacity to adapt positively to challenges and adversity. The findings of the present study suggest that music education supports precisely this network of protective factors. Through regular engagement in meaningful musical experiences, children gain access to developmental resources that simultaneously support emotional, social, creative, and psychological growth.

The Music-Informed Preventive School Counselling and Resilience Framework may therefore be summarised as operating across four interconnected ecological levels. At the individual level, music strengthens confidence, self-efficacy, emotional regulation, creativity, motivation, and self-expression. At the relational level, it promotes belonging, empathy, communication, cooperation, intercultural understanding, and positive peer relationships. At the school level, it contributes to inclusive educational environments, emotional safety, student engagement, participation, collaborative learning cultures, and positive classroom climate. Finally, at the policy level, it supports the integration of music within wellbeing initiatives, preventative educational strategies, teacher preparation programmes, and broader educational policies aimed at fostering resilience and holistic development.

The framework in **Figure 3**., conceptualises music education as a developmental and preventive resource operating across four interconnected ecological levels (individual, relational, school, and policy) that collectively support children's wellbeing, belonging, resilience, and inclusion through the strengthening of psychosocial protective factors. From this perspective, music education becomes more than an artistic experience; it functions as a mechanism through which protective processes are cultivated across individual, relational, institutional, and systemic levels. The Music-Informed Preventive School Counselling and Resilience Framework therefore provides a conceptual model capable of integrating music education, wellbeing promotion, resilience-building, and preventative school counselling within a unified theoretical perspective. Building upon the theoretical and empirical findings presented in the previous sections, the present framework offers an integrative conceptual model illustrating how music education may contribute to the promotion of wellbeing and resilience through multiple interconnected protective processes. Drawing on ecological systems theory, multisystemic resilience scholarship, and contemporary preventive approaches to school counselling, the framework conceptualises music as a developmental resource operating across individual, relational, institutional, and policy dimensions (Bronfenbrenner & Morris, 2007; Masten, 2021; Ungar, 2021; Southwick et al., 2023).

Figure 3. Music-Informed Preventive School Counselling and Resilience Framework

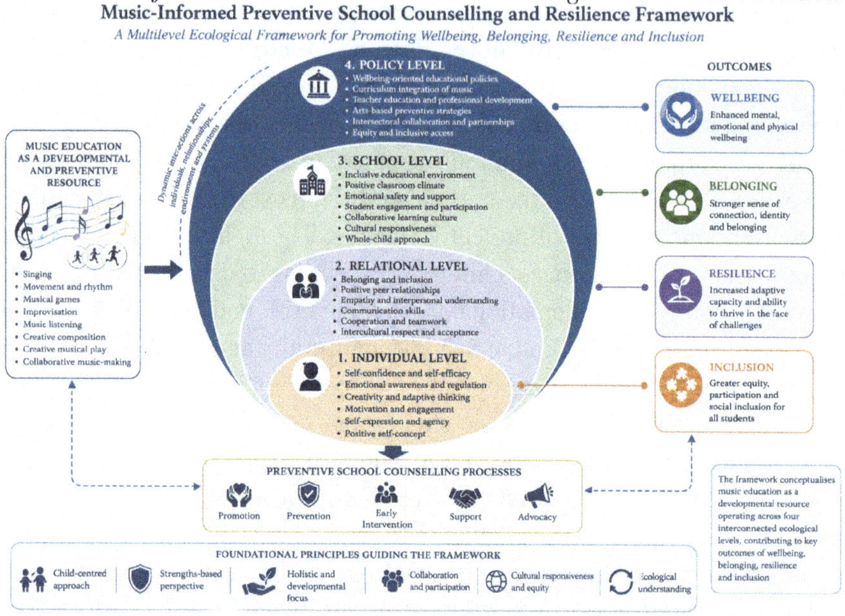

The framework synthesises the principal theoretical arguments and empirical insights developed throughout this chapter. Rather than positioning music education solely as an artistic or curricular domain, it conceptualises musical engagement as a mechanism through which protective factors associated with wellbeing and resilience may be strengthened. The model illustrates how emotional competence, confidence, belonging, social connectedness, creativity, participation, and positive identity development interact across ecological systems to support positive adaptation and holistic development. In doing so, the framework highlights the potential contribution of music education to contemporary wellbeing-oriented and preventive educational practices (Hallam & Himonides, 2022; Barrett et al., 2022; Goldstein & Brooks, 2023; Theron, 2023). By connecting these domains, the framework offers educators, school counsellors, educational leaders, researchers, and policymakers a new way of understanding the developmental significance of music and its potential contribution to holistic approaches to child wellbeing. Ultimately, the framework positions music as a valuable educational resource capable of supporting the creation of inclusive, resilient, and wellbeing-oriented educational environments that respond effectively to the developmental needs of children in contemporary societies.

8. IMPLICATIONS FOR EDUCATIONAL PRACTICE, SCHOOL COUNSELLING, LEADERSHIP, AND POLICY

The findings of the present study generate important implications for educational practice, school counselling, educational leadership, and policy development. Collectively, the results suggest that music education should be understood not merely as an artistic subject or enrichment activity but as a multidimensional developmental resource capable of supporting children's psychosocial wellbeing, resilience, and positive adaptation. Participants consistently associated music education with confidence-building, emotional competence, creativity, belonging, social participation, and positive engagement, all of which are recognised within contemporary literature as significant protective factors contributing to healthy developmental trajectories (Masten, 2021; Ungar, 2021).

From an educational perspective, the findings reinforce the importance of integrating music into everyday pedagogical practice rather than restricting musical experiences to occasional activities or isolated curricular events. Music-based learning experiences can be embedded across multiple areas of preschool education through singing, movement, storytelling, improvisation, rhythmic exploration, creative expression, and collaborative musical projects. Such approaches enable children to engage actively in learning while simultaneously supporting emotional expression, interpersonal communication, self-confidence, and social participation (American School Counselor Association, 2003; Barrett, Flynn, Brown & Welch, 2022; Hallam & Himonides, 2022). Furthermore, the findings suggest that music may be particularly effective when implemented through child-centred, participatory, and playful pedagogies that align with contemporary approaches to early childhood education emphasising exploration, creativity, agency, and holistic development (American School Counselor Association, 2003; Department of the Prime Minister and Cabinet, 2021; Department of Education, 2023).

At the same time, the study revealed a notable discrepancy between participants' recognition of the educational value of music and their confidence in implementing music-based pedagogies. Although respondents overwhelmingly acknowledged the developmental benefits of music, many reported limited practical experience and uncertainty regarding classroom implementation. This finding highlights the need for teacher education programmes to strengthen practical preparation in music pedagogy, enabling future educators to translate theoretical understanding into effective educational practice. Enhanced opportunities for experiential learning, classroom-based application, and interdisciplinary pedagogical training may contribute significantly to increasing educators' confidence and competence in utilising music as a developmental resource.

The findings also have important implications for school counselling and wellbeing promotion. Contemporary school counselling frameworks increasingly prioritise preventative and developmental approaches that seek to strengthen protective factors before difficulties emerge rather than focusing exclusively on remediation and intervention (Carey & Dimmitt, 2021). Within this context, music education appears particularly relevant because the developmental outcomes identified by participants correspond closely to many of the competencies targeted by preventative school counselling programmes. Emotional regulation, self-confidence, belonging, social connectedness, inclusion, empathy, and positive participation represent central objectives of both music education and contemporary wellbeing initiatives. Consequently, music may function as a valuable complementary resource within school-wide approaches designed to promote children's mental health, resilience, and psychosocial wellbeing.

Importantly, the framework proposed in this chapter does not advocate replacing counselling interventions with music-based activities. Rather, it suggests that music can strengthen many of the protective factors that underpin positive developmental outcomes and therefore contribute meaningfully to universal preventative strategies operating alongside counselling services and wellbeing programmes (Organisation for Economic Co-operation and Development, 2017; Cefai, Bartolo, Cavioni & Downes, 2018). Greater collaboration among educators, counsellors, psychologists, and wellbeing professionals may facilitate the development of integrated approaches that utilise music as part of broader efforts to promote emotional literacy, social-emotional learning, inclusion, and positive school climate (Kolbert, Crothers & Hughes, 2022).

The findings further highlight important implications for educational leadership. School leaders play a central role in shaping institutional cultures, establishing priorities, allocating resources, and creating conditions that support holistic development. Contemporary educational leadership increasingly recognises that schools are responsible not only for academic achievement but also for fostering wellbeing, inclusion, resilience, and positive educational experiences (Serrano, Fernändez & Marcos, 2024; Kakos, 2025; Selvitopu & Kaya, 2026)

The present findings suggest that music education may contribute substantially to these objectives by creating opportunities for participation, creativity, collaboration, and emotional engagement. Consequently, school leaders may wish to consider how music can be integrated into broader wellbeing strategies and school improvement initiatives.

Such integration may involve expanding opportunities for musical participation, encouraging interdisciplinary collaboration, supporting arts-based wellbeing programmes, and investing in professional development opportunities that strengthen educators' confidence in implementing music-based pedagogies. In addition, music-centred initiatives may contribute positively to school climate by fostering inclusion, community engagement, intercultural understanding, and collaborative learning cultures. These outcomes align closely with contemporary leadership models that emphasise whole-school wellbeing and the creation of supportive educational environments.

Finally, the findings raise important considerations for educational policy. International organisations such as Organisation for Economic Co-operation and Development (2016; 2017), United Nations Office for Disaster Risk Reduction (2023) and World Health Organization (2022) increasingly advocate for educational systems that prioritise wellbeing, mental health promotion, inclusion, creativity, and social-emotional development. Despite these priorities, arts education and music education -in particular- often remains marginal within policy discussions and curriculum planning. The present study suggests that such positioning may underestimate the broader developmental contributions of music. Rather than being viewed solely as an artistic subject, music may be understood as a strategic educational resource capable of simultaneously supporting multiple policy objectives related to wellbeing, resilience, inclusion, and holistic development.

Educational policy may therefore benefit from strengthening the role of music within early childhood curricula, promoting interdisciplinary approaches that connect music with wellbeing and social-emotional learning, expanding opportunities for music pedagogical training within teacher education programmes, encouraging collaboration among educators and wellbeing professionals, and recognising arts-based approaches as valuable components of preventative educational strategies (Carney, 2022; Theodoropoulou & Argyriou, 2026). Such developments would align closely with contemporary international priorities concerning whole-child education and would support the creation of educational systems capable of responding more effectively to the social, emotional, and developmental challenges facing children in the twenty-first century.

Taken together, these implications suggest that music education occupies a far more significant role within educational ecosystems than is often acknowledged. By contributing simultaneously to emotional, social, creative, relational, and developmental dimensions of learning, music offers considerable potential as a resource for promoting wellbeing, strengthening resilience, supporting preventative school counselling, and advancing holistic educational practice across multiple levels of the educational system (Saarikallio, Baltazar & Västfjäll, 2020; Makris, Welch & Himonides, 2022). Ultimately, the implications emerging from the present study extend beyond the domain of music education itself. The findings suggest that music may serve as a valuable developmental and preventative resource capable of supporting educational systems in addressing contemporary challenges related to children's wellbeing, inclusion, resilience, and psychosocial development. By fostering confidence, emotional competence, creativity, social connectedness, and meaningful participation, music contributes to many of the protective factors recognised within contemporary resilience and school counselling literature (Carey & Dimmitt, 2012; Goodman-Scott & Ockerman, 2023). Consequently, the integration of music-informed approaches into educational practice, wellbeing initiatives, leadership strategies, and policy development may offer a promising pathway towards more inclusive, supportive, and developmentally responsive educational environments. These implications provide the foundation for the concluding reflections of the chapter and reinforce the broader argument that music education should be recognised as an essential component of holistic approaches to child development and educational wellbeing (Burnard & Randles, 2022; Lorenzo de Reizabal, 2022; Goldstein & Brooks, 2023).

9. CONCLUSION AND FUTURE RESEARCH

The present chapter explored the contribution of music education to children's wellbeing and resilience through the perspectives of preservice preschool teachers. Drawing upon contemporary scholarship in music education, resilience theory, wellbeing research, and preventative school counselling, the study sought to examine whether music may be understood not only as an artistic discipline but also as a developmental resource capable of strengthening psychosocial protective factors associated with positive adaptation and holistic child development (Lindblad & de Boise, 2020; Welch, Biasutti, MacRitchie, McPherson & Himonides, 2020)

The findings revealed a remarkably consistent pattern across all investigated dimensions. Participants overwhelmingly perceived music education as contributing positively to children's confidence, emotional competence, creativity, social inclusion, sense of belonging, interpersonal relationships, and overall wellbeing. Music was consistently viewed as creating opportunities for emotional expression, meaningful participation, collaborative engagement, self-development, and positive social interaction. These findings reinforce a growing body of international research suggesting that music education contributes significantly to multiple dimensions of children's psychosocial development and educational experience (McFerran, Hense, Koike & Rickwood, 2018; Barrett et al., 2022; Hallam & Himonides, 2022).

Importantly, the findings align closely with contemporary resilience theory. The developmental outcomes most strongly associated with music education by participants correspond directly to the protective factors identified within resilience scholarship, including self-confidence, emotional regulation, positive relationships, belonging, creativity, and social connectedness (Masten, 2021; Ungar, 2021). Rather than functioning solely as an artistic activity, music appears to provide children with access to a network of developmental resources that support positive adaptation and wellbeing across multiple domains of experience.

The study further demonstrated that music education shares important objectives with contemporary preventative and developmental approaches to school counselling. Both fields seek to strengthen protective factors, foster positive relationships, support emotional competence, encourage participation, and promote healthy developmental trajectories. Consequently, the findings suggest that music may represent an underutilised resource within broader educational efforts aimed at promoting wellbeing, resilience, and mental health. This observation is particularly relevant at a time when educational systems worldwide are increasingly called upon to address complex challenges relating to children's psychological wellbeing, inclusion, and social-emotional development (Davidson & Wright, 2020; Akrami, Zali & Abbasi, 2022; Carney, 2022; Ravi, 2026).

Building upon these findings, the chapter proposed the Music-Informed Preventive School Counselling and Resilience Framework. The framework constitutes the principal theoretical contribution of the study by conceptualising music education as a multisystemic developmental resource operating across individual, relational, school, and policy levels. By integrating insights from resilience theory, ecological models of development, wellbeing research, and school counselling, the framework offers a novel perspective for understanding how music contributes to the cultivation of protective factors associated with positive developmental outcomes. In doing so, it extends existing discussions of music education beyond artistic learning and positions music as a valuable component of holistic and preventative educational practice (Katsarou, & Argyriou, 2026).

The study also carries important implications for educational practice, teacher education, school leadership, and policy development. The findings suggest that greater attention should be devoted to integrating music within wellbeing-oriented educational approaches and strengthening opportunities for future educators to develop practical music pedagogical competencies. Although participants overwhelmingly recognised the developmental value of music, many reported limited confidence in implementing music-based activities. This finding highlights the need for teacher preparation programmes that combine theoretical understanding with meaningful opportunities for practical application.

Several limitations should nevertheless be acknowledged. The study relied on self-reported perceptions obtained from a convenience sample of preservice preschool teachers within a single higher education institution. Consequently, the findings should be interpreted as perceptions rather than direct measures of children's developmental outcomes. Furthermore, the exploratory nature of the study and the absence of formal psychometric validation procedures limit the generalisability of the findings. These limitations do not diminish the value of the study but rather indicate areas requiring further investigation.

Future research should extend this line of inquiry in several directions. First, larger-scale studies involving multiple universities, educational contexts, and national settings would provide a broader understanding of educators' perceptions regarding the developmental role of music. Second, longitudinal investigations could examine how music-based experiences contribute to children's wellbeing and resilience over time. Third, mixed-methods and qualitative studies incorporating interviews, observations, and classroom-based evidence would offer richer insight into the mechanisms through which music influences psychosocial development. Fourth, future research should explore the implementation and effectiveness of music-informed preventative school counselling approaches in real educational settings. Finally, experimental and intervention-based studies may provide valuable evidence concerning the specific pathways through which music contributes to resilience-building and wellbeing promotion.

In conclusion, the present chapter argues that music education should be understood as a significant developmental and preventative resource within contemporary educational systems. By simultaneously supporting confidence, emotional competence, creativity, belonging, social connectedness, and positive engagement, music contributes to a network of protective factors that underpin children's wellbeing and resilience. As educational systems continue to prioritise holistic development, inclusion, and mental health promotion, music offers considerable potential as a means of fostering more supportive, participatory, and resilient educational environments. Recognising and utilising this potential may represent an important step towards developing educational practices that respond more effectively to the complex developmental needs of children in the twenty-first century.

REFERENCES

Akrami, F., Zali, A., & Abbasi, M. (2022). Entanglement of the rights of the child, well-being, and justice: A conceptual framework for child protection and well-being. *International Journal of Medical Toxicology and Forensic Medicine*, *12*(2), 1–11. DOI: 10.32598/ijmtfm.v12i2.36827

Aksoy, P. (2026). Art education in early childhood: Exploring pre-service teachers' perceptions of integrated art activities with natural and sustainable materials. *International Journal of Early Years Education*, *34*(2), 277–303. DOI: 10.1080/09669760.2026.2645343

American School Counselor Association. (2003). The ASCA National Model: A framework for school counseling programs. *Professional School Counseling*, *6*(3), 165–168. http://www.jstor.org/stable/42732424

Argyriou, M. (2021). *Applied music pedagogy: Educational frameworks and instructional design for preschool and primary education*. DiSIGMA Publications.

Argyriou, M. (2025a). Music and cultural identity in the early years: An empirical approach to intercultural learning. *European Journal of Education Studies*, *12*(8), 1–27. DOI: 10.46827/ejes.v12i8.6118

Argyriou, M. (2025b). Integrating technology-enhanced alternative assessment in special education: Pedagogical, cultural and structural dimensions for inclusive practice. *European Journal of Special Education Research*, *11*(6). Advance online publication. DOI: 10.46827/ejse.v11i6.6256

Argyriou, M. (2025c). The impact of action songs on gross motor skill development in preschool children: A Greek kindergarten case study. *International Journal of Education*, *13*(1), 53–69. DOI: 10.5121/ije.2025.13125

Argyriou, M., & Lici, E. (2026). Music education beyond technique: Cultural memory and intercultural pedagogy. *Rast Musicology Journal*, *14*(1), 53–92. DOI: 10.12975/rastmd.20261413

Argyriou, M., & Tapsis, N. (2025). Reframing multimodality in contemporary education: A critical review of research patterns and pedagogical shifts. *European Journal of Open Education and E-Learning Studies*, *10*(3), 1–24. DOI: 10.46827/ejoe.v10i3.6106

Argyriou, M., & Tapsis, N. (Eds.). (2026). *Educating through care: Music, the arts and the social value of cultural education in contemporary societies: RIAM 2026 abstract book*. University of the Aegean. https://doi.org/DOI: 10.26215/heal.uoa.11725

Atkinson, S., & Robson, M. (2012). Arts and health as a practice of liminality: Managing the spaces of transformation for social and emotional wellbeing with primary school children. *Health & Place, 18*(6), 1348–1355. DOI: 10.1016/j.healthplace.2012.06.017 PMID: 22840601

Aydoğdu, F., & Ayanoğlu, M. (2020). A review of the views of teacher candidates about art activities within the scope of teaching practice. *Gazi Üniversitesi Gazi Eğitim Fakültesi Dergisi, 40*(2), 699–726.

Bandura, A. (Ed.). (1997). *Self-efficacy in changing societies.* Cambridge university press.

Bandura, A., & Wessels, S. (1997). *Self-efficacy* (Vol. 10). Cambridge University Press.

Barrett, M. S., Flynn, L. M., Brown, J. E., & Welch, G. F. (2019). Beliefs and values about music in early childhood education and care: Perspectives from practitioners. *Frontiers in Psychology, 10,* 724. DOI: 10.3389/fpsyg.2019.00724 PMID: 31105608

Barrett, M. S., Flynn, L. M., Brown, J. E., & Welch, G. F. (Eds.). (2022). *The Oxford handbook of early childhood learning and development in music.* Oxford University Press., DOI: 10.1093/oxfordhb/9780190927521.001.0001

Becker, A. (2020). Post-collection Data Capture, Scoring, and Processing. In Wagemaker, H. (Ed.), *Reliability and Validity of International Large-Scale Assessment. IEA Research for Education, 10.* Springer., DOI: 10.1007/978-3-030-53081-5_9

Bhalerao, A. K. (2015). Application and performance of Google Forms for online data collection and analysis: A case of North Eastern Region of India. *Indian Journal of Extension Education, 51*(3–4), 49–53.

Bilir-Seyhan, G., & Ocak-Karabay, Ş. (2018). Early childhood pre-service teachers' views about visual arts education and aesthetics. *Eurasian Journal of Educational Research, 18*(73), 131–148. DOI: 10.14689/ejer.2018.73.8

Bronfenbrenner, U., & Morris, P. A. (2007). The bioecological model of human development. In Damon, W., & Lerner, R. M. (Eds.),; 6th ed., Vol. 1, pp. 793–828). Handbook of child psychology. Wiley., DOI: 10.1002/9780470147658.chpsy0114

Brown, C., Douthwaite, A., Donnelly, M., & Olaniyan, Y. D. (2025). Resilience Through Belonging: Schools' Role in Promoting the Mental Health and Well-Being of Children and Young People. *Behavioral Sciences (Basel, Switzerland), 15*(10), 1421. DOI: 10.3390/bs15101421 PMID: 41153211

Burnard, P. (2012). *Musical creativities in practice.* Oxford University Press. DOI: 10.1093/acprof:oso/9780199583942.001.0001

Burnard, P., & Randles, C. (2022). Reconfiguring the future of music education through pluralism, openness and authorship of new creativities. In Burnard, P., Ross, V., Minors, H., Powell, H., & Mackinlay, E. (Eds.), *The Routledge companion to creativities in music education* (pp. 3–13). Routledge., DOI: 10.4324/9781003248194-55

Çalış, Ş., Tan, E., Maç, S. D., & Turan, Ş. A. (2022). A critique of the internship measurement scales in higher education. *Educational Research Review, 37*, 100491. DOI: 10.1016/j.edurev.2022.100491

Campayo–Muñoz, E., & Cabedo–Mas, A. (2017). The role of emotional skills in music education. *British Journal of Music Education, 34*(3), 243–258. DOI: 10.1017/S0265051717000067

Carey, J., & Dimmitt, C. (2012). School counseling and student outcomes: Summary of six statewide studies. *Professional School Counseling, 16*(2), 146–153. DOI: 10.1177/2156759X0001600204

Cefai, C., Bartolo, P., Cavioni, V., & Downes, P. (2018). *Strengthening social and emotional education as a core curricular area across the EU: A review of the international evidence.* Publications Office of the European Union.

Cohen, L., Manion, L., & Morrison, K. (2018). *Research methods in education* (8th ed.). Routledge.

Crawford, R. (2020). Beyond the dots on the page: Harnessing transculturation and music education to address intercultural competence and social inclusion. *International Journal of Music Education, 38*(4), 537–562. DOI: 10.1177/0255761420921585

Creswell, J. W., & Creswell, J. D. (2024). *Research design: Qualitative, quantitative, and mixed methods approaches* (7th ed.). Sage Publications.

Davidson, E., & Wright, L. H. V. (2020). Realising children's rights in an ACE-aware nation. *Scottish Affairs, 29*(4), 538–555. DOI: 10.3366/scot.2020.0343

Department of Education. (2023). *State of the nation 2022: Children and young people's wellbeing.* Government Social Research.

Department of the Prime Minister and Cabinet. (2021). *Children and youth wellbeing strategy: Annual report for the year ending 30 June 2020.* New Zealand Government.

Dillman, D. A., Smyth, J. D., & Christian, L. M. (2014). *Internet, phone, mail, and mixed-mode surveys: The tailored design method* (4th ed.). John Wiley & Sons. DOI: 10.1002/9781394260645

Dollman, E. (2023). The Value of Music Education for Child Development and Wellbeing in the Post COVID-19 Landscape. In White, M. A., McCallum, F., & Boyle, C. (Eds.), *New Research and Possibilities in Wellbeing Education*. Springer., DOI: 10.1007/978-981-99-5609-8_7

European Observatory on Health Systems and Policies. Eriksen, A., De Bock, F., Alayli, A., Boode, K., et al. (2025). *Improving reach and access to health promotion and preventive services for vulnerable children and adolescents: Experiences from five European countries*. World Health Organization Regional Office for Europe.

Fegter, S., & Fattore, T. (2024). Child well-being als Zugang zu Lebenswelten, Lebenslagen und Bildungsräumen. In Schierbaum, A., Diederichs, M., & Schierbaum, K. (Eds.), *Kind(er) und Kindheit(en) im Blick der Forschung* (Vol. 30, pp. 145–166). Springer VS., DOI: 10.1007/978-3-658-42625-5_8

Feng, Y., & Wang, M. (2025). Effect of music therapy on emotional resilience, well-being, and employability: A quantitative investigation of mediation and moderation. *BMC Psychology*, *13*(1), 189. Advance online publication. DOI: 10.1186/s40359-024-02336-x PMID: 39825434

Goldstein, S., & Brooks, R. B. (Eds.). (2023). *Handbook of resilience in children* (3rd ed.). Springer., DOI: 10.1007/978-3-031-14728-9

Goodman-Scott, E., & Ockerman, M. S. (2023). Integrating school counseling and MTSS. In Goodman-Scott, E., & Ockerman, M. S. (Eds.), *The school counselor's guide to multi-tiered systems of support* (2nd ed., pp. 3–35). Routledge., DOI: 10.4324/9781003317454-1

Hallam, S., & Himonides, E. (2022). *The power of music: An exploration of the evidence* (2nd ed.). Open Book Publishers., DOI: 10.11647/OBP.0292

Head, G. (2020). Ethics in educational research: Review boards, ethical issues and researcher development. *European Educational Research Journal*, *19*(1), 72–83. DOI: 10.1177/1474904118796315

Henley, J. (2025). *Inclusive pedagogy in music education*. Routledge., DOI: 10.4324/9781003414261

Israel, M., & Hay, I. (2021). *Research ethics for social scientists* (3rd ed.). Sage Publications.

Jia, H. (2024). *Music supports social and emotional skills for small group activities in daycare settings* (Bachelor's thesis, Tampere University of Applied Sciences). TAMK University Repository. URL

Johnson, R. B., & Christensen, L. (2020). *Educational research: Quantitative, qualitative, and mixed approaches* (7th ed.). Sage Publications.

Kakos, M. (2025). Developing a holistic, rights-based model for the educational inclusion of migrant and refugee students. *Intercultural Education, 36*(2), 127–142. DOI: 10.1080/14675986.2024.2349473

Kanellou, D., & Argyriou, M. (2026). From training to pedagogical transformation: Preschool teachers' experiences of online professional development in creative music education. *European Journal of Open Education and E-Learning Studies, 10*(4). Advance online publication. DOI: 10.46827/ejoe.v10i4.6500

Katsarou, D., & Argyriou, M. (Eds.). (2026). *Groundbreaking approaches to early childhood development and therapy*. IGI Global., DOI: 10.4018/979-8-3373-3068-6

Keeley, B. (2021). [*On my mind—Promoting, protecting and caring for children's mental health*. UNICEF.]. *The State of the World's Children*, •••, 2021.

Khine, M. S., Zandvliet, D. B., & Fraser, B. J. (2021). Thirty years of learning environments: Looking back and looking forward. *Learning Environments Research, 24*(3), 537–539. DOI: 10.1007/s10984-021-09386-7

Koç, N., & Sungurtekin, Ş. (2023). Promoting preschool children's social-emotional learning skills through creative drama integrated music activities. *International Online Journal of Primary Education, 12*(3), 210–227. DOI: 10.55020/iojpe.1254401

Kolbert, J. B., Crothers, L. M., & Hughes, T. L. (2022). *Introduction to school counseling: Theory, research, and practice* (2nd ed.). Routledge., DOI: 10.4324/9781003167730

Kushwaha, R. K., Yadav, P. K., Sonker, J., & Devi, A. (2024). *Ethical frameworks in special education: A guide for researchers* (2nd ed.). Integrated Publications.

Learning, O. E., & Well-Being, C. (2020). *A Study of Five-year-old in England, Estonia, and the United States.*

Leriou, E. (2023). Understanding and measuring child well-being in the region of Attica, Greece: Round five: Understanding and measuring child well-being in the region of Attica, Greece: Round five. *Child Indicators Research, 16*(4), 1395–1451. DOI: 10.1007/s12187-023-10030-4 PMID: 37363702

Lici, E., Avdulaj, E., Argyriou, M., & Lamaj, I. (2026). The role of music education in fostering psychosocial and psychomotor development in children with ASD/ID: An interdisciplinary and inclusive approach. In Katsarou, D., & Argyriou, M. (Eds.), *Groundbreaking approaches to early childhood development and therapy* (pp. 43–86). IGI Global Scientific Publishing., DOI: 10.4018/979-8-3373-3068-6.ch003

Lindblad, K., & de Boise, S. (2020). Musical engagement and subjective wellbeing amongst men in the third age. *Nordic Journal of Music Therapy*, *29*(1), 20–38. DOI: 10.1080/08098131.2019.1646791

Masten, A. S. (2021). Resilience of children in disasters: A multisystem perspective. *International Journal of Psychology*, *56*(1), 1–11. DOI: 10.1002/ijop.12737 PMID: 33325580

McFerran, K. S., Hense, C., Koike, A., & Rickwood, D. (2018). Intentional music use to reduce psychological distress in adolescents accessing primary mental health care. *Clinical Child Psychology and Psychiatry*, *23*(4), 567–581. DOI: 10.1177/1359104518767231 PMID: 29669441

Nijs, L. (2025). Fostering a synergy between the development of well-being and musicianship: A kinemusical perspective. *Education Sciences*, *15*(9), 1245. DOI: 10.3390/educsci15091245

Organisation for Economic Co-operation and Development. (2016). *Education at a glance 2016: OECD indicators*. OECD Publishing., DOI: 10.1787/eag-2016-

Organisation for Economic Co-operation and Development. (2017). *PISA 2015 results (Volume III): Students' well-being*. OECD Publishing. https://doi.org/DOI: 10.1787/9789264273856-en

Organisation for Economic Co-operation and Development. (2020). *Early learning and child well-being: A study of five-year-olds in England, Estonia, and the United States*. OECD Publishing. https://doi.org/DOI: 10.1787/3990407f-en

Papageorgi, I., Saunders, J., Himonides, E., & Welch, G. F. (2022). Singing and social identity in young children. *Frontiers in Psychology*, *13*, 823229. DOI: 10.3389/fpsyg.2022.823229 PMID: 35719461

Pérez-Moreno, J., Lerma-Arregocés, D., & Dosaiguas, M. (2026). The role of music in young children's lives: Guide for adults seeking ways to interact. In Katsarou, D., & Argyriou, M. (Eds.), *Groundbreaking approaches to early childhood development and therapy* (pp. 87–118). IGI Global., DOI: 10.4018/979-8-3373-3068-6.ch004

Randles, C., & Burnard, P. (Eds.). (2023). *The Routledge companion to creativities in music education*. Routledge.

Ravi, R. (2026). Concepts, measures and policy problems: The case study of child wellbeing measurement in the UK between 2014 and 2024. *Child Indicators Research, 19*(3), 1393–1416. Advance online publication. DOI: 10.1007/s12187-026-10346-x

Saarikallio, S., Baltazar, M., & Västfjäll, D. (2020). Adolescents' musical relaxation: Understanding emotional self-regulation through music. *Psychology of Music, 48*(5), 653–667. DOI: 10.1177/0305735619854021

Selvitopu, A., & Kaya, M. (2026). Well-being and academic performance among students with an immigrant background: A meta-analysis. *Current Psychology (New Brunswick, N.J.), 45*(3), 256. DOI: 10.1007/s12144-025-08654-6

Serrano, I., Fernández, M., & Marcos, E. B. (2024). Building a set of indicators to assess migrant children's integration in Europe: A co-creation approach. *Child Indicators Research, 17*(6), 2389–2417. DOI: 10.1007/s12187-024-10165-y

Shen, L., & Yang, W. (2025). The intervention of music education on adolescents' subjective well-being from the perspective of sustainable development: A bibliometric review based on literature from 2000 to 2024. *Frontiers in Psychology, 16*, 1617097. DOI: 10.3389/fpsyg.2025.1617097 PMID: 40589882

Sink, C. A. (2005). *Contemporary school counseling: Theory, research, and practice*. Lahaska Press.

Smith, T. D. (2021). Music Education for Surviving and Thriving: Cultivating Children's Wonder, Senses, Emotional Wellbeing, and Wild Nature as a Means to Discover and Fulfill Their Life's Purpose. *Frontiers in Education, 6*, 648799. DOI: 10.3389/feduc.2021.648799

Southwick, S. M., Bonanno, G. A., Masten, A. S., Panter-Brick, C., & Yehuda, R. (2023). Resilience definitions, theory, and challenges: Interdisciplinary perspectives. *European Journal of Psychotraumatology, 14*(1), 2164790. DOI: 10.1080/20008198.2023.2164790 PMID: 25317257

Theodoropoulou, M., & Argyriou, M. (2026). Enhancing memory processes in early childhood through musical activities: A descriptive survey of preschool teachers' perceptions. *European Journal of Education Studies, 13*(4). Advance online publication. DOI: 10.46827/ejes.v13i4.6611

Theron, L. C. (2023). Resilience of children and adolescents in contexts of adversity: A social ecological perspective. *Child Abuse & Neglect, 138*, 106054. DOI: 10.1016/j.chiabu.2023.106054

Tian, L., Wu, T. L. Y., Robinson, N. L., Carreno-Medrano, P., Chan, W. P., Sakr, M., Abdi, E., Croft, E. A., & Kulić, D. (2025). Quantitative data collection and analysis. In Kulić, D., Croft, E., & Sakr, M. (Eds.), *Experimental methodology for human–robot interaction* (pp. xx–xx). CRC Press., DOI: 10.1201/9781032693682-7

Ungar, M. (2021). *Multisystemic resilience: Adaptation and transformation in contexts of change*. Oxford University Press., DOI: 10.1093/oso/9780190095888.001.0001

United Nations Office for Disaster Risk Reduction. (2023). *Global assessment report on disaster risk reduction 2023: Mapping resilience for the sustainable development goals*. UNDRR.

Váradi, J. (2022). A Review of the Literature on the Relationship of Music Education to the Development of Socio-Emotional Learning. *SAGE Open, 12*(1), 21582440211068501. Advance online publication. DOI: 10.1177/21582440211068501

Welch, G. F., Biasutti, M., MacRitchie, J., McPherson, G. E., & Himonides, E. (2020). Editorial: The impact of music on human development and well-being. *Frontiers in Psychology, 11*, 1246. DOI: 10.3389/fpsyg.2020.01246 PMID: 32625147

Welch, G. F., & McPherson, G. E. (2018). Commentary: Music education and the role of music in people's lives. In Welch, G. F., & McPherson, G. E. (Eds.), *Music and music education in people's lives: An Oxford handbook of music education* (pp. 3–18). Oxford University Press., DOI: 10.1093/oxfordhb/9780199730810.013.0002

World Health Organization. (2022). *World mental health report: Transforming mental health for all*. World Health Organization.

Zimba, O., & Gasparyan, A. Y. (2023). Designing, conducting, and reporting survey studies: A primer for researchers. *Journal of Korean Medical Science, 38*(48), e403. DOI: 10.3346/jkms.2023.38.e403 PMID: 38084027

Chapter 10
Psychological Resilience of Mothers of Children with ADHD:
An Empirical Study

Kyriaki Tasiou
http://orcid.org/0000-0001-8144-8090
University of the Aegean, Rhodes, Greece

Eleni Nikolaou
http://orcid.org/0000-0003-1840-3433
University of the Aegean, Rhodes, Greece

ABSTRACT

Attention-Deficit/Hyperactivity Disorder (ADHD) is one of the most common neurodevelopmental disorders of childhood, affecting not only the child but also the entire family system. Mothers of children with ADHD often experience increased levels of stress, parental burnout, and social pressure, while they are daily called upon to manage challenges related to their children's behavior. In this context, resilience constitutes a key factor in adaptation and psychosocial well-being. The present study investigates levels of resilience in a sample of 51 mothers of children with ADHD. The results indicated satisfactory levels of adaptive capacity. Additionally, resilience was found to be positively associated with specific coping strategies, particularly a positive approach. The findings suggest the presence of strong personal resources and stress-management abilities, despite the challenges associated with raising a child with ADHD. Strengthening resilience through targeted counseling and educational practices may significantly contribute to mothers' psychological empowerment.

DOI: 10.4018/979-8-3373-9420-6.ch010

INTRODUCTION

Attention-Deficit/Hyperactivity Disorder (ADHD) is a neurodevelopmental disorder that is primarily based on genetic and neurological factors (Olivier et al., 2009). Children with ADHD often display behaviors that make them difficult for parents to manage, resulting in higher levels of stress among parents compared to those raising children without any form of disability (Ringer, 2019).

In this context, the concept of resilience becomes particularly important, as psychological resilience is defined as the ability to effectively adapt to adversity and stressful conditions, as well as to recover from difficult experiences (American Psychological Association, 2013).

At the same time, the study of coping strategies, beyond examining their relationship with health and stress, highlights how individuals respond to their environment, as well as their role in shaping it (Lazarus, 1991). Investigating the relationship between resilience and coping strategies is especially important, as it can contribute to understanding how parents respond to everyday challenges.

Maternal resilience, in particular, has been associated with treatment outcomes in children with Attention-Deficit/Hyperactivity Disorder (Darling Rasmussen et al., 2020). However, the literature focusing specifically on mothers of children with ADHD remains limited, especially regarding the link between resilience and specific coping strategies. The present study aims to address this gap by exploring, on the one hand, possible differences in resilience between mothers of children with and without ADHD, and on the other hand, the relationship between resilience and coping strategies. The findings of this study are expected to contribute to a better understanding of the factors that enhance mothers' psychological adjustment and to provide guidance for the development of targeted support interventions.

Attention-Deficit/Hyperactivity Disorder (ADHD): Definition and Characteristics

ADHD is a widely recognized disorder in which symptoms appear early in development but may persist into adulthood and contribute to reduced functioning (Fayyad et al., 2018). According to the Diagnostic and Statistical Manual of Mental Disorders (DSM-5), ADHD is classified into three subtypes: predominantly inattentive presentation, predominantly hyperactive-impulsive presentation, and combined presentation (American Psychiatric Association, 2013). Based on DSM-5 diagnostic criteria, ADHD is estimated to occur in approximately 5% of children and 2.5% of adolescents (Centers for Disease Control and Prevention, 2003). In Greece, available epidemiological data on ADHD remain limited, as relevant studies are few. Indicatively, a study conducted in Crete by Skounti et al. (2006) reported a prevalence rate of 6.5% among 7-year-old children.

Hyperactive children are characterized by intense and continuous motor activity, a strong tendency to talk excessively, and difficulty remaining seated, as well as engaging in activities that require calmness and behavioral control. Impulsivity may also be present, manifested as impatience, difficulty waiting for one's turn, and challenges in following instructions. Regarding inattention, difficulties are observed in maintaining focus on a task for a sufficient period, with attention often being easily distracted by external stimuli and difficulty returning to the task (APA, 2000).

Impact of ADHD on the Family

It has been suggested that parents of children with ADHD often face significant difficulties (Tasiou & Nikolaou, 2023). At the same time, the effects of the disorder's symptoms on the daily functioning of children and their families have been the subject of extensive research (Harpin, 2005; Weiss, 2015; Faraone et al., 2015; Tasiou, 2024; Tasiou & Nikolaou, 2023; 2024; 2025a; 2025b).

Parents of children with ADHD may exhibit increased levels of stress, lower confidence in their parenting role, and feelings of reduced self-efficacy (Johnston & Mash, 2001). The diagnosis of ADHD in children may have significant effects not only on the child's functioning but also on the broader family system (Tasiou & Nikolaou, 2023; 2025).

Mothers of Children with ADHD

Among the various challenges faced by parents of children with ADHD, mothers often experience a particularly burdensome and multidimensional reality that warrants separate examination. Mothers of children with ADHD frequently encounter increased emotional strain, associated both with criticism they may receive regarding their child's disruptive behavior and with feelings of self-blame and limited support from the family environment (Harborne et al., 2004).

In this direction, George et al. (2024), in a sample of 40 mothers of children with ADHD (aged 6–14), found that mothers experience significantly elevated levels of stress. To cope with this stress, they were found to employ a variety of strategies. Similarly, in the study by Karimirad et al. (2019), 110 mothers of children with ADHD demonstrated a moderate level of resilience. Comparable findings were reported by Khdemloo et al. (2016), where, in a sample of 155 mothers of children with ADHD, lower mental health levels were observed compared to mothers of typically developing children, while a significant correlation was found between resilience and mental health in both groups.

The Concept of Psychological Resilience

Resilience is a fundamental process that arises from the proper functioning of an individual's core adaptive systems. Maintaining these systems in good condition contributes to stable development even under adverse circumstances. Conversely, their weakening - either before or after exposure to difficulties - increases the likelihood of developmental problems, especially when environmental risks persist (Masten, 2001).

This capacity of individuals to recover from adversity and adapt effectively is supported by both individual and environmental factors, such as personal strengths, support networks, and protective mechanisms (Hatzichristou et al., 2012). Protective factors can be categorized as internal and external. Internal factors may be biological or psychological, while external factors relate to the nature and quality of interpersonal relationships formed within and outside the family context. Within the family, key elements include the family climate, parenting practices, and the support provided by other family members (Mandleco & Peery, 2000).

In contrast, risk factors may lead to negative changes or maladaptive behaviors that can persist, produce adverse developmental outcomes, and are measurable (Keyes, 2004).

Coping Strategies

The ability to adapt requires persistence and commitment in order for individuals to manage personal and environmental difficulties (Lazarus & Lanier, 1978; Sorensen, 1993). It is of crucial importance for individuals' life course (Karadimas, 2005), while the strategies each person chooses to cope with difficulties vary. It has been noted that individuals - considered theoretically resilient - may struggle to adapt under conditions of extreme stress or severe adversity and may not immediately exhibit signs of resilience, even though it may exist, as their adaptive capacity is influenced by a set of interacting factors (Mandleco & Peery, 2000).

Coping strategies essentially describe the mechanisms (cognitive and behavioral) that individuals use to manage stressful situations. According to classical models of stress management, two main types of coping strategies are distinguished: problem-focused and emotion-focused strategies (Lazarus & Folkman, 1984). Problem-focused strategies aim at actively addressing the difficulty through problem-solving, information seeking, and action planning, whereas emotion-focused strategies concentrate on regulating and managing the emotional responses caused by stress.

It is worth noting the findings of Mustafa and Alwi (2021), who examined the relationship between parental stress, coping strategies, and depressive symptoms in mothers of children with ADHD, in a sample of 94 mothers from Malaysia. Their results indicated that higher levels of parental stress were associated with more intense depressive symptoms, which could, however, be reduced when problem-focused coping strategies were employed. Furthermore, both problem-solving strategies and seeking social support were associated with lower levels of depressive symptoms, highlighting their protective role in enhancing psychological resilience. In contrast, emotion-focused regulation strategies, such as attentional disengagement or emotional venting, did not appear to contribute to the reduction of depressive symptoms.

In the same direction, Berenguer et al. (2021) found that children's behavioral and emotional problems were strongly associated with levels of parental stress, as well as with specific coping strategies such as distancing and cognitive reappraisal, as reported by mothers of children with ADHD. Moreover, distancing emerged as a key mediating factor in the relationship between children's difficulties and maternal stress, as shown through mediation analysis.

METHODOLOGY

Sample

The findings presented in this study derive from a preliminary phase of a broader research project aimed at investigating resilience and coping strategies in parents of children with ADHD. The study was designed in accordance with ethical principles, ensuring confidentiality and voluntary participation. Mothers were included in the study if they were responsible for raising a child with a confirmed diagnosis of ADHD.

The sample consisted of 51 mothers of children diagnosed with ADHD. The children covered a wide age range and presented different subtypes of the disorder. For the purposes of comparative analysis, an additional group of mothers of children without ADHD or any other disability/disorder (control group) was included (N = 55). Participation was voluntary and anonymous.

Research Instruments

Data were collected using a structured questionnaire that included demographic information about parents and children (e.g., type of ADHD), as well as psychological variables (individual resilience and coping strategies).

Individual resilience was assessed using a self-report psychometric instrument, the Connor - Davidson Resilience Scale (CD-RISC-25) (Connor & Davidson, 2003; Connor et al., 2012), a five-point Likert scale consisting of 25 items. The total score ranges from 0 to 100, with higher scores indicating higher levels of resilience.

Coping strategies were assessed using a multidimensional instrument, the Stress Coping Strategies Scale (SCSS), based on the Greek adaptation of the "Ways of Coping" questionnaire (Lazarus & Folkman, 1984; Karadimas, 1998). This scale consists of 38 statements and includes the following distinct factors: (a) positive approach, (b) seeking social support, (c) avoidance/escape, (d) wishful thinking/daydreaming, and (e) assertive problem solving. It should be noted that both scales have been translated and adapted for the Greek population.

The internal consistency of the scales was assessed using Cronbach's alpha coefficient. The reliability of the resilience scale was very high for both mothers of children with ADHD (Cronbach's $\alpha = .879$) and mothers of children without ADHD (Cronbach's $\alpha = .904$). Similarly, the subscales of coping strategies demonstrated low to satisfactory levels of internal consistency (Cronbach's $\alpha = .57–.88$), supporting their use in the present analysis.

Data Collection Procedure

The study was approved by the Educational Research Committee of the University of the Aegean and was conducted in accordance with the ethical principles of the Declaration of Helsinki. Data were collected through anonymous questionnaires completed by the participants. Participation was voluntary, and the confidentiality of responses was ensured. The questionnaires were distributed in both printed and digital formats. Participants were informed about the purpose of the study and provided their consent to participate.

Data collection took place between February 2025 and February 2026.

Data Analysis Method Statistical Analysis

Statistical analysis of the data was carried out using PS IMAGO PRO software, version 10 (version 10, 2013–2024), which is based on IBM SPSS Statistics. The analyses were conducted using total scores of resilience and the factors of coping strategies, as derived from the standardized instruments.

Prior to the main analyses, the assumptions for applying parametric tests were examined. Normality of distributions was assessed using the Shapiro–Wilk test and visual inspection of Q–Q plots. The results indicated that individual resilience followed an approximately normal distribution in both groups (mothers of children with ADHD: $p = .192$; mothers without ADHD: $p = .361$). In contrast, some coping strategies showed deviations from normality, which was taken into account in the selection of statistical methods. Despite these deviations, both parametric and non-parametric analyses were conducted, as the sample size was considered sufficient for statistical testing.

Initially, descriptive statistics were calculated for all variables. Subsequently, independent samples t-tests were performed to examine potential differences in resilience levels between mothers of children with and without ADHD. Additionally, effect size (Cohen's d) was calculated to assess the practical significance of the differences. To investigate the relationship between resilience and coping strategies, Spearman's correlation coefficient was used. The level of statistical significance was set at $p < .05$.

RESULTS

Descriptive Statistics

Initially, descriptive statistics of the main study variables were examined. Regarding family type, the ADHD group sample mainly consisted of single-parent families (49%), followed by nuclear families (31.4%), extended families (15.7%), and reconstituted families (3.9%). In contrast, the majority of participants in the non-ADHD group came from nuclear families (63.6%), with smaller proportions from single-parent (14.5%), extended (20%), and reconstituted families (1.8%).

With regard to the area of residence, mothers of children with ADHD mainly came from island regions (41.2%), while notable percentages were also recorded in highly urban (21.6%) and urban areas (21.6%). A smaller percentage came from semi-urban areas (15.7%). Similarly, in the non-ADHD group, the majority of mothers came from island regions (85.5%), with significantly lower percentages in highly urban (5.5%), urban (5.5%), and semi-urban areas (3.6%).

In terms of children's gender, in the ADHD group 92.2% were boys and 7.8% were girls, while in the non-ADHD group the corresponding percentages were 40% boys and 60% girls.

Regarding age distribution, it was found that the majority of mothers of children with ADHD belonged to the middle age group (41–50 years), with smaller percentages in the 31–40 and 51–60 age groups. Very few participants belonged to the 20–30 age group. The age distribution of children with ADHD showed that most participants fell within the age ranges of 5.6–8.5 and 8.6–12.5 years, with smaller percentages in other categories—these were primarily school-aged children, with limited participation of adolescents.

Regarding mothers of children without ADHD, the majority fell within the 31–40 age group, while an equally substantial proportion of participants belonged to the 41–50 age group. The age distribution of children without ADHD showed that most participants were in the age groups 3–5.5, 5.6–8.5, and 8.6–12.5 years, with smaller percentages in the remaining categories.

With respect to the type of ADHD diagnosis, the majority of children presented the combined type (inattention and hyperactivity/impulsivity), accounting for 60.8%. This was followed by the hyperactive-impulsive type at 31.4%, while a small percentage (5.9%) exhibited the predominantly inattentive type. Finally, a minimal proportion (2.0%) had a diagnosis described as "features/indications of ADHD."

Subsequently, descriptive statistics of the study variables were calculated. The total sample of mothers ($N = 106$) showed a mean individual resilience score of $M = 95.93$ ($SD = 12.00$). The individual coping strategies displayed varying levels of use, with positive approach and social support showing relatively higher mean values compared to the others.

Comparison of Resilience Between Mothers of Children With and Without ADHD

This analysis was conducted on the subsample of mothers ($N = 51$) and the corresponding control group ($N = 55$). An independent samples t-test was performed to compare resilience between mothers of children with and without an ADHD diagnosis. The difference in individual resilience scores between the two groups was examined. The results indicated that there was no statistically significant difference between the groups, $t(104) = -0.32$, $p = .752$. The mean difference was small ($M_{diff} = -0.74$), suggesting similar levels of resilience between the groups. The effect size was negligible (Cohen's $d = -0.06$, 95% CI [-0.44, 0.32]). Mothers of children with ADHD ($M = 95.55$, $SD = 12.14$, $N = 51$) demonstrated similar levels of resilience compared to mothers without an ADHD diagnosis ($M = 96.29$, $SD = 11.98$, $N = 55$).

Correlation Between Resilience and Coping Strategies

This analysis was conducted only on the subsample of mothers ($N = 51$). Specifically, a correlation analysis (Spearman's rho) was applied to examine the relationships between individual resilience and the coping strategies used by mothers of children with Attention-Deficit/Hyperactivity Disorder.

The analysis showed that individual resilience scores had a statistically significant positive correlation with the positive approach strategy ($\rho = .541$, $p < .001$), while no significant correlations were found with social support, wishful thinking/daydreaming, avoidance/escape, or assertive problem solving.

Additionally, significant correlations were observed among the coping strategies themselves. Specifically, positive approach was positively correlated with social support ($\rho = .370$, $p = .007$) and assertive problem solving ($\rho = .321$, $p = .022$), with no significant relationship with wishful thinking/daydreaming or avoidance/escape. Social support also showed a positive correlation with wishful thinking/daydreaming ($\rho = .307$, $p = .028$) and a strong correlation with assertive problem solving ($\rho = .576$, $p < .001$). Furthermore, wishful thinking/daydreaming was positively correlated with both avoidance/escape ($\rho = .470$, $p < .001$) and assertive problem solving ($\rho = .418$, $p = .002$). Finally, avoidance/escape did not show statistically significant correlations with the other variables, except for its positive relationship with wishful thinking/daydreaming.

The subscales of coping strategies demonstrated significant intercorrelations, as expected due to their shared theoretical foundation.

DISCUSSION

The present study examined differences in individual resilience between mothers of children with and without an ADHD diagnosis. The results showed no statistically significant difference between the two groups, while the effect size was negligible. Mothers' resilience may be more strongly influenced by broader psychosocial factors and their overall mental state. This finding suggests that the presence of ADHD in the child does not appear to substantially differentiate levels of resilience among mothers in this sample. Mothers were found to have similar levels of resilience regardless of their child's ADHD diagnosis. In fact, the results indicated high levels of psychological resilience in both groups. Similar findings have been reported by Erginyavuz and Özdemir (2019), who, in a study of 163 mothers of children with ADHD, found low levels of depression and anxiety, along with good levels of psychological resilience. Moreover, a statistically significant relationship was identified between mothers' mental health and their children's level of adjustment.

One possible interpretation of these findings is that resilience constitutes a relatively stable psychological trait shaped by a range of factors, such as individual characteristics, interventions (e.g., family therapy, counseling), social support, and coping strategies, rather than solely by the challenges associated with raising a child with Attention-Deficit/Hyperactivity Disorder. From a systemic perspective, Walsh (2008) emphasizes the development of resilience as the result of interactions between genetic and environmental factors. At the same time, the dynamic interplay of multiple risk and protective factors - such as individual traits, family context, and sociocultural influences - has been highlighted.

Therefore, despite the increased demands that may accompany raising a child with ADHD, mothers appear to maintain similar levels of resilience. It is possible that, through long-term experience, they have developed more adaptive coping strategies, which may contribute to sustaining resilience at levels comparable to those of mothers without similar challenges.

The findings of this study contribute to the understanding of resilience in motherhood, suggesting that the presence of ADHD in a child is not necessarily associated with lower levels of maternal resilience. A particularly important finding is the positive correlation between resilience and the use of a positive approach as a coping strategy. These findings are consistent with those of Sobhani et al. (2024), who reported that emotion-focused coping strategies and those based on suppression or somatization of problems are negatively and significantly associated with resilience. In contrast, they found a positive and significant relationship between resilience and problem-focused coping strategies as well as those based on cognitive appraisal.

Additionally, the results showed that coping strategies among mothers of children with ADHD are interrelated to varying degrees. Some strategies demonstrated stronger positive correlations (e.g., social support, assertive problem solving, and positive reappraisal), while others, such as avoidance and wishful thinking/daydreaming, were more closely associated with each other as less adaptive patterns. Overall, adaptive coping strategies appear to co-occur and reinforce one another, whereas avoidance mechanisms tend to cluster together without strong links to more functional coping forms. Similarly, McKee et al. (2004) found that seeking social support was negatively correlated with avoidance and positively associated with coping strategies among mothers of children with ADHD.

Craig et al. (2020) concluded that further and more systematic investigation is needed into how parents of children with Attention-Deficit/Hyperactivity Disorder manage difficulties, in order to strengthen more effective and adaptive coping strategies. These findings also highlight the importance of enhancing positive coping strategies in interventions aimed at improving parental resilience. In this direction, Zabihollahzadeh et al. (2020), through an educational intervention with a sample of 30 mothers of children with ADHD, demonstrated that cognitive-behavioral intervention significantly contributes to strengthening both resilience and emotional regulation in mothers.

The results should be interpreted in light of certain limitations. First, the use of self-report instruments may be influenced by socially desirable responses. Additionally, the cross-sectional nature of the study does not allow for causal conclusions. Future research could examine the role of factors such as the level of social support or the severity of the child's symptoms.

Overall, the findings of the present study suggest that resilience is primarily associated with active and positive forms of coping and does not extend equally across all coping strategies. Notably, Podolski and Nigg (2001) reported that positive reappraisal is associated with lower levels of stress in both mothers and fathers, as well as greater satisfaction with the parenting role and fewer behavioral problems in children. Understanding these distinctions may contribute to the design of interventions that strengthen specific adaptive skills in mothers of children with developmental difficulties.

CONCLUSION

In conclusion, the present study contributes to the growing body of research on maternal resilience and coping in families of children with ADHD. Although mothers of children with ADHD are often confronted with increased daily stressors and caregiving demands, the findings did not reveal significant differences in resilience levels compared to mothers of children without ADHD, suggesting that resilience may function as a relatively stable personal resource independent of the child's diagnosis. Furthermore, resilience was positively associated with the use of adaptive coping strategies, particularly a positive approach, highlighting the importance of constructive cognitive and emotional management in fostering psychological adjustment.

The significant intercorrelations observed among coping strategies further indicate that mothers employ a multidimensional coping framework, combining emotional, cognitive, and problem-focused mechanisms in response to everyday challenges. Overall, the findings highlight the importance of adaptive coping and personal strengths in supporting maternal well-being. Interventions focusing on resilience enhancement, psychoeducation, and counseling support could help mothers manage stress more effectively, strengthen family relationships, and improve cooperation between families and the school community.

LIMITATIONS

Several limitations of the present study should be acknowledged. First, the relatively small sample size may limit the generalizability of the findings to the broader population of families with children with ADHD. In addition, the study included only mothers, excluding the perspectives of fathers or other caregivers who may experience and manage stress differently. Another limitation concerns the use of self-report measures, which may be influenced by social desirability or subjective interpretation. Furthermore, the cross-sectional design of the study does not allow conclusions about causal relationships between resilience and coping strategies. Future research could include larger and more diverse samples, longitudinal designs, and multiple family members in order to gain a more comprehensive understanding of resilience processes within families of children with ADHD.

REFERENCES

American Psychiatric Association. (2000). *Diagnostic and statistical manual of mental disorders* (4th ed., text rev.). American Psychiatric Association.

American Psychiatric Association. (2013). *Diagnostic and statistical manual of mental disorders* (5th ed.). American Psychiatric Publishing.

Berenguer, C., Roselló, B., & Miranda, A. (2021). Mothers' stress and behavioral and emotional problems in children with ADHD: Mediation of coping strategies. *Scandinavian Journal of Psychology*, *62*(2), 141–149. DOI: 10.1111/sjop.12680 PMID: 32920860

Centers for Disease Control and Prevention. (2005). Mental health in the United States: Prevalence of diagnosis and medication treatment for attention-deficit/hyperactivity disorder—United States, 2003. *MMWR. Morbidity and Mortality Weekly Report*, *54*(34), 842–847. PMID: 16138075

Connor, K. M., & Davidson, J. R. (2003). Development of a new resilience scale: The Connor–Davidson Resilience Scale (CD-RISC). *Depression and Anxiety*, *18*(2), 76–82. DOI: 10.1002/da.10113 PMID: 12964174

Connor, K. M., Davidson, J. R., Douzenis, A., Tsitas, N., & Tsigkaropoulou, E. (2012). Connor–Davidson Resilience Scale (CD-RISC-25) [Unofficial published translation of the Connor–Davidson Resilience Scale (CD-RISC)].

Craig, F., Savino, R., Fanizza, I., Lucarelli, E., Russo, L., & Trabacca, A. (2020). A systematic review of coping strategies in parents of children with attention deficit hyperactivity disorder (ADHD). *Research in Developmental Disabilities*, *98*, 103571. DOI: 10.1016/j.ridd.2020.103571 PMID: 31931455

Darling Rasmussen, P., Bilenberg, N., Kirubakaran, R., & Storebø, O. J. (2020). Mapping factors facilitating resilience in mothers—Potential clinical relevance for children with ADHD. *Nordic Journal of Psychiatry*, *74*(7), 541–544. DOI: 10.1080/08039488.2020.1748899 PMID: 32255402

Erginyavuz, K. A., & Özdemir, N. (2019). Determination of the anxiety, depression and psychological resilience levels of mothers with children diagnosed with attention deficit hyperactivity disorder: Anxiety, depression and psychological resilience levels of mothers with. *Medical Science and Discovery*, *6*(10), 249–256. DOI: 10.36472/msd.v6i10.306

Faraone, S. V., Asherson, P., Banaschewski, T., Biederman, J., Buitelaar, J. K., Ramos-Quiroga, J. A., & Franke, B. (2015). Attention-deficit/hyperactivity disorder. *Nature Reviews. Disease Primers*, *1*(1), 1–23. DOI: 10.1038/nrdp.2015.20 PMID: 27189265

Fayyad, J., Haro, J. M., Aguilar-Gaxiola, S., & Kessler, R. C. (2018). Attention-deficit. Mental Disorders Around the World: Facts and Figures from the WHO World Mental Health Surveys, 195.

George, B. B., Dangroo, A. A., Sahu, K. K., & Arun, P. (2024). Stress, coping, and resilience among mothers of children with attention deficit hyperactivity disorder. *Indian Journal of Psychiatric Social Work*, •••, 17–27.

Harborne, A., Wolpert, M., & Clare, L. (2004). Making sense of ADHD: A battle for understanding? Parents' views of their children being diagnosed with ADHD. *Clinical Child Psychology and Psychiatry*, *9*(3), 327–339. DOI: 10.1177/1359104504043915

Harpin, V. A. (2005). The effect of ADHD on the life of an individual, their family, and community from preschool to adult life. *Archives of Disease in Childhood*, *90*(suppl_1), i2–i7. DOI: 10.1136/adc.2004.059006 PMID: 15665153

Hatzichristou, C., Lampropoulou, A., & Adamopoulou, E. (2012). Psychological resilience: Basic issues of children's development and adjustment (pp. 1–6).

Johnston, C., & Mash, E. J. (2001). Families of children with attention-deficit/hyperactivity disorder: Review and recommendations for future research. *Clinical Child and Family Psychology Review*, *4*(3), 183–207. DOI: 10.1023/A:1017592030434 PMID: 11783738

Karadimas, E. H. (1998). The adaptation of a coping strategies measurement scale to the Greek population. *Psychologia*, *5*(3), 260–273.

Karadimas, E. H. (2005). *Health psychology: Theory and clinical practice*. Typothito.

Karimirad, M. R., Seyedfatemi, N., Hossein Oghli, S., Noorian, S., & Amini, E. (2019). Resilience of mothers of children with attention deficit hyperactivity disorder and its related underlying factors. *Journal of Preventive Epidemiology*, *4*(2), e11.

Keyes, C. L. M. (Ed.). (2004). *Risk and resilience in human development: A special issue of Research in Human Development*. Psychology Press., DOI: 10.4324/9780203764374

Lazarus, R., & Folkman, S. (1984). *Stress, appraisal, and coping*. Springer.

Lazarus, R., & Lanier, R. (1978). Stress-related transactions between person and environment. In L. A. Pervin & M. Lewis (Eds.), Perspectives in international psychology (pp. 287–327). Plenum Press.

Lazarus, R. S. (1991). *Emotion and adaptation*. Oxford University Press. DOI: 10.1093/oso/9780195069945.001.0001

Mandleco, B., & Peery, J. C. (2000). An organizational framework for conceptualizing resilience in children. *Journal of Child and Adolescent Psychiatric Nursing*, *13*(3), 99–111. DOI: 10.1111/j.1744-6171.2000.tb00086.x PMID: 11111503

Masten, A. S. (2001). Ordinary magic: Resilience processes in development. *The American Psychologist*, *56*(3), 227–238. DOI: 10.1037/0003-066X.56.3.227 PMID: 11315249

McKee, T. E., Harvey, E., Danforth, J. S., Ulaszek, W. R., & Friedman, J. L. (2004). The relation between parental coping styles and parent-child interactions before and after treatment for children with ADHD and oppositional behavior. *Journal of Clinical Child and Adolescent Psychology*, *33*(1), 158–168. DOI: 10.1207/S15374424JCCP3301_15 PMID: 15028550

Mustafa, Q. M., & Alwi, A. H. (2021). Stress experiences of mothers of children with ADHD: Significant coping strategies that safeguard their mental health. *Malaysian Journal of Medicine & Health Sciences*, *17*(3).

Olivier, M. A., Gomes, A. M., & Greyling, A. J. (2009). Attention deficit hyperactivity disorder (ADHD)—Dilemmas and solutions. *Journal of Psychology in Africa*, *19*(2), 237–241. DOI: 10.1080/14330237.2009.10820285

Podolski, C. L., & Nigg, J. T. (2001). Parent stress and coping in relation to child ADHD severity and associated child disruptive behavior problems. *Journal of Clinical Child Psychology*, *30*(4), 503–513. DOI: 10.1207/S15374424JCCP3004_07 PMID: 11708238

PS IMAGO. (2013–2024). PS IMAGO PRO Version 10 [Computer software].

Ringer, N. (2019). Young people's perceptions of and coping with their ADHD symptoms: A qualitative study. *Cogent Psychology*, *6*(1), 1608032. DOI: 10.1080/23311908.2019.1608032

Skounti, M., Philalithis, A., Mpitzaraki, K., Vamvoukas, M., & Galanakis, E. (2006). Attention deficit hyperactivity disorder in school children in Crete. *Acta Paediatrica (Oslo, Norway)*, *95*, 658–663. PMID: 16754545

Sobhani, S., Jamilian, H., & Paknejad, I. (2024). Prediction of resilience based on parenting and coping strategies in patients with psychosomatic disorders. *BMC Psychology, 12*(1), 280. DOI: 10.1186/s40359-024-01784-9 PMID: 38764081

Sorensen, E. (1993). *Children's stress and coping: A family perspective.* Guilford Press.

Tasiou, K. (2024). Experiences of stigma in a family with a child with ADHD: A case study. *International Journal of Educational Innovation, 6*(5), 1–15. DOI: 10.69685/VORM2511

Tasiou, K., & Nikolaou, E. N. (2023). The psychological resilience of families of children with attention deficit hyperactivity disorder. In Katsarou, D. V., Koundourou, C., & Reppa, G. P. (Eds.), *New trends and approaches in psychopathology and mental health of children and adults* (pp. 99–121). Gutenberg.

Tasiou, K., & Nikolaou, E. N. (2024). A family's experiences of raising a child diagnosed with ADHD: Family functioning and organization, sources of support and quality of life—A case study. In Katsarou, D. V. (Ed.), *Childhood developmental language disorders: Role of inclusion, families, and professionals* (pp. 116–133). IGI Global Scientific Publishing.

Tasiou, K., & Nikolaou, E. N. (2025a). Well-being among parents raising a child diagnosed with attention deficit hyperactivity disorder (ADHD) and intervention programs: A literature review. In Sofologi, M., Katsarou, D. V., & Efthymiou, E. (Eds.), *Exploring cognitive and psychosocial dynamics across childhood and adolescence* (pp. 229–248). IGI Global Scientific Publishing.

Tasiou, K. S., & Nikolaou, E. N. (2025b). Psychological resilience of parents of children with neurodevelopmental disorders during COVID-19 pandemic: A systematic review. *Emotional & Behavioural Difficulties, 30*(4), 1–15. DOI: 10.1080/13632752.2025.2536986

Walsh, F. (2008). Using theory to support a family resilience framework in practice. Social Work Now: The Practice Journal of Child, Youth and Family, 5–14.

Weiss, M. (2015). Functional impairment in ADHD. In Adler, L. A., Spencer, T. J., & Wilens, T. E. (Eds.), *Attention-deficit hyperactivity disorder in adults and children* (pp. 42–52). Cambridge University Press.

Zabihollahzadeh, F., Rashvand, P., & Nemattavosi, M. (2020). The effectiveness of cognitive behavioral therapy based on mindfulness on resilience and self-regulation emotional in mothers of adolescents attention deficit hyperactivity disorder (ADHD). [RRJ]. *Rooyesh-e-Ravanshenasi Journal, 8*(12), 31–38.

Chapter 11
Parenting Practices and Childhood Aggression:
Fostering Resilience through School Counseling

Eirini Tzovla
http://orcid.org/0000-0003-2611-2783
Neapolis University Pafos, Cyprus

Marilena Mousoulidou
http://orcid.org/0000-0002-3549-2522
Neapolis University Pafos, Cyprus

Andri Christodoulou
http://orcid.org/0000-0002-3281-3327
Neapolis University Pafos, Cyprus

George Tsitsas
Neapolis University Pafos, Cyprus

Angela Savvidou
Neapolis University Pafos, Cyprus

Theodoros Goutoglou
Neapolis University Pafos, Cyprus

ABSTRACT

This chapter explores the relationship between parenting practices and childhood aggression, highlighting the role of school counseling in fostering resilience. The authoritative parenting style (high warmth, reasonable control) functions protectively, limiting aggression and enhancing self-regulation. Conversely, the authoritarian style (low warmth, rigid control) and the permissive style (high warmth, absence of boundaries) constitute risk factors. Emphasis is placed on parental gender, family structure, and cultural context. Single parenthood, especially when accompanied by economic hardship, may lead to less effective parenting practices. School counseling emerges as a crucial intervention mechanism, supporting both parents and children while strengthening school-family collaboration in the prevention and management of aggression.

DOI: 10.4018/979-8-3373-9420-6.ch011

INTRODUCTION

Childhood aggression constitutes one of the most significant psychopathological risk factors in children and adolescents (Blok et al., 2022; Gin et al., 2021; Vaillancourt & Farrell, 2021) and refers to the interaction between the individual and their environment. It manifests through specific behaviors aimed at causing harm to people and/or objects (Dodge, 1991), is categorized as direct or indirect, verbal or nonverbal, and overt or covert (Buss, 1995), and presents in the form of physical (e.g., hitting), psychological (e.g., humiliation/degradation), and relational (e.g., social exclusion) aggressive behavior (Crick & Grotpeter, 1995).

Research indicates that aggression affects children's academic and social adjustment (Efrati-Virtzer & Margalit, 2009; Uludag, 2013) and reports that it is positively associated with non-completion of Secondary Education (Vitaro et al., 2005). Aggressive children are documented to be less accepted, have fewer friends, and are rejected more frequently by their peers (Efrati-Virtzer & Margalit, 2009), both in preschool (Crick et al., 2006) and in school-age children (Chen et al., 2012; Killen et al., 2013). Furthermore, studies link aggression to depression either directly (Blain-Arcaro & Vaillancourt, 2017; Chen et al., 2012) or indirectly through rejection (Morrow et al., 2006), and the depression-aggression relationship appears to be bidirectional (Beyers & Loeber, 2003).

Risk factors for childhood aggression also include gender, the child's reactive temperament (Joussemet et al., 2008), interparental conflict (Stover et al., 2016), parental separation, early onset of motherhood (Joussemet et al., 2008), parent-child conflict (Ostrov & Bishop, 2008), parental stress (Liu & Wang, 2015), and parenting type (Ehrenreich et al., 2014). The above demonstrates that the phenomenon is multifactorial. However, the role of parents is shown to be significant, and therefore the present effort will attempt to highlight the influence of parenting type on the manifestation of aggression in children, in relation to parental gender and family structure, while also emphasizing the need for family-school collaboration, as aggressive behaviors are also observed in the school environment, thus urgently necessitating school counseling interventions that enhance resilience, cooperation, and the overall mental health of students.

PARENTING TYPOLOGY

Parenting typology (or parenting type/style) is the combination of parental behaviors, derived from parents' attitudes, values, and beliefs about child development and upbringing (Baumrind, 1971; Darling & Steinberg, 1993), and influences the child's development of competencies, progression, and psychopathology (McKee et al., 2008). According to Baumrind's model (1966, 1967, 1971, 1978, 1989, 1991), three parenting types are identified: authoritative, authoritarian, and permissive. Each type is described by the dimensions of warmth/responsiveness and control/demandingness (Baumrind, 1991). The authoritative parent exhibits high control, reasonable demands, and high warmth. The authoritarian parent exhibits high control, high demands, and low warmth. The permissive parent exhibits high warmth and low control and demands (Baumrind, 1991).

In more detail, according to Baumrind (1966, 1967, 1971, 1978, 1989, 1991), parents who adopt the authoritative style seek to balance affection and discipline, and the use of disciplinary strategies ultimately aims to support rather than punish the child. Authoritative parents exercise reasonable levels of control and demonstrate flexibility in their stance (Masud et al., 2019). The authoritative parent attempts to guide the child's behavior in a rational manner without threats or coercion and encourages discussion when the child refuses to comply. The parent asserts their own perspective as an adult but recognizes the child's personal interests and views (Baumrind, 1989, 1991).

Conversely, the authoritarian parenting style represents traditional harsh child-rearing, in which children are obliged to obey their parents' directives and often face punitive consequences when they do not (Baumrind, 1971). Authoritarian parents are typically less warm and affectionate, have high demands, and possess limited flexibility. The authoritarian parenting style is associated with practices such as physical punishment, verbal hostility, and indifferent care (Schwerdtfeger et al., 2013). In this type, there is a predetermined and absolute desirable standard of behavior, based on which the child's behavior is evaluated and shaped. The authoritarian parent considers maintaining order and traditional structure very important. They do not encourage verbal communication, advocating that the child accept the parent's word as correct, and they use coercion and punitive disciplinary strategies when the child's actions or views differ from those of the parent's (Baumrind, 1966). The authoritarian type favors control and restriction of the child's self-will and autonomy, and compared to authoritative parents, authoritarian parents exercise higher levels of control to impose their will on children (Masud et al., 2019).

Parents who adopt a permissive parenting style display a tolerant, accepting attitude toward the child's impulses and desires, use minimal punishment, and avoid asserting authority or imposing controls and restrictions (Baumrind, 1971, 1991). This parenting style is characterized by high warmth and responsiveness, with low demandingness and control. Permissive parents tend to be warm and nurturing and usually have few or no expectations of the child, an attitude that typically leads to a lack of limit-setting (Baumrind, 1971, 1991). This parent presents themselves to the child as a resource rather than a role model or as a person responsible for shaping and changing the child's behavior (Baumrind, 1966), chooses to consult the child about family decisions and rules, provides excessive freedom and autonomy, and does not encourage obedience to established behavioral standards (Baumrind, 1966, 1967, 1971, 1978, 1989, 1991).

Research indicates that parenting typology is related to self-esteem (Hesari & Hejazi, 2011), self-confidence, responsibility, self-regulation (Piotrowski et al., 2013), academic achievement (Pong et al., 2010), and children's involvement in bullying incidents (Gómez-Ortiz et al., 2014; Martínez et al., 2019). Specifically, components of the authoritarian parenting type constitute risk factors for children's involvement in bullying (Gómez-Ortiz et al., 2014; Martínez et al., 2019). More specifically, children involved in bullying incidents report receiving greater behavioral control from their parents (Gómez-Ortiz et al., 2014), while children reported as perpetrating aggression state that they receive more psychological control and low levels of affection and communication from their parents (Gómez-Ortiz et al., 2014)—dimensions that fall within the authoritarian parenting style.

Regarding the permissive parenting style, these parents appear to develop better and longer-lasting relationships with their children compared to parents of other parenting styles (Ehrenreich et al., 2014), possibly because they often behave more like friends than parents (Sanvictores & Mendez, 2022). Consequently, the combination of low control and demandingness and high responsiveness that characterizes the permissive style facilitates the development of selfish/egocentric traits and hinders the development of self-regulation in children (Piotrowski et al., 2013)—elements that favor aggression.

Finally, the authoritative parenting style has been found to cultivate self-esteem (Hesari & Hejazi, 2011), self-confidence, and a sense of responsibility in children (Masud et al., 2019), to serve as a protective factor against children's involvement in bullying incidents (Gómez-Ortiz et al., 2014; Martínez et al., 2019), and to be positively related to their academic and social adjustment (Joussemet et al., 2005).

Relationship between Parenting Typology and Child Aggression

Parenting style appears to explain the development of internalizing and externalizing behavioral problems (Akhter et al., 2011; Gryczkowski et al., 2010; Pereira et al., 2009; Rinaldi & Howe, 2012) and to predict physical and relational aggression in children and adolescents (Baumrind et al., 2010; Carpenter & Mendez, 2013; Kuppens et al., 2009; Masud et al., 2019).

Initially, the authoritarian parenting style is a significant predictor of internalizing and externalizing behavior problems in preschool (Rankin Williams et al., 2009), school-age (Akhter et al., 2011; Underwood et al., 2009), and adolescence (Azimi et al., 2012; Batool, 2013). Parental aggression toward the child has a direct, long-term effect on the aggression the child subsequently displays (Benzies et al., 2009; Brook et al., 2001; Joussemet et al., 2008). It is documented that the authoritarian parenting style is associated with children's rebellious behaviors and the emergence of problematic behavior due to the high level of authority and control exercised by parents (Sarwar, 2016). Furthermore, authoritarian parenting is linked to several adverse emotional and behavioral outcomes in children and adolescents, including anxiety, depression, and suicidal ideation (Gorostiaga et al., 2019), and to low levels of self-control (Cecil et al., 2012)—factors associated with aggression (Cecil et al., 2012; Kofler et al., 2011).

In conclusion, among the permissive, authoritative, and authoritarian parenting styles, authoritarian strategies (coercion, violence, punishment) are the strongest predictor of aggression observed in children (Chan et al., 2018; Cleveland, 2014; Muñoz et al., 2017) and adolescents (Azimi et al., 2012). However, it is worth noting that although many studies present the authoritarian parenting type as a cause of childhood aggression, the relationship is bidirectional. On one hand, child aggression predicts the adoption of aggressive parental discipline strategies, and on the other hand, aggressive parental strategies predict children's aggressive behavior (Sheehan & Watson, 2008; Suzuki et al., 2016). Consequently, authoritarian strategies may result from the distress parents experience regarding their children's behavior (Fung et al., 2013).

Similarly, permissive parenting is associated with internalizing problems in preschool children (Rankin Williams et al., 2009) and with internalizing and externalizing behavior problems in school-age children (Akhter et al., 2011; Gryczkowski et al., 2010). It also predicts high aggression in children (Hosokawa & Katsura, 2019; Méndez et al., 2020; Underwood et al., 2009) and adolescents (Batool, 2013). In this context, a positive correlation is observed between permissive parenting and children’s relational aggression (Ehrenreich et al., 2014; Sandstrom, 2007), which appears to have long-term consequences for children's relationships (Ehrenreich et al., 2014). Permissive parents provide their children with ample opportunities to manipulate them and impose their desires (Sandstrom, 2007)—behaviors that children also adopt in their interactions with others. The high tolerance characteristic of permissive parenting increases children's aggressive behavior, as the absence of parental reaction and concessions is perceived by the child as approval of undesirable behavior (Baumrind, 1966). Consequently, children learn to expect permissive treatment from their parents and from others, which can lead to conflicts.

Conversely, the authoritative parenting style serves as a protective factor against aggression, as it is negatively related to children's behavioral problems (Akhter et al., 2011; Gómez-Ortiz et al., 2014; Martínez et al., 2019; Pinquart, 2017) and is associated with lower levels of aggression in children (Hesari & Hejazi, 2011; Trenas et al., 2013) and adolescents (Azimi et al., 2012; Llorca et al., 2017; Masud et al., 2019). The warmth dimension of this parenting style is linked to lower levels of physical and relational aggression in children (Lau, 2019), while high parental responsiveness has been found to reduce the risk of developing reactive aggression (Byrd et al., 2022). Furthermore, support for child autonomy, an element of the authoritative parenting style, enhances self-regulation capacity (Joussemet et al., 2005; Morris et al., 2007), which helps prevent aggressive behaviors, given that childhood aggression is related to emotion regulation (Byrd et al., 2022; Dodge, 1991; Röll et al., 2012). Additionally, it positively affects the child's self-esteem (Hesari & Hejazi, 2011), which acts preventively against aggression, since low self-esteem is associated with aggression (Amad et al., 2021; Taylor et al., 2007; Teng et al., 2015). Simultaneously, children subjected to authoritative parenting have higher social competence (Altay & Gure, 2012; Mensah & Kuranchie, 2013) and greater resilience (Kritzas & Grobler, 2005)—skills that function as protective factors against aggression (Boxer & Sloan-Power, 2013; Malti & Noam, 2009; Shayegh et al., 2021).

The above are also supported by Social Learning Theory, which holds that parental practices serve as behavioral models that children assimilate and adopt (Bandura, 1973). Consequently, parents who adopt behaviors characteristic of each parenting type will raise children who exhibit similar behavior toward others (Bandura, 1973). In conclusion, authoritative parenting appears to be the most beneficial and preventive against child and adolescent aggression (Masud et al., 2019; Rankin Williams et al., 2009); therefore, it could be categorized as the "positive or effective" parenting type. Correspondingly, due to their adverse consequences and negative impact on child and adolescent behavior (Batool, 2013; Masud et al., 2019), permissive and authoritarian parenting could be classified as "negative or ineffective" parenting types (Batool, 2013; Rankin Williams et al., 2009).

The Influence of Parenting Typology, Parental Relationships, and Cultural Factors on Childhood Aggression

Parenting typology appears to be related to child temperament; specifically, when the authoritative parenting style is applied to children with a "difficult" temperament, a reduction in problematic behaviors is observed, whereas the opposite occurs when authoritarian or permissive parenting is adopted (Propper & Moore, 2006). This is also supported by Rothbart and Bates (2006), who report that externalizing problems are more likely to develop when negative parental behavior coexists with a "difficult" child temperament (Joussemet et al., 2008).

Furthermore, marital relationships appear to significantly influence children's behavior (Tavassolie et al., 2016), and interparental conflict often negatively affects parental behavior, which in turn affects children's behavior (Stover et al., 2016).

More specifically, exposure to parental marital aggression during childhood predicts aggression toward peers in adolescence (McCloskey & Lichter, 2003; Stover et al., 2016; Tavassolie et al., 2016), and the adoption of aggressive problem-solving strategies by parents is related to children's tendency to propose aggressive solutions in disagreements with peers (Duman & Margolin, 2007). Additionally, research supports the idea that marital conflict increases childhood aggression (Stover et al., 2016), as these parents typically adopt harsh discipline strategies (Krishnakumar & Buehler, 2000), which align with an authoritarian parenting typology and favor the development of childhood aggression (Kuppens et al., 2009; Miner & Clarke-Stewart, 2008).

Consequently, cultural background plays a decisive role in the adoption of specific parenting practices (Bornstein & Cheah, 2006) and is linked to the society in which a child grows up, whether individualistic or collectivist (Hofstede, 2011). Western societies are characterized as individualistic, while Eastern and Southern societies are collectivist (Green et al., 2005). In the first type of society, greater emphasis is placed on individual independence, and autonomy, assertiveness, and self-reliance are encouraged, while each person is expected to care for themselves and their immediate family (Hofstede, 2011). Conversely, in the second type, greater emphasis is placed on conformism, compliance, respect for authority figures (e.g., parents), and interdependence (Hofstede, 2011). Furthermore, in collectivist societies, there is a tendency to apply stricter disciplinary methods than in individualistic ones (Davidov & Khoury-Kassabri, 2013); specifically, the authoritarian style is usually adopted in child-rearing by parents of Arab, Chinese, African, and Asian descent (Davidov & Khoury-Kassabri, 2013; Dwairy et al., 2006). The authoritarianism characterizing these parents is reflected in less acceptance and warmth in their parenting practices (Huntsinger & Jose, 2009), which may be due to the meaning they attribute to the acceptance/warmth dimension. For example, Chinese parents demonstrate acceptance and warmth through their involvement in and promotion of their children's education, whereas European and American parents express acceptance and warmth through verbal and physical acts such as praise and hugging (Chao & Tseng, 2002).

Additionally, it is observed that authoritarian parenting in collectivist societies does not necessarily have a negative impact on children. For instance, in Arab families, physical punishment is associated with lower levels of depressive symptoms (Davidov & Khoury-Kassabri, 2013) and higher levels of satisfaction in the parent-child relationship (Dwairy, 2004). Furthermore, in primary and secondary education, children from China, authoritarian parenting is negatively related to aggression (Gao et al., 2015), while in Greek families, it is linked to lower internalizing and externalizing problems (Bakoula et al., 2009). This may be because authoritarian disciplinary methods are perceived by children as having significant educational value (Davidov & Khoury-Kassabri, 2013). In this context, and regarding parental control, similar levels of control have been found to be exercised over children by parents of European and Chinese origin (Huntsinger & Jose, 2009), while in contrast to individualistic societies, psychological and behavioral control does not have the corresponding negative impact on children from collectivist cultures (Chao & Tseng, 2002; Dwairy, 2004; Greenfield et al., 2003; Pomerantz & Wang, 2009). The above may be explained because in collectivist societies, strict control is perceived by children as parental care, involvement, and love (Chao, 1995). Moreover, the authoritarian parenting style has been associated with negative consequences in collectivist contexts, such as Cyprus, where it is linked to bullying incidents (Georgiou et al., 2013). Similarly, in Asia, it is linked to low academic achievement (Pong et al., 2010), and in Chile, the use of physical punishment is associated with greater behavioral problems in adolescents (Ma et al., 2012).

Regarding the authoritative parenting style, it has been found to positively influence children's behavior and academic achievement (Ma et al., 2012; Pinquart & Kauser, 2018). However, in African American families, the authoritative parenting style is not characterized by the dimension of high responsiveness (Hill, 1995), while the promotion of autonomy and expression of warmth—key elements of authoritative parenting—are not considered positive parenting practices by adolescents of Arab origin (Dwairy et al., 2006). Permissive parenting is considered more effective and useful in collectivist cultures than in individualistic cultures (Barnhart et al., 2013). In conclusion, although the same parenting practices may appear in families from different ethnicities (Huntsinger & Jose, 2009), their interpretation may differ across cultural contexts.

Relationship between Parenting Typology and Parental Gender

Yaffe (2020) finds that women and men often adopt different approaches to raising their children, with mothers tending toward the authoritative style, whereas fathers are more likely to use authoritarian and permissive practices (Olivari et al., 2015; Pedro et al., 2015; Yaffe, 2020). Other scholars (Gaertner et al., 2007; Winsler et al., 2005) report that fathers judge themselves as more authoritarian than their partners, and mothers self-characterize as more authoritative than fathers.

Consequently, authoritarian fathers are associated with reduced involvement in daily care and children's play (Gaertner et al., 2007), and authoritative fathers with low involvement in direct care, which consists of tasks requiring direct contact and interaction with the child (e.g., dressing) (Monteiro et al., 2017). However, authoritative fathers are associated with greater participation in teaching and discipline, as well as in play and leisure activities outside the home (Monteiro et al., 2017). Studies also indicate that women usually cover more of their children's daily needs, whereas men are more likely to engage in their children's play (Lewis & Lamb, 2003; Pleck & Masciadrelli, 2004; Sayer et al., 2004).

Furthermore, fathers with higher educational levels are more involved in raising their children (Monteiro et al., 2017), perhaps because they hold less traditional views on gender roles, which facilitates taking on more responsibilities and greater engagement in childcare (Marks et al., 2009). The authoritative parenting style is not frequently found among men with low educational levels (Monteiro et al., 2017); however, when it does occur, it is associated with increased involvement of these fathers in direct care activities (Monteiro et al., 2017).

Regarding working hours, fathers who work long hours are less involved with their children (Monteiro et al., 2017) and have fewer interactions with them, especially during the workweek (Monteiro et al., 2017). However, adopting authoritative parenting practices mitigates the negative impact of long working hours, as fathers with many working hours (>40) who use authoritative parenting engage in teaching, discipline, and play activities (Monteiro et al., 2017). In conclusion, gender differences in child-rearing persist regardless of which parent works (Monteiro et al., 2017; Pakaluk & Price, 2020).

At this point, it should be noted that differences in parental behavior between women and men may be rooted in the social categorization of gender roles and social stereotypes about male and female behavior (Dufur et al., 2010). According to Sex-Role Socialization Theory, a large percentage of mothers are expected to adopt styles that are highly responsive and warm (permissive and authoritative), while fathers are expected to adopt styles characterized by high control and demandingness (authoritarian and authoritative) (Simons & Conger, 2007). These behaviors may be related, in the case of fathers, to ensuring the academic and social success of children (Chao & Tseng, 2002), while, in the case of mothers, to providing necessary emotional support through high responsiveness (Chao & Tseng, 2002). These attitudes align with what Baumrind (1991) calls "traditional parenting," in which the mother and father assume traditional gender roles. In this case, the mother responds significantly more than she demands, while the father is significantly more demanding than he responds (Baumrind, 1991). However, studies support the idea that the observed differences in parenting typologies stem from a need for balance (Simons & Conger, 2007), and for this reason, for example, the presence of two authoritarian parents is rarely encountered (Simons & Conger, 2007). Another explanation concerns how parental responsibilities are shared within the family. Specifically, the distribution of responsibilities is often influenced by mothers' protective stance, which can be detrimental because mothers may view themselves as more capable parents and criticize and replace their partners' parental behavior (Gaertner et al., 2007). In this context, fathers may be particularly vulnerable to their partners' lack of support and trust, which can lead to their withdrawal from active participation in raising their children (Gaertner et al., 2007; Tavassolie et al., 2016).

Interaction of Parenting Typology, Parental Gender, and Child Aggression

Studies support the view that the effects of negative parenting styles (authoritarian, permissive) on child development are similar, regardless of parental gender (Akhter et al., 2011; Ma et al., 2012; Tavassolie et al., 2016). However, other studies link an authoritarian maternal style to externalizing problems (Braza et al., 2015; Gershoff et al., 2010; Jewell et al., 2008), whereas fathers' authoritarian style is a better predictor of aggressive behavior (Tavassolie et al., 2016). Furthermore, fathers' permissive style is associated with externalizing problems at home and school (Jewell et al., 2008), whereas in female parents, the permissive style is often negatively related to childhood aggression (Azimi et al., 2012).

It is worth noting that the relationship between maternal and paternal parenting styles and the adoption of similar parenting strategies by both parents is a better predictor of aggression than either parent type alone (Kuppens et al., 2009; Trenas et al., 2013). For example, in families where both parents adopt a permissive parenting style, increased physical aggression in children is observed (Braza et al., 2015). Also, the combination of an authoritarian maternal type and a permissive paternal type is positively related to the presence of aggressive behavior (Braza et al., 2015). The same effect is observed when genders are reversed, with permissive strategies by mothers and authoritarian strategies by fathers linked to the emergence of problematic behavior in children (Rinaldi & Howe, 2012). However, maternal parenting style has a stronger influence on children's behavioral problems (Braza et al., 2015), perhaps because maternal influence on children's emotional regulation, empathy, and prosocial behavior is stronger (Davidov & Grusec, 2006).

The literature review showed no gender differences in the positive effect of the authoritative parenting style on children's psychosocial development. Indeed, regardless of parental gender, the presence of one authoritative parent is better than other parenting combinations that include no authoritative parent (Rinaldi & Howe, 2012). Therefore, the positive outcomes of the authoritative parenting style are enhanced when both parents adopt it (Simons & Conger, 2007).

Interaction of Family Structure, Parenting Typology, and Aggression

Research indicates that single-parent family structure is a risk factor for internalizing and externalizing behavior problems (Hosokawa & Katsura, 2019), which are associated with aggression in children (Benzies et al., 2009; Khan et al., 2014) and adolescents (Griffin et al., 2000), and this appears to hold true for both physical and relational aggression (Ehrenreich et al., 2014; Hosokawa & Katsura, 2019).

Single-parent family structure appears to be indirectly linked to aggression, as children from these families exhibit behaviors that promote it. Specifically, boys from single-parent families show high rates of substance use (Griffin et al., 2000), which is associated with aggressive and delinquent behavior (Griffin et al., 2000). Moreover, single-parent families often result from divorce, which is a significant risk factor for the development of aggression in children (Joussemet et al., 2008; Underwood et al., 2009). Additionally, single parents face financial difficulties due to a single income compared to two-parent families (Daryanani et al., 2016; Mistry et al., 2002; Vreeland et al., 2019), which contributes to the development of aggression in children, as there is a significant relationship between low income and high childhood aggression (Batool, 2013; Hosokawa & Katsura, 2019).

In this context, the link between low socioeconomic status and authoritarian parenting practices is also documented (Hadjicharalambous & Demetriou, 2020; Olivari et al., 2015; Talib et al., 2011), possibly because single parents experience increased stress and fatigue due to the difficulties they face (e.g., financial strain and increased childcare and rearing duties). Lower economic well-being and the consequent economic pressure experienced by many single parents may also indirectly affect their behavior through the adverse effects that financial strain has on their psychological well-being (Mistry et al., 2002; Underwood et al., 2009; Vreeland et al., 2019). For example, these parents are less affectionate and feel less effective and capable in interactions with their child, which can increase the child's behavioral problems (Mistry et al., 2002; Underwood et al., 2009).

Furthermore, a large percentage of single parents, especially those with low incomes, report symptoms of depression (Coiro, 2001; Lee et al., 2009) compared with parents in couples (Kim et al., 2018; Liang et al., 2019; Vreeland et al., 2019)—a condition that constitutes a risk factor for the development of aggressive behavior in the child (Letourneau et al., 2013) and influences the parenting strategies adopted, which are often non-beneficial (authoritarian, permissive) (Azak & Raeder, 2013; Lee et al., 2009; Vreeland et al., 2019). Consequently, the increased aggression observed in children raised in single-parent family structures appears to be mainly due to the influence of external factors on parental behavior.

In conclusion, single parents have been found to be more likely than parent couples to engage in non-beneficial parenting practices, such as psychological control, low involvement, rejecting behavior, and harsh discipline (Daryanani et al., 2016; Jackson et al., 2019), due to the circumstances and problems they face.

Interaction of Family Structure, Parental Gender, and Parenting Typology

Extending the above, the individualist and structuralist positions are two theories that predict parental behavior differently. Specifically, the individualist position argues that mothers and fathers raise their children very differently due to innate gender characteristics (Udry, 2000). Therefore, mothers and fathers will execute their parenting methods according to their gender, regardless of context. Conversely, the structuralist position holds that single parents, whether women or men, raise their children in a similar manner because they face analogous situations. Consequently, when the partner is absent, single parents also assume responsibilities usually performed by the opposite sex to fulfill both mother and father roles from a single parent (Dufur et al., 2010).

Proponents of individualist theory argue that mothers tend toward the authoritative style, showing more warmth, responsiveness, and support, whereas fathers are more likely to use authoritarian and permissive parenting practices (Hadjicharalambous & Demetriou, 2020; Pedro et al., 2015; Yaffe, 2020). Within this framework, the review of research on single-parent families appears to align with the literature on two-parent families. Specifically, the most widely used parenting style among female single parents appears to be authoritative (Anton et al., 2015; Ghani et al., 2014; Leung & Shek, 2018), while male single parents demonstrate less affection toward their children and report more negative feelings about their parental duties than female single parents (Dufur et al., 2010). They also appear to be stricter about setting limits and enforcing rules (e.g., bedtime, TV time) (Dufur et al., 2010). Furthermore, more frequent parent-child communication (Dufur et al., 2010) and involvement in parent-child activities (e.g., Hawkins et al., 2006) are observed in single mothers.

Nevertheless, these differences are sensitive to income disparities between women and men (Dufur et al., 2010). Even when socioeconomic characteristics are held constant, gender differences persist, with more single mothers than single fathers adopting more effective parenting practices, engaging actively with their children (Biblarz & Stacey, 2010), and spending more quality time with them (Biblarz & Stacey, 2010).

The structuralist position holds that when parents of both genders face similar conditions (e.g., incomes, living situations), they will also exhibit similar parenting behaviors (Dufur et al., 2010). Consequently, both male single parents (Biblarz & Stacey, 2010; Dufur et al., 2010) and female single parents (Daryanani et al., 2016; Dufur et al., 2010; Jackson et al., 2019) will use authoritarian strategies.

Interaction of Family Structure, Parental Gender, and Child Aggression

If the individualist approach to parental behavior is accurate, the well-being of children in families with single mothers and single fathers will vary significantly (Downey et al., 1998), and findings from studies of two-parent families will hold—that is, the authoritarian parenting style of both genders will be associated with externalizing and internalizing problems in children (Braza et al., 2015; Jewell et al., 2008; Tavassolie et al., 2016). The review found that, on average, children in maternal single-parent families had lower rates of delinquency and substance use in adolescence than children in single-father families (Biblarz & Stacey, 2010; Coles, 2015). Children living with single mothers also had fewer behavioral problems and higher academic achievement than those in paternal single-parent families (Biblarz & Stacey, 2010), possibly because fathers adopt a parenting style characterized by low involvement and warmth (Biblarz & Stacey, 2010). Furthermore, when single mothers have financial resources equal to those of single fathers, the parenting they provide (high responsiveness and demandingness) has a positive effect on the child's psychosocial and academic success (Leung & Shek, 2018).

Additionally, low involvement and high psychological control among single mothers are linked to externalizing problems in adolescents (Daryanani et al., 2016), and harsh parenting among children raised in maternal single-parent households is positively associated with behavioral problems the child presents during middle childhood (Jackson et al., 2019).

As previously mentioned, the income of single fathers tends to be significantly higher than that of single mothers (Dufur et al., 2010), and this parameter is associated with the adoption of authoritarian parenting strategies (Daryanani et al., 2016; Hadjicharalambous & Demetriou, 2020; Vreeland et al., 2019). Therefore, if single mothers are in a disadvantaged financial situation, they are likely to adopt authoritarian discipline strategies, which are associated with increased aggression in children and adolescents (Baumrind et al., 2010; Benzies et al., 2009; Joussemet et al., 2008). Furthermore, low income has been linked to depression in single mothers (Kim et al., 2018), who exhibit higher rates than women in parent couples (Kim et al., 2018; Liang et al., 2019). In turn, maternal depression can directly and indirectly affect children's psychosocial well-being through physical punishment (Eamon & Zuehl, 2001). Therefore, the negative effects on the child may be due to the challenges of the single-parent structure rather than the parent's gender.

Correspondingly, the structuralist position holds that women and men in similar contexts (e.g., single-parent contexts) will behave similarly, and children from single-parent families do not appear to benefit from one parent's gender over the other (Downey et al., 2006). In some studies, better academic achievement was observed among children with single fathers, but this finding was fully explained by the socioeconomic advantages offered by fathers (Dufur et al., 2010). In conclusion, the literature review reveals a multidimensional relationship among parenting typology, family structure, parental gender, and childhood aggression.

BRIDGING THE GAP: FOSTERING FAMILY RESILIENCE THROUGH SCHOOL-BASED COUNSELING

From the above, it becomes apparent that childhood aggression is a multifactorial and complex phenomenon, influenced by many factors and manifested not only within the family but also in the broader school community, as school and family have an interactive relationship and do not function in isolation (Widia & Bustomi, 2025). Investigating the relationship between parenting typology, parental gender, and family structure and childhood aggression yields valuable insights into children's psychosocial behavior in the school environment. Aggression, as a psychosocial indicator of dysfunction, affects not only the child's emotional and social development but also their educational trajectory and well-being within the school community.

In this context, identifying risk factors alone is insufficient for effective intervention. The challenge lies in translating this understanding into practice through the lens of Family Resilience. According to Walsh (2016), family resilience extends beyond individual traits to focus on the functional processes that enable the system to withstand and recover from challenges. As emphasized by Byrd et al. (2022), non-supportive parental reactions to children's negative emotions (often characteristic of authoritarian and permissive styles) increase the risk of emotional dysregulation, which constitutes a direct pathway to reactive aggression. Conversely, developing resilience enhances the family's capacity to regulate emotions and adapt to stressors, such as divorce or economic pressure, without resorting to dysfunctional behaviors.

At this point, the school community's contribution should be noted, as it serves as a critical microsystem that can either exacerbate or mitigate family stress. Counseling services, such as school counselors and support services within school units, including school psychologists and social workers, can identify patterns of dysfunctional parenting and, through targeted intervention programs, contribute to promoting positive parent-child relationships.

More specifically, school interventions can be vital because they can purposefully guide students from vulnerable, stressful family backgrounds (e.g., single-parent families) toward seeking psychological care (Cai et al., 2025). When schools act as "protective shields," they can mitigate the negative effects of dysfunctional parenting by providing corrective emotional experiences. Research confirms that active participation in school counseling programs not only improves academic performance but also promotes overall well-being, supports positive personal development, and cultivates a harmonious, inclusive school environment (Simbolon & Purba, 2022).

Targeted Interventions for Parental Empowerment and Student Resilience

To effectively promote resilience, interventions must be multi-leveled. At the student level, Guidance and Counseling interventions appear to enhance academic resilience, as they contribute to students' self-regulation, empower them, and strengthen cognitive restructuring (Widia & Bustomi, 2025). From a social learning theory perspective (Bandura, 1973), supportive counseling structures within school units can provide alternative, positive behavioral models that students can internalize to replace aggressive reactions.

At the family level, school counseling can support the three main areas of functioning outlined by Walsh (2016). The first is Reframing Belief Systems: for parents with authoritarian styles, counseling can help shift toward a "relational view of resilience" (Walsh, 2016). This includes training parents to respond supportively to negative emotions (Byrd et al., 2022) and to see the child's behavior as a developmental need for connection instead of a challenge. The second area is Enhancing Organizational Patterns: for permissive parents, counseling can highlight the protective role of authoritative guidance, which pairs nurturing with clear boundaries and offers structure in environments that tend to foster aggression (Walsh, 2016). The third is Improving Communication and Bonding: recognizing that single-parent stress often results in harsh parenting, counseling can help these parents manage their challenges. As Walsh (2016) emphasizes, involving extended family networks and mentors is vital to preventing aggression.

Parents and School: A Collaborative Path

In conclusion, addressing childhood aggression requires a fundamental shift: from blaming "negative" parenting styles to empowering families with resilience skills. In this context, school counseling can play a pivotal role in understanding and managing aggressive behavior, particularly when it is associated with dysfunctional parenting practices or vulnerable family structures, such as single-parent families. Cultivating children's resilience through targeted interventions—including support for emotional regulation, enhancement of self-esteem, and the development of positive relationships with adults in the school community—constitutes a key direction of school counseling practice (Cai et al., 2025; Simbolon & Purba, 2022).

The present chapter substantiates that the presence of supportive parental models can serve as a protective factor against the manifestation of aggressive behavior.

However, addressing childhood aggression requires multi-level interventions that involve the family and the school, with particular emphasis on strengthening positive parenting models and supporting vulnerable family structures. Consequently, the need to enhance skills such as emotional regulation, resilience, and self-esteem through school counseling emerges as imperative, as it can serve as a preventive factor in the manifestation of aggressive behavior and strengthen students' skills and their interpersonal relationships (Byrd et al., 2022).

This underscores the importance of counseling support not only for students but also for parents, thereby strengthening collaborative relationships between school and family. School counseling services can serve as the connecting link between family and school, providing individualized support and cultivating a school environment that enhances the resilience of all members of the school community. Therefore, the role of school counseling as a means of prevention and empowerment contributes to deepening understanding of the factors influencing aggression and to the prevention, management, and addressing of aggression problems within a systemic and inclusive intervention framework (Francis et al., 2022).

CONCLUSION

By adopting an early-intervention strategy, schools can proactively identify students' needs before problems escalate into more severe behavioral or emotional difficulties (Simbolon & Purba, 2022). This preventive approach enables timely support, reducing the likelihood that aggressive behaviors become entrenched and more resistant to change.

School counseling services act as a catalyst in this process, facilitating holistic collaboration among students, educators, and families. Within this collaborative framework, parents are neither pathologized nor blamed for their children's difficulties but are treated as essential partners in developing solutions. This strengths-based approach empowers parents to reflect on their parenting practices, acquire new skills, and become active agents of change within the family system.

Through this inclusive, resilience-oriented framework, the school becomes a safe, supportive base. It becomes an environment where students can form corrective emotional relationships with caring adults, learn to regulate their emotions, and develop prosocial coping strategies. In this way, the school helps break the intergenerational cycle of aggression, enabling every student, regardless of family background, to thrive both academically and emotionally.

REFERENCES

Akhter, N., Hanif, R., Tariq, N., & Atta, M. (2011). Parenting styles as predictors of externalizing and internalizing behavior problems among children. *Pakistan Journal of Psychological Research, 26*(1), 23–41.

Altay, F. B., & Gure, A. (2012). Relationship among the Parenting Styles and the Social Competence and Prosocial Behaviors of the Children Who are Attending to State and Private Preschools. *Educational Sciences: Theory & Practice, 12*(4), 2712–2718.

Amad, S., Gray, N. S., & Snowden, R. J. (2021). Self-esteem, narcissism, and aggression: Different types of self-esteem predict different types of aggression. *Journal of Interpersonal Violence, 36*(23-24), NP13296–NP13313. Advance online publication. DOI: 10.1177/0886260520905540 PMID: 32065011

Anton, M. T., Jones, D. J., & Youngstrom, E. A. (2015). Socioeconomic status, parenting, and externalizing problems in African American single-mother homes: A person-oriented approach. *Journal of Family Psychology, 29*(3), 405–415. DOI: 10.1037/fam0000086 PMID: 26053349

Azak, S., & Raeder, S. (2013). Trajectories of parenting behavior and maternal depression. *Infant Behavior and Development, 36*(3), 391–402. DOI: 10.1016/j.infbeh.2013.03.004 PMID: 23603820

Azimi, A. L., Vaziri, S., & Kashani, F. L. (2012). Relationship between maternal parenting style and child's aggressive behavior. *Procedia: Social and Behavioral Sciences, 69*, 1276–1281. DOI: 10.1016/j.sbspro.2012.12.062

Bakoula, C., Kolaitis, G., Veltsista, A., Gika, A., & Chrousos, G. P. (2009). Parental stress affects the emotions and behaviour of children up to adolescence: A Greek prospective, longitudinal study. *Stress (Amsterdam, Netherlands), 12*(6), 486–498. DOI: 10.3109/10253890802645041 PMID: 19206015

Bandura, A. (1973). *Aggression: A social learning analysis*. Prentice Hall.

Batool, S. S. (2013). Lack of adequate parenting: A potential risk factor for aggression among adolescents. *Pakistan Journal of Psychological Research*, •••, 217–238.

Baumrind, D. (1966). Effects of authoritative parental control on child behavior. *Child Development, 37*(4), 887–907. DOI: 10.2307/1126611

Baumrind, D. (1967). Childcare practices anteceding three patterns of preschool behavior. *Genetic Psychology Monographs, 75*(1), 43–88. PMID: 6032134

Baumrind, D. (1971). Current patterns of parental authority. *Developmental psychology, 4*(1), Pt.2), 1-103. https://doi.org/DOI: 10.1037/h0030372

Baumrind, D. (1978). Parental disciplinary patterns and social competence in children. *Youth & Society, 9*(3), 239–267. DOI: 10.1177/0044118X7800900302

Baumrind, D. (1989). Rearing competent children. In Damon, W. (Ed.), *Child development today and tomorrow* (pp. 349–378). Jossey-Bass/Wiley.

Baumrind, D. (1991). The influence of parenting style on adolescent competence and substance use. *The Journal of Early Adolescence, 11*(1), 56–95. DOI: 10.1177/0272431691111004

Baumrind, D., Larzelere, R. E., & Owens, E. B. (2010). Effects of preschool parents' power assertive patterns and practices on adolescent development. *Parenting, Science and Practice, 10*(3), 157–201. DOI: 10.1080/15295190903290790

Benzies, K., Keown, L. A., & Magill-Evans, J. (2009). Immediate and sustained effects of parenting on physical aggression in Canadian children aged 6 years and younger. *Canadian Journal of Psychiatry, 54*(1), 55–64. DOI: 10.1177/070674370905400109 PMID: 19175980

Beyers, J. M., & Loeber, R. (2003). Untangling developmental relations between depressed mood and delinquency in male adolescents. *Journal of Abnormal Child Psychology, 31*(3), 247–266. DOI: 10.1023/A:1023225428957 PMID: 12774859

Biblarz, T. J., & Stacey, J. (2010). How does the gender of parents matter? *Journal of Marriage and Family, 72*(1), 3–22. DOI: 10.1111/j.1741-3737.2009.00678.x

Blain-Arcaro, C., & Vaillancourt, T. (2017). Longitudinal associations between depression and aggression in children and adolescents. *Journal of Abnormal Child Psychology, 45*(5), 959–970. DOI: 10.1007/s10802-016-0204-2 PMID: 27671705

Blok, E., de Mol, C. L., van der Ende, J., Hillegers, M. H., Althoff, R. R., Shaw, P., & White, T. (2022). Stability and change of psychopathology symptoms throughout childhood and adolescence. *Child Psychiatry and Human Development, 53*(6), 1330–1339. DOI: 10.1007/s10578-021-01212-8 PMID: 34184159

Bornstein, M. H., & Cheah, C. S. L. (2006). The Place of "Culture and Parenting" in the Ecological Contextual Perspective on Developmental Science. In Rubin, K. H., & Chung, O. B. (Eds.), *Parenting beliefs, behaviours, and parent-child relations: A cross-cultural perspective* (pp. 3–33). Psychology Press.

Boxer, P., & Sloan-Power, E. (2013). Coping with violence: A comprehensive framework and implications for understanding resilience. *Trauma, Violence & Abuse, 14*(3), 209–221. DOI: 10.1177/1524838013487806 PMID: 23649832

Braza, P., Carreras, R., Muñoz, J. M., Braza, F., Azurmendi, A., Pascual-Sagastizábal, E., Cardas, J., & Sánchez-Martín, J. R. (2015). Negative maternal and paternal parenting styles as predictors of children's behavioural problems: Moderating effects of the child's sex. *Journal of Child and Family Studies, 24*(4), 847–856. DOI: 10.1007/s10826-013-9893-0

Brook, J. S., Zheng, L., Whiteman, M., & Brook, D. W. (2001). Aggression in toddlers: Associations with parenting and marital relations. *The Journal of Genetic Psychology, 162*(2), 228–241. DOI: 10.1080/00221320109597963 PMID: 11432607

Buss, A. H. (1995). *Personality: Temperament, Social Behavior, and the Self.* Allyn and Bacon.

Byrd, A. L., Vine, V., Frigoletto, O. A., Vanwoerden, S., & Stepp, S. D. (2022). A multi-method investigation of parental responses to youth emotion: Prospective effects on emotion dysregulation and reactive aggression in daily life. *Research on Child and Adolescent Psychopathology, 50*(2), 117–131. DOI: 10.1007/s10802-020-00754-0 PMID: 33856610

Cai, C., Mei, Z., Wang, Z., & Luo, S. (2025). School-based interventions for resilience in children and adolescents: A systematic review and meta-analysis of randomized controlled trials. *Frontiers in Psychiatry, 16*, 1594658. DOI: 10.3389/fpsyt.2025.1594658 PMID: 40458775

Carpenter, J., & Mendez, J. L. (2013). Adaptive and challenged parenting among low-income African American mothers: Parenting profiles relate to Head Start children's aggression and hyperactivity. *Early Education and Development, 24*(2), 1–20. DOI: 10.1080/10409289.2013.749762

Cecil, C. A., Barker, E. D., Jaffee, S. R., & Viding, E. (2012). Association between maladaptive parenting and child self-control over time: Cross-lagged study using a monozygotic twin difference design. *The British Journal of Psychiatry, 201*(4), 291–297. DOI: 10.1192/bjp.bp.111.107581 PMID: 22918964

Chan, J. Y., Harlow, A. J., Kinsey, R., Gerstein, L. H., & Fung, A. L. C. (2018). The examination of authoritarian parenting styles, specific forms of peer-victimization, and reactive aggression in Hong Kong Youth. *School Psychology International, 39*(4), 378–399. DOI: 10.1177/0143034318777781

Chao, R. (1995). Chinese and European American cultural models of the self are reflected in mothers' childrearing beliefs. *Ethos (Berkeley, Calif.), 23*(3), 328–354. DOI: 10.1525/eth.1995.23.3.02a00030

Chao, R., & Tseng, V. (2002). Parenting of Asians. In Bornstein, M. H. (Ed.), Handbook of parenting: Vol. 4. *Social conditions and applied parenting* (2nd ed., pp. 59–93). Erlbaum.

Chen, X., Huang, X., Wang, L., & Chang, L. (2012). Aggression, peer relationships, and depression in Chinese children: A multi-wave longitudinal study. *Journal of Child Psychology and Psychiatry, and Allied Disciplines, 53*(12), 1233–1241. DOI: 10.1111/j.1469-7610.2012.02576.x PMID: 22747770

Cleveland, E. S. (2014). Digit ratio, emotional intelligence, and parenting styles predict female aggression. *Personality and Individual Differences, 58*, 9–14. DOI: 10.1016/j.paid.2013.09.020

Coiro, M. J. (2001). Depressive symptoms among women receiving welfare. *Women & Health, 32*(1/2), 1–23. DOI: 10.1300/J013v32n01_01 PMID: 11459364

Crick, N. R., & Grotpeter, J. K. (1995). Relational aggression, gender, and social-psychological adjustment. *Child Development, 66*(3), 710–722. DOI: 10.2307/1131945 PMID: 7789197

Crick, N. R., Ostrov, J. M., Burr, J. E., Cullerton-Sen, C., Jansen-Yeh, E., & Ralston, P. (2006). A longitudinal study of relational and physical aggression in preschool. *Journal of Applied Developmental Psychology, 27*(3), 254–268. DOI: 10.1016/j.appdev.2006.02.006

Darling, N., & Steinberg, L. (1993). Parenting style as context: An integrative model. *Psychological Bulletin, 113*(3), 487–496. DOI: 10.1037/0033-2909.113.3.487

Daryanani, I., Hamilton, J. L., Abramson, L. Y., & Alloy, L. B. (2016). Single mother parenting and adolescent psychopathology. *Journal of Abnormal Child Psychology, 44*(7), 1411–1423. DOI: 10.1007/s10802-016-0128-x PMID: 26767832

Davidov, M., & Khoury-Kassabri, M. (2013). Recollections of harsh discipline in childhood and depressive feelings in adulthood: The roles of culture and gender. *Children and Youth Services Review, 35*(6), 1007–1014. DOI: 10.1016/j.childyouth.2013.03.009

Dodge, K. A. (1991). The structure and function of reactive and proactive aggression. *The development and treatment of childhood aggression, 16*(5), 201-218.

Dufur, M. J., Howell, N. C., Downey, D. B., Ainsworth, J. W., & Lapray, A. J. (2010). Sex differences in parenting behaviors in single-mother and single-father households. *Journal of Marriage and Family*, *72*(5), 1092–1106. DOI: 10.1111/j.1741-3737.2010.00752.x

Duman, S., & Margolin, G. (2007). Parents' aggressive influences and children's aggressive problem solutions with peers. *Journal of Clinical Child and Adolescent Psychology*, *36*(1), 42–55. DOI: 10.1207/s15374424jccp3601_5 PMID: 17206880

Dwairy, M., Achoui, M., Abouserie, R., Farah, A., Sakhleh, A. A., Fayad, M., & Khan, H. K. (2006). Parenting styles in Arab societies: A first cross-regional research study. *Journal of Cross-Cultural Psychology*, *37*(3), 230–247. DOI: 10.1177/0022022106286922

Eamon, M. K., & Zuehl, R. M. (2001). Maternal depression and physical punishment as mediators of the effect of poverty on socioemotional problems of children in single-mother families. *The American Journal of Orthopsychiatry*, *71*(2), 218–226. DOI: 10.1037/0002-9432.71.2.218 PMID: 11347362

Efrati-Virtzer, M., & Margalit, M. (2009). Student's behavior difficulties, sense of coherence and adjustment at school: Risk and protective factors. *European Journal of Special Needs Education*, *24*(1), 59–73. DOI: 10.1080/08856250802596758

Ehrenreich, S. E., Beron, K. J., Brinkley, D. Y., & Underwood, M. K. (2014). Family predictors of continuity and change in social and physical aggression from ages 9 to 18. *Aggressive Behavior*, *40*(5), 421–439. DOI: 10.1002/ab.21535 PMID: 24888340

Francis, J., Trapp, G., Pearce, N., Burns, S., & Cross, D. (2022). School Built Environments and Bullying Behaviour: A Conceptual Model Based on Qualitative Interviews. *International Journal of Environmental Research and Public Health*, *19*(23), 15955. DOI: 10.3390/ijerph192315955 PMID: 36498029

Fung, A. L. C., Gerstein, L. H., Chan, Y., & Hurley, E. (2013). Children's aggression, parenting styles, and distress for Hong Kong parents. *Journal of Family Violence*, *28*(5), 515–521. Advance online publication. DOI: 10.1007/s10896-013-9518-9

Gaertner, B. M., Spinrad, T. L., Eisenberg, N., & Greving, K. A. (2007). Parental childrearing attitudes as correlates of father involvement during infancy. *Journal of Marriage and Family*, *69*(4), 962–976. DOI: 10.1111/j.1741-3737.2007.00424.x PMID: 18174913

Gao, Y., Zhang, W., & Fung, A. L. C. (2015). The associations between parenting styles and proactive and reactive aggression in Hong Kong children and adolescents. *International Journal of Psychology, 50*(6), 463–471. DOI: 10.1002/ijop.12104 PMID: 25292156

Georgiou, S. N., Fousiani, K., Michaelides, M., & Stavrinides, P. (2013). Cultural value orientation and authoritarian parenting as parameters of bullying and victimization at school. *International Journal of Psychology, 48*(1), 69–78. DOI: 10.1080/00207594.2012.754104 PMID: 23390974

Gershoff, E. T., Grogan-Kaylor, A., Lansford, J. E., Chang, L., Zelli, A., Deater-Deckard, K., & Dodge, K. A. (2010). Parent discipline practices in an international sample: Associations with child behaviors and moderation by perceived normativeness. *Child Development, 81*(2), 487–502. DOI: 10.1111/j.1467-8624.2009.01409.x PMID: 20438455

Ghani, F. B. A., Roeswardi, S. I., & Aziz, A. A. (2014). Parenting styles and their relation to teenagers' personality profile in single-mother families: A case study. *Procedia: Social and Behavioral Sciences, 114*, 766–770. DOI: 10.1016/j.sbspro.2013.12.782

Gin, K., Stewart, C., & Jolley, S. (2021). A systematic literature review of childhood externalizing psychopathology and later psychotic symptoms. *Clinical Psychology & Psychotherapy, 28*(1), 56–78. DOI: 10.1002/cpp.2493 PMID: 32681551

Gómez-Ortiz, O., Del Rey, R., Casas, J. A., & Ortega-Ruiz, R. (2014). Parenting styles and bullying involvement. *C&E, Cultura y Educación, 26*(1), 132–158. DOI: 10.1080/11356405.2014.908665

Gorostiaga, A., Aliri, J., Balluerka, N., & Lameirinhas, J. (2019). Parenting styles and internalizing symptoms in adolescence: A systematic literature review. *International Journal of Environmental Research and Public Health, 16*(17), 3192. DOI: 10.3390/ijerph16173192 PMID: 31480548

Green, E. G., Deschamps, J. C., & Paez, D. (2005). Variation of individualism and collectivism within and between 20 countries: A typological analysis. *Journal of Cross-Cultural Psychology, 36*(3), 321–339. DOI: 10.1177/0022022104273654

Griffin, K. W., Botvin, G. J., Scheier, L. M., Diaz, T., & Miller, N. L. (2000). Parenting practices as predictors of substance use, delinquency, and aggression among urban minority youth: Moderating effects of family structure and gender. *Psychology of Addictive Behaviors, 14*(2), 174–184. DOI: 10.1037/0893-164X.14.2.174 PMID: 10860116

Gryczkowski, M. R., Jordan, S. S., & Mercer, S. H. (2010). Differential relations between mothers' and fathers' parenting practices and child externalizing behavior. *Journal of Child and Family Studies*, *19*(5), 539–546. DOI: 10.1007/s10826-009-9326-2

Hadjicharalambous, D., & Demetriou, L. (2020). The Relationship Between Parents' Demographic Factors and Parenting Styles: Effects on Children's Psychological Adjustment. *Psychology Research (Libertyville, Ill.)*, *10*(4), 125–138. DOI: 10.17265/2159-5542/2020.04.001

Hawkins, D. N., Amato, P. R., & King, V. (2006). Parent-adolescent involvement: The relative influence of parent gender and residence. *Journal of Marriage and Family*, *68*(1), 125–136. DOI: 10.1111/j.1741-3737.2006.00238.x

Hesari, N. K. Z., & Hejazi, E. (2011). The mediating role of self esteem in the relationship between the authoritative parenting style and aggression. *Procedia: Social and Behavioral Sciences*, *30*, 1724–1730. DOI: 10.1016/j.sbspro.2011.10.333

Hill, N. E. (1995). The relationship between family environment and parenting style: A preliminary study of African American families. *The Journal of Black Psychology*, *21*(4), 408–423. DOI: 10.1177/00957984950214007

Hofstede, G. (2011). Dimensionalizing Cultures: The Hofstede Model in Context. *Online Readings in Psychology and Culture*, *2*(1). Advance online publication. DOI: 10.9707/2307-0919.1014

Hosokawa, R., & Katsura, T. (2019). Role of Parenting Style in Children's Behavioral Problems Through the Transition from Preschool to Elementary School According to Gender in Japan. *International Journal of Environmental Research and Public Health*, *16*(1), 21–38. DOI: 10.3390/ijerph16010021 PMID: 30577659

Huntsinger, C. S., & Jose, P. E. (2009). Relations among parental acceptance and control and children's social adjustment in Chinese American and European American families. *Journal of Family Psychology*, *23*(3), 321–330. DOI: 10.1037/a0015812 PMID: 19586195

Jackson, A. P., Choi, J. K., & Preston, K. S. (2019). Harsh parenting and black boys' behavior problems: Single mothers' parenting stress and nonresident fathers' involvement. *Family Relations*, *68*(4), 436–449. DOI: 10.1111/fare.12373

Jewell, J. D., Krohn, E. J., Scott, V. G., Carlton, M., & Meinz, E. (2008). The Differential Impact of Mothers' and Fathers' Discipline on Preschool Children's Home and Classroom Behavior. *North American Journal of Psychology*, *10*(1), 173–188.

Joussemet, M., Vitaro, F., Barker, E. D., Côté, S., Nagin, D. S., Zoccolillo, M., & Tremblay, R. E. (2008). Controlling parenting and physical aggression during elementary school. *Child Development, 79*(2), 411–425. DOI: 10.1111/j.1467-8624.2007.01133.x PMID: 18366431

Killen, M., Mulvey, K. L., & Hitti, A. (2013). Social exclusion in childhood: A developmental intergroup perspective. *Child Development, 84*(3), 772–790. DOI: 10.1111/cdev.12012 PMID: 23170901

Kim, G. E., Choi, H. Y., & Kim, E. J. (2018). Impact of economic problems on depression in single mothers: A comparative study with married women. *PLoS One, 13*(8), e0203004. DOI: 10.1371/journal.pone.0203004 PMID: 30142180

Kofler, M. J., McCart, M. R., Zajac, K., Ruggiero, K. J., Saunders, B. E., & Kilpatrick, D. G. (2011). Depression and delinquency covariation in an accelerated longitudinal sample of adolescents. *Journal of Consulting and Clinical Psychology, 79*(4), 458–469. DOI: 10.1037/a0024108 PMID: 21787049

Krishnakumar, A., & Buehler, C. (2000). Interparental conflict and parenting behaviors: A meta-analytic review. *Family Relations, 49*(1), 25–44. DOI: 10.1111/j.1741-3729.2000.00025.x

Kritzas, N., & Grobler, A. A. (2005). The relationship between perceived parenting styles and resilience during adolescence. *Journal of Child and Adolescent Mental Health, 17*(1), 1–12. DOI: 10.2989/17280580509486586 PMID: 25868916

Kuppens, S., Grietens, H., Onghena, P., & Michiels, D. (2009). Associations between parental control and children's overt and relational aggression. *British Journal of Developmental Psychology, 27*(3), 607–623. DOI: 10.1348/026151008X345591 PMID: 19994571

Lau, E. Y. H. (2019). Parenting and childhood aggression in the Chinese context: An examination of parental responses, physical coercion, and warmth. *Early Years Journal of International Research and Development, 39*(1), 36–50. DOI: 10.1080/09575146.2017.1344195

Lee, C. Y. S., Anderson, J. R., Horowitz, J. L., & August, G. J. (2009). Family income and parenting: The role of parental depression and social support. *Family Relations, 58*(4), 417–430. DOI: 10.1111/j.1741-3729.2009.00563.x

Letourneau, N. L., Tramonte, L., & Willms, J. D. (2013). Maternal depression, family functioning, and children's longitudinal development. *Journal of Pediatric Nursing, 28*(3), 223–234. DOI: 10.1016/j.pedn.2012.07.014 PMID: 22940454

Leung, J. T., & Shek, D. T. (2018). Unbroken Homes: Parenting style and Adolescent Positive Development in Chinese single-mother families experiencing economic disadvantage. *Child Indicators Research, 11*(2), 441–457. DOI: 10.1007/s12187-016-9437-4

Lewis, C., & Lamb, M. E. (2003). Fathers' influences on children's development: The evidence from two-parent families. *European Journal of Psychology of Education, 18*(2), 211–228. DOI: 10.1007/BF03173485

Liang, L. A., Berger, U., & Brand, C. (2019). Psychosocial factors associated with symptoms of depression, anxiety, and stress among single mothers with young children: A population-based study. *Journal of Affective Disorders, 242*, 255–264. DOI: 10.1016/j.jad.2018.08.013 PMID: 30218920

Liu, L., & Wang, M. (2015). Parenting stress and children's problem behavior in China: The mediating role of parental psychological aggression. *Journal of Family Psychology, 29*(1), 20–28. DOI: 10.1037/fam0000047 PMID: 25438090

Llorca, A., Richaud, M. C., & Malonda, E. (2017). Parenting styles, prosocial, and aggressive behavior: The role of emotions in offender and non-offender adolescents. *Frontiers in Psychology, 8*, 1246. DOI: 10.3389/fpsyg.2017.01246 PMID: 28848459

Ma, J., Han, Y., Grogan-Kaylor, A., Delva, J., & Castillo, M. (2012). Corporal punishment and youth externalizing behavior in Santiago, Chile. *Child Abuse & Neglect, 36*(6), 481–490. DOI: 10.1016/j.chiabu.2012.03.006 PMID: 22766372

Malti, T., & Noam, G. G. (2009). A developmental approach to the prevention of adolescent's aggressive behavior and the promotion of resilience. *International Journal of Developmental Science, 3*(3), 235–246. DOI: 10.3233/DEV-2009-3303

Marks, J. L., Lam, C. B., & McHale, S. M. (2009). Family patterns of gender role attitudes. *Sex Roles, 61*(3), 221–234. DOI: 10.1007/s11199-009-9619-3 PMID: 22308059

Martínez, I., Murgui, S., Garcia, O. F., & García, F. (2019). Parenting in the digital era: Protective and risk parenting styles for traditional bullying and cyberbullying victimization. *Computers in Human Behavior, 90*, 84–92. DOI: 10.1016/j.chb.2018.08.036

Masud, H., Ahmad, M. S., Cho, K. W., & Fakhr, Z. (2019). Parenting styles and aggression among young adolescents: A systematic review of the literature. *Community Mental Health Journal, 55*(6), 1015–1030. DOI: 10.1007/s10597-019-00400-0 PMID: 31102163

McCloskey, L. A., & Lichter, E. L. (2003). The contribution of marital violence to adolescent aggression across different relationships. *Journal of Interpersonal Violence, 18*(4), 390–412. DOI: 10.1177/0886260503251179

McKee, L., Colletti, C., Rakow, A., Jones, D. J., & Forehand, R. (2008). Parenting and child externalizing behaviors: Are the associations specific or diffuse? *Aggression and Violent Behavior, 13*(3), 201–215. DOI: 10.1016/j.avb.2008.03.005 PMID: 19122818

Méndez, J. H. M., Sánchez, J. P. E., & Becerra, M. I. G. (2020). Role of parenting styles in internalizing, externalizing, and adjustment problems in children. *Salud Mental, 43*(2), 73–84. DOI: 10.17711/SM.0185-3325.2020.011

Mensah, M. K., & Kuranchie, A. (2013). Influence of parenting styles on the social development of children. *Academic Journal of Interdisciplinary Studies, 2*(3), 123-123. https://www.richtmann.org/journal/index.php/ajis/article/view/1397

Miner, J. L., & Clarke-Stewart, K. A. (2008). Trajectories of externalizing behavior from age 2 to age 9: Relations with gender, temperament, ethnicity, parenting, and rater. *Developmental Psychology, 44*(3), 771–736. DOI: 10.1037/0012-1649.44.3.771 PMID: 18473643

Mistry, R. S., Vandewater, E. A., Huston, A. C., & McLoyd, V. C. (2002). Economic well-being and children's social adjustment: The role of family process in an ethnically diverse low-income sample. *Child Development, 73*(3), 935–951. DOI: 10.1111/1467-8624.00448 PMID: 12038561

Monteiro, L., Fernandes, M., Torres, N., & Santos, C. (2017). Father's involvement and parenting styles in Portuguese families. The role of education and working hours. *Análise Psicológica, 35*(4), 513–528. DOI: 10.14417/ap.1451

Morris, A. S., Silk, J. S., Steinberg, L., Myers, S. S., & Robinson, L. R. (2007). The role of the family context in the development of emotion regulation. *Social Development, 16*(2), 361–388. DOI: 10.1111/j.1467-9507.2007.00389.x PMID: 19756175

Morrow, M. T., Hubbard, J. A., McAuliffe, M. D., Rubin, R. M., & Dearing, K. F. (2006). Childhood aggression, depressive symptoms, and peer rejection: The mediational model revisited. *International Journal of Behavioral Development, 30*(3), 240–248. DOI: 10.1177/0165025406066757

Muñoz, J. M., Braza, P., Carreras, R., Braza, F., Azurmendi, A., Pascual-Sagastizábal, E., Cardas, J., & Sánchez-Martín, J. R. (2017). Daycare center attendance buffers the effects of maternal authoritarian parenting style on physical aggression in children. *Frontiers in Psychology, 8*, 391. DOI: 10.3389/fpsyg.2017.00391 PMID: 28377733

Olivari, M. G., Wahn, E. H., Maridaki-Kassotaki, K., Antonopoulou, K., & Confalonieri, E. (2015). Adolescent perceptions of parenting styles in Sweden, Italy and Greece: An exploratory study. *Europe's Journal of Psychology, 11*(2), 244–258. DOI: 10.5964/ejop.v11i2.887 PMID: 27247655

Ostrov, J. M., & Bishop, C. M. (2008). Preschoolers' aggression and parent-child conflict: A multi-informant and multimethod study. *Journal of Experimental Child Psychology, 99*(4), 309–322. DOI: 10.1016/j.jecp.2008.01.001 PMID: 18299136

Pakaluk, C. R., & Price, J. (2020). Are mothers and father's interchangeable caregivers? *Marriage & Family Review, 56*(8), 784–793. DOI: 10.1080/01494929.2020.1778318

Pedro, M. F., Carapito, E., & Ribeiro, T. (2015). Parenting Styles and Dimensions Questionnaire – The Portuguese Self-Report Version/ Parenting Styles and Dimensions Questionnaire-versão portuguesa de autorrelato. *Psicologia: Reflexão e Crítica : Revista Semestral do Departamento de Psicologia da UFRGS, 28*(2), 302–312. DOI: 10.1590/1678-7153.201528210

Pereira, A. I., Canavarro, C., Cardoso, M. F., & Mendonça, D. (2009). Patterns of parental rearing styles and child behavior problems among Portuguese school-aged children. *Journal of Child and Family Studies, 18*(4), 454–464. DOI: 10.1007/s10826-008-9249-3

Pinquart, M. (2017). Associations of parenting dimensions and styles with externalizing problems of children and adolescents: An updated meta-analysis. *Developmental Psychology, 53*(5), 873–932. DOI: 10.1037/dev0000295 PMID: 28459276

Pinquart, M., & Kauser, R. (2018). Do the associations of parenting styles with behavior problems and academic achievement vary by culture? Results from a meta-analysis. *Cultural Diversity & Ethnic Minority Psychology, 24*(1), 75–100. DOI: 10.1037/cdp0000149 PMID: 28394165

Piotrowski, J. T., Lapierre, M. A., & Linebarger, D. L. (2013). Investigating correlates of self-regulation in early childhood with a representative sample of English-speaking American families. *Journal of Child and Family Studies, 22*(3), 423–436. DOI: 10.1007/s10826-012-9595-z PMID: 23525149

Pleck, J. H., Masciadrelli, B. P., & Lamb, M. E. (2004). Paternal involvement by US residential fathers. *The role of the father in child development, 4*, 222-271.

Pomerantz, E. M., & Wang, Q. (2009). The role of parental control in children's development in Western and East Asian countries. *Current Directions in Psychological Science, 18*(5), 285–289. DOI: 10.1111/j.1467-8721.2009.01653.x

Pong, S. L., Johnston, J., & Chen, V. (2010). Authoritarian parenting and Asian adolescent school performance: Insights from the US and Taiwan. *International Journal of Behavioral Development, 34*(1), 62–72. DOI: 10.1177/0165025409345073 PMID: 24850978

Propper, C., & Moore, G. A. (2006). The influence of parenting on infant emotionality: A multi-level psychobiological perspective. *Developmental Review, 26*(4), 427–460. DOI: 10.1016/j.dr.2006.06.003

Rankin Williams, L., Degnan, K. A., Perez-Edgar, K. E., Henderson, H. A., Rubin, K. H., Pine, D. S., Steinberg, L., & Fox, N. A. (2009). Impact of behavioral inhibition and parenting style on internalizing and externalizing problems from early childhood through adolescence. *Journal of Abnormal Child Psychology, 37*(8), 1063–1075. DOI: 10.1007/s10802-009-9331-3 PMID: 19521761

Rinaldi, C. M., & Howe, N. (2012). Mothers' and fathers' parenting styles and associations with toddlers' externalizing, internalizing, and adaptive behaviors. *Early Childhood Research Quarterly, 27*(2), 266–273. DOI: 10.1016/j.ecresq.2011.08.001

Röll, J., Koglin, U., & Petermann, F. (2012). Emotion regulation and childhood aggression: Longitudinal associations. *Child Psychiatry and Human Development, 43*(6), 909–923. DOI: 10.1007/s10578-012-0303-4 PMID: 22528031

Rothbart, M. K., & Bates, J. E. (2006). Temperament. In Eisenberg, N., Damon, W., & Lerner, R. M. (Eds.), *Social, emotional, and personality development* (pp. 99–166). Handbook of child psychology. John Wiley & Sons, Inc.

Sandstrom, M. J. (2007). A link between mothers' disciplinary strategies and children's relational aggression. *British Journal of Developmental Psychology, 25*(3), 399–407. DOI: 10.1348/026151006X158753

Sanvictores, T., & Mendez, M. D. (2022). Types of Parenting Styles and Effects on Children. In: StatPearls [Internet]. Treasure Island (FL): StatPearls Publishing; 2026 Jan-. Available from: https://www.ncbi.nlm.nih.gov/books/NBK568743/

Sarwar, S. (2016). Influence of parenting style on children's behaviour. *Journal of Education and Educational Development, 3*(2), 222–249. DOI: 10.22555/joeed.v3i2.1036

Sayer, L. C., Bianchi, S. M., & Robinson, J. P. (2004). Are parents investing less in children? Trends in mothers' and fathers' time with children. *American Journal of Sociology, 110*(1), 1–43. DOI: 10.1086/386270

Schwerdtfeger, K. L., Larzelere, R. E., Werner, D., Peters, C., & Oliver, M. (2013). Intergenerational transmission of trauma: The mediating role of parenting styles on toddlers' DSM-related symptoms. *Journal of Aggression, Maltreatment & Trauma*, *22*(2), 211–229. DOI: 10.1080/10926771.2013.743941

Shayegh, M., Bafrooei, K. B., & Rahimi, M. (2021). The role of family factors in aggression of preschool children by social skills intermediation. *Tulu-i Bihdasht*, *20*(1), 38–54. DOI: 10.18502/tbj.v20i1.6183

Sheehan, M. J., & Watson, M. W. (2008). Reciprocal influences between maternal discipline techniques and aggression in children and adolescents. *Aggressive Behavior*, *34*(3), 245–255. DOI: 10.1002/ab.20241 PMID: 18085532

Simbolon, R., & Purba, W. (2022). Evaluating the Impact of School Counseling Programs on Student Well-being and Academic Performance in the Educational Environment. *Jurnal Ilmu Pendidikan Dan Humaniora*, *11*(2), 118–137. DOI: 10.35335/jiph.v11i2.19

Simons, L. G., & Conger, R. D. (2007). Linking mother-father differences in parenting to a typology of family parenting styles and adolescent outcomes. *Journal of Family Issues*, *28*(2), 212–241. DOI: 10.1177/0192513X06294593

Stover, C. S., Zhou, Y., Kiselica, A., Leve, L. D., Neiderhiser, J. M., Shaw, D. S., Natsuaki, M. N., Scaramella, L. V., & Reiss, D. (2016). Marital hostility, hostile parenting, and child aggression: Associations from toddlerhood to school age. *Journal of the American Academy of Child and Adolescent Psychiatry*, *55*(3), 235–242. DOI: 10.1016/j.jaac.2015.12.008 PMID: 26903257

Suzuki, K., Kita, Y., Kaga, M., Takehara, K., Misago, C., & Inagaki, M. (2016). The association between children's behavior and parenting of caregivers: A longitudinal study in Japan. *Frontiers in Public Health*, *4*, 17. DOI: 10.3389/fpubh.2016.00017 PMID: 26913279

Talib, J., Mohamad, Z., & Mamat, M. (2011). Effects of parenting style on children development. *World Journal of Social Sciences*, *1*(2), 14–35.

Tavassolie, T., Dudding, S., Madigan, A. L., Thorvardarson, E., & Winsler, A. (2016). Differences in perceived parenting style between mothers and fathers: Implications for child outcomes and marital conflict. *Journal of Child and Family Studies*, *25*(6), 2055–2068. DOI: 10.1007/s10826-016-0376-y

Taylor, L. D., Davis-Kean, P., & Malanchuk, O. (2007). Self-esteem, academic self-concept, and aggression at school. *Aggressive Behavior*, *33*(2), 130–136. DOI: 10.1002/ab.20174 PMID: 17441013

Teng, Z., Liu, Y., & Guo, C. (2015). A meta-analysis of the relationship between self-esteem and aggression among Chinese students. *Aggression and Violent Behavior, 21*, 45–54. DOI: 10.1016/j.avb.2015.01.005

Trenas, A. F. R., Osuna, M. J. P., Olivares, R. R., & Cabrera, J. H. (2013). Relationship between parenting style and aggression in a Spanish children sample. *Procedia: Social and Behavioral Sciences, 82*, 529–536. DOI: 10.1016/j.sbspro.2013.06.304

Udry, J. R. (2000). Biological limits of gender construction. *American Sociological Review, 65*(3), 443–457. DOI: 10.1177/000312240006500307

Uludag, O. (2013). The influence of aggression on students' achievement: Evidence from higher education. *Procedia: Social and Behavioral Sciences, 89*, 954–958. DOI: 10.1016/j.sbspro.2013.08.963

Underwood, M. K., Beron, K. J., & Rosen, L. H. (2009). Continuity and change in social and physical aggression from middle childhood through early adolescence. *Aggressive Behavior, 35*(5), 357–375. DOI: 10.1002/ab.20313 PMID: 19685551

Vaillancourt, T., & Farrell, A. H. (2021). Mean kids become mean adults: Trajectories of indirect aggression from age 10 to 22. *Aggressive Behavior, 47*(4), 394–404. DOI: 10.1002/ab.21950 PMID: 33469944

Vitaro, F., Brendgen, M., Larose, S., & Trembaly, R. E. (2005). Kindergarten disruptive behaviors, protective factors, and educational achievement by early adulthood. *Journal of Educational Psychology, 97*(4), 617–629. DOI: 10.1037/0022-0663.97.4.617

Vreeland, A., Gruhn, M. A., Watson, K. H., Bettis, A. H., Compas, B. E., Forehand, R., & Sullivan, A. D. (2019). Parenting in context: Associations of parental depression and socioeconomic factors with parenting behaviors. *Journal of Child and Family Studies, 28*(4), 1124–1133. DOI: 10.1007/s10826-019-01338-3 PMID: 41583615

Walsh, F. (2016). Applying a family resilience framework in training, practice, and research: Mastering the art of the possible. *Family Process, 55*(4), 616–632. DOI: 10.1111/famp.12260 PMID: 27921306

Widia, A. P., & Bustomi, Y. I. (2025). The effectiveness of guidance and counseling interventions in improving students' academic resilience: A systematic literature review. *International Journal of Multidisciplinary Reseach, 1*(2), 250–259.

Winsler, A., Madigan, A. L., & Aquilino, S. A. (2005). Correspondence between maternal and paternal parenting styles in early childhood. *Early Childhood Research Quarterly, 20*(1), 1–12. DOI: 10.1016/j.ecresq.2005.01.007

Yaffe, Y. (2020). Systematic review of the differences between mothers and fathers in parenting styles and practices. *Current Psychology (New Brunswick, N.J.)*, •••, 1–14. DOI: 10.1007/s12144-020-01014-6

KEY TERMS AND DEFINITIONS

Authoritarian Parenting Style: A traditional, harsh child-rearing approach marked by low warmth, high control, and rigid demands, where children are expected to obey parental directives unconditionally, often facing punitive consequences and limited flexibility.

Authoritative Parenting Style: A parenting approach characterized by high warmth and responsiveness combined with reasonable control and demands, where parents guide children rationally, encourage discussion, and balance affection with discipline to support rather than punish.

Childhood Aggression: A multifactorial phenomenon referring to behaviors intended to cause harm to people or objects, manifesting in various forms such as physical, psychological, and relational aggression, and significantly impacting children's academic, social, and emotional adjustment.

Family Resilience: The capacity of the family system to withstand, adapt to, and recover from challenges and stressors through functional processes that enhance emotional regulation and problem-solving, rather than relying solely on individual traits.

Parenting Typology (or Parenting Style): The combination of parental behaviors, attitudes, values, and beliefs regarding child development and upbringing, which collectively influence the child's competencies, developmental progression, and psychological well-being.

Permissive Parenting Style: A tolerant and accepting parenting approach characterized by high warmth and responsiveness but low control and demands, where parents avoid asserting authority, set few limits, and present themselves as resources rather than role models.

School Counseling: Support services within educational settings that identify patterns of dysfunction, implement targeted intervention programs, and foster collaboration between family and school to promote students' mental health, emotional regulation, and resilience.

Compilation of References

Aarons, G. A., Hurlburt, M., & Horwitz, S. M. (2011). Advancing a conceptual model of evidence-based practice implementation in public service sectors. *Administration and Policy in Mental Health, 38*(1), 4–23. DOI: 10.1007/s10488-010-0327-7

Adolphus, K., Lawton, C. L., & Dye, L. (2013). The effects of breakfast on behavior and academic performance in children and adolescents. *Frontiers in Human Neuroscience, 7*, 425. DOI: 10.3389/fnhum.2013.00425 PMID: 23964220

Aelterman, A., Engels, N., Van Petegem, K., & Verhaeghe, J. P. (2007). The wellbeing of teachers in Flanders: The importance of a supportive school culture. *Educational Studies, 33*(3), 285–298. DOI: 10.1080/03055690701423085

Aguilar, E. (2013). *The art of coaching: Effective strategies for school transformation*. John Wiley & Sons.

Ainsworth, S., & Oldfield, J. (2019). Quantifying teacher resilience: Context matters. *Teaching and Teacher Education, 82*, 117–128. DOI: 10.1016/j.tate.2019.03.012

Akhter, N., Hanif, R., Tariq, N., & Atta, M. (2011). Parenting styles as predictors of externalizing and internalizing behavior problems among children. *Pakistan Journal of Psychological Research, 26*(1), 23–41.

Akrami, F., Zali, A., & Abbasi, M. (2022). Entanglement of the rights of the child, well-being, and justice: A conceptual framework for child protection and well-being. *International Journal of Medical Toxicology and Forensic Medicine, 12*(2), 1–11. DOI: 10.32598/ijmtfm.v12i2.36827

Aksoy, P. (2026). Art education in early childhood: Exploring pre-service teachers' perceptions of integrated art activities with natural and sustainable materials. *International Journal of Early Years Education, 34*(2), 277–303. DOI: 10.1080/09669760.2026.2645343

Alagaraja, M. (2020). Wellbeing in the workplace: A new conceptual model and implications for practice. In Dhiman, S. (Ed.), *The Palgrave handbook of workplace well-being* (pp. 1–22). Palgrave Macmillan. DOI: 10.1007/978-3-030-02470-3_69-1

Allergy & Anaphylaxis Australia. (2024). *Support dogs in school and the risk to students with allergy.* https://allergyfacts.org.au/support-dogs-in-school-and-the-risk-to-students-with-allergy/

Al-Mahdi, O. (2019). *Family–School Connections: Different Theoretical Perspectives and their Implications for Teacher Education. Humanities and Social Sciences Review, 2*(4), 13–23. https://j.ideasspread.org/index.php/hssr/article/view/350

Aloia, L. S., & McTigue, M. (2019). Buffering against sources of academic stress: The influence of supportive informational and emotional communication on psychological well-being. *Communication Research Reports, 36*(2), 126–135. DOI: 10.1080/08824096.2019.1590191

Altay, F. B., & Gure, A. (2012). Relationship among the Parenting Styles and the Social Competence and Prosocial Behaviors of the Children Who are Attending to State and Private Preschools. *Educational Sciences: Theory & Practice, 12*(4), 2712–2718.

Alzouebi, K., Al Hammadi, D. Y., Ankit, A., & Abu Khurma, O. (2025). School innovation: Building a culture through leadership and stakeholder engagement. *Societies (Basel, Switzerland), 15*(4), 77. DOI: 10.3390/soc15040077

Amad, S., Gray, N. S., & Snowden, R. J. (2021). Self-esteem, narcissism, and aggression: Different types of self-esteem predict different types of aggression. *Journal of Interpersonal Violence, 36*(23-24), NP13296–NP13313. Advance online publication. DOI: 10.1177/0886260520905540 PMID: 32065011

Ameli, K., Braun, T. F., & Krämer, S. (2023). Animal-assisted interventions and animal welfare—An exploratory survey in Germany. *Animals (Basel), 13*(8), 1324. Advance online publication. DOI: 10.3390/ani13081324

American Psychiatric Association. (2022). *Diagnostic and statistical manual of mental disorders* (5th ed., text rev.). American Psychiatric Publishing.

American School Counselor Association. (2003). The ASCA National Model: A framework for school counseling programs. *Professional School Counseling, 6*(3), 165–168. http://www.jstor.org/stable/42732424

American Veterinary Medical Association. (n.d.). *Animal-assisted interventions: Guidelines.* https://www.avma.org/resources-tools/animal-health-and-welfare/service-emotional-support-and-therapy-animals/animal-assisted-interventions-guidelines

Anastassopoulos, A. (2018). *Teacher well-being: Dimensions and interconnections with the role of the principal-leader and the school climate* (Master's thesis, Hellenic Open University, School of Humanities, Studies in Education Program).

Angantyr, M., Hansen, E. M., Eklund, J. H., & Malm, K. (2016). Reducing sex differences in children's empathy for animals through a training intervention. *Journal of Research in Childhood Education*, *30*(3), 273–281. DOI: 10.1080/02568543.2016.1178198

Angelakou, E.-P. (2018). *School development as a self-referential process of improvement of the organizational learning and intelligence: The example of post - dictatorship Greece.* [Doctoral dissertation, University of the Aegean]. National Archive of PhD Theses. https://doi.org/DOI: 10.12681/eadd/43701

Angelakou, E.-P. (2019). The communication system in school operation and development: The case of Greek educational legislation. In C. Kalloniatis, C.-N. Anagnostopoulos, D. Papageorgiou, A. Kitsiou, & M. Sideri (Eds.), *International Conference on Cultural Informatics, Communication & Media Studies e-Proceedings*, *1*(1). National Documentation Center. http://dx.doi.org/DOI: 10.12681/cicms.2733

Angelakou, E.-P. (2020). Commitments of the educational legal framework to the communication system: A systemic study of the "communication complexity" of Greek primary educational organizations. In A. Kodakos & P. Stamatis (Eds.), *Communication and education, Vol. 3: Issues of theory and research methodology of communication in education* (pp. 187–205). Diadrasi.

Angelakou, E.-P. (2021). The "adaptation" of Greek primary school to a social environment of increasing communicative complexity. In A. Kodakos & F. Kalavasis (Series Eds.), *Topics in Educational Design, Vol 12: Educational engineering of communication and its media in the design and development of educational organizations* (pp. 182–200). Diadrasi.

Angner, E. (2011). The evolution of eupathics: The historical roots of subjective measures of wellbeing. *International Journal of Wellbeing*, *1*(1), 4–41. https://doi.org/XXXX. DOI: 10.5502/ijw.v1i1.14

Anton, M. T., Jones, D. J., & Youngstrom, E. A. (2015). Socioeconomic status, parenting, and externalizing problems in African American single-mother homes: A person-oriented approach. *Journal of Family Psychology, 29*(3), 405–415. DOI: 10.1037/fam0000086 PMID: 26053349

Argyriou, M. (2021). *Applied music pedagogy: Educational frameworks and instructional design for preschool and primary education.* DiSIGMA Publications.

Argyriou, M. (2025a). Music and cultural identity in the early years: An empirical approach to intercultural learning. *European Journal of Education Studies, 12*(8), 1–27. DOI: 10.46827/ejes.v12i8.6118

Argyriou, M. (2025b). Integrating technology-enhanced alternative assessment in special education: Pedagogical, cultural and structural dimensions for inclusive practice. *European Journal of Special Education Research, 11*(6). Advance online publication. DOI: 10.46827/ejse.v11i6.6256

Argyriou, M. (2025c). The impact of action songs on gross motor skill development in preschool children: A Greek kindergarten case study. *International Journal of Education, 13*(1), 53–69. DOI: 10.5121/ije.2025.13125

Argyriou, M., & Lici, E. (2026). Music education beyond technique: Cultural memory and intercultural pedagogy. *Rast Musicology Journal, 14*(1), 53–92. DOI: 10.12975/rastmd.20261413

Argyriou, M., & Tapsis, N. (2025). Reframing multimodality in contemporary education: A critical review of research patterns and pedagogical shifts. *European Journal of Open Education and E-Learning Studies, 10*(3), 1–24. DOI: 10.46827/ejoe.v10i3.6106

Argyriou, M., & Tapsis, N. (Eds.). (2026). *Educating through care: Music, the arts and the social value of cultural education in contemporary societies: RIAM 2026 abstract book.* University of the Aegean. https://doi.org/DOI: 10.26215/heal.uoa.11725

Argyris, C. (1999). *On organizational learning* (2nd ed.). Blackwell Publishers.

Argyris, C., & Schön, D. A. (1974). *Theory in practice: Increasing professional effectiveness.* Jossey-Bass.

Argyris, C., & Schön, D. A. (1978). *Organizational learning: A theory of action perspective.* Addison-Wesley.

Armitage, R. (2021). Bullying in children: Impact on child health. *BMJ Paediatrics Open, 5*(1), e001336. DOI: 10.1136/bmjpo-2020-000939 PMID: 33782656

Arnsten, A. F. T. (2009). Stress signalling pathways that impair prefrontal cortex structure and function. *Nature Reviews. Neuroscience*, *10*(6), 410–422. DOI: 10.1038/nrn2648

Artinopoulou, B., Theodoros Babalis, T., & Vasilios Nikolopoulos, V. (2016). *Nationwide survey on school violence and bullying in primary and secondary education*. Ministry of Education, Research and Religious Affairs.

Ascione, F. R. (1997). Humane education research: Evaluating efforts to encourage children's kindness and caring toward animals. *Genetic, Social, and General Psychology Monographs*, *123*(1), 57–77. https://api.semanticscholar.org/CorpusID: 142398952

Ascione, F. R., & Weber, C. V. (1996). Children's attitudes about the humane treatment of animals and empathy: One-year follow-up of a school-based intervention. *Anthrozoos*, *9*(4), 188–195. DOI: 10.2752/089279396787001455

Ashkanasy, N. M., Broadfoot, L. E., & Falkus, S. (2000). Questionnaire measures of organizational culture. In Ashkanasy, N. M., Wilderom, C. P. M., & Peterson, M. F. (Eds.), *Handbook of organizational culture and climate* (pp. 131–145). Sage.

Athanasoula-Reppa, A. (2008). *Educational administration and organizational behavior: The pedagogy of educational administration*. Ellin.

Atkinson, P. A., Martin, C. R., & Rankin, J. (2009). Resilience revisited. *Journal of Psychiatric and Mental Health Nursing*, *16*(2), 137–145. DOI: 10.1111/j.1365-2850.2008.01341.x

Atkinson, P., & Hammersley, M. (1994). Ethnography and participant observation. In Denzin, N. K., & Lincoln, Y. S. (Eds.), *Handbook of qualitative research* (pp. 248–261). Sage.

Atkinson, S., & Robson, M. (2012). Arts and health as a practice of liminality: Managing the spaces of transformation for social and emotional wellbeing with primary school children. *Health & Place*, *18*(6), 1348–1355. DOI: 10.1016/j.healthplace.2012.06.017 PMID: 22840601

Auerbach, S. (2012, Ed.). *School Leadership for Authentic Family and Community Partnerships: Research Perspectives for Transforming Practice*. Routledge.

Aydoğdu, F., & Ayanoğlu, M. (2020). A review of the views of teacher candidates about art activities within the scope of teaching practice. *Gazi Üniversitesi Gazi Eğitim Fakültesi Dergisi*, *40*(2), 699–726.

Azak, S., & Raeder, S. (2013). Trajectories of parenting behavior and maternal depression. *Infant Behavior and Development*, *36*(3), 391–402. DOI: 10.1016/j.infbeh.2013.03.004 PMID: 23603820

Azimi, A. L., Vaziri, S., & Kashani, F. L. (2012). Relationship between maternal parenting style and child's aggressive behavior. *Procedia: Social and Behavioral Sciences*, *69*, 1276–1281. DOI: 10.1016/j.sbspro.2012.12.062

Babbie, E. (2011). *Introduction to social research* (G. Vogiatzis, Trans.; K. Zafeiropoulos, Ed.-Intro.). Kritiki.

Baird, R., Berger, E., & Grové, C. (2023). Therapy dogs and school wellbeing: A qualitative study. *Journal of Veterinary Behavior*, *68*, 15–23. DOI: 10.1016/j.jveb.2023.08.005

Bakker, A. B., & Demerouti, E. (2017). Job demands–resources theory: Taking stock and looking forward. *Journal of Occupational Health Psychology*, *22*(3), 273–285. https://psycnet.apa.org/doi/10.1037/ocp0000056. DOI: 10.1037/ocp0000056

Bakoula, C., Kolaitis, G., Veltsista, A., Gika, A., & Chrousos, G. P. (2009). Parental stress affects the emotions and behaviour of children up to adolescence: A Greek prospective, longitudinal study. *Stress (Amsterdam, Netherlands)*, *12*(6), 486–498. DOI: 10.3109/10253890802645041 PMID: 19206015

Ballard, H. L., Dixon, C. G. H., & Harris, E. M. (2017). Youth-focused citizen science: Examining the role of environmental science learning and agency for conservation. *Biological Conservation*, *208*, 65–75. DOI: 10.1016/j.biocon.2016.05.024

Ball, S. J. (2003). The teacher's soul and the terrors of performativity. *Journal of Education Policy*, *18*(2), 215–228. DOI: 10.1080/0268093022000043065

Bandura, A. (1973). *Aggression: A social learning analysis*. Prentice Hall.

Bandura, A. (1990). Perceived self-efficacy in the exercise of personal agency. *Journal of Applied Sport Psychology*, *2*(2), 128–163. DOI: 10.1080/10413209008406426

Bandura, A. (1997). *Self-efficacy: The exercise of control*. W H Freeman/Times Books/ Henry Holt & Co.

Bandura, A. (Ed.). (1997). *Self-efficacy in changing societies*. Cambridge university press.

Bandura, A., & Wessels, S. (1997). *Self-efficacy* (Vol. 10). Cambridge University Press.

Baraldi, C., & Gavioli, L. (2023). Mediation and dialogue in multilingual and multicultural contexts. In Gavioli, L., & Wadensjö, C. (Eds.), *The Routledge Handbook of Public Service Interpreting* (pp. 1–14). Routledge.

Barrett, M. S., Flynn, L. M., Brown, J. E., & Welch, G. F. (2019). Beliefs and values about music in early childhood education and care: Perspectives from practitioners. *Frontiers in Psychology*, *10*, 724. DOI: 10.3389/fpsyg.2019.00724 PMID: 31105608

Barrett, M. S., Flynn, L. M., Brown, J. E., & Welch, G. F. (Eds.). (2022). *The Oxford handbook of early childhood learning and development in music*. Oxford University Press., DOI: 10.1093/oxfordhb/9780190927521.001.0001

Basch, C. E. (2011). Healthier Students Are Better Learners: A Missing Link in School Reforms to Close the Achievement Gap. *The Journal of School Health*, *81*(10), 593–598. DOI: 10.1111/j.1746-1561.2011.00632.x PMID: 21923870

Bassette, L. A., & Taber-Doughty, T. (2013). The effects of a dog reading visitation program on academic engagement behavior in three elementary students with emotional and behavioral disabilities: A single case design. *Child and Youth Care Forum*, *42*(3), 239–256. DOI: 10.1007/s10566-013-9197-y

Batool, S. S. (2013). Lack of adequate parenting: A potential risk factor for aggression among adolescents. *Pakistan Journal of Psychological Research*, •••, 217–238.

Baumrind, D. (1971). Current patterns of parental authority. *Developmental psychology, 4*(1), Pt.2), 1-103. https://doi.org/DOI: 10.1037/h0030372

Baumrind, D. (1966). Effects of authoritative parental control on child behavior. *Child Development*, *37*(4), 887–907. DOI: 10.2307/1126611

Baumrind, D. (1967). Childcare practices anteceding three patterns of preschool behavior. *Genetic Psychology Monographs*, *75*(1), 43–88. PMID: 6032134

Baumrind, D. (1978). Parental disciplinary patterns and social competence in children. *Youth & Society*, *9*(3), 239–267. DOI: 10.1177/0044118X7800900302

Baumrind, D. (1989). Rearing competent children. In Damon, W. (Ed.), *Child development today and tomorrow* (pp. 349–378). Jossey-Bass/Wiley.

Baumrind, D. (1991). The influence of parenting style on adolescent competence and substance use. *The Journal of Early Adolescence*, *11*(1), 56–95. DOI: 10.1177/0272431691111004

Baumrind, D., Larzelere, R. E., & Owens, E. B. (2010). Effects of preschool parents' power assertive patterns and practices on adolescent development. *Parenting, Science and Practice*, *10*(3), 157–201. DOI: 10.1080/15295190903290790

Becker, J. L. (2014). Presence of a dog on executive functioning and stress in children with emotional disorders. *ETD Collection for Fordham University.* https://research.library.fordham.edu/dissertations/AAI3629239

Becker, A. (2020). Post-collection Data Capture, Scoring, and Processing. In Wagemaker, H. (Ed.), *Reliability and Validity of International Large-Scale Assessment. IEA Research for Education, 10.* Springer., DOI: 10.1007/978-3-030-53081-5_9

Becker, M. C., & Haunschild, A. (2003). The impact of boundaryless carries on organizational decision making. An analysis from the perspective of Luhmann's theory on social system. *International Journal of Human Resource Management, 14*(5), 713–727. DOI: 10.1080/0958519032000080767

Beetz, A. (2013). Socio-emotional correlates of a schooldog-teacher-team in the classroom. *Frontiers in Psychology, 4.* Advance online publication. DOI: 10.3389/fpsyg.2013.00886

Beetz, A., Uvnäs-Moberg, K., Julius, H., & Kotrschal, K. (2012). Psychosocial and psychophysiological effects of human-animal interactions: The possible role of oxytocin. *Frontiers in Psychology, 3.* Advance online publication. DOI: 10.3389/fpsyg.2012.00234

Bela, G., Peltola, T., Young, J. C., Balázs, B., Arpin, I., Pataki, G., Hauck, J., Kelemen, E., Kopperoinen, L., van Herzele, A., Keune, H., Hecker, S., Suškevičs, M., Roy, H. E., Itkonen, P., Külvik, M., László, M., Basnou, C., Pino, J., & Bonn, A. (2016). Learning and the transformative potential of citizen science. *Conservation Biology, 30*(5), 990–999. DOI: 10.1111/cobi.12762 PMID: 27185104

Beltman, S., Mansfield, C., & Price, A. (2011). Thriving not just surviving: A review of research on teacher resilience. *Educational Research Review, 6*(3), 185–207. DOI: 10.1016/j.edurev.2011.09.001

Benevene, P., De Stasio, S., & Fiorilli, C. (2020). Well-being of school teachers in their work environment. *Frontiers in Psychology, 11,* 1239. Advance online publication. DOI: 10.3389/fpsyg.2020.01239 PMID: 32903655

Benzies, K., Keown, L. A., & Magill-Evans, J. (2009). Immediate and sustained effects of parenting on physical aggression in Canadian children aged 6 years and younger. *Canadian Journal of Psychiatry, 54*(1), 55–64. DOI: 10.1177/070674370905400109 PMID: 19175980

Berenguer, C., Roselló, B., & Miranda, A. (2021). Mothers' stress and behavioral and emotional problems in children with ADHD: Mediation of coping strategies. *Scandinavian Journal of Psychology*, *62*(2), 141–149. DOI: 10.1111/sjop.12680 PMID: 32920860

Bermejo-Toro, L., Prieto-Ursua, M., & Hernandez, V. (2016). Towards a model of teacher well-being: Personal and job resources involved in teacher burnout and engagement. *Educational Psychology*, *36*(3), 481–501. DOI: 10.1080/01443410.2015.1005006

Bert, F., Gualano, M. R., Camussi, E., Pieve, G., Voglino, G., & Siliquini, R. (2016). Animal assisted intervention: A systematic review of benefits and risks. *European Journal of Integrative Medicine*, *8*(5), 695–706. DOI: 10.1016/j.eujim.2016.05.005

Best, J. R., & Miller, P. H. (2010). A developmental perspective on executive function. *Child Development*, *81*(6), 1641–1660. DOI: 10.1111/j.1467-8624.2010.01499.x

Beyers, J. M., & Loeber, R. (2003). Untangling developmental relations between depressed mood and delinquency in male adolescents. *Journal of Abnormal Child Psychology*, *31*(3), 247–266. DOI: 10.1023/A:1023225428957 PMID: 12774859

Bhalerao, A. K. (2015). Application and performance of Google Forms for online data collection and analysis: A case of North Eastern Region of India. *Indian Journal of Extension Education*, *51*(3–4), 49–53.

Biblarz, T. J., & Stacey, J. (2010). How does the gender of parents matter? *Journal of Marriage and Family*, *72*(1), 3–22. DOI: 10.1111/j.1741-3737.2009.00678.x

Bigge, M. (1990). *Learning theories for teachers* (Kantas, A., & Chantzi, A., Trans.). Patakis.

Bilir-Seyhan, G., & Ocak-Karabay, Ş. (2018). Early childhood pre-service teachers' views about visual arts education and aesthetics. *Eurasian Journal of Educational Research*, *18*(73), 131–148. DOI: 10.14689/ejer.2018.73.8

Blain-Arcaro, C., & Vaillancourt, T. (2017). Longitudinal associations between depression and aggression in children and adolescents. *Journal of Abnormal Child Psychology*, *45*(5), 959–970. DOI: 10.1007/s10802-016-0204-2 PMID: 27671705

Blair, C., & Raver, C. C. (2015). School readiness and self-regulation: A developmental psychobiological approach. *Annual Review of Psychology*, *66*(1), 711–731. DOI: 10.1146/annurev-psych-010814-015221

Blok, E., de Mol, C. L., van der Ende, J., Hillegers, M. H., Althoff, R. R., Shaw, P., & White, T. (2022). Stability and change of psychopathology symptoms throughout childhood and adolescence. *Child Psychiatry and Human Development*, *53*(6), 1330–1339. DOI: 10.1007/s10578-021-01212-8 PMID: 34184159

Bonney, R., Cooper, C. B., Dickinson, J., Kelling, S., Phillips, T., Rosenberg, K. V., & Shirk, J. (2009). Citizen science: A developing tool for expanding science knowledge and scientific literacy. *Bioscience*, *59*(11), 977–984. DOI: 10.1525/bio.2009.59.11.9

Bonney, R., Shirk, J. L., Phillips, T. B., Wiggins, A., Ballard, H. L., Miller-Rushing, A. J., & Parrish, J. K. (2014). Next Steps for Citizen Science. *Science*, *343*(6178), 1436–1437. DOI: 10.1126/science.1251554 PMID: 24675940

Boonk, L., Gijselaers, H. J. M., Ritzen, H., & Brand-Gruwel, S. (2018). A review of the relationship between parental involvement indicators and academic achievement. *Educational Research Review*, *24*, 10–30. DOI: 10.1016/j.edurev.2018.02.001

Bordalba, M. M., & Bochaca, J. G. (2019). Digital media for family–school communication? Parents' and teachers' beliefs. *Computers & Education*, *132*, 44–62. DOI: 10.1016/j.compedu.2019.01.006

Bornstein, M. H., & Cheah, C. S. L. (2006). The Place of "Culture and Parenting" in the Ecological Contextual Perspective on Developmental Science. In Rubin, K. H., & Chung, O. B. (Eds.), *Parenting beliefs, behaviours, and parent-child relations: A cross-cultural perspective* (pp. 3–33). Psychology Press.

Bosacki, S., Tardif-Williams, C. Y., & Roma, R. P. S. (2022). Children's and adolescents' pet attachment, empathy, and compassionate responding to self and others. *Adolescents (Basel, Switzerland)*, *2*(4), 493–507. DOI: 10.3390/adolescents2040039

Bourdieu, P. (1991). *Language and symbolic power (J. B. Thompson* (Raymond, G., & Adamson, M. Eds. & Trans.). Harvard University Press., https://monoskop.org/images/4/43/Bourdieu_Pierre_Language_and_Symbolic_Power_1991.pdf

Bouvier, A. (2013). *Management and cognitive sciences (A. Kodakos & F. Kalavasis* (Theofylaktopoulou, E., Koitsanou, E., & Papazachariou, T. Eds. & Trans.). Diadrasi.

Boxer, P., & Sloan-Power, E. (2013). Coping with violence: A comprehensive framework and implications for understanding resilience. *Trauma, Violence & Abuse*, *14*(3), 209–221. DOI: 10.1177/1524838013487806 PMID: 23649832

Brackett, M. A., Palomera, R., Mojsa-Kaja, J., Reyes, M. R., & Salovey, P. (2010). Emotion-regulation ability, burnout, and job satisfaction among British secondary-school teachers. *Psychology in the Schools*, *47*(4), 406–417. DOI: 10.1002/pits.20478

Brandão, C., Sampaio, M., Sousa-Gomes, V., Fávero, M., & Moreira, D. (2025). Effects of animal-assisted therapy for anxiety reduction in children and adolescents: A systematic review. *Journal of Clinical Medicine*, *14*(1), 287. DOI: 10.3390/jcm14010287

Braun, V., & Clarke, V. (2012). Thematic analysis. In H. Cooper, P. M. Camic, D. L. Long, A. T. Panter, D. Rindskopf, & K. J. Sher (Eds.), *APA handbook of research methods in psychology: Vol. 2. Research designs: Quantitative, qualitative, neuropsychological, and biological* (pp. 57–71). American Psychological Association. https://doi.org/DOI: 10.1037/13620-004

Braun, V., & Clarke, V. (2006). Using thematic analysis in psychology. *Qualitative Research in Psychology*, *3*(2), 77–101. DOI: 10.1191/1478088706qp063oa

Braza, P., Carreras, R., Muñoz, J. M., Braza, F., Azurmendi, A., Pascual-Sagastizábal, E., Cardas, J., & Sánchez-Martín, J. R. (2015). Negative maternal and paternal parenting styles as predictors of children's behavioural problems: Moderating effects of the child's sex. *Journal of Child and Family Studies*, *24*(4), 847–856. DOI: 10.1007/s10826-013-9893-0

Brelsford, V. L., Dimolareva, M., Gee, N. R., Rowan, E., & Meints, K. (2022). Can dog-assisted and relaxation interventions boost spatial ability in children with and without special educational needs? A longitudinal, randomized controlled trial. *Frontiers in Pediatrics*, *10*, 886324. Advance online publication. DOI: 10.3389/fped.2022.886324

Brelsford, V. L., Meints, K., Gee, N. R., & Pfeffer, K. (2017). Animal-assisted interventions in the classroom—A systematic review. *International Journal of Environmental Research and Public Health*, *14*(7), 669. DOI: 10.3390/ijerph14070669

Brelsford, V. L., Meints, K., Gee, N. R., & Pfeffer, K. (2020). Best practice standards in animal-assisted interventions: How the field can move forward. *Animals (Basel)*, *10*(10), 1853. DOI: 10.3390/ani10101853

Brinia, V. (2008). *Management of educational units and education*. Stamoulis.

British Society for Allergy & Clinical Immunology. (2024). *Model policy for allergy management at school*. https://www.bsaci.org/wp-content/uploads/2024/01/Model-Policy-for-allergy-at-management-at-school-v2.1-090124.pdf

Bronfenbrenner, U., & Morris, P. A. (2007). The bioecological model of human development. In Damon, W., & Lerner, R. M. (Eds.),; 6th ed., Vol. 1, pp. 793–828). Handbook of child psychology. Wiley., DOI: 10.1002/9780470147658.chpsy0114

Brook, J. S., Zheng, L., Whiteman, M., & Brook, D. W. (2001). Aggression in toddlers: Associations with parenting and marital relations. *The Journal of Genetic Psychology, 162*(2), 228–241. DOI: 10.1080/00221320109597963 PMID: 11432607

Brown, C., Douthwaite, A., Donnelly, M., & Olaniyan, Y. D. (2025). Resilience Through Belonging: Schools' Role in Promoting the Mental Health and Well-Being of Children and Young People. *Behavioral Sciences (Basel, Switzerland), 15*(10), 1421. DOI: 10.3390/bs15101421 PMID: 41153211

Brownett, T., Wilson, V., & Bowden, A. (2021). Wellbeing at work. In Manley, K., Wilson, V., & Oye, C. (Eds.), *International practice development in health and social care* (2nd ed., pp. 220–236). John Wiley & Sons. DOI: 10.1002/9781119698463.ch16

Brunzell, T., Waters, L., & Stokes, H. (2015). Teaching with strengths in trauma-affected students: A new approach to healing and growth in the classroom. *The American Journal of Orthopsychiatry, 85*(1), 3–9. DOI: 10.1037/ort0000048 PMID: 25642652

Bryk, A. S. (2010). Organizing schools for improvement. *Phi Delta Kappan, 91*(7), 23–30. DOI: 10.1177/003172171009100705

Bryk, A. S., & Schneider, B. (2002). *Trust in schools: A core resource for improvement.* Russell Sage Foundation.

Bryk, A. S., & Schneider, B. (2002). *Trust in Schools: A Core Resource for Improvement.* Russell Sage Foundation.

Burnard, P. (2012). *Musical creativities in practice.* Oxford University Press. DOI: 10.1093/acprof:oso/9780199583942.001.0001

Burnard, P., & Randles, C. (2022). Reconfiguring the future of music education through pluralism, openness and authorship of new creativities. In Burnard, P., Ross, V., Minors, H., Powell, H., & Mackinlay, E. (Eds.), *The Routledge companion to creativities in music education* (pp. 3–13). Routledge., DOI: 10.4324/9781003248194-55

Burton, P. (2005). *Suffering at school: Results of the Malawi gender-based violence in schools survey.* National Statistics Office.

Buss, A. H. (1995). *Personality: Temperament, Social Behavior, and the Self.* Allyn and Bacon.

Byrd, A. L., Vine, V., Frigoletto, O. A., Vanwoerden, S., & Stepp, S. D. (2022). A multi-method investigation of parental responses to youth emotion: Prospective effects on emotion dysregulation and reactive aggression in daily life. *Research on Child and Adolescent Psychopathology, 50*(2), 117–131. DOI: 10.1007/s10802-020-00754-0 PMID: 33856610

Cai, C., Mei, Z., Wang, Z., & Luo, S. (2025). School-based interventions for resilience in children and adolescents: A systematic review and meta-analysis of randomized controlled trials. *Frontiers in Psychiatry, 16*, 1594658. DOI: 10.3389/fpsyt.2025.1594658 PMID: 40458775

Çalış, Ş., Tan, E., Maç, S. D., & Turan, Ş. A. (2022). A critique of the internship measurement scales in higher education. *Educational Research Review, 37*, 100491. DOI: 10.1016/j.edurev.2022.100491

Campayo–Muñoz, E., & Cabedo–Mas, A. (2017). The role of emotional skills in music education. *British Journal of Music Education, 34*(3), 243–258. DOI: 10.1017/S0265051717000067

Cann, R. F., Riedel-Prabhakar, R., & Powell, D. (2021). A model of positive school leadership to improve teacher wellbeing. *International Journal of Applied Positive Psychology, 6*(3), 195–218. DOI: 10.1007/s41042-020-00045-5

Carey, J., & Dimmitt, C. (2012). School counseling and student outcomes: Summary of six statewide studies. *Professional School Counseling, 16*(2), 146–153. DOI: 10.1177/2156759X0001600204

Carpenter, J., & Mendez, J. L. (2013). Adaptive and challenged parenting among low-income African American mothers: Parenting profiles relate to Head Start children's aggression and hyperactivity. *Early Education and Development, 24*(2), 1–20. DOI: 10.1080/10409289.2013.749762

Carroll, C., Patterson, M., Wood, S., Booth, A., Rick, J., & Balain, S. (2007). A conceptual framework for implementation fidelity. *Implementation Science : IS, 2*(1), 40. Advance online publication. DOI: 10.1186/1748-5908-2-40

Cecil, C. A., Barker, E. D., Jaffee, S. R., & Viding, E. (2012). Association between maladaptive parenting and child self-control over time: Cross-lagged study using a monozygotic twin difference design. *The British Journal of Psychiatry, 201*(4), 291–297. DOI: 10.1192/bjp.bp.111.107581 PMID: 22918964

Cefai, C., Bartolo, P., Cavioni, V., & Downes, P. (2018). *Strengthening social and emotional education as a core curricular area across the EU: A review of the international evidence*. Publications Office of the European Union.

Cefai, C., & Cavioni, V. (2014). *Social and emotional education in primary school: Integrating theory and research into practice*. Springer. DOI: 10.1007/978-1-4614-8752-4

Centers for Disease Control and Prevention. (2005). Mental health in the United States: Prevalence of diagnosis and medication treatment for attention-deficit/hyperactivity disorder—United States, 2003. *MMWR. Morbidity and Mortality Weekly Report*, *54*(34), 842–847. PMID: 16138075

Centers for Disease Control and Prevention. (2009). *Appendix D: Guidelines for animals in school and child-care settings. In Compendium of measures to prevent disease associated with animals in public settings.* https://www.cdc.gov/mmwr/preview/mmwrhtml/rr5805a5.htm

Centers for Disease Control and Prevention. (2024). Resources for schools and daycares. *Healthy Pets, Healthy People.* https://www.cdc.gov/healthy-pets/schools-daycares/index.html

Century, J., Rudnick, M., & Freeman, C. (2010). A framework for measuring fidelity of implementation: A foundation for shared language and accumulation of knowledge. *The American Journal of Evaluation*, *31*(2), 199–218. DOI: 10.1177/1098214010366173

Chan, J. Y., Harlow, A. J., Kinsey, R., Gerstein, L. H., & Fung, A. L. C. (2018). The examination of authoritarian parenting styles, specific forms of peer-victimization, and reactive aggression in Hong Kong Youth. *School Psychology International*, *39*(4), 378–399. DOI: 10.1177/0143034318777781

Chao, R. (1995). Chinese and European American cultural models of the self are reflected in mothers' childrearing beliefs. *Ethos (Berkeley, Calif.)*, *23*(3), 328–354. DOI: 10.1525/eth.1995.23.3.02a00030

Chao, R., & Tseng, V. (2002). Parenting of Asians. In Bornstein, M. H. (Ed.), Handbook of parenting: Vol. 4. *Social conditions and applied parenting* (2nd ed., pp. 59–93). Erlbaum.

Chen, J. J., & Rivera-Vernazza, D. E. (2023). Communicating Digitally: Building Preschool Teacher–Parent Partnerships via Digital Technologies during COVID-19. *Early Childhood Education Journal*, *51*(7), 1189–1203. DOI: 10.1007/s10643-022-01366-7 PMID: 35789788

Chen, X., Huang, X., Wang, L., & Chang, L. (2012). Aggression, peer relationships, and depression in Chinese children: A multi-wave longitudinal study. *Journal of Child Psychology and Psychiatry, and Allied Disciplines*, *53*(12), 1233–1241. DOI: 10.1111/j.1469-7610.2012.02576.x PMID: 22747770

Cherkowski, S. (2018). Positive teacher leadership: Building mindsets and capacities to grow wellbeing. *International Journal of Teacher Leadership*, *9*(1), 63–78.

Cho, H. J., Levesque-Bristol, C., & Yough, M. (2021). International students' self-determined motivation, beliefs about classroom assessment, learning strategies, and academic adjustment in higher education. *Higher Education*, *81*(6), 1215–1235. DOI: 10.1007/s10734-020-00608-0

Chow, A. R. W., Pingault, J.-B., & Baldwin, J. R. (2022). Early risk factors for joint trajectories of bullying victimization and perpetration. *European Child & Adolescent Psychiatry*, *32*(9), 1723–1731. DOI: 10.1007/s00787-022-01989-6 PMID: 35469033

Chu, L., Li, P., & Yu, M. (2020). The longitudinal effect of children's self-regulated learning on reading habits and well-being. *International Journal of Educational Research*, *104*, 101673. Advance online publication. DOI: 10.1016/j.ijer.2020.101673

Cilek, A., Kılınç, A. Ç., Erdoğan, O., Arslan, K., & Sezgin, F. (2025). Linking principal support and teacher resilience to teacher leadership in Türkiye: The mediating role of teacher work engagement. *Educational Management Administration & Leadership*, •••, 17411432241308679.

Cleveland, E. S. (2014). Digit ratio, emotional intelligence, and parenting styles predict female aggression. *Personality and Individual Differences*, *58*, 9–14. DOI: 10.1016/j.paid.2013.09.020

Coffman, A. N., Bernstein, E. R., Davies, S. C., & Justice, A. F. (2023). The Impact of a Canine-Assisted Reading Program on Readers Needing Extra Practice. *The Reading Teacher*, *76*(6), 724–734. DOI: 10.1002/trtr.2192

Cohen, L., Manion, L., & Morrison, K. (2008). *Research methods in education (5th compl* (Kyranakis, S., Mavrakis, M., & Mitsopoulou, C. Eds. & Trans.). Metaichmio.

Cohen, L., Manion, L., & Morrison, K. (2008). *Research methods in education* (Kyrianakis, S., Mavrakis, M., Mitsopoulou, C., Bithara, P., & Filopoulou, M., Trans.). Metaichmio Publications.

Cohen, S., & Wills, T. A. (1985). Stress, social support, and the buffering hypothesis. *Psychological Bulletin*, *98*(2), 310–357. DOI: 10.1037/0033-2909.98.2.310

Coiro, M. J. (2001). Depressive symptoms among women receiving welfare. *Women & Health*, *32*(1/2), 1–23. DOI: 10.1300/J013v32n01_01 PMID: 11459364

Collaborative for Academic, Social, and Emotional Learning (CASEL). (2020). *CASEL's SEL framework* (CASEL 5). https://casel.org/casel-sel-framework-11-2020/

Collie, R. J., Shapka, J. D., & Perry, N. E. (2015). School climate and social–emotional learning: Predicting teacher stress, job satisfaction, and teaching efficacy. *Journal of Educational Psychology*, *104*(4), 1189–1204. DOI: 10.1037/a0029356

Collinson, V., Cook, T. F., & Conley, S. (2006). Organizational learning in schools and school systems: Improving learning, teaching, and leading. *Theory into Practice*, *45*(2), 107–116. DOI: 10.1207/s15430421tip4502_2

Connell, R. W. (2006). *Social gender*. Epikentro.

Conner, T., & Walker, A. (2025). Reciprocal Mentoring: The Secret to Thriving Change Leadership Partnerships. *Alabama Journal of Educational Leadership*, *12*, 74–93.

Connor, K. M., Davidson, J. R., Douzenis, A., Tsitas, N., & Tsigkaropoulou, E. (2012). Connor–Davidson Resilience Scale (CD-RISC-25) [Unofficial published translation of the Connor–Davidson Resilience Scale (CD-RISC)].

Connor, K. M., & Davidson, J. R. (2003). Development of a new resilience scale: The Connor–Davidson Resilience Scale (CD-RISC). *Depression and Anxiety*, *18*(2), 76–82. DOI: 10.1002/da.10113 PMID: 12964174

Conus, X., & Fahrni, L. (2017). Routine communication between teachers and parents from minority groups: An endless misunderstanding? *Educational Review*, *71*(2), 234–256. DOI: 10.1080/00131911.2017.1387098

Corcoran, R. P., Cheung, A. C. K., Kim, E., & Xie, C. (2018). Effective universal school-based social and emotional learning programs for improving academic achievement: A systematic review and meta-analysis of 50 years of research. *Educational Research Review*, *25*, 56–72. https://api.semanticscholar.org/CorpusID:149185325. DOI: 10.1016/j.edurev.2017.12.001

Cornell, D., & Huang, F. (2016). Authoritative school climate and high school student risk behavior: A cross-sectional multi-level analysis of student self-reports. *Journal of Youth and Adolescence*, *45*(11), 2246–2259. DOI: 10.1007/s10964-016-0424-3 PMID: 26781806

Correale, C., Crescimbene, L., Borgi, M., & Cirulli, F. (2017). Development of a dog-assisted activity program in an elementary classroom. *Veterinary Sciences*, *4*(4), 62. DOI: 10.3390/vetsci4040062

Council of Europe. (2019). *Gender mainstreaming toolkit for education*. Council of Europe.

Craig, F., Savino, R., Fanizza, I., Lucarelli, E., Russo, L., & Trabacca, A. (2020). A systematic review of coping strategies in parents of children with attention deficit hyperactivity disorder (ADHD). *Research in Developmental Disabilities*, *98*, 103571. DOI: 10.1016/j.ridd.2020.103571 PMID: 31931455

Crawford, C., & Burns, R. (2022). School culture, racial composition, and preventing violence: Evaluating punitive and supportive responses to improving safety. *Social Sciences (Basel, Switzerland)*, *11*(7), 270. DOI: 10.3390/socsci11070270

Crawford, R. (2020). Beyond the dots on the page: Harnessing transculturation and music education to address intercultural competence and social inclusion. *International Journal of Music Education*, *38*(4), 537–562. DOI: 10.1177/0255761420921585

Creswell, J. W., & Creswell, J. D. (2024). *Research design: Qualitative, quantitative, and mixed methods approaches* (7th ed.). Sage Publications.

Creswell, J. W., & Plano Clark, V. L. (2018). *Designing and conducting mixed methods research* (3rd ed.). Sage.

Crick, N. R., & Grotpeter, J. K. (1995). Relational aggression, gender, and social-psychological adjustment. *Child Development*, *66*(3), 710–722. DOI: 10.2307/1131945 PMID: 7789197

Crick, N. R., Ostrov, J. M., Burr, J. E., Cullerton-Sen, C., Jansen-Yeh, E., & Ralston, P. (2006). A longitudinal study of relational and physical aggression in preschool. *Journal of Applied Developmental Psychology*, *27*(3), 254–268. DOI: 10.1016/j.appdev.2006.02.006

Crisp, R. (2014). Well-being. In Zalta, E. N. (Ed.), *The Stanford encyclopedia of philosophy*. Stanford University., https://plato.stanford.edu/archives/win2014/entries/well-being/

Cui, L. (2022). The role of teacher-student relationships in predicting teachers' occupational wellbeing, emotional exhaustion, and enthusiasm. *Frontiers in Psychology*, *13*, 896813. Advance online publication. DOI: 10.3389/fpsyg.2022.896813 PMID: 35664194

Cyert, R. M., & March, J. G. (1963). *A behavioral theory of the firm*. Prentice-Hall.

Dalin, P. (1998). *School development: Theories and strategies: An international handbook*. Cassell.

Daly, B., & Suggs, S. (2010). Teachers' experiences with humane education and animals in the elementary classroom: Implications for empathy development. *Journal of Moral Education, 39*(1), 101–112. DOI: 10.1080/03057240903528733

Damschroder, L. J., Aron, D. C., Keith, R. E., Kirsh, S. R., Alexander, J. A., & Lowery, J. C. (2009). Fostering implementation of health services research findings into practice: A consolidated framework for advancing implementation science. *Implementation Science : IS, 4*(1), 50. DOI: 10.1186/1748-5908-4-50

Daniilidou, A., & Platsidou, M. (2018). Teachers' resilience scale: An integrated instrument for assessing protective factors of teachers' resilience. *Hellenic Journal of Psychology, 15*(1), 15–39.

Darling Rasmussen, P., Bilenberg, N., Kirubakaran, R., & Storebø, O. J. (2020). Mapping factors facilitating resilience in mothers—Potential clinical relevance for children with ADHD. *Nordic Journal of Psychiatry, 74*(7), 541–544. DOI: 10.1080/08039488.2020.1748899 PMID: 32255402

Darling, N., & Steinberg, L. (1993). Parenting style as context: An integrative model. *Psychological Bulletin, 113*(3), 487–496. DOI: 10.1037/0033-2909.113.3.487

Daryanani, I., Hamilton, J. L., Abramson, L. Y., & Alloy, L. B. (2016). Single mother parenting and adolescent psychopathology. *Journal of Abnormal Child Psychology, 44*(7), 1411–1423. DOI: 10.1007/s10802-016-0128-x PMID: 26767832

Datnow, A., & Park, V. (2018). *Professional collaboration with purpose: Teacher learning towards equitable and excellent schools*. Routledge., DOI: 10.4324/9781351165884

Davenport, T. H., & Prusak, L. (2000). *Working knowledge: How organizations manage what they know*. Harvard Business School Press.

Davidov, M., & Khoury-Kassabri, M. (2013). Recollections of harsh discipline in childhood and depressive feelings in adulthood: The roles of culture and gender. *Children and Youth Services Review, 35*(6), 1007–1014. DOI: 10.1016/j.childyouth.2013.03.009

Davidson, E., & Wright, L. H. V. (2020). Realising children's rights in an ACE-aware nation. *Scottish Affairs, 29*(4), 538–555. DOI: 10.3366/scot.2020.0343

Day, C., & Gu, Q. (2009). Teacher emotions: Well being and effectiveness. In Schutz, P. A., & Zembylas, M. (Eds.), *Advances in teacher emotion research: The impact on teachers' lives* (pp. 15–31). Springer. DOI: 10.1007/978-1-4419-0564-2_2

Day, C., & Gu, Q. (2013). *Resilient teachers, resilient schools: Building and sustaining quality in testing times*. Routledge. DOI: 10.4324/9780203578490

Deal, T., & Kennedy, A. (1982). *Corporate cultures: The rites and rituals of corporate life*. Wesley.

Deci, E. L., & Ryan, R. M. (2000). The "what" and "why" of goal pursuits: Human needs and the self-determination of behavior. *Psychological Inquiry*, *11*(4), 227–268. DOI: 10.1207/S15327965PLI1104_01

Delle Fave, A., Brdar, I., Freire, T., Vella-Brodrick, D., & Wissing, M. P. (2011). The eudaimonic and hedonic components of happiness: Qualitative and quantitative findings. *Social Indicators Research*, *100*(2), 185–207. DOI: 10.1007/s11205-010-9632-5

Denham, S. A. (2006). Social–emotional competence as support for school readiness: What is it and how do we assess it? *Early Education and Development*, *17*(1), 57–89. https://psycnet.apa.org/doi/10.1207/s15566935eed1701_4. DOI: 10.1207/s15566935eed1701_4

Denzin, N. K. (1978). *The research act: A theoretical introduction to sociological methods* (2nd ed.). McGraw-Hill.

Department of Education. (2023). *State of the nation 2022: Children and young people's wellbeing*. Government Social Research.

Department of the Prime Minister and Cabinet. (2021). *Children and youth wellbeing strategy: Annual report for the year ending 30 June 2020*. New Zealand Government.

Desimone, L. M., & Garet, M. S. (2015). Best practices in teachers' professional development in the United States. Psychology. *Social Education*, *7*(3), 252–263. DOI: 10.25115/psye.v7i3.515

Devos, G., Bouckenooghe, D., Engels, N., Hotton, G., & Aelterman, A. (2007). An assessment of well- being of principals in Flemish primary schools. *Journal of Educational Administration*, *45*(1), 33–61. DOI: 10.1108/09578230710722449

Diamond, A. (2013). Executive functions. *Annual Review of Psychology*, *64*(1), 135–168. DOI: 10.1146/annurev-psych-113011-143750

Dietz, T. J., Davis, D., & Pennings, J. (2012). Evaluating animal-assisted therapy in group treatment for child sexual abuse. *Journal of Child Sexual Abuse, 21*(6), 665–683. DOI: 10.1080/10538712.2012.726700

Dignath, C., Buettner, G., & Langfeldt, H. P. (2008). How can primary school students learn self-regulated learning strategies most effectively? A meta-analysis on self-regulation training programmes. *Educational Research Review, 3*(2), 101–129. DOI: 10.1016/j.edurev.2008.02.003

Dignath, C., & Büttner, G. (2008). Components of fostering self-regulated learning among students. A meta-analysis on intervention studies at primary and secondary school level. *Metacognition and Learning, 3*(3), 231–264. DOI: 10.1007/s11409-008-9029-x

Dillman, D. A., Smyth, J. D., & Christian, L. M. (2014). *Internet, phone, mail, and mixed-mode surveys: The tailored design method* (4th ed.). John Wiley & Sons. DOI: 10.1002/9781394260645

Dimitra Sakka, D., & Aris Markos, A. (2013). From the adolescents' perspective: Violence and aggression at school in relation to ethnocultural background and gender. *Scientific Yearbook of the School of Philosophy. Developmental Psychology, 1*, 127–162.

Dixon, N. (1994). *The organizational learning cycle: How we can learn collectively*. McGraw-Hill.

Dodge, K. A. (1991). The structure and function of reactive and proactive aggression. *The development and treatment of childhood aggression, 16*(5), 201-218.

Dollarhide, C. T., & Saginak, K. A. (2011). *Comprehensive school counseling programs: K-12 delivery systems in action*. Pearson Higher Ed.

Dollman, E. (2023). The Value of Music Education for Child Development and Wellbeing in the Post COVID-19 Landscape. In White, M. A., McCallum, F., & Boyle, C. (Eds.), *New Research and Possibilities in Wellbeing Education*. Springer., DOI: 10.1007/978-981-99-5609-8_7

Domitrovich, C. E., Durlak, J. A., Staley, K. C., & Weissberg, R. P. (2017). Social-emotional competence: An essential factor for promoting positive adjustment and reducing risk in school children. *Child Development, 88*(2), 408–416. DOI: 10.1111/cdev.12739

Dor, A. (2018). Parent–teacher Communication: The Case of Diverse Family Patterns. *Education and Society (Melbourne), 36*(1), 5–20. DOI: 10.7459/es/36.1.02

Dreer, B. (2024). Teachers' well-being and job satisfaction: The important role of positive emotions in the workplace. *Educational Studies*, *50*(1), 61–77. DOI: 10.1080/03055698.2021.1940872

Dreer-Goethe, B. (2026). Moments that matter: How critical incidents shape the well-being of student teachers during their practicum. *Research Papers in Education*, •••, 1–25. DOI: 10.1080/02671522.2026.2659788

DuFour, R., & Eaker, R. (1998). *Professional learning communities at work: Best practices for enhancing student achievement*. National Education Service.

DuFour, R., & Fullan, M. (2013). *Cultures built to last: Systemic PLCs at work TM*. Solution Tree Press.

Dufur, M. J., Howell, N. C., Downey, D. B., Ainsworth, J. W., & Lapray, A. J. (2010). Sex differences in parenting behaviors in single-mother and single-father households. *Journal of Marriage and Family*, *72*(5), 1092–1106. DOI: 10.1111/j.1741-3737.2010.00752.x

Duman, S., & Margolin, G. (2007). Parents' aggressive influences and children's aggressive problem solutions with peers. *Journal of Clinical Child and Adolescent Psychology*, *36*(1), 42–55. DOI: 10.1207/s15374424jccp3601_5 PMID: 17206880

Durlak, J. A., Weissberg, R. P., Dymnicki, A. B., Taylor, R. D., & Schellinger, K. B. (2011). The Impact of Enhancing Students' Social and Emotional Learning: A Meta-Analysis of School-Based Universal Interventions. *Child Development*, *82*(1), 405–432. DOI: 10.1111/j.1467-8624.2010.01564.x PMID: 21291449

Dwairy, M., Achoui, M., Abouserie, R., Farah, A., Sakhleh, A. A., Fayad, M., & Khan, H. K. (2006). Parenting styles in Arab societies: A first cross-regional research study. *Journal of Cross-Cultural Psychology*, *37*(3), 230–247. DOI: 10.1177/0022022106286922

Eamon, M. K., & Zuehl, R. M. (2001). Maternal depression and physical punishment as mediators of the effect of poverty on socioemotional problems of children in single-mother families. *The American Journal of Orthopsychiatry*, *71*(2), 218–226. DOI: 10.1037/0002-9432.71.2.218 PMID: 11347362

Edmondson, A. (1999). Psychological safety and learning behavior in work teams. *Administrative Science Quarterly*, *44*(2), 350–383. DOI: 10.2307/2666999

Edmondson, A. C., & Lei, Z. (2014). Psychological safety: The history, renaissance, and future of an interpersonal construct. *Annual Review of Organizational Psychology and Organizational Behavior*, *1*(1), 23–43. DOI: 10.1146/annurev-orgpsych-031413-091305

Education Support Partnership. (2019). *Health survey 2017: The mental health and wellbeing of education professionals in the UK*. YouGov. https://www.educationsupport.org.uk/sites/default/files/education_staff_health_survey_2017.pdf

Efrati-Virtzer, M., & Margalit, M. (2009). Student's behavior difficulties, sense of coherence and adjustment at school: Risk and protective factors. *European Journal of Special Needs Education*, *24*(1), 59–73. DOI: 10.1080/08856250802596758

Eger, R. J., & Maridal, J. H. (2015). A statistical meta-analysis of the wellbeing literature. *International Journal of Wellbeing*, *5*(1), 45–74. DOI: 10.5502/ijw.v5i2.4

Ehrenreich, S. E., Beron, K. J., Brinkley, D. Y., & Underwood, M. K. (2014). Family predictors of continuity and change in social and physical aggression from ages 9 to 18. *Aggressive Behavior*, *40*(5), 421–439. DOI: 10.1002/ab.21535 PMID: 24888340

Ein, N., Li, L., & Vickers, K. (2018). The effect of pet therapy on the physiological and subjective stress response: A meta-analysis. *Stress and Health*, *34*(4), 477–489. DOI: 10.1002/smi.2812

Elbers, E., & de Haan, M. (2014). Parent–teacher conferences in Dutch culturally diverse schools: Participation and conflict in institutional context. *Learning, Culture and Social Interaction*, *3*(4), 252–266. DOI: 10.1016/j.lcsi.2014.01.004

Elias, M. J., Zins, J. E., & Weissberg, R. P. (1997). *Promoting social and emotional learning: Guidelines for educators*. Association for Supervision and Curriculum Development.

Epstein, J. L. (2018). *School, Family, and community Partnerships: Preparing Educators and Improving Schools*. Routledge., DOI: 10.4324/9780429494673

Epstein, J. L., & Sheldon, S. B. (2019). The importance of evaluating programs of school, family, and community partnerships. *Aula Abierta*, *48*(1), 31–42. DOI: 10.17811/rifie.48.1.2019.31-42

Erez, M., & Gati, E. (2004). A dynamic, multi-level model of culture: From the micro level of the individual to the macro level of a global culture. *Applied Psychology*, *53*(4), 583–598. DOI: 10.1111/j.1464-0597.2004.00190.x

Erginyavuz, K. A., & Özdemir, N. (2019). Determination of the anxiety, depression and psychological resilience levels of mothers with children diagnosed with attention deficit hyperactivity disorder: Anxiety, depression and psychological resilience levels of mothers with. *Medical Science and Discovery*, *6*(10), 249–256. DOI: 10.36472/msd.v6i10.306

European Observatory on Health Systems and Policies. Eriksen, A., De Bock, F., Alayli, A., Boode, K., et al. (2025). *Improving reach and access to health promotion and preventive services for vulnerable children and adolescents: Experiences from five European countries.* World Health Organization Regional Office for Europe.

Fan, X., & Chen, M. (2001). Parental Involvement and Students' Academic Achievement: A Meta-Analysis. *Educational Psychology Review, 13*(1), 1–22. DOI: 10.1023/A:1009048817385

Faraone, S. V., Asherson, P., Banaschewski, T., Biederman, J., Buitelaar, J. K., Ramos-Quiroga, J. A., & Franke, B. (2015). Attention-deficit/hyperactivity disorder. *Nature Reviews. Disease Primers, 1*(1), 1–23. DOI: 10.1038/nrdp.2015.20 PMID: 27189265

Farrand, K. M., & Jung, J. Y. (2025). Exploring how a therapy dog intervention in a Tier 3 classroom influences mental health components of well-being: A case study. *Behavioral Sciences (Basel, Switzerland), 15*(11), 1585. DOI: 10.3390/bs15111585

Fayyad, J., Haro, J. M., Aguilar-Gaxiola, S., & Kessler, R. C. (2018). Attention-deficit. Mental Disorders Around the World: Facts and Figures from the WHO World Mental Health Surveys, 195.

Fedor, J. (2018). Animal-assisted therapy supports student connectedness. *NASN School Nurse, 33*(6), 355–358. DOI: 10.1177/1942602X18776424

Fegter, S., & Fattore, T. (2024). Child well-being als Zugang zu Lebenswelten, Lebenslagen und Bildungsräumen. In Schierbaum, A., Diederichs, M., & Schierbaum, K. (Eds.), *Kind(er) und Kindheit(en) im Blick der Forschung* (Vol. 30, pp. 145–166). Springer VS., DOI: 10.1007/978-3-658-42625-5_8

Feng, Y., & Wang, M. (2025). Effect of music therapy on emotional resilience, well-being, and employability: A quantitative investigation of mediation and moderation. *BMC Psychology, 13*(1), 189. Advance online publication. DOI: 10.1186/s40359-024-02336-x PMID: 39825434

Fernandez-Molina, M., Hernandez-Prados, M. A., & Belmonte, M. L. (2019). Teacher emotional competence and well-being in the educational context. *International Journal of Environmental Research and Public Health, 16*(20), 4065. Advance online publication. DOI: 10.3390/ijerph16204065

Filias, V. (1996). *Introduction to the methodology and techniques of social research.* Gutenberg.

Finger, L., Sprinks, J., van den Born, R. J. G., & van den Berg, L. (2023). The science of citizen science: A systematic literature review on educational and scientific outcomes. *Frontiers in Education, 8*, 1226529. DOI: 10.3389/feduc.2023.1226529

Fisher, J. W. (2020). Reconsidering spiritual well-being: Complexity, plurality and practice. *Religions, 11*(1), 26. Advance online publication. DOI: 10.3390/rel11010026

Fishstrom, S., Capin, P., Fall, A. M., Roberts, G., Grills, A. E., & Vaughn, S. (2024). Understanding the relation between reading and anxiety among upper elementary students with reading difficulties. *Annals of Dyslexia, 74*(1), 123–141. DOI: 10.1007/s11881-024-00299-7

Fixsen, D. L., Naoom, S. F., Blase, K. A., Friedman, R. M., & Wallace, F. (2005). *Implementation research: A synthesis of the literature*. University of South Florida, Louis de la Parte Florida Mental Health Institute, National Implementation Research Network. https://fpg.unc.edu/sites/fpg.unc.edu/files/resource-files/NIRN-MonographFull-01-2005.pdf

Flick, U. (2014). *An introduction to qualitative research* (5th ed.). Sage.

Flood, R. L., & Romm, N. R. A. (1996). Contours of diversity management and triple-loop learning. *Kybernetes, 25*(7/8), 154–163. DOI: 10.1108/03684929610149747

Forman, S. G., Olin, S. S., Hoagwood, K. E., Crowe, M., & Saka, N. (2009). Evidence-based interventions in schools: Developers' views of implementation barriers and facilitators. *School Mental Health, 1*(1), 26–36. DOI: 10.1007/s12310-008-9002-5

Forsström, S., Morten, M., Munthe, E., Alvarez-Galvan, J.-L., & Houldsworth, L. (2025). The impact of digital technologies on students' learning: Results from a literature review. *OECD Education Working Paper No. 335*. https://dx.doi.org/ DOI: 10.1787/19939019

Fossati, P. (2026). Correlated subjects: Relational ethics and veterinary legal accountability in animal-assisted interventions. *Animals (Basel), 16*(1), 92. DOI: 10.3390/ani16010092

Francis, J., Trapp, G., Pearce, N., Burns, S., & Cross, D. (2022). School Built Environments and Bullying Behaviour: A Conceptual Model Based on Qualitative Interviews. *International Journal of Environmental Research and Public Health, 19*(23), 15955. DOI: 10.3390/ijerph192315955 PMID: 36498029

Fredricks, J. A., Blumenfeld, P. C., & Paris, A. H. (2004). School engagement: Potential of the concept, state of the evidence. *Review of Educational Research, 74*(1), 59–109. DOI: 10.3102/00346543074001059

Fredrickson, B. L. (2001). The role of positive emotions in positive psychology: The broaden-and-build theory of positive emotions. *The American Psychologist*, *56*(3), 218–226. DOI: 10.1037/0003-066X.56.3.218

Friedman, N. P., & Miyake, A. (2017). Unity and diversity of executive functions: Individual differences as a window on cognitive structure. *Cortex*, *86*, 186–204. DOI: 10.1016/j.cortex.2016.04.023

Fuchs, C., & Hofkirchner, W. (2009). Autopoiesis and critical social theory. *Kybernetes*, *38*(6), 1112–1129.

Fujisawa, H., Kumasaka, T., & Kudo, K. (2022). Effects of animal-assisted activities on stress reduction in nursery school teachers. *International Medical Journal*, *29*(5), 269–272. DOI: 10.1016/j.pedn.2017.05.006

Fullan, M. (1996). Turning systemic thinking on its head. *Phi Delta Kappan*, *77*(6), 420–423.

Fullan, M. (2005). The Meaning of Educational Change: A Quarter of a Century of Learning. In Lieberman, A. (Ed.), *The Roots of Educational Change: International handbook of educational change* (pp. 202–216). Springer., DOI: 10.1007/1-4020-4451-8_12

Fullan, M. (2007). *The new meaning of educational change* (4th ed.). Teachers College Press.

Fullan, M. (2020). *Leading in a culture of change* (2nd ed.). Jossey-Bass.

Fung, A. L. C., Gerstein, L. H., Chan, Y., & Hurley, E. (2013). Children's aggression, parenting styles, and distress for Hong Kong parents. *Journal of Family Violence*, *28*(5), 515–521. Advance online publication. DOI: 10.1007/s10896-013-9518-9

Fung, S.-C. (2019). Effect of a canine-assisted read aloud intervention on reading ability and physiological response: A pilot study. *Animals (Basel)*, *9*(8), 474. DOI: 10.3390/ani9080474

Gaertner, B. M., Spinrad, T. L., Eisenberg, N., & Greving, K. A. (2007). Parental childrearing attitudes as correlates of father involvement during infancy. *Journal of Marriage and Family*, *69*(4), 962–976. DOI: 10.1111/j.1741-3737.2007.00424.x PMID: 18174913

Gaffney, H., Farrington, D. P., & Ttofi, M. M. (2021). School-based anti-bullying programs: A meta-analysis. *Aggression and Violent Behavior*, *58*, 101611. DOI: 10.1016/j.avb.2020.101611

Gagné, R. M. (1975). *Essentials of learning for instruction*. Dryden Press.

Gámez-Genovart, M., Oliver-Trobat, M. F., & Rosselló-Ramon, M. R. (2025). Research on teacher well-being: A systematic review. *Teaching and Teacher Education, 168*, 105264. DOI: 10.1016/j.tate.2025.105264

Gao, Y., Zhang, W., & Fung, A. L. C. (2015). The associations between parenting styles and proactive and reactive aggression in Hong Kong children and adolescents. *International Journal of Psychology, 50*(6), 463–471. DOI: 10.1002/ijop.12104 PMID: 25292156

Garcés-Prettel, M., Santoya-Montes, Y., & Jiménez-Osorio, J. (2020). Influence of family and pedagogical communication on school violence. *Media Education Research Journal, 63*(28), 73–82. DOI: 10.3916/C63-2020-07

Gee, N. R., Crist, E. N., & Carr, D. N. (2010). Preschool children require fewer instructional prompts to perform a memory task in the presence of a dog. *Anthrozoos, 23*(2), 173–184. DOI: 10.2752/175303710X12682332910051

Gee, N. R., Griffin, J. A., & McCardle, P. M. (2017). Human–animal interaction research in school settings: Current knowledge and future directions. *AERA Open, 3*(3), 1–9. DOI: 10.1177/2332858417724346

Gee, N. R., Sherlock, T. R., Bennett, E. A., & Harris, S. L. (2009). Preschoolers' adherence to instructions as a function of presence of a dog and motor skills task. *Anthrozoos, 22*(3), 267–276. DOI: 10.2752/175303709X457603

Geertz, C. (1973). *The interpretation of cultures*. Basic Books.

Gehle, M., Trautner, M., & Schwinger, M. (2023). Motivational self-regulation in children with mild learning difficulties during middle childhood: Do they use motivational regulation strategies effectively? *Journal of Applied Developmental Psychology, 84*, 101487. Advance online publication. DOI: 10.1016/j.appdev.2022.101487

Gehle, R., Dörrenbächer, S., & Perels, F. (2023). Teachers' promotion of self-regulated learning in inclusive classrooms: Current developments and future directions. *Teaching and Teacher Education, 125*, 104054. DOI: 10.1016/j.tate.2023.104054

Geissler, H. (1995). *Organisationslernen und Wissensmanagement* [Organizational learning and knowledge management]. R. Oldenbourg Verlag.

Gelfer, J. I. (1991). Teacher–Parent Partnerships: Enhancing Communications. *Childhood Education, 67*(3), 164–167. DOI: 10.1080/00094056.1991.10521602

George, B. B., Dangroo, A. A., Sahu, K. K., & Arun, P. (2024). Stress, coping, and resilience among mothers of children with attention deficit hyperactivity disorder. *Indian Journal of Psychiatric Social Work*, •••, 17–27.

Georgiou, S. N., Fousiani, K., Michaelides, M., & Stavrinides, P. (2013). Cultural value orientation and authoritarian parenting as parameters of bullying and victimization at school. *International Journal of Psychology*, *48*(1), 69–78. DOI: 10.1080/00207594.2012.754104 PMID: 23390974

Gershoff, E. T., Grogan-Kaylor, A., Lansford, J. E., Chang, L., Zelli, A., Deater-Deckard, K., & Dodge, K. A. (2010). Parent discipline practices in an international sample: Associations with child behaviors and moderation by perceived normativeness. *Child Development*, *81*(2), 487–502. DOI: 10.1111/j.1467-8624.2009.01409.x PMID: 20438455

Ghani, F. B. A., Roeswardi, S. I., & Aziz, A. A. (2014). Parenting styles and their relation to teenagers' personality profile in single-mother families: A case study. *Procedia: Social and Behavioral Sciences*, *114*, 766–770. DOI: 10.1016/j.sbspro.2013.12.782

Ghinea, V. M., & Bratianu, C. (2012). Organizational culture modeling. *Management & Marketing*, *7*(2), 257–276.

Gibson, E. M., Certion, C. B., & Aldridge, L. D. (2022). The ASCA national model. In Edwards, C. N., & Graham, M. A. (Eds.), *Foundations of School Counseling: Innovation in Professional Practice* (pp. 57–72). Springer Publishing., DOI: 10.1891/9780826187536.0004

Gillett-Swan, J., & Baroutsis, A. (2023). Student voice and teacher voice in educational research: A systematic review of 25 years of literature. *Oxford Review of Education*, *50*(4), 533–551. DOI: 10.1080/03054985.2023.2257132

Gin, K., Stewart, C., & Jolley, S. (2021). A systematic literature review of childhood externalizing psychopathology and later psychotic symptoms. *Clinical Psychology & Psychotherapy*, *28*(1), 56–78. DOI: 10.1002/cpp.2493 PMID: 32681551

Gisewhite, R. A., Jeanfreau, M. M., & Holden, C. L. (2021). A call for ecologically-based teacher–parent communication skills training in pre-service teacher education programmes. *Educational Review*, *73*(5), 597–616. DOI: 10.1080/00131911.2019.1666794

Glenk, L. M., & Foltin, S. (2021). Therapy dog welfare revisited: A review of the literature. *Veterinary Sciences*, *8*(10), 226. DOI: 10.3390/vetsci8100226

Goldstein, S., & Brooks, R. B. (Eds.). (2023). *Handbook of resilience in children* (3rd ed.). Springer., DOI: 10.1007/978-3-031-14728-9

Gómez-Ortiz, O., Del Rey, R., Casas, J. A., & Ortega-Ruiz, R. (2014). Parenting styles and bullying involvement. *C&E, Cultura y Educación, 26*(1), 132–158. DOI: 10.1080/11356405.2014.908665

Goodall, J., & Montgomery, C. (2014). Parental involvement to parental engagement: A continuum. *Educational Review, 66*(4), 399–410. DOI: 10.1080/00131911.2013.781576

Goodman-Scott, E., & Ockerman, M. S. (2023). Integrating school counseling and MTSS. In Goodman-Scott, E., & Ockerman, M. S. (Eds.), *The school counselor's guide to multi-tiered systems of support* (2nd ed., pp. 3–35). Routledge., DOI: 10.4324/9781003317454-1

Goodmon, L. B., Burnett, P. R., Pack, R., & Powell, R. (2021). The effect of a dog assisted reading program on the reading ability and motivation of children with dyslexia. *Human Animal Interactions Bulletin, 9*(2), 1–26. DOI: 10.1079/hai.2021.0031

Gorostiaga, A., Aliri, J., Balluerka, N., & Lameirinhas, J. (2019). Parenting styles and internalizing symptoms in adolescence: A systematic literature review. *International Journal of Environmental Research and Public Health, 16*(17), 3192. DOI: 10.3390/ijerph16173192 PMID: 31480548

Grant, C. A., Gardner, K., Cavendish, W., & Moltzen, R. (2021). The professional wellbeing of educators: A review. *Educational Research Review, 34*, 100411. Advance online publication. DOI: 10.1016/j.edurev.2021.100411

Graziano, P. A., Reavis, R. D., Keane, S. P., & Calkins, S. D. (2007). The role of emotion regulation in children's early academic success. *Journal of School Psychology, 45*(1), 3–19. DOI: 10.1016/j.jsp.2006.09.002

Green, E. G., Deschamps, J. C., & Paez, D. (2005). Variation of individualism and collectivism within and between 20 countries: A typological analysis. *Journal of Cross-Cultural Psychology, 36*(3), 321–339. DOI: 10.1177/0022022104273654

Griffin, J. A., Hurley, K., & McCune, S. (2019). Human–animal interaction research: Progress and possibilities. *Frontiers in Psychology, 10*, 2803. Advance online publication. DOI: 10.3389/fpsyg.2019.02803

Griffin, K. W., Botvin, G. J., Scheier, L. M., Diaz, T., & Miller, N. L. (2000). Parenting practices as predictors of substance use, delinquency, and aggression among urban minority youth: Moderating effects of family structure and gender. *Psychology of Addictive Behaviors, 14*(2), 174–184. DOI: 10.1037/0893-164X.14.2.174 PMID: 10860116

Grimmett, H., Forgasz, R., Williams, J., & White, S. (2018). Reimagining the role of mentor teachers in professional experience: Moving to I as fellow teacher educator. *Asia-Pacific Journal of Teacher Education, 46*(4), 340–353. DOI: 10.1080/1359866X.2018.1437391

Griva, E., & Stamou, A. G. (2014). *Investigating bilingualism in the school environment: Perspectives of teachers, students, and immigrant parents.* Kyriakidis Publications.

Groenewoud, D., Enders-Slegers, M. J., Leontjevas, R., van Dijke, A., de Winkel, T., & Hediger, K. (2023). Children's bond with companion animals and associations with psychosocial health: A systematic review. *Frontiers in Psychology, 14*, 1120000. DOI: 10.3389/fpsyg.2023.1120000

Grové, C., Henderson, L., Lee, F., & Wardlaw, P. (2021). Therapy dogs in educational settings: Guidelines and recommendations for implementation. *Frontiers in Veterinary Science, 8*, 655104. DOI: 10.3389/fvets.2021.655104

Gryczkowski, M. R., Jordan, S. S., & Mercer, S. H. (2010). Differential relations between mothers' and fathers' parenting practices and child externalizing behavior. *Journal of Child and Family Studies, 19*(5), 539–546. DOI: 10.1007/s10826-009-9326-2

Gugel, G. (2018). Warum sind Menschen gewalttätig? Ursachen von Aggression und Gewalt. *Bürger & Staat, 68*(3), 113–119. https://www.buergerundstaat.de/3_18/gewalt.pdf

Gunnar, M., & Quevedo, K. (2007). The neurobiology of stress and development. *Annual Review of Psychology, 58*(1), 145–173. DOI: 10.1146/annurev.psych.58.110405.085605

Gu, Q. (2014). The role of relational resilience in teachers' career-long commitment and effectiveness. *Teachers and Teaching, 20*(5), 502–529. DOI: 10.1080/13540602.2014.937961

Gu, Q., & Day, C. (2013). Challenges to teacher resilience: Conditions count. *British Educational Research Journal, 39*(1), 22–44. DOI: 10.1080/01411926.2011.623152

Habermas, J. (1987). *The theory of communicative action, Volume 2: Lifeworld and system.* Beacon Press.

Hackman, J. R., & Oldham, G. R. (1980). *Work redesign.* Addison-Wesley.

Hadjicharalambous, D., & Demetriou, L. (2020). The Relationship Between Parents' Demographic Factors and Parenting Styles: Effects on Children's Psychological Adjustment. *Psychology Research (Libertyville, Ill.), 10*(4), 125–138. DOI: 10.17265/2159-5542/2020.04.001

Hagemann-White, C. (2020). *Gewalt und Geschlecht: Gewaltverhältnisse & Gewaltdynamiken*. Universitätsklinikum Ulm, Klinik für Kinder- und Jugendpsychiatrie/ Psychotherapie (KJPP). https://www.academia.edu/71972478/Hagemann_White _2020_Gewalt_und_Geschlecht

Hallam, S., & Himonides, E. (2022). *The power of music: An exploration of the evidence* (2nd ed.). Open Book Publishers., DOI: 10.11647/OBP.0292

Hallinger, P. (2003). Leading educational change: Reflections on the practice of instructional and transformational leadership. *Cambridge Journal of Education, 33*(3), 329–352. DOI: 10.1080/0305764032000122005

Hallinger, P., & Heck, R. H. (2010). Collaborative leadership and school improvement: Understanding the impact on school capacity and student learning. *School Leadership & Management, 30*(2), 95–110. DOI: 10.1080/13632431003663214

Hall, S. S., Gee, N. R., & Mills, D. S. (2016). Children Reading to Dogs: A Systematic Review of the Literature. *PLoS One, 11*(2), e0149759. Advance online publication. DOI: 10.1371/journal.pone.0149759

Hamm, J. E., & Mousseau, A. D. S. (2023). Predicting Parent Trust Based on Professionals' Communication Skills. *Education Sciences, 13*(4), 350. DOI: 10.3390/ educsci13040350

Hamre, B. K., & Pianta, R. C. (2001). Early teacher–child relationships and the trajectory of children's school outcomes through eighth grade. *Child Development, 72*(2), 625–638. DOI: 10.1111/1467-8624.00301

Harborne, A., Wolpert, M., & Clare, L. (2004). Making sense of ADHD: A battle for understanding? Parents' views of their children being diagnosed with ADHD. *Clinical Child Psychology and Psychiatry, 9*(3), 327–339. DOI: 10.1177/1359104504043915

Hargreaves, A. (2019). *Teacher well-being: Its meaning and its measurement* (OECD Education Working Papers No. 213). OECD Publishing. https://doi.org/ DOI: 10.1787/c1aa7a2d-en

Hargreaves, A. (2001). *Changing teachers, changing times: Teachers' work and culture in the postmodern age*. Teachers College Press.

Hargreaves, A. (2005). Educational change takes ages: Life, career and generational factors in teachers' emotional responses to educational change. *Teaching and Teacher Education, 21*(8), 967–983. DOI: 10.1016/j.tate.2005.06.007

Hargreaves, A., & O'Connor, M. T. (2018). *Collaborative professionalism: When teaching together means learning for all.* Corwin. DOI: 10.4135/9781506328133

Harpin, V. A. (2005). The effect of ADHD on the life of an individual, their family, and community from preschool to adult life. *Archives of Disease in Childhood, 90*(suppl_1), i2–i7. DOI: 10.1136/adc.2004.059006 PMID: 15665153

Harris, A., & Jones, M. (2020). COVID-19 – School leadership in disruptive times. *School Leadership & Management, 40*(4), 243–247. DOI: 10.1080/13632434.2020.1811479

Harris, A., Jones, M., & Ismail, N. (2022). Distributed leadership: Taking a retrospective and contemporary view of the evidence base. *School Leadership & Management, 42*(5), 438–456. DOI: 10.1080/13632434.2022.2109620

Harrison, H. F., Kinsella, E. A., Loftus, S., DeLuca, S., McGovern, G., Belanger, I., & Eugenio, T. (2024). "Nurturing a trusting learning community": Perceptions of relationships in a health professions education peer mentorship program. *International Journal of Mentoring and Coaching in Education, 13*(1), 55–72. DOI: 10.1108/IJMCE-08-2022-0065

Harter, J. K., Schmidt, F. L., & Keyes, C. L. M. (2002). Well-Being in the workplace and its relationship to Business Outcomes: A review of the Gallup studies. In Keyes, C. L., & Haidt, J. (Eds.), *Flourishing: The positive person and the good life* (pp. 205–224). American Psychological Association.

Hascher, T., Beltman, S., & Mansfield, C. (2021). Teacher wellbeing and resilience: Towards an integrative model. *Educational Research, 63*(4), 416–439. DOI: 10.1080/00131881.2021.1980416

Hattie, J. (2009). *Visible learning: A synthesis of over 800 meta-analyses relating to achievement.* Routledge.

Hatzichristou, C., Lampropoulou, A., & Adamopoulou, E. (2012). Psychological resilience: Basic issues of children's development and adjustment (pp. 1–6).

Hawkins, D. N., Amato, P. R., & King, V. (2006). Parent-adolescent involvement: The relative influence of parent gender and residence. *Journal of Marriage and Family, 68*(1), 125–136. DOI: 10.1111/j.1741-3737.2006.00238.x

Hawkins, R. D., & Williams, J. M. (2017). Assessing effectiveness of a nonhuman animal welfare education program for primary school children. *Journal of Applied Animal Welfare Science, 20*(3), 240–256. DOI: 10.1080/10888705.2017.1305272

Hawkins, R. D., & Williams, J. M. (2017). Childhood attachment to pets: Associations between pet attachment, attitudes to animals, compassion, and humane behaviour. *International Journal of Environmental Research and Public Health, 14*(5), 490. DOI: 10.3390/ijerph14050490

Head, G. (2020). Ethics in educational research: Review boards, ethical issues and researcher development. *European Educational Research Journal, 19*(1), 72–83. DOI: 10.1177/1474904118796315

Hedberg, B. (1981). How organizations learn and unlearn. In Nystrom, P. C., & Starbuck, W. H. (Eds.), *Handbook of organizational design: Adapting organizations to their environment* (Vol. 1, pp. 3–27). Oxford University Press.

Hediger, K., Meisser, A., & Zinsstag, J. (2019). A One Health research framework for animal-assisted interventions. *International Journal of Environmental Research and Public Health, 16*(4), 640. DOI: 10.3390/ijerph16040640

Hediger, K., & Turner, D. C. (2014). Can dogs increase children's attention and concentration performance? A randomised controlled trial. *Human Animal Interactions Bulletin, 2*(2), 21–39. DOI: 10.1079/hai.2014.0010

Heiliger, A. (2001). Gewalt in der Schule: Geschlechterdifferenzierung und Handlungsperspektiven. *Pädagogisches Forum, 6*, 448–453.

Heinla, E., & Kuurme, T. (2024). The impact of school culture, school climate, and teachers' job satisfaction on the teacher-student relationship: A case study in four Estonian schools. *Research Papers in Education, 39*(3), 439–465. DOI: 10.1080/02671522.2022.2150883

Helliwell, J. F., Layard, R., Sachs, J., & De Neve, J. E. (2020). World happiness report 2020. *Sustainable Development Solutions Network.* https://worldhappiness.report/ed/2020

Henderson, L., Grové, C., Lee, F., Trainer, L., Schena, H., & Prentice, M. (2020). An evaluation of a dog-assisted reading program to support student wellbeing in primary school. *Children and Youth Services Review, 118*, 105449. Advance online publication. DOI: 10.1016/j.childyouth.2020.105449

Henley, J. (2025). *Inclusive pedagogy in music education.* Routledge., DOI: 10.4324/9781003414261

Hergovich, A., Monshi, B., Semmler, G., & Zieglmayer, V. (2002). The effects of the presence of a dog in the classroom. *Anthrozoos*, *15*(1), 37–50. DOI: 10.2752/089279302786992775

Hesari, N. K. Z., & Hejazi, E. (2011). The mediating role of self esteem in the relationship between the authoritative parenting style and aggression. *Procedia: Social and Behavioral Sciences*, *30*, 1724–1730. DOI: 10.1016/j.sbspro.2011.10.333

Hidayat, H., & Arini, F. D. (2022). Exploring Factors of the Parent–Teacher Partnership Affecting Learning Outcomes: Empirical Study in the Early Childhood Education Context. *International Journal of Instruction*, *15*(4), 411–434. https://www.e-iji.net/dosyalar/iji_2022_4_23.pdf. DOI: 10.29333/iji.2022.15423a

Hill, N. E. (1995). The relationship between family environment and parenting style: A preliminary study of African American families. *The Journal of Black Psychology*, *21*(4), 408–423. DOI: 10.1177/00957984950214007

Hill, N. E., & Tyson, D. F. (2009). Parental involvement in middle school: A meta-analytic assessment of the strategies that promote achievement. *Developmental Psychology*, *45*(3), 740–763. DOI: 10.1037/a0015362 PMID: 19413429

Hirst, J. C. (2021). *Perspectives on the Use of Technology as a Home–School Communication and Parent Partnership Tool*. Walden University Scholar Works. https://scholarworks.waldenu.edu/cgi/viewcontent.cgi?article=11992&context=dissertations

Hoagwood, K. E., Acri, M., Morrissey, M., & Peth-Pierce, R. (2017). Animal-assisted therapies for youth with or at risk for mental health problems: A systematic review. *Applied Developmental Science*, *21*(1), 1–13. DOI: 10.1080/10888691.2015.1134267

Hoang, K., Grow, H. M., Rooholamini, S. N., McPhillips, H., Selling, S. K., Rassbach, C. E., & Blankenburg, R. (2024). Impact of longitudinal coaching on pediatric residents' professional identity formation: A multi-institution qualitative study. *Academic Pediatrics*, *24*(5), 866–874. DOI: 10.1016/j.acap.2024.04.012

Hoffmann, T. C., Glasziou, P. P., Boutron, I., Milne, R., Perera, R., Moher, D., Altman, D. G., Barbour, V., Macdonald, H., Johnston, M., Lamb, S. E., Dixon-Woods, M., McCulloch, P., Wyatt, J. C., Chan, A.-W., & Michie, S. (2014). Better reporting of interventions: Template for intervention description and replication (TIDieR) checklist and guide. *BMJ (Clinical research ed.), 348*. DOI: 10.1136/bmj.g1687

Hofherr, S., & Kindler, H. (2018). Sexuelle Übergriffe in Schulen aus der Sicht von Schülerinnen und Schülern: Zusammenhänge zum Erleben von Schule und der Bereitschaft zur Hilfesuche. In Andresen, S., & Tippelt, R. (Eds.), *Sexuelle Gewalt in Kindheit und Jugend: Theoretische, empirische und konzeptionelle Erkenntnisse und Herausforderungen erziehungswissenschaftlicher Forschung* (pp. 95–110). Beltz Juventa., DOI: 10.25656/01:22311

Hofstede, G. (2011). Dimensionalizing Cultures: The Hofstede Model in Context. *Online Readings in Psychology and Culture*, *2*(1). Advance online publication. DOI: 10.9707/2307-0919.1014

Hogue, B., Xue, M., & Wessel-Powell, C. (2025). A self-study of bi-directional mentoring relationships within an early literacy methods course. *Studying Teacher Education*, *21*(3), 318–341. DOI: 10.1080/17425964.2025.2552649

Hone, L., Schofield, G., & Jarden, A. (2016). Conceptualizations of wellbeing: Insights from a prototype analysis on New Zealand workers. *New Zealand Journal of Human Resource Management*, *12*(1), 97–118.

Hosokawa, R., & Katsura, T. (2019). Role of Parenting Style in Children's Behavioral Problems Through the Transition from Preschool to Elementary School According to Gender in Japan. *International Journal of Environmental Research and Public Health*, *16*(1), 21–38. DOI: 10.3390/ijerph16010021 PMID: 30577659

Hostinar, C. E., Sullivan, R. M., & Gunnar, M. R. (2014). Psychobiological mechanisms underlying the social buffering of the hypothalamic–pituitary–adrenocortical axis: A review of animal models and human studies across development. *Psychological Bulletin*, *140*(1), 256–282. DOI: 10.1037/a0032671

Howell, T. J., Nieforth, L., Thomas-Pino, C., Samet, L., Agbonika, S., Cuevas-Pavincich, F., Fry, N. E., Hill, K., Jegatheesan, B., Kakinuma, M., MacNamara, M., Mattila-Rautiainen, S., Perry, A., Tardif-Williams, C. Y., Walsh, E. A., Winkle, M., Yamamoto, M., Yerbury, R., Rawat, V., & Bennett, P. (2022). Defining Terms Used for Animals Working in Support Roles for People with Support Needs. *Animals (Basel)*, *12*(15), 1975. Advance online publication. DOI: 10.3390/ani12151975

Hoyland, A., Dye, L., & Lawton, C. L. (2009). A systematic review of the effect of breakfast on the cognitive performance of children and adolescents. *Nutrition Research Reviews*, *22*(2), 220–243. DOI: 10.1017/S0954422409990175 PMID: 19930787

Hoy, W. K., & Miskel, C. G. (2005). *Educational administration: Theory, research, and practice* (7th ed.). McGraw-Hill.

Hoy, W. K., & Tschannen-Moran, M. (1999). Five faces of trust: An empirical confirmation in urban elementary schools. *Journal of School Leadership*, *9*(3), 184–208. DOI: 10.1177/105268469900900301

Hsu, P. C., & Chen, R. S. (2023). Analyzing the Mechanisms by Which Digital Platforms Influence Family–School Partnerships among Parents of Young Children. *Sustainability (Basel)*, *15*(24), 16708. Advance online publication. DOI: 10.3390/su152416708

https://www.ungei.org/sites/default/files/A-whole-school-approach-to-prevent-school-related-gender-based-violence-Minimum-Standards-and-Monitoring-Framework-2019-eng.pdf

Huber, G. P. (1991). Organizational learning: The contributing processes and the literatures. *Organization Science*, *2*(1), 88–115. DOI: 10.1287/orsc.2.1.88

Huntsinger, C. S., & Jose, P. E. (2009). Relations among parental acceptance and control and children's social adjustment in Chinese American and European American families. *Journal of Family Psychology*, *23*(3), 321–330. DOI: 10.1037/a0015812 PMID: 19586195

Immordino-Yang, M. H., & Damasio, A. (2007). We Feel, Therefore We Learn: The Relevance of Affective and Social Neuroscience to Education. *Mind, Brain and Education : the Official Journal of the International Mind, Brain, and Education Society*, *1*(1), 3–10. DOI: 10.1111/j.1751-228X.2007.00004.x

International Association of Human-Animal Interaction Organizations. (2018). *The IAHAIO definitions for animal assisted intervention and guidelines for wellness of animals involved in AAI* (White paper; updated for 2018). https://iahaio.org/wp/wp-content/uploads/2021/01/iahaio-white-paper-2018-english.pdf

International Association of Human-Animal Interaction Organizations. (2022). *IAHAIO international guidelines for minimum standards for education and training in animal-assisted interventions (AAI).* https://iahaio.org/wp/wp-content/uploads/2022/11/iahaio-educational-standards_final.pdf

Iosifidis, T. (2003). *Analysis of qualitative data in the social sciences.* Kritiki Publications.

Isaacs, W. N. (1993). Taking flight: Dialogue, collective thinking, and organizational learning. *Organizational Dynamics, 22*(2), 24–39. [REMOVED HYPERLINK50 FIELD] https://doi.org/DOI: 10.1016/0090-2616(93)90051-2

Isari, F., & Michalis Pourkos, M. (2015). *Qualitative research methodology*. Association of Greek Academic Libraries. https://hdl.handle.net/11419/5826

Isaris, P., & Pourkos, M. (2015). *Qualitative research in the social sciences*. National and Kapodistrian University of Athens, Department of Philosophy, Pedagogy and Psychology.

Israel, M., & Hay, I. (2021). *Research ethics for social scientists* (3rd ed.). Sage Publications.

Iváncsik, R., Podráczky, J., Molnár, M., Stromájer, G. P., & Csima, M. (2025). The role of animal-assisted intervention in supporting the preschool-to-school transition. *International Journal of Early Childhood*, *57*(3), 667–686. DOI: 10.1007/s13158-024-00414-0

Jacelon, C. S. (1997). The trait and process of resilience. *Journal of Advanced Nursing*, *25*(1), 123–129. DOI: 10.1046/j.1365-2648.1997.1997025123.x

Jackson, A. P., Choi, J. K., & Preston, K. S. (2019). Harsh parenting and black boys' behavior problems: Single mothers' parenting stress and nonresident fathers' involvement. *Family Relations*, *68*(4), 436–449. DOI: 10.1111/fare.12373

Jacobson, M. J., & Wilensky, U. (2006). Complex systems in education: Scientific and educational importance and implications for the learning sciences. *Journal of the Learning Sciences*, *15*(1), 11–34. DOI: 10.1207/s15327809jls1501_4

Jalongo, M. R. (2005). "What are all these dogs doing at school?": Using therapy dogs to promote children's reading practice. *Childhood Education*, *81*(3), 152–158. DOI: 10.1080/00094056.2005.10522259

Jarden, A., & Roache, A. (2023). What is wellbeing? *International Journal of Environmental Research and Public Health*, *20*(6), 5006. Advance online publication. DOI: 10.3390/ijerph20065006 PMID: 36981914

Jennings, P. A., & Greenberg, M. T. (2009). The prosocial classroom: Teacher social and emotional competence in relation to student and classroom outcomes. *Review of Educational Research*, *79*(1), 491–525. DOI: 10.3102/0034654308325693

Jewell, J. D., Krohn, E. J., Scott, V. G., Carlton, M., & Meinz, E. (2008). The Differential Impact of Mothers' and Fathers' Discipline on Preschool Children's Home and Classroom Behavior. *North American Journal of Psychology*, *10*(1), 173–188.

Jeynes, W. H. (2017). A Meta-Analysis on the Relationship between Character Education and Student Achievement and Behavioral Outcomes. *Education and Urban Society*, *51*(1), 33–71. DOI: 10.1177/0013124517747681

Jia, H. (2024). *Music supports social and emotional skills for small group activities in daycare settings* (Bachelor's thesis, Tampere University of Applied Sciences). TAMK University Repository. URL

Ji, Y. (2022). Teacher well-being: A literature review. *Frontiers in Psychology, 13*, 903513. Advance online publication. DOI: 10.3389/fpsyg.2022.903513

Johns, G., & Saks, A. M. (2005). *Organizational Behaviour* (6th ed.). Pearson Education Canada Inc.

Johnson, D. W., & Johnson, R. T. (2009). An educational psychology success story: Social interdependence theory and cooperative learning. *Educational Researcher, 38*(5), 365–379. DOI: 10.3102/0013189X09339057

Johnson, R. B., & Christensen, L. (2020). *Educational research: Quantitative, qualitative, and mixed approaches* (7th ed.). Sage Publications.

Johnston, C., & Mash, E. J. (2001). Families of children with attention-deficit/hyperactivity disorder: Review and recommendations for future research. *Clinical Child and Family Psychology Review, 4*(3), 183–207. DOI: 10.1023/A:1017592030434 PMID: 11783738

Jones, S. M., & Bouffard, S. M. (2012). Social and emotional learning in schools: From programs to strategies and commentaries. *Child Policy Nexus, 26*(4), 1–33. DOI: 10.1002/j.2379-3988.2012.tb00073.x

Joshi, A., Eberly, J., & Konzal, J. (2005). Dialogue across cultures: Teachers' perceptions about communication with diverse families. *Multicultural Education, 13*(2), 11–15. https://www.researchgate.net/publication/286896219_Dialogue_across_cultures_Teachers'_perceptions_about_communication_with_diverse_families

Joussemet, M., Vitaro, F., Barker, E. D., Côté, S., Nagin, D. S., Zoccolillo, M., & Tremblay, R. E. (2008). Controlling parenting and physical aggression during elementary school. *Child Development, 79*(2), 411–425. DOI: 10.1111/j.1467-8624.2007.01133.x PMID: 18366431

Juríčková, V., Bozděchová, A., Machová, K., & Vadroňová, M. (2020). Effect of animal assisted education with a dog within children with ADHD in the classroom: A case study. *Child & Adolescent Social Work Journal, 37*(6), 677–684. DOI: 10.1007/s10560-020-00716-x

Kakos, M. (2025). Developing a holistic, rights-based model for the educational inclusion of migrant and refugee students. *Intercultural Education, 36*(2), 127–142. DOI: 10.1080/14675986.2024.2349473

Kalavasis, F. (2013). Routes of networks and/or reasoning. In A. Kodakos & F. Kalavasis (Series Eds.), *Topics in Educational Planning* (Vol. 6: *Social networking and schools: Bridges and meanings)* (pp. 129–148). Atrapos.

Kanellou, D., & Argyriou, M. (2026). From training to pedagogical transformation: Preschool teachers' experiences of online professional development in creative music education. *European Journal of Open Education and E-Learning Studies, 10*(4). Advance online publication. DOI: 10.46827/ejoe.v10i4.6500

Kapetanovic, S., & Skoog, T. (2021). The Role of the Family's Emotional Climate in the Links between Parent–Adolescent Communication and Adolescent Psychosocial Functioning. *Research on Child and Adolescent Psychopathology, 49*(2), 141–154. DOI: 10.1007/s10802-020-00705-9 PMID: 32960375

Kaplan, S. (1995). The restorative benefits of nature: Toward an integrative framework. *Journal of Environmental Psychology, 15*(3), 169–182. DOI: 10.1016/0272-4944(95)90001-2

Karadimas, E. H. (1998). The adaptation of a coping strategies measurement scale to the Greek population. *Psychologia, 5*(3), 260–273.

Karadimas, E. H. (2005). *Health psychology: Theory and clinical practice*. Typothito.

Karasek, R. A. (1979). Job demands, job decision latitude, and mental strain: Implications for job redesign. *Administrative Science Quarterly, 24*(2), 285–308. DOI: 10.2307/2392498

Karasek, R., & Theorell, T. (1990). *Healthy work: Stress, productivity, and the reconstruction of working life*. Basic Books.

Karimirad, M. R., Seyedfatemi, N., Hossein Oghli, S., Noorian, S., & Amini, E. (2019). Resilience of mothers of children with attention deficit hyperactivity disorder and its related underlying factors. *Journal of Preventive Epidemiology, 4*(2), e11.

Karsten, J. (2004). *Teaching about complexity in primary and secondary schools: An exploration of new approaches to ecosystem education* [Doctoral dissertation, McGill University]. McGill University Repository.

Kassotakis, M., & Flouris, G. (2018). *School and family: Dimensions of cooperation and communication*. Gutenberg.

Katidou, E. (2019). *Teachers' well-being: Shaping factors and dimensions in primary education* (Master's thesis, University of Western Macedonia, School of Education, Department of Primary Education, Postgraduate Program).

Katsarou, D. (2024). The Play as a Mediator of Learning and Psychosocial Empowerment of Children with Learning Difficulties. In L. Ioannidou & a. Argyriadi (Eds), *Building Mental Resilience in Children: Positive Psychology, Emotional Intelligence, and Play* (pp 332-346). IGI Global. DOI: 10.4018/979-8-3693-8312-4.ch013

Katsarou, D., & Argyriou, M. (Eds.). (2026). *Groundbreaking approaches to early childhood development and therapy*. IGI Global., DOI: 10.4018/979-8-3373-3068-6

Katsarou, D., Mantsos, E., Papadopoulou, S., Sofologi, M., Efthymiou, E., Vasileiou, I., Megari, K., Theodoratou, M., & Kougioumtzis, G. (2025). Exploring AI technology in grammar performance testing for children with learning disabilities. *Education Sciences*, *15*(3), 351–365. DOI: 10.3390/educsci15030351

Keeley, B. (2021). [*On my mind—Promoting, protecting and caring for children's mental health.* UNICEF.]. *The State of the World's Children*, •••, 2021.

Kelsey, R. M. (2021). Teachers' lived experiences regarding the use of therapy dogs as a behavior management strategy: A phenomenological study (Doctoral dissertation, Drexel University). DOI: 10.17918/00000359

Keravnos, N., & Lipsou, E. (2026). Relational trust and principal well-being: Extending the job demands–resources framework in school leadership. *Educational Management Administration & Leadership*, *17411432261446399*, 17411432261446399. Advance online publication. DOI: 10.1177/17411432261446399

Kertes, D. A., Liu, J., Hall, N. J., Hadad, N. A., Wynne, C. D. L., & Bhatt, S. S. (2017). Effect of pet dogs on children's perceived stress and cortisol stress response. *Social Development*, *26*(2), 382–401. DOI: 10.1111/sode.12203

Keyes, C. L. M. (Ed.). (2004). *Risk and resilience in human development: A special issue of Research in Human Development.* Psychology Press., DOI: 10.4324/9780203764374

Keyes, C. L. M., & Waterman, M. B. (2022). Pathways to flourishing: The dynamic interplay of psychological and social well-being. *The Journal of Positive Psychology*, *17*(2), 100–115. DOI: 10.1080/17439760.2021.1884477

Khamisa, N., Oldenburg, B., Peltzer, K., & Ilic, D. (2015). Work related stress, burnout, job satisfaction and general health of nurses. *International Journal of Environmental Research and Public Health*, *12*(1), 652–666. DOI: 10.3390/ijerph120100652

Khine, M. S., Zandvliet, D. B., & Fraser, B. J. (2021). Thirty years of learning environments: Looking back and looking forward. *Learning Environments Research*, *24*(3), 537–539. DOI: 10.1007/s10984-021-09386-7

Killen, M., Mulvey, K. L., & Hitti, A. (2013). Social exclusion in childhood: A developmental intergroup perspective. *Child Development, 84*(3), 772–790. DOI: 10.1111/cdev.12012 PMID: 23170901

Kim, E. M., Sheridan, S. M., Kwon, K., & Koziol, N. (2013). Parent beliefs and children's social-behavioral functioning: The mediating role of parent–teacher relationships. *Journal of School Psychology, 51*(2), 175–185. DOI: 10.1016/j.jsp.2013.01.003 PMID: 23481083

Kim, G. E., Choi, H. Y., & Kim, E. J. (2018). Impact of economic problems on depression in single mothers: A comparative study with married women. *PLoS One, 13*(8), e0203004. DOI: 10.1371/journal.pone.0203004 PMID: 30142180

Kim, H., Doiron, K., Warren, M. A., & Donaldson, S. I. (2018). The international landscape of positive psychology research: A systematic review. *International Journal of Wellbeing, 8*(1), 50–70. DOI: 10.5502/ijw.v8i1.651

Kim, J. H., & Callahan, J. L. (2013). Finding the intersection of the learning organization and learning transfer: The significance of leadership. *European Journal of Training and Development, 37*(2), 183–200. DOI: 10.1108/03090591311301680

King, M., & Winn, D. (2017). Cross institutional peer coaching: A case study. In *Beyond mentoring* (pp. 93–106). Chandos Publishing., DOI: 10.1016/B978-0-08-101294-9.00008-8

Kioussi, S. (2025). A systems approach to school culture as a factor in effective school development [Doctoral dissertation, University of the Aegean]. National Archive of PhD Theses. https://doi.org/DOI: 10.12681/eadd/60580

Kirk, M. A., Kelley, C., Yankey, N., Birken, S. A., Abadie, B., & Damschroder, L. (2015). A systematic review of the use of the Consolidated Framework for Implementation Research. *Implementation Science : IS, 11*(1), 72. DOI: 10.1186/s13012-016-0437-z PMID: 27189233

Kirk, S., VanMeter, C., & van Asselt, K. W. (2025). School Counselor and Principal Relationship as a Predictor of ASCA National Model Implementation. *Professional School Counseling, 29*(1b), 2156759X251365244. Advance online publication. DOI: 10.1177/2156759X251365244

Kirnan, J. P., Siminerio, S., & Wong, Z. (2016). The impact of a therapy dog program on children's reading skills and attitudes toward reading. *Early Childhood Education Journal, 44*(6), 637–651. DOI: 10.1007/s10643-015-0747-9

Klar, H. W., & Brewer, C. A. (2013). Successful leadership in high-needs schools: An examination of core leadership practices enacted in challenging contexts. *Educational Administration Quarterly, 49*(5), 768–808. DOI: 10.1177/0013161X13482577

Klassen, R. M., & Chiu, M. M. (2010). Effects on teachers' self-efficacy and job satisfaction: Teacher gender, years of experience, and job stress. *Journal of Educational Psychology, 102*(3), 741–756. DOI: 10.1037/a0019237

Kluchert, G. (2009). Schulkultur(en) in historischer Perspektive: Einführung in das Thema. *Zeitschrift für Pädagogik, 55*(3), 326–333.

Kluckhohn, C. (2017). *Mirror for man: The relation of anthropology to modern life* (1st ed.). Routledge., DOI: 10.4324/9781315107127

Knight, J. (2017). *The impact cycle: What instructional coaches should do to foster powerful improvements in teaching*. Corwin Press.

Koç, N., & Sungurtekin, Ş. (2023). Promoting preschool children's social-emotional learning skills through creative drama integrated music activities. *International Online Journal of Primary Education, 12*(3), 210–227. DOI: 10.55020/iojpe.1254401

Kodakos, A. (2010). Systemic educational leadership. In F. Kalavasis & A. Kodakos (Series Eds.), *Topics in educational planning, Vol. 4: Communication and governance of educational systems,* (pp. 75–92). Diadrasi.

Kodakos, A., & Angelakou, E.-P. (2016). From school theories to school development. In A. Kodakos & F. Kalavasis (Series Eds.), *Topics in educational planning, Vol. 8: Systemic educational development: Technological and pedagogical interweaving,* (pp. 29–65). Diadrasi.

Kodakos, A., & Angelakou, E.-P. (2017). The portrait of an intelligent school: The example of Greece. In A. Kodakos & F. Kalavasis (Series Eds.), *Topics in educational planning, Vol. 9: The school as an intelligent, hybrid, and moral entity* (pp. 85–117). Diadrasi.

Kodakos, A., Angelakou, E.-P., & Oikonomidi, E. (2017, August 22–25). *School development as development of organizational learning and change: A systemic approach* [Conference presentation]. *European Conference on Educational Research (ECER)*, Copenhagen, Denmark.

Kofler, M. J., McCart, M. R., Zajac, K., Ruggiero, K. J., Saunders, B. E., & Kilpatrick, D. G. (2011). Depression and delinquency covariation in an accelerated longitudinal sample of adolescents. *Journal of Consulting and Clinical Psychology, 79*(4), 458–469. DOI: 10.1037/a0024108 PMID: 21787049

Kolbert, J. B., Crothers, L. M., & Hughes, T. L. (2022). *Introduction to school counseling: Theory, research, and practice* (2nd ed.). Routledge., DOI: 10.4324/9781003167730

Kools, M., & Stoll, L. (2016). *What makes a school a learning organisation?* OECD Publishing., DOI: 10.1787/5jlwm62b3bvh-

Kotrschal, K., & Ortbauer, B. (2003). Behavioral effects of the presence of a dog in a classroom. *Anthrozoos*, *16*(2), 147–159. DOI: 10.2752/089279303786992170

Kotsikis, V. (2003). *Educational administration and policy*. Ellin.

Kourkouni, A. (2020). *Professional well-being and factors affecting it: Perceptions of permanent and substitute primary education teachers* (Master's thesis, Hellenic Open University, Patras, Greece).

Kraft, M. A., & Dougherty, S. M. (2013). The Effect of Teacher–Family Communication on Student Engagement: Evidence from a Randomized Field Experiment. *Journal of Research on Educational Effectiveness*, *6*(3), 199–222. DOI: 10.1080/19345747.2012.743636

Kraft, M. A., & Rogers, T. (2015). The underutilized potential of teacher-to-parent communication: Evidence from a field experiment. *Economics of Education Review*, *47*, 49–63. DOI: 10.1016/j.econedurev.2015.04.001

Krishnakumar, A., & Buehler, C. (2000). Interparental conflict and parenting behaviors: A meta-analytic review. *Family Relations*, *49*(1), 25–44. DOI: 10.1111/j.1741-3729.2000.00025.x

Kritzas, N., & Grobler, A. A. (2005). The relationship between perceived parenting styles and resilience during adolescence. *Journal of Child and Adolescent Mental Health*, *17*(1), 1–12. DOI: 10.2989/17280580509486586 PMID: 25868916

Kröger, C., Klann, N., & Kaps, M. (2009). „Stark ohne Gewalt“: Evaluation eines innovativen Ansatzes zur schulischen Gewaltprävention. *Beratung Aktuell*, *10*(2), 3–23.

Kuppens, S., Grietens, H., Onghena, P., & Michiels, D. (2009). Associations between parental control and children's overt and relational aggression. *British Journal of Developmental Psychology*, *27*(3), 607–623. DOI: 10.1348/026151008X345591 PMID: 19994571

Kushwaha, R. K., Yadav, P. K., Sonker, J., & Devi, A. (2024). *Ethical frameworks in special education: A guide for researchers* (2nd ed.). Integrated Publications.

Kusma, B., Groneberg, D. A., Nienhaus, A., & Mache, S. (2012). Determinants of day care teachers' job satisfaction. *Central European Journal of Public Health, 20*(3), 191–198. DOI: 10.21101/cejph.a3700 PMID: 23285519

Kuusimäki, A.-M., Uusitalo-Malmivaara, L., & Tirri, K. (2019). Parents' and Teachers' Views on Digital Communication in Finland. *Education Research International, 2019*(9), 1–7. DOI: 10.1155/2019/8236786

Kvale, S., & Brinkmann, S. (2009). *InterViews: Learning the craft of qualitative research interviewing* (2nd ed.). Sage.

Kyriacou, C. (2000). *Stress-busting for teachers.* Nelson Thornes.

Kyriacou, C. (2001). Teacher stress: Directions for future research. *Educational Review, 53*(1), 27–35. DOI: 10.1080/00131910120033628

Laal, M., & Laal, M. (2012). Collaborative learning: What is it? *Procedia: Social and Behavioral Sciences, 31*, 491–495. DOI: 10.1016/j.sbspro.2011.12.092

Laermans, R. (2007). Theorizing culture, or reading Luhmann against Luhmann. *Cybernetics & Human Knowing, 14*(2–3), 67–83.

Langford, R., Bonell, C. P., Jones, H. E., Pouliou, T., Murphy, S. M., Waters, E., Komro, K. A., Gibbs, L. F., Magnus, D., & Campbell, R. (2014). The WHO Health Promoting School framework for improving the health and well-being of students and their academic achievement. *Cochrane Database of Systematic Reviews, 2014*(4), CD008958. Advance online publication. DOI: 10.1002/14651858.CD008958.pub2 PMID: 24737131

Lau, E. Y. H. (2019). Parenting and childhood aggression in the Chinese context: An examination of parental responses, physical coercion, and warmth. *Early Years Journal of International Research and Development, 39*(1), 36–50. DOI: 10.1080/09575146.2017.1344195

Lave, J., & Wenger, E. (1991). *Situated learning: Legitimate peripheral participation.* Cambridge University Press. DOI: 10.1017/CBO9780511815355

Lazarus, R., & Lanier, R. (1978). Stress-related transactions between person and environment. In L. A. Pervin & M. Lewis (Eds.), Perspectives in international psychology (pp. 287–327). Plenum Press.

Lazarus, R. S. (1991). *Emotion and adaptation.* Oxford University Press. DOI: 10.1093/oso/9780195069945.001.0001

Lazarus, R., & Folkman, S. (1984). *Stress, appraisal, and coping.* Springer.

le Roux, M. C., Swartz, L., & Swart, E. (2014). The effect of an animal-assisted reading program on the reading rate, accuracy and comprehension of Grade 3 students: A randomized control study. *Child and Youth Care Forum*, *43*(6), 655–673. DOI: 10.1007/s10566-014-9262-1

le Roux, M., Swartz, L., & Swart, E. (2015). The effect of an animal-assisted reading programme on word recognition and spelling skills of grade 3 children. *Tydskrif vir Geesteswetenskappe*, *55*(2), 289–303. DOI: 10.17159/2224-7912/2015/V55N2A9

Leach, F. (2008). Gender violence in schools in the developing world. *Commonwealth Education Partnerships*, *2008*, 28–31.

Learning, O. E., & Well-Being, C. (2020). *A Study of Five-year-old in England, Estonia, and the United States*.

Leat, D., Reid, A., & Lofthouse, R. (2015). Teachers' experiences of engagement with and in educational research: What can be learned from teachers' views? *Oxford Review of Education*, *41*(2), 270–286. DOI: 10.1080/03054985.2015.1021193

Lee, C. Y. S., Anderson, J. R., Horowitz, J. L., & August, G. J. (2009). Family income and parenting: The role of parental depression and social support. *Family Relations*, *58*(4), 417–430. DOI: 10.1111/j.1741-3729.2009.00563.x

Leithwood, K., Harris, A., & Hopkins, D. (2008). Seven strong claims about successful school leadership. *School Leadership & Management*, *28*(1), 27–42. DOI: 10.1080/13632430701800060

Leithwood, K., & Jantzi, D. (2005). A Review of Transformational School Leadership Research 1996–2005. *Leadership and Policy in Schools*, *4*(3), 177–199. DOI: 10.1080/15700760500244769

Lenihan, D., McCobb, E., Diurba, A., Linder, D., & Freeman, L. (2016). Measuring the effects of reading assistance dogs on reading ability and attitudes in elementary schoolchildren. *Journal of Research in Childhood Education*, *30*(2), 252–259. DOI: 10.1080/02568543.2016.1143896

Leontopoulos, S., Skenderidou, I., Stafylis, N., Papageorgiou, K., & Skenderidis, P. (2025). MENTORING AND COACHING IN EDUCATIONAL LEADERSHIP: FOSTERING REFLECTIVE AND STRATEGIC SCHOOL LEADERS. *European Journal of Education Studies*, *12*(12). Advance online publication. DOI: 10.46827/ejes.v12i12.6341

Leos, R. A., Cuccaro, P. M., Herbold, J. R., & Hernandez, B. F. (2022). Exploring School Staff Perceptions Relating to Animals and Their Involvement in Interventions to Support Mental Health. *International Journal of Environmental Research and Public Health, 19*(12), 7126. DOI: 10.3390/ijerph19127126

Leriou, E. (2023). Understanding and measuring child well-being in the region of Attica, Greece: Round five: Understanding and measuring child well-being in the region of Attica, Greece: Round five. *Child Indicators Research, 16*(4), 1395–1451. DOI: 10.1007/s12187-023-10030-4 PMID: 37363702

Letourneau, N. L., Tramonte, L., & Willms, J. D. (2013). Maternal depression, family functioning, and children's longitudinal development. *Journal of Pediatric Nursing, 28*(3), 223–234. DOI: 10.1016/j.pedn.2012.07.014 PMID: 22940454

Leung, J. T., & Shek, D. T. (2018). Unbroken Homes: Parenting style and Adolescent Positive Development in Chinese single-mother families experiencing economic disadvantage. *Child Indicators Research, 11*(2), 441–457. DOI: 10.1007/s12187-016-9437-4

Lewis, C., & Lamb, M. E. (2003). Fathers' influences on children's development: The evidence from two-parent families. *European Journal of Psychology of Education, 18*(2), 211–228. DOI: 10.1007/BF03173485

Lewis, H., Godfrey Oostendorp, J., & Knight, C. (2023). Tales of the unexpected: Teacher's experiences of working with children and dogs in schools. *Human-Animal Interactions, 11*(1), 1–11. DOI: 10.1079/hai.2023.0040

Liang, L. A., Berger, U., & Brand, C. (2019). Psychosocial factors associated with symptoms of depression, anxiety, and stress among single mothers with young children: A population-based study. *Journal of Affective Disorders, 242*, 255–264. DOI: 10.1016/j.jad.2018.08.013 PMID: 30218920

Liargovas, P. (2023). *Introduction to scientific research.* Papazisis Publications.

Liargovas, P., Dermatis, Z., & Komninos, D. (2023). *Research methodology and scientific writing* (2nd ed.). Tziolas Publications.

Li, L.-W., Ochoa, W., McWayne, C. M., Priebe Rocha, L., & Hyun, S. (2023). "Talk to me": Parent–teacher background similarity, communication quality, and barriers to school-based engagement among ethnoculturally diverse Head Start families. *Cultural Diversity & Ethnic Minority Psychology, 29*(2), 267–278. DOI: 10.1037/cdp0000497 PMID: 34735169

Lincoln, Y. S., & Guba, E. G. (1985). Naturalistic inquiry. *Sage (Atlanta, Ga.).*

Lindblad, K., & de Boise, S. (2020). Musical engagement and subjective wellbeing amongst men in the third age. *Nordic Journal of Music Therapy*, *29*(1), 20–38. DOI: 10.1080/08098131.2019.1646791

Linder, D. E., Mueller, M. K., Gibbs, D. M., Siebens, H. C., & Freeman, L. M. (2017). Animal-assisted interventions: A national survey of health and safety policies in hospitals, eldercare facilities, and therapy animal organizations. *American Journal of Infection Control*, *45*(8), 883–887. DOI: 10.1016/j.ajic.2017.04.287

Lipton, L., & Wellman, B. (2024). *Mentoring Matters: A Practical Guide to Learning-Focused Relationships, (Establish a learning-focused mentor-teacher relationship)*. Solution Tree Press.

Liu, L., & Wang, M. (2015). Parenting stress and children's problem behavior in China: The mediating role of parental psychological aggression. *Journal of Family Psychology*, *29*(1), 20–28. DOI: 10.1037/fam0000047 PMID: 25438090

Liu, S., & Hallinger, P. (2018). Principal instructional leadership, teacher self-efficacy, and teacher professional learning in China: Testing a mediated-effects model. *Educational Administration Quarterly*, *54*(4), 501–528. DOI: 10.1177/0013161X18769048

Liu, Z. (2023). Transforming teaching: Wellbeing and professional practice. *Frontiers in Psychology*, *14*, 1192148. DOI: 10.3389/fpsyg.2023.1192148 PMID: 37397297

Llorca, A., Richaud, M. C., & Malonda, E. (2017). Parenting styles, prosocial, and aggressive behavior: The role of emotions in offender and non-offender adolescents. *Frontiers in Psychology*, *8*, 1246. DOI: 10.3389/fpsyg.2017.01246 PMID: 28848459

Lomas, T., Waters, L., Williams, P., Oades, L. G., & Kern, M. L. (2021). The dynamics of wellbeing: A systems approach. *The Lancet. Public Health*, *6*(7), e508–e513. DOI: 10.1016/S2468-2667(21)00025-9

López-Cepero, J. (2020). Current status of animal-assisted interventions in scientific literature: A critical comment on their internal validity. *Animals (Basel)*, *10*(6), 985. Advance online publication. DOI: 10.3390/ani10060985

Louis, K. S. (2010). *Learning from leadership: Investigating the links to improved student learning*. Wallace Foundation.

Luhmann, N. (1984). *Soziale Systeme: Grundriss einer allgemeinen Theorie*. Suhrkamp.

Luhmann, N. (1992). Organisation. In Küpper, W., & Ortmann, G. (Eds.), *Mikropolitik: Rationalität, Macht und Spiele in Organisationen* (pp. 165–185). Westdeutscher Verlag.

Luhmann, N. (1995a). *Social Systems* (Bednarz, J.Jr, & Baecker, D., Trans.). Stanford University Press.

Luhmann, N. (1995b). *Theory of social systems* (Karkatsoulis, P., & Makrydimitris, A., Eds.). Sakkoulas. (Original work published 1984)

Luhmann, N. (1995c). Kultur als historischer Begriff. In Luhmann, N. (Ed.), *Gesellschaftsstruktur und Semantik IV* (pp. 31–54). Suhrkamp.

Luhmann, N. (1995d). The paradox of observing systems. *Cultural Critique*, *31*(31), 37–55. DOI: 10.2307/1354444

Luhmann, N. (1997). *Die Gesellschaft der Gesellschaft*. Suhrkamp.

Luhmann, N. (2000a). *Organisation und Entscheidung*. Westdeutscher Verlag. DOI: 10.1007/978-3-322-97093-0

Luhmann, N. (2000c). *Organization and decision*. Cambridge University Press.

Luhmann, N. (2003a). Organization. In Bakken, T., & Hernes, T. (Eds.), *Autopoietic organization theory: Drawing on Niklas Luhmann's social systems perspective* (pp. 31–52). Copenhagen Business School Press.

Luhmann, N. (2003b). *The reality of the mass media* (Zeri, P., Trans.). Metaichmio. (Original work published 1996)

Luhmann, N. (2003c). *Funktionen und Folgen formaler Organisation* (4th ed.). Suhrkamp Verlag.

Luhmann, N. (2005). *Soziale Systeme: Grundriß einer allgemeinen Theorie* (7th ed.). Suhrkamp.

Luhmann, N. (2012). *Theories of distinction: Redescribing the descriptions of modernity*. Stanford University Press.

Luhmann, N. (2018). *Organization and decision (D. Baecker* (Barrett, R. Ed. & Trans.). Cambridge University Press. (Original work published 2000), DOI: 10.1017/9781108560672

Lunenburg, F. C. (2010). Schools as open systems. *Schooling*, *1*(1), 1–5.

Luong, G. Y. (2025). The effectiveness of mentoring, coaching, and induction practices for early career teachers: A scoping review. *Teaching and Teacher Education*, *163*, 105065. DOI: 10.1016/j.tate.2025.105065

Luthar, S. S. (2015). Resilience in development: A synthesis of research across five decades. In Cicchetti, D., & Cohen, D. J. (Eds.), *Wiley*. Developmental psychopathology, DOI: 10.1002/9780470939406.ch20

MacBeath, J., & McGlynn, A. (2004). *Self-evaluation. What's in it for schools?* RoutledgeFalmer., DOI: 10.4324/9780203018668

MacBeath, J., Schratz, M., Meuret, D., & Jakobsen, L. B. (2005). *Self-evaluation in the European school: How things have changed* (Deligianni, M., Trans.). Metaixmio.

MacGilchrist, B., Myers, K., & Reed, J. (2004). *The intelligent school* (2nd ed.). Sage. DOI: 10.4135/9781446216484

Magklaras, V. (2013). *Theories of social systems: Parsons, Luhmann, Habermas.* Sideris.

Ma, J., Han, Y., Grogan-Kaylor, A., Delva, J., & Castillo, M. (2012). Corporal punishment and youth externalizing behavior in Santiago, Chile. *Child Abuse & Neglect, 36*(6), 481–490. DOI: 10.1016/j.chiabu.2012.03.006 PMID: 22766372

Malti, T., & Noam, G. G. (2009). A developmental approach to the prevention of adolescent's aggressive behavior and the promotion of resilience. *International Journal of Developmental Science, 3*(3), 235–246. DOI: 10.3233/DEV-2009-3303

Mandleco, B., & Peery, J. C. (2000). An organizational framework for conceptualizing resilience in children. *Journal of Child and Adolescent Psychiatric Nursing, 13*(3), 99–111. DOI: 10.1111/j.1744-6171.2000.tb00086.x PMID: 11111503

Mansfield, C. F., Beltman, S., Broadley, T., & Weatherby-Fell, N. (2016). Building resilience in teacher education: An evidenced informed framework. *Teaching and Teacher Education, 54*, 77–87. DOI: 10.1016/j.tate.2015.11.016

Mantzourani, E., Chang, H., Desselle, S., Canedo, J., & Fleming, G. (2022). Reflections of mentors and mentees on a national mentoring programme for pharmacists: An examination into relationships, personal and professional development. *Research in Social & Administrative Pharmacy, 18*(3), 2495–2504. DOI: 10.1016/j.sapharm.2021.04.019

March, J. G., & Simon, H. A. (1993). *Organizations* (2nd ed). Oxford.

March, J. G. (1991). Exploration and exploitation in organizational learning. *Organization Science, 2*(1), 71–87. DOI: 10.1287/orsc.2.1.71

March, J. G., & Simon, H. A. (1958). *Organizations*. Wiley.

Maria Kokkidou, M., & Georgios Mygdanis, G. (2024). School bullying, victimization and intervention proposals. *Culture - Journal of Culture in Tourism. Art Education*, *4*(2), 33–43. DOI: 10.12681/hjre.19440

Maria Kouroutsidou, M., & Nikolaos Raptis, N. (2021). *Gender violence and educational institutions: Teachers as social reformers. The case of the Dodecanese*. Goni Publications.

Marks, J. L., Lam, C. B., & McHale, S. M. (2009). Family patterns of gender role attitudes. *Sex Roles*, *61*(3), 221–234. DOI: 10.1007/s11199-009-9619-3 PMID: 22308059

Marquardt, M. J. (1996). *Building the learning organization: Mastering the five elements for corporate learning*. Davies-Black Publishing.

Marsden, N., Link, J., & Büllesfeld, E. (2015). Personas und stereotype Geschlechterrollen. In Marsden, N., & Kempf, U. (Eds.), *Gender-UseIT: HCI, usability und UX unter Gendergesichtspunkten* (pp. 91–104). De Gruyter Oldenbourg.

Marsick, V. J., & Watkins, K. E. (2003). Demonstrating the value of an organization's learning culture: The dimensions of the learning organization questionnaire. *Advances in Developing Human Resources*, *5*(2), 132–151. DOI: 10.1177/1523422303005002002

Martens, W. (2006). The distinctions within organizations: Luhmann from a cultural perspective. *Organization*, *13*(1), 83–108. DOI: 10.1177/1350508406059643

Martens, W., & Ortmann, G. (2006). Organisationen in der Systemtheorie Niklas Luhmanns. *Zeitschrift für Soziologie*, *35*(2), 115–139.

Martínez, I., Murgui, S., Garcia, O. F., & García, F. (2019). Parenting in the digital era: Protective and risk parenting styles for traditional bullying and cyberbullying victimization. *Computers in Human Behavior*, *90*, 84–92. DOI: 10.1016/j.chb.2018.08.036

Marzano, R. J. (2003). *What works in schools: Translating research into action*. ASCD.

Maschke, S., & Stecher, L. (2021). *Sexualisierte Gewalt in der Erfahrung Jugendlicher: Erweiterungsstudie Berufliche Schulen. Kurzbericht*. Arbeitsgruppe „Speak". https://www.uni-marburg.de/de/fb21/erzwinst/arbeitsbereiche/aew/forschung/speak/kurzbericht-speak-berufliche-schulen_maschke-stecher.pdf

Maslowski, R. (2001). *School culture and school performance: An explorative study into the organizational culture of secondary schools and their effects* [Doctoral dissertation, University of Twente]. Twente University Press.

Maslowski, R. (2006). A review of inventories for diagnosing school culture. *Journal of Educational Administration*, *44*(1), 6–35. DOI: 10.1108/09578230610642638

Mason, J. (2011). *Conducting qualitative research* (E. Dimitriadou, Trans., & N. Kyriazi, Ed.). Pedio.

Masten, A. (2025). *Ordinary magic. Resilience in development* (2nd ed.). Guilford Press.

Masten, A. S. (2001). Ordinary magic: Resilience processes in development. *The American Psychologist*, *56*(3), 227–238. DOI: 10.1037/0003-066X.56.3.227 PMID: 11315249

Masten, A. S. (2016). Resilience in developing systems: The promise of integrated approaches. *European Journal of Developmental Psychology*, *13*(3), 297–312. DOI: 10.1080/17405629.2016.1147344

Masten, A. S. (2021). Resilience of children in disasters: A multisystem perspective. *International Journal of Psychology*, *56*(1), 1–11. DOI: 10.1002/ijop.12737 PMID: 33325580

Masten, A. S., & Barnes, A. J. (2018). Resilience in children: Developmental perspectives. *Children (Basel, Switzerland)*, *5*(7), 98. DOI: 10.3390/children5070098

Masten, A. S., & Motti-Stefanidi, F. (2020). Multisystem Resilience for Children and Youth in Disaster: Reflections in the Context of COVID-19. *Adversity and Resilience Science*, *1*(2), 95–106. DOI: 10.1007/s42844-020-00010-w PMID: 32838305

Masud, H., Ahmad, M. S., Cho, K. W., & Fakhr, Z. (2019). Parenting styles and aggression among young adolescents: A systematic review of the literature. *Community Mental Health Journal*, *55*(6), 1015–1030. DOI: 10.1007/s10597-019-00400-0 PMID: 31102163

Matsaggouras, H. (2007). *Theory and practice of teaching: The school classroom—Space, group, discipline, method.* Grigoris.

Maturana, H. R., & Varela, F. J. (1980). *Autopoiesis and cognition: The realization of the living*. Reidel. DOI: 10.1007/978-94-009-8947-4

Maurer, K. (2010, February). Communication and language in Niklas Luhmann's systems theory. *Pandaemonium Germanicum*, 1–21. https://doi.org/DOI: 10.1590/S1982-88372010000200002

Mavrogiorgos, G. (2016). School-family cooperation in the modern educational context. *Review of Educational Issues*, *22*, 45–60. https://ejournals.epublishing.ekt.gr/index.php/epaggelmatiki/article/view/12645

Ma, X., & Marion, R. (2024). How does leadership affect teacher collaboration? Evidence from teachers in US schools. *School Effectiveness and School Improvement*, *35*(2), 116–141. DOI: 10.1080/09243453.2024.2330533

McArdle, K., & Coutts, N. (2010). Taking teachers' continuous professional development (CPD) beyond reflection: Adding shared sense-making and collaborative engagement for professional renewal. *Studies in Continuing Education*, *32*(3), 201–215. DOI: 10.1080/0158037X.2010.517994

McCance-Katz, E. F. (2018). The Substance Abuse and Mental Health Services Administration (SAMHSA): New Directions. *Psychiatric Services (Washington, D.C.)*, *69*(10), 1046–1048. DOI: 10.1176/appi.ps.201800281 PMID: 30099944

McCloskey, L. A., & Lichter, E. L. (2003). The contribution of marital violence to adolescent aggression across different relationships. *Journal of Interpersonal Violence*, *18*(4), 390–412. DOI: 10.1177/0886260503251179

McCullough, A., Ruehrdanz, A., Garthe, R., Hellman, C., & O'Haire, M. (2021). Measuring the social, behavioral, and academic effects of classroom pets on third and fourth-grade students. *Human Animal Interactions Bulletin*, *9*(1), 1–21. DOI: 10.1079/hai.2021.0023

McEwen, B. S. (2007). Physiology and neurobiology of stress and adaptation: Central role of the brain. *Physiological Reviews*, *87*(3), 873–904. DOI: 10.1152/physrev.00041.2006

McFerran, K. S., Hense, C., Koike, A., & Rickwood, D. (2018). Intentional music use to reduce psychological distress in adolescents accessing primary mental health care. *Clinical Child Psychology and Psychiatry*, *23*(4), 567–581. DOI: 10.1177/1359104518767231 PMID: 29669441

McKee, L., Colletti, C., Rakow, A., Jones, D. J., & Forehand, R. (2008). Parenting and child externalizing behaviors: Are the associations specific or diffuse? *Aggression and Violent Behavior*, *13*(3), 201–215. DOI: 10.1016/j.avb.2008.03.005 PMID: 19122818

McKee, T. E., Harvey, E., Danforth, J. S., Ulaszek, W. R., & Friedman, J. L. (2004). The relation between parental coping styles and parent-child interactions before and after treatment for children with ADHD and oppositional behavior. *Journal of Clinical Child and Adolescent Psychology, 33*(1), 158–168. DOI: 10.1207/S15374424JCCP3301_15 PMID: 15028550

McNeely, C. A., Nonnemaker, J. M., & Blum, R. W. (2002). Promoting School Connectedness: Evidence from the National Longitudinal Study of Adolescent Health. *The Journal of School Health, 72*(4), 138–146. DOI: 10.1111/j.1746-1561.2002.tb06533.x PMID: 12029810

McNicholas, J., & Collis, G. M. (2000). Dogs as catalysts for social interactions: Robustness of the effect. *British Journal of Psychology, 91*(1), 61–70. DOI: 10.1348/000712600161673

Meints, K., Brelsford, V. L., Dimolareva, M., Maréchal, L., Pennington, K., Rowan, E., & Gee, N. R. (2022). Can dogs reduce stress levels in school children? effects of dog-assisted interventions on salivary cortisol in children with and without special educational needs using randomized controlled trials. *PLoS One, 17*(6), e0269333. Advance online publication. DOI: 10.1371/journal.pone.0269333

Meissner, H. (2008). *Die soziale Konstruktion von Geschlecht: Erkenntnisperspektiven und gesellschaftstheoretische Fragen*. Freie Universität Berlin. https://www.fu-berlin.de/sites/gpo/soz_eth/Geschlecht_als_Kategorie/Die_soziale_Konstruktion_von_Geschlecht_____Erkenntnisperspektiven_und_gesellschaftstheoretische_Fragen/hanna_meissner.pdf

Meixner, J., & Kotrschal, K. (2022). Animal-assisted interventions with dogs in special education—A systematic review. *Frontiers in Psychology, 13*, 876290. Advance online publication. DOI: 10.3389/fpsyg.2022.876290

Mellor, D. J., Beausoleil, N. J., Littlewood, K. E., McLean, A. N., McGreevy, P. D., Jones, B., & Wilkins, C. (2020). The 2020 Five Domains Model: Including Human–Animal Interactions in assessments of animal welfare. *Animals (Basel), 10*(10), 1870. Advance online publication. DOI: 10.3390/ani10101870

Meltzer, L. (Ed.). (2018). *Executive function in education: From theory to practice*. Guilford Publications.

Melzer, W., & Schubarth, W. (2006). *Gewalt als soziales Problem an Schulen: Untersuchungsergebnisse und Präventionsstrategien.* Verlag Barbara Budrich. https://doi.org/DOI: 10.25656/01:16061

Méndez, J. H. M., Sánchez, J. P. E., & Becerra, M. I. G. (2020). Role of parenting styles in internalizing, externalizing, and adjustment problems in children. *Salud Mental, 43*(2), 73–84. DOI: 10.17711/SM.0185-3325.2020.011

Mensah, M. K., & Kuranchie, A. (2013). Influence of parenting styles on the social development of children. *Academic Journal of Interdisciplinary Studies, 2*(3), 123-123. https://www.richtmann.org/journal/index.php/ajis/article/view/1397

Mercer, S., & Gregersen, T. (2020). *Teacher wellbeing*. Oxford University Press.

Merriam, S. B. (2009). *Qualitative research: A guide to design and implementation*. Jossey-Bass.

Meyer, A., Rose, D. H., & Gordon, D. (2014). *Universal design for learning: Theory and practice*. CAST.

Meyer, J. W., & Rowan, B. (1977). Institutionalized organizations: Formal structure as myth and ceremony. *American Journal of Sociology*, *83*(2), 340–363. DOI: 10.1086/226550

Meyers, D. C., Domitrovich, C. E., Dissi, R., Trejo, J., & Greenberg, M. T. (2019). Supporting systemic social and emotional learning with a schoolwide implementation model. *Evaluation and Program Planning*, *73*, 53–61. DOI: 10.1016/j.evalprogplan.2018.11.005

Michaelson, J., Mahony, S., & Schifferes, J. (2012). *Measuring wellbeing: A guide for practitioners*. New Economics Foundation.

Miner, J. L., & Clarke-Stewart, K. A. (2008). Trajectories of externalizing behavior from age 2 to age 9: Relations with gender, temperament, ethnicity, parenting, and rater. *Developmental Psychology*, *44*(3), 771–736. DOI: 10.1037/0012-1649.44.3.771 PMID: 18473643

Mingers, J. (2002). Can social systems be autopoietic? Assessing Luhmann's social theory. *The Sociological Review*, *50*(2), 278–299. DOI: 10.1111/1467-954X.00367

Mistry, R. S., Vandewater, E. A., Huston, A. C., & McLoyd, V. C. (2002). Economic well-being and children's social adjustment: The role of family process in an ethnically diverse low-income sample. *Child Development*, *73*(3), 935–951. DOI: 10.1111/1467-8624.00448 PMID: 12038561

Modecki, K. L., Minchin, J., Harbaugh, A. G., Guerra, N. G., & Runions, K. C. (2020). Bullying and victimization across contexts. *The Journal of Adolescent Health*, *66*(2), 203–210. DOI: 10.1016/j.jadohealth.2014.06.007 PMID: 25168105

Moe, I., Ho, P. J., Andersson, M., Karlberg, S., Lidfors, L., Sampaio, F., & Feldman, I. (2025). Effectiveness of animal-assisted services for school-aged children: A systematic review. *European Child & Adolescent Psychiatry, 34*(10), 3017–3033. DOI: 10.1007/s00787-025-02740-7

Moloi, K. C. (2010). How can schools build learning organisations in difficult education contexts? *South African Journal of Education, 30*(4), 621–633. DOI: 10.15700/saje.v30n4a392

Mombeck, M. M., & Albers, T. (2024). The Impact of a School Dog on Children's Social Inclusion and Social Climate in a School Class. *European Journal of Investigation in Health, Psychology and Education, 14*(1), 1–17. DOI: 10.3390/ejihpe14010001

Montague, M. (2008). Self-regulation strategies to improve mathematical problem solving for students with learning disabilities. *Learning Disability Quarterly, 31*(1), 37–44. DOI: 10.2307/30035524

Monteiro, L., Fernandes, M., Torres, N., & Santos, C. (2017). Father's involvement and parenting styles in Portuguese families. The role of education and working hours. *Análise Psicológica, 35*(4), 513–528. DOI: 10.14417/ap.1451

Moore, G. F., Audrey, S., Barker, M., Bond, L., Bonell, C., Hardeman, W., Moore, L., O'Cathain, A., Tinati, T., Wight, D., & Baird, J. (2015). Process evaluation of complex interventions: *Medical Research Council guidance. BMJ (Clinical Research Ed.), 350*(mar19 6), h1258. Advance online publication. DOI: 10.1136/bmj.h1258

Morcom, V., & MacCallum, J. (2022). Mentoring experienced teachers to change their practice: A sociocultural perspective for professional learning and development. *Learning, Culture and Social Interaction, 34*, 100627. DOI: 10.1016/j.lcsi.2022.100627

Morgan, D. L. (1997). *Focus groups as qualitative research* (2nd ed.). Sage. DOI: 10.4135/9781412984287

Morgan, S. (2024). Animal assisted education and social communication competency: Systematic literature review. *Discover Education, 3*(1), 258. Advance online publication. DOI: 10.1007/s44217-024-00357-7

Morris, A. S., Silk, J. S., Steinberg, L., Myers, S. S., & Robinson, L. R. (2007). The role of the family context in the development of emotion regulation. *Social Development, 16*(2), 361–388. DOI: 10.1111/j.1467-9507.2007.00389.x PMID: 19756175

Morrow, M. T., Hubbard, J. A., McAuliffe, M. D., Rubin, R. M., & Dearing, K. F. (2006). Childhood aggression, depressive symptoms, and peer rejection: The mediational model revisited. *International Journal of Behavioral Development, 30*(3), 240–248. DOI: 10.1177/0165025406066757

Mortimore, P. (1993). School effectiveness and the management of effective Learning and teaching. *School Effectiveness and School Improvement, 4*(4), 290–310. DOI: 10.1080/0924345930040404

Munezero, E., Tóth, E., & Hódi, Á. (2026). A systematic review on teacher resilience assessment: Trends, foci, and implications. *Hungarian Educational Research Journal*, 063-2026. DOI: 10.1556/063.2026.00425

Muñoz, J. M., Braza, P., Carreras, R., Braza, F., Azurmendi, A., Pascual-Sagastizábal, E., Cardas, J., & Sánchez-Martín, J. R. (2017). Daycare center attendance buffers the effects of maternal authoritarian parenting style on physical aggression in children. *Frontiers in Psychology, 8*, 391. DOI: 10.3389/fpsyg.2017.00391 PMID: 28377733

Murgor, J. C., Korir, R. R., & Ogoma, S. O. (2020). In-school gender-based violence in public primary schools in one municipality, Kenya. *International Journal of Education and Research, 8*(6), 1–16.

Murray, E., McFarland-Piazza, L., & Harrison, L. J. (2015). Changing patterns of parent–teacher communication and parent involvement from preschool to school. *Early Child Development and Care, 185*(7), 1031–1052. DOI: 10.1080/03004430.2014.975223

Mustafa, Q. M., & Alwi, A. H. (2021). Stress experiences of mothers of children with ADHD: Significant coping strategies that safeguard their mental health. *Malaysian Journal of Medicine & Health Sciences, 17*(3).

National Association of State Public Health Veterinarians Animal Contact Compendium Committee. (2023). *Compendium of measures to prevent disease associated with animals in public settings.* https://nasphv.org/Documents/AnimalsInPublicSettings2023.pdf

National Research Council. (2012). *Education for life and work: Developing transferable knowledge and skills in the 21st century.* The National Academies Press. https://www.nationalacademies.org/projects/DBASSE-CFE-10-06

New York State Department of Agriculture and Markets. (2019). *Guidance for handlers and facilities using therapy dogs.* https://agriculture.ny.gov/system/files/documents/2020/03/therapydogguidance.pdf

Ngai, J. T. K., Yu, R. W. M., Chau, K. K. Y., & Wong, P. W. C. (2021). Effectiveness of a school-based programme of animal-assisted humane education in Hong Kong for the promotion of social and emotional learning: A quasi-experimental pilot study. *PLoS One*, *16*(3), e0249033. Advance online publication. DOI: 10.1371/journal.pone.0249033

Nicoll, K., Trifone, C., & Samuels, W. E. (2008). An in-class, humane education program can improve young students' attitudes toward animals. *Society & Animals*, *16*(1), 45–60. DOI: 10.1163/156853008X269881

Niesler, A., Ścigała, G., & Łudzeń-Izbińska, B. (2016). Cat (Fel d 1) and dog (Can f 1) allergen levels in cars, dwellings and schools. *Aerobiologia*, *32*(3), 571–580. DOI: 10.1007/s10453-016-9433-7

Nijs, L. (2025). Fostering a synergy between the development of well-being and musicianship: A kinemusical perspective. *Education Sciences*, *15*(9), 1245. DOI: 10.3390/educsci15091245

Nikolaou, E. N., & Stamatis, P. J. (2022). Preservice Preschool Teachers' perspectives on the Psychological Well-being of Pre-schoolers. *The International Journal of Childbirth Education*, *3*(2), 1–8. DOI: 10.33422/ijce.v3i2.313

Nikolaou, E. N., & Stamatis, P. J.Eleni N. NikolaouPanagiotis J. Stamatis. (2023). Promoting Teacher Psychological Well-Being: Implications for School Mental Health and Teacher Training. *US-China Education Review B*, *13*(4), 213–222. DOI: 10.17265/2161-6248/2023.04.001

Nind, M., Wiles, R., Bengry-Howell, A., & Crow, G. (2021). Ethical challenges in the researcher-participant relationship: Reflective ethical decision-making in qualitative research. *Qualitative Research*, *21*(2), 261–276. DOI: 10.1177/1468794118796365

Nitschke, P. (2024). Berger & Luckmann (1966): The Social Construction of Reality. In Hoffjann, O., & Sandhu, S. (Eds.), *Schlüsselwerke für die Strategische Kommunikationsforschung*. Springer VS., DOI: 10.1007/978-3-658-45292-6_29

Nonaka, I., & Takeuchi, H. (1995). *The knowledge-creating company: How Japanese companies create the dynamics of innovation*. Oxford University Press. DOI: 10.1093/oso/9780195092691.001.0001

Ntavlamanou, M. (2024). Occupational Burnout of Greek Primary Education Teachers. European. *Journal of Education and Pedagogy*, *5*(6), 46–51. DOI: 10.24018/ejedu.2024.5.6.893

O'Haire, M. E., Guérin, N. A., & Kirkham, A. C. (2015). Animal-assisted intervention for trauma: A systematic literature review. *Frontiers in Psychology*, *6*. Advance online publication. DOI: 10.3389/fpsyg.2015.01121

O'Haire, M. E., McKenzie, S. J., Beck, A. M., & Slaughter, V. (2013). Social behaviors increase in children with autism in the presence of animals compared to toys. *PLoS One*, *8*(2), e57010. Advance online publication. DOI: 10.1371/journal.pone.0057010

O'Haire, M. E., McKenzie, S. J., McCune, S., & Slaughter, V. (2013). Effects of animal-assisted activities with guinea pigs in the primary school classroom. *Anthrozoos*, *26*(3), 445–458. DOI: 10.2752/175303713X13697429463835

OECD. (2013). *Synergies for better learning: An international perspective on evaluation and assessment*. OECD Publishing.

OECD. (2018). *Education at a glance 2018: OECD indicators*. OECD Publishing., DOI: 10.1787/eag-2018-

OECD. (2020). *Supporting teachers' well-being: Insights from TALIS 2018*. OECD Publishing., DOI: 10.1787/53e2b1bd-

OECD. (2024). Nurturing Social and Emotional Learning Across the Globe: Findings from the OECD Survey on Social and Emotional Skills 2023. OECD Publishing. https://www.oecd.org/en/publications/nurturing-social-and-emotional-learning-across-the-globe_32b647d0-en.html

OECD. (2025). *Education at a Glance 2025: OECD Indicators*. OECD Publishing.

Olivari, M. G., Wahn, E. H., Maridaki-Kassotaki, K., Antonopoulou, K., & Confalonieri, E. (2015). Adolescent perceptions of parenting styles in Sweden, Italy and Greece: An exploratory study. *Europe's Journal of Psychology*, *11*(2), 244–258. DOI: 10.5964/ejop.v11i2.887 PMID: 27247655

Olivier, M. A., Gomes, A. M., & Greyling, A. J. (2009). Attention deficit hyperactivity disorder (ADHD)—Dilemmas and solutions. *Journal of Psychology in Africa*, *19*(2), 237–241. DOI: 10.1080/14330237.2009.10820285

Ollila, J., Mankki, V., & Räihä, P. (2025). Collaboration and control: Insights into principals' role in establishing teacher mentoring in Finnish schools. *Professional Development in Education*, •••, 1–18. DOI: 10.1080/19415257.2025.2567260

Organisation for Economic Co-operation and Development. (2016). *Education at a glance 2016: OECD indicators*. OECD Publishing., DOI: 10.1787/eag-2016-

Organisation for Economic Co-operation and Development. (2017). *PISA 2015 results (Volume III): Students' well-being*. OECD Publishing. https://doi.org/DOI: 10.1787/9789264273856-en

Organisation for Economic Co-operation and Development. (2020). *Early learning and child well-being: A study of five-year-olds in England, Estonia, and the United States*. OECD Publishing. https://doi.org/DOI: 10.1787/3990407f-en

Ostrov, J. M., & Bishop, C. M. (2008). Preschoolers' aggression and parent-child conflict: A multi-informant and multimethod study. *Journal of Experimental Child Psychology, 99*(4), 309–322. DOI: 10.1016/j.jecp.2008.01.001 PMID: 18299136

Özmen, F., Akuzum, C., Zincirli, M., & Selcuk, G. (2016). The Communication Barriers between Teachers and Parents in Primary Schools. *Eurasian Journal of Educational Research, 16*(66), 27–46. https://dergipark.org.tr/en/pub/ejer/issue/42424/510769. DOI: 10.14689/ejer.2016.66.2

Pagán-Castaño, E., Sánchez-García, J., Garrigos-Simon, F. J., & Guijarro-García, M. (2021). The influence of management on teacher well-being and the development of sustainable schools. *Sustainability (Basel), 13*(6), 2909. DOI: 10.3390/su13052909

Pakaluk, C. R., & Price, J. (2020). Are mothers and father's interchangeable caregivers? *Marriage & Family Review, 56*(8), 784–793. DOI: 10.1080/01494929.2020.1778318

Pakarinen, E., Kiuru, N., Lerkkanen, M., Poikkeus, A., Siekkinen, M., & Nurmi, J. (2010). Classroom organization and teacher stress predict learning motivation in kindergarten children. *European Journal of Psychology of Education, 25*(3), 281–300. DOI: 10.1007/s10212-010-0025-6

Palts, K., & Harro-Loit, H. (2015). PARENT-TEACHER COMMUNICATION PATTERNS CONCERNING ACTIVITY AND POSITIVE-NEGATIVE ATTITUDES. *Trames, 19*(2), 139–154. https://www.kirj.ee/public/trames_pdf/2015/issue_2/Trames-2015-2-139-154.pdf

Panadero, E. (2017). A review of self-regulated learning: Six models and four directions for research. *Frontiers in Psychology, 8*, 422. DOI: 10.3389/fpsyg.2017.00422 PMID: 28503157

Panagiotopoulos, G., & Moysidou, E. (2014). Conclusions. In Vergidis, D., Panagiotopoulos, G., & Moysidou, E. (Eds.), *Violence in the school environment: A journey through the schools of the Regional Directorate of Education of Western Greece* (pp. 255–266). Peloponnisos.

Papageorgi, I., Saunders, J., Himonides, E., & Welch, G. F. (2022). Singing and social identity in young children. *Frontiers in Psychology, 13*, 823229. DOI: 10.3389/fpsyg.2022.823229 PMID: 35719461

Pashiardis, P. (2004). *Educational leadership: From the period of benevolent indifference to the modern era.* Metaichmio Publications.

Patti, J., Senge, P., Madrazo, C., & Stern, R. (2015). Developing socially, emotionally, and cognitively competent school leaders and learning communities. In Durlak, J. A., Domitrovich, C. E., Weissberg, R. P., & Gullotta, T. P. (Eds.), *Handbook of social and emotional learning: Research and practice* (pp. 438–452). Guilford Press.

Patton, M. Q. (1990). Qualitative evaluation and research methods. *Sage (Atlanta, Ga.).*

Patton, M. Q. (2002). *Qualitative research and evaluation methods* (3rd ed.). Sage.

Pedler, M., Burgoyne, J., & Boydell, T. (1997). *The learning company: A strategy for sustainable development* (2nd ed.). McGraw-Hill.

Pedro, M. F., Carapito, E., & Ribeiro, T. (2015). Parenting Styles and Dimensions Questionnaire – The Portuguese Self-Report Version/ Parenting Styles and Dimensions Questionnaire-versão portuguesa de autorrelato. *Psicologia: Reflexão e Crítica : Revista Semestral do Departamento de Psicologia da UFRGS, 28*(2), 302–312. DOI: 10.1590/1678-7153.201528210

Peña-Jorquera, H., Hernández-Jaña, S., Sanchez-Martinez, J., Espinoza-Puelles, J. P., Martínez-Flores, R., Barreto-Schuch, F., Yáñez-Sepúlveda, R., Delgado-Floody, P., Ferrari, G., Sadarangani, K. P., Cancino-López, J., Bento-Torres, J., Espinoza-Salinas, A., Stamatakis, E., & Cristi-Montero, C. (2025). Dog companionship and cortisol levels in youth: A systematic review and meta-analysis. *Social Science & Medicine, 369*, 117815. Advance online publication. DOI: 10.1016/j.socscimed.2025.117815

Pereira, A. I., Canavarro, C., Cardoso, M. F., & Mendonça, D. (2009). Patterns of parental rearing styles and child behavior problems among Portuguese school-aged children. *Journal of Child and Family Studies, 18*(4), 454–464. DOI: 10.1007/s10826-008-9249-3

Peter, M., Diekötter, T., & Kremer, K. (2019). Participant Outcomes of Biodiversity Citizen Science Projects: A Systematic Literature Review. *Sustainability (Basel), 11*(10), 2780. DOI: 10.3390/su11102780

Peura, P., Aro, T., Viholainen, H., Räikkönen, E., Usher, E. L., Sorvo, R., & Aro, M. (2019). Reading self-efficacy and reading fluency development among primary school children: Does specificity of self-efficacy matter? *Learning and Individual Differences, 73*, 67–78. DOI: 10.1016/j.lindif.2019.05.007

Pianta, R. C., Hamre, B. K., & Allen, J. P. (2012). Teacher–student relationships and engagement: Conceptualizing, measuring, and improving the capacity of classroom interactions. In Christenson, S. L., Reschly, A. L., & Wylie, C. (Eds.), *Handbook of research on student engagement* (pp. 365–386). Springer., DOI: 10.1007/978-1-4614-2018-7_17

Piekarczyk, A. (2017). Organisation Culture from Systems Theory of Organisation Perspective. In Nedelko, Z., & Brzozowski, M. (Eds.), *Exploring the Influence of Personal Values and Cultures in the Workplace* (pp. 39–52). IGI Global., DOI: 10.4018/978-1-5225-2480-9.ch003

Pinquart, M. (2017). Associations of parenting dimensions and styles with externalizing problems of children and adolescents: An updated meta-analysis. *Developmental Psychology, 53*(5), 873–932. DOI: 10.1037/dev0000295 PMID: 28459276

Pinquart, M., & Kauser, R. (2018). Do the associations of parenting styles with behavior problems and academic achievement vary by culture? Results from a meta-analysis. *Cultural Diversity & Ethnic Minority Psychology, 24*(1), 75–100. DOI: 10.1037/cdp0000149 PMID: 28394165

Pinto, L. E., & Foulkes, D. (2015). Well-Being and Human-Animal Interactions in Schools: The Case of "Dog Daycare Co-Op". *Brock Education Journal, 24*(2). Advance online publication. DOI: 10.26522/brocked.v24i2.395

Pintrich, P. R. (2004). A conceptual framework for assessing motivation and self-regulated learning in college students. *Educational Psychology Review, 16*(4), 385–407. DOI: 10.1007/s10648-004-0006-x

Piotrowski, J. T., Lapierre, M. A., & Linebarger, D. L. (2013). Investigating correlates of self-regulation in early childhood with a representative sample of English-speaking American families. *Journal of Child and Family Studies, 22*(3), 423–436. DOI: 10.1007/s10826-012-9595-z PMID: 23525149

Pleck, J. H., Masciadrelli, B. P., & Lamb, M. E. (2004). Paternal involvement by US residential fathers. *The role of the father in child development, 4*, 222-271.

Podolski, C. L., & Nigg, J. T. (2001). Parent stress and coping in relation to child ADHD severity and associated child disruptive behavior problems. *Journal of Clinical Child Psychology, 30*(4), 503–513. DOI: 10.1207/S15374424JCCP3004_07 PMID: 11708238

Polheber, J. P., & Matchock, R. L. (2014). The presence of a dog attenuates cortisol and heart rate in the Trier Social Stress Test compared to human friends. *Journal of Behavioral Medicine, 37*(5), 860–867. DOI: 10.1007/s10865-013-9546-1

Pomaki, G., & Anagnostopoulou, T. (2003). A test and extension of the demand/control/social support model: Prediction of wellness/health outcomes in Greek teachers. *Psychology & Health, 18*(4), 537–550. DOI: 10.1080/0887044031000147256

Pomerantz, E. M., & Wang, Q. (2009). The role of parental control in children's development in Western and East Asian countries. *Current Directions in Psychological Science, 18*(5), 285–289. DOI: 10.1111/j.1467-8721.2009.01653.x

Pong, S. L., Johnston, J., & Chen, V. (2010). Authoritarian parenting and Asian adolescent school performance: Insights from the US and Taiwan. *International Journal of Behavioral Development, 34*(1), 62–72. DOI: 10.1177/0165025409345073 PMID: 24850978

Pot, F. D. (2017). Workplace innovation and wellbeing at work. In Oeij, P., Rus, D., & Pot, F. (Eds.), *Workplace innovation: Aligning perspectives on health, safety and well-being* (pp. 95–110). Springer. DOI: 10.1007/978-3-319-56333-6_7

Proctor, E., Silmere, H., Raghavan, R., Hovmand, P., Aarons, G., Bunger, A., Griffey, R., & Hensley, M. (2011). Outcomes for implementation research: Conceptual distinctions, measurement challenges, and research agenda. *Administration and Policy in Mental Health, 38*(2), 65–76. DOI: 10.1007/s10488-010-0319-7

Propper, C., & Moore, G. A. (2006). The influence of parenting on infant emotionality: A multi-level psychobiological perspective. *Developmental Review, 26*(4), 427–460. DOI: 10.1016/j.dr.2006.06.003

PS IMAGO. (2013–2024). PS IMAGO PRO Version 10 [Computer software].

Psyrras, N. (2026). Leadership 4.0 in education: Beyond technology. *Management in Education, 08920206261440720*, 08920206261440720. Advance online publication. DOI: 10.1177/08920206261440720

Pushor, D. (2015). Walking Alongside: A Pedagogy of Working with Parents and Family in Canada. *Teaching Education, 42*(4), 5–26. DOI: 10.1108/S1479-368720150000025008

Pushor, D., & Ruitenberg, C. (2005). *Parent engagement and leadership*. Dr. Stirling McDowell Foundation for Research into Teaching., https://mcdowellfoundation.ca/wp-content/uploads/2025/08/134_parent_engagement.pdf

Quinn, J. F., Cola, P. A., Cooper, M., & Miller, C. (2025). Development of a survey tool to assess emotional and social behavioral competencies of science technology engineering math and medicine (STEMM) graduate students. *PLoS One*, *20*(9), e0328308. DOI: 10.1371/journal.pone.0328308

Qvortrup, L. (2005). Society's education system: An introduction to Niklas Luhmann's pedagogical theory. *Seminar. International Journal (Toronto, Ont.)*, *1*(1), 1–21.

Ramage, M., & Shipp, K. (2009). *Systems thinkers*. Springer., DOI: 10.1007/978-1-84882-525-3

Rankin Williams, L., Degnan, K. A., Perez-Edgar, K. E., Henderson, H. A., Rubin, K. H., Pine, D. S., Steinberg, L., & Fox, N. A. (2009). Impact of behavioral inhibition and parenting style on internalizing and externalizing problems from early childhood through adolescence. *Journal of Abnormal Child Psychology*, *37*(8), 1063–1075. DOI: 10.1007/s10802-009-9331-3 PMID: 19521761

Raptis, N. G., & Psyrras, N. (2026). Integrating artificial intelligence in primary education: empirical insights of school leadership perspectives. In *Artificial Intelligence in Education* (Vol. 2, No. 3, pp. 18-32). Emerald Publishing Limited. DOI: 10.1108/AIIE-06-2025-0149

Ravi, R. (2026). Concepts, measures and policy problems: The case study of child wellbeing measurement in the UK between 2014 and 2024. *Child Indicators Research*, *19*(3), 1393–1416. Advance online publication. DOI: 10.1007/s12187-026-10346-x

Reeve, J., & Cheon, S. H. (2021). Autonomy-supportive teaching: Its malleability, benefits, and potential to improve educational practice. *Educational Psychologist*, *56*(1), 54–77. DOI: 10.1080/00461520.2020.1862657

Reilly, K. M., Adesope, O. O., & Erdman, P. (2020). The effects of dogs on learning: A meta-analysis. *Anthrozoos*, *33*(3), 339–360. DOI: 10.1080/08927936.2020.1746523

Rickard, M., Ackermann, D. M., Schnitzler, M., & Kozlowski, D. (2025). Emotional intelligence as a component of surgical coaching: A scoping review. *Journal of Surgical Education*, *82*(1), 103316. DOI: 10.1016/j.jsurg.2024.103316

Rinaldi, C. M., & Howe, N. (2012). Mothers' and fathers' parenting styles and associations with toddlers' externalizing, internalizing, and adaptive behaviors. *Early Childhood Research Quarterly*, *27*(2), 266–273. DOI: 10.1016/j.ecresq.2011.08.001

Ringer, N. (2019). Young people's perceptions of and coping with their ADHD symptoms: A qualitative study. *Cogent Psychology*, *6*(1), 1608032. DOI: 10.1080/23311908.2019.1608032

Robson, C. (2007). *Real world research: A resource for social scientists and practitioner-researchers*. Gutenberg - G. & K. Dardanos.

Rolff, H.-G. (1993). *Wandel durch Selbstorganisation: Theoretische Grundlagen und praktische Hinweise für eine bessere Schule*. Juventa.

Rolff, H.-G. (2013). Schulleitung und Schulentwicklung. In Rolff, H.-G. (Ed.), *Schulentwicklung kompakt: Modelle, Instrumente, Perspektiven* (pp. 10–29). Beltz.

Röll, J., Koglin, U., & Petermann, F. (2012). Emotion regulation and childhood aggression: Longitudinal associations. *Child Psychiatry and Human Development*, *43*(6), 909–923. DOI: 10.1007/s10578-012-0303-4 PMID: 22528031

Romanovska, L., & Novak, M. (2024). THE ROLE OF TEACHER-STUDENT RELATIONSHIPS IN PROVIDING SOCIAL AND PSYCHOLOGICAL SUPPORT TO PARTICIPANTS OF THE EDUCATIONAL PROCESS. *Social Work Education*, *11*(2), 308–319. DOI: 10.25128/2520-6230.24.2.11

Ross, S. W., Romer, N., & Horner, R. H. (2012). Teacher well-being and the implementation of schoolwide positive behavior interventions and supports. *Journal of Positive Behavior Interventions*, *20*(10), 1–12.

Rothbart, M. K., & Bates, J. E. (2006). Temperament. In Eisenberg, N., Damon, W., & Lerner, R. M. (Eds.), *Social, emotional, and personality development* (pp. 99–166). Handbook of child psychology. John Wiley & Sons, Inc.

Roth, S. (2011). Les deux révolutions de l'autopoïèse: De la biologie à l'organisation. *Revue Internationale de Psychosociologie*, *17*(43), 179–204.

Rud, A. G.Jr, & Beck, A. M. (2003). Companion animals in Indiana elementary schools. *Anthrozoos*, *16*(3), 241–251. DOI: 10.2752/089279303786992134

Rusk, R. D., & Waters, L. E. (2013). Tracing the size, reach, impact, and breadth of positive psychology. *The Journal of Positive Psychology*, *8*(3), 207–221. DOI: 10.1080/17439760.2013.777766

Russell, W., & Qiu, H. (2024). The Dynamics of Parent–Teacher Relationships and Their Impact on Student Success. *Iranian Journal of Educational Sociology*, *7*(1), 212–218. DOI: 10.61838/kman.ijes.7.1.21

Rutter, M. (2006). Implications of resilience concepts for scientific understanding. *Annals of the New York Academy of Sciences*, *1094*(1), 1–12. DOI: 10.1196/annals.1376.002

Ryan, R. M., & Deci, E. L. (2000). Self-determination theory and the facilitation of intrinsic motivation, social development, and well-being. *The American Psychologist*, *55*(1), 68–78. DOI: 10.1037/0003-066X.55.1.68

Ryan, R. M., & Deci, E. L. (2017). *Self-determination theory: Basic psychological needs in motivation, development, and wellness*. Guilford Press. DOI: 10.1521/978.14625/28806

Ryan, R. M., & Deci, E. L. (2020). Intrinsic and extrinsic motivation from a self-determination theory perspective: Definitions, theory, practices, and future directions. *Contemporary Educational Psychology*, *61*, 101860. DOI: 10.1016/j.cedpsych.2020.101860

Ryff, C. D. (1989). Happiness is everything, or is it? Explorations on the meaning of psychological well-being. *Journal of Personality and Social Psychology*, *57*(6), 1069–1081. DOI: 10.1037/0022-3514.57.6.1069

Ryff, C. D., & Singer, B. H. (2015). Know thyself and become what you are: A eudaimonic approach to psychological well-being. *Journal of Happiness Studies*, *16*(1), 3–20. DOI: 10.1007/s10902-013-9504-1

Saaranen, T., Tossavainen, K., Turunen, H., & Vertio, H. (2007). Occupational well-being of school staff members: A structural equation model. *Health Education Research*, *22*(2), 248–260. DOI: 10.1093/her/cyl073 PMID: 16880218

Saarikallio, S., Baltazar, M., & Västfjäll, D. (2020). Adolescents' musical relaxation: Understanding emotional self-regulation through music. *Psychology of Music*, *48*(5), 653–667. DOI: 10.1177/0305735619854021

Sadownik, A. R. (2023). Bronfenbrenner: Ecology of human development in ecology of collaboration. In Sadownik, A. R., & Višnjić Jevtić, A. (Eds.), *Re) theorising more-than-parental involvement in early childhood education and care* (pp. 83–95). Springer., DOI: 10.1007/978-3-031-38762-3_4

Sahlberg, P., & Stringer, A. (2023). Coaching for professional learning of early career teachers. In *International Encyclopedia of Education* (pp. 144–152). Elsevier Ltd., DOI: 10.1016/B978-0-12-818630-5.04011-2

Samuels, W. E., & Onuoha-Jackson, N. (2023). Learning to care: An in-school humane education program improves affective and cognitive empathy among lower-elementary students. *International Journal of Educational Research Open*, *5*, 100292. Advance online publication. DOI: 10.1016/j.ijedro.2023.100292

Sandstrom, M. J. (2007). A link between mothers' disciplinary strategies and children's relational aggression. *British Journal of Developmental Psychology*, *25*(3), 399–407. DOI: 10.1348/026151006X158753

Sankalaite, S., Huizinga, M., Dewandeleer, J., Xu, C., De Vries, N., Hens, E., & Baeyens, D. (2021). Strengthening executive function and self-regulation through teacher-student interaction in preschool and primary school children: A systematic review. *Frontiers in Psychology*, *12*, 718262. DOI: 10.3389/fpsyg.2021.718262 PMID: 34489822

Santaniello, A., Dicé, F., Carratú, R. C., Amato, A., Fioretti, A., & Menna, L. F. (2020). Methodological and terminological issues in animal-assisted interventions: An umbrella review of systematic reviews. *Animals (Basel)*, *10*(5), 759. DOI: 10.3390/ani10050759

Sanvictores, T., & Mendez, M. D. (2022). Types of Parenting Styles and Effects on Children. In: StatPearls [Internet]. Treasure Island (FL): StatPearls Publishing; 2026 Jan-. Available from: https://www.ncbi.nlm.nih.gov/books/NBK568743/

Sarwar, S. (2016). Influence of parenting style on children's behaviour. *Journal of Education and Educational Development*, *3*(2), 222–249. DOI: 10.22555/joeed.v3i2.1036

Savaş, G., Arslan, K., Dolapcı, E., Erdoğan, O., & Kılınç, A. Ç. (2025). Leadership for learning, teacher epistemic curiosity and psychological safety: Promoting professional learning. *Educational Management Administration & Leadership*, *17411432251355389*, 17411432251355389. Advance online publication. DOI: 10.1177/17411432251355389

Sayer, L. C., Bianchi, S. M., & Robinson, J. P. (2004). Are parents investing less in children? Trends in mothers' and fathers' time with children. *American Journal of Sociology*, *110*(1), 1–43. DOI: 10.1086/386270

Scandurra, C., Santaniello, A., Cristiano, S., Mezza, F., Garzillo, S., Pizzo, R., Menna, L. F., & Bochicchio, V. (2021). An animal-assisted education intervention with dogs to promote emotion comprehension in primary school children—The Federico II model of healthcare zooanthropology. *Animals (Basel)*, *11*(6), 1504. Advance online publication. DOI: 10.3390/ani11061504

Schaufeli, W. B. (2015). Engaging leadership in the job demands-resources model. *Career Development International*, *20*(5), 446–463. DOI: 10.1108/CDI-02-2015-0025

Scheerens, J. (1992). *Effective schooling*. Cassell.

Schein, E. H. (1985). *Organizational culture and leadership*. Jossey-Bass.

Schina, E. M. (2016). *The professional well-being of primary education teachers and the factors determining it* (Master's thesis, University of Peloponnese, Department of Social and Educational Policy, Postgraduate Program: Educational Programs and Material - Formal, Informal and Distance Education).

Schön, D. A. (2017). *The reflective practitioner: How professionals think in action*. Routledge., DOI: 10.4324/9781315237473

Schonert-Reichl, K. A. (2017). Social and emotional learning and teachers. *The Future of Children*, *27*(1), 137–155. DOI: 10.1353/foc.2017.0007

Schröttle, M. (2010). Kritische Anmerkungen zur These der Gendersymmetrie bei Gewalt in Paarbeziehungen. *Gender – Zeitschrift für Geschlecht. Kultur und Gesellschaft*, *2*(1), 133–151.

Schuck, S. E. B., Emmerson, N. A., Fine, A. H., & Lakes, K. D. (2015). Canine-assisted therapy for children with ADHD: Preliminary findings from the Positive Assertive Cooperative Kids Study. *Journal of Attention Disorders*, *19*(2), 125–137. DOI: 10.1177/1087054713502080

Schuck, S. E. B., Johnson, H. L., Abdullah, M. M., Stehli, A., Fine, A. H., & Lakes, K. D. (2018). The role of animal assisted intervention on improving self-esteem in children with attention deficit/hyperactivity disorder. *Frontiers in Pediatrics*, *6*, 300. Advance online publication. DOI: 10.3389/fped.2018.00300

Schuck, S. E. B., Zeiler, C. N., Stehli, A., Steinhoff, L. A., Stokes, R. Y., Jeffrey, S. E., & Granger, D. A. (2024). Acute salivary cortisol response in children with ADHD during psychosocial intervention with and without therapy dogs. *Frontiers in Psychiatry*, *15*, 1476522. Advance online publication. DOI: 10.3389/fpsyt.2024.1476522

Schultes, M. T. (2023). An introduction to implementation evaluation of school-based interventions. *European Journal of Developmental Psychology*, *20*(1), 189–201. DOI: 10.1080/17405629.2021.1976633

Schwerdtfeger, K. L., Larzelere, R. E., Werner, D., Peters, C., & Oliver, M. (2013). Intergenerational transmission of trauma: The mediating role of parenting styles on toddlers' DSM-related symptoms. *Journal of Aggression, Maltreatment & Trauma, 22*(2), 211–229. DOI: 10.1080/10926771.2013.743941

Seidl, D. (2005a). Organisational change and the concept of autopoiesis. In Czarniawska, B., & Sevón, K. (Eds.), *Global ideas: How ideas, objects and practices travel in the global economy* (pp. 133–146). Copenhagen Business School Press.

Seidl, D. (2005b). The basic concepts of Luhmann's theory of social systems. In Seidl, D., & Becker, K. H. (Eds.), *Niklas Luhmann and organization studies*. Liber & Copenhagen Business School Press.

Seidl, D. (2005c). *Organisational Identity and Self-Transformation: An Autopoietic Perspective*. Liber & Copenhagen Business School Press.

Seidl, D. (2007). Organisational identity and self-transformation: An autopoietic perspective. In Berthoin Antal, A., Dierkes, M., Child, J., & Nonaka, I. (Eds.), *Handbook of organizational learning and knowledge* (pp. 85–107). Oxford University Press.

Seidl, D., & Becker, K. H. (2006). Organizations as distinction generating and processing systems: Niklas Luhmann's contribution to organization studies. *Organization, 13*(1), 9–35. DOI: 10.1177/1350508406059635

Seidl, D., & Mormann, H. (2015). Niklas Luhmann as organization theorist. In Adler, P., du Gay, P., Morgan, G., & Reed, M. (Eds.), *The Oxford Handbook of Sociology, Social Theory, and Organization Studies: Contemporary Currents* (pp. 125–157). Academic., DOI: 10.1093/oxfordhb/9780199671083.013.0007

Seidman, I. (2013). *Interviewing as qualitative research: A guide for researchers in education and the social sciences*. Teachers College Press.

Selvitopu, A., & Kaya, M. (2026). Well-being and academic performance among students with an immigrant background: A meta-analysis. *Current Psychology (New Brunswick, N.J.), 45*(3), 256. DOI: 10.1007/s12144-025-08654-6

Selwyn, N. (2016). *Education and Technology: Key Issues and Debates* (2nd ed.). Bloomsbury Academic.

Senge, P. M. (1990). *The fifth discipline: The art and practice of the learning organization*. Century / Doubleday.

Serrano, I., Fernández, M., & Marcos, E. B. (2024). Building a set of indicators to assess migrant children's integration in Europe: A co-creation approach. *Child Indicators Research, 17*(6), 2389–2417. DOI: 10.1007/s12187-024-10165-y

Shanker, S. (2016). *Self-reg: How to help your child (and you) break the stress cycle and successfully engage with life*. Penguin.

Shao, X. (2021). *The implementation of digital communication (DC) in parent–teacher partnership in China: teachers' and parents' views*. Oxford University Research Archive. https://ora.ox.ac.uk/objects/uuid:ea270492-e1d2-4f14-ad66-8dae0f021c28

Shayegh, M., Bafrooei, K. B., & Rahimi, M. (2021). The role of family factors in aggression of preschool children by social skills intermediation. *Tulu-i Bihdasht, 20*(1), 38–54. DOI: 10.18502/tbj.v20i1.6183

Sheehan, M. J., & Watson, M. W. (2008). Reciprocal influences between maternal discipline techniques and aggression in children and adolescents. *Aggressive Behavior, 34*(3), 245–255. DOI: 10.1002/ab.20241 PMID: 18085532

Sheehan, W. J., Permaul, P., Petty, C. R., Coull, B. A., Baxi, S. N., Gaffin, J. M., Lai, P. S., Gold, D. R., & Phipatanakul, W. (2017). Association Between Allergen Exposure in Inner-City Schools and Asthma Morbidity Among Students. *JAMA Pediatrics, 171*(1), 31–38. DOI: 10.1001/jamapediatrics.2016.2543

Sheldon, S. B., & Van Voorhis, F. L. (2004). Partnership programs in U.S. schools: Their development and relationship to family involvement outcomes. *School Effectiveness and School Improvement, 15*(2), 125–148. DOI: 10.1076/sesi.15.2.125.30434

Shen, J., Shi, Q., & Zhang, S. (2026). Teacher induction and collaboration: Investigating the role of school instructional leadership, mentoring, and collaborative school culture. *Journal of Educational Change, 27*(1), 1–29. DOI: 10.1007/s10833-026-09541-y

Shen, L., & Yang, W. (2025). The intervention of music education on adolescents' subjective well-being from the perspective of sustainable development: A bibliometric review based on literature from 2000 to 2024. *Frontiers in Psychology, 16*, 1617097. DOI: 10.3389/fpsyg.2025.1617097 PMID: 40589882

Sheridan, S. M., Smith, T. E., Kim, E. M., Beretvas, S. N., & Park, S. (2012). A Meta-Analysis of Family–School Interventions and Children's Social–Emotional Functioning: Moderators and Components of Efficacy. *Review of Educational Research, 89*(2), 296–332. DOI: 10.3102/0034654318825437

Shields, C. M. (2010). Transformative leadership: Working for equity in diverse contexts. *Educational Administration Quarterly, 46*(4), 558–589. DOI: 10.1177/0013161X10375609

Shields, G. S., Sazma, M. A., & Yonelinas, A. P. (2016). The effects of acute stress on core executive functions: A meta-analysis and comparison with cortisol. *Neuroscience and Biobehavioral Reviews*, *68*, 651–668. DOI: 10.1016/j.neubiorev.2016.06.038

Shu, K. (2022). Teachers' commitment and self-efficacy as predictors of work engagement and well-being. *Frontiers in Psychology*, *13*, 850204. DOI: 10.3389/fpsyg.2022.850204

Silkenbeumer, M., & Vazquez Perez, R. (2010). *Gewalt und Geschlecht an Schulen: Analysen, Positionen, Praxishilfen*. Max-Traeger-Stiftung. https://www.gew.de/index.php?eID=dumpFile&t=f&f=24453&token=f77ae32eff309a4d6110e1c8a350aaeab5fb4d4f&sdownload=

Silverii, H., Cain, M. P., Ahn, J., Fernandez, N., Lendvay, T., Gupta, A., Joyner, B., Kieran, K., Shnorhavorian, M., & Merguerian, P. (2024). Putting the coach in the game: Current and future state of surgical coaching in pediatric urology. *Journal of Pediatric Urology*, *20*(4), 608–e1. DOI: 10.1016/j.jpurol.2024.03.004

Simbolon, R., & Purba, W. (2022). Evaluating the Impact of School Counseling Programs on Student Well-being and Academic Performance in the Educational Environment. *Jurnal Ilmu Pendidikan Dan Humaniora*, *11*(2), 118–137. DOI: 10.35335/jiph.v11i2.19

Simon, F. B. (2010). *Introduction to the systems theory of organizations* (Makrydimitris, A., Trans.). Sakkoulas.

Simon, H. A. (1957). *Administrative behavior: A study of decision-making processes in administrative organization* (2nd ed.). Macmillan.

Simons, L. G., & Conger, R. D. (2007). Linking mother-father differences in parenting to a typology of family parenting styles and adolescent outcomes. *Journal of Family Issues*, *28*(2), 212–241. DOI: 10.1177/0192513X06294593

Sink, C. A. (2005). *Contemporary school counseling: Theory, research, and practice*. Lahaska Press.

Skaalvik, E. M., & Skaalvik, S. (2017). Motivated for teaching? Associations with school goal structure, teacher self-efficacy, job satisfaction and emotional exhaustion. *Teaching and Teacher Education*, *67*, 152–160. DOI: 10.1016/j.tate.2017.06.006

Skaalvik, E. M., & Skaalvik, S. (2018). Job demands and job resources as predictors of teacher motivation and well-being. *Social Psychology of Education*, *21*(5), 1251–1275. DOI: 10.1007/s11218-018-9464-8

Skivington, K., Matthews, L., Simpson, S. A., Craig, P., Baird, J., Blazeby, J. M., Boyd, K. A., & Moore, L. (2021). A new framework for developing and evaluating complex interventions: Update of Medical Research Council guidance. *BMJ (Clinical Research Ed.)*, *37*, n2061. Advance online publication. DOI: 10.1136/bmj.n2061

Skounti, M., Philalithis, A., Mpitzaraki, K., Vamvoukas, M., & Galanakis, E. (2006). Attention deficit hyperactivity disorder in school children in Crete. *Acta Paediatrica (Oslo, Norway)*, *95*, 658–663. PMID: 16754545

Smith, T. D. (2021). Music Education for Surviving and Thriving: Cultivating Children's Wonder, Senses, Emotional Wellbeing, and Wild Nature as a Means to Discover and Fulfill Their Life's Purpose. *Frontiers in Education*, *6*, 648799. DOI: 10.3389/feduc.2021.648799

Smith, T. E., Thompson, A. M., & Maynard, B. R. (2022). Self-management interventions for reducing challenging behaviors among school-age students: A systematic review. *Campbell Systematic Reviews*, *18*(1), e1223. DOI: 10.1002/cl2.1223 PMID: 36913185

Sobhani, S., Jamilian, H., & Paknejad, I. (2024). Prediction of resilience based on parenting and coping strategies in patients with psychosomatic disorders. *BMC Psychology*, *12*(1), 280. DOI: 10.1186/s40359-024-01784-9 PMID: 38764081

Sofologi, M., Katsarou, D., Efthymiou, E., Kougioumtzis, G., Argyriadis, A., Kamari, A., Mantsos, E., & Megari, K. (2025). Unrevealing the pattern of interrelationships among learning behaviors, executive functions and social functioning in preschool age children. In Megari, K. (Ed.), *Clinical applications of pediatric neuropsychology from infancy to adolescence* (pp. 107–118). IGI Global. DOI: 10.4018/979-8-3693-9689-6.ch005

Solano, M. (2022). *Communicating Effectively: An Exploration of Communication Methods between Parents and Teachers with Mixed Methods*. West Chester University. https://digitalcommons.wcupa.edu/all_doctoral/156/

Sorensen, E. (1993). *Children's stress and coping: A family perspective*. Guilford Press.

Sorin, R., Brooks, T., & Lloyd, J. (2015). The impact of the Classroom Canines program on children's reading, social and emotional skills, and motivation to attend school. *The International Journal of Literacies*, *22*(2), 23–35. DOI: 10.18848/2327-0136/CGP/v22i02/48840

Southwick, S. M., Bonanno, G. A., Masten, A. S., Panter-Brick, C., & Yehuda, R. (2023). Resilience definitions, theory, and challenges: Interdisciplinary perspectives. *European Journal of Psychotraumatology, 14*(1), 2164790. DOI: 10.1080/20008198.2023.2164790 PMID: 25317257

Spillane, J. P. (2006). Towards a theory of leadership practice: A distributed perspective. In *Rethinking schooling* (pp. 208–242). Routledge.

Stake, R. E. (1995). The art of case study research. *Sage (Atlanta, Ga.).*

Stalmach, A., D'Elia, P., Di Sano, S., & Casale, G. (2023). Digital learning and self-regulation in students with special educational needs: A systematic review of current research and future directions. *Education Sciences, 13*(10), 1051. DOI: 10.3390/educsci13101051

Stamatis, P. J. & Nikolaou, E. N. (2016). Communication and collaboration between school and family for addressing bullying. *International Journal of Criminology and Sociology, 5, 99-104. Special Issue "Adjustment of Learners' Violent Behaviour in a School Context".* Lifescience Global https://doi.org/DOI: 10.6000/1929-4409.2016.05.09

Stamatis, P. J. (2013). *Communication in Education.* Diadrassi Publications.

Stamatis, P. J. (2015). *Preschool and Early Elementary School Pedagogy: Communicative Dimensions of Educational Procedure.* Diadrassi Publications.

Stamatis, P. J. (2015a). From Kindergarten to Primary School: Communication Activities for a Smoother Transition of Preschoolers. *The International Journal of Early Childhood Learning, 21*(3-4), 1–8. DOI: 10.18848/2327-7939/CGP/v21i3-4/48449

Stamatis, P. J. (2019). Communication relations among parents and preschoolers: Thoughts, comments and suggestions. In Nata, R. V. (Ed.), *Progress in Education* (Vol. 60, pp. 83–106). Nova Science Publishers.

Stamatis, P. J., & Chatzinikola, M. (2021). Advantages and Reasons Hindering the Communication between Teachers and Parents: An Empirical Study. *European Journal of Education and Pedagogy, 2*(2), 43–48. DOI: 10.24018/ejedu.2021.2.2.79

Stamatis, P. J., & Nikolaou, E. N. (2019). Parents' Perceptions about Bullying. In Ancho, I. V., & Krizna, K. R. (Eds.), *School Violence: Risk factors, prevention and challenges* (pp. 97–115). Nova Science Publishers.

Stamatis, P. J., & Nikolaou, E. N. (2020). *Communication and Mental Health Promotion in Early Childhood Education.* Nova Science Publishers. DOI: 10.52305/QXVD5566

Stamatis, P. J., & Nikolaou, E. N. (2022). *The 21st-century Kindergarten. Communication and counselling issues in preschool and early elementary school education*. Gutenberg.

Stamatis, P. J., & Nikolaou, E. N. (2022a). *Counseling and Communication in Education*. Diadrassi Publications.

Stamatis, P. J., & Stavropoulou, E. J. (2018). Communication styles of preschool and early primary school teachers during teaching activities. In Stamatis, P. J., & Nikolaou, E. N. (Eds.), *Violent Communication and Bullying in Early Childhood Education* (pp. 35–55). Nova Science Publishers.

Steel, J. (2024). Children's wellbeing and reading engagement: the impact of reading to dogs in a Scottish Primary 1 classroom. *Education 3-13, 52*(3), 375–390. https://doi.org/DOI: 10.1080/03004279.2022.2100442

Steel, J. (2023). Reading to Dogs in schools: A controlled feasibility study of an online Reading to Dogs intervention. *International Journal of Educational Research, 117*, 102117. Advance online publication. DOI: 10.1016/j.ijer.2022.102117

Steel, J. (2024). Reading to Dogs as a form of animal-assisted education: Are positive outcomes supported by quality research? *Literacy*, *58*(1), 102–119. DOI: 10.1111/lit.12345

Steel, J., Williams, J. M., & McGeown, S. (2021). Reading to dogs in schools: An exploratory study of teacher perspectives. *Educational Research*, *63*(3), 279–301. DOI: 10.1080/00131881.2021.1956989

Stefanova, E., & Nikolova, N. (2019). Overcoming the barriers in teacher–parent communication. In *Proceedings of EDULEARN19 Conference* (pp. 1107–1116). https://doi.org/DOI: 10.21125/edulearn.2019.0349

Stokes, P., Fatien Diochon, P., & Otter, K. (2021). "Two sides of the same coin?" Coaching and mentoring and the agentic role of context. *Annals of the New York Academy of Sciences*, *1483*(1), 142–152. DOI: 10.1111/nyas.14316

Stoll, L., & Fink, D. (1996). *Changing our schools: Linking school effectiveness and school improvement*. Open University Press.

Stover, C. S., Zhou, Y., Kiselica, A., Leve, L. D., Neiderhiser, J. M., Shaw, D. S., Natsuaki, M. N., Scaramella, L. V., & Reiss, D. (2016). Marital hostility, hostile parenting, and child aggression: Associations from toddlerhood to school age. *Journal of the American Academy of Child and Adolescent Psychiatry*, *55*(3), 235–242. DOI: 10.1016/j.jaac.2015.12.008 PMID: 26903257

Štremfel, U., Šterman Ivančič, K., & Peras, I. (2024). Addressing the sense of school belonging among all students? A systematic literature review. *European Journal of Investigation in Health, Psychology and Education*, *14*(11), 2901–2917. DOI: 10.3390/ejihpe14110190

Sun, P., & Scott, J. (2003). Exploring the divide: Organizational learning and learning organization. *The Learning Organization*, *10*(4), 202–215. DOI: 10.1108/09696470310476972

Sutton, P., & Shouse, A. W. (2016). Building a culture of collaboration in schools. *Phi Delta Kappan*, *97*(7), 69–73. DOI: 10.1177/0031721716641653

Suzuki, K., Kita, Y., Kaga, M., Takehara, K., Misago, C., & Inagaki, M. (2016). The association between children's behavior and parenting of caregivers: A longitudinal study in Japan. *Frontiers in Public Health*, *4*, 17. DOI: 10.3389/fpubh.2016.00017 PMID: 26913279

Sweeney, P. J., & LeBoeuf, J. (2023). Enabling Medical Leaders Through Mentoring. *Clinics in Sports Medicine*, *42*(2), 219–231. DOI: 10.1016/j.csm.2022.11.006

Tahir, A., & Safder, M. (2025). Relationship between Reflective Teaching and Teachers' Burnout at Public Secondary School Level. *Journal of Sustainable Education*, 15-24. DOI: 10.71257/jse.v2i2.4743

Talib, J., Mohamad, Z., & Mamat, M. (2011). Effects of parenting style on children development. *World Journal of Social Sciences*, *1*(2), 14–35.

Tasiou, K. (2024). Experiences of stigma in a family with a child with ADHD: A case study. *International Journal of Educational Innovation*, *6*(5), 1–15. DOI: 10.69685/VORM2511

Tasiou, K. S., & Nikolaou, E. N. (2025b). Psychological resilience of parents of children with neurodevelopmental disorders during COVID-19 pandemic: A systematic review. *Emotional & Behavioural Difficulties*, *30*(4), 1–15. DOI: 10.1080/13632752.2025.2536986

Tasiou, K., & Nikolaou, E. N. (2023). The psychological resilience of families of children with attention deficit hyperactivity disorder. In Katsarou, D. V., Koundourou, C., & Reppa, G. P. (Eds.), *New trends and approaches in psychopathology and mental health of children and adults* (pp. 99–121). Gutenberg.

Tasiou, K., & Nikolaou, E. N. (2024). A family's experiences of raising a child diagnosed with ADHD: Family functioning and organization, sources of support and quality of life—A case study. In Katsarou, D. V. (Ed.), *Childhood developmental language disorders: Role of inclusion, families, and professionals* (pp. 116–133). IGI Global Scientific Publishing.

Tasiou, K., & Nikolaou, E. N. (2025a). Well-being among parents raising a child diagnosed with attention deficit hyperactivity disorder (ADHD) and intervention programs: A literature review. In Sofologi, M., Katsarou, D. V., & Efthymiou, E. (Eds.), *Exploring cognitive and psychosocial dynamics across childhood and adolescence* (pp. 229–248). IGI Global Scientific Publishing.

Tasis, T. (2012, April–June). The dialogue between Habermas and Luhmann. *Theseis*, 119.

Tavassolie, T., Dudding, S., Madigan, A. L., Thorvardarson, E., & Winsler, A. (2016). Differences in perceived parenting style between mothers and fathers: Implications for child outcomes and marital conflict. *Journal of Child and Family Studies*, *25*(6), 2055–2068. DOI: 10.1007/s10826-016-0376-y

Taylor, L. D., Davis-Kean, P., & Malanchuk, O. (2007). Self-esteem, academic self-concept, and aggression at school. *Aggressive Behavior*, *33*(2), 130–136. DOI: 10.1002/ab.20174 PMID: 17441013

Taylor, R. D., Oberle, E., Durlak, J. A., & Weissberg, R. P. (2017). Promoting positive youth development through school-based social and emotional learning interventions: A meta-analysis of follow-up effects. *Child Development*, *88*(4), 1156–1171. DOI: 10.1111/cdev.12864

Teng, Z., Liu, Y., & Guo, C. (2015). A meta-analysis of the relationship between self-esteem and aggression among Chinese students. *Aggression and Violent Behavior*, *21*, 45–54. DOI: 10.1016/j.avb.2015.01.005

Tennessee Department of Education. (2025). *School therapy dog implementation guide.* https://www.tn.gov/content/dam/tn/education/health-%26-safety/School_Therapy_Dog_Implementation_Guide.pdf

Tepper, D., Shnookal, J., Howell, T., & Bennett, P. (2023). Can interacting with animals improve executive functions? A systematic review. *Animals (Basel)*, *13*(13), 2080. Advance online publication. DOI: 10.3390/ani13132080

Thapa, A., Cohen, J., Guffey, S., & Higgins-D'Alessandro, A. (2013). A Review of School Climate Research. *Review of Educational Research*, *83*(3), 357–385. DOI: 10.3102/0034654313483907

Theodoropoulou, M., & Argyriou, M. (2026). Enhancing memory processes in early childhood through musical activities: A descriptive survey of preschool teachers' perceptions. *European Journal of Education Studies*, *13*(4). Advance online publication. DOI: 10.46827/ejes.v13i4.6611

Theron, L. C. (2023). Resilience of children and adolescents in contexts of adversity: A social ecological perspective. *Child Abuse & Neglect*, *138*, 106054. DOI: 10.1016/j.chiabu.2023.106054

Thompson, B. (2019). Characteristics of Parent–Teacher E-Mail Communication. *Communication Education*, *57*(2), 201–223. DOI: 10.1080/03634520701852050

Thompson, K. L., & Gullone, E. (2003). Promotion of empathy and prosocial behaviour in children through humane education. *Australian Psychologist*, *38*(3), 175–182. DOI: 10.1080/00050060310001707187

Thurmond, V. A. (2001). The point of triangulation. *Journal of Nursing Scholarship*, *33*(3), 253–258. DOI: 10.1111/j.1547-5069.2001.00253.x

Tian, L., Wu, T. L. Y., Robinson, N. L., Carreno-Medrano, P., Chan, W. P., Sakr, M., Abdi, E., Croft, E. A., & Kulić, D. (2025). Quantitative data collection and analysis. In Kulić, D., Croft, E., & Sakr, M. (Eds.), *Experimental methodology for human–robot interaction* (pp. xx–xx). CRC Press., DOI: 10.1201/9781032693682-7

Tillmann, K.-J., Holler-Nowitzki, B., Holtappels, H. G., Meier, U., & Popp, U. (1999). *Schülergewalt als Schulproblem: Verursachende Bedingungen, Erscheinungsformen und pädagogische Handlungsperspektiven*. Juventa.

Trautner, M., & Schwinger, M. (2020). Integrating the concepts self-efficacy and motivation regulation: How do self-efficacy beliefs for motivation regulation influence self-regulatory success? *Learning and Individual Differences*, *80*, 101890. Advance online publication. DOI: 10.1016/j.lindif.2020.101890

Trautner, M., Schwinger, M., & Otterpohl, N. (2020). Effects of school-based self-regulation interventions on academic outcomes: A meta-analytic review. *Metacognition and Learning*, *15*(3), 315–344. DOI: 10.1007/s11409-020-09232-1

Travers, C. J. (2010). Current knowledge on the nature, prevalence, sources and potential impact of teacher stress. In Leka, T., & Houdmont, J. (Eds.), *Occupational health psychology* (pp. 23–54). Wiley-Blackwell.

Trenas, A. F. R., Osuna, M. J. P., Olivares, R. R., & Cabrera, J. H. (2013). Relationship between parenting style and aggression in a Spanish children sample. *Procedia: Social and Behavioral Sciences*, *82*, 529–536. DOI: 10.1016/j.sbspro.2013.06.304

Tristiana, R. D., Pratiwi, I. N., Wulansari, D., Yusuf, A., & Sulistyono, R. E. (2023). Adolescents' experience of gender-based violence: A qualitative study. *International Journal of Public Health Science, 12*(2), 822–830. DOI: 10.11591/ijphs.v12i2.22614

Tschannen-Moran, M. (2014). *TRUST MATTERS: LEADERSHIP for SUCCESSFUL SCHOOLS*. Jossey-Bass.

Tschannen-Moran, M., & Hoy, W. K. (2000). A multidisciplinary analysis of the nature, meaning, and measurement of trust. *Review of Educational Research, 70*(4), 547–593. DOI: 10.3102/00346543070004547

Tsoukas, H. (2005). *Complex knowledge: Studies in organizational epistemology*. Oxford University Press.

U.S. Department of Justice, Civil Rights Division. (2011). *ADA requirements: Service animals*. ADA.gov. https://www.ada.gov/resources/service-animals-2010-requirements/

Uchida, Y., Ogihara, Y., & Fukushima, S. (2015). Cultural construal of wellbeing: Theories and empirical evidence. In Glatzer, W., Camfield, L., Møller, V., & Rojas, M. (Eds.), *Global handbook of quality of life*. Springer. DOI: 10.1007/978-94-017-9178-6_38

Udry, J. R. (2000). Biological limits of gender construction. *American Sociological Review, 65*(3), 443–457. DOI: 10.1177/000312240006500307

Ulrich, R. S. (1984). View through a window may influence recovery from surgery. *Science, 224*(4647), 420–421. DOI: 10.1126/science.6143402

Uludag, O. (2013). The influence of aggression on students' achievement: Evidence from higher education. *Procedia: Social and Behavioral Sciences, 89*, 954–958. DOI: 10.1016/j.sbspro.2013.08.963

Underwood, M. K., Beron, K. J., & Rosen, L. H. (2009). Continuity and change in social and physical aggression from middle childhood through early adolescence. *Aggressive Behavior, 35*(5), 357–375. DOI: 10.1002/ab.20313 PMID: 19685551

UNESCO & UN Women. (2016). *Global guidance on addressing school-related gender-based violence*. UNESCO., DOI: 10.54675/VFOP6248

UNESCO, Global Education Monitoring Report Team. (2020). *Global education monitoring report 2020: Gender report – A new generation: 25 years of efforts for gender equality in education*. UNESCO. https://unesdoc.unesco.org/ark:/48223/pf0000374514

UNESCO. (2019). *Behind the numbers: Ending school violence and bullying*. UNESCO., DOI: 10.54675/TRVR4270

UNESCO. (2021). *Reimagining our futures together: a new social contract for education*. International Commission on the Futures of Education., DOI: 10.54675/ASRB4722

UNESCO. (2021). *The journey towards comprehensive sexuality education: Global status report*. UNESCO. https://unesdoc.unesco.org/ark:/48223/pf0000377963

Ungar, M. (2011). The social ecology of resilience: Addressing contextual and cultural ambiguity of a nascent construct. *The American Journal of Orthopsychiatry*, *81*(1), 1–17. https://psycnet.apa.org/doi/10.1111/j.1939-0025.2010.01067.x. DOI: 10.1111/j.1939-0025.2010.01067.x

Ungar, M. (2012). *The Social Ecology of Resilience: A Handbook of Theory and Practice*. Springer., DOI: 10.1007/978-1-4614-0586-3

Ungar, M. (2018). Systemic resilience: Principles and processes for a science of change in contexts of adversity. *Ecology and Society*, *23*(4), art34. Advance online publication. DOI: 10.5751/ES-10385-230434

Ungar, M. (2021). *Multisystemic resilience: Adaptation and transformation in contexts of change*. Oxford University Press., DOI: 10.1093/oso/9780190095888.001.0001

United Nations Girls' Education Initiative. (2020). *Frequently asked questions: School-related gender-based violence.* UNGEI. https://www.ungei.org/publication/frequently-asked-questions-school-related-gender-based-violence

United Nations Girls' Education Initiative. (2024). *Prevention of sexual violence in education settings: White paper.* UNGEI. https://www.ungei.org/sites/default/files/202410/Prevention%20Of%20Sexual%20Violence%20In%20Education%20Settings%20White%20Paper.pdf

United Nations Office for Disaster Risk Reduction. (2023). *Global assessment report on disaster risk reduction 2023: Mapping resilience for the sustainable development goals*. UNDRR.

United Nations. (2006). *World report on violence against children.* United Nations. https://violenceagainstchildren.un.org/sites/violenceagainstchildren.un.org/files/document_files/world_report_on_violence_against_children.pdf

Unrau, N. J., Rueda, R., Son, E., Polanin, J. R., Lundeen, R. J., & Muraszewski, A. K. (2017). Can reading self-efficacy be modified? A meta-analysis of the impact of interventions on reading self-efficacy. *Review of Educational Research, 88*(2), 167–204. DOI: 10.3102/0034654317743199

Vaillancourt, T., & Farrell, A. H. (2021). Mean kids become mean adults: Trajectories of indirect aggression from age 10 to 22. *Aggressive Behavior, 47*(4), 394–404. DOI: 10.1002/ab.21950 PMID: 33469944

Van Horn, J., Taris, T. W., Schaufeli, W. B., & Schreurs, P. J. G. (2004). The structure of occupational well-being: A study among Dutch teachers. *Journal of Occupational and Organizational Psychology, 77*(3), 365–375. DOI: 10.1348/0963179041752718

Váradi, J. (2022). A Review of the Literature on the Relationship of Music Education to the Development of Socio-Emotional Learning. *SAGE Open, 12*(1), 21582440211068501. Advance online publication. DOI: 10.1177/21582440211068501

Varela, F. G. (1979). *Principles of biological autonomy*. North Holland.

Verhoeven, R., Butter, R., Martens, R., & Enders-Slegers, M.-J. (2023). Animal-assisted education: Exploratory research on the positive impact of dogs on behavioral and emotional outcomes of elementary school students. *Children (Basel, Switzerland), 10*(8), 1316. Advance online publication. DOI: 10.3390/children10081316

Vickers, H. S., & Minke, K. M. (1995). Exploring parent–teacher relationships: Joining and communication to others. *School Psychology Quarterly, 10*(2), 133–150. DOI: 10.1037/h0088300

Vitaro, F., Brendgen, M., Larose, S., & Trembaly, R. E. (2005). Kindergarten disruptive behaviors, protective factors, and educational achievement by early adulthood. *Journal of Educational Psychology, 97*(4), 617–629. DOI: 10.1037/0022-0663.97.4.617

Vogel, S., & Schwabe, L. (2016). Learning and memory under stress: Implications for the classroom. *npj Science of Learning, 1*. DOI: 10.1038/npjscilearn.2016.11

Vogus, T. J., & Sutcliffe, K. M. (2007). Organizational resilience: Toward a theory and research agenda. In *Proceedings of the 2007 IEEE International Conference on Systems, Man and Cybernetics* (pp. 3418–3422). IEEE. https://doi.org/DOI: 10.1109/ICSMC.2007.4414160

Vrasidas, C. (2014). *Introduction to qualitative research*. CARDET Press.

Vreeland, A., Gruhn, M. A., Watson, K. H., Bettis, A. H., Compas, B. E., Forehand, R., & Sullivan, A. D. (2019). Parenting in context: Associations of parental depression and socioeconomic factors with parenting behaviors. *Journal of Child and Family Studies*, *28*(4), 1124–1133. DOI: 10.1007/s10826-019-01338-3 PMID: 41583615

Vygotsky, L. S. (1978). *Mind in society: The development of higher psychological processes.* Harvard University Press.

Walsh, F. (2008). Using theory to support a family resilience framework in practice. Social Work Now: The Practice Journal of Child, Youth and Family, 5–14.

Walsh, F. (2016). Applying a family resilience framework in training, practice, and research: Mastering the art of the possible. *Family Process*, *55*(4), 616–632. DOI: 10.1111/famp.12260 PMID: 27921306

Walsh, J. P., & Ungson, G. R. (1991). Organizational memory. *Academy of Management Review*, *16*(1), 57–91. DOI: 10.2307/258607

Wang'ombe, T. (2023). The role of educational leadership in fostering a positive school culture and enhancing teacher retention. *European Journal of Education*, *1*(1), 31–43.

Wang, F., Guo, J., & Yang, G. (2023). Study on positive psychology from 1999 to 2021: A bibliometric analysis. *Frontiers in Psychology*, *14*, 1101157. DOI: 10.3389/fpsyg.2023.1101157 PMID: 36935984

Wang, M. T., & Degol, J. L. (2016). School climate: A review of the construct, measurement, and impact on student outcomes. *Educational Psychology Review*, *28*(2), 315–352. DOI: 10.1007/s10648-015-9319-1

Warr, P. (1990). The measurement of well-being and other aspects of mental health. *Journal of Occupational Psychology*, *63*(3), 193–210. DOI: 10.1111/j.2044-8325.1990.tb00521.x

Warr, P. (2007). *Road improvement and poverty reduction in Laos.* Australian Agricultural and Resource Economics Society.

Watkins, T. J. (1997). Teacher Communications, Child Achievement, and Parent Traits in Parent Involvement Models. *The Journal of Educational Research*, *91*(1), 3–14. DOI: 10.1080/00220679709597515

Wefald, A. J., Mills, M. J., Smith, M. R., & Downey, R. G. (2012). A comparison of three job engagement measures: Examining the factorial and criterion-related validity. *Applied Psychology. Health and Well-Being*, *4*(1), 67–90. DOI: 10.1111/j.1758-0854.2011.01059.x PMID: 26286971

Weick, K. E. (1995). *Sensemaking in organizations.* Sage Publications.

Weissberg, R. P. (2019). Promoting the social and emotional learning of millions of school children. *Perspectives on Psychological Science, 14*(1), 65–69. DOI: 10.1177/1745691618817756

Weiss, M. (2015). Functional impairment in ADHD. In Adler, L. A., Spencer, T. J., & Wilens, T. E. (Eds.), *Attention-deficit hyperactivity disorder in adults and children* (pp. 42–52). Cambridge University Press.

Weist, M. D., Evans, S. W., & Lever, N. A. (Eds.). (2003). *Handbook of school mental health: Advancing practice and research* (pp. 1–7). Kluwer Academic/Plenum Publishers. DOI: 10.1007/978-0-387-73313-5

Welch, G. F., Biasutti, M., MacRitchie, J., McPherson, G. E., & Himonides, E. (2020). Editorial: The impact of music on human development and well-being. *Frontiers in Psychology, 11*, 1246. DOI: 10.3389/fpsyg.2020.01246 PMID: 32625147

Welch, G. F., & McPherson, G. E. (2018). Commentary: Music education and the role of music in people's lives. In Welch, G. F., & McPherson, G. E. (Eds.), *Music and music education in people's lives: An Oxford handbook of music education* (pp. 3–18). Oxford University Press., DOI: 10.1093/oxfordhb/9780199730810.013.0002

Wenger, E. (1998). *Communities of practice: Learning, meaning, and identity.* Cambridge University Press. DOI: 10.1017/CBO9780511803932

Wentzel, K. R. (1998). Social relationships and motivation in middle school: The role of parents, teachers, and peers. *Journal of Educational Psychology, 90*(2), 202–209. https://psycnet.apa.org/doi/10.1037/0022-0663.90.2.202. DOI: 10.1037/0022-0663.90.2.202

Wentzel, K. R. (2015). Teacher-Student Relationships, Motivation, and Competence at School. In Rubie-Davies, C. M. (Ed.), *The Routledge International Handbook of Social Psychology of the Classroom* (pp. 167–176). Routledge.

Wescott, S., & Roberts, S. (2025). On the utility of the concept of 'school-related gender-based violence' (SRGBV) in the context of escalating gendered violence in schools. *Critical Studies in Education*, 1–19. Advance online publication. DOI: 10.1080/17508487.2025.2514278

Widia, A. P., & Bustomi, Y. I. (2025). The effectiveness of guidance and counseling interventions in improving students' academic resilience: A systematic literature review. *International Journal of Multidisciplinary Reseach, 1*(2), 250–259.

Wiener, N. (1948). *Cybernetics: Or, Control and Communication in the Animal and the Machine*. MIT University Press.

Wilder, S. (2014). Effects of parental involvement on academic achievement: A meta-synthesis. *Educational Review, 66*(3), 377–397. DOI: 10.1080/00131911.2013.780009

Wilkins, A., & Ouchi, W. (1983). Efficient cultures: Exploring the relationship between culture and organizational performance. *Administrative Science Quarterly, 28*(3), 468–8. DOI: 10.2307/2392253

Willemse, T. M., Thompson, I., Vanderlinde, R., & Mutton, T. (2018). Family–school partnerships: A challenge for teacher education. Journal of Education for Teaching. *Journal of Education for Teaching, 44*(4), 1–6. DOI: 10.1080/02607476.2018.1465545

Williams, J. M., Padilla Cardoso, M., Zumaglini, S., & Finney, A. L. (2022). "Rabbit Rescuers": A school-based animal welfare education intervention for young children. *Anthrozoos, 35*(1), 55–73. DOI: 10.1080/08927936.2021.1944561

Willke, H. (1996). *Introduction to Systems Theory* (Livos, N., Trans.). Kritiki Publications.

Willke, H. (2007). *Smart governance: Governing the global knowledge society*. Campus Verlag.

Wilson Heenan, I., De Paor, D., Lafferty, N., & Mannix McNamara, P. (2023). The impact of transformational school leadership on school staff and school culture in primary schools—A systematic review of international literature. *Societies (Basel, Switzerland), 13*(6), 133. DOI: 10.3390/soc13060133

Wilson, E. O. (1984). *Biophilia*. Harvard University Press. DOI: 10.4159/9780674045231

Winsler, A., Madigan, A. L., & Aquilino, S. A. (2005). Correspondence between maternal and paternal parenting styles in early childhood. *Early Childhood Research Quarterly, 20*(1), 1–12. DOI: 10.1016/j.ecresq.2005.01.007

Wintermantel, L., Grové, C., Henderson, L., & Laletas, S. (2024). Social and emotional therapy dog-assisted interventions in mainstream school settings: A systematic review. *Educational and Developmental Psychologist, 41*(1), 74–90. DOI: 10.1080/20590776.2023.2256444

Wohlfarth, R., Mutschler, B., Beetz, A., & Schleider, K. (2014). An investigation into the efficacy of therapy dogs on reading performance in 6–7 year old children. *Human Animal Interactions Bulletin, 2*(2), 60–73. DOI: 10.1079/hai.2014.0013

Wolf, S., Torrente, C., McCoy, M., Rasheed, D., & Aber, J. L. (2015). Cumulative risk and teacher well-being in the Democratic Republic of the Congo. *Comparative Education Review*, *59*(4), 717–742. DOI: 10.1086/682902

Wolgast, A., & Fischer, N. (2017). You are not alone: Colleague support and goal-oriented cooperation as resources to reduce teachers' stress. *Social Psychology of Education*, *20*(1), 97–114. DOI: 10.1007/s11218-017-9366-1

Women, U. N. (2015). *A framework to underpin action to prevent violence against women.* UN Women. https://www.unwomen.org/sites/default/files/Headquarters/Attachments/Sections/Library/Publications/2015/Prevention_Framework_unwomen_nov2015.pdf

World Health Organization. (2002). *World report on violence and health* (Krug, E., Dahlberg, L., Mercy, J., Zwi, A., & Lozano, R., Eds.). World Health Organization., https://apps.who.int/iris/handle/10665/42495

World Health Organization. (2015). [*A European policy framework supporting action across government and society for health and well-being.* World Health Organization, Regional Office for Europe.]. *Health*, •••, 2020.

World Health Organization. (2022). *World mental health report: Transforming mental health for all.* World Health Organization.

Yaffe, Y. (2020). Systematic review of the differences between mothers and fathers in parenting styles and practices. *Current Psychology (New Brunswick, N.J.)*, •••, 1–14. DOI: 10.1007/s12144-020-01014-6

Yang, D., Chen, P., Wang, H., Wang, K., & Huang, R. (2022). Teachers' autonomy support and student engagement: A systematic literature review of longitudinal studies. *Frontiers in Psychology*, *13*, 925955. DOI: 10.3389/fpsyg.2022.925955 PMID: 36072024

Yin, R. K. (2018). *Case study research and applications: Design and methods* (6th ed.). Sage.

Yu, G., & Wang, C. (2023). Teacher as Mediator: How Teacher Interacts with Parents of the Victim and Agent in School Conflict. *Contrastive Pragmatics*, *4*(1), 1–30. DOI: 10.1163/26660393-bja10070

Zabihollahzadeh, F., Rashvand, P., & Nemattavosi, M. (2020). The effectiveness of cognitive behavioral therapy based on mindfulness on resilience and self-regulation emotional in mothers of adolescents attention deficit hyperactivity disorder (ADHD). [RRJ]. *Rooyesh-e-Ravanshenasi Journal*, *8*(12), 31–38.

Zenner, C., Herrnleben-Kurz, S., & Walach, H. (2014). Mindfulness-based interventions in schools—A systematic review and meta-analysis. *Frontiers in Psychology*, *5*, 603. DOI: 10.3389/fpsyg.2014.00603 PMID: 25071620

Zhao, Q. (2022). On the role of teachers' professional identity and well-being in their professional development. *Frontiers in Psychology*, *13*, 913708. DOI: 10.3389/fpsyg.2022.913708 PMID: 35719489

Zimba, O., & Gasparyan, A. Y. (2023). Designing, conducting, and reporting survey studies: A primer for researchers. *Journal of Korean Medical Science*, *38*(48), e403. DOI: 10.3346/jkms.2023.38.e403 PMID: 38084027

Zimmerman, B. J. (2000). Attaining self-regulation: A social cognitive perspective. In Boekaerts, M., Pintrich, P. R., & Zeidner, M. (Eds.), *Handbook of self-regulation* (pp. 13–39). Academic Press., DOI: 10.1016/B978-012109890-2/50031-7

Zimmerman, B. J., & Schunk, D. H. (2011). *Self-regulated learning and performance: An introduction and an overview. Handbook of self-regulation of learning and performance*. Routledge.

Zoogman, S., Goldberg, S. B., Hoyt, W. T., & Miller, L. (2015). Mindfulness interventions with youth: A meta-analysis. *Mindfulness*, *6*(2), 290–302. DOI: 10.1007/s12671-013-0260-4

About the Contributors

Eleni Nikolaou is an Associate Professor at the Department of Sciences of Preschool Education and Educational Design, University of the Aegean. She has been teaching at the Department since 2006. She has worked for almost fifteen consecutive years in a counseling and mental health service for children, adolescents and their families in Rhodes, Greece. Eleni Nikolaou holds a Ph.D from the Department of Preschool Education and Educational Design, University of the Aegean (2005). She completed her postgraduate studies (Master Program) at City University, London (M.Sc. in Counseling Psychology, 1999). She holds a Bachelor's Degree in Psychology from the University of Crete (1996). Her articles have been published in reputable scientific peer reviewed journals and Conferences, either in national or international level. She participates as a reviewer in Greek as well as in International Journals. She has also co-edited several collective volumes in Greek and international level. Her research interests include school counselling, psychological resilience, psychological wellbeing, mental health promotion, bullying and issues of developmental psychopathology.

***

Edu Abao, RGC, RPm, LPT, is a Guidance Counselor III at Cebu Normal University, where he provides counseling services, facilitates developmental programs, and supports students' academic, personal, and psychosocial growth. He previously taught Psychology at University of the Visayas and Cebu Technological University, contributing to the preparation of future professionals in psychology and the social sciences. He also has over six years of teaching experience in the Department of Education, including five years serving as a Guidance Designate, where he integrated counseling and education in school-based practice. He earned his Master of Arts in Guidance and Counseling from Cebu Normal University and is currently pursuing a Master of Arts in Clinical Psychology at Cebu Institute of

Technology University. His professional interests include school counseling, student well-being, psychosocial resilience, and Gestalt-informed therapeutic practice. He also collaborates with Psychosomatherapia Clinic in facilitating psychotherapeutic activities, mental health trainings, and therapeutic adventure-based programs. He is an active member of the Psychological Association of the Philippines and remains committed to advancing mental health awareness through counseling, teaching, and community engagement.

Maria Argyriou (Postdoctoral Researcher) is a laboratory teaching academic faculty in applied music pedagogy at the Department of Pre-school Education and Educational Design, School of Humanities, University of the Aegean (Rhodes, Greece). She holds a Ph.D. in Cultural Policy and Music Education from the Department of Music Studies at the Ionian University, as well as two master's degrees in education, including one in education leadership and school unit assessment. Her research focuses on music education policy, early childhood music pedagogy, cultural identity, lifelong professional learning, and digitally mediated music education. Her work has appeared in peer-reviewed journals and edited volumes addressing music education, intercultural pedagogy, early childhood education, and multimodal learning. Dr. Argyriou co-edits the open-access Hellenic Journal of Music, Education, and Culture and serves as editor-in-chief of the national digital textbook Music in the First Grade. In 2024, she was awarded one of the three Kiveli–Y. Horn Scholarships / Special Grants for archival research at the Music Library of Greece "Lilian Voudouri," focusing on a specialized collection of children's songs by Minos Dounias (1900–1962). She is an active member of the International Society for Music Education (ISME), serving in the SIG Practice and Research Group in Integrated Music Education (PRIME), and participates in the European Music Council (EMC).

Charistoula Chatzinikola is a postdoctoral researcher at the University of the Aegean, specializing in nutrition and sustainability within the interdisciplinary fields of culture and education. Her research focuses on innovative approaches to food and nutrition literacy and on promoting sustainable development in early childhood education settings. Her work explores the intersection of education, sustainability, and health promotion, with particular emphasis on early childhood learning environments.

Andri Christodoulou is an Assistant Professor of Clinical Psychology at Neapolis University Pafos. She holds a Doctorate (Psy.D.) in Psychology and Master's degrees in Psychology from Pace University, USA. Her work focuses on clinical psychology, counseling, and mental health, and she has contributed to research on psychological well-being and related psychosocial issues.

Theodoros Goutoglou holds a Bachelor's degree in Psychology from Neapolis University Pafos and is currently pursuing a Master's degree in Counselling Psychology at the same university. His interests include decision-making, psychosocial development, and mental health. He has research experience and experience in academic writing and has co-authored work on psychosocial development in children and adolescents exhibiting aggressive behaviour.

Emmanuel Hernani, PhD, RPsy, ICAP III, CSEE, is a clinical psychologist, psychotherapist, educator, and Gestalt therapy practitioner based in the Philippines. He has been a faculty member of Cebu Normal University since 2002 and has served in several leadership roles, including University Counselor, Dean of Student Affairs, Chair of the Psychology Department, and Chair of the Research Ethics Committee. Dr. Hernani is the founder and director of Psychosomatherapia, a clinic specializing in psychological assessment, psychotherapy, consultation, and research. With more than two decades of professional practice, he has provided individual, group, family, and couples psychotherapy, particularly for clients experiencing trauma, substance use concerns, relational crises, and psychosocial distress. His clinical and scholarly work is strongly informed by Gestalt therapy, with additional integration of play, arts, movement, breathing, awareness-based practices, and other experiential approaches. He has delivered numerous workshops, training programs, and conference presentations in the Philippines and abroad on psychotherapy, counseling, mental health, relational engagement, and psycho-legal issues. Dr. Hernani has also published book chapters and scholarly works on mental health, embodiment, awareness, and psychosocial support, including contributions to internationally recognized academic publications. His research and professional interests include school mental health, Gestalt-informed counselling, psychosocial resilience, relational pedagogy, and holistic approaches to human development.

Katerina Karanikola is a German language teacher in Greek public secondary education, where she has been serving since 2009. She holds a degree in German Language and Literature from the University of Essen, Germany, and a Master of Education (M.Ed.) in New Forms of Education and Learning from the University of the Aegean. Her postgraduate studies focused on educational sciences, lifelong learning, adult education, e-learning, educational research methodology, and gender in education. Her research interests include gender-based violence in education, school violence, gender studies, gender equality, gender stereotypes, discrimination, and the social construction of gender identities within educational settings.

She is particularly interested in the ways gender influences students' experiences, relationships, and participation in school life.

Dimitra Katsarou is a Permanent Assistant Professor of Developmental Psychopathology and Language Disorders in the Department of Sciences of Preschool Education Sciences and Educational Design, University of the Aegean, Greece. Her academic and research work focuses on developmental psychopathology, language development and disorders, developmental language disorder, learning difficulties, neurodevelopmental disorders, Down syndrome and other genetic syndromes, psycholinguistics, bilingualism, literacy, and inclusive education. She has extensive teaching and research experience in higher education and has participated in undergraduate and postgraduate programmes in psychology, special education, language development, and developmental disorders. Her research adopts an interdisciplinary perspective, integrating psychological, linguistic, neuropsychological, and educational approaches to the study of child development.

Stamatina Kioussi is an educator and researcher specializing in educational leadership and systems thinking. She holds a PhD from the Department of Pre-school Education Sciences and Educational Design at the University of the Aegean (2025), where her doctoral research investigated "A systems approach to school culture as a driving factor in effective school development". She also holds an M.Ed. in Educational Leadership and School Improvement from the University of Manchester (2003) and a BA in English Language and Literature from the National and Kapodistrian University of Athens (2000). Dr. Kioussi has served as a researcher at the University of the Aegean and has more than two decades of teaching experience within Greek secondary education. Her primary research interests include systems approaches to education, organizational school culture, and school improvement.

Anastassios Kodakos is a Professor at the Department of Sciences of Preschool Education and Educational Design (D.S.P.E.D.) of the University of the Aegean, in the field of "History and Theory of School Development". He is Director of the Postgraduate Program "Models of Design and Development of Educational Units" and Deputy Director of the MSc "Children's book and Pedagogical Material". His research interests include History and Theory of Education, Development of Educational Systems and Units, Educational Design, Pedagogical Communication, Media and Information Pedagogy, Systems Theory, Pedagogy of Imagination. He has participated with presentations in many international and Greek conferences, has edited a series of collective volumes and published books on the above issues.

Maria Kouroutsidou is an Associate Professor at the Department of Preschool Education and Educational Design (TEPAES), University of the Aegean, Greece.

She teaches undergraduate and postgraduate courses on social exclusion, gender role formation, and research methodology. She also teaches in the Distance Learning Master's Programme in Public Administration at Neapolis University Pafos, Cyprus. For many years, she has served as a research associate in research projects and initiatives conducted by the Laboratory of Educational and Social Research at TEPAES. Her research interests focus on social exclusion, gender, family and school, adult education, and formal and non-formal learning. She is the author of three books, the editor of two edited volumes, and has published numerous scientific articles in both Greek and English.

Georgios Kritikos is an Assistant Professor and member of the Learning Technology and Educational Engineering Laboratory at the Department of Preschool Education Sciences and Educational Design, University of the Aegean. His research interests include Science and Mathematics Education, Educational Engineering, STEAM Education, Systems Theory in Education, Reflection and Metacognition, and Education for Sustainable Development. His work further explores interdisciplinary approaches to teaching and learning, with particular emphasis on conceptual representations and innovative educational practices.

Marilena Mousoulidou is an Assistant Professor of Cognitive Psychology at the Department of Psychology at Neapolis University Pafos and serves as the Coordinator of the BSc in Psychology. She earned a PhD in Cognitive Psychology from the University of Leicester (UK) and a BSc in Psychology from the University of Derby (UK). Her research focuses on cognitive psychology, reading comprehension, and issues related to mental health.

Meropi Ntavlamanou is an Elementary School Headteacher. She holds a BA in Elementary Education, a BA in Preschool Education and a MA in School Management. She has great experience in elementary school administration. She also has published research and theoretical papers in international journals.

Afroditi Ntouka is a postdoctoral researcher in the Department of Sciences of Preschool Education and Educational Design, at the University of the Aegean. She has been working as a kindergarten teacher for six years in Rhodes, Greece. She holds a bachelor's degree in Preschool Education from the University of the Aegean (2013) and she has completed her postgraduate studies, also at the University of the Aegean (2016). She holds a Ph.D. in Instructional Communication from the Department of Sciences of Preschool Education and Educational Design, University of the Aegean (2021). She has participated in conferences, at Greek and international level and her research interests include instructional communication, the effects of vocalics in instructional procedure and teachers' wellbeing.

Vasileios Papavasileiou is a Professor at the Department of Preschool Education Sciences and Educational Design, University of the Aegean, specializing in Environmental Education in Educational Sciences. He currently serves as Chair of the Department. His teaching and research focus on environmental education, education for sustainability, educational planning, research methodology, local sustainable development, and environmental awareness. He has taught at both undergraduate and postgraduate levels and has participated in research and educational projects related to sustainability and environmental education. His published work includes books, edited volumes, journal articles, collective-volume chapters, and conference papers.

Nikolaos Psyrras is a PhD candidate at the University of the Aegean, Department of Preschool Education and Educational Planning, with a research focus on educational leadership, digital transformation, and educational policy. He is a permanent primary school teacher in Greek public education with extensive experience in school leadership and management. He holds postgraduate degrees in Educational Management and Leadership and in New Forms of Education and Learning, as well as a Bachelor's degree in Sociology, supporting an interdisciplinary approach to educational research. His academic interests include educational leadership, new technologies and artificial intelligence in education, professional development, and knowledge management. He has published in peer-reviewed international journals and conference proceedings, and his work on school leadership and digital advancement has received a Best Paper Award at an international scientific conference.

Nikolaos Raptis is Associate Professor at the Department of Preschool Education and Educational Design ("TEPAES" in Greek) of the University of the Aegean (Rhodes, Greece), where he is serving as the Director of Post-Graduate Program "New Forms of Education & Learning" (NFEL). He has many years of professional experience having worked as an education executive in several institutional positions, such as: Head and Director of a School Unit, Director of Education, School Counselor and Regional Director of Primary and Secondary Education. He has been serving since 2019 at the University of the Aegean. His research and writing focus mainly on Leadership and Management of Schools and Systems. He has written seven books and several research papers / studies, including: "Cooperative Leadership in Education", "The role of the Head and the Teachers' Association, "Leadership of Educational Units" and "Managing innovation by School Leadership" etc. He has participated in 16 funded research programs at national and regional level.

Angela Savvidou is a Master's degree in Counselling Psychology from Neapolis University Pafos. Her research interests focus broadly on mental health and psychological well-being. She has research experience and experience in academic writing.

Maria Sofologi is an Adjunct Ass. Professor at the Department of Early Childhood and Education at the University of Ioannina in Greece. She delivers the courses "Cognitive Psychology", and "Developmental Psychology". She is also a postdoctoral researcher at the University of Ioannina in Greece. She holds a Ph.D. in Cognitive Psychology from the Aristotle University of Thessaloniki. She also holds a Master of Science degree in Cognitive Psychology from the Aristotle University of Thessaloniki. During her master's degree years she trained and practiced different assessment cognitive tools to evaluate all cognitive functions like memory, attention, language, executive functions both in adults and children. She is the key speaker in many European and Hellenic conferences concerning cognitive psychology, educational psychology, special education in children and adults, as well. Her academic work includes a series of many scientific publications, books, and book chapters concerning Cognitive Psychology, Special Education, Educational Psychology, and Cognitive impairments in children and adults as well.

Panagiotis Stamatis (PhD) is a Professor of Communication Pedagogy at the Department of Preschool Education Sciences and Educational Design at the University of the Aegean, Greece. He has great experience in teaching, research and international collaboration, especially in tertiary education. He has published noumerous of research and theoretical papers in international journals and books focused on issues of communication in education in Greece and USA.

Kyriaki Tasiou is a teacher and works for the last 14 years at a primary school as a special education teacher. She holds a Master's degree on the topic: "Gender and New Educational and Working Environments in the Information Society" of the T.E.P.A.E.S.-University of the Aegean and Master's degree with the title: "Sciences of Education: Special Education and Education of Persons with Problems of Oral and Written Communication" of the Inter-University MSc of the EAP with the University of Thessaly. She has been trained in Greek Sign Language. She is a PhD candidate at the T.E.P.A.E.S of the University of the Aegean.

George Tsitsas is an Assistant Professor in Counseling Psychology at the Department of Psychology at Neapolis University Pafos. He holds a PhD in Counseling Psychology from the National and Kapodistrian University of Athens and an MSc in Counseling Psychology from City University London. His work focuses on counseling psychology, family and couple therapy, and mental health, and he has extensive experience in university counseling services and psychological support.

Eirini Tzovla is PhD holder in utilization of ICT in education from Democritus University of Thrace, Master Master's degrees in Pedagogy and Master's degrees in Adult Education. Her research interests focus on the utilization of ICT in education, counseling, psychosocial development and Adult Education. She collaborates with universities and has written books and published in scientific journals.

Index

A

C

D

E

F

G

K

M

O

P

R

S

T

W

www.ingramcontent.com/pod-product-compliance
Lightning Source LLC
LaVergne TN
LVHW062028101126
852251LV00005B/53